AF769869

THE TREATY OF NICE

Constitutional Law Library

1. F. Laursen (Ed.), *The Treaty of Nice: Actor Preferences, Bargaining and Institutional Choice* (2006)

2. T. Barkhuysen and S.D. Lindenbergh (Eds), *Constitutionalisation of Private Law* (2006)

3. J. Nergelius (Ed.), *Nordic and Other European Constitutional Traditions* (2006)

The Treaty of Nice

Actor Preferences, Bargaining and Institutional Choice

Edited by

Finn Laursen

MARTINUS NIJHOFF PUBLISHERS
LEIDEN / BOSTON
2006

A C.I.P. record for this book is available from the Library of Congress.

Printed on acid-free paper.

ISSN 1871-4110
ISBN 90-04-14820-5
© 2006 Koninklijke Brill NV, Leiden, The Netherlands

Koninklijke Brill NV incorporates the imprints Brill Academic Publishers, Martinus Nijhoff Publishers and VSP.

http://www.brill.nl

All rights reserved. No part of this publication may be reproduced, stored in a retrieval system, or transmitted in any form or by any means, electronic, mechanical, photocopying, microfilming, recording or otherwise, without written permission from the Publisher.

Authorization to photocopy items for internal or personal use is granted by Brill Academic Publishers provided that the appropriate fees are paid directly to The Copyright Clearance Center, 222 Rosewood Drive, Suite 910, Danvers MA 01923, USA.
Fees are subject to change.

PRINTED AND BOUND IN THE NETHERLANDS.

CONTENTS

SECTION 3
INTERSTATE BARGAINING

SECTION 4
THE PARALLEL PROCESSES

SECTION 5
CONCLUSIONS

PREFACE

This book is about the Treaty of Nice, negotiated during 2000, signed in 2001 and in force since 1 February 2003.

The book can be seen as a sequence to the two books I co-edited together with Sophie Vanhoonacker while I was based at the European Institute of Public Administration (EIPA), Maastricht, namely *The Intergovernmental Conference on Political Union: Institutional Reforms, New Policies and International Identity of the European Community* (Maastricht: EIPA, and Dordrecht: Nijhoff, 2002), and *The Ratification of the Maastricht Treaty: Issues, Debates and Future Implications* (Maastricht: EIPA, and Dordrecht: Nijhoff, 1994), as well as the book I edited after moving to the University of Southern Denmark, namely *The Amsterdam Treaty: National Preference Formation, Interstate Bargaining and Outcome* (Odense: Odense University Press, 2002).

In the research for this book, the authors were asked to analyse why the Member States went into the Intergovernmental Conference (IGC), which negotiated the Treaty of Nice in 2000, with certain positions (national preferences) and why the negotiations within the IGC eventually had the outcome they had in December 2000. No specific theories were imposed on the authors, but Andrew Moravcsik's liberal intergovernmentalism was mentioned as a possible approach to the issues of national preference formation and inter-state bargaining. In the end some authors have ignored liberal intergovernmentalism and some have used and some have criticised it.

Concretely the book has chapters on the 15 Member States and the two Community actors, the Commission and the European Parliament. One chapter also deals with the role of the Council Secretariat. Three chapters deal with the most important issues in the negotiations, namely re-weighting of votes in the Council, extended use of qualified majority voting (QMV), and changes in the provisions concerning the use of enhanced cooperation. The book further includes two chapters on what we have termed the parallel processes, namely important developments concerning European Security and Defence Policy (ESDP) and the negotiation of a Charter of Fundamental Rights by a Convention. This Charter was accepted as a political document in 2000. Finally there are two concluding chapters by the editor, one discussing explanations, including the limits of liberal intergovernmentalism, the other looking towards the future, the so-called post-Nice agenda, which has since then produced a draft Constitutional Treaty through a new Convention in 2002-2003 and the IGC 2003-04. The Constitutional Treaty is now going through the process of ratification, but this process has been put on hold after the French and Dutch voted No in referendums on 29 May and 1 June 2005 respectively. The less than satisfactory solution of the institutional issues in Nice in connection with the major enlargement of the EU in 2004 called—it was felt in 2000—for yet another treaty reform. This post-Nice process has now come to a halt, at least for the moment. Without knowing the contents of the Treaty of Nice and how it was negotiated it is not possible to fully understand the Constitutional Treaty as it was negotiated. We hope this book will contribute to such an understanding. And as long as the Constitutional Treaty cannot be ratified, the EU will have to live with the Treaty of Nice analysed in this book.

Finn Laursen
Odense, August 2005.

LIST OF CONTRIBUTORS

Esko Antola	Professor, Jean Monnet Chair, University of Turku, Finland
Felipe Basabe Lloréns	Administrative Director, Instituto Cervantes, Centre Culturel Espagnol, Paris, France
Derek Beach	Assistant Professor, Department of Political Science, Aarhus University, Aarhus, Denmark
Federiga Bindi	Jean Monnet Professor of European Integration and Director of the European Office, University of Roma 'Tor Vergata', Rome, Italy
Kathrin Blanck	Research Assistant, Europainstitut, University of Economics and Business Administration, Vienna, Austria
Spyros Blavoukos	Ph.D.-Candidate, Department of Government, University of Essex, United Kingdom
Monica den Boer	Director of Research, Police Academy of the Netherlands, Apeldoorn, and Vrije Universiteit Amsterdam, The Netherlands
Christian Engel	Unit Head in charge of bilateral relations with EU countries, State Chancellery of Northrhine-Westfalia, Düsseldorf, Germany
Christer Karlsson	Research Fellow and Lecturer, Department of Political Science, Uppsala University, Sweden
Bart Kerremans	Associate Professor of International Relations and American Politics, Department of Political Science, Katholieke Universiteit Leuven, Leuven, Belgium
Henrik Larsen	Associate Professor in International Relations and Jean Monnet Chair, Department of Political Science, University of Copenhagen, Copenhagen, Denmark

Finn Laursen	Professor of International Politics and Jean Monnet Chair, Department of Political Science, and Director, Centre for European Studies, University of Southern Denmark, Odense, Denmark
Sander Luitwieler	Ph.D.-student, Department of Political Science, Erasmus University Rotterdam, the Netherlands
Nicolas Mackel	Permanent Representation of Luxembourg to the European Union, Brussels, Belgium
Ana M. Guerra Martins	Professor, Law Faculty of the University of Lisbon, European Institute, Lisbon, Portugal
Andreas Maurer	Head of Unit I – EU-Integration, German Institute for International and Security Affairs (SWP), Berlin, and Lecturer, Free University of Berlin, Germany
Christine Neuhold	Assistant Professor, European Studies Programme, University of Maastricht, Maastricht, The Netherlands
Laura Lund Olsen	Research Assistant, Centre for European Studies and Graduate student, Department of Political Science, University of Southern Denmark, Odense, Denmark
Alfred Pijpers	Senior Research Fellow, Clingendael European Studies Programme (CESP), The Hague; Assistant Professor, Department of Political Science, University of Leiden, The Netherlands
Christina Pineda Polo	Policy Analyst, The European Policy Centre, Brussels, Belgium
Sten Rynning	Associate Professor, Department of Political Science, University of Southern Denmark, Odense, Denmark

Adriaan Schout — Associate Professor, European Institute of Public Administration, Maastricht, The Netherlands, and Senior Research Fellow, Clingendael European Studies Programme (CESP), The Hague, The Netherlands

Anna-Carin Svensson — Deputy Director, Division for Police Issues, incl. Public Order and Safety, Ministry of Justice, Stockholm, Sweden

Ben Tonra — Jean Monnet Professor of European Foreign, Security and Defence Policy, Academic Director and Senior Lecturer, Dublin European Institute (DEI), University College Dublin, Dublin, Ireland

Panos Tsakaloyannis — Associate Professor and Jean Monnet Chair, Department of European Economic Studies, Athens University of Economics and Business, Athens, Greece

Sophie Vanhoonacker — Associate Professor, Faculty of Arts and Culture, University of Maastricht, Maastricht, The Netherlands

Maciej Wilga — Ph.D.-Student, Department of Political Science, University of Southern Denmark, Odense, Denmark

ACKNOWLEDGMENTS

This book is the outcome of a project which received financial support from the Danish Social Science Research Council. This support is gratefully acknowledged. The editor would also like to acknowledge the co-operation with the Department of Political Science and the Centre for European Studies (CFES) at the University of Southern Denmark.

Part of the project was an international conference organized by the CFES in Odense, 6-7 September 2002, where early drafts of some of the chapters in this book were presented. Special thanks are due to student assistants, Morten Møller Iversen, Berenice Lara Laursen and Laura Lund Olsen for organisational and research assistance.

At the secretariat of the Department of Political Science special thanks go to Vibeke Pierson for her invaluable help. I am particularly indebted to her for her diligent linguistic assistance with this book. Berenice Lara Laursen is thanked for preparing the index.

Odense, August 2005.
Finn Laursen

CHAPTER 1

INTRODUCTION: OVERVIEW OF THE INTERGOVERNMENTAL CONFERENCE 2000 AND THE TREATY OF NICE

INTRODUCTION

The Treaty of Nice was negotiated by an Intergovernmental Conference (IGC), which ran through most of the year 2000. The European Council in Nice, France, concluded the negotiations in December 2000. This treaty introduced a number of institutional changes in the EU. The changes were related to future enlargements, which took membership to 25 in May 2004. The treaty determines the number of votes in a future EU-27. The 12 future members are 10 countries from Central and Eastern Europe (CEECs) as well as Cyprus and Malta. Turkey is also a candidate for membership but no future number of votes in the Council was assigned to Turkey in Nice.

Nice dealt with three related issues known as the Amsterdam 'leftovers' because the Treaty of Amsterdam in 1997 had failed to solve them (Laursen, 2002):

1. Re-weighting of votes in the Council
2. Increased use of Qualified Majority Voting (QMV) in the Council
3. Size and composition of the Commission.

It was the large Member States that demanded a re-weighting of votes, claiming that they were relatively underrepresented according to the old weighting, and that this would become a bigger issue in a much enlarged Union, since most new Member States are relatively small, with the main exception of Poland. A re-weighting of votes they hoped would increase the legitimacy of the system.

An increased use of QMV should improve the decision-making capacity of the Union. As long as unanimity is required, one single Member State can veto decisions. With a QMV it will take a small group of states—a so-called blocking minority—to block a decision. The size of this group depends on the definition of the QMV, which in Nice was closely linked to the re-weighting of votes.

The third question, the size and composition of the Commission, was also difficult because most Member States wish to be represented in the College of Commissioners. At the time, in EU-15, there were 20 Commissioners, two from each of the big five and one from each of the 10 smaller

Member States. But was the Commission not already becoming too big to function as a collegial body and for leaving meaningful portfolios for all members?

It took a lot of 'horse-trading' in Nice in December 2000 to solve these issues. And in the end most of the Heads of State or Government meeting in Nice were rather unhappy about the outcome.

In many ways Nice was unique. Past IGCs had usually dealt with both substantive policy issues and some institutional issues. This time the agenda was largely limited to institutional issues. These were to include a fourth issue that was added during the conference, viz. 'closer' (or 'enhanced') cooperation or 'flexibility.' The Treaty of Amsterdam had introduced clauses allowing a group of Member States to go further in the integration process than the more hesitant and slow Member States, but the conditions for such 'closer cooperation' were rather strict (Stubb, 2002). The issue in the Nice negotiations was whether the conditions should be made less strict. This would make it easier for pro-integration members to move faster than integration-sceptical Member States and possibly form an *avant garde*.

The IGC 2000

The Luxembourg summit in December 1997 decided to start membership negotiations with six applicant states. So the enlargement was under way and it might be faster and bigger than first expected. Given the protocol on institutions from Amsterdam, which allowed for enlargement with up to five new members on condition of a reduction of the size of the Commission to one member per Member State and some modification of the weighting of votes in the Council, it looked as if the number of five might be exceeded in a first enlargement. The Amsterdam Protocol foresaw a new IGC "to carry out a comprehensive review of the provisions of the Treaties on the composition and functioning of the institutions" before the EU could take in more than five new members (Galloway, 2001; Church, 2001).

The meeting of the European Council in Cologne in June 1999 therefore decided to convene an IGC in 2000 to deal with the 'Amsterdam leftovers':

> In order to ensure that the European Union's institutions can continue to work efficiently after enlargement, the European Council confirms its intention of convening a Conference of the Representatives of the Governments of the Member States early in 2000 to resolve the institutional issues left open in Amsterdam that need to be settled before enlargement. The Conference should be completed and the necessary amendments to the treaties agreed upon at the end of 2000 (European Council, 1999a).

Preparation this time was left to the Finnish Presidency during the second half of 1999. The Commission also had a report prepared by Jean-Luc

Dehaene, Richard von Weizsäcker and David Simon on "The Institutional implications of enlargement." The report was presented to the Commission on 18 October 1999. The Commission issued its own Communication on 10 November 1999 (Commission 1999).

The meeting of the European Council in Helsinki in December 1999 confirmed the relatively narrow agenda of the IGC leaving open the possibility of adding other topics later. In the Presidency Conclusions we read:

> Following the Cologne Conclusions and in the light of the Presidency's report, the Conference will examine the size and composition of the Commission, the weighting of votes in the Council, as well as other necessary amendments to the Treaties arising as regards the European institutions in connection with the above issues and in implementing the Treaty of Amsterdam. The incoming Presidency will report to the European Council on progress made in the Conference and may propose additional issues to be taken on the agenda of the Conference (European Council, 1999b).

The idea was now to convene the IGC in February 2000 and complete it by December 2000. It thus was to run through the Portuguese and French Presidencies of that year.

As to organization of the IGC, the Foreign Ministers would have the "overall political responsibility." Preparatory work was to be the responsibility of "a Group composed of a representative of each Member State's Government." The Commission would take part in the IGC at both the political and preparatory level. The Council Secretariat would provide secretariat support.

The European Parliament would be "closely associated and involved" in the IGC. The EP would have two observers in the Preparatory Group. Sessions of foreign ministers were to be "preceded by an exchange of views with the President of the European Parliament, assisted by two representatives" of the EP. "Meetings at the level of Heads of State or Government dealing with the IGC will be preceded by an exchange of views with the President of the European Parliament" (Ibid.).

Helsinki also called for the start of accession negotiations with the next six applicants and gave Turkey the status of an applicant without, however, setting a date for the start of negotiations. Candidate states would be regularly briefed during the IGC.

Helsinki decided to follow up on another decision from Cologne, namely to develop the Union's defence policy. The summit underlined the "determination to develop an autonomous capacity to take decisions, and, where NATO as a whole is not engaged, to launch and conduct EU-led military operations in response to international crises." In particular, the European Council agreed that "cooperating voluntarily in EU-led operations, Member States must be able, by 2003, to deploy within 60 days and sustain for at least one year military forces of up to 50,000-60,000 persons capable of the full range of Petersberg tasks," i.e. various peace-keeping and peace-enforcing activities.

The idea of consolidating "the fundamental rights applicable at Union level" in a charter had also been accepted at the Cologne summit. It was decided that "a draft of such a Charter of Fundamental Rights of the European Union should be elaborated by a body composed of representatives of the Heads of State and Government and the President of the Commission as well as of members of the European Parliament and national parliaments." The body, later known as a Convention, should present a draft document "in advance of the European Council in December 2000" (European Council, 1999a).

So these two questions, defence policy and fundamental rights, were kept separate from the IGC and dealt with in parallel processes.

The formal initiative for the IGC went out from the Finnish Presidency on 14 December 1999. The proposal went to hearings in the Commission and European Parliament on 17 December as required by Article 48 TEU.

The Commission issued its positive recommendation on 26 January 2000 in the form of an opinion entitled "Adapting the Institutions to make a Success of Enlargement" (Commission, 2000a).

The European Parliament followed on 3 February with the required resolution. Objecting to the "excessively narrow agenda adopted in Helsinki," the EP called for "an ambitious reform of the Treaty" (European Parliament, 2000).

Having heard from the Commission and the European Parliament the Council could formally call the IGC, which started 14 February 2000. During the following 10 months, the Group of Representatives met about twice a month. The Foreign Ministers met about once a month. And the Heads of State or Government met in Santa Maria da Feira, Portugal, 19-20 June, in Biarritz, France, 13-14 October, and finally in Nice 7-10 December, 2000. The concluding negotiations in Nice actually finished at 4:15 on Monday 11 December.

By the time of the Feira summit in June, the Portuguese Presidency put forward a report on the IGC, giving an overview of the discussions, listing options and some concrete proposals (CONFER 4750). In the Presidency Conclusions the Heads of State or Government talked about "significant headway," and said "The European Council considers in particular that the provisions on closer cooperation introduced into the Treaty of Amsterdam should form part of the Conference's future work, while respecting the need for coherence and solidarity in an enlarged Union" (European Council, 2000a). So closer or 'enhanced cooperation', as it was eventually to be called in the Treaty of Nice, was now on the agenda.

The question of increased application of QMV was one of the issues debated during the Portuguese Presidency. At the outset there were 73 areas requiring unanimity. How many of these could be transferred to QMV?

In their report to the Feira summit, the Portuguese mentioned 39 areas that might be moved to QMV and eight areas where QMV could be considered for only certain specific aspects. This latter group included measures to provide freedom of movement for workers and self-employed workers (Article 42 TEC), certain tax measures (Article 93 TEC), certain specific provisions on social matters (Article 137 TEC), and arrangements for participation by the EU in WTO proceedings, where a new protocol was suggested (Annex 3.1 in CONFER 4750). Also listed were 24 constitutional, quasi-constitutional or organic provisions for which unanimity is required in the Council, and for which no QMV was envisaged (Annex 3.7).

When the French Presidency put forward its first progress report on 3 November the "List of Provisions to be examined with a view to a possible move to qualified majority voting" had been increased to 47, including Articles 42, 93 and 137 (CONFER 4790). It also included Article 133(1) or (4) TEC – conclusion of international agreements on intellectual property and services. A draft protocol would move the sectors covered by the General Agreement on Trade in Services (GATS) and the Agreement on Trade-related Aspects of Intellectual Property Rights (TRIPS) under Article 133 (4) which stipulates QMV. Sea transport would remain under the Common Transport Policy (Title V of TEC).

The French proposal for QMV also included that several of the Justice and Home Affairs (JHA) areas be transferred from Pillar III to Pillar I in the Amsterdam Treaty (parts of Articles 62, 63, 65 and 66) as well as structural funds (Article 161).

Since some of these proposals were unacceptable for some Member States, the politics of QMV became an important part of the IGC endgame up to Nice. As we shall see later, in the end about 30 areas were moved to QMV.

Size and composition of the Commission also turned out to be a very controversial issue. It pitted smaller Member States who insisted on retaining a Commissioner of their nationality against larger Member States, led by France who insisted on a smaller Commission in the future and some system of rotation.

Most dramatic was the issue of weighting of votes in the Council. The French Presidency put forward its first proposal on 9 December in Nice. The proposal was to triple the number of votes for the big four to 30 votes and double the votes for most medium-sized and smaller Member States. Spain would move from eight to 28, more than a tripling. Luxembourg would move from two to three, less than a doubling.

Since the first proposal was violently criticized by the medium-sized and smaller Member States, the French put forward a second proposal on 10 December. Most smaller and medium-sized members would get an additional vote in this proposal, but the Netherlands would get two extra, thus creating a differentiation between Belgium and the Netherlands. In the end, the Presidency had to offer the medium-sized members one additional vote and reduce the big Member States' votes by one.

All kinds of linkages were brought into the negotiations. Portugal felt that Spain was treated too generously. The treatment of the Netherlands upset the Belgians. Some of the countries upset then got extra seats in the European Parliament and Belgium was promised that future summits would take place in Brussels. Germany was won over by the stipulation that a QMV must also represent 62% of the population in the EU. Germany further avoided a reduction in the number of seats in the European Parliament, which all other Member States, except Luxembourg, had to accept.

Institutional Choices

Re-Weighting of Votes

In the end a reweighting took place. The four biggest states, which currently have 10 votes, will get 29 in the future. If we only concentrate on population, Germany should have had more votes. Spain, which currently has eight votes, will get 27, a very good result for that country. Spain then pulled Poland up to the same level. There will be a differentiation between the Netherlands getting 13 and Belgium getting 12 votes.

The Treaty of Nice also assigned new numbers of seats in the European Parliament. Here a differentiation between Germany and France has existed since a mini-reform took place after the Maastricht Treaty negotiations in 1992. In the future Germany will retain its 99 seats. France, Italy and the UK will go down from 87 to 72 seats.

Qualified Majority Vote (QMV)

The second main issue was the increased use of QMV. When the IGC2000 started there were about 70 areas left that still required unanimity according to the treaty. The IGC discussed about 45 of these with a view to a possible transfer to QMV. In the end it was decided to transfer 23 areas from the entry into force of the treaty and 12 areas later to QMV.

More than 20 areas, mainly constitutional or quasi-constitutional provisions, were considered too sensitive from the outset. It was agreed early on not to touch them.

The more controversial areas in these discussions about increased use of QMV included visa, asylum and immigration, where some issues will be transferred to QMV in 2004 and others later.

Another controversial area was trade policy where the introduction of QMV for trade in services and trade-related aspects of intellectual property rights (TRIPS) takes place with some exemptions, including culture and the audiovisual area. Especially France insisted on that exemption.

Next, social policy was controversial. This included article 42, where no change will take place, and Article 137, where a limited move to QMV is to be decided by unanimity later. The UK and Denmark were among the countries that had problems with the proposed changes in these two articles.

The treaty also leaves taxation policies untouched. This satisfied the UK, among other states.

Size and Composition of Commission

Concerning the third issue, size and composition of the Commission the Treaty of Nice only found a partial solution. From 1 January 2005, the Commission will consist of one national from each Member State. When the EU reaches 27 members a reduction in the size of the Commission will have to be agreed and a system of rotation found, all this by unanimity. So, at some point in time the Member States will not always have a Commissioner of their own nationality.

Nice has also strengthened the role of the President of the Commission. In the future he/she may decide the internal organization of the Commission and reallocate responsibilities among the Commissioners during the Commission's term of office. The President may also call on a member of the Commission to resign after obtaining the collective approval of the Commission.

Enhanced Cooperation

Nice makes 'enhanced cooperation' easier especially by now only requiring an absolute minimum number of states of eight, where the Treaty of Amsterdam required a majority of the Member States. The exact rules vary between the three pillars and remain rather complex.

The Treaty of Amsterdam had enabling clauses for closer cooperation in the first and third pillars. It provided the possibility of using a veto against such cooperation. This veto is now removed for those two pillars. Nice introduces enabling clauses for enhanced cooperation in the second pillar but with a veto possibility. The general conditions remain rather restrictive.

ANALYSING THE IGC 2000

Andrew Moravcsik has developed a model for studying the major decisions in European integration. He calls it 'liberal intergovernmentalism.' When he first developed his approach, he suggested a two-step analysis of integration, first national preference formation and then interstate bargaining (Moravcsik, 1993). Later he added a third step, institutional choice (Moravcsik, 1998). The framework is summarized in table 1.1.

The first stage is to try to explain national preferences. The central question asked by Moravcsik here is whether it is economic or geopolitical interests that dominate when Member States form their preferences. The answer based on major decisions in the European integration process is that economic interests are the most important ones.

The second stage, interstate bargaining, seeks to explain the efficiency and distributional outcomes from EU negotiations. Here two possible explanations of agreements on substance are contrasted: asymmetrical interdependence or supranational entrepreneurship. Moravcsik arrives at the conclusion that asymmetrical interdependence has the most explanatory power. Some Member States have more at stake than others. They will work harder to influence outcomes. The entrepreneurial role of the Commission is not considered very important. Concerning the outcomes of interstate bargaining three factors are likely to be decisive:

1. The value of unilateral policy alternatives, relative to the status quo, which underlies credible threats to veto,
2. The value of alternative coalitions, which underlies credible threats to exclude, and
3. The opportunities for issue linkage or side-payments, which underlie "package deals" (Moravcsik, 1998, 63).

Summarizing the discussion of the first point, Moravcsik says: "those who more intensely desire the benefits of cooperation will concede more to get them." Summarizing the discussion of the second point he says: "the credible threat of exclusion is likely to generate an even more powerful pressure on recalcitrant states than does the threat of nonagreement." In respect to linkage strategies Moravcsik observes that the major constraint lies in their domestic distributional implications. Concessions often create domestic losers. This will limit the use of package deals (Moravcsik, 1998, 63-67).

Table 1.1: International cooperation: A rationalist framework

Stages of Negotiation	National Preference	Interstate Bargaining	Institutional Choice Formation
Alternative independent variables underlying each stage	What is the source of underlying national preferences?	Given national preferences what explains the efficiency and distributional outcomes of inter-state bargaining?	Given substantive agreement, what explains the transfer of sovereignty to interantional institutions?
	Economic interests or Geopolitical interests? or More credible commitment?	Asymmetrical interdependence or Supranational entrepreneurship?	Federalist ideology or Centralized technocratic management
Observed outcomes at each stage	Underlying national preferences	Agreements on substance	Choice to delegate or pool decision-making in international institutions

Source: Moravcsik (1998), p. 24.

The third stage explores the reasons why states choose to delegate or pool decision-making in international institutions. Delegation in the EU refers to the powers given to the Commission and the European Court of Justice (ECJ). Pooling of sovereignty refers to the application of majority decisions, including QMV. To explain institutional choice, Moravcsik contrasts three possible explanations: Federalist ideology, centralized technocratic management or more credible commitment. The answer he gives is that states delegate and pool sovereignty to get more credible commitment. Pooling and delegation is a rational strategy adopted by the Member States to pre-commit governments to future decisions, to encourage future cooperation and to improve future implementation of agreements (Moravcsik, 1998, 73).

Using theories of decision-making, negotiations and international political economy in combination has allowed Moravcsik to construct an parsimonious framework for the study of international cooperation including international integration.

The Moravcsik framework has been used to structure this book. However, it has been left to individual authors how to approach the analysis of actor preferences, bargaining and institutional choice.

Moravcsik's scheme seems most applicable to the question about increased use of QMV. Here size was probably not an important variable in determining attitudes. Specific national socio-economic interests, such as taxation and social policy in the UK, shipping interests in Greece and Denmark, film industry interests in France, labour market interests in Denmark, and banking interests in Luxembourg, would probably go far in explaining national preferences and positions during the negotiations.

Concerning preferences in respect to re-weighting of votes, the most important variable was size. These issues were largely pitting the big against the small Member States. The big wanted a re-weighting in their favour. The small resisted this. Many big countries wanted to reduce the size of the Commission. Many small countries wanted to retain 'their' Commissioner. Using Moravcsik's terms, this might to a large extent fall more under geopolitics than economic interests as such. The questions concerning the Council and Commission were fundamental questions about institutional design. What kind of considerations do actors make when they design institutions? Since institutional reforms affect future decision-making, actors are interested in using such reforms to increase their influence and control in the future. Voting weights are directly linked to influence. Control is linked to the 'blocking minority' that follows from the definition of a QMV.

Influence, power and control are relative factors. The states look at relative gains and relative losses. They compare themselves with the other Member States.

The end game in Nice became a tough bargaining process, with questions of national prestige playing an unusual role. The French wanted to get as many votes as the Germans. The Belgians wanted to get as many votes as the Dutch. But the Germans and the Dutch pointed to differences in population.

The Spanish argued that there was a special Spanish problem. When Spain joined in 1986 it got fewer votes in the Council than the other big countries against getting two Commissioners. Losing one Commissioner in connection with enlargement, Spain expected compensation in the form of more votes in the Council.

The Germans in the end were compensated by the rule that a QMV should also represent 62% of the EU population. Since Germany will have about 17% of the total population in EU-27 it will have nearly half of a blocking minority in terms of population making it a very attractive coalition partner in the future.

As mentioned earlier, Nice was mainly about institutional choice (or design) and not so much about substance. If there was a broader question of substance it was enlargement. The Member States favouring speedy enlargement may therefore have been in a weaker bargaining position than those who did not mind enlargement being postponed. This may have weakened Germany and the Nordic members. It strengthened the cohesion countries, especially Spain who not only got relatively many votes in the Council but also succeeded in getting QMV for structural funds postponed until 2007 or later.

The Post-Nice Agenda

In a Declaration on the Future of the Union, the Heads of State or Government meeting in Nice said that important reforms had been decided and that the ratification of the Nice Treaty would complete the institutional changes necessary for the accession of new Member States. They called for "a deeper and wider debate about the future development of the European Union." They went on to mention the following points on the agenda of that future debate: a more precise delimitation of competencies between the European Union and the Member States, the status of the Charter of Fundamental Rights of the European Union, a simplification of the Treaties, and the role of the national Parliaments in the European architecture.

The Declaration also talked about "the need to improve and to monitor the democratic legitimacy and transparency of the Union and its institutions, to bring them closer to the citizens of the Member States." Nice linked this agenda with the decision that a new IGC would be convened in 2004 to discuss the above issues.

So Nice was not the end of the road. The nature of the EU is still very much on the agenda. What kind of Union is it? What kind of Union should it become? The issues suggest such a (re)new(ed) debate of a constitutional kind.

Ratification

The adopted treaty then had to be ratified by all Member States to enter into force. The first to deposit the ratification instrument was Denmark on 13 June 2001. Denmark this time ratified without a referendum. The last to finish the ratification process was Ireland. In the Irish case a referendum was considered necessary. The Irish voters surprised by voting 'no' in a referendum on 7 June 2001 with 53.87% of the votes. Eventually a second referendum took place on 19 October 2002. This time there was a 'yes' vote of 62.89% (see table 1.1).

The Treaty of Nice entered into force on 1 February 2003. But a number of stipulations in the treaty will only be applied gradually.

Table 1.2: Ratification of the Treaty of Nice

	Procedure	Stages of ratification	Date of lodging ratification instrument
Belgium	Parliamentary (ratification by the seven parliaments at the various levels of authority (Federal level [Senate and Chamber] + 2 Communities and 3 Regions)	Adopted by the Senate on 7 March 2002. Adopted by the Chamber on 28 March (106 for, 24 against, 7 abstentions). Adopted by the Conseil de la Communauté française on 23 April. Adopted by the Conseil régional wallon on 29 May. Adopted by the Vlaamse Raad on 19 June. Adopted by the Rat der Deutschsprachigen Gemeinschaft on 24 June. Adopted by the Parlement de la Région de Bruxelles-Capitale on 2 July 2002	26 August 2002
Denmark	Parliamentary (Folketing)	Draft ratification law adopted by the Folketing on 1 June 2001 (98 for, 14 against, 1 abstention). Signed by the Queen on 7 June 2001	13 June 2001
Germany	Parliamentary (Bundestag + Bundesrat)	Adopted by the Bundestag on 18 October 2001 (570 for, 32 against, 2 abstentions). Adopted by the Bundesrat on 9 November 2001 (unanimously). Signed by the President on 21 December 2001.	11 February 2002
Greece	Parliamentary	Adopted by the Chamber on 20 March 2002 (253 for, 10 against, 3 abstentions)	3 June 2002
Spain	Parliamentary (Congreso + Senado)	Adopted by the Congreso on 4 October 2001 (290 for, 6 abstentions). Adopted by the Senado on 24 October 2001 (213 for, 2 abstentions). Royal assent given on 10 December 2001.	27 December 2001

France	Parliamentary (Assemblée nationale + Sénat)	Draft ratification law adopted by the Assemblée Nationale on 12 June 2001 (407 for, 27 against, 113 abstentions) Adopted by the Sénat on 28 June 2001 (288 for, 8 against)	19 October 2001
Ireland	Parliamentary (Seanad + Dáil) and referendum	Publication of the ratification bill on 29 March 2001. Referendum (7 June 2001): NO (53,87%). National debate. Second referendum on 19 October 2002: YES (62,89%). Adopted by the Seanad on 20 November. Adopted by the Dáil on 28 November. Signed by the President and the Taoiseach on 10 December 2002	18 December 2002
Italy	Parliamentary (Camera + Senato)	Submission of the draft ratification law to the Camera on 17 September 2001. Adopted by the Camera on 26 March 2002 (298 for, 7 against, 6 abstentions). Adopted by the Senato by a very large majority (show of hands) on 7 May 2002	9 July 2002
Luxembourg	Parliamentary (Chamber of Deputies)	Adopted by the Chamber of Deputies on 12 July 2001 (57 for, 1 against, 2 abstentions). Act sanctioned by the Grand Duke on 1 August 2001.	24 September 2001
Netherlands	Parliamentary (Eerste Kamer + Tweede Kamer)	Draft ratification law submitted to the Tweede Kamer on 18 June 2001. Adopted by the Tweede Kamer on 22 November 2001 (vote by show of hands: very large majority "for"). Adopted by the Eerste Kamer on 19 December 2001.	28 December 2001
Austria	Parliamentary (Nationalrat + Bundesrat)	Draft constitutional law adopted unanimously by the Nationalrat on 23 October 2001 and by the Bundesrat on 8 November 2001. Draft ratification law adopted unanimously by the Nationalrat on 21 November 2001 and adopted by the Bundesrat on 6 December 2001. Signed by the President on 14 December 2001.	8 January 2002

Portugal	Parliamentary (Assembleia da República)	Draft ratification law adopted by the Assembleia da República on 25 October 2001 (211 for, 19 against). Signed by the President of the Republic on 11 December 2001.	18 January 2002
Finland	Parliamentary (Eduskunta)	Adopted by Eduskunta on 14 December 2001 (170 for, 9 against, 20 abstentions). Signed by the President on 4 January 2002. Adopted by the Åland Assembly on 25 January 2002.	29 January 2002
Sweden	Parliamentary (Riksdag)	Draft ratification law presented in September 2001. Adopted by Riksdag on 6 December 2001 (249 for, 51 against, 4 abstentions)	25 January 2002
United Kingdom	Parliamentary (House of Commons + House of Lords)	Presentation of ratification bill and 1st reading in the House of Commons on 21 June 2001. Second reading on 4 July 2001. Adopted by the House of Commons on 17 October 2001 (392 for, 158 against). Second reading in the House of Lords 1 November 2001 (no vote). Adopted by the house of Lords at third reading (no vote) on 28 January 2001. Royal assent: 26 February 2002.	25 July 2002

Source: http://europa.eu.int/comm/nice_treaty/ratiftable_en.pdf

BIBLIOGRAPHY

Best, Edward (2000), "Crossing the Bridge of Size: Reaching a Deal at Nice," *Eipascope*, No. 2000/3, pp. 2-9.

— (2001), "The Treaty of Nice: Not Beautiful but It'll Do," *Eipascope* No. 2001/1, pp. 2-9.

—, Mark Gray and Alexander Stubb (eds.) (2000), *Rethinking the European Union: IGC 2000 and Beyond.* Maastricht: European Institute of Public Administration.

Church, Clive (2001), "Intergovernmental Conferences and Treaty Reform: The Nice Experience," in Martyn Bond and Kim Feus (eds.), *The Treaty of Nice explained.* London: Federal Trust and Kogan Page, pp. 75-95.

CONFER 4750/00: Conference of the Representatives of the Governments of the Member States, "Intergovernmental Conference on Institutional Reform. Presidency report to the Feira European Council," Brussels, 14 June 2000.

— 4790/00: Conference of the Representatives of the Governments of the Member States, "Summary: Progress report on the Intergovernmental Conference on institutional reform," Brussels, 3 November 2000.

— 4795/00: Conference of the Representatives of the Governments of the Member States, "Presidency note: Extension of qualified majority voting," Brussels, 9 November 2000.

— 4810/00: Conference of the Representatives of the Governments of the Member States, "Revised Summary," Brussels, 23 November 2000.

— 4815/00: Conference of the Representatives of the Governments of the Member States, "Revised Summary," Brussels, 30 November 2000.

— 4816/00: Conference of the Representatives of the Governments of the Member States, "Draft Treaty of Nice," Brussels, 6 December 2000.

Dinan, Desmond and Sophie Vanhoonacker (2000a), "IGC 2000 Watch (Part I): Origin and Preparation," *ECSA Review*, Vol. 13, No. 2 (Spring, pp. 19-21.

— (2000b), "IGC 2000 Watch (Part 2): The Opening Round," *ECSA Review*, Vol. 13, No. 3 (Summer), pp. 7-9.

— (2000c), "IGC Watch (Part 3): Pre- and Post-Nice," *ECSA Review*, Vol. 13, No. 4 (Fall), pp. 1-2.

— (2001), "IGC Watch (Part4): Long Live the IGC," *ECSA Review*, Vol. 14, No. 1 (Winter), pp. 1 + 20-21.

Duke, Simon (2000), "From Feira to Nice: more *bonnes paroles*?, *Eipascope*, No. 2000/3, pp. 14-18.

— (2001), "After the Applause Stops: Nice's Aftermath and the Prospects for CESDP," *Eipascope*, No. 2001/1, pp. 24-26.

European Commission (1999), "Adapting the Institutions to make a success of enlargement: Contribution by the European Commission to preparations for the Intergovernmental Conference on institutional issues. Presented by the President and Mr Barnier," 10 November.
http://www.europa.eu.int/comm/archives/igc2000/offdoc/prep_igc.en.pdf

— (2000a), "Adapting the institutions to make a success of enlargement: Commission Opinion in accordance with Article 48 of the Treaty on European Union on the calling of a Conference of Representatives of Governments of the Member States to amend the Treaties," COM (2000) 34, 26 January.
http://www.europa.eu.int/comm/archives/igc2000/offdoc/opin_igc_en.pdf

— (2000), "Conférence 2000: Fiches thématiques, »
http://europa.eu.int/comm/igc2000/geninfo/fact-sheets/index_fr.htm

European Council (1999a), "Presidency Conclusions. Cologne European Council, 3 and 4 June." Presidency Conclusions can be downloaded from
http://ue.eu.int/newsroom/newmain.asp?lang=1

— (1999b), "Presidency Conclusions. Helsinki European Council 10 and 11 December."

— (2000a), "Presidency Conclusions. Santa Maria Da Feira European Council 19 and 20 June 2000."

—— (2000b), "Presidency Conclusions. Nice European Council Meeting 7, 8 and 9 December."
European Parliament (2001), "Resolution of the European Parliament on the convening of the Intergovernmental Conference (14094/1999 – C5-0341/1999 – 1999/0825(CNS))," http://www.europarl.eu.int/igc2000/offdoc/pdf/res03022000_en.pdf
——, Commission des Affaires Constitutionelles (2001), "Projet du Traité de Nice (première analyse), " PE 294.737. Bruxelles, 10 January.
European Union (1997), *Consolidated Treaties*. Luxembourg: Office for Official Publications of the European Communities.
—— (2001), *Treaty of Nice*. Luxembourg: Office for Official Publications of the European Communities. Also in *Official Journal* C80 (10.03.2001). Downloadable from http://www.europa.eu.int/eur-lex/en/treaties/index.html
Friis, Lykke og Niels-Jørgen Nehring (2000), "Den permanente regeringskonference," *Fokus* No.3.
—— and Trine Strøbech (eds.) (2001), *Towards a Nice Treaty? The Inter-governmental Conference 2000. Report from the DUPI Conference 21 November 2000.* Copenhagen: Danish Institute of International Affairs.
Galloway, David (2001), *The Treaty of Nice and Beyomd: Realities and Illusions of Power in the EU.* Sheffield: Sheffield Academic Press.
Kerremans, Bart (1998), "The Problem of Capacity and Control in an Enlarged EU Council," in Pierre-Henri Laurant and Marc Maresceau (eds.), *The State of the European Union*, Vol. 4, pp. 87-109.
Laursen, Finn (2001a), "EU Enlargement: Intersts, Issues and the Need for Institutional Reform," in Svein S. Andersen and Kjell A. Eliassen (eds.), *Making Policy In Europe*. 2nd ed. London: SAGE, pp. 206-228.
—— (2001b), *Guide til Nice-traktaten: Baggrund, kommentarer og perspektiver*. Copenhagen: The Danish European Movement.
—— (2002), "Institutions and Procedures: The Limited Reforms," in Finn Laursen (ed.), *The Amsterdam Treaty: National Preference Formation, Interstate Bargaining and Outcome.* Odense: Odense University Press, pp. 565-590.
Ludlow, Peter (2001), "The Treaty of Nice: Neither Triumph nor Disaster," *ECSA Review,* Vol. 14, No 2 (Spring), pp. 1 + 3-4.
Meunier, Sophie and Kalypso Nicolaïdis (2001), "Trade Competence in the Nice Treaty," *ECSA Review*, Vol. 14, No. 2 (Spring 2001), pp. 7-8.
Moe, Terry (1990), "Towards a Theory of Public Bureaucracy," in Oliver E. Williamson (ed.), *Organization Theory*. Oxford: Oxford University Press, pp. 116-153.
Moravcsik, Andrew (1993), "Preferences and Power in the European Community: A Liberal Intergovernmentalist Approach," *Journal of Common Market Studies*, Vol. 31, No. 4 (December), pp. 473-524.
—— (1998), *The Choice for Europe.* Ithaca, NY: Cornell University Press.
Nehring, Niels-Jørgen (2001), "Europæisk jeopardy – EU's regeringskonferencer siden 1990," *Politologiske Studier*, 4. årg, nr. 1 (marts), pp. 6-13.
Nicolaides, Phedon (2000), "The Feira European Council and the Process of Enlargement of the European Union," *Eipascope*, No. 2000/3, pp. 9-13.
Phillippart, Eric (2001), "The New Provisions on "Closer Cooperation": A Call for Prudent Politics," *ECSA Review*, Vol. 14, No. 2 (Spring), pp. 6-7.
Ross, George (2001), "France's European Tour of Duty, or Caution – One Presidency May Hide Another," *ECSA Review*, Vol. 14, No. 2 (Spring), pp. 4-6.
SN 511/00: "Meeting Document. Subject: Elements for an overall agreement," Nice, 9 December 2000. Kindly provided by the Danish Foreign Ministry.
—— 514/00: "Mødedokument. Vedr.: Elementer til en samlet aftale," Nice, 9. december 2000. Kindly provided by the Danish Foreign Ministry.

—— 521/00: Konferencen mellem repræsentanterne for medlemsstaternes regeringer, "Arbejdsdokument Vedr.: RK 2000 – Formandskabets endelige kompromisforslag," Nice, 10. december 2000. Kindly provided by the Danish Foreign Ministry.

—— 522/00: "Protocol on the Enlargement of the European Union and Declaration on the Enlargement of the European Union to be included in the Final Act of the Conference (This Annex Cancels and Replaces pages 88-96 of CONFER 4816/00)," Nice, 10 December 2000. Kindly provided by the Danish Foreign Ministry.

—— 533/00: "Treaty of Nice. Provisional text approved by the Intergovernmental Conference on institutional reform," Brussels, 12 December 2000. http://www.deltur.cec.eu.int/english/nicetreaty.pdf

Stubb, Alexander (2002), *Negotiating Flexibility in the European Union: Amsterdam, Nice and Beyond*. Houndsmills: Palgrave, 2002.

Von Kyaw, Dietrich (2001), "Nice Summit Sets the Course," *Internationale Politik (Transatlantic Edition)* Vol. 2, No. 1 (Spring), pp. 33-39.

Wessels, Wolfgang (2001), "Nice results: The Millenium IGC in the EU's evolution," *Journal of Common Market Studies*, Vol. 39, No. 2 (June), pp. 197-219.

Yataganas, Xenophon A. (2001), "The Treaty of Nice: The Sharing of Power and the Institutional Balance in the European Union – A Continental Perspective," Working Papers, The Jean Monnet Chair, Harvard Law School, 23 April 2001. http://www.jeanmonnetprogram. org/papers/01/010101.html

SECTION 1

NATIONAL PREFERENCE FORMATION

CHAPTER 2

AUSTRIA: BETWEEN SIZE AND SANCTIONS

INTRODUCTION

A fortnight before the start of the IGC in 2000, the Portuguese Presidency issued a *statement* containing a direct warning addressed to Austria that diplomatic sanctions would be introduced against it should the right-wing FPÖ party under Jörg Haider participate in the formation of the new government (Statement, 2000). When the new coalition-cabinet of Mr. Schüssel, including members of the conservative ÖVP party and the FPÖ,[1] was formally installed by the President of the Republic on 4 February 2000, these sanctions became effective.

Ten days later, on 14 February 2001, the IGC was officially launched. During the following seven months of 'quarantine' (Hummer and Pelinka, 2002), the Austrian public debate on Europe and the EU Treaty revision were eclipsed by biased indignation among the population (either with regard to the sanctions or with regard to the government) and official endeavours of the incriminated government to restore Austria's European relations and to regain its international standing.

Against this background, Austria's main contribution to the IGC leading to a new Treaty of Nice concentrated on procedural improvements of Article 7 of the TEU, together with a few sensitive national issues such as the environment and social protection. Notwithstanding its modest impact on the final output of the conference, Austria successfully realised most of its objectives.

CONSTITUTIONAL IMPLICATIONS OF AUSTRIA'S MEMBERSHIP OF THE EU/ CHARACTERISTICS OF THE AUSTRIAN GOVERNMENTAL SYSTEM

Before analysing the Austrian position in the IGC, it is important to draw attention to the particularities of the underlying constitutional system governing Euro-Austrian relations. The act of joining the European Union in 1995 implied a total revision (*Gesamtänderung*) of the Austrian Constitution. A number of fundamental principles of the Constitution (*Baugesetze*),

---

[1] The four parties represented in the Austrian Parliament are the Christian Democratic Austrian People's Party (ÖVP), the Austrian Social Democratic Party (SPÖ), the Austrian Freedom Party (FPÖ) and the Austrian Green Party (Die Grünen).

such as those concerning democracy, the rule of law, federalism and the separation of powers were substantially affected by the massive transfer of sovereign rights to the EU. According to the Constitution a total revision necessitates not only a 2/3 majority in Parliament but equally requires a positive vote in a popular referendum., The referendum which took place on 12 June 1994 and produced a significant majority in favour of EU accession, was notably not about the issue of a total revision of the Constitution, but about the government's authority to conclude the accession treaty (Griller, 1995; Öhlinger and Potacs, 1998; Seidl-Hohenveldern, 1995).

On a general basis the Constitution only allows for transfers of singular national competences (Article 9 para. 2 B-VG), which falls short of covering acts such as the accession to the European Union and its *acquis communautaire*. As a result the Austrian government opted for a particular constitutional act (the so-called EU-Accession-Act) to legally anchor the accession to the Union.[2] This somewhat complicated procedure has since been used consistently after each Treaty revision,[3] except for the popular referendum, as the degree of legal implication on the Constitution, resulting from both the Treaty of Amsterdam and the Treaty of Nice, did not amount to a total revision. In other words, the conclusion of the constitutional acts on the accession to the Treaty of Amsterdam and to the Treaty of Nice required a qualified approval each time by both chambers of Parliament (*Nationalrat* and *Bundesrat*).

In addition to the authorisation of the total revision of the Constitution, the accession to the Union also entailed changes in Austrian constitutional law. Effectively, a number of new constitutional provisions had to be stipulated, dealing with procedural matters, covering aspects of nomination, participation and decision-making competences as well as the limitation of the discretionary powers of Austrian organs by the European Union institutions. For the sake of coherence a specific section on the European Union was introduced into the Constitution encompassing the relevant provisions.[4] The ratification of the Treaty of Amsterdam necessitated a further amendment of the Constitution, particularly due to Austria's unconditional obligation to fully implement the Common Foreign and Security Policy (CFSP) including active execution of the so-called Petersberg tasks.[5] The Austrian commit-

[2] Bundesverfassungsgesetz über den Beitritt Österreichs zur Europäischen Union, BGBl (Federal Law Gazette). 744/1994 of 09.09.1994.

[3] For the Treaty of Amsterdam see BGBl. I No. 76/1998; for the Treaty of Nice see BGBl. I No. 120/2001.

[4] Articles 23a – 23f B-VG.

[5] BGBl. I Nr. 83/1998. This constitutional act lead to an amendment of Article 23f B-VG.

ment to carry out crisis management operations touches upon the delicate issue of permanent neutrality, which is, however, not a fundamental principle of the Constitution and will not be analysed in further detail in this chapter.

Within the sphere of Euro-Austrian relations, the most fundamental characteristics of the constitutional system in Austria—compared to other national systems in the European Union—are twofold. On the one hand there is an important *federal* element, due to the significant role of the *Länder* and also to a lesser extent by the decreasingly important position of the formerly powerful *Sozialpartner* in the governmental decision making process.[6] On the other hand, the Austrian Parliament takes a strong stance with regard to controlling and influencing European affairs, at least following the wording of the Constitution, which we will summarise as the *parliamentary* element.

Starting with the federal aspect, Article 23d of the Austrian Constitution (B-VG) confers direct participation rights to the nine *Länder.* In case any issue negotiated at the European level correlates with the constitutionally guaranteed legislative competences of the *Länder,* they can issue a common opinion which is binding on the federal government. Moreover, in such a case the federal government may even entrust decision-making powers in the Council to a representative of the *Länder.* In practice, however, this instrument is hardly ever used and the number of opposing opinions by the *Länder* are negligible.

With regard to the parliamentary aspect, among the EU Member States, Austria has the strongest constitutional provisions for parliamentary participation and control in EU policy making. Both chambers of the Parliament are legally entitled to assert extensive rights to information on EU matters from the government,[7] and the *Nationalrat* is empowered to adopt opinions that are binding on the Austrian government in all negotiations and voting in the EU (Falkner, 2000). In practice, most parliamentary work on European issues is prepared in the Main Committee on European Affairs (*Hauptausschuss*), which, since 1999, is assisted by a Standing Sub-Committee on European Affairs. In return, following a vote in the Council the respective federal minister has to forward a report to the *Nationalrat.* Deviation from this procedure is restricted to cases where there are imperative foreign and

[6] The informal construction of social partners in Austria is composed of the following institutions: Chamber of Business (Wirtschaftskammer Österreich), the Chamber of Labour (Bundesarbeiterkammer), the Conference of Presidents of the Chambers of Agriculture (PRÄKO) and the Austrian Trade Union Confederation (ÖGB).

[7] Actually the Austrian Parliamentary Administration receives between 17,000 and 22,000 documents a year, which in 2001 amounted to around 60 documents a day. In practice, the extensive transmission of (uncommented) information by the executive to the Parliament comes nearer to a deliberate overloading than to supportive information sharing.

integration policy reasons and only if the *Nationalrat* does not object within an appropriate period of time to such departure.[8] However, similar to the *Länder*, the Austrian Parliament exercises its influential rights with care and reservation, striking a balance between effective democratic control and necessary flexibility for the minister negotiating in Brussels.

In concrete figures this means that while the main Committee adopted 18 binding opinions in the first year of EU membership, it adopted only one in 1998 and 1999 and two in 2001 (Pollack and Slominski, 2003). This considerable shift in the numbers of parliamentary opinions clearly reflects the decreasing intensity of co-operation between the political parties in EU affairs and, at the same time, a growing importance of the classical intra-governmental deals between the legislative and executive branch.[9] In other words, as Pollack and Slominski put it: "the decline of binding opinions can best be explained by the salience of the intragovernmental mode, i.e. the maintenance of party discipline in EU affairs and by the perception of MPs that binding opinions are narrowing the room for manoeuvre for the Austrian representative in the Council" (Pollack and Slominski, 2003). Moreover, one has to take into consideration that effective control and participation of the Parliament, which is confronted with an abundance of EU legislation, requires respective experts and permanent structures. In Austria, discussions in the Main Committee on EU affairs are limited to monthly meetings, which impressively mirrors the intrinsic contradiction between formal strength and active output.

The Impact of the Sanctions Against Austria

Although an overwhelming majority of 66.58% of the Austrian population voted in favour of EU accession in June 1994, public support and confidence in the system of the Union almost immediately lost ground and gave way to wide-spread scepticism. The declining popularity of EU membership was clearly reflected by the substantial gains of the EU-sceptic party, the FPÖ, in the 1999 governmental elections (21.9% in 1995 and 26.9% in 1999). In

[8] Article 23e para. 2 B-VG; The German original version speaks of "zwingende außen- und integrationspolitische Gründe."

[9] Another reason refers to a bad experience concerning an EC directive on animal transport. In this case Austria was outvoted in the Council of Ministers because the *Nationalrat* could not be consulted in time. As a consequence Austria not only had to accept considerably lower standards than those already guaranteed at the national level, it also failed to give way to a more acceptable compromise which was under discussion.

2001, only 34% of the Austrians believed that EU membership was beneficial for the country (Pelinka, 2002).[10]

The imposition of the sanctions against Austria aggravated the negative stance towards the EU. A general *statement* issued on 31 January 2000 by the Portuguese Presidency[11] on behalf of the EU-14 declared that these Member States "will not promote or accept any official bilateral contacts at political level with an Austrian government integrating the FPÖ," moreover that "there will be no support for Austrian candidates seeking positions in international organisations" and, finally, that "Austrian Ambassadors in EU capitals will only be received at a technical level." Through a special declaration issued one day later, the European Commission took note of the *statement* and explicitly added its voice to the expressions of concern about the underlying political situation in Austria.[12] In its function as guardian of the Treaties the Commission emphasised its obligation to preserve and guarantee the principles anchored in Articles 6 and 7 of the TEU. However, the Commission did not opt for any rupture of working relations with Austria, but announced it would closely observe the political situation in the country.

Similarly the European Parliament issued a resolution explicitly referring to the *statement* of the Portuguese Presidency of 31 January 2000 and the declaration of the Commission dated 1 February 2000.[13] The European Parliament explicitly warned about potential repercussions when accepting parties of the extreme right within coalition governments in EU Member States, particularly in light of the rigid Maastricht criteria in terms of democratic values and the rule of law, which the candidate countries are obliged to respect. Effectively, the European Parliament was the first to concretely associate the participation of the FPÖ with the general legitimation of extreme right governments in Europe. Against this background, the European Parliament requested that the Council and the Commission together survey future developments in Austria, paying particular attention to incidents of racism and xenophobia. In case of grave and continuous breaches of the principles stipulated in Article 6 TEU, both institutions would, after the approval of the European Parliament, take the necessary measures according to Article 7

---

[10] Eurobarometer 55 (spring 2001) printed in *Pelinka* (2002).

[11] "Statement from the Portuguese Presidency of the European Union on behalf of XIV Member States" of 31.01.2000, in: *Bulletin Quotidien Europe* No. 7645 of 31.1/1.2. 2000, 9. The fact that the *statement* was written on official notepaper of the Presidency may indicate that the threat of sanctions against Austria was not only of a bilateral nature.

[12] European Commission, Austria: Declaration by the Commission, Brussels, 1 February 2000, IP/00/93.

[13] European Parliament, Resolution of 3 February 2000, PE 284.656.

TEU. When, on 4 February 2000 the Austrian President formerly installed the ÖVP-FPÖ cabinet, the sanctions as set out in the *statement* of the Presidency became effective.

However, two main problems overshadowed the whole procedure of implementing the sanctions. First of all, diplomatic sanctions were imposed, on the one hand, by the EU-14 without any confirmation or proof of breaches of the agreed values incorporated in Article 6 TEU attributable to the new government, and on the other hand, by simply ignoring Austria's right to be heard. According to Article 7 TEU no such hearing was legally required, but such an obligation is implied, at least implicitly, in the reference in Article 6 para. 1 TEU, according to which the "Union is founded (...) on the principle of (...) the rule of law, principles which are common to the Member States." Moreover, in the given context the right to be heard belongs to the sphere of public international law known as *international courtoisie* (Hummer, 2001). Since the declaration of the EU-14 was neither issued by the Council nor by the Commission and was not legally based on Article 7 TEU, one has to conclude that the initiative can not be qualified as an EU-act but as an act of international public law. In other words, since the conditions for launching the procedure of Article 7 TEU have never existed (or have never been proven to exist) one may conclude that the collective set of bilateral actions taken by the EU-14 were not covered by the Treaties, but belonged exclusively to the sphere of intergovernmental co-ordination.

The second problem regards the absolute lack of the fourteen foreseeing any exit strategy. Apparently, the EU-14 relied exclusively on the deterrent effect of their collective threat of diplomatic sanctions, so they did not even consider that they should prepare for the actual reality of FPÖ participation in the Austrian government. In return, there was no chance for the Austrian government to improve its standing except by its collective removal from office, which was in direct opposition to the intentions of the government.

The policy of deliberate isolation used by the EU-14 was perceived by the Austrian population as an act of unlawful interference by the *Union* in national affairs. It is argued that this interpretation reveals the general conviction among the Austrian population that Austria still unconditionally disposes of its sovereign rights (Pelinka, 2002). On the other hand, it seems necessary to adopt a more differentiated view. In Austria it is commonly agreed—not only among the population but also at the political and academic level—that the fact of EU membership does not prejudice core elements of the Austrian constitutional system. These elements are, among others, the commitment to neutrality and to human rights. The decision by the EU-14 to challenge the legitimacy of the democratically elected Austrian government was perceived in Austria as directly affecting the protected constitutional sphere.

In addition, reactions varied between the governmental parties and the opposition. The EU-friendly ÖVP and the FPÖ, which then formed the government, described the sanctions as a discrimination against the country and against European law. This stance was especially prevalent because at the instance of Austria's President Mr. Klestil, the new coalition had added a specific declaration labelled "Verantwortung für Österreich—Zukunft im Herzen Europas" ("Responsibility for Austria—Future in the heart of Europe") to the preamble of their coalition pact, in order to demonstrate their full commitment to the European project. In addition, Mr. Haider, the leader of the FPÖ had announced that he would resign from office, a promise he realised shortly afterwards.

The opposition however, in the form of the Social-Democrat party SPÖ, expressed their sympathy towards the measures pursued by the EU-14; particularly, they welcomed the explicit rejection of xenophobia and the position adopted with regard to the dangers of any participation of the FPÖ in the Austrian government.[14]

Since every attempt by the Austrian political parties to collectively repudiate the *statement* by the EU-14 during the preliminary stages of the sanctions had failed,[15] the latent discord between the former coalition partners finally came to the surface. As a consequence of the internal political antagonism, Austria was deprived of a unified political response to the sanctions (Hummer, 2001),[16] while the EU-14 increasingly felt the pressure of a missing back door.

It was finally the European Parliament which resolved the impasse by issuing a resolution on 13 June 2000, charging the Portuguese Presidency with assessing the relations between the EU-14 and Austria and with developing a strategy which might eventually lead to an acceptable solution. Already before, the Austrian government had announced a plan of action according to which it would organise a public opinion poll *(Volksbefragung)*[17] in accordance with the Constitution, in case the sanctions would not be lifted

---

[14] See the declarations of the respective parties: 105/AE XXI.GP and 106/AE XXI.GP.

[15] At the occasion of the last ministerial meeting of the former SPÖ-ÖVP government, the ÖVP tried in vain to persuade its coalition partner to adopt a "Declaration on behalf of the federal government" aiming at collectively rejecting the reproaches expressed in the statement of the 14.

[16] Only the *Landeshauptleutekonferenz* ("Conference of the regional governors") succeeded in issueing a declaration in unanimity, in which they proposed to introduce a more transparent system to survey the compliance of Member States with regard to the principles of democracy, the rule of law and fundamental rights.

[17] Article 49b B-VG.

by the end of the Portuguese Presidency.[18] Most controversially the government did not only intend to enquire about the sanctions, but equally about whether the Austrians still wished to uphold EU-membership. It is interesting to observe, that even at this point, after months of international isolation there was no political agreement in Austria.[19]

Two days before the end of its term, the Portuguese Presidency tabled a proposal. It contained an exit-strategy which envisaged the empowering of the President of the European Court for Human Rights, Mr. Luzius Wildhaber, to appoint three prominent persons and to give them a mandate to compile a report on Austria. The report was to include the results arrived at after close scrutiny of the Austrian position towards European values, particularly those concerning the protection of minorities, refugees and immigrants and also after an examination of the political nature of the FPÖ. After a period of barely two months, the three so called 'Wise Men' Martii Ahtisaari, Jochen Frowein and Marcelino Oreja forwarded their results to the French Presidency.

They confirmed that European values were fully applied and defended by the Austrian government.[20] As to the nature of the FPÖ, they sustained in principle the objection to a populist right-wing party containing radical elements. However, it was stated that the respective representatives of the FPÖ in the government generally aligned themselves to the pre-defined obligations, which might eventually lead to a process of the re-orientation of the party.[21] In their conclusions—and thereby exceeding their original mandate—they recommended that the sanctions should be lifted because of their counterproductive effects. As a consequence and because of massive pressure by Denmark, which feared negative side effects for its Euro-Referendum,[22] the French Presidency formerly terminated the sanctions on 12 September 2000. However, in its declaration the Presidency insisted that

---

[18] See *Die Presse [Online-Archiv]* of 06.05.2000, Lenkt EU bis Juni nicht ein kommt eine Volksbefragung.

[19] See Report of the Main Committee of 11.07.2001, in: *268 Beilagen zu den Stenographischen Protokollen des Nationalrates, XXI. GP;* see also *Die Presse [Online-Archiv]* of 05.05.2000, EU-Sanktionen: Keine gemeinsame Linie, auch nicht zur Volksbefragung.

[20] Report by Martii Ahtisaari, Jochen Frowein and Marcelino Oreja [*Weisenbericht*], Paris, 8 September 2000, para. 108-109.

[21] Report by Martii Ahtisaari, Jochen Frowein and Marcelino Oreja [*Weisenbericht*], Paris, 8. September 2000, para. 110-113.

[22] See *Die Presse [Online-Archiv]* of 19.05.2000, Rasmussen für Abbau der Sanktionen.

the EU-14 maintained a sort of collective monitoring of the further development of the FPÖ.

AUSTRIA'S POSITIONS IN THE IGC

Given the predefined agenda of the IGC 2000 containing the so-called Amsterdam *leftovers,*[23] the basic principles of Austria's position as adopted by the Austrian government and presented a few days before the official start of the IGC, clearly reflected the concerns of a small country on these issues.[24] However, not only due to its size but also as a direct neighbour to four out of ten candidate countries, Austria's approach towards the IGC 2000 was driven by an interest in preparing the Union's institutions for enlargement and safeguarding its own interests with regard to the decision making process. More concretely, the Austrian position was underpinned by the following considerations:

- "Efficient and transparent institutions and meaningful decision making processes in the EU make for greater confidence and involvement in the Union and its institutions on the part of the citizen.
- Because of its concern for the Union to be capable of action and able to assume its responsibility for stability throughout Europe, Austria is in favour of consolidating the institutional structure of the European Union and will accordingly oppose any weakening of the current degree of integration. The most important aim of the forthcoming Intergovernmental Conference is to create the conditions for the EU institutions to remain operational and efficient in an enlarged Union.
- On the issue of taking account of population size, Austria's interests naturally coincide with those of the smaller and medium-sized Member States. The way the institutional set-up of the European Union enables these countries to share in decision-making and to look after their own interests is for Austria a vital feature of European integration.
- The forthcoming Intergovernmental Conference should concentrate on its essential task of preparing the Union's institutions for enlargement. Community policies do not enter into the negotiations. The work on a European security and defence policy and on the Charter of Fundamental Rights of the Union running concurrently with the Intergovernmental Conference might require Treaty amendments that could be dealt with by the Intergovernmental Conference at a later date."

---

[23] The Amsterdam *leftovers* are summarised in the 'Protocol on the institutions with the prospect of enlargement of the European Union' appended to the Treaty of Amsterdam. They refer to the size and composition of the Commission, the weighting of votes in the Council, the possible extension of qualified majority voting in the Council as well as other necessary amendments to the Treaties arising as regards the European institutions in connection with the above issues and in implementing the Treaty of Amsterdam.

[24] Basic principles of Austria's position, CONFER 4712/00.

In the position paper, particular attention was paid to the position of the Commission as a strong and independent institution. Despite the fact that Commissioners are not supposed to act as representatives of their country of origin, an exclusion would be received by the public as an illegitimate act against the principle of equality. Against this background, Austria insisted on the right of every Member State to appoint at least one member of the Commission. Accordingly, Austria rejected any idea of 'junior commissioners,' firmly claiming that the collegial nature of the Commission and the equal status of all its members be maintained. To support the argument Austria insisted that "it is not the size of the Commission that determines the capacity to act,"[25] pointing at the necessity of a structural reorganisation of the Commission. However, these kind of reforms were not on the agenda of the IGC, since they did not imply any amendment to the Treaties. The final solution to accept one commissioner per country from January 2005 until the 27th Member State has joined the Union, constitutes an interim arrangement which already includes future concessions by all Member States as to the size and composition of the College.

In return Austria expressed its willingness to accept a modest adjustment of Council votes provided that it would not undermine the relative strength of the small EU Member States in the decision-making process. In this respect Austria pleaded for the establishment of "objective, verifiable criteria that the European public can easily grasp," which would be of a definitive and reform-resistant nature. From an Austrian perspective, any new voting model should come into force at the same moment as the new Member States accede to the Union.

With regard to the extension of qualified majority voting in the Council, Austria generally adopted a positive stance. On the other hand, it outlined a number of "particularly sensitive areas," where unanimity should be maintained, specifying water resources, regional planning, land use and choice of energy sources. Austrians particularly fear any kind of compulsory sale of its rich water resources as soon as it foregoes its sovereign rights to them. This argument was frequently put forward by the FPÖ together with the explicit threat to refuse the necessary ratification of the final Treaty of Nice should it contain any regulation that it opposed.[26] In this respect the final Article 175 para. 2 TEC incorporated into the Treaty of Nice is even more explicit than

---

[25] Basic principles of Austria's position, CONFER 4712/00.

[26] Similarly the FPÖ announced its decision to block the Austrian ratification process of the Accession Treaties regarding the ten new EU Member States, should the open question of the Czech Benes-Decrees and the Slovenian Avnoj-Decrees not be resolved beforehand. For further information see http://www.modernpolitics.at/de/europa/avnoj_benes.php [19.04.2004].

its predecessor, providing for i.a., an exemption from the rule of qualified majority voting in the sphere of environmental policy with regard to "quantitative management of water resources or affecting, directly or indirectly, the availability of those resources." Similarly, due to massive opposition to nuclear power among the Austrian population, any deviation from the still exclusive right to chose the form of energy generation at the national level, which might allow for EU-wide nuclear power plants, would strengthen anti-European voices in Austria. Once again these concerns were met in Article 175 para. 2 lit. c TEC by excluding qualified majority voting for "measures significantly affecting a Member State's choice between different energy sources and the general structure of its energy supply."

Additionally, Austria stressed the importance of closing some legal gaps in the Treaties, such as the question of individual responsibility of the members of the Commission. To this end it supported the idea of conferring on the President of the European Commission the right to dismiss individual members. Moreover, Austria upheld the position to generally extend the co-decision procedure to those areas where qualified majority voting is applied, including matters relating to economic and monetary union. Finally, Austria pleaded for cautious reforms of the European Court of Justice, aiming at improving its efficiency in order to adapt it to increased responsibilities and the resulting increased workload, which most probably will get even heavier after enlargement. In this respect Austria also advocated the idea to vest the Court of First Instance with additional powers. Similarly, Austria raised the question of the future allocation of seats in the EU institutions, above all in the European Parliament. In this respect Austria's contingent was reduced from 21 to 17 MEPs by the Treaty of Nice. This outcome was roughly aligned to the model of degressive proportionality, which was generally applied except with regard to Luxembourg and Germany which both maintained their number of deputies, although for different reasons. However, Austria did not adopt any clear position as regards the incorporation of the Charter of Fundamental Rights into the Treaties or with regard to the future development of the European Security and Defence Policy. Referring these questions to the discussion at the IGC as a whole, Austria simply asked that the IGC "maintain an open position on these issues also."

Apart from the general position paper, Austria only issued two more contributions during the IGC. These were, however, closely linked to crucial issues at the national level. First of all due to its own experiences during the period of sanctions, Austria was particularly concerned about setting up an early warning system for potential and actual breaches of human rights in the European Union. Already at the beginning of May 2000, the Belgian Delegation, which was one of the most active proponents of the sanctions against Austria, had raised the issue. One month later Austria presented a counter-proposal for a reworded Article 7 TEU to the IGC, with the objective of anchoring the principle of a fair hearing and, in case of necessity, to ensure that any kind of countermeasure is appropriate and proportionate. The whole procedure should also be subject to judicial review by the European Court of Justice.[27] Against this background, one should bear in mind that already in March 2000 the Austrian President had addressed a letter to the then President of the Council, A. Guterres, proposing a reform of Article 7 TEU allowing for preventive measures in case of potential breaches of the above mentioned rule.[28] Additional substance was given to these claims by the final report on Austria by the three 'Wise Men' which was published on 8 September 2000.[29] Following the informal summit of the European Council in Biarritz on 13 to14 October 2000, the mandate of the IGC was officially extended to this question (Schorkopf, 2002).[30]

The final version incorporated into the Treaty of Nice closely followed the Austrian proposal. According to the new rule, any decision by the Council on sanctions against a Member State would require a previous determination by the Council—acting by unanimity and after obtaining assent from the European Parliament—of the "existence of a serious and persistent breach by a Member State of the principles mentioned in Article 6 (1)." In the preliminary stages of this process the Council, acting by a majority of four-fifths of its members, and equally with assent from the European Parliament, may determine that "there is a clear risk of a serious breach" of the principles in question. Moreover, as it happened in the case of sanctions against Austria, the Council may appoint independent persons to submit a report on the situation in the Member State in question. Additionally, the Council is obliged to regularly verify the validity of its determination. However, Austria had to accept one reservation: the European Court's competence to review measures taken under Article 7 TEU is restricted to "purely procedural stipulations,"[31] and therefore excludes substantial questions from judicial control.

---

[27] ONFER 4748/00 Draft amendments to Articles 7 and 46 of the TEU.

[28] An abstract of the letter is to be found in Bulletin Quotidien Europe, No. 7683 of 24 March 2000.

[29] Report on Austria by *Ahtisaari, Frohwein* and *Oreja.*

[30] All together there had been four proposals regarding an amendment to Article 7 TEU: Proposal by the Belgian Delegation CONFER 4739/00 of 2 May 2000; Proposal by the Austrian Delegation CONFER 4748/00 of 7 June 2000; Proposal by the Portuguese Presidency CONFER 4750/00 of 14 June 2000 and proposal by the Commission IP/00/1116 and CONFER 4782/00 of 5 October 2000.

[31] Article 46 lit. 3 TEU.

A second contribution forwarded during the IGC was aimed at clarifying the applicability of Article 42 TEC on self-employed persons, even pushing for an extension to other categories of people than those already covered by the legal norm.[32]

THE IGC PROCESS AND NEGOTIATIONS

During the negotiation process Austria was truly committed to carrying through its position. In return, it became apparent that the most controversial questions, such as the composition of the Commission, the re-weighting of votes in the Council and the extension of qualified majority voting in certain areas would be postponed to high-level discussions at the European Council summit in Nice. In the meantime, Austria successfully built alliances with other small and medium-sized countries, particularly with regard to its most sensitive issues.

After the informal summit in Biarritz of 13-14 October 2000, when even the large countries had to admit that they would not maintain their initial position of capping the Commission, due to the massive front of smaller countries, Austria was among those firmly defending their mandate. It cannot be qualified as a victory since in this battle national interests strongly prevailed over European or common interests, but it confirmed the strategy of active coalition building among equals to eventually win in European bargaining. However, the arrangement adopted at Nice is limited in time. It will be upheld until 2009. From then on, following a Council decision based on unanimity, the College will be reduced on the basis of equal rotation. Furthermore, the Member States agreed on a stronger position for the President of the Commission and the inclusion of a right to dismiss individual commissioners.

Concerning the extension of qualified majority voting Austria, together with Greece, firmly upheld the rejection of any loosening of the unanimity principle with regard to environmental issues, namely water resources, regional planning and the choice of the energy supply. By contrast, Austria conceded to accept qualified majority voting in the field of environment policy with regard to taxation (Article 175 para. 2 TEC), which however met with strong opposition from Great Britain, Luxembourg, Spain and Greece. Although Austria generally adopted a positive stance towards applying qualified majority voting in the area of social policy, its Delegation insisted on safeguarding unanimity concerning social security for workers [Article

[32] CONFER 4769/00 of 11 September 2000.

137 para. 3 (1) TEC]. Furthermore, Austria pleaded for the explicit extension of the scope of social protection to the self-employed. Austria failed to fulfil this objective, mainly because of the fact that due to relevant secondary law, the EU rules on social protection are already equally applicable to the self-employed.[33]

Furthermore, Austria together with Italy supported the idea to generally apply qualified majority voting in the realm of taxation. The Austrian Delegation also proposed the introduction of an enabling clause into the Treaties allowing for harmonisation of direct taxes. This competence should become effective not only for the sole reason of guaranteeing the functioning of the internal market, but should equally be triggered when confronted with arguments in support of a comprehensive European economic policy based on economic growth and employment.

More generally speaking, it was at the informal summit in Biarritz that most of the participants and observers had to admit that due to substantial but still unresolved questions, the IGC was facing a crisis, which most probably would lead to a virtual failure of the original mandate. Against this background, the proposal of a *post-Nice-process* was voiced for the first time. A process which should not only tackle the *left-overs* originating from the IGC 2000, but should go further in preparing grounds for a European Constitution. It was Germany in particular, and to a certain extent Austria, that openly referred to the post-Nice-process as a remedy to resolving questions such as the limitation of competences between the Union and the Member States (Fischer, 2003).

Concerning issues which did not appear on the IGC agenda, Austria was particularly interested in adding the question of EU accession to the European Convention on Human Rights. This intention clearly overlapped with the unresolved question about the fate of the EU Charter of Fundamental Rights and any further discussion was thus postponed. Similarly without any success, the Austrian Delegation advanced arguments in favour of an adaptation of the Euratom Treaty. The issue of nuclear energy use is closely linked to Austrian opposition to the operationalization of the Czech nuclear power plant in Temelin.

The Nice Summit and the Ratification Process

[33] See Regulation (EEC) No 1408/71 of the Council of 14 June 1971 on the application of social security schemes to employed persons and their families moving within the Community, OJ (1971) L 149/2.

After ten months of intensive discussion, the IGC closed with the summit of the European Council in Nice on 7-11 December 2000.[34] In the time after, the Treaty of Nice underwent a technical and linguistic revision and was officially signed by the Head of States and Government on 26 February 2001. In order to respect the timetable on enlargement determined at the European Council summit in Helsinki, it was necessary to ratify the Treaty of Nice by the end of 2002. In a first declaration issued by the Chancellor of the Republic at the address of the *Nationalrat* in January 2001, he emphasised that despite the sanctions most objectives had been accomplished, at least from an Austrian perspective. Moreover he also pointed at the necessity to prepare for the post-Nice-process, however without giving any details.[35] The ratification process itself started in June 2001, after the respective governmental bill had been presented to the Parliament.[36]

Beforehand, according to the Austrian specific method of first providing a constitutional act on which to base the final ratification, a method which had already been applied during the ratification process of the Accession Treaty and the Treaty of Amsterdam, the Constitutional Committee of the Austrian Parliament issued its proposal on 25 April 2001. The proposal was passed in both of the parliamentary chambers, successfully fulfilling the required qualified majorities. Despite the unanimous approval by all parties represented in the Austrian Parliament, the Social Democratic party and the Green party openly criticised the Treaty of Nice qualifying it as an imperfect compromise. However, the common awareness as to the importance of having the Treaty in force before the pending enlargement, constituted a pressing argument in favour of positive votes.

Following this, the Constitutional Committee unanimously proposed to the *Nationalrat* on 14 November 2001 that the Treaty of Nice be ratified, which effectively happened one week later, again without any opposing vote. The second chamber of the Parliament likewise approved the ratification of the Treaty of Nice by unanimity. Although the Treaty of Nice was not received as a substantial improvement to the project of the European Union, it constituted however a partial success for smaller countries in general and for Austria in particular. According to the Chancellor, Mr. Schüssel, the Treaty of Nice constitutes 'real progress' and provides the necessary institu-

[34] See *Conclusions by the Presidency*, in: Bull. EU 12-2000, no. I.6.11.

[35] *Erklärung des Bundeskanzlers gemäß §19 Abs. 2 GOG zum Thema "Ergebnisse des Europäischen Gipfels von Nizza",* Stenographisches Protokoll des Nationalrates, XXI. Gesetzgebungsperiode, 55. Sitzung, 53 ff.

[36] 600. Beilage zu den Stenographischen Protokollen, XXI. Gesetzgebungsperiode.

tional adaptations for enlargement. Furthermore, he emphasised that it is possible "to think as a European and to represent national interests at the same time."[37] The leader of the opposition party, Mr. Gusenbauer, however pointed at the disappointing results with regard to institutional reform, but generally joined in with the positive conclusions. In other words, the Austrian objective to fully rehabilitate as an equal partner on the European stage and to adapt the Union for enlargement had gained such paramount importance that members of governmental and opposition parties did not even dare challenge the ratification process.

Conclusions and Looking Forward to the Post-Nice-Process

From an Austrian perspective the Treaty of Nice can be summarised as a successful project, despite the restricted agenda of the IGC and its modest output. One may critically observe that Austria's position did not go beyond the official mandate, leaving aside the parallel discussion on European Security and Defence Policy[38] and even abstaining from any official contribution to the issue of flexibility adopted by the IGC at the informal European Council summit in June 2000 in Feira. Despite starting from a most unfavourable position, Austria finally managed to achieve satisfactory results.

First, from the outset the general objective of preparing the EU institutions for enlargement was reached. Austria, always a keen supporter of opening the European Union to the countries of Central and Eastern Europe, welcomed the Treaty of Nice as a precondition for keeping to the enlargement schedule. However, Austria equally pleaded for a number of transitional measures, hoping to minimize at the national level some collateral effects resulting from the right of free movement of services or workers after the enlargement. In order to mitigate the firm position adopted by the Austrian government in this respect, it also proposed to conclude bilateral 'strategic partnerships' with candidatae countries, a proposal which was not, however,

---

[37] Plenarsitzung des Nationalrates, in: Parlamentskorrespondenz/01/11.05.2001/Nr. 349. In the German original version: "Das Ergebnis habe auch bewiesen dass man europäisch denken und zugleich nationale Interessen vertreten könne."

[38] On the national level however, the government commissioned a group of experts in January 2001, to elaborate a comprehensive security policy analysis. Following intensive discussions in a parliamentary sub-committee specifically set up for this purpose in 2001, the National Assembly adopted by majority on 12 December 2001 a new Security and Defence Doctrine on the basis of this analysis. In the Doctrine it was explicitly stated that Austria——as recently as by its unreserved participation in the EU's CFSP——has radically changed its status from a permanently neutral to a non-allied country; see *Austrian Security and Defence Doctrine*, edited by Federal Chancellery, Vienna 2002.

received with the expected enthusiasm.[39] From a broader perspective the record of the Treaty of Nice is rather mixed. The IGC 2000 failed to complete institutional reform, which is impressively illustrated by the complicated and time limited modifications of the Commission's composition set out in the Protocol on Enlargement appended to the Treaty, and by the almost immediate start of a new revision process formally institutionalised by the Laeken Declaration of 15 December 2001.[40] The choice of the innovative Convention method indicated the attempt to ensure participation and transparency and to combine diplomatic and parliamentary styles, it was, however, also designed to prevent a recurrence of the Nice debacle.

Secondly, the final result with regard to the weighting of the votes in the Council represents a fundamental success for the small and medium-sized countries, including Austria. Although one might suggest that this achievement to a great extent is based on national interests and a policy of continuous obstruction during the IGC against a more realistic or 'European' compromise (above all in an enlarged Union), it remains a diplomatic victory for the small EU members.

Thirdly, the period of sanctions, which overlapped exactly with the time schedule of the IGC, left a deep and lasting impression on Austria. Positive aspects of this were a comprehensive reanimation of the debate on the European Union within the country and also a reorientation of the governmental system having for too long covered any open controversy by an almost institutionalised "grand coalition" system. Moreover, it finally led to an improvement of Article 7 TEU in terms of clarity and functionality. Since the coming into force of the Treaty of Nice, the rule leading to sanctions expressly foresees—as it has been proposed and supported by Austria—a preliminary hearing of the 'incriminated' Member States and a pre-defined early-warning mechanism. Austria had had the doubtful role of constituting a failed example of how not to meet populist polemics and nationalistic trends in a Member State's party-spectrum. However, any formal improvement will have to be proven in practice, not at least depending on how the precondition of a "serious and persistent breach by a Member State of principles mentioned in Article 6 (1)" will be interpreted in a given future case.

Fourthly, Austria's positions with regard to the extension of qualified majority voting touching upon crucial issues such as water resources, regional planning and energy supply have been successfully upheld and defended. Again, from the outset this may be interpreted as relying upon purely national motivations of self-interest, however the preservation of these prerogatives, which mainly belong to the sphere of competences of the *Länder,*

[39] Österreich will Beziehungen zu den Staaten Ost- und Mitteleuropas intensivieren. Wien sucht Partner unter den EU-Kandidaten, *Handelsblatt,* 4 June 2001.
[40] Document SN 300/1/01/REV1 of 15 December 2001.

successfully strikes a balance between the European and the federal aspect of the Austrian constitutional system. The objective to make the extended scope of recipients which are provided by Article 42 TEC more explicit, could not be realised. However this concern has only been of a formal and not of a substantial nature.

Finally, the domestic ratification process of the Treaty of Nice has been both, most uncontroversial and smooth, allowing for quick and effective implementation. The underlying reasons have been analysed earlier, but may be summarised as the common objective to prepare the Union for enlargement and as an effort to present the country as a fully-fledged partner to the European project. Furthermore, the prospect of a more substantial post-Nice-process calmed critical voices and shifted the debate to the broader context of constitutionalising the European Union.

BIBLIOGRAPHY

Falkner, Gerda (2000), "How Pervasive are Euro-Politics? Effects of EU Membership on a New Member State," *Journal of Common Market Studies*, Vol. 38, No. 2, 223-250.

Fischer, Klemens (2003) (2nd ed.), *Der Vertrag von Nizza*. Baden-Baden: Nomos.

Griller, Stefan (1995), "Verfassungsfragen der österreichischen EU-Mitgliedschaft," *Zeitschrift für Rechtsvergleichung und Europarecht*, 89-115.

— and Hummer, Waldemar (eds.) (2002), *Die EU nach Nizza. Ergebnisse und Perspektiven*. Wien / New York: Springer.

Hummer, Waldemar (2001), "Eine Verfassung für die Europäische Union – eine Sicht aus Österreich," in Heiner Timmermann (ed.), *Eine Verfassung für die Europäische Union*. Opladen: Leske+Budrich, 107-145.

— and Anton Pelinka (2002), *Österreich unter „EU-Quarantäne": die "Maßnahmen der 14" gegen die österreichische Bundesregierung aus politikwissen-schaftlicher und juristischer Sicht ; Chronologie, Kommentar, Dokumentation*. Wien: Linde Verlag.

IGC (2000), *Intergovernmental Conference 2000. Basic Principles of Austria's position*, Brussels, 15 February 2000 (Doc. CONFER 4712/00).

— (2000), *Intergovernmental Conference 2000. Draft amendments to Articles 7 and 46 TEU*, Brussels, 7 June 2000 (Doc. CONFER 4748/00).

— (2000), *Intergovernmental Conference 2000. Proposed amendment to Article 42 of the TEU*, Brussels, 11 September 2000 (Doc. CONFER 4769/00).

Köck, Heribert Franz and Margit Hintersteininger (2000), "Zu den Sanktionen der vierzehn EU-Partnerstaaten gegen Österreich," in Köck and Hintersteininger, *Europa als Sicherheits- und Wertegemeinschaft*. Wien: Verlag Österreich, 477-510.

Nationalrat der Republik Österreich (2001), *Regierungsvorlage betreffend Bundesverfassungsgesetz über den Abschluss des Vertrages von Nizza*, 565. der Beilagen zu den Stenographischen Protokollen, XXI. Gesetzgebungsperiode.

— (2001), *Regierungsvorlage betreffend Vertrag von Nizza*, 600. der Beilagen zu den Stenographischen Protokollen, XXI. Gesetzgebungsperiode.

— (2001), Verfassungsausschuss ebnet Weg für Ratifikation des Nizza-Vertrages, *Parlamentskorrespondenz/02/17.10.2001/Nr. 682.*

Neisser, Heinrich and Sonja Puntscher Riekmann (eds.) (2002), *Europäisierung der österreichischen Politik*. Vienna: Universitätsverlag.

Theodor Öhlinger and Michael Potacs (2001), *Gemeinschaftsrecht und nationales Recht*. Vienna: Orac.

Pelinka, Anton (2002), "Innenansicht: Rollenbild und Rollenwahrnehmung Österreichs als Akteur in der EU," in Heinrich Neisser and Sonja Puntscher Riekmann (eds.), *Europäisierung der österreichischen Politik*. Vienna: Universitätsverlag, 17-36.

Pollack, Johannes and Peter Slominski (2003), "Influencing EU Politics? The Case of the Austrian Parliament," *Journal of Common Market Studies*, 41, 707-729.

Report by Martii Ahtisaari, Jochen Frowein and Marcelino Oreja [*Weisenbericht*], Paris, 8 September 2000.

Schorkopf, Frank (2002), "Der Frühwarnmechanismus bei Verletzung der ‚EU-Verfassungsgrundsätze,'" in Stefan Griller and Waldemar Hummer (eds.), *Die EU nach Nizza. Ergebnisse und Perspektiven*. Vienna / New York: Springer, 103-130.

Seidl-Hohenveldern (1995), "Constitutional Problems involved in Austria's Accession to the EU," *Common Market Law Review*, 727-741.

Statement from the Portuguese Presidency of the European Union on behalf of XIV Member States of 31.01.2000, *Bulletin Quotidien Europe* No. 7645 of 31.1/1.2. 2000, 9.

Timmermann, Heiner (ed.) (2001), *Eine Verfassung für die Europäische Union*. Opladen: Leske+Budric

CHAPTER 3

BELGIUM: MORE CATHOLIC THAN THE POPE?

INTRODUCTION

During the previous IGC's—such as those that resulted in the Maastricht and Amsterdam treaties—Belgium belonged to the most orthodox pro-federalist Member States. In fact, during the run-up to the 1996-97 IGC, the official Belgian position on the negotiations explicitly referred to this federalist vocation of Belgium's policy on European integration. And to a large extent, if criticisms were ushered during parliamentary debates on the ratification of previous EU Treaties, it was not because they went too far in strengthening the supranational characteristics of the European construction, but rather, because they did not go far enough in doing so. The purpose of this chapter is to answer the question of whether Belgium resorted to this orthodox pro-federalist approach again and whether, at the end of the day, it showed the same pragmatism as it had done during the IGC that resulted in the Amsterdam Treaty.

From more than just one perspective, the intergovernmental conference of 2000 was particularly interesting in raising this question. First, there was an external cause. As one of the discussions concerned the re-weighting of the votes in the Council of Ministers, one could wonder whether Belgium would follow a policy to preserve its own voting power in the Council rather than preserving the Council's capacity to act decisively after the upcoming EU's enlargements. The Amsterdam Summit provided grounds to conclude that at least on this point, Belgium would behave in a more 'intergovernmental' way than it usually did (Kerremans 2002, 57-58).

Second, the same question could be raised concerning the composition of the Commission. Would Belgium stick to its position of keeping its one commissioner, even if this would be to the detriment of the Commission's efficiency in an enlarged EU of twenty-seven or more members?

Third, for the first time since the negotiation of the EEC Treaty between 1955 and 1957, the Belgian government coalition did not include the Christian-Democrats, traditionally the strongest ideological proponent of a Belgian EU policy based on federalist principles. This time, the coalition—nicknamed the 'purple-green' coalition—consisted of the following six parties: the Flemish Liberals, the Francophone Liberals, the Flemish Socialists, the Francophone Socialists, the Flemish Greens, and the Francophone Greens. Especially the Greens—both Flemish and Francophone—had been vocal critics of European integration in the past, not because Europe integrated too much, but because it did not integrate sufficiently.

Fourth, when the new IGC commenced in February 2000, the new Belgian prime minister, Guy Verhofstadt, did not yet have clear EU credentials. The big question then became whether he would follow in the footsteps of his Christian-Democratic predecessors by trying to play a prominent pro-integration role in the EU, or whether the EU would be of only secondary interest to him. A related question was also, how this would work in combination with the pro-active foreign policy of Deputy Prime Minister Louis Michel, Belgium's new federal foreign minister and most powerful member of the government.

There may have been a certain discontinuity in terms of government members, but there was also a level of continuity. First, even if the new government could have decided to take another permanent representative to the EU than the one during the previous government, it decided not to do so. Indeed, Frans Van Daele, Ambassador of the Permanent Representation of Belgium, had closely cooperated with the previous Prime Minister, Jean-Luc Dehaene. But at the same time, his close involvement in negotiations on both the Maastricht Treaty (not as permanent representative but as senior foreign ministry official), and the Amsterdam Treaty (this time as permanent representative) had given him the kind of knowledge and experience about the intricacies of the IGC's and the sensitivities of the other Member States, that the new government could use very well when defining and developing its European policy, especially on the IGC (cf. Kerremans and Beyers 2001). After all, the left-overs of Amsterdam were also to a certain extent the left-overs of a Belgian mission unaccomplished. This was clearly demonstrated by the French-Italian-Belgian Declaration, attached to the Amsterdam Treaty, which linked the re-weighting of the votes of the Council of Ministers to the scope of Qualified Majority Voting (QMV) in the EU. Consequently, the re-weighting issue—legally one of the left-overs—almost automatically entailed the inclusion of the QMV-scope as an Amsterdam left-over as well. And this scope would quickly prove to be one of the central concerns of both the previous and the new governments.

But there was another—maybe even more remarkable—aspect of continuity as well. When preparations for the new IGC began, the European Commission created a group of three 'wise men' on the institutional implications of enlargement in view of the forthcoming intergovernmental conference. One of the members of that group was former Belgian Prime Minister Jean-Luc Dehaene. And even if Dehaene was not appointed by the new Belgian government, the positions he defended in that group, and which he included in the report published by that group on 18 October 1999, largely reflected a consensus that exists among Belgian political elites on questions of European integration. That the new government had no problems working with a former prime minister on European integration even if his party was now in the opposition was also demonstrated a year after the 2000 IGC, when the Belgian government proposed Jean-Luc Dehaene as vice-chairman of the European Convention.

Given all these elements, despite the government change in Belgium, one could expect a high level of continuity in Belgium's European policy in general, and its approach to the 2000 IGC in particular. This continuity consisted of a strong pro-federal approach to European integration and the concomitant institutional reforms. From the start of the IGC on, this was quite clear. There were exceptions, however. First, on the composition of the Commission, and second on the re-weighting of the Council's votes, as we will see.

The IGC's Agenda

Almost from day one of the new IGC, the Belgian government stressed its intense desire to use the conference to push forward the process of European integration, partly from the observation that only a maximalist attitude by some Member States could avoid a situation where the IGC would fail to make any progress. The first issue on the Belgian IGC agenda, therefore, was the agenda of the IGC. Belgium did not want to limit the IGC's scope to the so-called Amsterdam left-overs, but wanted to use the IGC to push for a broader agenda. In a certain way, one issue that was included already went beyond the formal Amsterdam left-overs: the scope of the QMV. As mentioned above, this was due to the "Belgian-French-Italian Declaration on the Institutions with the Prospect of Enlargement of the European Union" (Declaration no. 6, attached to the Amsterdam Treaty). That Declaration, referring to the "Protocol on the Institutions of the Treaty", clearly stated that:

> "[Belgium, France, and Italy] are determined to give the fullest effect appropriate to the Protocol as regards the composition of the Commission and the weighting of votes and consider that a significant extension of recourse to qualified majority voting forms part of the relevant factors which should be taken into account."

But neither the Belgian government, nor the Belgian federal parliament, believed that this was sufficient to prepare the EU for its enlargement. Both requested an extension of the IGC's agenda beyond the left-overs, so as to utilise the last chance to thoroughly reform the EU before enlargement would make this much more difficult, if not impossible. The emphasis, therefore, was on the need to use this IGC to make the EU more efficient, more democratic, and more transparent. In order to achieve these three goals in an EU of 27 or 28 members, it was necessary that the EU be organized along federal principles. But Belgium realized that this approach was not shared by many, much less most, other Member States. That is why for Belgium, an important focus of the non-left-over issues of this IGC consisted of the enhanced (or closer) cooperation. Belgium sought to make it easier for a limited number of Member States to start such cooperation, and therefore wanted to change the treaty provisions—themselves the result of the Amsterdam Treaty—with respect to this. Likewise, Belgium preferred to include in the Treaty the Charter on Fundamental Rights that since June 1999 was being negotiated in a European convention, and to grant the European Union legal personality.

In addition to these issues, Belgium also sought to amend Article 7 of the Treaty on European Union. This effort arose out of concern for the conflict that had pitted Austria against the remaining fourteen Member States with respect to the coalition negotiations between the Austrian ÖVP (Die Österreichische Volkspartei) and the FPÖ (Freiheitliche Partei Österreichs) of Jörg Haider.

But Belgium's ambition to include more issues in the negotiations went further. In this sense, it shared the European Parliament's and the European Commission's concerns. But since most Member States preferred to stick to the Amsterdam left-overs, the IGC largely restricted itself to these until the European Council in Feira (19 June 2000). At the first Ministerial meeting of the IGC on 10 April 2000, for instance, Belgium and Luxembourg were the only Member States favouring an extensive agenda as requested by the European Parliament. The European Council of Feira decided, however, to include the enhanced cooperation as well. This was partly—but not completely—the consequence of intensive lobbying of the other Member States by Belgium, primarily Portugal, which as IGC president during the first semester of 2000 exerted considerable influence on the IGC's agenda. The Feira European Council equally included the amendment of Article 7 in the IGC. The Charter of Fundamental Rights was not included due to strong opposition by the UK, Spain, Ireland, Denmark and Sweden.

The Feira European Council's decision to essentially limit the IGC's scope to the Amsterdam left-overs, enhanced cooperation, and Article 7 resulted in the German proposal for a new IGC to be organized in 2003 or 2004. This proposal was enthusiastically supported by the Belgian government, who pleaded for a 'bolder' IGC than the ongoing one, but simultaneously stressed that this did not imply that the ambitions of the latter had to be scaled down. As Ambassador Frans Van Daele observed in the 27 June 2000 hearing of the European Parliament's Committee on Constitutional Affairs, Nice "had to be ambitious enough to deal with the enlargement process with a clear conscience" (*Agence Europe* 28 June 2000).

The idea of a new IGC after the ongoing one was picked up by Prime Minister Guy Verhofstadt, who pleaded for a preparatory stage that would be completed with a declaration to be adopted at the end of the 2001 Belgian EU Presidency, the so-called Laeken Declaration. In this sense, a continuous process of deliberations on EU institutional reform would take place from the start of the 2000 IGC until the end of the one of 2004.

The Issues

Enhanced Cooperation

From the outset, it was clear that Belgium would favour amendments to the treaty provisions on enhanced cooperation. Three issues were central here. The first concerned the question of the minimum number of Member States required to start such cooperation. The second issue concerned how decisions on the enhanced cooperation would be taken, a discussion which arose from the Amsterdam Treaty about the right of veto. The third issue dealt with the scope of the enhanced cooperation. Would it be extended to the second pillar and if so, would its conditions be similar to those of the first and the third pillar?

The Belgian position on the enhanced cooperation was made clear through a number of documents related to the IGC. The first such document was the Benelux Memorandum of 7 March 2000, in which point 4 referred to this issue. The Memorandum clearly defined the objective of the enhanced cooperation—called the reinforced collaboration—as the creation of a group of Member States that would "act as pioneers in pushing forward this Community work in a first phase" (CONFER 4721/00), and thus "guarantee the momentum of the Union's further development" (Ibid.). Decisions on initiating enhanced cooperation should not require unanimity because "the interests of the non-participants are guaranteed, among other things, thanks to the Commission's role" (Ibid.). Finally, the Memorandum provided that even after an enlargement, the current minimum of eight involved states would remain.

Following the Feira European Council's acceptance of enhanced cooperation as an issue for the IGC, the Belgian government submitted its own proposal (CONFER 4765/00, 28 August 2000). This proposal—which largely reflected the principles included in the Benelux Memorandum—contained a more detailed argumentation in favour of changing the provisions of the Amsterdam Treaty, and more detailed proposals for new provisions on the enhanced cooperation. In its argumentation, the Belgian government stressed the difficulties to start enhanced cooperation under the unanimity requirement— even if only through an appeal at the European Council level—especially in a future enlarged EU. It pointed at similar difficulties in case the minimum threshold would be kept at one half of the Member States. Belgium proposed, therefore, to maintain the minimum requirement of eight Member States—even in an enlarged EU—and to introduce QMV when deciding on acceding to the enhanced cooperation.

Following the logic expounded in the Benelux Memorandum, the Belgian government advocated granting the Commission the right and monopoly of initiative for the enhanced cooperation in the first pillar and to eventually extend that privilege to the third pillar as well. As far as the second pillar was concerned, it was proposed to make the role of the High Representative 'decisive' whenever it concerned enhanced cooperation related to the implementation of the CFSP.

The Belgian proposal also indicated that the Belgian government wanted to maintain the safeguards on enhanced cooperation provided by the Amsterdam Treaty so as to avoid enhanced cooperation acting to the detriment of the EU and its *acquis*. In addition, the open nature of the cooperation was stressed—so that all Member States wishing to join would be able to do so—as was the flexibility of its composition. In the words of the Belgian proposal: "the participants must not always be the same (otherwise Europe would be split into two set groups)."

On the issue of enhanced cooperation for the second pillar, the Belgian government indicated that it only wanted to have such cooperation as far as the CFSP implementation was concerned. It was therefore stressed that such cooperation could be particularly useful in the area of diplomatic action and in the military sphere. The former would consist of some Member States that would make their know-how available to the High Representative for a particular action. The latter already existed in the area of armaments and indirectly operational matters, but provisions could be 'fleshed out' here.

Article 7

The question of enhanced cooperation may have been related to the almost traditional concern of Belgium for the political aspects and objectives of the process of European integration. Hence, the issue of Article 7 showed up as a consequence of the discussion about the coalition talks between the Austrian Christian-Democrats and the FPÖ of Jörg Haider. Of all the EU Member States, Belgium belonged to the most vocal proponents of sanctions taken by the 'fourteen' against Austria. Belgian foreign minister Louis Michel made it almost a personal crusade. This had as much to do with the values included in Article 6 of the Treaty on European Union as with Belgian domestic politics. As in Belgium, one extreme right-wing party—the *Vlaams Blok*—had become increasingly popular because of its success in Flanders. Hence, the question about what to do with extreme right-wing parties in Austria or in Italy was not without direct relevance for the principal stance taken by the remaining Belgian political parties to create a *cordon sanitaire* against the *Vlaams Blok*. None of the traditional parties would govern at whatever level—federal, regional, or local—with the *Vlaams Blok* or would even tacitly rely on this party for legislative majorities. The Austrian case and Louis Michel's reaction against it, therefore, was a means of creating a situation for all traditional Flemish political parties to honour the *cordon sanitaire* principle, especially in a year of municipal elections where in some Flemish cities it was expected that support for the *Vlaams Blok* would be so large that all other parties would be compelled to form a coalition against it (as was already the case in the largest Flemish city: Antwerp). Belgium's proposal on Article 7 was just a step further in that direction. That article would make it as difficult for Austria as it would be for Belgium to include extreme right-wing parties in government coalitions.

In its proposal of 2 May 2000, Belgium suggested to amend Article 7 Treaty of the European Union (TEU) so as to include an early warning mechanism (CONFER 4739/00, 2 May 2000). That mechanism would alert a Member State in case it was about to breach the principles enumerated in article 6 (1) TEU.[1] According to the Belgian proposal, the Council would trigger this alert acting by QMV on a proposal submitted by one-third of the Member States or by the Commission. In addition, instead of acting by unanimity, the Council, meeting in the composition of the heads of state or government, would decide by QMV to determine the existence of a serious and persistent breach of the principles of Article 6 (1) TEU.

The Belgian proposal triggered a counter proposal by Austria stressing the need to consult the Member State that was considered to be on the verge of breaching the principles, as well as the European Parliament. The other Member States—as Agence Europe observed (*Agence Europe* 5 June 2000, 5)—took a cautious position.

The Composition of the Commission

The question of the composition of the European Commission expounded a certain contradiction in Belgium's approach to the IGC. On the one hand,

[1] Article 6 (1) TEU contains the observation that the EU is founded on the principles of liberty, democracy, respect for human rights and fundamental freedoms, and the rule of law.

given Belgium's pro-federalist stance on European integration, one would have expected that it would not stick to a Commission in which nationals from each of the Member States would have a seat. After all, the Commission's members are not supposed to act as the representative of their Member State. On the other hand, if there was one issue on which Belgium was not prepared to concede, it was on the principle that indeed, nationals from each of the Member States had to have a seat in the EU's executive body. The Governmental Coalition Agreement—the basis of any new government coalition—clearly stated that Belgium would plead for the "maintenance of the principle that each Member State is entitled to at least one commissioner" (Federale Regering 1999, 30). Proposals by France to limit the number of commissioners were rejected out of hand, therefore, as was the idea of senior and junior commissioners (the so-called 'hierarchisation'). The Belgian reasoning, presented at different occasions, consisted of the legitimacy of the Commission. As articulated by Ambassador Van Daele in the EP Committee on Constitutional Affairs hearing of 27 June 2000, Belgium argued that all Member States had to provide at least one commissioner "to help ensure the institutional legitimacy in the eyes of the general public" (*Agence Europe* 28 June 2000, 5-6).

Gradually, however, a shift in the Belgian position started to emerge. In the Belgian federal parliament, the first indications of such a shift emerged in May 2000 when a resolution—submitted by the Advisory Committee on European Affairs—was approved in which it was stated that each Member State had to be represented "(…) in the same way and on an equal footing" (Kamer van Volksvertegenwoordigers 2000a, 3; Belgische Senaat 2000b, 3). This language was less stringent than a position which insisted on one commissioner from each Member State. In the ensuing parliamentary debates, gradually and steadily, the point of view was being expressed that given the increase in Members States, the Commission's membership had to be restricted in order to keep this institution manageable and efficient. Two conditions were attached to this. The first was the principle of equality (as mentioned above). If a rotation system were to be applied, all Member States—large and small—would have to rotate at the same rhythm. If, for instance, the rotation would imply that each Member State would have a commissioner in five of seven consecutive Commissions, this would have to be the case for all the Member States, not just the small ones (cf. Belgische Senaat 2000a, 7-9). The second condition was that a ceiling could only be accepted as part of a larger process of constitutionalization of the EU, including the 'presidentialization' of the Commission itself.

The Belgian government was not immediately prepared to follow suit and continued to stick to the position of one commissioner per Member State, as was made clear by foreign minister Louis Michel in his response to the Senate debate on the parliamentary resolution (Belgische Senaat 2000a, 23). It was only in November—in an interview with the newspaper *Les Echos*—that Prime Minister Guy Verhofstadt indicated that Belgium was prepared to accept a ceiling on the number of commissioners and on the condition that such a Commission would be part of a European constitution in which a Europe would exist with powers on defence, foreign policy, and economic and social policy. He added: "We speak of a Europe where the Commission president would be elected and in which nationality would not be important" (*Agence Europe* 5 June 2000, 5).

The Re-Weighting of the Votes

The question of the Commission's composition was inextricably linked to the re-weighting of the votes in the Council. That linkage was not just political but also legal because of the provisions of the "Protocol on the Institutions with the Prospect of Enlargement of the European Union", attached to the Amsterdam Treaty. Article 1 of that Protocol provided the basis of a trade-off between the loss by the large Member States of 'their' nationals in the Commission, and a modification of the voting weights in the Council of Ministers. The large Member States would have to be compensated for 'their' losses in the Commission. The question of the linkage also erupted in the context of Article 2 of the Protocol. What the EU was doing in the 2000 IGC was going beyond Article 1—which applied to an enlarged EU with 21 members—as it was preparing itself institutionally for an EU of 25, 27 or 28. If that preparation would entail a 'loss' of commissioners by the smaller Member States—in the sense that they would not always have one of their nationals in the Commission – they would have to be compensated in the Council as well, which would mean that the whole re-weighting—which was an endeavour to benefit the larger states—could be in jeopardy. Conversely—and more importantly from the Belgian point of view—a re-weighting of the Council votes to the benefit of the larger Member States could only be accepted on condition that all Member States—large and small—would be treated equally as far as their representation in the Commission was concerned. This could be done either by maintaining the principle 'One Member State/One Commissioner', or by creating a rotation system that would apply equally to all Member States, both large and small.

A second even more intricate question arose, however, about the differentiation of the Council votes. This was an issue that specifically concerned four Member States: France, Germany, The Netherlands, and Belgium. And of these four, especially France and Belgium raised the point. In the case of Belgium, this came as no surprise. Already during the 1996-97 IGC, especially during the Amsterdam Summit, it had stuck to the position that Belgium and the Netherlands should have a similar number of votes in the Council despite the disparity of their populations (10 million versus 16 million). By tying the question to that of the votes of France and Germany (with populations, respectively, of 58 and 81 million), Belgium hoped that French resistance against the differentiation of its votes compared with those of Germany would be sufficient to avoid a differentiation between Belgium and its northern neighbour. An important element of the Belgian reasoning was the December 1989 'gentlemen's agreement' between Helmut Kohl and François Mitterrand. In that agreement, in exchange for France's acceptance of German reunification, Kohl accepted Mitterrand's demand for the maintenance of voting power in the Council (not in the European Parliament) despite the fact that as a consequence of the reunification, the German population would significantly exceed that of France. This seemingly watertight commitment would help Belgium in its resistance to a differentiation with the Netherlands.

In the run-up to the Nice Summit, this Belgian position was made clear in two respects. First, Belgium insisted that the problem of the underrepresentation of the large Member States had to be resolved by introducing a double majority system in which, besides the existing QMV measures would be taken to ensure that a significant majority of the EU population was represented in such a qualified majority. To pre-empt possible German pressure on the issue of differentiation—Germany did indeed take a low profile on differentiation—Belgium readily accepted Germany's proposal to apply a 62% criterion. Calculations had indeed made clear that with such a threshold, only one Member State would benefit compared to the existing system, and that was Germany. By readily acquiescing with the 62%, Belgium hoped that Germany would be more willing to accept an equal voting weight like France, and Belgium could then legitimately ask that no Belgian-Dutch differentiation would be created. There was one problem with this approach, however, and that was Spain.

During its accession negotiations with the European Community in the 1980s, Spain had insisted on being treated equally with the large Member States of that moment: France, West-Germany, the UK, and Italy. In arduous negotiations, the compromise reached was that Spain would not receive as many votes as these four in the Council, but—as compensation—would receive the same number of commissioners. Since the reform of the Commission would result in a loss of that compensation—Spain would 'lose' one commissioner—it was predictable that the differentiation in Council votes would be questioned as well. This opened a window of opportunity for the Netherlands, however. If differentiation would be maintained for Spain—which was probable, given the large population discrepancy with Germany—why would the Dutch have to accept a lack of differentiation with Belgium, Portugal, and Greece? This Dutch question was all the more legitimate, since the discrepancy between the populations of Spain and those of France, Italy and the UK was almost identical—namely a 62/100 ratio—to that of Belgium (and Portugal and Greece) compared with the Netherlands. So whatever the reasoning —Germany/France or Spain/largest Member States—the issue of differentiation between Belgium and the Netherlands was difficult to avoid. In political terms, however, fewer Belgian than Dutch votes would be seen in Belgium as a real defeat, or at least that was the perception. How would the population assess the predictable newspaper headlines "The Netherlands—Belgium: 12-10", especially in Flanders, where an ambivalent relationship with the Dutch (admiration and irritation) is entertained, even if only at the level of folklore.

In the Benelux, the whole problem was evaded by relatively complicated references to the re-weighting question that left all options open. In the Benelux Memorandum of 7 March 2000, for instance, point 7 makes the following reference:

> Concerning the vote consideration in the Council, the Benelux countries declare themselves open to discuss formulas mentioned in the Protocol of the Treaty of Amsterdam: a reconsideration of the votes or a double majority (or a combination of both). Irrespective of the chosen formula, the Benelux countries are of the opinion that it is essentially a matter of taking into account the global balance between the bigger and smaller countries when revising the relative weight of the Member States, in order to guarantee this balance in the framework of the extension, with, as much as possible, equal differentiation application to similar situations, as well as the representativeness of the decisions (CONFER 4721/00, 7 March 2000).

Similarly, but more concisely, the Benelux Memorandum (submitted on 19 October 2000) referred to this question as follows (point 14):

> The Member States' votes in the Council should be re-weighted to take account of relative population size, with comparable solutions being applied in comparable situations. The Benelux countries would emphasise that the general balance between large and small Member States should be preserved after enlargement. The new weighting could be achieved by re-weighting existing votes or by introducing a double majority (CONFER 4787/00, 19 October 2000).

Belgian decision-makers increasingly realized that one way or the other, there was no escape from a re-weighting of the votes. After the Biarritz Summit (13-14 October 2000), it became quite clear that the Dutch would go for a re-weighting coupled to a differentiation. So even if Belgium and The Netherlands shared an interest in the intensifying debate between the large and small Member States – despite the fact that those involved stressed that in day-to-day decision-making, there had never been an opposition between large and small—the question of differentiation pitted one against the other. It was only at the Nice Summit itself that a way out of this problem could be found, and this was largely because the Belgian prime minister seized it as an opportunity to demonstrate to his EU partners—and Belgian public opinion—his European credentials and his statesmanship. Instead of sticking to the equality in votes, Belgium became the protector of the voting interests of the prospective Member States. It—somewhat surprisingly—coupled its acceptance of differentiation with the number of votes for Lithuania and the differentiation between the votes of Romania and those of the Netherlands. In addition, together with Portugal, it increased the pressure on the larger Member States to restrict the voting ratio between the category of largest Member States and that of the medium group (to which Belgium belongs) to less than 3 (29 against 10). And in order to avoid an increase in the qualified majority threshold as a consequence of the maintenance of the blocking minority at its current level after future enlargements, Verhofstadt played a large role in including in the new Treaty the principle that the QMV-threshold would not exceed the current level of 73.4% of the votes.[2]

The Scope of the Qualified Majority Voting

It is obvious that the question of the re-weighting of the votes was not only politically linked to the Commission's composition but also to the scope of the qualified majority itself. From the Belgian perspective, one could describe this issue as an—almost perpetually—ongoing struggle. From the 1985 IGC (resulting in the Single European Act), to the one of 1991 (the Maastricht Treaty), and the one of 1996-97 (the Amsterdam Treaty), Belgium, together with some other Member States, has been struggling to extend the scope of QMV as much as possible. This does not mean that Belgium has never asked for exceptions. It did so, but only exceptionally. One such exception is the cultural paragraph (Article 151 TEC) where despite the co-decision procedure, the Council requires unanimity in order to be able to act. This can be explained by the language question and Flemish sensitivities on this issue (see also the unanimity rule in Article 290 TEC).

---

[2] See Article3 (2) of the Protocol on the Enlargement of the European Union, annexed to the Nice Treaty and its reference to the Declaration in which the maximum threshold has been indicated. As a matter of fact, the threshold would rise slightly from the current 72% to 73.4% (see the Declaration on the Qualified Majority Threshold and the Number of Votes for a Blocking Minority in the Context of Enlargement to be Included in the Final Act of the Conference, known in Belgium as the "Verhofstadt Declaration").

The extension of the QMV's scope was considered by the Belgian federal government to be one of the most important issues of the 2000 IGC. As the Belgian EU ambassador indicated in his introduction to the Belgian proposal on this issue (21 November 2000): "In my Government's opinion, this is the most important of the subjects on the agenda for the Intergovernmental Conference" (21 November 2000, doc. CONFER 4809/00). It was not a surprise, therefore, that Belgium wanted again to extend the QMV's scope as much as possible. Domestic criticisms against previous treaties had indeed been that the scope had not been sufficiently extended. And two areas where increasingly concerns about the lack of QMV were being raised consisted of social policy and tax harmonization. Given past criticisms about a lack of QMV in these areas, it was no surprise that even though a new government coalition was now in power, Belgium would insist on QMV. In so doing, a clear distinction was being made between basic regulations concerning the aims, principles, general policy lines, and the Union's institutional framework, where unanimity had to be preserved, and the other regulations dealing with the wide array of policy fields of the first pillar, which should be governed by QMV principles. For the third pillar, an acceleration of the so-called 'passerelles' of the Treaty of Amsterdam was called for (cf. Article 67 TEC).

Belgium's position on the QMV's scope (together with that of the Netherlands, and Italy) was not made any easier by the fact that most Member States did not want to go that far and by the fact that almost all of them requested the maintenance of unanimity in some issues so that the requests of all Member States combined resulted in a relatively short list of issues where QMV could be introduced. The consequence was that rather than on full policy areas or even treaty provisions, the negotiations gradually shifted to areas where QMV would be accepted but where some issues would be decided upon by unanimity. A decision in that respect was taken by the Preparatory Group (the so-called Vimont Group) in its meeting of 23 October 2000. It applied to the politically most sensitive issues in the discussion on the QMV's scope. These concerned the measures against discrimination (Article 13 TEC), tax harmonization (Article 93 TEC), provisions affecting social security (Articles 42 and 137(3) TEC), trade in services and trade-related intellectual property rights (Article 133 TEC), and issues related to visa, immigration, and asylum (Articles 63-67 TEC).

As soon as the Vimont Group took its decision to introduce QMV while 'ring-fencing' it with unanimity decisions, the Belgian government submitted a proposal in which it indicated that it wanted to limit the range of unanimity issues as much as possible. Instead of 'ring-fencing' QMV, what had been the idea behind the Vimont Group decision of October, the Belgian proposal tried to ring-fence unanimity (CONFER 4809/00, 21 November 2000). This was initially the case with Article 13 TEC, in which it was proposed to apply QMV to the entire article. In the area of social policy, the Belgian delegation accepted that QMV would apply only to the protection of workers where their employment contract is terminated, and to the conditions for employment for third country nationals legally residing in Community territory (Article 137(3) d & g TEC). In the areas of asylum, immigration policy, and judicial cooperation in civil matters, it was proposed to provide for an automatic transition to QMV after a period shorter than the five years provided by the Amsterdam Treaty (Article 67 TEC). Finally, on tax harmonization, the Belgian delegation proposed to extend the EU's competence to the approximation of the laws and regulations of the Member States on direct taxation, to the extent necessary for the establishment and functioning of the internal market, but to do so by unanimity.[3] QMV (and co-decision) would be applied to three kinds of measures: (1) to measures to update, for the purpose of simplifying, existing Community rules on turnover tax, excise duties, and other forms of indirect taxation; (2) to measures to coordinate the provisions of the Member States to prevent discrimination and double taxation;[4] (3) to cover regulations aimed at preventing fraud, tax evasion, and the circumvention of Community rules and regulations. Fourth, it would include the provisions necessary for the mutual assistance, information exchange, and cooperation between tax authorities within the EU. Belgium also proposed to provide for a provision in which—on the basis of QMV (and co-decision) —the Council would be able (but would not be obliged) to adopt measures "the main objective of which is to protect the environment"

It is obvious that Belgium did not succeed in getting everything it wanted on the QMV's scope. And despite its satisfaction with the fact that reference to unanimity was replaced by QMV in about 30 different Treaty provisions, it did not succeed in achieving its QMV objectives in the area of social policy and tax harmonization. The failure to achieve environmental taxation in Article 93 TEC was especially frustrating. As was observed in a hearing organized in the Flemish Parliament on the IGC, both Jacques Chirac and Tony Blair were not prepared to make any concessions on these areas (Vlaams Parlement 2001, 7).

[3] Article 93 TEC provided for such approximation and harmonization on turnover taxes, excise duties, and other forms of indirect taxation only.

[4] With a view to the detailed clarification of this provision, Belgium also proposed a Protocol on Article 93(2) TEC.

CONCLUSION

Was Belgium more Catholic than the Pope during the 2000 IGC? As a principled pro-federalist Member State, this seemed to be the case. Nevertheless, cracks showed up in this nice federalist picture. First, there was Belgium's insistence on the principle of one commissioner per Member State even if the commissioners are not supposed to represent the Member States. At the end of the day, Belgium conceded on this point, even if it could not achieve the linkage with a smaller (or less extensive) Commission in a federalized Union.[5]

Second, there was the struggle against differentiation. This struggle seemed to have reflected a kind of petty nationalism, which was difficult, if not impossible, to reconcile with a federalist approach to the European project.

Is it fair to expect an unswerving federalist stance on all issues under all circumstances? It probably is not in a European Union that, despite federalist dreams, remains an organization with a very strong intergovernmental component.

Is it relevant to point to the 'cracks' in Belgian Euro-federalism? Perhaps. It may indeed indicate that within the Belgian elite, the concern is growing that in an enlarged EU, the risks of dilution become tremendously high. In such a situation, there are two alternatives. Either, to radically federalize (and constitutionalize) the Union before it is enlarged, or to accept the EU with its strong, albeit not predominant, intergovernmental component and to try and protect one's own interests within such a system. Belgium sought a compromise between these two alternatives, a middle road. The compromise indeed consisted of the concession it ultimately made on the Commission's composition and on the re-weighting of the votes, while assuring that after Nice, a next step would be taken (the Laeken Declaration followed by a Convention, and by a new IGC).

The middle road consisted of facilitating the enhanced cooperation. That cooperation would provide a tool to seduce the reluctant Member States to follow the pioneers, or at least to incapacitate the former to obstruct the latter. In this sense, Belgium's approach to the 2000 IGC reflected the dilemmas a Euro-federalist Member State has to face in an enlarging union with a potentially larger number of Euro-sceptic Member States. It is a dilemma between being more Catholic than the Pope, and converting oneself to more intergovernmental approaches to the process of European integration.

---

[5] See Article 4(2) of the Protocol on the Enlargement of the European Union.

BIBLIOGRAPHY

Kamer Van Volksvertegenwoordigers (2000a), *Voorstel van resolutie betreffende de Intergouvernementele Conferentie van 2000*, Brussels, Doc. 50 0680/002.

Kerremans, B. (2000), "Belgium: From Orthodoxy to Pragmatism," in F. Laursen (ed.), *The Amsterdam Treaty. National Preference Formation, Interstate Bargaining and Outcome*. Odense: Odense University Press, pp. 43-70.

— and J. Beyers (2001), "The Belgian Permanent Representation to the European Union: Mail Box, Messenger, or Representative?" in H. Kassim, A. Menon, B.G. Peters, V. Wright (eds.), *National Coordination in the EU: The EU Level*. Oxford: Oxford University Press, pp. 191-210.

Belgische Senaat (2000a), "Voorstel van resolutie betreffende de Intergouvernementele Conferentie van 2000: Bespreking," in *Belgische Senaat: Handelingen*, Gewone Zitting 1999-2000, Plenaire vergaderingen, 7 June 2000, pp. 4-27.

— (2000b), *Voorstel van resolutie betreffende de Intergouvernementele Conferentie van 2000*, Brussels, Doc. 2-451/2.

Vlaams Parlement (2001), *Gedachtewisseling met ambassadeur Frans Van Daele, permanent vertegenwoordiger van België bij de Europese Unie, in het kader van de opvolging en voortgang van standpuntbepaling inzake Europese aangelegenheden*. Brussels: Vlaams Parlement. Stukken, Zitting 2000-2001, Stuk 680, nr. 1, pp. 1-29.

CHAPTER 4

DENMARK: THE BATTLE TO AVOID A REFERENDUM

INTRODUCTION

The Danish political establishment went to the Intergovernmental Conference (IGC) 2000 with some apprehension. Could a referendum be avoided this time? The fear was a repetition of the 1992 referendum where a small majority of the Danish electorate voted against the Maastricht Treaty despite the fact that it had wide support in the Parliament. The Maastricht Treaty was eventually accepted in a second referendum in May 1993 after Denmark had secured four exemptions from the Treaty at the Edinburgh meeting of the European Council in December 1992. During the 1996-97 IGC the Danish government worked very hard to influence the future Amsterdam Treaty along lines that were expected to make it more popular among the Danish voters and to avoid developments that could be hard to sell in Denmark. The Danish people accepted the Amsterdam Treaty in a referendum in May 1998. But when the government sent one of the Danish exemptions from the Maastricht Treaty, the question of participation in the euro, to a referendum in September 2000 the Danish people voted 'no'. This took place during the IGC 2000. It increased anxiety about the future Treaty of Nice, eventually adopted in December 2000.

In this chapter we shall outline the Danish policy in respect to the IGC 2000 and see how the ensuing Nice Treaty was received in Denmark, by the government and the political parties. Since the government succeeded in avoiding a referendum this time, we do not know how the electorate would have reacted to the Treaty, if it had been put to a popular vote. In the end, Denmark was the first Member State to ratify the Treaty of Nice. The bill to authorize ratification was passed by the Danish Parliament, the *Folketing*, on 1 June 2001. The Queen signed it on 7 June as Law number 499. The instrument of ratification was deposited on 13 June 2001.

Parties and Public Opinion[1]

Referenda

Attitudes to European integration in Denmark are very complex. A majority of the Danish people support economic integration in Europe as long as it does not affect Danish autonomy too much. Denmark joined the EEC in 1973 after a referendum in October 1972 where 63.4 per cent of the Danish people supported membership. The Single European Act (SEA) was ratified after being supported by 56.2 per cent of the Danish voters it in a referendum on 27 February 1986. But the Maastricht Treaty was first voted down by a narrow majority of 50.7 per cent on 2 June 1992. When it was accepted in a second referendum on 18 May 1993 by 56.7 per cent of the electorate, Denmark had secured four exemptions, or opt-outs, at the Edinburgh summit in December 1992 (Laursen, 1994). One of these dealt with Economic and Monetary Union (EMU), where Denmark decided not to take part in the third phase.

The three other exemptions dealt with Citizenship of the Union, Justice and Home Affairs (JHA) co-operation and defence policy. Denmark would not join the Western European Union (WEU) and only take part in intergovernmental JHA co-operation. The four areas of exemptions were those where a deepening of integration was taking the process closer to the traditional symbols of the nation state: citizenship, money and defence.

The hesitancy of the Danish public should be contrasted with an economic and political elite who are much more pro-integration. 141 members of the Danish parliament voted in favour of membership in 1972, against 34 'no' votes. In 1992 and 1993 there were quite large majorities in the Parliament, too. The only exception from the rule was January 1986, when the opposition denied the Liberal-Conservative government a majority in favour of the Single European Act (SEA). But after a referendum, where a majority of the people supported the SEA, a substantial majority of MPs did vote for the treaty.

On 12 May 1992, the *Folketing* authorised ratification of the Maastricht Treaty with 130 votes in favour, with only 25 voting against. After the four Edinburgh exemptions had been accepted by Denmark's partners, prior to the second referendum in 1993, 154 members of the Folketing voted for ratification of the Maastricht Treaty as supplemented with the four exemptions. An important difference compared with 1992 was the support from the Socialist People's Party, which had been actively involved in finding the so-

---

[1] Parts of this paper have relied on earlier writings by the author, especially Laursen 2002 and Laursen 2003a.

called national compromise, which became the basis for the Edinburgh exemptions. The Progress Party remained opposed, but the total number of 'No' votes was only 16.

The Amsterdam Treaty was accepted by 92 votes after the third reading on 7 May 1998 in the Parliament (Social Democrats, Liberals, Conservatives, Centre-Democrats, Social Liberals and Christian People's Party) against 22 votes (Socialist People's Party, Danish People's Party, the Unity List, the Progress Party and one Conservative MP, Frank Dahlgaard) (*Folketingets Forhandlinger*, no. 6, 1997-98 (2. samling), p. 1275).

To transfer sovereignty (or competences) to the EU Article 20 of the Danish Constitution requires a five-sixths' majority in the *Folketing* or an ordinary majority in the *Folketing* followed by a decisive referendum. Given the fact that there was not a five-sixths majority in the Parliament, the referendum was necessary for Danish ratification of the Amsterdam Treaty in 1998.

The referendum on Amsterdam on 28 May 1998 resulted in a 'yes' vote of 55.1 per cent. The turnout was 74.8 per cent, lower than earlier EU referenda.[2] Maybe the Treaty did not spark the imagination of the Danes? Or maybe they were a little tired after the two Maastricht referenda (Laursen, 2002).

The last referendum was about Danish participation in the euro. It took place on September 2000, i.e. during the IGC 2000. It gave a shocking 'no' of 53.1% (Jakobsen, Reinert and Risbjerg Thomsen, 2001; Laursen, 2003b).

In relation to the Treaty of Nice coming so soon after the 'no' to the euro, the central question was, could a referendum be avoided? As we shall see, the government tried actively to avoid changes that would fall under the Constitution's Art. 20 and thus require a referendum.

Table 4.1: Danish referenda on EC/EU questions

Date	Topic	Participation in %	Yes in %	No in %
2 October 1972	Danish membership	90.1	*63.3*	36.7
17 February 1986	Single European Act	75.8	*56.2*	43.8
2 June 1992	The Maastricht Treaty	83.1	49.3	*50.7*
18 May 1993	The Maastricht Treaty and The Edinburgh Agreement	86.5	*56.7*	43.3
28 May 1998	The Amsterdam Treaty	74.8	*55.1*	44.9
28 September 2000	Adherence to the Euro	87.5	46.9	*53.1*

Source: Branner and Kelstrup, 2000, p. 17, and *Morgenavisen Jyllands-Posten*, 30 September 2000, 2nd section, p. 5.

[2] As reported in the Danish press, e.g. *Jyllands-Posten*, 30 May 1998.

The Political Parties

The election to the *Folketing* on 11 March 1998 just prior to the referendum on the Amsterdam Treaty resulted in a Parliament where the following parties opposed the Amsterdam Treaty: Socialist People's Party, Danish People's Party, the Unity List (Red-Green Alliance) and the Progress Party. The Socialist People's Party, however, was split on the issue.

At the election to the European Parliament in June 1999, the June Movement took 16.1 per cent, the People's Movement against the EC Union 7.3 per cent and the Danish People's Party 5.8 per cent of the votes. The anti-EU vote thus remained very large. The Social Democrats, who received 36 per cent of the votes at the Folketing election in March 1998, could only muster 16.5 per cent in the EP election in June 1999.

During the IGC 2000 and Nice summit, Denmark had a Social-Democrat-led government which also included the Social Liberal Party. As is normal in Denmark it was a minority government in the sense that the two parties did not have an absolute majority in the *Folketing*. Prime Minister was Poul Nyrup Rasmussen.

The hesitancy of the Danish public has in many ways made Denmark a 'minimalist' state in European integration. Danish EU-policy is domestic-politics driven. Pro-integration parties fear retribution at the polls if they become too pro-European.

Whereas Denmark's original reasons for joining the EEC were based on the interests of Danish agriculture and industry there is now, however, increasingly an agenda of issues where Denmark actively seeks European solutions, viz. the environment, consumer protection, social policy and employment. During the period 1993-2001 Denmark had governments led by the Social Democratic Party, which actively sought to give the EU a more 'progressive' face in the hope of making the two-level game between the domestic constituents and the European partners easier. This also included support for increased transparency in EU decision-making and support for subsidiarity—or nearness—as it is usually translated into Danish.

The basic attitudes of the established political parties did not change fundamentally during the late 1990s. The Liberal Party and the smaller Centre Democrats remained the most pro-integration parties. The Social Democrats and Social Liberals were in favour of integration, but had minority factions that were sceptical. These two parties remained committed to the four Edinburgh exemptions through the Amsterdam process. The first effort to abolish the exemptions, the euro referendum in September 2000 ended in failure.

Table 4.2: Parliamentary Representation of Danish Parties and Groups at the time of Nice

	EUROPEAN PARLIAMENT ELECTION 10 JUNE 1999		FOLKETING ELECTION 11 MARCH 1998	
Seats won in the election and % of the total votes in Denmark	Seats	% of vote	Seats	% of vote
Social Democrats	3	16.5	63	36.0
Liberal Party	5	23.4	42	24.0
Conservative Party	1	8.5	16	8.9
Socialist People's Party	1	7.1	13	7.5
Danish People's Party	1	5.8	13	7.4
Centre Democrats	0	3.5	8	4.3
Social-Liberal Party	1	9.1	7	3.9
Unity List (Red-Green Alliance)	NP		5	2.7
Christian People's Party	0	2.0	4	2.5
Progress Party	0	0.7	4	2.4
June Movement	3	10.1	NP	
People's Movement Against the EC Union	1	7.3	NP	
Greenland*			2	
Faroe Islands*			2	
Total number of seats	16		179	

NP: did not participate
* Greenland and the Faroe Islands have home rule and are not members of the European Union.
Source: Ministry of Foreign Affairs, "Political Parties in Denmark" http://www.um.dk/english/danmark/om_danmark/partier/, and "The referendum in Denmark on 28 May 1998 on the ratification of the Amsterdam Treaty," http://www.um.dk/english/udenrigspolitik/europa/vurderinguk/ "Europa-Parlamentsvalget den 10. juni 1999," http://www.im.dk/ev1999/evland.htm.

The Conservative Party was also pro-integration, but less so than the Liberal Party. It was the smaller parties on both the left and the right wings that tried to exploit the public's scepticism by advocating anti-integration policies. These smaller parties have sometimes been very successful in setting the agenda of the Danish EU debate.

Policy-Making Mechanisms

The most direct 'lesson' of the difficulties of getting the Maastricht Treaty ratified was an increased Danish emphasis on policies that could make the whole integration process more legitimate. This led to more emphasis on environment policy, consumer protection, social policy and employment policy as well as openness and subsidiarity. Indeed, the trauma from 1992 affected the way the Amsterdam Treaty and Nice Treaty negotiations were prepared in Denmark

In connection with the Amsterdam Treaty negotiations a special mechanism was established for preparation of a Danish policy. All interested ministries were represented in the 'EC Committee in special session' (*EF-udvalget i særlig samling*) at the level of head of office (*kontorchef*) and chaired by the Head of the Northern division in the Ministry of Foreign Affairs. Above this was the Summit Committee (*Topmødeudvalget*), in which Heads of Department (*departementschef*) represented all interested ministries. The interesting thing was that the Head of Department from the Prime Minister's Office chaired this committee. This meant a somewhat weakened position of the Ministry of Foreign Affairs. About half the ministers took part in the government's own Summit Committee (*Regeringens topmødeudvalg*).[3] All in all this lead to a broader involvement in policy preparation compared with earlier IGCs. The purpose was to capture as many of the domestic implications as possibly and to avoid the problems of the Maastricht Treaty ratification. Prime Minister Poul Nyrup Rasmussen's personal interest may also help explain the greater involvement by the Prime Minister and his Office in EU policy (Petersen, 1998). This same mechanism was used during IGC 2000 (information from the Foreign Ministry to the author).

The government's interest in central control is clear. It wanted to control the politically sensitive aspects of the EU decision-making process. Since even technical details, such as which food additives are allowed or prohibited, can become political issues, getting input from experts and affected interests is important. An elaborate system of co-ordination has therefore been set up to assure these relevant inputs. The central role normally played by the Foreign Ministry can be explained by Denmark's efforts to get as much influence in Brussels as possible. Thus there are both consensus and efficiency considerations behind the established co-ordination mechanisms.

The Government's Main Priorities

The Danish government outlined its 'Basis for negotiations' in a document in February 2000. It was forwarded to the IGC in March 2000 (as CONFER 4722/00). In this document the Danish government says that the EU faces the biggest task after the fall of the Berlin Wall, "creating a united Europe to

[3] Foreign Ministry, 'Den danske beslutningsprocedure i EU-sager,' (Copenhagen, August 1997) gives the following group of participants: Prime Minister (chairman), and Ministers of Economy, Finance, Foreign Affairs, Environment and Energy, Business and Industry, Justice, and Food, Agriculture and Fisheries.

pave the way for freedom, peace, welfare and secure living conditions for all European citizens" (Danish Government, 2000). This was seen as an essential task. To succeed both the Central and Eastern European Countries (CEECs) and the EU had homework to do. On the EU side the preparation for enlargement included the institutional changes necessary to become a Union of 27 Member States or more. The IGC should focus upon "the adjustments in the Council, the Commission, the European Parliament, the Court of Justice and the Court of Auditors etc." These were the "issues not settled in Amsterdam." By implication Denmark favoured a narrow agenda.

The government had been ready to settle these institutional issues in Amsterdam. So the government's Basis for Negotiations from December 1995 was still a good basis for negotiations. The new Basis for negotiations did not replace but elaborate the earlier Basis from 1995.

Denmark wanted the IGC to be concluded in December 2000 so that the EU would be ready to welcome new members from the end of 2002.

From the outset the government also stated clearly: "The Danish opt-outs contained in the Edinburgh Decision and the Amsterdam Treaty are not up for negotiation at the Conference. They have been determined by referendum and can only be altered by the Danish population by a further referendum."

Re-Weighting of Votes and QMV

Concerning institutional changes the government took a conservative position on most issues. On the re-weighting of votes in the Council we read in the Basis for Negotiations:

> The Danish Government will work to ensure that the balance between small, medium-sized and large countries is not altered. One solution could for example be that decisions should require not only a qualified majority in the Council of Ministers but a majority which also represents at least half the total population of the EU—a so-called double majority of both Member States and citizens.

The threshold for QMV "should be maintained around the current level," the government said.

The Danish government realized that the question of extended use of QMV was on the agenda in connection with enlargement: "The Danish Government is prepared to discuss further areas where qualified majority voting can be applied (Pillar I)." Nothing was said about Pillar II or III, where we may presume that the Danish government wanted unanimity to remain the rule. The Danish government took a case-by-case approach to extended use of QMV: The IGC "should carefully assess the specific Treaty provisions as well as parts of these provisions with a view to considering the possibility of transferring these provisions to qualified majority voting in whole or in part." Denmark only mentioned green taxes explicitly as an area where Denmark wanted QMV.

Among areas that should remain under unanimity, the government mentioned "provisions on revision of the Treaty, other fundamental institutional provisions and the own resources system." Further, "each Member State shall also in the future be permitted to pursue its own policy with regard to distribution of income and maintain or improve social welfare benefits." Reference was made to the declaration to this effect from the Edinburgh European Council in December 1992, when the Danish opt-outs from the Maastricht Treaty were accepted.

Commission and the EP

Denmark wanted the IGC to reconfirm the principle mentioned in the protocol on Institutions attached to the Treaty of Amsterdam: "Each Member State must be represented in the Commission by one Commissioner."

Denmark was aware that enlargement would lead to an increase in the number of Commissioners. Changes in the functioning of the Commission were therefore called for. The government also said "It is important that the individual Commissioner can be held politically accountable for the administration of his or her portfolio." But the government added "A revision of the Treaty provisions in this regard should respect the institutional balance and must not undermine the collective character of the Commission."

In respect to the European Parliament Denmark was ready to discuss an extended use of the co-decision procedure, again on a case-by-case basis. Once more the conservative proviso followed: "The overall result should not alter the balance between the institutions." Denmark made no concrete proposals. So the country did not signal a wish to strengthen the EP despite the rhetoric about making the EU more democratic. The Danish attitude to the EP has remained rather ambivalent over the years since the EP represents a supranational element in the institutional system.

The Danish government wanted to keep the limit of number of seats in the EP to 700 as agreed in Amsterdam. Also, "the current principles for allocating the seats in the European Parliament should be maintained." The government was of course aware that this would lead to a reduction in the number of members from existing Member States as enlargement progresses.

Other Topics

It was noted that the workload of the European Court of Justice (ECJ) and the Court of First Instance had been increasing in recent years. The government was therefore ready to discuss changes in organisation, functioning, etc., but stressed that "each Member State should have one judge" in both courts. The same applied to the Court of Auditors.

The Basis for Negotiations also mentioned the parallel negotiations about European defence and crisis management and the Charter of Fundamental Rights. On the former: "The Danish Government will monitor carefully the developments in this area and will participate actively in all discussions to safeguard Danish interests and positions in the ongoing process—with due respect for Denmark's opt-out."

On the Charter: "Denmark will play a constructive and active role in this work. It is important to demonstrate that the EU exists for the citizens and that they have rights in relation to the institutions of the EU. The contents of the Charter should express the fundamental freedoms and human values we all share." But, "The Danish Government holds the view that the Charter should be a political document." So Denmark was not ready to incorporate the Charter into the Treaty in such a way as to make it a legally binding document.

Again, we notice a relatively conservative approach. The strategy seems to have been to limit reforms as much as possible to avoid a difficult ratification debate. These efforts to avoid what became known as knots (*knaster*) in the Danish debate became even more outspoken after the 'no' in the Danish euro referendum on 28 September, about halfway through the IGC.

Denmark in the IGC End-Game

The euro-no led to a call from the no-parties for a stricter negotiation mandate for the Danish government in the IGC. The Unity List and the Danish People's Party wanted the government to use its veto against more QMV, especially QMV which might undermine the Danish arrangements concerning welfare and labour market policies. The Socialist People's Party, however, was willing to give the government some leeway in the negotiations. So the negotiation mandate was not changed (Emborg, 11 October 2000; Ipsen, 12 October 2000). The leader of the Socialist People's Party, Holger K. Nielsen, explained that for security policy reasons his party put higher priority on Eastern enlargement of the EU than the Unity List and the Danish People's Party (Ipsen, 13 October 2000).

As the IGC went into the more hectic final negotiations it became apparent that Denmark was under pressure on especially three points, viz. the question of QMV in the area of social policy, easier use of flexibility (or enhanced cooperation) and the introduction of some surveillance mechanism concerning fundamental rights in the treaty.

The questions relating to social policy included Art. 42 and 137. The former deals with social security measures necessary to provide freedom of movement for workers. The Danish government opposed QMV for arrangements for migrant workers and their dependants. The official explanation was that the Danish welfare state is tax based, while most other European countries have insurance-type systems of obligatory individual contributions. The fear was that migrant workers and their dependants might be able to undermine the Danish tax base (Rostrup, 4 October 2000). The other social policy related article, where Denmark was under pressure, was Art. 137, which required unanimity for questions relating to social security and social protection of workers, protection of workers when their employment contract is terminated, representation and collective defence of the interests of workers and employers, including co-determination, and conditions of employment for third-country nationals legally residing in Community territory. Given the fact that labour market conditions in Denmark to a large extent are determined by agreements between the employers and employees and not by legislation, Denmark has a special labour market system that it wanted to be able to maintain.

The Danish welfare state system had been an important ingredient in the euro referendum debate in September 2000, so the government was under extra pressure to prove that the EU was not a threat to the Danish welfare and labour market systems.

Denmark had been against making 'closer cooperation' easier, fearing marginalisation. The no-parties argued that flexibility would mean more union. But after the euro-no in September the government realized that it would be difficult to maintain a non-compromising position on this issue. With the Danish opt-outs it was difficult to argue about the speed of other member states (Rostrup, 10 October 2000). Instead of opposing a change in the treaty's provisions on 'closer cooperation' the government turned to the details of the new proposed rules, emphasising especially that any member state should be able to join 'enhanced cooperation' at a later stage (Klarskov, 13 October 2000).

The third issue for Denmark followed from the Austrian case. The decision by 14 EU members to sanction Austria had not been well received in Denmark and may even have contributed to the euro-no in September. The government was therefore against introducing an internal surveillance mechanism in the treaty fearing that it could create more anti-EU sentiment in Denmark and be exploited by the no-parties.

At the time of the Biarritz summit it became clearer where Denmark stood in relation to other actors.

Prime Minister Poul Nyrup Rasmussen confirmed that Denmark had moved on enhanced cooperation. He emphasized three conditions: it should be open for others to join, it should not affect existing achievements, including the internal market, and it had to take place within the treaties (Nielsen and Rostrup, 14 October 2000). So no new institutions should be created for an *avant guard*.

Concerning social policy Denmark maintained its opposition to QMV for the specific points in Art. 42 and 137. The Prime Minister claimed to have met some understanding from the French Presidency, but foresaw intensive work ahead (Nielsen and Rostrup, 14 October 2000).

Opposition against a surveillance procedure in relation to Art. 7 was also maintained. However, back in Copenhagen representatives of the Conservative and Liberal parties let it be understood that they could accept such a procedure. It would hinder the other member states from taking the law into their own hands (*selvtægt*) said Per Stig Møller (Conservative). There should be objective criteria, said Charlotte Antonsen (Liberal) (Østergaard and Justsen, 15 October 2000). This eased the two-level pressure on the government in this respect.

A new issue emerged, however. Biarritz saw massive pressure from France and other large member states concerning the composition of the Commission. Germany came out in support of the French idea of a smaller Commission and the Benelux countries for the first time seemed willing to consider the matter. But most of the smaller member states, led by Portugal, kept insisting on retaining a Commissioner in the future. So did Denmark. Poul Nyrup Rasmussen gave two reasons why it was important for each member state to have a Commissioner: It would ensure the legitimacy of the Commission and it would make it easier to solve conflicts between the Commission and a member state (Nielsen and Bostrup, 14 October 2000).

Two veteran Danish officials, Niels Ersbøll and Jens Christensen, now entered the debate about QMV.[4] In a newspaper article they argued that unanimity gives the member states an 'uncivilized veto.' With QMV they do retain a 'civilized veto.' Fundamentally the EU is voluntary cooperation. If a member state has serious problems with some proposals the other member states will not press such proposal through since it would lead to unsolvable conflicts. So the Luxembourg compromise is not completely dead, and coun-

[4] Niels Ersbøll had been Secretary General of the Council and Jens Christensen had been involved in negotiating Danish membership in 1972.

tries like Denmark wanting a reasonably effective Union should not fear QMV (Ersbøll and Christensen, 2000).

On 3 November the French Presidency published a "Progress report on the Intergovernmental Conference on institutional reform" (CONFER 4790/00). In relation to Art. 137 the report suggested QMV for "minimum requirements in the field of representation and collective defence of the interests of workers and employers, including co-determination." This the Danish foreign minister, Niels Helveg Petersen, found unacceptable even if the proposal contained the proviso that measures "shall not affect the right of Member States to define the fundamental principles of their social security systems and must not significantly affect the financial equilibrium thereof." The rule could threaten the special Danish labour market model it was claimed. Nor did the foreign minister like the proposed Art. 42, which, apart from QMV for rights to benefits for migrant workers, now also included "self-employed persons and students who are nationals of Member States and for workers who are covered by agreements concluded with third States, stateless persons and refugees." For other persons, i.e. workers from third countries without agreements, unanimity was maintained. This proposal also had the important proviso that measures "may not significantly affect the financial equilibrium of Member States' social security schemes" (Nielsen, 4 November 2000a; Justsen, 4 November 2000; and Bang Nielsen, 4 November 2000).

The foreign minister also commented on two other parts of the Presidency report. It was confirmed that Denmark was accepting easier flexibility, but enhanced cooperation should remain open for non-participants to join. According to the French report the Commission would decide on others joining closer cooperation in the first pillar while the Council would decide in the second and third pillars. The government would have to take a closer look at this. Finally, concerning the new Art. 7 the government now felt isolated and adapted accordingly. Helveg Petersen noted that a country which might risk a serious breach of the fundamental principles should be heard before the other states could make recommendations and take actions. Therefore with the new rule another Austria case could be avoided (Nielsen, 4 October 2000b).

At a week-end meeting in Paris 4-5 November, the Danish chief negotiator Poul Skytte Christoffersen put forward a proposal which would solve the Danish problems. Afterwards he reported to the press that the proposal was well-received. Basically Denmark was willing to accept QMV for social benefits already covered by EU rules and for the group of persons already covered. According to the proposal, persons from third countries should fall under the EU's policy on immigration, where Denmark has an opt-out. By avoiding an extension of EU competences on social benefits, Denmark could avoid a referendum about the Nice Treaty. Denmark was also willing to accept QMV for taxation as long as it was limited to environmental taxes, cooperation about tax fraud and adjustment of existing VAT rules. Christoffersen now added a new argument in favour of QMV. As long as unanimity is the rule, the ECJ often has to intervene to fill in gaps. "Sometimes the Court makes the 'right' decision, sometimes not," he said (Bostrup, 6 November 2000).

On November 9, 2000, the French Presidency issued a note on extension of qualified majority voting (CONFER 4795/00). Concerning Art. 42 it suggested a protocol which would list the areas and persons covered by Art. 42. The proposal mentioned "stateless persons and refugees residing within the territory of one of the Member States", suggesting that there was no automatic right of moving around between member states for refugees. Further the protocol would "confirm that social security for workers from third countries is governed by the provisions of Article 63(4) TEC." According to Prime Minister Nyrup Rasmussen this proposal would solve Denmark's problem. Art. 63 (4) TEC is covered by the Danish exemption concerning supranational Justice and Home Affairs cooperation. By thus excluding Denmark from new social security requirements for immigrants, Denmark could avoid a referendum (Bostrup, 10 November 2000). Were Art. 42 to be extended to migrating workers from third countries□ such as Turkish workers in Berlin who had kept their Turkish citizenship□ it would be an extension of competences falling under the Danish Constitution's Art. 20.

Some days later chief negotiator Poul Skytte Christoffersen told the Danish press that it now seemed that the other member states had accepted the Danish view concerning social benefits for immigrants. The biggest problem had been Sweden and Finland which did not share the Danish fear of an influx. Instead they were fighting for a stronger social policy in the EU by extending QMV as much as possible (Bostrup, 15 November 2000).

In respect to retaining a Commissioner, Denmark remained under pressure. Various leading European politicians visited Copenhagen to press for a smaller Commission with a rotation system including both the large and small member states. On the occasion of a visit by the German chancellor Gerhard Schröder on 17 November, both the Prime Minister Nyrup Rasmussen and the Foreign Minister Helveg Petersen sent out signals that Denmark might have to accept such a proposal (Pittelkow, 19 November 2000). But representatives of the other political parties reacted critically to the new government signals, saying that Denmark should keep fighting with other small states for a Commissioner. This included representatives of the Liberal and Conservative opposition parties. Also the chairman of the European Affairs Committee Claus Larsen-Jensen (Soc. Dem.) said that Denmark should keep fighting for a Commissioner. That is part of the negotiation mandate, he said (Elbæk Maressa, 19 November 2000).

Another issue then cropped up in the Danish debate, namely the proposed new Art. 229a concerning the creation of EU industrial property rights. Some legal experts argued that conferring jurisdiction on the ECJ would fall under the Danish constitution's Art. 20. But how would the Danes react to a referendum about patents? Could the Parliament find a 5/6th majority, or could such a step be interpreted as a minor measure thus avoiding a referendum? (Thobo-Carlsen, 22 November 2000). Holger K. Nielsen, the leader of the Socialist People's Party said that the demand for a referendum was coming closer. But Minister of Industry, Pia Gjellerup, suggested that transfer of sovereignty would only take place later, if the Council were to decide to use the possibility of conferring jurisdiction on the ECJ (Madsen and Thobo-Carlsen, 24 November 2000).

On 23 November 2000, the French Presidency put forward a "revised summary" of the negotiations (CONFER 4810/00). The Danish representative Poul Skytte Christoffersen expressed the view that the document did not include a transfer of sovereignty. He had been in touch regularly with the experts in the Ministry of Justice. He had worked to avoid a referendum. But he had only used the referendum argument once in the negotiations with his colleagues, viz. in connection with Art. 42. According to Art. 42 in the proposal, unanimity would be required in the Council "when it extends the material or personal field of application of Community regulations ... of social security schemes to persons moving within the Community, as such regulations stand on the date of entry into force of the Nice Treaty, to cover other social security benefits and other citizens of the Union and their dependants." In Art. 137 the French still suggested QMV for "representation and collective defence of the interests of workers and employers," which Denmark kept opposing, but the proposal was not considered to imply a transfer of sovereignty (Bang Nielsen and Rostrup, 28 November 2000). The ambassador did not comment on the proposed Art. 229a on the possibility of conferring jurisdiction on the ECJ in respect to industrial property rights.

As the Nice summit approached, the question of the Commission kept being discussed by Danish politicians. As it seemed more and more likely that a deferred ceiling on number of members and a rotation system would be adopted in Nice the EU spokesman of the Unity List, Keld Albrechtsen, said that such a decision would mean a transfer of sovereignty and require a referendum. But Prime Minister Nyrup Rasmussen disagreed and said that it would not fall under Art. 20 of the Danish Constitution (Seidelin, 30 November 2000). Also Holger K. Nielsen, leader of the Socialist People's Party, suggested that Denmark might have to have a referendum. Having a

Commissioner was a precondition of Danish membership in 1972 he said, and he still saw problems with Art. 42 (Seidelin, 2 December 2000).

On 30 November, the French produced yet a document (CONFER 4815/00), which did not include important changes from a Danish perspective.

On 1 December, the Danish government got a broad negotiating mandate in the Parliament. It was clear that the political establishment still considered the question of a Danish Commissioner in the future a very important question (Seidelin, 5 December 2000).

When the foreign ministers met on 3 December the last time prior to the Nice summit, the Danish foreign minister Helveg Petersen felt obliged to explain to his colleagues that the right solution was one Commissioner per country. He also found the rotation system now proposed by the French Presidency imprecise. But he insisted with the Danish press that an adoption of the French proposal would not lead to a referendum in Denmark (Bang Nielsen, 4 December 2000)

On 6 December, *Berlingske Tidende* reported a poll from the Gallup Institute which showed that 77% of the Danes agreed with the statement that "All Member States should continue to have a member of the EU Commission – also after the countries of Eastern Europe have joined". This could only reinforce the pressure already coming from the *Folketing.* The Foreign Minister now mentioned the possibility of trying to postpone the decision until after enlargement with a number of the candidate countries (Madsen and Thobo-Carlsen, 6 December 2000).

On December 6, the day before the start of the Nice summit the French Presidency published the Draft Treaty of Nice (CONFER 4816/00). The same day the Danish government went through the Draft in the European Affairs Committee in the *Folketing.* Afterwards the Prime Minister announced that he would use all his energy to secure a permanent Commission post for Denmark. There had been a strong demand from the political parties to that effect. Nyrup Rasmussen had also told the parties represented in the European Affairs Committee that this question was linked with the question of voting weights in the Council. His promise on that point was more airy: He would fight for a good result. On questions relating to QMV, enhanced cooperation, and democracy surveillance the Danish government and much of the political establishment seemed to have moved towards accepting the proposals from the French Presidency (Madsen and Thobo-Carlsen, 7 December 2000).

Just prior to the Nice summit, the question of referendum remained high on the agenda. The Danish People's Party, the Christian People's Party and the Unity List called for a referendum in any case. The Socialist People's Party said it would depend on the final result. The party still had doubts in relation to social policy and should Denmark lose its Commissioner that would be such a fundamental change that the treaty should be sent to a referendum. But the Prime Minister said that for him it was the Constitution that was decisive. It would be up to the government's lawyers to determine whether the changes would fall under Art. 20 of the Constitution. But what was proposed did not point in the direction of a referendum Nyrup Rasmussen said (Thobo-Carlsen and Madsen, 7 December 2000).

Before the negotiation began in Nice the British upset the Danes. British diplomats contacted Danish media claiming that the Danish interpretation of the proposal in relation to social security rights was wrong. The British claimed that the proposal would give immigrants to other EU countries access to the Danish social security system. Denmark denied this and found support from the Commission (Bostrup, Seidelin and Nielsen, 8 December 2000).

The negotiations in Nice about the new treaty started Friday evening with 'confessionals' with President Chirac. Nyrup Rasmussen and Helveg Petersen were among the first to get a twenty-minute audience with the French President. The Danes told Chirac what they could accept and what they could not accept. Concerning QMV they mentioned Art. 42 and 137, but also MEP salaries and services aspects of international trade negotiations (Art. 133—where the Danish problem was shipping) should be decided by unanimity. The demand for a permanent Commissioner was repeated and Denmark supported a double majority in the Council (Madsen, Rostrup and Bang Nielsen, 9 December 2000; and Seidelin, Nielsen and Bostrup, 9 December 2000).

On Saturday 9 December the French Presidency put forward two meeting documents of relevance for the Danish situation. One document put forward in the morning proposed to keep Art. 42 and 137 as proposed in the Draft Treaty of 6 December. This included QMV for "representation and collective defence of the interests of workers and employers." The document also had the first Presidency proposal for the Commission and weighting of votes. For the Commission the proposal was a two-stage solution. From 2005 one national from each Member State. From 2010 or when the Union has 27 Member States the Commission would be composed of 20 members, with a rotation system based on the principle of equality. The proposed weighting of votes in the Council would increase the four large countries' votes from 10 to 30 with a relatively lower increase for smaller states. Denmark would go from 3 to 6 votes (Meeting Document SN 511). The Danish reaction was one of resisting the rotation system in the Commission and the proposed weighting of votes in the Council was also unacceptable (Ulla Østergaard, 10 December 2000). The Danish Prime Minister further found it unacceptable that Spain should have 28 votes and Poland only 26 despite the fact that the two countries have about the same population and he wowed to speak for Poland (Rostrup, Madsen and Bang Nielsen, 10 December 2000).

In another document, put forward late Saturday afternoon, the French proposed to keep unanimity for "representation and collective defence of the interests of workers and employers" (Meeting document SN 514). This meant progress on this issue seen from a Danish perspective. So Art. 42 and 137 were becoming acceptable. So was Art. 133 which retained unanimity for shipping (Nielsen, Bostrup and Seidelin, 10 December 2000). The new document retained the idea of a smaller Commission once country number 27 joins, but did neither mention the year 2010 nor the figure 20.

On Sunday 10 December, the Presidency put forward its final compromise proposal in two documents. The first had a new proposal concerning the Commission. The idea was still to limit the size of the Commission below the number of member states when member number 27 joins and to introduce a system of rotation. But the new proposal had an important proviso. This new system would be adopted by unanimity (SN 521). This first document had no number for votes in the Council. Such a document followed later the same day. The proposal retained 30 for the big four. But the numbers were increased slightly for smaller member states. Denmark would get 7 votes (SN 522).

Denmark's response to the French proposals was positive. The interpretation was that Denmark would keep its Commissioner. Changes in that situation would require negotiations later where Denmark would have a veto. The Prime Minister was happy (Nielsen, Bostrup and Seidelin 11 December 2000). The response in Copenhagen from the Liberal Party and Conservative Party was also positive. Even Holger K. Nielsen said that it looked reasonable (Klarskov, 11 December 2000). Denmark was also satisfied with the new proposed voting weights (Seidelin, Bostrup and Nielsen, 11 December 2000).

The Nice summit continued Monday morning until about 4:15 a.m. The big member states accepted 29 votes in the Council instead of 30. Some medium-sized states got an additional vote. But Denmark was not directly affected by this. About 5 a.m. a satisfied Danish Prime Minister met the press. An enlargement treaty had been adopted, he said. The Union was becoming more democratic. It was his estimation that there was no transfer of Danish sovereignty. Consequently, no referendum would be needed – but the final decision on this was up to the legal experts in the Ministry of Justice. Somewhat disappointingly for the Danes, the British in the end vetoed any QMV in Art 42. After all the Danish work to find a balanced improvement, no changes at all! (Bang Nielsen and Rostrup, 12 December 2000).

THE DANISH GOVERNMENT'S RECEPTION OF NICE

After the many referenda about EU questions in Denmark, and given the unpredictability of referenda, the government was happy to conclude after the Nice summit that it looked as if a referendum could be avoided this time.

The Ministry of Justice was asked to evaluate the Treaty from a legal point of view. Did it involve a transfer of sovereignty according to Art. 20 of the Danish Constitution? The answer given in a report on 27 February was 'no' (Denmark, Ministry of Justice, 2001). The Parliament could therefore authorize ratification as for any other international treaty according to Art. 19 in the Constitution. This meant a simple majority in the Parliament and no referendum.

How did the Ministry of Justice reach such conclusion? The interpretation given was that a transfer of sovereignty takes place when EU competence is extended to new policy areas. This did not happen in the Nice Treaty. The institutional changes that took place in the Treaty of Nice were not interpreted as transfer of sovereignty. Nor was the extended use of QMV seen as transfer of sovereignty. As we shall see, this interpretation was later criticised by the Danish People's Party and the Unity List. They called for an interpretation by independent legal experts. But the government decided to trust its own lawyers in the Ministry of Justice.

The Ministry of Justice did mention one possible problem in the Treaty, viz. the new Art. 229A, which deals with a possible future transfer of competence to the ECJ for industrial property rights. If such a transfer does take place Denmark will, at that point in time, have to apply Art. 20 of the Constitution.

On 2 March 2001, the new Foreign Minister, Mogens Lykketoft, proposed the bill authorising Danish ratification of Nice.[5] The bill excluded Denmark from Art. 67 and the Protocol attached to it. Denmark was kept outside supranational JHA co-operation by this procedure. It was in accordance with the Danish exemption. Further, Denmark did not adhere to the new Art. 229A through its ratification of Nice.

In the remarks to the bill the government called the Treaty of Nice an enlargement treaty and argued that enlargement will be good for Europe and Denmark. Enlargement will increase European stability and help secure the security-political gains that followed the ending of the Cold War. Enlargement would also be economically beneficial to Denmark. Especially small and medium-sized companies would get new markets. The participation of the CEECs in the internal market would be good for investors and export-

[5] In the meantime Niels Helveg Petersen had resigned, saying that he could no longer administer the Danish opt-outs.

ers.[6]

Looking at Nice from a broader political perspective, the political establishment could be relieved that Nice did not really question the Danish exemptions. Nor did the extended use of QMV touch upon very sensitive areas from a Danish point of view, with unanimity largely retained for social and taxation policies. But the developments in the JHA area and the parallel developments in the area of defence policy, did put pressure on the Danish exemptions.

THE RATIFICATION DEBATE IN THE *FOLKETING*

How then did the political parties receive the Treaty of Nice? The *Folketing* had a first reading on 21 March 2001.

Claus Larsen-Jensen spoke on behalf of the Social Democrats. He called the Treaty a technical treaty, which had finalised the Treaty of Amsterdam and made the EU ready for enlargement. But he did not go into very many details. He mentioned a new balance of power between the Member States, referring to new weights of votes. He mentioned increased QMV "so that the EU does not lose its capacity to make decisions after enlargement." As member of the leading government party he of course supported ratification of the Treaty.

Also the other major political parties were in favour of ratification of the Nice Treaty. Charlotte Antonsen, speaking on behalf of the Liberal Party, said that the substance of the matter was Eastern enlargement. A more efficient decision-making process was needed. This required more QMV. Referring to the new rules of 'enhanced cooperation' she said that Denmark could not oppose these because Denmark moves slowly because of the exemptions from 1992.

Lene Espersen, speaking on behalf on the Conservatives, also saw Nice as an enlargement treaty, considered the changed voting weights and increased use of QMV as necessary. She accepted the new rules of flexibility because there were still limitations. She referred to changes relating to Art. 7 as a 'never again Austria' article.

Elisabeth Arnold, speaking on behalf of the Social Liberals, saw Eastern enlargement as Europe's big chance. The Amsterdam Treaty had left some unresolved problems. These problems had now been solved by Nice. As a matter of fact, the Social Liberals would have liked to see more QMV, in-

---

[6] The bill and the parliamentary debates can be located at the home page of the Parliament: www.folketinget.dk as well as from the Parliament's EU information www.eu-oplysningen.dk

cluding environmental taxes and company taxation.

The Socialist People's Party, represented in the debate by Anne Baastrup, came out in favour of the Treaty. We recall that the party had been against the Amsterdam Treaty (but internally split). The party emphasised that Nice was an enlargement treaty. The party recognised the need for more QMV in an enlarged Union, as long as such extensions would not undermine the Danish welfare society. This would not be the consequence of Nice. Concerning the new Art. 133 (including services under trade policy) she argued that it could not be used to force privatisation in the areas of environment and health as feared by some. The Party found the new Art. 7 unnecessary; but this was not enough to vote against the Treaty. On balance the Socialist People's Party supported the Treaty. This of course was important for the government.

There was also support for Nice from the Centre Democrats, represented by Susanne Clemensen, and the Christian People's Party, represented by Jann Sjursen.

Two parties spoke against Nice, viz. the Unity List on the left and the Danish People's Party on the right wing. In reality, the debate was between these two parties and the rest.

Kristian Thulesen Dahl spoke on behalf of the Danish People's Party. He argued that the Treaty would move competences from the Member States to the EU. The increased use of QMV meant such a transfer because Member States would lose their veto. He specifically spoke against the changes in Art. 7 and Art. 133. Enhanced co-operation in the Treaty was about some states moving further. There was nothing about some states dropping out of part of the existing co-operation. So it was one-sided flexibility. The Danish People's Party wanted a much slimmer Union. That would be the way to prepare for enlargement.

Keld Albrechtsen from the Unity List suggested that a 'no' to Nice could lead to a new agenda in Europe. He called for a slowdown in integration. At the moment the governments were building a federation without popular support. That is why they did not dare send the Treaty to a referendum. Why shouldn't Poland be able to have the same exemptions as Denmark? What about the membership of Ukraine? He questioned the whole philosophy behind the EU, including its enlargement strategy.

After the first reading, the bill was sent to the European Affairs Committee, which produced a report. The final version of the report was made public on 15 May 2001 (*Folketinget*, European Affairs Committee, 2001b). It confirmed that all parties, except the Danish People's Party and the Unity List, were in favour of ratification of the Treaty of Nice.

During the work on the bill on ratification of the Nice Treaty the European Affairs Committee had five meetings. The Foreign Minister answered six oral and fourteen written questions. The Social Democrats, the Social Liberals, the Liberals, the Conservatives and the Centre Democrats were in favour of the bill. The Socialist People's Party was also in favour of ratification, but included a minority statement explaining their reasoning. They welcomed the expanded use of QMV, but stressed that the Danish welfare society should not be undermined. They therefore welcomed the fact that unanimity had been retained in Art. 42 and Art. 137. Concerning Art. 133, which had worried them, they had concluded that it could not be used to force Denmark to liberalise public services in the environmental and health areas. They found the changes in Art. 7 unnecessary, but did not want to vote against the Treaty because of them. They would have liked to see QMV for company taxes and environmental taxes, better rules for the environment and food policy and more openness in decision-making processes. But they accepted the Treaty as it was because they did not want to postpone enlargement.

The Socialist People's Party also stated that they were of the opinion that the Treaty ought to be sent to a referendum because of its political importance even if it did not formally involve a transfer of sovereignty in the sense of Art. 20 of the Danish constitution.

The Danish People's Party mainly criticised Art. 7, surveillance of democracy they called it. They demanded a referendum, claiming that the increased use of QMV and the Danish loss of a Commissioner once the EU reaches 27 members will mean a transfer of sovereignty to the EU. They also criticised the Treaty's provisions on European parties, claiming that this part of the treaty would lead to discrimination of the Danish anti-EU members of the European Parliament.

The Unity List called for a referendum. The Treaty would lead to transfer of power from the small states to the large states and the Commission. Art. 133 would have negative consequences for public services.

The two opposing parties suggested various changes, including for instance postponing the ratification of the Treaty of Nice until the EU had accepted five new members, claiming that the existing treaty easily could handle 20 members.

The second reading in the plenary session of the *Folketing* followed on 17 May 2001. Some of the earlier arguments were repeated.

Part of the discussion was about the referendum question, with those who were against the Treaty claiming that it was undemocratic not to send it to a referendum. Jann Sjursen from the Christian People's Party, which was not represented in the European Affairs Committee, stated that his party also was in favour of a referendum, but like the Socialist People's Party he did not find that the fact that there would not be a referendum enough reason to vote against the Treaty.

During the debate, the Foreign Minister Mogens Lykketoft stated that the best way to deal with EU treaties is to follow the constitution. So no referendum would take place if not required formally! Kristian Thulesen Dahl from the Danish People's Party and Keld Albrechtsen from the Unity List claimed that this was a major change in Danish practice since 1986 according to which important EU decisions have to be sent to a referendum. The government's interpretation of the Constitution was criticised. Keld Albrechtsen claimed that the government's interpretation would allow radical changes in the EU institutions without a referendum, even the introduction of a federal constitution in 2004. The Foreign Minister denied this, but also said that the EU will never become a federal state in the American sense.

The second reading finished with a rejection of the various amendments from the Danish People's Party and the Unity List.

The third and final reading took place on 1 June 2001. It was a relatively short debate, with the Danish People's Party and the Unity List repeating their opposition. The major parties chose not to take part in the debate. This was criticised by the opponents. The government was again criticised for the alleged change in the tradition of sending major EU decisions to a referendum. Maybe, if the Danes had accepted the euro on 28 September 2000, the Danes would have had a referendum on Nice, it was suggested. The major parties were criticised for not being ready for a debate, neither in the Parliament nor with the people.

In the end the *Folketing* authorised ratification of the Treaty of Nice with 98 votes in favour (Social Democrats, Liberals, Conservatives, Socialist People's Party, Centre-Democrats and Christian People's Party) and 14 against (Danish People's Party, Unity List and three independents, former members of the Progressive Party, which had split up and ceased to exist as a parliamentary party). One member, Frank Dahlgaard, independent, abstained.

Conclusion

Danish policy-makers drew certain lessons from the Maastricht debacle (Laursen, 1997). They tried actively to avoid a repetition of the 1992 referendum by working to influence the Amsterdam Treaty in certain directions, while at the same time retaining the Danish exemptions from 1993. In the case of Nice, the government worked very hard to avoid changes that could be interpreted as a transfer of sovereignty according to Article 20 of the Danish Constitution. In that it succeeded. The Treaty of Nice was accepted by the Parliament without a referendum. This happened largely without public debate despite the government's declared wish for such a debate.

BIBLIOGRAPHY

Bang Nielsen, Ole (2000), "Ambitiøst fransk udspil til EU-traktat," *Berlingske Tidende*, 4 November.

—— (2000), "EU hvæsser sanktions-våbnet," *Berlingske Tidende*, 5 November.

—— (2000), "EU-kerne vil forcere udenrigspolitikken," *Berlingske Tidende*, 7 November.

—— (2000), "Danmark står fast på sin kommissærpost," *Berlingske Tidende*, 4 December.

—— and Ask Rostrup (2000), "Nyrup ser bæstet i øjnene," *Berlingske Tidende*, 14 October.

—— and Ask Rostrup (2000), "Ingen ny afgivelse af suverænitet," *Berlingske Tidende*, 28 November.

—— and Ask Rostrup (2000), "Poul Nyrup fjernede de danske ligtorne," *Berlingske Tidende*. 12 December.

Bostrup, Jens (2000), "Dansk forslag om traktatkompromis mødt med velvilje," *Politiken*, 6 November.

—— (2000), "Dansk sejr i ny EU-traktat," *Politiken*, 10 November.

—— (2000), "Ingen dansk pension til EU's indvandrere," *Politiken*, 15 November.

—— , Michael Seidelin and Jakob Nielsen (2000), "Beskidte britiske kneb mod Nyrup," *Politiken*, 8 December.

Branner, Hans and Morten Kelstrup (2000), "Denmark's Policy towards Europe in a Historical and Theoretical Perspective," in Hans Branner and Morten Kelstrup (eds.), *Denmark's Policy towards Europe after 1945*. Odense: Odense University Press, pp. 9-38.

CONFER 4722/00: Conference of the Representatives of the Governments of the Member States, "Information Note. Subject: IGC 2000: Contribution from the Danish Government: Basis for negotiations," Brussels, 7 March 2000.

—— 4790/00: Conference of the Representatives of the Governments of the Member States, "Summary: Progress report on the Intergovernmental Conference on institutional reform," Brussels, 3 November 2000.

—— 4795/00: Conference of the Representatives of the Governments of the Member States, "Presidency note: Extension of qualified majority voting," Brussels, 9 November 2000.

—— 4810/00: Conference of the Representatives of the Governments of the Member States, "Revised Summary," Brussels, 23 November 2000.

—— 4815/00: Conference of the Representatives of the Governments of the Member States, "Revised Summary," Brussels, 30 November 2000.

—— 4816/00: Conference of the Representatives of the Governments of the Member States, "Draft Treaty of Nice," Brussels, 6 December 2000.

Danish Government (1995), "Basis for Negotiations. Open Europe: The 1996 Intergovernmental Conference," SN 522/95 (REFLEX 23), 11 December.

—— (2000), "IGC 2000: Contribution from the Danish Government: Basis for negotiations," CONFER 4722/00, 7 March.

Denmark, Foreign Ministry (1995), *Dagsorden for Europa. Sammendrag*. Copenhagen, August.

—— (2001a), *Danmark og Europa: Udvidelse, globalisering, folkelig forankring*. Copenhagen: Schultz Information.

—— (2001b), *Europas Fremtid – et dansk bud*, 23 August.

Denmark, Ministry of Justice (2001), "Redegørelse for visse forfatningsretlige spørgsmål i forbindelse med Danmarks ratifikation af Nice-Traktaten", 27 februar. www.jm.dk/publikationer/nice/index.htm

Danmark, "L 179 (som fremsat): Forslag til lov om ændring af lov om Danmarks tiltrædelse af De Europæiske Fællesskaber og Den Europæiske Union. (Danmarks ratifikation af Nicetraktaten). Fremsat den 2. marts 2001 af udenrigsministeren (Mogens Lykketoft)," http://www.folketinget.dk/samling/2001/lovforslag_som_fremsat/1179.htm

Eising, Jesper (2000), "Intet dansk nej ved Nice," *Berlingske Tidende*, 22 November.

Elbæk Maressa, Jette (2000), "EU-udspil isolerer regeringen," *Jyllands-Posten*, 19 November.

Emborg, Rasmussen (2000), "Holger freder Nice-mandat," *Politiken*, 11 October.

Ersbøll, Niels and Jens Christensen (2000), "Enstemmighed og flertal," *Politiken*, 18 October.
European Union (1997), *Consolidated Treaties*. Luxembourg: Office for Official Publications of the European Communities.
— (2001), *Treaty of Nice*. Luxembourg: Office for Official Publications of the European Communities.
Folketinget, European Affairs Committee (2001a), "Beretning om Europaudvalgets fremtidige arbejde." Beretning afgivet af Europaudvalget den 10. maj.
—, European Affairs Committee (2001b), "Betænkning over Forslag til lov om ændring af lov om Danmarks tiltrædelse af De Europæiske Fællesskaber og Den Europæiske Union (Danmarks ratifikation af Nicetraktaten), (L 179 – bilag 15), 15 May.
Helveg Petersen, Niels (2000), "Uden Nice ingen udvidelse," *Jyllands-Posten*, 19 November.
Ipsen, Jens-Martin (2000), "Nyrup splitter nej-partierne," *Berlingske Tidende*, 12 October.
— (2000), "Nej-sigere skyder på SF," *Berlingske Tidende*, 13 October.
Jakobsen, Mogens Storgaard, Regin Reinert og Søren Risbjerg Thomsen, "Afstemningen om den fælles mønt – social baggrund og holdninger," *Politica*, Vol. 33, No. 1 (2001), pp. 66-88.
Justsen, Klaus (2000), "Godt og dårligt nyt i udkast til EU-traktat," *Jyllands-Posten*, 4 November.
Klarskov, Kristian (2000), "Dansk kovending: Ja til fleksibelt EU," *Politiken*, 13 October.
— (2000), "Tilfredshed med løsning," *Politiken*, 11 December.
Laursen, Finn (1992), "Denmark and European Political Union," in Finn Laursen and Sophie Vanhoonacker, eds., *The Intergovernmental Conference on Political Union*. Dordrecht: Martinus Nijhoff, pp. 63-78.
— (1994), "Denmark and the Ratification of the Maastricht Treaty," in Finn Laursen and Sophie Vanhoonacker (eds.), *The Ratification of the Maastricht Treaty* Dordrecht: Nijhoff, pp. 61-86.
— (1997), 'The Lessons of Maastricht,' in Geoffrey Edwards and Alfred Pijpers (eds.), *The Politics of European Treaty Reform: The 1996 Intergovernmental Conference and Beyond.* London: Pinter, pp. 59-73.
— (2001), "Dansk EU-politik i europæisk perspektiv: Nice og Post-Nice," *Økonomi og Politik*, No. 2 (June), pp. 2-13.
— (2001c), "The Danish Folketing and its European Affairs Committeee: Strong Players in the National Policy Cycle," in Andreas Maurer and Wolfgang Wessels (eds.), *National Parliaments on their Ways to Europe: Losers or Latecomers?* Baden-Baden: Nomos Verlagsgesellschaft, pp. 99-115.
— (2002), "Denmark: The Battle for a Better Treaty," in Finn Laursen (ed.), *The Amsterdam Treaty: Preference Formation, Interstate Bargaining and Outcome*. Odense: Odense University Press, pp. 71-91.
— (2003a), "Denmark: In Pursuit of Influence and Legitimacy," in Wolfgang Wessels, Andreas Maurer and Jürgen Mittag (eds.), *Fifteen into One? The European Union and the Member States*. Manchester: Manchester University Press, pp. 99-114.
— (2003b), "The Danish 'No' to the Euro and its implications: Towards more Variable Geometry?" *CFES Working Paper* (Odense) No. 9/2003.
Lykketoft, Mogens (2001), "Europa i verden," speech to The Foreign Policy Society, Copenhagen, 23 August.
Madsen, Jens Jørgen and Jesper Thobo-Carlsen (2000), "Patent presser ny EU-traktat," *Berlingske Tidende*, 24 November.
— (2000), "Krav om dansk kommissær," *Berlingske Tidende*, 6 December.
— (2000), "Regeringen kæmper for kommissærpost," *Berlingske Tidende*, 7 December.
Madsen, Jens Jørgen, Ask Rostrup and Ole Bang Nielsen (2000), "EU-opgøret skudt i gang," *Berlingske Tidende*, 9 December.
Nielsen, Jakob (2000a), "Veto under pres i Nice," *Politiken*, 4 November.
— (2000b), "Fransk plan om todelt EU," *Politiken*, 4 November.
—, Jens Bostrup and Michael Seidelin (2000), "Øget pres mod dansk EU-kommissær,"

Politiken, 14 October.
—— (2000), "Bister Nyrup fik ret i Nice," *Politiken*, 10 December.
—— (2000), "Dansk glæde over kompromis," *Politiken*, 11 December.
Pittelkow, Ralf (2000), "Om EU-kommissæren," *Jyllands-Posten*, 19 November.
Rostrup, Ask (2000), "Stærkt EU-pres på Danmark," *Berlingske Tidende*, 4 October.
—— (2000), "Det umuliges kunst," *Berlingske Tidende*, 10 October.
Rostrup, Ask and Ole Bang Nielsen (2000), "Søluften klarede tankerne," *Berlingske Tidende*, 15 October.
Seidelin, Michael (2000), "Fortsat strid om Nice," *Jyllands-Posten*, 30 November.
—— (2000), "Holger K. truer med folkeafstemning," *Politiken*, 2 December.
—— (2000), "Dansk kommissær hovedemne," *Politiken*, 5 December.
——, Jakob Nielsen and Jens Bostrup (2000), "De store lande kæmper for vetoretten i EU," *Politiken*, 9 December.
—— (2000), "Magtkamp om stemmer," *Politiken*, 11 December.
SN 511/00: "Meeting Document. Subject: Elements for an overall agreement," Nice, 9 December 2000. Kindly provided by the Danish Foreign Ministry.
—— 514/00: "Mødedokument. Vedr.: Elementer til en samlet aftale," Nice, 9 December 2000. Kindly provided by the Danish Foreign Ministry.
—— 521/00: Konferencen mellem repræsentanterne for medlemsstaternes regeringer, "Arbejdsdokument Vedr.: RK 2000 – Formandskabets endelige kompromisforslag," Nice, 10 December 2000. Kindly provided by the Danish Foreign Ministry.
—— 522/00: "Protocol on the Enlargement of the European Union and Declaration on the Enlargement of the European Union to be included in the Final Act of the Conference (This Annex Cancels and Replaces pages 88-96 of CONFER 4816/00)," Nice, 10 December 2000. Kindly provided by the Danish Foreign Ministry.
—— 533/00: "Treaty of Nice. Provisional text approved by the Intergovernmental Conference on institutional reform," Brussels, 12 December 2000.
Thobo-Carlsen, Jesper (2000), "Expert: Forslag kan udløse ny afstemning," *Berlingske Tidende*, 22 November.
—— and Jens Jørgen Madsen (2000), "Næppe ny folkeafstemning," *Berlingske Tidende*, 7 December.
Østergaard, Ulla (2000), "Lang vej til dansk sejr," *Jyllands-Posten*, 10 December.
—— and Klaus Justsen (2000), "Danmark må bøje sig," *Jyllands-Posten*, 14 October.
—— (2000), "Danmark klar til ny EU-overvågning," *Jyllands-Posten*, 15 October.

CHAPTER 5

GERMANY: A STORY OF SAVING FACE [1]

INTRODUCTION – EUROPEAN TREATY NEGOTIATIONS IN GERMANY

Traditionally, the Federal Republic of Germany belongs to the group of Member States in which European Treaty negotiations have not led to serious domestic conflict. Bearing in mind controversial and partisan debates—e.g. about EMU—and the well-known tension between the federal and regional governments—the *Länder*—with regard to past Treaty changes, this statement may come as a surprise and deserves some elaboration.

On the occasion of the Single European Act (SEA) of 1986, the German *Länder* first started raising objections with regard to a further transfer of powers to the European Community and were concerned, in particular, with the impact of the internal market programme on the domestic allocation of competences and powers. Their concerns and their threat to block ratification of the SEA in the Upper House, or Federal Chamber (*Bundesrat*), however, were accommodated through new and, for the first time, legally binding rules concerning their participation in EU decision-making at both the domestic and the European level. These were enshrined in Art. 2 of the ratification law (EEAG; see Hrbek and Thaysen, 1986, with regard to the debate around the SEA and the domestic ratification process). Throughout the controversial debate, however, ratification of the SEA had never seriously been in doubt.

Much the same can be said with regard to the Treaty of Maastricht. Although Monetary Union and the prospect of giving up the *D-Mark* were heavily contested and gave rise to a wide public and academic debate, the Treaty as such was not seriously challenged at the *political* level. Both houses of Parliament—the *Bundesrat* and the *Bundestag*—ratified the Treaty with a reserve implying that the decision to take part in the final phase of Monetary Union would require a new examination at a later stage, and that they could still block the process if the criteria for entry into the final phase were not met. Green light, however, was finally given by both *Bundestag*

---

[1] This chapter was finalized while the author worked at the European Institute of Public Administration (EIPA) in Maastricht, the Netherlands. The views in the chapter are those of the author and they do not necessarily represent the views of EIPA or the current employer of the author.

and *Bundesrat*[2] and all major political parties in 1997 with overwhelming majorities (despite considerable doubts with regard to the number of Member States participating and their performance in meeting the EMU entry criteria). The Treaty of Amsterdam, for its part, was accompanied by partisan debates centring on the new Treaty chapter on employment (see Beuter, 2002), but again ratification was not in danger at any moment.

Both the Treaties of Maastricht and Amsterdam also gave rise to renewed tensions between the federal and regional governments. As during negotiations leading to the Single Act, the *Länder* had presented new claims with regard to their participation in EU affairs and were concerned with new powers being transferred to the European level (see Bauer, 1991; Borkenhagen et al., 1992). But, as before, non-ratification of the Treaties by the Federal Chamber was never considered a serious political option and the domestic struggle was solved through increased rights of participation in EU affairs at the domestic level in particular (see Borkenhagen et al., 1992; Borkenhagen, 1998).

Renewed threats to block the ratification process in face of new powers being transferred to the Union were—and continue to be—misunderstood in the public and academic debate; in reality the *Länder* never seriously thought of vetoing a continuation of the integration process. Typical accounts of German federal governments being openly pro-integrationists, whatever the colour of the government in power, and of German *Länder* far less enthusiasts (see van Schendelen, 2002: 122), miss the reality of domestic political structures, ties and constraints and have tended, over the past 15 years or so, to clearly overestimate the degree of domestic inter-governmental struggle over European Treaty negotiations.

One of the characteristic features of the German political system is the high level of vertical integration of the party system or, to put it differently, the fact that German federalism has not led to the emergence of regional political parties (De Winter and Türsan, 1998) or to a significant amount of political careers at the regional level (Stolz, 2000)—the Bavarian Christian Social Union (CSU) being the only relevant exception. Unlike in other federalised or strongly regionalised European countries, political issues involving tensions between federal and regional interests are mainly discussed and solved *within* political parties. Conflicts with regard to European Treaty negotiations, in particular, are moderated and softened by political party ties that are, in the eyes of the political actors, of much stronger relevance and endurance than tensions over, in particular, European issues. If European

[2] In the Federal Chamber, only the Free State (*Freistaat*) of Saxonia voted against, whereas Bavaria—also very critical towards the entry decision—in the last minute decided not to vote against.

issues, including Treaty negotiations, give rise to conflicts, the particular domestic features of multi-level policy-making and territorial political exchange (Parri, 1989) will force actors to compromise and to find solutions accommodating the views of both sides. In contrast, the threat of vetoing European Treaty changes is a tool that may be used in the political and public arena, but is not a serious option in practical terms. To use the picture, it would imply using a political atomic bomb to deal with a limited situation of conflict. In a nutshell, the domestic struggle between federal and regional—or state—governments over European integration, and its consequences with regard to the distribution of powers has placed a burden on German federal government's freedom of negotiation, but has often been misinterpreted and overestimated.

At the same time, public opinion—with the one exception regarding the threat to lose the *Deutschmark*—equally has not, in the past, been a factor that strongly has reduced the latitude of German Treaty negotiators. Even compared to other EU Member States, the German public is on the whole neither well informed of European policies nor interested. The degree of affective or utilitarian support for the whole European enterprise and the trust in European institutions today belongs to the lowest in the EU—the degree of trust in the European Commission, for instance, has been shown to be at the bottom end of Member States, together with public opinion in the UK (Niedermayer, 1998). After 50 years of European integration, the famous 'permissive consensus' underlying German integration policy clearly has vanished or, as one may be inclined to say, the thrill has gone.

Seeking to find an explanation, we are usually inclined to believe that the end of the cold war and German unification, in particular, have led to a new perception of Germany's role in Europe and in the world—to the perception of Germany as an ordinary country like any other, the foreign and European policy of which is now led more by national 'interests' than by a rather abstract wish to integrate into the Western world and its institutions and to contribute to this process even where German 'interests' might suggest a more cautious approach. Research with regard to Germany's approaches to European policy-making (Schneider et al., 2001) has shown that this argument—although evidence can be found—must be treated cautiously. The unification of Germany has had its impact and has partly led to the public perception of a 'new normality' of the country, and thus to a general public perception or belief that the country now is—or should be—less restricted in its foreign policy than it was in the past. This development does influence the perception of European policies and does contribute to a stronger emphasis on, or a more pronounced defence of, national 'interests' and to a changed general view on European integration.

These developments, however, cannot fully explain the on the whole clearly negative trend in public opinion with regard to European integration. Personally, the author believes that changes in public perception and opinion of European integration can mainly be explained by the changing nature of the impact of European policies since the late 1980s—i.e. a much deeper, much more visible impact and an impact more immediately and directly felt. What is relevant to our debate, however, is that—although clearly less favourable to European integration then in the past—German public opinion on Europe is mainly characterised by disinterest, certainly with regard to the constitutional development of the Union, and thus on the whole indifferent and hardly places clear restrictions on the way Treaty negotiations are conducted at the European level. Negotiators may be led to be more prudent when it comes to shifting new powers to the EU level and may insist, perhaps more strongly than in the past, on issues such as subsidiarity, but clear restrictions are hard to discern (see also Korte and Maurer, 2001).

In a nutshell: At the domestic level, German politicians are forced to negotiate European Treaties with and 'sell' Treaty outcomes to their peers, but not so much to the public. Politicians in Germany also find it difficult to 'score' on European issues, let alone when these are 'theoretical' constitutional issues. Due to a lack of public interest, media attention also remains at a very modest level. The freedom politicians and civil servants thus enjoy at the European level remains formidable, and domestic debates by and large remain confined to the political and administrative arena.

In this contribution, I will first discuss the domestic negotiation framework (the initial definition of objectives and the organisational structure of inner-domestic negotiations, chapter 1) and the evolving German position in view of the main negotiation items to finally review the conclusions of the negotiations at Nice, the domestic debate with regard to the results and the simple and quick ratification process. Some concluding reflections will close the contribution.

The Domestic Negotiation Framework

The Organisational Structure

The German system for co-ordinating European policy-making at the domestic level is usually described as a complex and decentralised system of intermediation without a dominant centre or authoritative arbitration (see for instance Petiteville, 1999; Mayer, 2002). 'Failing successfully' (Derlien, 2000) is a typical description of a system geared more towards accommodating different actors' interests ('successful' co-ordination) and towards avoiding a plurality of voices at the European level than towards developing clear and sound strategies and positions that are negotiable and can be defended at the European level (ultimate 'failure' of the system).

The German system of European policy co-ordination has undergone considerable changes over the years, and has again been significantly modified under the current governmental coalition in power since 1998. The position of the Foreign Office in European policy co-ordination has been strengthened, and global responsibility for co-ordinating the whole range of economic policies was transferred from the Ministry of Economy to the Ministry of Finance. Both Ministries now share overall responsibility for European policy co-ordination (broadly speaking: the Foreign Office for COREPER II and the respective Council formations, the Ministry of Finance for COREPER I), whereas the tradition that responsibility for working out German negotiation positions and for seeking agreement across Government lies with the 'lead' Ministry (*federführendes Ressort*) competence in substance was not put into question. The lead Ministry is also, in principle, responsible for involving the German *Länder* and other interested parties. The Federal Chancellery (*Bundeskanzleramt*), finally, plays a role in ensuring the global orientation of Germany's European strategies and policies and becomes involved more actively only in the run-up to meetings of the European Council (for the German system of European policy-co-ordination, see Derlien, 2000; Bulmer et al., 2001; Mayer, 2002). The responsibility for overall strategy and direction has over the years—at some stages more, at some stages less—given rise to tensions between the Foreign Office and the Chancellery, in particular when the latter assumed a more visible role (e.g. in the Kohl era under the Director of the International Department in the Chancellery, Mr. Bitterlich). Recently, the old issue of vesting a stronger and more formal power for European policy co-ordination in the Chancellery, advocated by some observers (e.g. Janning and Meyer, 1998; Mayer, 2002), was openly discussed before the general elections of 2002 when both candidates for the office of Federal Chancellor publicly expressed dissatisfaction with the way EU business is conducted (i.e. by the Foreign Office in particular) and with the way German interests are articulated and defended in Brussels.[3] In the end, the system of European policy co-ordination was not modified after the federal elections of 22 September 2002, but the struggle continues.[4]

---

[3] "Schröder macht Fischer die Europapolitik streitig", FAZ vom 19.3.2002; "Schröder plant Neuordnung der Europapolitik", FAZ vom 20 March 2002; "Schröder will Europa zur Chefsache machen—auf Kosten des Außenministers", Handelsblatt vom 20 March 2002.

[4] The system remained unchanged due to the electoral success of Mr. Fischer's Green Party. For the first time, however, a 'European' department (*Europaabteilung*) was set up within the Chancellery, demonstrating an increased will to keep an eye on and influence

Intergovernmental Conferences, for their part, have in Germany traditionally been co-ordinated by the Foreign Office, in close consultation with the Chancellery that assumed the lead role in the run-up to European Council meetings (Thurner and Stoiber, 2001). The structure of the IGC 2000 followed this tradition: the Foreign Office had the overall responsibility for developing and co-ordinating Germany's initial negotiation positions as well as for ensuring the ongoing co-ordination between the federal government and the Länder, and for the development of negotiation positions in the light of the IGC proceedings. It did this through a specially created task force 'IGC' that organised inter-departmental meetings almost weekly and—where necessary□ through the political steering body of European policy-making, the Secretaries of State for European Affairs existing in all federal government ministries (*Europa-Staatssekretäre*). The Foreign Office's lead role was even clearer than in the past due to the scope of the IGC's agenda, limited—in principle—to institutional issues. From a distance, but visible enough to those involved, the Chancellery oversaw the direction of the country's negotiation orientations, and assumed a more visible role where domestic (with the *Länder*) and bilateral (mainly with France) negotiations became politically sensitive. Only towards the closing stages of the IGC did the Chancellery finally take control of negotiations (Wiedmann, 2001: 196).

As for the *Länder*, their involvement in IGCs has since the Single European Act been a sensitive and precarious issue. On a purely formal basis, participation of the *Länder* in IGCs is covered by chapter VII, §2 of the agreement between the federal government and state governments of 29 October 1993, laying down the details of co-operation in European affairs.[5] According to these rules, the *Länder*□ through the Federal Council□ are to be kept informed of IGC proceedings to the extent that their interests are concerned. Opinions of the Federal Council (*Bundesrat*) will be taken into ac-

European strategies and policy-making at the domestic and European level. See Eckart Lohse, "Schröders Europa", *FAZ,* 19 September 2003, p. 3.

[5] *Vereinbarung vom 29. Oktober 1993 zwischen der Bundesregierung und den Regierungen der Länder über die Zusammenarbeit in Angelegenheiten der Europäischen Union in Ausführung von §9 des Gesetzes vom 12. März 1993 über die Zusammenarbeit von Bund und Ländern in Angelegenheiten der Europäischen Union*, Bundesanzeiger 1993, No. 226 of 2 December 1993, p. 10425. Involvement of the *Länder* in European affairs is governed by a complex set of rules at three levels: the foundations are laid down in Art. 23, § 4-6 of the Basic Law, an implementing law specifying these provisions, adopted on 12 March 1993, and finally an inter-governmental agreement between federal and regional governments, of 29 October 1993, covering the details of co-operation such as the transfer of documents, etc. (the so-called *Bund-Länder-Vereinbarung* (BLV)). It is this latter agreement that I refer to. For a detailed and mainly still up-to-date description and analysis of co-operation between the federal and regional governments in European affairs see Morawitz and Kaiser, 1994.

count in accordance with the general rules (i.e. depending on the extent to which domestic interests and powers of the *Länder* are concerned), and the *Länder* may take part, with a maximum number of two observers, at the level of domestic preparatory meetings as well as directly—to the extent that this is possible—in IGCs (as part of the German delegation). Formal opinions of the *Länder* thus have to be issued through the Federal Council, in principle by a simple majority of weighted votes, and will be treated just like opinions with regard to day-to-day European policies. It is the *direct* involvement of the *Länder* in IGCs that to some extent has been a controversial issue ever since the 1991 IGC. Although in the end direct participation by the *Länder* through two observers—representing the two major political parties, or one *Land* ruled by Christian Democrats and one ruled by Social Democrats[6]—has always been accepted, federal governments, independent of their colour, have never really accepted the idea that the *Länder* are to be directly involved in European-level negotiations, even if it were only with a status of observer. If European policy co-ordination between the federal and state governments quite regularly has led to *substance*-related conflicts, such conflicts have tended to be both substance and *process*-related in the context of IGCs (when the Foreign Office, in particular, emphasises traditional diplomacy and seeks to reduce the role of both other government departments and the *Länder*). During the IGC 2000, this conflict became public when, at the beginning of the French Presidency, the Minister of State in the Foreign Office in charge of European integration, Christoph Zöpel, officially declared in March 2000 that he would no longer take part in IGC meetings (at the level of personal representatives) on the grounds that he believed the Foreign Office should represent, within the ICG, the Federal *Republic* of Germany and not only the federal *government*.[7]

Although the *Länder* formally have to act through the *Bundesrat* and may thus, in defining their interests, work with the majority principle, they have in practice ever since sought to develop a unanimous position with regard to the most important and politically sensitive European issues, including IGCs. In practice, IGCs are thus—at the level of the *Länder*—extensively discussed and prepared in all the relevant sectoral Conferences of Ministers (*Fachministerkonferenzen*). The Conference of Ministers for European Affairs (EMK, *Europaministerkonferenz*, see Gerster, 1993) of the Länder is responsible for co-ordination and for preparing, ultimately, decisions of the

[6] In the case of the 1991 IGC, these *Länder* were Baden-Württemberg and Northrhine-West-falia (for the IGC on Political Union) and Bavaria and Hamburg (for the IGC on EMU); in the 1996/1997 IGC the *Länder* were represented by Bavaria and Rhineland-Palatinate, and in the 2000 IGC by Baden-Württemberg and Rhineland-Palatinate.

[7] "Machtkampf im Auswärtigen Amt", TAZ, 13 July 2000.

Conference of Prime Ministers (MPK; *Ministerpräsidentenkonferenz*) at the apex of domestic inter-regional co-ordination. Only then—when unanimous agreement is reached at this level—is a position of the *Länder* formally adopted—or 'ratified'—by the Federal Council. Consequently, reaching agreement between the *Länder* is a time-consuming affair, more particularly when it comes to details such as identifying areas selectable for QMV. Moreover, modifying or developing positions that have once been accepted by all becomes an even more burdensome matter.

Domestic co-ordination of IGCs thus is made more complex by the fact that the federal government may find it difficult, if not impossible, to obtain a clear and reliable position of the *Länder* even while negotiations at the European level are under way or close to come to an end, and that representatives of the *Länder* invited to take part in domestic negotiations to fix the German negotiation position may not be fully prepared or entitled to actually speak on behalf of the *Länder* as a whole. These have sought to overcome these problems by preparing for the IGC at a very early stage in 1999, well before the agenda of the IGC had been agreed, and by adopting a first formal opinion of the Federal Council before real negotiations started, in February 2000 (Bundesrat, 2000). The early preparation and adoption of a formal position, however, had two side-effects that made domestic co-ordination of the IGC perhaps more difficult instead of easier at a later stage:

- The first opinion of the *Bundesrat* was a framework statement that needed to be filled in with details, in particular with regard to the issue of moving towards QMV in sensitive areas. The opinion did not contain specific statements that would have allowed *Länder* representatives to agree or disagree with individual Treaty articles being subject to QMV in the future.
- As the first formal opinion of the *Bundesrat* started to be prepared in early 1999, it also covered at least two items of major political sensitivity that were not part of the European agenda but nevertheless could not simply be treated as irrelevant by the federal government: a better delimitation of competences (*Kompetenzabgrenzung*) and a guarantee for services of general interest (*Daseinsvorsorge*). Early preparation set in motion a self-referential logic that to some extent was decoupled from the IGC agenda-setting process at the European level.

Following the first statement of the *Bundesrat*, it was obvious to both the federal and the state level that addressing the politically sensitive issues that went beyond the scope of the IGC required an ongoing and flexible *political* consultation process not foreseen by existing, strongly formalised domestic co-operation agreements and structures in the area of European policy-making. Such a consultation process was needed also because—unlike during most previous IGCs—the *Länder* were internally divided and because both political and administrative negotiations with the federal government could hardly be taken care of by just two state governments representing the totality of the *Länder*.

To solve this impasse, the Prime Ministers of the *Länder* early in 2000 agreed, with the Chancellor, to launch an informal political dialogue that was to operate both at the official and the political level to discuss political differences with regard to the IGC 2000 and that was to be organised on an irregular basis whenever required (Wiedmann, 2001: 199). This so-called 'Bund-Länder Working Party IGC', or also 'Pleuger-Hoffmann round' (*Pleuger-Hoffmann-Runde*[8]), was composed of representatives of 8 German *Länder* and—depending on the issue—a number of representatives of the federal government (including the Foreign Office co-presiding the meetings together with the *Land* holding the Presidency of the Conference of Prime Ministers, the Chancellery and other Ministries). It subsequently assumed a major role in finding solutions to the pending political issues surrounding the IGC and in further developing the positions of the *Länder*, whereas their regular domestic involvement in the IGC took place in the framework of the ordinary inter-departmental co-ordination meetings organised and chaired by the Foreign Office. The new working practice of irregular and flexible meetings at the political level later was considered to be so fruitful that it was maintained after the IGC and continues to date (although today with mainly different actors and topics).

If the federal Parliament, the *Bundestag*, is discussed only at the end, then this is because not in theory but in practice—and the 2000 IGC was no exception to this rule—it plays only a minor role in the domestic decision-making process with regard to European affairs, or indeed in European Treaty negotiations. The involvement of the *Bundestag* in European policy-making has its foundation in the Basic Law (Art. 23 §3) and in an ordinary law[9] and is based on the simple principle that Parliament is given the possibility of issuing statements that will be taken into account by the government. The position of the specialised European Committee of the *Bundestag* has also been solidified over the years, and it occupies a unique position in comparison with other parliamentary committees (Fuchs, 2001; Kövel, 2000; Rath, 2001). Yet the practical influence of the *Bundestag* on European policy-making at the domestic level remains limited. The description of its position as 'benevolent weakness' moving towards 'supportive scrutiny' (Hölscheidt, 2001; see also Sterzing and Tidow, 2001) is an adequate summary

---

[8] Named after the then State Secretary for European Affairs in the Foreign Office, Gunter Pleuger, and the State Secretary in the Prime Ministers Office of the Land Bremen holding the Presidency of the *Ministerpräsidentenkonferenz* at that time.

[9] *Gesetzes vom 12. März 1993 über die Zusammenarbeit von Bundesregierung und Deutschem Bundestag in Angelegenheiten der Europäischen Union*, Bundesgesetzblatt (BGBl.) I 1993, S. 311.

hardly disguising the fact that its ability—or perhaps even willingness—to significantly influence the government's European policy-making is hardly formidable. In practise, the European Committee closely followed the IGC 2000 and was kept informed by the federal government at all stages but, contrary to the Federal Council, never proceeded towards issuing formal statements, let alone 'mandates', that would have restricted the government's ability to negotiate.

As a conclusion, the organisational framework for negotiations placed the Foreign Office—guided by the Federal Chancellery at critical moments—at the centre and mainly focused on making sure that other federal ministries would remain on board and that the German *Länder* were, first, closely involved and would not be able to argue that they had had no opportunity to influence the German position, and, second, would be able to find themselves in the final outcome, or at least to argue that their interests had been taken into account. The organisational framework clearly concentrated on the executive branch of government and otherwise did not seriously have to take account of parliamentary or other 'external' interests.

Clear Objectives and a Limited Scope

As far as the federal government was concerned, Germany entered the IGC with the pronounced objective to limit the agenda of the IGC to what was strictly necessary to reform the institutions in order to pave the way for enlargement. Or, more precisely, the objective was to focus—if not to limit—the agenda to the issues mentioned in the conclusions of the Cologne European Council (June 1999), i.e. to the 'left-overs' from Amsterdam and 'other institutional arrangements' necessary to reform the institutions before enlargement. The initial German position before the Helsinki European Council in December 1999 did include a number of other points to be addressed by the IGC: the individual responsibility of Commissioners (following the demise of the Santer Commission earlier in 1999), institutional issues linked to the CFSP and the composition and working of the Court of Justice. These items were believed, however, not to undermine the clear focus on the 'left-overs' of Amsterdam and were considered both as urgent and linked to the core agenda of the IGC (e.g. the individual responsibility of Commissioners was to be treated in context with the future composition of the Commission). By contrast, other possible items, according to the German position, were to be treated either in their relation to the extension of QMV (flexibility) or in the context of accession negotiations (the composition and the size of the European Parliament).

This rather restricted objective was clearly spelled out by Chancellor Schröder in his governmental statement (*Regierungserklärung*) given to the Bundestag on 3 December 1999, a week before the Helsinki European Council.[10] The official reason given was that only a limited agenda would allow to conclude the IGC by the end of 2000 under the French Presidency. Other political considerations, however, clearly contributed to the fact that the federal government spoke out in favour of a restricted agenda and provided additional arguments.

In the course of 1999, it became clear that relevant domestic actors would place additional demands on the agenda, demands that could—not only in the eyes of the federal government – not realistically be satisfied. The German *Länder*, although focusing on the institutional issues at stake, again started raising the issue of a better, or clearer, division of tasks and competences between the European and the domestic level of government (*Kompetenzabgrenzung*), and were also, again, seeking to strengthen direct regional involvement at the European level, in line with regional or 'federal' claims they had first, and after all rather successfully, presented during the 1991 IGC (strengthening of the Committee of the Regions, direct access of regions with legislative powers to the Court of Justice, a more rigorous definition of the subsidiarity principle; see Bauer, 1991). As the federal government was invited to take part in the *Länder* working party set up to prepare their position with regard to the IGC, it was well informed of what was discussed amongst these.

To make things more complicated, the main opposition party, the Christian Democrats, presented on 3 May 1999, a strategy paper arguing that the EU was in need of a constitutional debate and a 'constitutional Treaty' (*Verfassungsvertrag*) and that, in the perspective of enlargement, the values, structures and policies of the Union had to be clarified and rethought beyond what was agreed in the Agenda 2000 and beyond what was to be negotiated during the forthcoming IGC (Schäuble and Lamers, 1999). Later, prior to the Helsinki European Council, two key issues discussed in this paper—new and strengthened institutional rules with regard to 'flexibility' and a better division of tasks based on the principle of subsidiarity—were singled out by opposition spokesmen as items that needed to be added to the agenda of the IGC.[11] Both the *Länder* and the main opposition party, in their attempts to enlarge the agenda of the IGC, were also backed by the most important

---

[10] *Regierungserklärung des Bundeskanzlers zum bevorstehenden Europäischen Rates in Helsinki am 10./11. Dezember 1999*, Stenographischer Bericht des Deutschen Bundestages, 14. Wahlperiode, 77. Sitzung am 3. Dezember 1999, pp. 7061-7065.

[11] Stenographischer Bericht des Deutschen Bundestages, 14. Wahlperiode, 77. Sitzung am 3. Dezember 1999, pp. 7061-7098. See also Ausschuss für Angelegenheiten der Europäischen Union, 2000: 33; 35.

European think-tank, the Bertelsmann Foundation, and by other public comments.

Faced with some political pressure to expand the agenda of the IGC to issues of a more clearly constitutional character that, at least partly, would raise little if any support by other Member States, the federal government´s strategic choice therefore was to strictly limit the agenda of the IGC. Any extension of the agenda suggested by other Member States would at the domestic level have raised the question of why, then, the wider agenda discussed domestically was not reflected in the Helsinki agreement. And although the government in reality knew that the demand for a wider, and more constitutional, agenda was part of the political game and was only partly to be taken seriously, the *Länder* were in practice not united behind their claims, and the opposition which was in power at the time of the 1991 and 1996/1997 IGCs, had itself sought to avoid a more constitutional agenda, the best possible option to avoid any embarrassing and potentially dangerous domestic debate was to limit the new agenda. This line was also advocated from the start by the governmental coalition in the Federal Diet that was far from enthusiastic on the issue of flexibility and against adding the division of powers on agenda (Ausschuss für Angelegenheiten der Europäischen Union, 2000: 35; 37).

To take into account both the domestic and the European debate, the initial German position with regard to the mandate of the IGC, however, also included the proposal that the current IGC should already pave the way for future reforms with a clear timetable. This opening for other and more far-reaching reforms was a particular concession that was made to the Länder in order to satisfy their demands that were otherwise—as far as the federal government was concerned—part of the so-called 'crazy box' of the Portuguese Presidency in the first half of 2000.

On the whole, the German government was satisfied with the conclusions of the Helsinki European Council. The only noteworthy adaptation of the initial position that was made before the official opening of the IGC on 9 February 2000 concerned the issue of 'flexibility.' Where the initial position was that flexibility 'should' not be treated as an isolated issue in its own right, the basic negotiation brief later stated that flexibility 'must not necessarily' be treated in an isolated way, reflecting the fact that some other countries had shown a stronger interest in the issue.

The 'Neue Normalität' and the Defence of National Interests

In preparing the agenda of the IGC, a second, politically more sensitive issue marked the domestic debate; it also—as the future would show—placed a heavy burden on the IGC and strongly contributed to the near-failure at Nice.

Since the 1991 IGC, the defence of 'national interests' in Brussels started to become a domestic political issue and the decision to give up the *Deutschmark* in favour of EMU. The issue became more pronounced, however, in the electoral campaign of 1998 when Gerhard Schröder—taking up popular views and challenging Chancellor Kohl on his distinctly pro-European attitude – sharply criticised the government in power for not defending national interests in Brussels and argued that the times of Germany paying the bill for other countries (*'Checkbuchdiplomatie'*) had to come to an end. The catchword used by Schröder during and after the electoral campaign—the 'new normality' (*'neue Normalität'*) of the (equally new) *'Berliner Republik'* and its foreign relations—indeed seemed to stand in clear contrast to the tradition of German European policy which was on the whole marked by the congruence or 'symbiotic' relation (Hellmann, 2002) between national and European 'interests'. The insistence with which Schröder proclaimed a 'new normality' and the need to emphasise 'national interests' drew heavy criticism by many, including former Chancellor Helmut Schmidt, and was indeed seen as a major challenge to Germany's traditionally pro-integrationist approach.[12]

In the context of our discussion, the government's, and in particular the Chancellor's, emphasis on the fact that other partners had to understand that Germany, like any other country, also had 'legitimate national interests'[13] in practice has left its traces on the conduct of European policies by Germany since 1998.[14] Just before the IGC 2000, the 'new' public debate concerning national interests had particularly focused on the outcome of the Agenda 2000, which was severely criticised also by opposition parties, and on the role France had played in securing the deal at the Berlin European Council on 25 March 1999. It was thus not surprising that the issue of 'national interests' had some impact on the German conduct of negotiations during the IGC 2000.

---

[12] See e.g. *Der Spiegel* Nr. 52 of 21 December 1998; *Der Spiegel* Nr. 53 of 28 December 1998.

[13] See Interview with Gerhard Schröder in *Die Welt am Sonntag*, 27 February 1999.

[14] Examples of Schröder's 'new'—but not necessarily successful—way of defending 'national interests' in Brussels are abundant, e.g. the events around the vehicles end-of-life directive, the takeover directive or several cases in the area of competition policy (Holtzmann and others).

Before the Helsinki European Council, Chancellor Schröder emphasised that unanimity in the Council had to be maintained on 'key issues of national interest.'[15] Subsequently, the insistence on the 'demographic' dimension in the future weighting of votes in the Council became the pivotal issue for Germany in the IGC—Chancellor Schröder's statement before the *Bundestag* right ahead of the Nice European Council was clear in this respect[16]—and was at the heart of the rift that divided Germany and France. Whoever was to blame for the subsequent developments, the origins can be traced back to a perhaps not so new, but clearly more outspoken and public emphasis on national interests by Chancellor Schröder in particular. Opposition parties, for their part, also played an important role in this context. Although Christian Democrats, in particular, warned that Germany had been well served by its traditional 'careful diplomacy' at the EU level and that the Chancellor's European rhetoric was dangerous and not backed by a clear concept (Schäuble and Lamers, 1999), this overall criticism—raised throughout and after the conclusion of the IGC—found little reflection in the way they defined their own approach to the IGC. Not only did the opposition in substance support the government's approach to the IGC (e.g. with regard to the weighting of votes in the Council; see Ausschuss für Angelegenheiten der Europäischen Union, 2000, 30), their main spokesman in the parliamentary debate ahead of the Helsinki European Council, Bavarian Prime Minister Edmund Stoiber, even criticised the government for having failed to take into account national interests when negotiating in Brussels.[17]

In the eyes of the author, the domestic debate with regard to defending national interests in Brussels—re-launched ahead of the 2002 federal elections—had little if anything to do with substance, but all the more with policy style and public rhetoric. In any case it placed a burden upon Germany's negotiating position during the IGC as the government had to come back home with an outcome that could be sold in the light of this debate.

STRIKING THE BALANCE – THE MAIN NEGOTIATION CHAPTERS

From the German point of view, following the logic of the declaration on the functioning of institutions annexed to the Treaty of Amsterdam, the issues under examination by the IGC were closely interrelated: QMV as general

[15] Stenographischer Bericht des Deutschen Bundestages, 14. Wahlperiode, 77. Sitzung am 3. Dezember 1999, p. 7063—he did not, however, mention which issues he was referring to.

[16] Stenographischer Bericht des Deutschen Bundestages, 14. Wahlperiode, 135. Sitzung am 28. November 2000, pp. 13026sq.

[17] Stenographischer Bericht des Deutschen Bundestages, 14. Wahlperiode, 77. Sitzung am 3. Dezember 1999, pp. 7065sq.

voting rule was seen as the best possible option with a view to increasing the efficiency of decision-making in the Council under the condition of a satisfactory solution to the weighting of votes; QMV was seen as particularly profitable to Germany if the country's voting power could be increased to bypass that of other larger Member States. Reducing the number of Commissioners was seen as an option not only to streamline decision-making in the College but also—bearing in mind that larger Member States would have to give up their second Commissioner—as a sacrifice to be made to smaller Member States. A sacrifice that was perhaps not too difficult to make since Germany shared the perception that the role of the Commission within the institutional triangle had declined rather than increased over the last years. Or, to put it differently, the readiness of larger Member States, including Germany, to give up their second Commissioner also was a clear signal that they did not believe that the Commission was likely to regain the political weight it had enjoyed under Jacques Delors.

Germany, like the other Member States, thus entered the IGC with the ambition to strike the best possible balance between the different negotiation boxes from a domestic point of view. These main boxes will now be examined one by one.

Reforming the Commission

Together with the other large Member States, Germany entered the IGC with the firm intention—already defended during the 1996 IGC (Beuter, 2002)—to reduce the size of the College and to fix a ceiling to the number of Commissioners. Domestically, this position was broadly shared by all political parties, with the CDU emphasising that the number of Commissioners should be based on the actual tasks of the College and not a 'theoretical' number (Ausschuss für Angelegenheiten der Europäischen Union, 2000: 29). Having in mind, the two groups of countries identified in the 'options paper' of December 1999 preparing the Helsinki European Council, Germany thus clearly belonged to the second group suggesting that a Commission consisting of a limited and fixed number of members was "the best way of enabling it to fulfil effectively its functions as a College" (Council of the European Union, 1999: 5).

Once the IGC had officially started, it soon became clear that the position with regard to the limitation of the number of Commissioners shared by the larger Member States could not be maintained and that Germany—along with the other large Member States—would, in the end, have to give in to the overwhelming majority of smaller Member States insisting on the principle of one Commissioner per Member State. As stated in an internal position paper of May 2000, of all the small countries only the Netherlands had, in bilateral talks, indicated that at the end of the day they could accept the idea of a fixed ceiling below the number of Member States, provided that the actual composition of the College would be based on a rotation system with equal treatment of all Member States. German negotiators thus in practice concentrated on the conditions under which the country was prepared to give up its official position and accept the idea of one Commissioner per Member State. These conditions were essentially two: a satisfactory solution to the allocation of votes in the Council, and an efficient internal structure of the Commission, including an element of hierarchy between Commissioners. This was to be realised for instance through an increased number of Vice-Presidents with a reinforced role[18] or through a distinction between full members of the Commission (with own portfolio) and Junior Commissioners (with a right to vote but without portfolio). The German position on the issue—including the conditions under which it would compromise—was from the outset well co-ordinated with the other large Member States.

The official position of the larger Member States, including Germany, was maintained until the European Council of Nice. However, it was already following the Foreign Ministers' meeting of 19 September 2000, the last IGC meeting at this level before the Biarritz Summit, that some of the larger Member States, including Germany, indicated that the hypothesis of a 'restricted College' was probably unrealistic and that internal reforms would have to safeguard the effectiveness of the College in the future.[19] Just two days before Biarritz, Chancellor Schröder had indicated that from the German perspective the 'battle' for the position of the large Member States with regard to the composition of the Commission was a lost cause.[20]

As described by Galloway (2001, 48 sq.), the Biarritz informal summit of 13/14 October 2000—despite its poisoned atmosphere and the fact that it brought about no real progress—represented the turning point of the debate concerning the size of the Commission. It still saw the 5 largest Member States officially united in their suggestion of a College still restricted in size, but now composed on the basis of a system of rotation placing all Member States on an equal footing, meaning that they accepted the idea of temporarily giving up not only one but their two Commissioners, whereas some smaller Member States started to accept the idea that the size of the College

[18] At the domestic level, the ideas that were developed suggested that, for instance, the increased number (7-8) of Vice-Presidents could have certain co-ordinating functions with regard to other Commissioners, or that they could form an "inner cabinet".

[19] See Agence Europe of 20 September 2000, p. 3.

[20] See Hartmut Hausmann, Fehlender Wille zur Einigung, Das Parlament No. 44, 27 October 2000.

would have to be capped at some point in the future (so-called 'deferred capping'). Among the larger Member States, Germany had played a leading role in adapting—or clarifying—their initial position; on several occasions, Chancellor Schröder himself had publicly declared that he would have no problem with a Commission that temporarily included no German citizen.

If Biarritz marked the turning point, the final agreement, although close at hand, had to wait until Nice. From a German point of view, the size of the Commission by then, however, was no longer a top priority as it was realised that the block of smaller Member States would not compromise over the maintenance of one Commissioner per country for the years to come. The agreement reached in Nice was not ideal but acceptable to Germany in that the size of the Commission was going to be reduced somewhere in the future and in that the sub-optimal agreement included internal reforms of the Commission that were included in the initial German position. At the end, Germany had helped reach an agreement by internally accepting, at a rather early stage, that the initial position of the larger Member States—among which Spain was not a strong ally and tended to side with the small countries—could not be maintained, and by putting forward compromise. On the other hand, Germany—and the Chancellor personally—had strongly contributed, together with France, to the ideological character concerning the future composition and role of the Commission through a new kind of popular 'Commission bashing' in particular over the latter's state aid and competition policy. Germany thus had clearly played a major role in giving the impression that the larger Member States wanted to downsize rather than strengthen the Commission.

QMV in the Council

When setting out the country's agenda for the IGC before the *Bundestag* on 3 December 1999, Chancellor Schröder explicitly pointed out that, although a more pronounced move towards QMV and co-decision with the European Parliament was one of the main goals of his government, Germany would insist on unanimity voting on 'key issues' of national interest.[21] This ambiguity, it can be argued, characterised the German position towards QMV throughout the IGC and was—due to circumstances—never fully resolved.

Throughout negotiations, Germany's position towards QMV in the Council thus to some extent remained both clear and ambiguous. From the political and strategic point of view, there was hardly any opposition towards

[21] Stenographischer Bericht des Deutschen Bundestages, 14. Wahlperiode, 77. Sitzung am 3. Dezember 1999, p. 7063.

QMV as a generalised voting rule; a more pronounced move towards QMV had for some time indeed been part of Germany's political preferences and was shared by all relevant political parties (Ausschuss für Angelegenheiten der Europäischen Union, 2000: 31). If there was a degree of *open* scepticism, this was—like during previous IGCs—voiced by the German *Länder*. In its initial resolution on the opening of the IGC, of 4 February 2000 (Bundesrat, 2000), the *Bundesrat* had spoken in favour of QMV as a general rule, but had also pointed out that the rule of unanimity could, in individual cases, be a means to safeguard the powers of the *Länder*—or national interests—at the European level. The *Länder* also pointed out that, where QMV was considered, the attributions of the Union had to be clarified more precisely, and thus linked the issue of QMV to the issue of *Kompetenzabgrenzung*. The wording of the resolution of the *Bundesrat* was a compromise between those *Länder* that were pronounced spokesmen of QMV (and opposed to the *Kompetenzabgrenzungs*-debate) and others more concerned with a clearer delimitation of competences and, in reality, less interested in QMV.

Within the federal government, the position on QMV was not as clear as it would seem at first sight. From the beginning, the Foreign Office tried to avoid a substantial or policy-related domestic debate with regard to QMV and got the principle accepted that Germany would be in favour of the principle that unanimity in the Council should be restricted to the few cases of decisions of constitutional (requiring ratification by the Member States) or quasi-constitutional character (such as decisions based on Article 308 TEC), turning integration backward (e.g. Art. 93 §2 allowing the Council to agree that by exception a state aid measure is compatible with the Common Market) or related to defence matters. In all other cases, Ministries in fact need to justify why a decision should remain within the scope of unanimity. This methodology for separating different types of decisions was even more rigorous than the category-based approach chosen by the Portuguese Presidency in preparing the negotiations on this sensitive issue (Galloway, 2001: 99sq.) and effectively put the burden on those Ministries aiming at keeping 'their' policies under the rule of unanimity. The objective of the Foreign Office was clear, and also proved to be rather successful: a substantial debate in the course of which individual Ministries would raise their traditional concerns was to be avoided as far as possible.

At the same time, the Foreign Office urged the *Länder* to identify as quickly as possible the areas in which, from their point of view, the rule of unanimity was to be maintained, so that Germany could enter European negotiations with a clear position. The urgency to clarify the position of the *Länder* was in some contrast with the desire to avoid substantial discussions between federal government Ministries, and based on the knowledge that the *Länder* would find it extremely difficult if not impossible to reach unanimous agreement over individual Treaty articles that were to remain within the scope of unanimity.

When the French Presidency submitted its initial list of 49 Treaty provisions that could be considered for QMV (IGC document *CONFER 4770/00*), German negotiators found themselves in a rather comfortable but at the same time not so easy situation. On the one hand, they had a large room of manoeuvre and could signal a wide-ranging willingness to move towards QMV. On the other hand, they had not yet received a formal position from the *Länder*—this was only to come at the end of October 2000—and, due to the chosen approach to QMV, case-by-case examination of some sensitive provisions at the federal level had started rather late and was not concluded. Germany's position thus was highly favourable towards QMV but at the same time lacked, to some extent, a firm and agreed foundation at the domestic level. In the early negotiations under the French Presidency, Germany thus did not raise objections to a single one of the articles proposed for QMV by the Presidency, but had reservations about a considerable number of items (14 out of 49) where discussions with the *Länder* and/or within the federal government had not been closed. While retaining a positive attitude, Germany's position was less clear than that of other delegations.

Early in September 2000, the German government was close to finalising an internal list of Treaty articles that could move towards QMV.[22] While domestic negotiations with the Ministry of Employment and Social Affairs and the Ministry of the Interior over QMV in their areas were still under way and discussions with the German *Länder* were to be continued, the overall approach agreed within the government and bilateral discussions with the Foreign Office had led most federal government Ministries to accept QMV in their areas or convinced them that QMV would increase rather than diminish the likelihood of defending German interests in Brussels. A clear point in case was the proposal—put forward together with France in November 2000—to move to QMV in some areas of taxation (IGC Document *CONFER 4808/00* of 21 November 2000). Altogether, several sensitive issues such as provisions concerning structural funds, areas of taxation, CSFP (excluding defence matters), police co-operation and others were seen as candidates for QMV. Domestically, German negotiators aimed at closing all the chapters by the time of the last meeting of Personal Representatives before the informal Biarritz Summit, on 25 September 2000.

As negotiations progressed and it became increasingly clear—following the stalemate at the Biarritz Summit—that substantial progress in sensitive

---

[22] See *Handelsblatt* of 6 September 2000, p. 9: "Berlin legt Liste für EU-Mehrheitsentscheidungen vor."

policy areas would not be achieved because other delegations were firmly opposed to QMV in core areas, domestic negotiations concentrated on reaching an agreement between the federal government and the *Länder* on the limited number of areas in which the *Länder* would refuse QMV but where progress seemed possible at the European level. The position of the *Länder* was not firmly agreed before the yearly conference of Prime Ministers from 25-27 October 2000 in Schwerin (Ministerpräsidentenkonferenz, 2000), the outcome of which was later transformed into a second resolution of the Federal Council on the IGC.[23] Prime Ministers identified seven key Treaty Articles that according to them had to remain within the scope of unanimity, while agreement between the *Länder* on the areas of taxation and social policy had still not been reached.[24]

In the closing stages of the IGC, just two areas, or Treaty articles, were still problematic from the German point of view, namely Art. 47 §2 TEC (principles governing the professions with regard to training and conditions of access for natural persons) and Art. 151 §5 TEC (cultural support programmes). Unanimity in both areas was demanded by the *Länder*, whereas the federal government itself could maintain a very open and favourable position towards QMV; the areas where individual Ministries were not or not fully prepared to move towards QMV were already 'covered' by a sufficient degree of resistance from other Member States (taxation, social policy, Justice and Home Affairs). Germany was able to secure unanimity in both of the aforementioned areas, in the case of Art. 151 §5 acting alone (all other delegations, or so it seemed, accepted QMV in the area of cultural support programmes). The fact that the federal government on these two issues was acting on behalf of the *Länder* made it easier to secure unanimity; the pending threat of non-ratification of the Treaty was a formidable argument understood by other delegations. Both areas were, moreover, not generally seen as major policy areas in which progress needed to be made.

Throughout the negotiations and notwithstanding some domestic reservations, Germany was able to maintain a positive tone on QMV and was seen as a 'demander' for QMV rather than as a blocking force (unlike during the closing stages of the European Convention in June and July 2003). One of the prime arguments that allowed the country to be generally open to QMV was the fact that with a new weighting of votes in the Council larger Mem-

---

[23] Bundesratsentschließung of 10 November 2000 (Drs. 680/00).

[24] Art. 13 TEC (actions to combat discrimination), Art. 47 § 2 TEC (principles governing the professions with respect to training and conditions of access for natural persons), measures in the area of visa, asylum and migration (Arts. 62 and 63 TEC), Art. 151 §5 (cultural support programmes), Art. 159 §3 TEC (specific actions outside of structural funds), Art. 175 §2 TEC (specific environmental provisions and measures) and Art. 308 TEC or new specific Community attributions replacing Art. 308.

ber States and Germany in particular had more to gain than to lose from QMV.

The Weighting of Votes in the Council

It need not be emphasised that the weighting of votes in the Council—the voting power of Member States—was not only, with the composition of the Commission, the most sensitive issue of the IGC and the Nice European Council, but that Germany played a major part in it.

When defining its initial position for the IGC in November and December 1999, the federal government limited itself to setting as objective a voting system that would better reflect the demographic weight of Member States without specifying what such a system had to look like. Domestically, this position was not challenged and even found explicit support from the *Länder*. For tactical reasons, Germany remained open to different possible scenarios, always provided they would reflect the size of the population. More precisely, Germany was open to a simple re-weighting of votes —with France and the UK as main allies which, however, were openly against de-coupling the voting power of Germany—as well as to a system of double majority—preferred by smaller Member States—or even to a combined solution. The Commission's proposal for a system of double but simple majority was met with scepticism although it included the demographic aspect; it would have implied the possibility of forming majorities against a too large number of countries.

The number of different possible 'models' for dealing with the weighting of votes in the Council proliferated in the course of the IGC, and even entering the Nice European Council a solution was not in sight. While in principle siding with the larger Member States in preference of a 'simple' re-weighting of votes, in the course of negotiations Germany remained open to other solutions for a very long time. In the parliamentary debate of 25 October following the European Council of Biarritz, Foreign Minister Fischer continued to state that the government was open to different models provided these included the demographic factor.[25] He also repeated Chancellor Schröder's statement that the weighting of votes was not a 'mathematical' but a political question, indicating that Germany was prepared to negotiate a solution but needed a satisfactory outcome at least from an 'optical' perspective.

Fischer's statement reflected not only Germany's initial intentions but also the awareness that the country found itself in an awkward position. Although some understanding for the German position had been reached with

[25] Stenographischer Bericht des Deutschen Bundestages, 14. Wahlperiode, 126. Sitzung am 25. Oktober 2000, p. 12109.

some Member States, France—now exercising the Presidency—remained firmly opposed to any solution explicitly referring to the demographic weight of Member States, let alone a decoupling of votes. Bilateral talks even at the highest level had not led to an agreement between the countries (although they continued to work together on other IGC items). Germany therefore also stayed open to solutions preferred by smaller Member States as its stated interests were not entirely backed by its 'natural' allies, the larger countries.

Towards mid November 2000, reflected in a Presidency note of 16 November 2000 (IGC 2000a), a compromise accepted by a clear majority of Member States was reached on the principle of a simple re-weighting of votes that would have to take into account both the population and the number of Member States—a 'model' in line with the kind of 'combined solution' that had been reflected in Germany's initial position. The Presidency note of 16 November included three basic 'models' that all—to a different extent—took into account the German position. Among these, the 'Swedish' model that proposed a clear de-coupling of the votes of larger Member States was most strongly in line with German interests and showed that indeed the preferred outcome was not necessarily one suggested by a large Member State. An alternative 'Italian' model was acceptable with regard to the voting power of larger Member States but would have kept Germany in line with the other three most powerful countries.

A solution to the weighting of votes in the Council was not in sight before Nice. What made things difficult for Germany was that the outcome it preferred—a pronounced re-weighting including a decoupling of Germany's votes from those of France, Italy and the UK—was matched neither by the group of larger Member States—generally not in favour of decoupling but more 'relaxed' and hiding behind France—nor by the smaller countries opposed to a pronounced re-weighting. Germany thus found itself without a 'natural' or evident ally ahead of Nice. Finally, the stake for the outcome at Nice with regard to the demographic factor had been raised so high by the government—and by Chancellor Schröder in particular—that it needed to come back from Nice with a result it could sell to the public. The domestic media had by then clearly focused their attention on the weighting power in the Council and the 'battle' between Chirac and Schröder; neither of both could in fact give in at Nice. For German negotiators, however, the agreement to the whole reform package depended upon a satisfactory solution to the weighting of votes.

The 'Future of the Union' and Other Issues

From the German perspective, reaching, in Nice, an agreement over a future and wider reform agenda turned out to be the second most important issue at stake. To take and to keep the German *Länder* on board, the idea to fix a future—and wider—reform agenda had been part of the German negotiation package from the beginning, but the outcome remained open until the Nice European Council.

The main reason for Germany's insistence on reaching an agreement over a more constitutional reform agenda came from the need to accommodate, in one way or another, the strong demand for a clearer and more transparent division of tasks and competences between the European and the national level, a division the *Bundesrat* had (once again) expressed in its initial statement on the IGC 2000, of 4 February 2000. Although the tone of this demand was more careful than it had been in the past and had been linked to QMV, the *Länder* had made it clear that progress on the issue of *Kompetenzabgrenzung* was going to be one of the essential criteria over which they would assess the outcome of the IGC in the Federal Council.[26]

From the point of view of the federal government, *Kompetenzabgrenzung* was, from the outset, an issue belonging to the so-called 'crazy box'. Experience from past Treaty reforms as well as bilateral preparatory talks had convinced the Foreign Office at a very early stage that there would be no opening for this highly sensitive issue during the IGC. At an early stage, the Foreign Office thus started looking for an alternative way to offer something to the *Länder* that would allow them to accept the final outcome of the IGC without it being unacceptable to other Member States. In March/April 2000, a first written proposal to adopt, in Nice, a declaration on further Treaty reforms was presented to the German *Länder* in bilateral talks at the political level (in the 'Pleuger-Hoffmann-group'). Domestic agreement was quickly reached on the principle of an 'opening declaration', but not on the character—binding or non-binding—or on the content of such a declaration. The *Länder* insisted on a declaration that would be part of the new Treaty and that would clearly spell out the objectives—or the content—of a next round of Treaty reforms, whereas the federal government suggested that it might not be possible to obtain more than a vague political statement to be inserted into the Presidency conclusions at Nice.

Foreign Office negotiators proved to be right in their assumption that it would be highly difficult, if not impossible, to convince other delegations of the proposal to already pave the way for a next round of Treaty reforms. Joschka Fischer's now 'famous' speech of 12 May 2000—held not as Minister

[26] The second difficult and sensitive issue brought up by the *Länder*, the '*Daseinsvorsorge*' (services of general economic interest), will not be dealt with here. It was solved by a joint input of the federal and state governments to the Commission′s communication on this topic issued on 20 September 2000.

of Foreign Affairs but as a private person□ can to some extent also be seen as an attempt to see what kind of reactions a 'federal' vision for the future of the European Union, including a clearer allocation of competences, would provoke in other Member States (Fischer, 2000). There were indeed many reactions, in particular from France which, at least initially, felt completely overridden and was annoyed, in particular, by the fact that the views expressed had no relation with the agenda of the IGC and disturbed the sensitive negotiations. Indeed Fischer's move can only be understood in the light of the domestic debate and his wish to signal that he was aware and supportive of the wider reform agenda proposed both by the *Länder* and by the parliamentary opposition.

The Presidency report to the Feira European Council, however, refrained from even mentioning the idea of a new Treaty reform agenda and merely pointed out that some 'other questions' has been raised at the Conference—including the allocation of powers between the Union/Community and Member States—but that "at this stage of the discussion there are neither objective reasons nor sufficient support to justify the inclusion of these issues in the Conference agenda" (IGC, 2000b: 50; 118). In the subsequent deliberations and bilateral talks in the run-up to the Nice European Council, it turned out that it proved to be extremely difficult to convince either the new French Presidency or a larger number of other delegations of the need to agree to the agenda of further, and more far-reaching, Treaty reforms. Although political support for the idea was broad at the domestic level, as demonstrated by parliamentary debates following the Biarritz European Council and just before the Nice European Council,[27] and seemed to build up in other countries (if we consider the series of speeches given following Fischer's ideas, including the speech of President Chirac before the *Bundestag* in July 2000), no real progress had been made in the IGC, and it remained uncertain whether a solution satisfying German needs could be found in Nice.

Compared to the issue of *Kompetenzabgrenzung,* or the wider constitutional debate, other issues outside of the core agenda of the IGC were of lesser importance to Germany. The German *Länder* officially continued to put forward their claims in view of strengthening the third—or regional—level of government but were in reality divided over the issue and never suggested progress was imperative in this area. Although they officially did support the demands issued by the Committee of the Regions, a widely shared feeling of frustration with the work of the Committee considerably reduced their ardour.

---

[27] Stenographischer Bericht des Deutschen Bundestages, 14. Wahlperiode, 126. Sitzung am 25. Oktober 2000, pp. 12102sq., and 135. Sitzung am 28. November 2000, pp. 13023sq.

STRIKING THE DEAL AND RATIFICATION

The Nice European Council

When the European Council met in Nice to conclude the IGC, German negotiators had to deal with mainly two issues upon the satisfaction of which their consent to the whole package depended. Except for the odd cases mentioned, the composition of the Commission and QMV remained important issues, but they were a) not of individual relevance to Germany, and b) the outline of a likely outcome was rather clear but depended on the solution to the weighting of votes. The country's weight in the Council—in particular in comparison with other larger Member States—and a satisfactory solution to the question of a new reform agenda that would include the allocation of powers between the Union and Member States thus were essential issues on which Chancellor Schröder needed to bring back home an outcome that could be 'sold'.

The conflict between Germany and France—the other larger Member States appeared to be 'fairly relaxed' (Galloway, 2001: 82) but were also hiding behind the Presidency—over "decoupling" their voting power in the Council has been much discussed and hardly needs to be emphasised once again. Both countries had, in their last attempt during the 76th Franco-German consultations in Vittel on 10 November 2000, proven to be unable to find a bilateral compromise. This 'mésentente cordiale'[28]—a solution to which would have helped solve other conflicts, e.g. between Belgium and the Netherlands—thus loomed heavily over the whole negotiations in Nice. Germany was in a comfortable position in the sense that the French President, holding the Presidency, had to come up with suggestions and had to present the first draft of an overall compromise at the beginning of the Nice European Council, a draft that was in many ways disappointing, heavily criticised by many delegations with regard to the weighting of votes and was responsible for the negative atmosphere of the hole Council meeting (Wiedmann, 2001: 188). On the other hand, Germany lacked a natural ally on the weighting of votes, and because the stakes had been raised very high also could hardly contribute to reaching a deal.

The deal ultimately struck in Nice on the last night—and which included horse-trading over the number of seats in the European Parliament—was not

---

[28] Libération, 11 November 2000.

based on any clear and understandable principle but a pure matter of 'power poker' (*Machtpoker*).[29] As far as France and Germany were concerned, however, it allowed both chief negotiators, Chancellor Schröder and President Chirac, to save face. Although "in a somewhat less than transparent manner" (Galloway, 2001: 89), Germany effectively obtained, one could argue, more than it could have hoped for. The 62% population threshold agreed in Nice puts the country in a position to form a blocking minority together with just two other large Member States even in an EU of 27 Member States; the Nice solution also clearly left its imprint on the debates of the European Convention.[30]

More interesting is the solution found to the 'Post-Nice-agenda' that had also remained open until Nice. Even in Nice it was only towards the end of the negotiations that the French Presidency proposed a very short and not very substantial text that would have only slightly opened the window for a next round of reforms, without specifying the agenda of further reform steps nor the objectives. The text was unacceptable to the German *Länder*—present in Nice through two observing *Länder* (Baden-Württemberg and Rheinland-Pfalz)—which then set down themselves to draft a more substantial proposal, together with the Italian and the Belgian delegation both of which had been won over for the idea (in the case of Belgium, regional governments played an essential role on this issue). The new draft placed the issue of allocation of powers in the context of a broader constitutional debate including the simplification of the Treaties, the Charter of Fundamental Rights and the role of national Parliaments (a traditional 'French' topic) and subsequently, after being presented by Chancellor Schröder as a joint initiative from Belgium, Germany and Italy, found a place in the final compromise.

It would be difficult to argue that Germany—or perhaps any country indeed—played a very constructive role in Nice. In the case of Germany, the rhetorical emphasis that had been put on 'national interests' and that had been translated into the necessity to decouple its own voting power from that of other large Member States, and—as has partly been suggested—a certain degree of willingness to let France 'pay' for the way in which it had defended its (agricultural) interests during the negotiations over the Agenda 2000 under the German Presidency had placed the country in an uncomfortable position to help find a compromise on the most sensitive issue, the allocation of votes in the Council.

---

[29] See FAZ vom 13. Dezember 2000.

[30] The draft Constitutional Treaty in Art. 1-24.1 sets the threshold for QMV at the majority of Member States representing at least 60% of the population.

The Domestic Debate

At the domestic level, the Treaty of Nice was—like in other Member States—hardly received with enthusiasm. The results of the IGC were on the whole criticised by the media, in the academic debate (see among others Hatje, 2001; Wessels, 2001; Wiedmann, 2001), by relevant interest groups such as the Trade Unions (Deutscher Gewerkschaftsbund, 2001) and industry (Bundesverband der Deutschen Industrie, 2001) and—last but not least—in the political debate. The overall tone of the domestic debate can be summarised in a criticism of the Treaty of Nice as a compromise at the lowest common denominator and as a Treaty hardly understandable and of byzantine complexity. As far as the content is concerned, the main criticism focused on the fact that decision-making was rendered more difficult instead of easier, that the move towards QMV was only modest and that, on the whole, the reform of institutions was just—but only just—sufficient to pave the way for enlargement. Even Chancellor Schröder, in an article written for the *Handelsblatt* on 29 December 2000[31] and in his official statement with regard to the results of the Nice European Council given before the *Bundestag* on 19 January 2001, refrained from giving an all too positive account of the conclusion of the IGC and—while drawing a globally positive picture of the new Treaty—placed emphasis on the fact that Germany had expected 'more' from Nice.[32]

Reviewing the domestic debate following the European Council of Nice and in the course of the ratification process, however, one of the striking features is that, despite wide-spread criticism of a 'failure' at Nice, it is virtually impossible to identify any fundamental or substantial objection to the Treaty or to the conduct of negotiations by the German government. In the main parliamentary debate analysing the results of the Nice European Council, on 19 January,[33] and in the first parliamentary reading of the ratification law, on 28 June 2001,[34] collective failure to give substantial answers to the issues at stake, the dominance of national egoisms and of *Besitzsstandswahrung*

[31] Gerhard Schröder, *Impulse für ein zukunftsfähiges Europa*, Handelsblatt, 29 December 2000.

[32] *Regierungserklärung der Bundesregierung zu den Ergebnissen des Europäischen Rates von Nizza*, Stenographischer Bericht des Deutschen Bundestages, 14. Wahlperiode, 144. Sitzung am 19. Januar 2001, pp. 14111-14114.

[33] Stenographischer Bericht des Deutschen Bundestages, 14. Wahlperiode, 144. Sitzung am 19. Januar 2001, pp. 14111 14133.

[34] Stenographischer Bericht des Deutschen Bundestages, 14. Wahlperiode, 179. Sitzung am 28. Juni 2001, pp. 17613-17630.

(maintenance of acquired rights) and the minimal results were criticised by speakers of the major opposition parties. The tone of the criticism, however, was marked by an apprehension for the complexity of the negotiation agenda and by a positive appraisal that—with the Declaration on the Future of the Union—the door seemed to have been opened for a far more substantial constitutional debate at the European level.

In its internal analysis of the Treaty of Nice, the main opposition party, the Christian Democrats, concluded that, on the whole, the Treaty showed a "positive balance in bonsai format" (CDU/CSU Fraktion, 2001: 1); and in analysing individual objectives associated with the IGC, they identified more positive than negative elements in the Treaty, with the exception of the objective of increasing transparency and clearness of the Treaties. As a consequence, the paper suggested that a refusal to ratify the Treaty was no real option as it would not help addressing the main challenges at the European level. They did point out that a number of political commitments by the federal government—an earlier launching of the next reforms, the inclusion of 'left-overs' from Nice to the post-Nice-agenda and initiatives to make use of the possibilities, provided by the Nice Treaty in some areas, to move towards QMV following a unanimous decision by the Council—would make it easier to vote in favour of the ratification law, but these demands were not formulated as necessary preconditions. Two other aspects are of even greater interest: First, the paper identified the French Presidency as the main source of horse-trading at Nice and, in particular, criticised French insistence on maintaining the voting parity between the two countries by even misusing the prerogatives of the Presidency (CDU/CSU Fraktion, 2001: 8), whereas we find no word of criticism directed at the German government or Chancellor Schröder personally. Second, whereas the issues of subsidiarity and *Kompetenzabgrenzung* have consistently been raised by opposition parties in the political arena, the paper fails to take up the matter and to blame the Treaty for not addressing it.

The brief review of the internal analysis of the Nice Treaty undertaken by the main opposition party that had itself experienced three consecutive IGCs in the past allows us to better understand the domestic debate after Nice. The public criticism—voiced mainly in the *Bundestag*, but also in press statements—was mainly window dressing. And where critical remarks were directly aimed at the government and Chancellor Schröder in particular, they were only to a limited extent backed by a real belief that negotiations could have been conducted in a better way. Schröder was attacked, in particular, by the parliamentary leader of the opposition, Friedrich Merz, and the spokesman on Europe, Peter Hintze, for having raised the issue of Germany's voting power to a question of prestige and to becoming the decisive yardstick at Nice, and for thus having placed a burden on the Nice European Council that had strongly contributed to the horse-trading negotiation style and to the failure; Schröder was also attacked for a failure to show leadership qualities and for having, since assuming the Chancellorship in 1998, forgotten to show real interest in Franco-German relations and to develop a joint Franco-German understanding of and approach to the issues at stake in Nice.[35] In reality, however, the government's stance on the distribution of votes in the Council, in particular, had from the beginning been supported by the opposition parties which would have heavily criticised the government for failing to take into account national interests should the government have defined Germany's position on this issue in a different way.

The character of the domestic debate in the *political* arena became even clearer in the Federal Council, the first of both chambers to discuss the ratification law, on 11 May 2001.[36] Whereas the *Bundesrat* has a long tradition of political debate and statements on major European events, and Treaty negotiations in particular, the first reading of the ratification law featured just one speaker (and two statements given as written protocols) who, on top, just gave a very brief statement; none of the Prime Ministers, usually seizing such opportunities to convey their European credence to the public, considered taking the floor. The sole speaker, Bavaria's Minister for European Affairs Reinhold Bocklet (a former MEP), just made a short general reference to the shortcomings of the Treaty, and then went on to show his satisfaction with the fact that the institutional reforms agreed in Nice paved the way for enlargement and, in particular, with the Declaration on the Future of the Union and the post-Nice-process that now, according to him, mainly had to be used to address the issue of a clearer description and delimitation of the Union's tasks. Whereas no other *Land* had insisted on *Kompetenz-abgrenzung* in the preparation of the IGC and during negotiations with the same ardour as Bavaria, the fact that Nice had brought no real progress on this issue no longer seemed to pose a major problem.

As a conclusion it can be said that, although the Treaty of Nice received strong public criticism and although even the government itself was merely defending it as a realistic outcome sufficient to go ahead with enlargement, the domestic ratification debate from the outset was marked by a broad agreement that there were no alternatives to the Nice Treaty and that, in reality, German interests had been taken into account to a rather satisfactory degree.

---

[35] Stenographischer Bericht des Deutschen Bundestages, 14. Wahlperiode, 144. Sitzung am 19. Januar 2001, pp. 14115;14128.

[36] Bundesrat, Stenografischer Bericht, 763. Sitzung, 11 May 2001, pp. 234sq.

The Ratification Process

Following what has been said above, it is not surprising that the ratification process itself was smooth and easy except for an unnecessary domestic constitutional conflict between the federal government and, mainly, the Federal Council. When introducing its ratification bill following the signing of the Nice Treaty on 26 February 2001, the federal government based it on Art. 23 §1, second sentence and Art. 59 §2, first sentence of the Basic Law. This implied that the bill would have to obtain the consent of both Houses of Parliament by a simple majority only, whereas Art. 23 §1, third sentence of the Basic Law foresees the need of a constitutional majority of two thirds of the votes in both Houses of Parliament for modifications to the European Treaties if these modifications change or supplement the substance of the Basic Law. Although politically sure to obtain the consent of both the *Bundesrat* and the *Bundestag*, the federal government planned a simple—or, as the opposition spokesman on Europe suggested, 'low-level'[37]—ratification and made a principle out of its conviction that the Treaty of Nice did not effectively change the substance of the German Basic Law. This approach to the ratification process was criticised not only by the Federal Council but also by all political parties in the Federal Diet (where agreement among all parties was reached in the European Committee to proceed to a ratification with constitutional majorities). The insistence of the federal government on a disputable principle moreover was a strategic failure as it allowed opposition parties to imply that the low-quality ratification suggested by the government corresponded to the low level of quality of the Treaty.

Apart from this unnecessary—and somewhat typically German—constitutional debate, ratification proceeded without any obstacles. The Federal Council unanimously approved the ratification bill in its first reading on 11 May 2001[38] by emphasising the relevance of what was by then already called the 'Post-Nice-process' and again in its second reading on 9 November 2001.[39] For its part, the *Bundestag* had its first reading of the ratification bill—and its second major political debate on the Treaty of Nice—on 28 June 2001, when the bill was referred to the European Committee (leading

[37] Stenographischer Bericht des Deutschen Bundestages, 14. Wahlperiode, 179. Sitzung am 28. Juni 2001, p. 17617.

[38] Bundesrat, Stenografischer Bericht, 763. Sitzung, 11 May 2001, pp. 234sq.

[39] Bundesrat, Stenografischer Bericht, 769. Sitzung, 9 November 2001, pp. 600sq; the votes of the individual *Länder* are recorded on p. 607.

committee) and other committees for closer examination.[40] After examination by the committees, the second and third readings, when actual voting was conducted, took place on 18 October 2001. Following the near unanimous recommendation issued by the European Committee[41] to approve the ratification bill, the latter was adopted with an overwhelming majority—Social Democrats, Christian Democrats, Liberal Democrats and Greens unanimously voted in favour of the bill, only most (but not all) MPs of the Party of Democratic Socialism (PDS) voted against.[42] Following the necessary examination and signature by the Federal President, the ratification law ultimately came into force shortly before Christmas on 21 December 2001.[43]

Conclusions – A Process of Saving Face

By nearly all standards, the negotiations leading to the Nice Treaty, and the final result obtained, can be described as a success story from a German perspective, and German negotiators themselves have not hidden their satisfaction (Pleuger, 2002). Success indicators are easy to identify and abundant:

- The domestic ratification process was unusually smooth and quick, and—for the first time since the Single European Act—did not really give rise to a controversial domestic debate. Opposition parties stressed the critical points or shortcomings of the Nice Treaty and partly put the blame on the federal government and Chancellor Schröder personally—emphasising his inability to maintain close ties with France and criticising the way in which he had defined and defended national interests, but their criticism remained moderate, and they saw no alternative to ratification. They could even argue—and did so—that the IGC had, in the end, taken on board two of their main objectives, i.e. new rules on 'flexibility' and an opening of a broader constitutional debate.
- Germany could claim that its main objectives had been reached: the door for enlargement was open, the position of the larger Member States in the Council, and thus 'democracy'—at least in quantitative terms—more generally, was strengthened at the European level. Where progress had been less significant—on the reform of the Commission and on QMV in the Council, Germany was not to blame (or at least had not been a major blocking factor).

---

[40] Stenographischer Bericht des Deutschen Bundestages, 14. Wahlperiode, 179. Sitzung am 28. Juni 2001, p. 17617; Bundestags-Drucksache 14/6146 of 25 May 2001.

[41] Bundestags-Drucksache 14/7172 of 17 Oktober 2001.

[42] Stenographischer Bericht des Deutschen Bundestages, 14. Wahlperiode, 195. Sitzung am 28. Oktober 2001, p. 19008.

[43] Gesetz vom 21. Dezember 2001 zum Vertrag von Nizza vom 26. Februar 2001, Bundesgesetzblatt II, p. 1666.

- The positions Germany had defended could to a large extent be presented as 'European' instead of purely national. On the whole, the country had played a positive role in breaking the deadlock between smaller and larger Member States with regard to the Commission, it had 'fought' for more QMV, and it had given the main impetus to the "Declaration on the Future of the Union" that would lead to a kind of constitutional process. Also, from a European perspective, it seemed that it was France rather than Germany which was to blame for the power struggle between both countries, and France rather than Germany which was to blame for the power struggle between smaller and larger countries.
- Domestically, the *Länder* raised no objections to the results but congratulated themselves for having obtained—or so it would seem—a clear guarantee that their concern with a more precise delimitation of competences would now finally be on the European political agenda. The federal government, on the other hand, had made no real promises or concessions to the *Länder*, had kept its freedom in view of the next IGC and would be able to argue that it had fought for the issue of *Kompetenzabgrenzung* but that 'unfortunately', no one else had really been open to the issue.

From a domestic point of view, the Treaty of Nice, although clearly not a formidable masterpiece of statesmanship, thus had the advantage that it allowed all actors to save face and to argue that their main concerns were reflected by the Treaty, despite the fact that no significant progress had been made on any dimension.

BIBLIOGRAPHY

Ausschuss für die Angelegenheiten der Europäischen Union (2000), *Der Europaausschuss und die institutionellen Reformen der Europäischen Union – Texte und Materialien*, Bd. 15, Berlin.

Bauer, Joachim, ed. (1991), *Europa der Regionen. Aktuelle Dokumente zur Rolle und Zukunft der deutschen Länder im europäischen Integrationsprozeß*. Berlin: Duncker & Humblot.

Beuter, Rita (2002), "Germany," in Finn Laursen (ed.), *The Amsterdam Treaty. National Preference Formation, Interstate Bargaining and Outcome*. Odense: Odense University Press, pp. 93-120.

Borkenhagen, Franz H.U., et al., eds. (1992), *Die deutschen Länder in Europa. Politische Union und Wirtschafts- und Währungsunion*. Baden-Baden: Nomos.

—— , ed. (1998), *Europapolitik der deutschen Länder. Bilanz und Perspektiven nach dem Gipfel von Amsterdam*. Opladen: Leske + Budrich.

Bulmer, Simon, et al. (2001), "Das Entscheidungs- und Koordinationssystem deutscher Europapolitik: Hindernis für eine neue Politik?", in Schneider et al. (eds.) pp. 231-266.

Bundesrat (2000), *Entschließung des Bundesrates zur Eröffnung der Regierungskonferenz zu institutionellen Fragen (Beschluss)*, BR-Drucksache 61/00, 4 February 2000.

Bundesverband der Deutschen Industrie (2001), *Der Vertrag von Nizza – Institutionelle Veränder-ungen und Post-Nizza-Prozess*. Brussels: BDI.

CDU/CSU Fraktion (2001), *CDU/CSU Fraktion im Deutschen Bundestag, Arbeitsgruppe Europe: Der Vertrag von Nizza – eine kritische Analyse*, 15 January.

Council of the European Union (1999), *Efficient Institutions after Enlargement. Options for the Intergovernmental Conference*, Brussels, 7 December 1999 (Doc. No. 13636/99 – LIMITE).

De Winter, Lieven and Huri Türsan, eds. (1998), *Regionalist Parties in Western Europe*. London and New York: Routledge.

Derlien, Hans-Ulrich (2000), "Co-ordinating German EU Policy. Failing Successfully?" in Hussein Kassim, Guy B. Peters and Vincent Wright (eds.), *National Co-ordination of EU Policy: the domestic level*, Oxford: Oxford University Press, pp. 54-78.

Deutscher Gewerkschaftsbund (2001), *Stellungnahme des Deutschen Gewerkschaftsbundes (DGB) zur Organisation der Debatte über die Zukunft Europas. Vorschläge für den EU-Ratsgipfel in Laeken (Belgien), im Dezember 2001*, Berlin, Oktober.

Fischer, Joschka (2000), *Vom Staatenverbund zur Föderation – Gedanken über die Finalität der Europäischen Integration*, Rede am 12. Mai 2000 in der Humboldt-Universität in Berlin.

Fuchs, Michael (2001), *Der Ausschuss für die Angelegenheiten der Europäischen Union des Deutschen Bundestages: kein Ausschuss wie jeder andere*, Ms., Bundestag.

Galloway, David (2001), *The Treaty of Nice and Beyond. Realities and Illusions of Power in the EU*. Sheffield: Sheffield Academic Press.

Gerster, Florian (1993), "Die Europaministerkonferenz der deutschen Länder: Aufgaben – Themen – Selbstverständnis," *integration* 16, No. 2, pp. 61-67.

Hatje, Armin (2001), "Die institutionelle Reform der Europäischen Union – der Vertrag von Nizza auf dem Prüfstand," *Europarecht* 36, No. 2, pp. 143-184.

Hellmann, Gunther (2002), "Deutschland in Europa: Eine symbiotische Beziehung," *Aus Politik und Zeitgeschichte*, Nr. B 48/2002.

Hölscheidt, Sven (2001), "The German Bundestag: From Benevolent "Weakness" Towards Supportive Scrutiny", in Andreas Maurer and Wolfgang Wessels (eds.), *National Parliaments on their Ways to Europe: Losers or Latecomers?*, Baden-Baden: Nomos, pp. 129-162.

Hrbek, Rudolf, and Uwe Thaysen, eds. (1986), *Die deutschen Länder und die Europäischen Gemeinschaften*. Baden-Baden: Nomos.

IGC (2000a), *Intergovernmental Conference on Institutional Reform. Weighting of votes in the Council*, Brussels, 16 November 2000 (Doc. CONFER 4801/00).

—— (2000b), *Intergovernmental Conference on Institutional Reform. Presidency Report to the Feira European Council*, Brussels, 14 June 2000 (Doc. CONFER 4750/00).

Janning, Josef, and Patrick Meyer (1998), *Deutsche Europapolitik. Vorschläge zur Effektivierung*. Gütersloh: Verlag Bertelsmann Stiftung.

Kövel, Svea (2000), *Die Mitwirkung des Deutschen Bundestages in Angelegenheiten der Europäischen Union unter besonderer Berücksichtigung der Mitwirkung am und der Veränderung durch den Vertrag von Amsterdam*. München: UTZ Wissenschaft.

Korte, Karl-Rudolf, and Maurer, Andreas (2001), "Innenpolitische Grundlagen der deutschen Europapolitik. Konturen der Kontinuität und des Wandels," in Schneider et al. (eds.), pp. 195-230.

Mayer, Franz C. (2002), "Nationale Regierungsstrukturen und europäische Integration. Verfassungsrechtliche Vorgaben für den institutionellen Rahmen der Europapolitik auf nationaler und europäischer Ebene," *Europäische Grundrechte-Zeitschrift* 29, 5-8, pp. 111-124.

Ministerpräsidentenkonferenz (2000), *Jahreskonferenz der Ministerpräsidenten der Länder vom 25-27 Oktober 2000 in Schwerin, Ergebnisprotokoll*, TOP 2.1./2.2.: "Institutionelle Reformen und Weiterentwicklung der EU."

Morawitz, Bruno, and Kaiser, Wilhelm (1994), *Die Zusammenarbeit von Bund und Ländern bei Vorhaben der Europäischen Union*. Bonn: Europa Union Verlag.

Niedermayer, Oskar (1998), "Die Entwicklung der öffentlichen Meinung zu Europa", in Mathias Jopp et al. (eds.), *Europapolitische Grundverständnisse im Wandel. Analyse und Konsequenzen für die politische Bildung*. Bonn: Europa Union Verlag, pp. 419-448.

Parri, Leonardo (1989), "Territorial Political Exchange in Federal and Unitary Countries," *West European Politics* 12, No. 3, pp. 197-213.

Petiteville, Franck (1999), *La face nationale de la gouvernance communautaire. L'élaboration des "positions nationales" des Etats membres sur les propositions d'actes communautaires*. Maastricht: EIPA.

Pleuger, Gunter (2001), "Der Vertrag von Nizza: Gesamtbewertung der Ergebnisse," *integration* 24, No. 1, pp. 1-7.

Rath, Christian (2001), *Entscheidungspotenziale des Deutschen Bundestages in EU-Angelegenheiten. Mandatsgesetze und parlamentarische Stellungnahmen im Rahmen der unionswärtigen Gewalt*. Baden-Baden: Nomos.

Schäuble, Wolfgang, and Lamers, Karl (1999), *Europa braucht einen Verfassungsvertrag. Überlegungen zur europäischen Politik II – zum Fortgang des europäischen Einigungsprozesses*. Bonn, 3 May.

Schneider, Heinrich, et al., eds. (2001), *Eine neue deutsche Europapolitik? Rahmenbedingungen – Problemfelder – Optionen*. Bonn: Europa Union Verlag.

Sterzing, Christian, and Stefan Tiedow (2001), "Die Kontrolle der deutschen Europapolitik durch den EU-Ausschuss des Deutschen Bundestages: Bilanz und Reformpotentiale", *integration* 3/2001, pp. 274-288.

Stolz, Klaus (2000), *The Regional Political Class in Comparative Perspective: Career Patterns in Western Democracies*. Paper presented at the tri-annual congress of the International Political Science Association, Quebec, 1-5 August.

Thurner, Paul W., and Michael Stoiber (2001), *Interministerielle Netzwerke: Formale und informale Koordinationsstrukturen bei der Vorbereitung der deutschen Verhandlungspositionen zur Regierungskonferenz 1996*, Arbeitspapiere des Mannheimer Zentrums für Europäische Sozialforschung, No. 37. Mannheim: MZES.

Van Schendelen, Marinus (2002), *Machiavelli in Brussels*, Amsterdam: Amsterdam University Press.

Wessels, Wolfgang (2001), "Die Vertragsreformen von Nizza – Zur institutionellen Erweiterungsreife," *integration* 24, No. 1, pp. 8-25.

Wiedmann, Thomas (2001), "Der Vertrag von Nizza – Genesis einer Reform", *Europarecht* 36, No. 2, pp. 185-215.

CHAPTER 6

FINLAND: "WE HAVE TO LIVE WITH THIS RESULT"[1]

LESSONS FROM AMSTERDAM

Finland applied for membership of the European Union for three main reasons. The Finnish 'three-S-strategy' emphasised stability, security and say. Stability as an element of the Finnish strategy aimed at enhancing a firm economy in a country with a small national economy, highly dependent on external trade in a periphery of Europe. Security interests were seen indirectly. The Finns hoped that being part of a strong economic and political union would contribute to Finland's security although no collective security commitments were offered by the European Union. Finally 'say' as an element of the Finnish approach, pointed at the aim of having a seat at the table where decisions affecting vital Finnish interests are taken.

Finland established itself as a new Member State of the European Union through the Amsterdam process. The learning process offered by the Amsterdam negotiations took Finland to the group of traditional small states of the Union. The Finnish identity of a neutral country in the Cold War period and its traditional Nordic identity were replaced by the identity of a small EU Member State in the core of the European Union. The IGC preceding the Amsterdam Treaty was a learning process. For Finland, keeping the European Union as an association of independent states was a fundamental premise and basis of the negotiation process (Antola 2002, 121-138).

During the process of the IGC96, Finland moved from its initially cautious and reserved position towards the mainstream of small Member States. In the end, Finland was less intergovernmentalistic than in the opening stage. A logical explanation to this change is that at the same time Finland deliberately moved towards the EMU and into the 'hard core' of the European Union. The thrust to the EMU core had an impact on the overall approach of the country as well.

When introducing the new Treaty of Amsterdam to the Finnish Parliament the Prime Minister argued that in the end Finland was successful in its achievements if measured against its background of a new and small Member State. The Finnish strategy was based on a 'constructive approach'

---

[1] Prime Minister Paavo Lipponen to the press, December 10th, 2000.

which enhanced the image of Finland as a Member State actively contributing to the development of the European Union (Lipponen 1998).

SIX FACTORS SHAPING THE FINNISH APPROACH

Amsterdam experiences laid the foundations to the Finnish approach to the IGC2000. It was initially shaped by five factors. First, Finland took a decision to join the Economic and Monetary Union in the first wave of members in 1999. Secondly, Finland held its first Presidency during the latter part of 1999 which gave the country access to shape the process of the IGC in its early stages. Thirdly, Finland experienced the first wave of a national debate on the future of Europe. As a part of that Prime Minister Lipponen offered a personal contribution to the European debate with his speech in Bruges in November 2000. Finally, the perspective of enlargement was seen as an influential factor in the Finnish debate. Again the Presidency widened the perspective. The Helsinki Summit took the decision to open negotiations with the rest of the applicants from Central and Eastern Europe. The Helsinki Summit also recognised a new position for Turkey as a candidate country. Naming the new countries entering negotiations as a Helsinki Group certainly made Finland consider enlargement as an important element of the IGC2000.

During the last five months of negotiations a sixth factor emerged. In particular after the Council meeting in Biarritz, the tension between large and small Member States was openly recognised by the Finnish negotiating team. Towards the Nice Council and in particular in comments after Nice the divisions emerged as a dominant element in Finnish comments.

During the period between the Amsterdam Council and the opening of the Nice process, Finland established itself as a member of the core in the European Union. The main reason for the choice was to maximise influence, which was emphasised in the deliberate wish to be in the first wave of countries entering into the third stage of the Economic and Monetary Union. The motivation for being in the core was that the single currency would bring about economic stability and undermine the very unstable economic environment to which Finland belongs in terms of geography.

The Finnish Treaty of Accession did not contain any reservation concerning the EMU. The Finnish Government in its economic policy put the highest priority on EMU Membership. The economic and monetary policy was targeted to meet the convergence criteria by the time of the final decision concerning the members of the EMU.

In November 1996, the Prime Minister of Finland appointed an expert working group of nine professors to study the significance and consequences of the EMU for the Finnish economy. The expert group was asked to pay special attention to the production structure of Finland, the labour market, public finances and economic policy.

The expert group published its report in the Spring of 1997 (Finland and EMU 1997). Its overall conclusion was positive towards the EMU although the report recognised the difficulties that the Membership in the EMU would bring to Finland and pointed as well to tasks of structural reforms needed in Finland. The report, however, outlined very clearly the political motivation for the Finnish Membership in the EMU. The Expert Group argued: (Finland and EMU 1997, 27)

> "The opportunity to exert influence is one of the arguments for joining in Stage Three in the first wave. The Maastricht Treaty ties participation in decision-making to the degree of participation. Only those Member States which join the first wave will be entitled to share the decision-making concerning the start of Stage Three."

Through the decision to join the EMU in the first wave, Finland established itself in the core of the European Union. This was a landmark decision in the Finnish EU Strategy and also formed the basis of the Nice negotiations. Finland entered the Nice process with a commitment to be in the core of the EU. This commitment also distanced Finland from its traditional Nordic reference group. Both Denmark and Sweden opted out of the first wave.

Yet the Nordic caucus still functions on specific issues. Finland and Sweden have co-operated successfully on matters on which they have common interests. Two outstanding examples are their joint proposal at Amsterdam concerning crisis management provisions and their support for the inclusion of the employment provisions in the Treaty. In relation to crisis management they share a common interest as militarily non-aligned countries with a strong background in peace keeping. The employment question is another typical regional issue rooted in the Nordic welfare model.

The first Presidency of Finland in the EU during the Second Part of 1999 marked another important starting point to the Finnish approach. The Presidency was in some ways a litmus test for the Finnish Membership. Finland assumed its first presidency of the European Union in the midst of a major international crisis. Whatever the priorities were in the planning groups for the presidency, the crisis in Kosovo and the stability pact for the Western Balkans had top priority. This reflects the harsh reality of the Presidency's work: the world around the Union but also within the Union is unpredictable. The latter fact also shaped the Finnish presidency. First of all the implementation of the Amsterdam Treaty was in its early phases. The treaty entered into force in May 1999, two months before the beginning of the Finnish presidency.

The crisis brought about by the resignation of the Commission in March 1999 had an impact on the Finnish Presidency. Finland could not rely on the initiative role of the Commission as the motor of the Union decision-making for the major part of its term. The new composition of the European Parliament was established as a result of European elections in June and the nomination process of the new Commission dominated the first half of the Finnish term.

For Austria and Finland, holding the first Presidency has been the most important experience of their EU Membership. Although they probably could not perform high national profiles, the Presidency was an important element of socialisation of new Member States into the work and dynamics of the EU. Socialisation is not only important for civil servants attached to the running of a Presidency. The Presidency and the preparation of it drew considerable public attention to EU issues. For the first time since the referendum debates EU matters penetrated the public awareness.

The third element of the Finnish approach was a contribution to the debate about the future of Europe. The Finnish contribution was channelled into the debate by a speech given by the Prime Minister of Finland, Paavo Lipponen at the College of Europe in November 2000 (Lipponen 2000). When outlining his personal views on the future of Europe, Lipponen at the same time summed up the cornerstones of the Finnish European policy. After listing the key elements of the Finnish views (extension of qualified majority voting, closer cooperation, strong Commission and effective Council), Lipponen put a strong emphasis on the external activities. Lipponen strongly argued that the European Union should be made an effective global player.

Lipponen took part in the European debate of 2000 by placing himself among those who regretted the tendency towards increasing intergovernmentalism. Lipponen saw growing intergovernmentalism as a threat to the institutional balance and the equality of Member States, European citizens and European companies. Lipponen's contribution was an opening to the issues of equality between Member States which at the Nice Summit emerged as a dominant issue.

In the domestic debate, Lipponen's speech was seen as a plea for federalism. At least a glimpse of federalism could be sensed in his approach. Lipponen argued in favour of an established division of labour between the supranational institutions and the Member States. He argued:

> "For this reason it is widely considered that policies like those relating to the internal market, international trade, the common currency, foreign and security policy, external boarders and security in the Union and the global environment are the best dealt with on the EU level."

Lipponen argued in favour of a federal-type constitution which should produce an institutional structure that "would permanently secure the equality of member states by transforming the Council" in order to avoid a "permanent haggling over the weighting of votes in the Council". In the framework of the constitution, the Parliament should represent the democratic legitimacy and the Commission should enjoy the confidence of the Parliament.

Lipponen also outlined his agenda to Nice consisting of six issues. Issue number one was granting a legal status of fundamental rights. Secondly, he proposed the establishment of a political guideline on the division of competence. The third issue on Lipponen's list was a restructuring of the treaties followed by the re-examination of the institutional balance, the principle of good governance. The sixth issue on Lipponen's list was a claim that the agenda should also contain deliberations that aimed at strengthening the European Union as an international actor.

Perhaps the most far-reaching proposal in the Lipponen speech was a proposal to establish a Convention to prepare the agenda of the future of Europe. Lipponen outlined an idea of a Convention that should include the governments and national parliaments of the Member States and the Candidate States as well as EU institutions and representatives. A plea for a Convention was later adopted in the Laken declaration.

The core arguments of the Brussels speech reflected the overall European policy line of his second Government. General elections in March 1999 gave support to the European policy line of the Government coalition that was formed in April 1996. The composition of the coalition remained unchanged and continued the European policy line that was shaped during the Amsterdam negotiations. In the passage on European policy in its program, the Government emphasised first of all Nordic themes: transparency, responsibility and administrative effectiveness. The Government also indicated its commitment to strengthen the European Union as an international economic and political actor.

From an institutional point of view, the programme indicated the Government's readiness to "to support the extension of qualified majority voting to ensure the proper functioning of the Union and to preserve a balance among the Institutions of the Union and to ensure joint cooperation". The commitment to the extension of qualified majority voting placed Finland in the position of a traditional small state in the EU and further distanced Finland from its Nordic partners in institutional matters.

The Domestic Platform

As in the course of the Amsterdam process, a permanent dialogue between the Government and the Parliament was established for the Nice process too. Political inquiries in Parliament rest on two main committees: the Grand Committee and the Foreign Affairs Committee. Towards the end of the process also the Constitutional Committee took an active part in the dialogue. The procedure is based on Section 54 of the Parliament Act.

The dialogue was opened by a Government report to the Parliament in February 2000. (CONFER 4723/00). The report outlined the cornerstones of the Finnish overall strategy. The Government report evaluated the results of the Amsterdam Treaty by noting that the previous IGC did not succeed in resolving the most difficult institutional issues: the size and composition of the Commission and the weighting of votes in the Council. The overall evaluation of the Amsterdam results was rather positive from Finland's point of view.

During the Nice negotiations, the Government submitted 14 written documents to the Parliament. They covered a wide range of issues but the emphasis was on the extension of the use of qualified majority voting, the use and modification of the flexibility clause and decision-making rules in general. (HE 93/2001, point 2.4.2).

From the Finnish perspective, an important step from Amsterdam to Nice was the Finnish Presidency and in particular the IGC Report drafted by the Presidency in December 1999 (Efficient Institutions after Enlargement. Options for the Intergovernmental Conference 1999). The Presidency report set three main ambitions for the coming IGC: the agenda of the IGC should be focused on the institutional reforms necessary for enlargement, the conference should come up with a politically defendable and balanced outcome which should be acceptable also to the public and, thirdly, the Conference should end its work by the end of 2000.

The Presidency report was presented to the Grand Committee of the Finnish Parliament before the Helsinki European Council. Its final version and the results of the Helsinki European Council were reported to the same body as well. The Presidency Report is the foundation of the Government Report of February 2000 as well. The Government was thus exceptionally well prepared for the Nice process.

The Government report to the Parliament reflected the ideas of the Presidency Report. It repeats the main content and ideas of the Presidency Report as the foundation of the national strategy. The main aim of Finland in the coming IGC was stated as follows (CONFER 4723/00, 7):

> "The Government's objective is to arrive at a comprehensive and logical long-term solution. It is essential that the outcome be balanced and that the interests

> of all Member States be taken into account in a manner which contributes to the consolidation of the Union's legitimacy in all Member States and to effective decision-making."

The starting point is in line with the approach that emerged during the Amsterdam negotiations. It is the view of a small Member State. It emphasises the need to reach a balanced outcome that contributes to the legitimacy of the EU. It aims to ensure effective decision-making that takes into account the interests of all Member States. The approach stresses that the interests of all Member States should be taken into consideration. Equality of Member States and the institutional issues emerged as two main themes of the Finnish strategy.

Effectiveness of the decision-making, a strengthening of the institutional balance and equality between Member States are profile themes in the Government's first report. The size and composition of the Commission, the weighting of votes in the Council, the extension of qualified majority voting and the inter-institutional issues were at the forefront of the Finnish approach. In the course of the negotiation process, in particular after the Biarritz European Council, the balance between large and small Member States emerged as a parallel, if not the dominant topic.

Concerns about the rise of intergovernmentalism became also evident in the Finnish strategy. After Biarritz, Finland concluded that large Member States were united in their aim to change the decision-making rules in order to secure their power in an enlarged Union. Finland saw that large states emphasised intergovernmentalism at the expense of the community method. In the final weeks of the negotiation process this greatly influenced its strategy.

NEGOTIATION STRATEGY

Finland was not among the high profile countries in the negotiations. The emphasis was not on making formal proposals but rather on shaping the process through a constructive profile as suggested by the Government's initial report. Finland contributed in its own name only with documents to the Intergovernmental Conference. (The Competence to Accede to the European Convention of Human Rights and Fundamental Freedoms, signed in Rome, 4 November 1950: CONFER 4775/00, Intellectual property rights and services under Article 133: CONFER 4807/00 and on the inclusion of environmental and energy taxation into the Treaty under Art. 93: CONFER 4814/00). This was somewhat less than during the Amsterdam negotiations (eight proposals).

It is difficult to judge whether this reflects any changes in the negotiation strategy. For the Nice negotiations, the Finnish contribution was made in the

Presidency Report and through this the country was able to shape the themes from the initial stages. Finland also approached these consultations as a Member State having a position at the core of the EU. Finnish negotiators approached the Nice process with much more confidence and experience than they approached the Amsterdam process as a new Member States. It is tempting to conclude therefore that the influence of Finland on the end result was seen more as influencing the negotiation process through diplomacy.

The most visible example of this is the active and rather constructive role that Finland played to the end of negotiations concerning the issues of Article 133. The end result was a success in the eyes of Finland although French resistance at the Nice Summit prevented the achievement of the full aims of Finland. In Article 133 questions, a like-minded group of small Member States (Finland, Luxembourg, Ireland and Belgium seconded by Italy) worked together. Finland was also an active promoter of the extension of qualified majority voting to taxation (Art. 93), in particular in energy and environmental questions but without success. In a similar way, Finland took an offensive strategy in social policy issues (Art. 42, 137).

The composition of the Commission, the weighting of votes in the Council and the overall balance of the institutions were the key elements of the institutional issues. Throughout the negotiation process, Finland stressed that even in an enlarged Union the Commission should comprise one national member from each State with equal status (CONFER 4723/00, 8). The Government expressed its opinion that “the Commission can operate efficiently as a college in this composition even after enlargements”. This approach aimed at ensuring both the legitimacy of the Commission and the equality among the Member States.

In analysing the weighting of votes, Finland was from the beginning more flexible than in the composition of the Commission. The Government Report recognized that successive enlargements without structural reforms of the system have contributed to a situation where Member States with a small population have “a proportionally larger number of votes compared with the larger Member States.”

On this ground and anticipating the enlargement, Finland was ready to accept changes in the weighting of votes as a starting point. However, the Government linked the re-weighting to satisfactory results in other institutional issues. The overall solution of institutional reforms should be balanced and the interests of all Member States needed to be taken into consideration (ibid. 9). The report stressed also the need to create a simple solution that would be applicable in every phase of enlargement.

Institutional balance and a fair representation of Member States are dominant themes too in the evaluation of other institutional issues. These elements were in particular stressed in reforming the Parliament. Finland accepted an upper ceiling of 700 Members of the Parliament provided an appropriate representation of the Member States would be safeguarded (ibid 12). The same argumentation was repeated in provisions of the Court of Justice and the Court of Auditors (ibid. 12-13).

Qualified majority voting is the key instrument in enhancing effectiveness of decision-making in the Finnish approach. "The Government supports the extension of qualified majority voting as the key to preserving efficiency in an enlarging Union," the Government report argues (ibid. 10). Throughout the negotiation process Finland stressed that the extension of QMV was the most important issue on the table. It was a paramount issue for two reasons. It was needed to improve the effectiveness of the Union and it was a necessity in order to meet the challenge of enlargement. This approach was maintained to the end. Finland also saw a close link between the use of QMV and co-decision. The main principle in the Finnish approach was that whenever QMV is used, the issue should be moved to co-decision.

In its initial report to the Parliament, the Government listed an extensive number of topics where QMV could be applied. These include i.a. issues related to Union citizenship and the free movement of persons, approximation of legislation and budget issues directly linked to the operation of the internal market. The report also included Community policies such as industry, culture and the environment. A special Finnish topic was trade policy where Finland later profiled in the final stages of negotiations.

In all, the Finish approach to QMV was that "issues related to the basic nature of the Union which do not concern increasing the efficiency of decision-making should remain subject to unanimous decision-making" (CONFER 4723/00, 10). Amendments to the Treaties, changes to the common institutional system, the division of competences, certain budgetary decisions as well as defence policy were among the issues which Finland wanted to keep outside QMV. In many ways Finland thus belonged to the 'radicals' in the extension of QMV.

In the name of effectiveness Finland also had a positive attitude towards the more extensive use of *flexibility*. Flexibility was not on the initial agenda of the IGC, but gradually emerged on it. Initially also Finland regarded that "thorough changes in the flexibility provisions of the Treaty of Amsterdam are not needed" (CONFER 4723/00, 17). In the end, the reform of the flexibility clause appeared as one of the most remarkable achievements of the process. As a reaction to the Presidency Report on flexibility (CONFER 4737/00) Finland changed its attitude and started actively to take part in the debate.

The basic understanding of Finland reflected the idea of flexibility as 'oil in the gearbox': the use of flexibility is accepted if it helps the Union to overcome or bypass a deadlock in attempts to deepen integration. The baseline of the Finnish Government was, however, that a deepening should take place within the institutional structure of the Union (HVK 2000: Vahvistettu yhteistyö, 2000).

Finland emphasised that the flexibility clause should offer a lucrative alternative if compared to the alternative of working outside the institutions. It should offer a platform for willing and able Member States to work within the institutions with commonly accepted rules rather than take actions outside the institutional framework. The Government memo saw flexibility as an instrument of a last resort for the deepening of cooperation. A precondition for its use should be that it is open to all willing and able Members in the existing institutional framework respecting the *acquis*. Finland also stressed that if used flexibility should be as open as possible and take into consideration the rights of Members staying out.

The flexibility doctrine echoes the grand strategy of Finland in the Nice negotiations. If used, flexibility must take into consideration the equality between the Member States, must contribute to a deepening of integration and respect the existing institutional structure of the Union. The Government memo also emphasised that the decision to apply the principle ought to be taken by a qualified majority, and in the first pillar the Community method should be applied. In addition, Finland supported the abolition of the 'emergency break' introduced in the Amsterdam Treaty, i.e. the abolition of the right of a single Member State to prevent the use of flexibility. In the Second Pillar issues Finland took a more cautious approach. The main alternative there should have been the use of qualified majority decision-making where the Treaty allows it.

Throughout the negotiation process the Finnish agenda had its focus on qualified majority and the role and composition of the Commission. In extending the qualified majority voting Finland favoured its extensive application. Finland had two motives: an extensive use of QMW would strengthen the communitarian dimension of the Union and is an inevitable necessity for a successful enlargement. Finland had two specific interests in QMW: widening its use in Article 133 and extending it into taxation. The Finnish priority was to extend the use of QMV and to apply flexibility only as the last instrument.

Finland was not satisfied with the progress of negotiations during the first weeks of the French Presidency. This became evident in the comments after the Biarritz European Council. Biarritz made public the divide between large and small states. The official Finnish position was that the divide is artificial in the sense that it never surfaces in actual decision-making situations in the Council.

In his press report after the Biarritz Council, Prime Minister Lipponen noted the emerging divide in institutional matters. Basically Finland was ready to accept a redefinition of the voting power in the Council but within modest limits. Finland saw the redefinition as an element of improving the effectiveness of the Union and as compensation to larger Member States for the reform of the composition of the Commission.

During the last weeks of negotiations the institutional issues consisted of four interrelated topics: the extension of QMV, flexibility, the composition of the Commission and the reweighting of votes.

CFSP: More Flexibility

When applying for membership of the European Union, Finland emphasised that accession would not essentially change its basic foreign policy line. At the same time a general recognition prevailed that membership of the European Union called for new interpretations of neutrality. By joining the European Union, participation in foreign policy co-ordination was seen as an element of wider co-operation. As vital interests in other policy areas spoke for membership, the costs of taking part in previously encapsulated areas of foreign policy co-ordination constituted a tolerable side effect.

During the accession negotiations Finland stressed that with reservations it accepted the *acquis* also in the field of the CFSP. Whatever reservations there were among the other Member States concerning the role of Finland in the CFSP before the accession, they did not materialise. Traces of old neutralism were not identified in the behaviour of Finland. Participation in the CFSP became the major framework of Finnish foreign policy. Finland has for instance reformed the structure of its Foreign Ministry primarily to improve its capacity to accommodate participation in CFSP work.

In the same spirit, Finland has also supported the strengthening of the crises management capacity of the Union and indeed, the defence dimension. The joint Finnish-Swedish proposal for the establishment of a crises management facility in the Treaty of Amsterdam was an important step. At the end of the Finnish presidency the Helsinki Headline Goals were established for the crises management capacity. The role of the Presidency was naturally important in achieving the result. Finnish input to the process was recently emphasised when a former Chief of Staff of the Finnish Armed Forces was nominated to the post of chairman of the Military Committee.

In its primary policy paper to the Parliament in the early part of 2000, Finland took a cautious approach to the CFSP. It expressed the opinion that the evolution of the crises management capabilities of the Union would not automatically require amendments to the Treaty (CONFER 4723/00, 15). In the Nice negotiations, Finland made no reservations about the line finally adopted. Finland was ready to extend the use of the flexibility clause into the

ESDP and even to matters having defence implications. Flexibility was not the first choice but was acceptable. Finland stressed throughout the negotiations that in all possible applications of flexibility, the position of Member States outside the action must be secured.

EVALUATION

Finland entered the Nice process with the aim of reaching a new Treaty which would accommodate new Member States. In its proposal to the Parliament for the ratification of the Treaty, the Government of Finland notes that this aim was reached. In meeting the primary aim, the Conference was successful although the end result does not meet the Finnish aim in its entirety (HE 93/2001, 11). However, the Government was ready to propose the ratification. The Treaty was ratified on 14th December 2001 with a convincing majority of 170 out of 200 Members of the Parliament. Nine votes only were cast against and 20 Members abstained.

The introduction of the Treaty to the Parliament was briefly delayed by the Government because of dissatisfaction with the post-Nice quarrels over the finalisation of the Summit results. Finland postponed acceptance, because there was some uncertainty about the qualified majority decisions and the text containing the idea of moving EU summit meetings to Brussels. Finland insisted that the country holding the Presidency should be allowed to hold informal meetings on its own territory. These meetings would not be called European Councils, however. The Nice solution was accepted under the condition that it will be reconsidered at the next Inter-Governmental Conference.

The Finnish Government maintained its strong position concerning the provision of moving the European Councils to Brussels until the General Affairs Council on 22nd January 2001. This made possible the unanimous, final signature to the Treaty on the 26th of February. It is difficult to say whether the Finnish position was a reaction to the actual decision or whether it should be seen as a reaction to the style of the Presidency in the final hours of the Nice negotiations. As a matter of principle, Finland expressed concerns that the decision could lead to the undermining of the principle of a rotating Presidency (*Helsingin Sanomat,* January 15, 2001).

Among the elements where the aims of the Government were not met in a satisfactory manner was first of all the weighting of votes. In the eyes of the Finnish Government, the outcome was not balanced and was not based on objective criteria. Finland considered also that the result did not meet the criteria of effectiveness and clarity. The Finnish idea of a simple double-majority was realised only by the inclusion the criterion of the majority of the member States behind the QMV. The triple majority solution is far from the initial Finnish idea of a simple majority (Lipponen, PTK 82/2001).

Finland was ready to accept the solution although it marked a shift of power in favour of large Member States. In his speech to the Parliament, presenting the Government proposal for ratification, Prime Minister Paavo Lipponen defended the solution by explaining that the increased power to larger Member States would in practical terms only increase their power to prevent a decision through the 62 per cent rule. He argued that the majority of Member States–rule, advocated by Finland, works in the opposite direction (Lipponen 2001.) Under heavy pressure from the Presidency, and supported by other Member States, the Finnish model lost the battle.

The decision-making system in the Council was made too complicated with too many criteria. Finland complained that power in the Council voting was altered too much in the interest of large Member States. Finland, and in particular Prime Minister Lipponen, profiled during the negotiation after Biarriz as a defender of the interests of small Member States. During the last hours of intensive negotiations in Nice, Lipponen together with the Prime Ministers of Portugal, Austria, Sweden and Greece fought for a more equitable solution but lost (Ludlow 2001, 10). The Autumn of 2000 placed Finland at the core of the group of small Member States reinforcing its small state identity.

The extension of the use of QMV did not meet Finnish interests. In the Finnish view, the Treaty is not as ambitious in extending QMV as Finland would have considered necessary for the efficient functioning of the Union. Finland was ready to accept a wider extension of its use and was in particular unhappy about the modest progress in Article 133. A slow progress in the coordination of social policy (Art. 42), a lack of progress in the field of taxation as well as a modest advance in Justice and Home Affairs are listed as items where Finland saw too little improvement.

In other institutional modifications the Finnish aims were more or less met according to the Government proposal. The composition of the Commission as well as its nomination process satisfy the Finnish aims. In particular Finland is satisfied with the reforms made to the nomination process of the Commission President. The new rotation system introduced by the Treaty is 'satisfactory' in the eyes of Finland. Finland has no reservations either about the reforms concerning the role and composition of the Parliament.

A major change to the initial position was made on flexibility issues. Finland entered negotiations with an argument that no changes were needed in the Amsterdam provisions. However, during the Spring of 2000, Finland changed its attitude and during the Autumn of 2000 flexibility was seen as one of the key elements in effective working of the institutions. No explanation can be traced for this. One reason may be that in preparing the Government position, Finland preferred a limited agenda for the IGC. This preference is seen in the Presidency Report for instance. Finland was initially reluctant to expand the agenda but when new issues emerged, was ready to modify its strategy. Similar elements can be seen as well in its attitude towards the CFSP agenda. Flexibility in the strategy is clearly visible in the Finnish negotiation strategy.

The main conclusion could be that Finland profiled as an institution specific country in the Nice negotiation. In this regard its approach was the 'classical' small-state-approach traditionally adopted by the Benelux group. The line established during the first years of the Membership seems to prevail for the future as well. The experiences from being in the core are reassuring from the Finnish perspective. Finland also emphasises that the community method and the balance of the institutions are preserved.

For small states in particular, institutions offer a reliable forum in which they can gain information about the actions and preferences of other states - large and small. Institutions also give small countries the opportunity to influence that powerful states comply with joint decisions and rules while emphasising their own input in common projects. They believe that states will adhere to international treaties monitored and executed by institutions more effectively than in cases where there are treaties without institutions. In this latter case, relative differences in size and power assume greater importance.

Finland is also a believer in the power of the Commission as "a friend of small Member States." In her 'classical' small-state-approach Finland sees growing elements of intergovernmentalism as an alarming sign, which must be rejected. Intergovernmentalism gives more room for larger Members and invites them to exercise their power at the expense of small Members. Equality of Member States is threatened if this trend prevails.

Although the overall evaluation of the results of Nice was seen as satisfactory by Finland, new challenges were brought up as well. One of the key lessons of the negotiation process was that the Nordic group became even more dispersed than before the negotiation process. Institutionally, Finland distanced itself from Denmark and Sweden by joining the EMU. In a number of issues Finland and Sweden had different views in the Nice negotiations. The extension of the QMV, the highest priority to Finland, was not welcomed by Sweden. In particular, Swedish opposition to the inclusion of environmental taxation into QMV caused dissatisfaction in Finland.

Finland and Sweden also offered different models for the weighting of votes. The Finnish double majority model was contrasted by the Swedish square root model which remained on the table until the final moments of negotiations. In the Nice negotiations, Finland and Sweden did not act together in the CFSP matters as they did in the Amsterdam negotiations.

BIBLIOGRAPHY

Antola, Esko (2002), "Finland: From Cautious to Hard-Core Member," in Finn Laursen (ed.), *The Amsterdam Treaty. National Preference Formation, Interstate Bargaining and Outcome*. Odense: Odense University Press, pp. 121-138.

CONFER 4723/00: IGC 2000: Contribution from the Finnish Government: Background and Objectives in the IGC 2000., Brussels 7 March.

Efficient Institutions after Enlargement. Options for the Intergovernmental Conference. Presidency Report. Press Release, Nr. 13636/99, Brussels 7.12.1999.

Finland and EMU. The Prime Ministers Office, Publication 1997/26.

HE 93/2001 vp. Hallituksen esitys Euroopan unionista tehdyn sopimuksen sekä Euroopan yhteisöjen perustamissopoimusten ja niihin liittyvien tiettyjen asiakirjojen muuttamisesta tehdyn Nizzan sopimuksen lainsäädännön alaan kuuluvien määräysten voimaansaatta-misesta.

Helsingin Sanomat, January 15, 2001.

HVK 2000: Vahvistettu yhteistyö. Ministerial Committee on EU Affairs, 3 November.

Lipponen, Paavo (1998), Introduction to the ratification of the Treaty of Amsterdam to the Parliament, February.

—— (2000), Speech in the Council of Europe, Bruge, 10 November.

—— (2001), Speech to the Parliament of Finland, June 18, 2001. (PKT 82/2001 vp)

Ludlow, Peter (2001), The European Council at Nice: Neither Triumph nor Disaster. Brussels: CEPS.

CHAPTER 7

FRANCE: PRESIDENCY ROLES AND NATIONAL INTERESTS

THE IGC 2000 AND THE PROBLEM OF EVALUATING PRESIDENCIES

Contrary to most of the other chapters in this volume, this contribution is not about the role of a particular Member State or an EU institution in the IGC 2000 but about that of the French Presidency. France was the country that held the chair during the last six months of the IGC negotiations and it played a crucial role in forging the final agreement. It is appropriate to distinguish the role of France from that of the French Presidency because the chair is an office that imposes certain duties and raises institutional expectations that have an important impact on the behaviour of the country in question. The role of the chair is quite different from that of the national delegations around the table since it cannot merely defend its national interests but also has to look for the general interest. Presiding and setting the agenda at every level from the meetings of the personal representatives to those of the European Council, it is in a particularly privileged position to influence the direction of the debate and the final outcome. An examination of the Presidency's role in the negotiations may therefore be helpful to better understand the IGC process. So far studies on IGCs have paid little attention to the Presidency.[1]

The conduct of the French Presidency has been one of the most debated features of Nice as the French chair did not quite behave as was expected. The press and the EU literature depicted its performance as chaotic, biased, arrogant and lacking in ambition (*Le Monde*, 12 December 2000; Stubb and Gray, 2001, *European Voice*, 14-20 December 2000). The question arises whether France can indeed be blamed for everything that went wrong during the IGC. What is the impact and the influence of the chair on the final outcome and what should be the criteria for evaluating the Presidency?

Using contingency theory, this chapter elaborates a framework for understanding and evaluating the Presidency. As a first step, we make the roles of the Presidency explicit and argue that in addition to organiser and broker it also has the—admittedly controversial—roles of political leader and representative of national interests. Secondly, we link the four roles to the conditions of the environment in which the chair operates and posit that the ap-

[1] An exception is Bobby McDonagh (1998).

propriateness of Presidency styles is contingent on the situation. This leads to a set of hypotheses about the relationship between behaviour and environmental circumstances. They address the internal and external situational variables affecting the behaviour of the chair. External conditions 'demand' specific Presidency roles and the internal Presidency environment pushes towards a particular 'supply'. By allowing a comparison between behaviour and needs, our contingency theory offers a tool to assess the performance of the Presidency.

The model is used to examine the conduct of the French Presidency during the Intergovernmental Conference of 2000. We will examine the situational variables that played a role in the four items on the IGC agenda: flexibility, the extension of qualified majority voting (QMV), the composition of the Commission, and the re-weighting of votes. Each of these items made special claims on France and presented it with particular national sensitivities. For each dossier we examine to what extent the Presidency supplied the required style.

A number of caveats are in place. This chapter presents a single sample case study. As only one Presidency is studied, in the specific setting of an IGC, we have to be careful with generalising the findings. Further research will have to find out whether the findings can be applied to the Presidency in general and to the day-to-day decision-making process in the Union. Whatever the restrictions of limiting this chapter to a single case, n=1 studies allow constructing concepts (King *et al.*, 1984; Yin, 1984)—and that is how the case of Nice is used. Secondly, this research is based on reports, books, articles, Presidency papers and interviews with the actors involved.[2] The interviewees and written information show strong opinions. The question arises whether such subjective sources are reliable and to which extent they merely reflect the spirit of the moment? By consulting as many sources and voices as possible, we have tried to get a best possible feel for what happened. We are, however, conscious of the limitations when trying to get an insight into such a complex event as a Treaty negotiation.

This contribution consists of three parts: firstly, the main roles fulfilled by the country in the chair are outlined (see Table 7.1); secondly, the factors that influence the demand and supply of Presidency styles are identified; and finally, the framework is applied to the performance of the French Presidency during the IGC 2000.

---

[2] Interviews have been held with representatives of the following bodies: European Commission (2); Council General Secretariat (2); Dutch Permanent Representation (1); Portuguese Permanent Representation (2); Finnish Permanent Representation (1); French Permanent Representation (1); Quai d'Orsay (3); French Prime Minister Office (1).

THE ROLES OF THE PRESIDENCY

Discussing the roles of the Presidency is no easy matter. The office developed over time and in different directions (O'Nuallain, 1985). Emerging gaps in the EU's institutional design demanded organisational as well as political responsibilities from the Presidency. Most scholars mention the following tasks: management of day-to-day Council business, co-ordination, chairing, mediation, spokesperson and external representation, acting as contact point, taking political initiatives (e.g. Kirchner, 1992; Westlake, 1995; Wurzel, 1996; Hayes-Renshaw and Wallace, 1997; Sherrington, 2000). This list can be presented at different levels of detail (see e.g. the Council Guide, 1997). To get at the essence of the Presidency, the various tasks are grouped together into a limited number of core dimensions (*roles*). This was also the approach taken by the Three Wise Men in their report on the reform of the institutions (1979). They referred to the Presidency's "dual role of organisational control and political impetus" (Report of the Three Wise Men 1979, p. 35).[3] In addition, we distinguish the roles of broker and representative of the national position/interests (see Table 7.1). This leads to a more complex set of roles which the Presidency has to juggle (Schout, 1998). The Presidency *style* is the combination of its roles. The actual style in a particular situation can be a balanced package of roles or it can be dominated by one or more roles.

The four roles are not chosen arbitrarily but have specific conceptual origins. The first three roles relate to three key roles in leadership theory (as e.g. reviewed by Yukl, 1998): task-oriented leadership, group-oriented leadership and transformational leadership. Task-oriented leadership is about taking the steps necessary to get the job done. Group-oriented leadership is concerned with the atmosphere and with facilitating problem solving. Task-oriented leadership and group-oriented leadership aim at getting results and serving group processes. As one member of a Presidency team said: "I don't mind whether they decide to paint the room black or white, as long as the decision is taken in the correct way".[4] In contrast, the purpose of transformational leadership is not to arrive at just any common position. It is long term and vision-oriented and aims at moving away from friction and at finding new solutions.

In addition, our classification includes a fourth role, which is to represent national positions and interests. Although the chair should, in the first place,

---

[3] The same distinction can be found in Kirchner (1992); see also Sherrington (2000), p. 3.

[4] Quote by senior official of the Council General Secretariat during Presidency seminar organised by the European Institute of Public Administration (EIPA) in preparation of the Swedish Presidency, Stockholm.

look for a common denominator, it is an illusion to assume that a country at the helm can simply ignore its interests. In our view, the question is not so much whether a country ignores its national position but how it handles it. We advocate to consider this role in its own right because it is an important element when evaluating the performance of a chair.

The classification of the roles calls for additional remarks. Firstly, it is a heuristic device. As discussed in more detail below, the boundaries between the roles of organiser, broker, political leader and representative of national interests are not always sharp and they are not mutually exclusive. Especially with regard to the role of representative of the national position, one could argue that it is part of the broker role and of the role of political leader (e.g. long term visions may be highly biased by national interests). However, we consider national interests separately so that we are able to explicitly address the question of how the chair handled its national position and how this affected its performance.

Secondly, the roles can be mutually supportive as well as conflicting. Political leadership will generally require the organiser and broker roles. The role of broker, for example, can be very inefficient and interfere with the focus of the organiser role. Similarly, transformational leadership may spoil the atmosphere but this does not mean that the output will be less.

Thirdly, the fact that the roles are interrelated also implies that the chair has to play different roles at the same time, e.g. acting as broker, providing transformational leadership and defending national interests (Gibson *et al.*, 1996; Schout, 1998). Finally, not all roles are necessary in every dossier.

Organiser: Task-Oriented Leadership

Getting results in an efficient way during the six months' Presidency requires thorough preparation. Ministers and national officials come from far to negotiate. Hence, meetings have to be organised so that a maximum use is made of everyone's time. Moreover, six months is a short time and the heavy agendas require careful planning of meetings, the organisation of discussions, anticipation of resistance, efficient chairing, the arranging of rooms and the preparation and distribution of documents. These are the immediate tasks to be undertaken. The organiser however also needs a long-term perspective. In order for meetings to be efficient, complex issues have to be broken up into manageable parts, background studies need to be made so that the real issues are identified and less relevant topics filtered out, overviews are needed of alternatives and implications, etc. The Secretariat will help with the immediate tasks related to efficient chairing (Council Guide,

1997, and the Council's Rules of Procedure, 2004). The long-term preparations, however, have to be taken care of by the Presidency itself.

Even though these are primarily administrative tasks, their importance should not be underestimated. With the involvement of all Member States, the Commission, and the EP, it is important that meetings are adequately prepared. If done well, the organisational work is hardly noticed but if neglected, e.g. if papers are too late, it may greatly hamper the meeting and cause a lot of frustration.

Brokerage: Group-Oriented Leadership

The broker role receives a lot of emphasis in literature and is seen by many as the core function of the chair (Ludlow, 1993; Weyland, 1993; Galloway, 2001). It is about facilitating problem solving and involves sounding out Member States, creating a good atmosphere and unearthing directions for compromises on which Member States can agree. The chair has to support the conditions for finding common positions. Brokerage requires trust. This can be gained by lending a receptive ear to problems and objections and by not favouring particular delegations.

The broker role has short-term and long-term dimensions. In the short term, diplomatic skills are required and the positions of each party have to be respected. It is important to empathise with the concerns that are expressed. This will often require long-term preparations so as to become familiar with everyone's position, to show that the Presidency understands the dilemmas and to ensure that the partners see that the chair takes account of their problems.

The mediating role is not exclusive; usually, there is multiple brokerage in EU negotiations. The Commission, the Council General Secretariat (particularly in the case of an IGC)[5] and other delegations may also fulfil this role.

Political Leadership: Transformational Leadership

In terms of the transaction costs theory, the organiser and broker roles facilitate the exchange of information, communication and problem solving. Political leadership on the contrary is concerned with the long-term viability of proposals and solutions. It involves making deliberate efforts to move solutions beyond the lowest common denominator and recasting short-term na-

[5] See chapter by Derek Beach in this volume.

tional interests in terms of 'what is best for Europe in the long term'. This always involves a degree of subjectivity but there are criteria such as legitimacy, effectiveness and efficiency that facilitate discussions about directions to be taken. Moreover, debates about what is best for Europe are not necessarily related to a specific outcome but should aim to move away from preconceived interests and to search for common, long-term solutions.[6] It involves giving full consideration to the consequences of proposals and finding innovative solutions.

Political leadership requires thorough preparation. In addition to familiarisation with national positions and elements of friction, it demands an understanding of future trends and the possession of skills to persuade delegations to give up national stakes for wider EU interests. Not all dossiers lend themselves to such an approach and not all countries in the chair have similar transformational ambitions.

The older literature on the Presidency warns against political leadership. It would create resistance, make the Presidency part of the problem and erode the trust in the chair (e.g. Verbeke and Van de Voorde, 1994). Moreover, it is argued that one should not overrate what can be achieved in six months. A political Presidency undoubtedly presents a number of pitfalls but when provided properly, it can lead to a more ambitious outcome than if the role of the chair were limited to serving group processes. At a time when there is general concern about the lack of transformational leadership in the EU (e.g. Grant, 2002), the Presidency's potential to make a difference should not be downplayed.

National Positions and Interests

The fourth is the most controversial role. Generally, the representation of national interests is regarded as the task of the national delegate. The chair is expected to ignore national interests, even to the point of making heavy sacrifices so as to have its hands free to serve EU decision making.[7] The argument is that showing national preferences reduces the Presidency's credibility as a broker and creates distrust. Giving up national positions allegedly sets the right example and raises its prestige. Ludlow (1995) emphasises that the Presidency is first and foremost an office of the Union and not an instrument to pursue national objectives.

---

[6] See the concept of integrative bargaining in Walton and Dutton (1969).

[7] See e.g. the Presidency handbook of the Secretariat General of the Council: "The Presidency must, by definition, be *neutral and impartial*" in Presidency Handbook 1997, p. 5 (original emphasis).

However important it is that the Presidency operates in terms of general interest, one cannot simply ignore that the chair too, has interests at stake from which it often cannot dissociate itself. The national interests can take two forms. The Presidency may add hobbyhorses to or remove sensitive topics from the agenda. Moreover, it often uses its formal and informal positional powers to incorporate its own positions and interests in the negotiations (Tallberg, 2003). Tallberg's argument is based on the high coordination costs in EU negotiations, which make it possible to include national interests in compromises. We concur with this possibility. However, rather than viewing influencing agendas and outcomes as manipulating negotiations, we see the defence of national interests as a legitimate role for each Member State—including the Presidency. Moreover, partiality need not be intrusive but is often openly a part of negotiations without being a cause of problems (e.g. Mazzucelli, 2003). Countries around the table usually know where the Presidency stands and understand the pressure it is under as they have been or can be in similar positions. The domestic pressure not to give in may be considerable when an issue is very sensitive for a chair. The price of concessions may sometimes be high and politically unacceptable. Having to come back to the negotiating table after the six months' term because the national parliament does not accept the concessions is not very conducive to building a legitimate Union either.

Evidently, national interests can easily compromise trust and Presidencies have to be careful, but they need not always be problematic or tabooed. As argued in the next section, it will depend on the situation whether there is scope for national views. The art of the Presidency does not require neutrality, but it is essential that the partners remain convinced of its fairness (see Gibson *et al.*, 1996).

Table 7.1: Presidency roles

	Organiser	Broker	Political leadership	National positions / interests
Conceptual origin	Task-oriented leadership	Group-oriented leadership	Transformational leadership	Traditional role of Member States in negotiations
Tasks	Planning meetings External representation Arranging rooms Drafting agendas of meetings (listing the agenda items) Chairing meetings (i.e. organising the debates) Preparing and distributing documents Mapping the various aspects of the topic Separating the issues, devising a strategy for moving forward Carrying out background studies	Sounding out Member States Creating a good atmosphere Creating understanding for each other's problems Identifying mainstreams Identifying bargains and trade-offs Formulating compromises Serving group pro-cesses	Putting current discussions in a long term perspective of EU challenges Steering the debate in specific directions Convincing delegations to abandon short-term interests Not necessarily moving towards new vistas for the EU, but at least moving away from frictions by recasting the debate in a long-term perspective	Short-term orientation on national gains and values Influencing the political agenda by adding or removing topics
Focus	Effectiveness in the search for a common position	Fairness in the search for a common position (guarding trust)	Moving towards long-term objectives	Including national preferences in the negotiations

TOWARDS A CONTINGENCY THEORY FOR THE PRESIDENCY

It is well established in organisation theory that there is no one best way to organise (Lawrence and Lorsch, 1969; Schout, 1999). This insight has triggered research on relations between specific types of complexity and dynamism and the way in which organisations are structured and behave. The environment may 'demand' certain types of organisations.

It is important to state up front that the resulting body of contingency theory does not lead to fixed patterns of structures and behaviour. There are many—overlapping and conflicting—environmental variables that pull organisations in different directions. Moreover, there is also an element of choice. Different strategists have different preferences and well-chosen actions can change the characteristics of the environment. Hence, structure and behaviour are determined by external conditions (demand, D) and are shaped by choices and actions of the organisation (supply, S). Due to these options, contingency theory cannot predict or prescribe organisational behaviour (see Child, 1972, 1975). Nor is contingency theory sufficient for examining empirical phenomena. However, it can indicate which patterns will be feasible under specific circumstances. Therefore, it is a powerful tool when it comes to planning and evaluation. Contingency theory does not lead to a set of cast-iron rules, but offers a framework for mapping relevant variables and causalities. Its value is that it helps to bring the environment into discussions on Presidency behaviour.

This section applies contingency theory to the Presidency. The approach can lead to more insights into the usefulness of its roles in specific situations. The assumption is that, depending on the circumstances, different roles will be demanded or be appropriate. At the same time, the roles supplied will be influenced by internal contingencies.

An Effective Presidency: D=S

Because of the complexity of 'effectiveness', performance evaluations are inherently multi-dimensional (e.g. Powell, 1987). There are many definitions of an effective chair. To mention just a few: a chair that concludes negotiations, one that ensures that the outcome meets quality standards (e.g. of subsidiarity, implementability and legal clarity), one that maintains a good atmosphere or one that achieves its objectives. Each of these definitions is hard to substantiate as outcomes relate to many factors such as efforts of previous Presidencies, the sensitivity of the issue, the Commission's flexibility, personal styles, etc.

Contingency theory leads to a particular definition of an effective chair: one that matches the demand and supply of Presidency styles. For example, a Presidency will be counterproductive if brokerage is needed because the chair only focuses on national interests. There may also be circumstances in which a national position will not be problematic – e.g. when there are multiple brokers in the system. There is no direct link with the output of Council meetings. However, following the logic of contingency theory, the appropriate Presidency style will at least make it easier to reach agreement. The advantage of the D=S definition of effectiveness is that it captures a set of input and output elements and therefore offers a multivariate analysis.[8]

Contingency Factors

To develop a contingency approach to the Presidency, we have to identify the factors that influence the demand and supply of roles. In addition, the forces in EU decision making that help to align supply and demand need to be specified. The external and internal factors that steer the demand and supply of the roles are shown in Tables 7.2 and 7.3. External contingencies refer to the EU context in which the chair works, and exert pulls on the chair, e.g. towards a specific type of leadership. Internal contingencies are related to the domestic environment of the Presidency. They push the chair in certain directions, for example to raise problems in European integration related to the legitimacy of the EU in the home country.

One could argue that the roles of organiser and broker are needed in any negotiation, whatever the environment. We are however addressing the question of the dominant demand, i.e. the extent to which a role is determining for the success of the negotiations. If all issues have already been mapped by the previous Presidency e.g., we argue that there is no dominant demand for the organiser role. Similarly there is no dominant demand for the broker role when there are other brokers ready to take over from the chair (see infra).

The external variables included in this study are the following: the degree to which a topic has been explored (new versus old), the level of trust in the chair, the presence of other brokers in the system, the shadow of the future, and the political sensitivity of a topic.[9] The internal variables are the importance of the topic to the country in the chair, preferences and commitments

[8] Even though the suggested approach for assessing effectiveness is broad, there are evidently additional perspectives on output that would be useful to include, such as the quality of policy decisions (see e.g. the White Paper on European Governance, 2001). However, this would require, among others, cost-benefit analyses and falls outside the scope of this chapter.

[9] Given the complexity of social and political processes, the tables of demand and supply factors are not exhaustive. The factors listed resulted from brainstorming at the start of the study about potentially relevant situational conditions for Presidencies. At the end of the study, the initial causalities could be elaborated and adjusted, whereas others could be dropped as they added little to these IGC negotiations (e.g. the influence of unanimity and the technicality of the topic). The selection of the contingency factors and the elaboration of the causalities were part of the interviews with senior national and European officials involved in the IGC.

of key players, the level of preparations, and sensitivities between coalition partners.

For each of the variables we examine how it affects the demand or the supply of a Presidency style. Starting with the external contingency factors, we argue that a topic that has extensively been explored (Table 7.2.1a) will not be demanding in terms of task-oriented, group-oriented or political leadership and that there will be scope for presenting the national position. A new issue on the other hand (Table 7.2. 1b) needs exploration of the various positions (organiser), identification of possible bargains (broker), and provides more scope for steering the debate away from short-term friction (political leadership). Defence of national interests may be possible but will have to be handled carefully. Low trust in the chair (Table 7.2. 2) will be demanding in terms of organisation and brokerage. Political leadership and the defence of national interests are not appropriate in this case. The presence of other brokers such as the European Commission, other Member States and the Council General Secretariat (Table 7.2. 3) reduces the demand for organisation, brokerage and political leadership. When others show willingness to step in for the chair, there is scope for the defence of the national position. What we have called 'the shadow of the future' is a fourth variable that influences the demand for the Presidency style (Table 7.2. 4). A deadline, or negative repercussions on the broader process of European integration, makes high demands on the chair in terms of organisation and brokerage and leaves little scope for national interests. This variable says little about the need for political leadership. Finally, sensitive issues (Table 7.2. 5b) are very demanding in terms of organisation and brokerage, leaving little scope for national interests. Such issues may or may not demand a political leadership approach, but one has to realise that recasting the debate in terms of European interest will be difficult.

Table 7.3 formulates a series of hypotheses on the internal contingency factors. When a topic is important for the country in the chair (Table 7.3. 1), this will positively affect the supply of the roles of organiser, broker and political leader. The chair will also try to take into account the national interest. When high level players in the country at the helm are committed to a certain dossier, they will invest in providing different types of leadership from task- and group oriented to political leadership. Their involvement also increases the chances that national positions will be defended. A thorough preparation of the Presidency term (Table 7.3. 3) will positively affect the provision of task-oriented, group-oriented and political leadership. It also helps to create an understanding for the chair's national sensitivities. The variable of competing coalition partners (Table 7.3. 4) makes it difficult for the chair to act as an organiser and broker and makes political leadership unlikely as there is no agreed direction. Domestic politics may lead to a competition for the strongest representation of national interests.

A couple of points need to be made about the Tables. The rows cannot be seen in isolation. For example, the demand in the case of an old sensitive topic (rows 1 and 5) is different from that relating to a new sensitive issue (rows 1 and 5). When analysing the behaviour of the chair, due regard for the interrelations between contingency factors is indispensable. Contingency factors can be mutually reinforcing but may also be conflicting. For example, a transparent topic with low levels of trust suffers from opposing pulls. Furthermore, some variables will clearly be stronger than others ('dominant contingency factors'). Which Presidency style is the most useful needs to be considered on an issue-by-issue basis.

Secondly, the list of factors is not complete. There have only been a few seminal attempts to introduce a contingency approach into European integration theory (e.g. Elgström, 2000). The five demand and four supply variables below are clearly a simplification of elements that have to be taken into account when analysing political and social interactions in the EU. Compared to their richness in private sector management theory (e.g. Ansoff, 1985), contingency approaches in EU studies are still in their infancy.

Drivers for D=S

Contingency theory does not lead to cast-iron rules due to the many and often conflicting pulls and pushes. Moreover, the directions in which variables pull is not always unidirectional but depend on the situation. Nevertheless, there are a number of mechanisms that contribute to the approximation of demand and supply. These are:

a) *rational* processes: Presidency teams analyse situations, map scenarios and decide on the optimal behaviour (using worst-case and optimal scenarios).

b) *institutional expectations*: there is a tendency in EU negotiations to gravitate D and S towards both the organisational and the broker role. EU decision making involves many trained diplomats who are well versed in running and chairing international meetings. This helps to contain the pressure from ministers to be transformational (but may also lead to colourless Presidencies).

c) *political EU pressure*: every situation puts specific pressures on the Presidency. New topics demand an exploration of countries' positions; brokerage or steering the outcome in a particular direction only becomes relevant at later stages. Deadlines, on the other hand, demand goal orientation and provoke political involvement. Upcoming elections in the county holding the Presidency will invoke a whole set of different pressures.

d) *personal experience*: chairpersons and their teams benefit from experience obtained in EU negotiations and may be expected to have developed a feeling for how far they can go or when to stir up the heat.

Despite these equilibrating forces there is no guarantee that D will be S. The pulls and pushes may be too strong.

Table 7.2: External contingency factors: The dominant demand for a Presidency style

	Organiser	Broker	Political leadership	National positions/ interests
1) Degree to which a topic has been explored *a) Old/transparent topic*	- Issues and positions are already mapped out.	- Well known positions facilitate formulation of bargains.	- Little room for novel solutions.	+ Position of country at helm is well known.
b) New topic	+ Need to study key issues and alternatives.	+ Need to identify possible bargains.	+ Scope for steering debates away from short-term interests.	+ or - Pushing of national position has to be handled carefully.
2) Lack of trust in the chair	+ Good organisation can increase trust.	+ Compromises taking into account various positions reinforce trust.	- Strong arguing in favour of a particular solution, even if in Europe's long-term interest, raises suspicion.	- Representation and defence of national interests further reduce trust.
3) Multiple brokerage	- Others play a role in mapping out issues.	- Other players compensate lack of brokerage by the chair.	- Others may put the debate in a long-term/ European perspective.	+ Others can defend the general interest.
4) Shadow of the future	+ Efficient use of valuable time is needed.	+ Pressures to reach agreement leads to a high demand for brokerage.	+ or - It will depend on other factors whether or not political leadership will be needed.	- Pushing for national interest will further complicate the negotiation process.

5) Political sensitivity *a) Non-sensitive issue*	- It will be easy to map the various positions.	- Lack of sensitivity makes it easier to find a compromise.	+ Countries are more willing to move away from their short-term national interests.	+ Other delegations are more open to national interests.
b) Sensitive issue	+ Bad organisation will add to further irritation.	+ Building a good atmosphere and compromise-building are crucial.	+ or - Recasting the debate towards long-term European interests may or may not be demanded but will be diffcult	- Defence of national interest will further complicate the negotiations.

- : not relevant or to be avoided.

+ : this role is demanded. (As regards national interests: the environment does not demand national interests, but in some cases the environment leaves scope to include the national interest in the negotiations.)

As explained in the text, the variables are interdependent so that the influence, as presented in the Table, can differ depending on the circumstances.

Table 7.3: Internal contingency factors: The dominant supply of a Presidency style

	Organiser	Broker	Political leadership	National positions/interests
1) Important topic for the chairing country	+ The Presidency will invest in preparations and mapping the issues.	+ The Presidency will formulate compromises to move things forward.	+ The Presidency will be motivated to argue its position in European terms.	+ The Presidency will try to take national interests into account.
2) Commitments of key players / politicians at national level	+ Commitment will positively affect the development of a strategy to move forward.	+ Commitment of key players will promote brokerage.	+ or - The chair may try to sell its own preferred solution as the best option for Europe.	+ Preferences of national politicians or high-level officials increase the chances that national positions/interests will be defended.

3) Preparations	+ If well prepared, the efficiency of meetings will increase.	+ Thorough preparations increase the chances of brokerage being supplied.	+ Preparations are a precondition for the supply of transformational leadership.	+ Explaining the national position prior to the Presidency period will create an understanding for the chair's national sensitivities.
4) Sensitivity between the coalition partners in the government	- Internal fights negatively affect task-oriented leadership.	- Internal disagree-ments negatively affect the supply of brokerage.	- The partners risk immobilising each other.	+ The coalition partners are likely to defend positions that serve their national audience.

-: This style will be difficult or impossible to offer.
+: This style will be possible or is likely to be offered.

THE CONTINGENCY FRAMEWORK AND THE IGC 2000

After the preparations made by the Finnish and Portuguese Presidencies, France chaired the IGC 2000 during the final six months of the negotiations. The way it handled its term in office resulted in strong accusations of mismanagement. The Swedish Prime Minister Göran Persson criticised the Nice Summit for being organised '*à la italienne*' (*Le Monde*, 12 December 2000). Gray and Stubb (2001), both insiders to the IGC, regretted the lack of continuity with the previous Presidencies. Others criticised the chair for being highly biased. President Chirac was charged of an "unashamed championing of his country's own interest" (*European Voice*, 14-20 December 2000) and of not listening to the views of others, particularly those of the small Member States (*Le Monde*, 12 December 2000). The French were blamed for being arrogant, antagonising partners, seriously hampering the search for compromises and lacking ambition. As a result, Paris was accused of bearing responsibility for the poor outcome (Gray and Stubb, 2001).

Did France do such a poor job as most observers and insiders claim? We will answer this question by examining the extent to which the Presidency style matched the demand as regards the four items on the IGC agenda.10

[10] For details on the four topics see, among others, Galloway (2001), Gray and Stubb (2001) and Ludlow (2001).

Flexibility

Enhanced or flexible cooperation between the Member States within the Union's institutional framework was one of the achievements of the IGC negotiations in Amsterdam. However, the conditions were defined so strictly that flexibility was hardly an option. The IGC 2000 aimed to simplify the procedures.

Demand

The biggest challenge for the flexibility dossier was to get the issue on the IGC agenda. The Benelux countries and Italy had already been lobbying actively in Helsinki (December 1999) and the Portuguese Presidency (Feira, June 2000) added it officially to the agenda. By the time the French took over, flexibility was, in terms of situational variables, an 'old' or 'transparent' issue. The positions of the Member States were well known. A majority supported a relaxation of the conditions but it remained a sensitive issue for Denmark, Spain and the United Kingdom, who feared that flexibility would reduce their influence (Galloway, 2001, p.134). Belgium, Germany and Italy gave it priority.

Due to the transparency there was little need for task-oriented leadership. Limited brokerage was required as a majority of Member States thought along the same lines. The main task consisted in convincing the opposing minority that relaxation of the conditions would not lead to their isolation. Moreover, the pressure on the Presidency was reduced by the presence of other brokers. Multiple brokerage and transparency also provided scope for the chair's national position. The situation did not call for political leadership.

Supply

Both parties of the *cohabitation* favoured the relaxation of the flexibility clauses but initially opposed placing the question on the agenda. France wanted to concentrate on the three leftovers of Amsterdam and was wary of further burdening the IGC negotiations. However, once it had lost this battle, the chair—with the help of Germany and Italy—worked hard to reach a breakthrough.

The dominant Presidency style was that of organiser and broker. France prepared the meetings well by presenting various papers and structuring the debate around five questions. The French Permanent Representative, Pierre Vimont, devoted considerable time to the issue during the first eight meetings of the Preparatory Group (Gray and Stubb, 2001, p.11) and contributed to the creation of a good atmosphere. 'Ring-fencing', i.e. excluding important areas such as the internal market and economic and social cohesion, was one of France's key contributions to brokering a compromise. It met the concerns of those fearing that enhanced cooperation would exclude them from core policies and allowed all delegations to agree that they would no longer be able to veto enhanced cooperation in the first and third pillars (Galloway 2001, p.134). A political agreement on flexibility was already reached at the European Summit of Biarritz (Gray and Stubb 2001, p.12).

D=S?

The flexibility dossier did not place huge demands on the chair. The positions of the Member States were well known (transparency), there was multiple brokerage and although the relaxation of the flexibility conditions struck a sensitive chord with some Member States, it was not a major issue on the IGC agenda. Even if the demand for brokerage was limited, the agreement was primarily forged at the instigation of the chair.

Table 7.4: Flexibility

FLEXIBILITY	Organiser	Broker	Political leader	National positions/ interests
Dominant demand	- Old and transparent topic	Limited demand Multiple brokerage Majority in favour of relaxation	- Old topic.	+ Multiple brokerage
Dominant supply	+ Meetings were well prepared; issues were mapped out clearly	+ Chair developed compromises. Co-operation of chair with Germany and Italy.	-	+ France favoured relaxation but not a priority.
D=S	The supply fitted the demand			

Extension of Qualified Majority Voting (QMV)

Qualified majority voting had already been on the agenda of various IGCs and dated back to the Single European Act. All Member States agreed that enlargement required its extension, but there was no consensus on the articles to which this should apply. The Commission's proposal to make QMV the general rule and to limit the negotiations to an agreement on the exceptions was considered by most as a non-starter. As a result, the negotiations focused on the articles that could move from unanimity to QMV (Galloway, 2001, p. 99-100).

Demand

The dossier had already been prepared under the Portuguese Presidency and by the time France took over, the positions of the various delegations were transparent. Having grouped the different provisions into categories such as "provisions associated with the internal market", "institutionally anomalous decisions" etc., Portugal had drawn up a list of approximately 50 articles which could be accepted (Galloway, 2001, p. 100). However, taxation, social security, asylum and migration, common commercial policy, structural and cohesion funds and environment remained sensitive (Gray and Stubb, 2001, p.16; Ludlow, 2001, p.15-17). One way out was to limit the extension of QMV to only part of the articles.

The QMV dossier needed a broker who mastered the technicalities of the dossiers and who could formulate compromise proposals taking account of the sensitivities of the Member States. The chair was in a good position to assume this role, but there were also other brokers—such as the Commission and some Member States—who were well versed in the issues and ready to contribute. The presence of multiple brokers offered scope for a French national position. There was no room for political leadership since the option of making QMV the general decision-making rule had already been explicitly excluded during the Portuguese Presidency. Given the extensive preparations under previous Presidencies, also the demand for task-oriented leadership was limited.

Supply

France favoured further extension of QMV. As Portugal had already forged agreement on the 'easy' dossiers, France had to concentrate on the sensitive issues. The QMV dossier was largely dealt with at the level of the Vimont preparatory group in which the Presidency emphasised brokerage. It listed the positions and tried to take into account the different national concerns—including the French. The attempts to forge agreement on social security and taxation were without result, despite strong support from the Commission (social security) and the German delegation (taxation). Denmark opposed an agreement on social security, and the taxation article was a bridge too far for several delegations.

In the case of the common commercial policy, France itself was the strongest opponent of introducing QMV. This had to do with national sensitivities about QMV in trade in cultural matters, audio-visual services and education. A large lobby group of actors and media personalities had mobilised the press and exerted strong pressure on the government not to let down French and European culture. Given the high visibility of the topic, neither Chirac nor Jospin wanted to be seen as too soft. At the same time, several other delegations pushed hard for QMV in the area of trade.

The lack of progress on these very sensitive areas in Nice was primarily due to the intransigent positions of the Member States, but key actors also estimate that in Nice the chair did not sufficiently develop the potential for progress. Some suspect that Chirac gave in too quickly because it was more important to safeguard French interests on the 'weighting of votes dossier' (see infra).

As regards the trade dossier, France itself was the strongest opponent of an extension of QMV. When it appeared that the chair was incapable of distancing itself from its national position, the Commission and the Finnish delegation stepped in and hammered out an agreement in Nice. The defence of the French national position did not prevent a deal but it delayed the negotiations. In Nice precious time was lost on a dossier that should have been settled at a lower level. Moreover, it negatively affected the trust in the Presidency.

D=S?

The QMV dossier demanded primarily a broker. The Presidency played a key role in formulating compromises—except in the case of trade. France's opposition to QMV in this field did not prevent an agreement as the Commission and Finland filled the vacuum. It would however have been preferable if this question could have been addressed before Nice.

Table 7.5: QMV

QMV	Organiser	Broker General	Trade	Political leader	National positions/ interests
Dominant demand	- Old and transparent topic	+ Sensitive issue - Multiple brokerage	+ Sensitive issue - Multiple brokerage	- Old topic; option to make QMV the general rule was a non-starter	+ Scope for national position because of multiple brokerage

Dominant supply	+ Meetings were well prepared; issues were mapped out clearly	+ Chair played key role in developing compromises	- France did not broker; Brokerage by Com-mission and Finland.	-	+ Important for France and its political top, especially in the case of trade
D=S	France brokered heavily. The fact that France was weak on brokerage in the field of trade did not prevent an agreement but delayed the negotiations eating into the precious time of Nice.				

Size of the Commission

Demand

Having been on the agenda in Amsterdam, the positions of the different delegations regarding the size of the Commission were well known (transparent). The issue was highly sensitive because it was linked with the influence of Member States. The division between small and large delegations further complicated the situation and the atmosphere was one of distrust. Large countries wanted to be compensated for losing their second Commissioner and the small states feared that their Commissioners would rotate while the large countries would always be represented.

When France took over the chair, the two options of one Commissioner per country or a capped College were still on the table. The first option was supported by the small Member States (the majority) and was easier to sell to national parliaments and the public. The second one was preferred by most of the large countries and could well be argued from a European point of view: a small Commission would be more efficient, more independent and stronger. The sensitivity of the dossier and the polarisation of views required ample brokerage. As the national delegations as well as the Commission were divided, brokerage had to be ensured primarily by the chair (no multiple brokerage). The option of a small and strong Commission lent itself for a leadership approach. Given the sensitivity and the atmosphere of distrust, such anapproach needed careful preparation. The chair would have to move the Member States away from frictions between small and large, recast the debate in a long-term perspective and ensure that it would be trusted. The fact that the model of a small Commission coincided with the French national position made such approach all the more challenging.

Supply

France was unmistakably in favour of a capped Commission (10 to 12 members) and had already defended this view in Amsterdam. The small countries, however, saw the appeal for a 'small and effective' Commission as a way to push for the French position and mistrusted the 'best for Europe' arguments. They feared that a small Commission would lead to the introduction of a Security Council model in which only the large countries would always be represented. France did nothing to eliminate these concerns. On the contrary, by initially refusing to inscribe the principle of equal rotation into the Treaty, it fuelled suspicions of a hidden agenda.

Contrary to the flexibility and the QMV dossiers in which the French Permanent Representation had taken the lead, the Commission file was handled at the political level of the Council and the European Council. Especially during the first months of the negotiations, the small Member States felt that France was hardly interested in listening to or meeting their objections. At the first ministerial conclave of 24 July, the chair was accused of being biased and failing to take into account the views of the majority. This spoiled the atmosphere. The defence of a capped Commission was not seen in terms of political leadership but as an abuse of the Presidency position. The Luxembourg Prime Minister Juncker described the informal European Council of Biarritz as "a crazy trench warfare between small and large Member States" (*Bulletin Quotidien Europe* 2000, p.5).

Nevertheless, it was in Biarritz that the first foundations for a compromise between small and large Member States were laid (Gray and Stubb, 2001, p.12). The Dutch proposal to postpone the introduction of a small Commission was an important breakthrough. Following the models of the Council Secretariat for rotation on an equal basis, France finally accepted to write this principle into the Treaty and convinced the other large countries to follow. Deferred capping and equal rotation also convinced some of the smaller Member States. Finally, the outcome was more ambitious than many had expected.[11]

D=S?

The dossier demanded a broker and had potential for political leadership. Given the earlier debates in Amsterdam, the organiser role was less needed. Giving France the benefit of the doubt, one can argue that by pushing for a small and independent Commission, the Presidency tried to provide political

[11] "The fact that the Conference agreed to cap the Commission, albeit at a later date, was a far more ambitious outcome than could have been envisaged even half way through the negotiations. Before the IGC began, this outcome was discounted as a non-starter." (Galloway, p. 57).

leadership. Due to lack of preparation and strategy, the chair did however not succeed in elevating the debate in terms of what is best for the EU. On the contrary, its behaviour was primarily seen as a defence of the national position. The broker role was only assumed in the last months of the negotiations and was triggered by proposals from The Netherlands and the Council Secretariat.

Table 7.6: Size and Composition of Commission

SIZE AND COMPOSITION COMMISSION	Organiser	Broker	Political leader	National positions/ interests
Dominant demand	- Old and transparent topic.	+ Lack of trust in the chair. No other brokers. Sensitive issue.	+ Option of small Commission could well be argued in European terms.	Limited Old and transparent topic. Sensitive. Lack of trust in chair.
Dominant supply	-	- Discussion papers were seen as being biased. + Only from Biarritz onwards following proposals from others.	- France tried but did not succeed.	+ Top priority for France.
S only partly met D	France tried to provide political leadership but was not successful. Its pushing for a small Commission was primarily interpreted as a defence of the national position. In the early phase of the negotiations, brokerage was poor but from Biarritz onwards, it was very active in forging a compromise.			

Re-Weighting of Votes

The re-weighting of votes in the Council, which had already been a stumbling block in Amsterdam was also the most sensitive question in the IGC 2000. It is a typical example of zero-sum negotiations: more votes for one Member State imply a decrease in the relative position of others. Moreover, it polarised large and small states. Large countries wanted sufficient compensation for the loss of their second Commissioner; the small ones were afraid to become marginalised in an enlarged EU.

Demand

For the Presidency this dossier was undoubtedly the most challenging one. In terms of contingency it was an example of conflicting pulls. Lack of trust in the chair, the absence of multiple brokerage and the shadow of the future (no agreement in Nice being a negative signal for enlargement) pulled towards group-oriented leadership. The sensitivity of the issue made it all the more important to invest in the creation of a good atmosphere. At the same time however, there were also factors restricting the scope for brokerage. Arguments had been repeated over and over again (old topic) and prior to Nice, Member States would not make major concessions. It was a typical case where agreement would only be reached under pressure of a deadline and a waiting press. After Amsterdam, Europe could not afford another failure.

The dossier did not demand a political leadership approach. Member States were so obsessed with securing their own interests that, according to insiders, it was a non-starter to elevate the debate to a discussion on principles of efficiency and transparency.

There was some scope for the representation of national interest. For any country in the chair the interests at stake were too high to be simply ignored. The lack of trust in the chair and the absence of other brokers implied however that France had to handle the defence of its national position carefully.

Supply

France had two main priorities. Firstly, it wanted to reinforce the position of the large Member States who had given up their second Commissioner. It considered that a simple re-weighting was the best way to achieve this. Secondly, it aimed to maintain parity with Germany. The latter question was widely discussed in the French press. None of the coalition parties wanted to be seen as selling out French interests and they closely observed each other's moves—ready to take political advantage whenever the other partner was too soft. In adopting such a rigid position, Paris manoeuvred itself in a difficult situation vis-à-vis both its own public and the other Member States. Not the slightest attempt was made to explain to the French public that, given the considerably higher number of inhabitants in Germany, a differentiation in votes would be justified. The obsession with parity aroused the other delegations' suspicion, they feared that Paris' first objective was to secure a good deal for itself.

The Presidency's pushing for a simple re-weighting of votes, while refusing to seriously consider the option of double majority, reinforced the misgivings. Despite bilateral summits, France did not manage to settle the parity issue with Germany prior to Nice. Rather than being a facilitator, the chair was one of the central problems at the European Summit and spent valuable time on working out a compromise with Germany. The Presidency's proposal to maintain parity between France and Germany but to differentiate between The Netherlands and Belgium, further eroded the chair's credibility. Spain, among others, cleverly exploited the situation by extracting as many concessions as possible. As mentioned before, it also affected the Presidency's position in the QMV negotiations.

The poor performance of the chair blackened the spirit of the partners but it did not prevent the Fifteen from reaching an agreement. All realised that failure would lead to a deadlock in the EU and no one wanted to take the blame.

D=S?

The weighting of votes dossier was subject to conflicting pulls. Its sensitive character, lack of multiple brokerage and distrust in the chair demanded group leadership. At the same time, the scope for brokerage was restrained because it was a topic that had already been extensively discussed in Amsterdam and Member States would postpone concessions until the final moments of Nice. There was some room for national interest but seeing the distrust towards the chair it had to be handled carefully. In terms of supply, France invested little in group leadership and did not handle its national interest well. It mishandled the divergence of views with Germany and by refusing to give up parity while asking it from others, it reinforced the impression of bias. In the end agreement was reached. This had not so much to do with the performance of the chair but with the fact that none of the Member States wanted the IGC to fail.

Table 7.7: Re-weighting of Votes

RE-WEIGHTING OF VOTES	Organiser	Broker	Political leader	National positions/interests
Dominant demand	- Old and transparent topic	+ sensitive lack of multiple brokerage lack of trust in the chair - old and transparent topic	- Old topic	+ Old topic: setting the example by abandoning national interests will not change positions of others - Sensitive issue Lack of other brokers Lack of trust in the chair

Dominant supply	- Poor preparations	- Little investment in creation of good atmosphere Poor performance as regards identification of bargains.	-	+ Highly important for France and its political top. Sensitive issue among coalition partners: none of the parties wants to be seen as giving in too much.
D ≠ S	France performed poorly as broker and overplayed the scope for defending its national position. The chair can however not take the full blame for the painful process as factors such as the zero-sum character of the negotiations restricted the scope for brokerage by the chair.			

CONCLUSION

This chapter proposes a model to evaluate Presidencies based on contingency theory. It starts from the assumption that countries in the chair fulfil four different roles: those of organiser, broker, political leader and representative of national positions and interests (Table 1). Secondly, it states that the demand and the supply of these roles are contingent on the situation. Depending on the environment, certain roles may be demanded whereas others are not. Sometimes only one or two roles may be necessary; in other cases there is scope for all four of them. The internal Presidency environment can make it more or less easy for the chair to provide the required roles.

Studying the Presidency in terms of the demand and supply of roles has the advantage that it offers clear criteria for evaluation. A successful Presidency is defined as one that is able to supply the role(s) that are needed. The challenge of such an approach is to define the impact of the external environment on the demand and that of the internal (i.e. Presidency) environment on the supply. As a first step we have formulated a series of hypotheses on how external and internal situational variables affect the demand and supply of the four Presidency roles (Tables 7.2 and 7.3). Secondly, we tested the model in a case study on the performance of the French Presidency during the IGC 2000.

The question we address is not whether France was well-organised and created a good atmosphere but whether and how it supplied the required Presidency style.

Table 7.8: Summary

	Organiser	Broker	Political Leadership	National position/ interest
Flexibility	/	+	/	+
QMV	/	+	/	+
Composition Commission	/	+ from Biarritz onwards	-	-
Re-weighting of votes	/	-	/	-

+: demand fits supply
-: demand does not fit supply
/: not relevant

As can be seen from the above Table, the balance sheet for France is mixed. As concerns the organiser role, the case study learns that there was no dominant demand for task-oriented leadership during the IGC 2000. The issues on the agenda had already been discussed extensively in Amsterdam and under the Finnish and the Portuguese Presidencies. The positions of the Member States were to a large extent already mapped.

As regards brokerage, the analysis of the four topics shows that the chair did well in the cases of flexibility and QMV. The lack of brokerage in the case of trade (QMV dossier) delayed the negotiations but did not lead to a vacuum as there was multiple brokerage. In the Commission dossier, France initially performed poorly but in the last two months prior to the summit, it played an active role in the formulation of a compromise. The chair's brokerage role in the re-weighting of votes was problematic. Rather than identifying bargains and trade-offs, the chair was in the first place concerned with its own problems and failed to be an honest broker.

The IGC 2000 offered little scope for transformational leadership. The dossiers were 'old' and the directions for solutions had already largely emerged under the previous Presidencies. The composition of the Commission was an exception. However, the Presidency did not manage to 'sell' the option of a capped Commission as the solution that best served Europe's long-term interests. On the contrary by not taking into account the sensitivities of the smaller countries it reinforced the suspicion that France was abusing its position to push for its national rather than the European interest.

The way France handled its national position and interests was problematic in two of the four cases. By pushing too hard for its preferred option of a capped Commission, it failed to convince its partners of the many strengths of this option. In the case of the re-weighting of votes, it badly managed its problems with Germany and by proposing solutions to others that it was not willing to accept itself, the Presidency lost credibility. Every country at the helm would have had a hard job but the distrust of France had the effect that the Presidency, rather than facilitating the outcome, became part of the problem.

An analysis based on contingency theory arrives at a different conclusion than the evaluations based on general impressions. The performance of France during the IGC 2000 was not optimal but is was definitely more positive than many suggested. The chair did well with regard to flexibility and QMV. It started off poorly in the Commission dossier but radically improved its performance in the final stage of the negotiations. It was in the reweighting of votes dossier that the performance of the chair was the poorest. Its obsession with parity and the incapacity to address the Franco-German tensions prior to Nice had the effect that it was hardly in a position to provide the much-needed broker role.

One could argue that the poor performance of the chair in the reweighting of votes dossier negatively affected the other issues on the IGC agenda. The 'contamination' risk is particularly high towards the end of the negotiations when the various issues come together in the European Council. If the behaviour of the chair leads to distrust in one dossier, it will affect the general attitude towards the chair. At the same time however, one should be cautious not to downgrade the entire Presidency just because of the poor performance in one dossier. It is the strength of the contingency approach that it allows to look beneath the surface and to examine individual topics in their own right.

Evaluating Presidencies is a difficult exercise. Those directly involved see only part of the picture and outsiders have to rely on public documents or the events that are highlighted in the press. Contingency theory provides us with an instrument to map and to get a better insight into the external and internal constraints under which a chair is operating. It elucidates to which extent the different Presidency roles are needed and provides us with clear criteria for evaluation.

BIBLIOGRAPHY

Ansoff, I. (1985), *Corporate strategy*. London: Penguin Books.

Beach, D. (2003), "The vital cog: agenda-shaping and brokerage by the Council Secretariat in the IGC negotiations." Paper presented at the EUSA 8th Biennial International Conference, March 27-29, Nashville Tennessee.

Bulletin Quotidien Europe, Sunday, 15 October, 2000, No 7821.

Child, J. (1972), "Organizational structure, environment and performance; the role of strategic choice", *Sociology*, Vol. 6, pp.1-22.

Id. (1975), "Managerial and organizational factors associated with company performance; part II A: contingency analysis", *Journal of Management Studies*, Vol.12, pp. 12-27.

Council Decision of 22 March 2004 adopting the Council's Rules of Procedure, *Official Journal*, L 106/22, 15 April 2004.

Council Guide (1997), Vol. 1. Presidency Handbook. Luxembourg: Office for Official Publications of the European Communities.

Elgström, O. (2000), "Negotiating in the European Union: Bargaining or problem solving", *Journal of European Public Policy*, Vol. 7, No. 5, pp. 684-704.

— , ed. (2003), *European Union Council Presidencies. A ComparativePerspective.* London: Routledge.

Galloway, D. (2001), *The Treaty of Nice and Beyond. Realities and Illusions of Power in the EU.* Sheffield: Sheffield Academic Press.

Gibson, K., L. Thompson, M. Bazerman (1996), "Shortcomings of neutrality in mediation: solutions based on rationality", *Negotiation Journal*, Vol.12, No.1, pp. 69-80.

Grant, Ch. (2002), "Restoring leadership to the European Council". *Policy Brief.* London: Centre for European Reform.

Gray, M. and A. Stubb (2001), "Keynote Article: The Treaty of Nice – Negotiating a Poisoned Chalice?", *Journal of Common Market Studies*, Vol. 39, Annual Review, pp. 5-23.

Hayes-Renshaw, F., and H. Wallace (1997), *The Council of Ministers*. New York: Macmillan.

King, G., R. Keohane and S. Verba (1994), *Designing social enquiry: scientific inference in qualitative research.* New Jersey: Princeton University Press.

Kirchner, E. (1992), *Decision-making in the European Community: The Council presidency and European integration*. Manchester: Manchester University Press.

Lawrence, P., and J. Lorsch (1969), *Organization and Environment: Managing differentiation and integration.* Homewood: R.D. Irwin.

Ludlow, P. (1993), "The UK Presidency: A View from Brussels", *Journal of Common Market Studies,* Vol. 31, No. 2, pp. 246-268.

— (1995), *Preparing for 1996 and a larger European Union: principles and priorities.* Brussels: Centre for European Policy Studies.

— (2001), "The European Council at Nice: Neither Triumph nor Disaster", *A View from Brussels. A commentary on the EU,* No. 10. Brussels: Centre for European Policy Studies.

Macdonagh, B. (1998), *Original sin in a brave new world: the paradox of Europe. An account of the negotiations of the Treaty of Amsterdam.* Dublin: Institute of European Affairs.

Mazzucelli, C. (2003), "Understanding the Dutch presidency's influence at Amsterdam: a constructivist analysis." Paper presented at the EUSA 8th Biennial International Conference, March 27-29, Nashville Tennessee.

Moravcsik, A. (1999), "A new statecraft? Supranational entrepreneurs and international cooperation", *International Organization*, Vol. 53, No. 2, pp. 267-306.

Notre Europe: Discours prononcé par Monsieur Jacques Chirac, Président de la République Française devant le B*undestag* allemand, Berlin, 27 June 2000.

O'Nuallain, C., ed. (1985), *The Presidency of the European Council of Ministers; impacts and implications for national governments.* London-Maastricht: Croom Helm/European Institute of Public Administration.

Peel, Q. (2000), "Rebuilding Europe's Office. French plans for closer cooperation may make the EU more bureaucratic and less responsive to democratic control", *Financial Times*, 26 June.

Powell, V. (1987), *Improving Public Enterprise Performance: Concepts and Techniques*. Geneva: International Labour Office.

Report of the Three Wise Men (1979), *Report on European Institutions*, presented by the Committee of Three to the European Council. Luxembourg: Office for Official Publications of the European Communities.

Schout, J.A. (1998), "The Presidency as juggler; managing conflicting expectations", *Eipascope*, No. 2, pp. 2-9.

Sherrington, Ph. (2000), *The Council of Ministers – Political Authority in the European Union*. London and New York: Pinter.

Tallberg, J. (2003), "The agenda-shaping powers of the EU Council Presidency", *Journal of European Public Policy*, Vol. 10, No.1, p 1-19.

Vanhoonacker, S. and J.A. Schout (2003), "The reform of the Presidency: towards a third life of the EU presidency? Paper presented at the EUSA 8th Biennial International Conference, March 27-29, Nashville, Tennessee.

Verbeke J. and W. van de Voorde (1994), "The Presidency of the European Union: some reflections on current practice and recent evolutions", *Studia Diplomatica*, Vol. 47, No. 3, pp. 29-40.

Walton, R.E. and J.M. Dutton (1969), "The management of interdepartmental conflict; a model and review", *Administrative Science Quarterly*, Vol. 14, No. 1, pp. 73-84.

Westlake, M. (1999), *The Council of the European Union*. London: John Harper.

Weyland, J. (1993), "Strategies and perspectives of the Luxembourg Presidency", in E. Kirchner and A. Tsagkari (eds.), *The EC Council Presidency. The Dutch and Luxembourg Presidencies*. London: University Association for Contemporary European Studies (UACES), pp. 15-21.

Wurzel, R. (1996), "What role can the presidency play in coordinating European Union environmental policy-making? An Anglo-German comparison", *European Environmental Law Review*, Vol. 3, No. 2, pp. 1350-1763.

Yin, R.K. (1989), *Case study research: design and methods*. London: Sage Publications.

Yukl, G. (1998), *Leadership in organisations*. Fourth Edition. Upper Saddle River: Prentice-Hall.

CHAPTER 8

GREECE: CONTINUITY AND CHANGE

GREECE FROM MAASTRICHT TO NICE

The 1990s marked a major transformation of Greece's attitude to the European Community-Union. While in the 1980s Greece had acquired a reputation as the EC's 'enfant terrible' and a 'foot note' partner, going it alone on East-West relations, the Middle East, and other issues discussed in the framework of European Political Cooperation (EPC), by the end of the decade she was making concerted efforts to shed her old image and join the mainstream of European developments.

The reasons for this change of outlook were manifold. To begin with, the economic benefits from Greece's accession to the EC were becoming too obvious, especially with the inflow of Community funds from the Integrated Mediterranean Programmes (IMPs) and the cohesion funds initiated in the mid-1980s. And this at a time when the Greek economy was coming under increasing strain, with mounting budget deficits and recurring devaluations of the Drachma. At the same time institutional reforms in the EC, not least the Single European Act and the EC's Mediterranean enlargement, presented Athens with the opportunity to play a more active role in EC affairs and to make a common cause with other Mediterranean partners. The fact that the southern flank of the EC, headed by Mitterrand's France, was governed by Socialist Parties, strengthened the impression of a common Mediterranean caucus within the Community.

Hence when in April 1990 the Twelve agreed to convene an IGC on Economic, Monetary and Political Union, which led to Maastricht, the New Democracy Conservative Government of C. Mitsotakis, an old political opponent of Andreas Papandreou, saw in it the opportunity to testify his European credentials. It should be noted that in the preceeding months (1989-90) Greece was beset by political instability, as the PASOK administration was faltering, beset by alleged scandals and other misdemeanours attributed to its ailing leader, Andreas Papandreou. The domestic political crisis had undermined further the Greek economy which, by the late 1980s, appeared to be on the verge of collapse. As Greece was plunging into a political and economic morass, the post-war European and world order was crumbling, with the fall of the Berlin Wall and the ensuing dismantling of the Cold War order.

From that point of view, the IGC of Maastricht offered a unique opportunity for the Greek government to enter the mainstream of European developments. As the prospects for Greece joining the Monetary Union appeared remote in the early 1990s, Athens focused its attention on the IGC on Political Union. In the ensuing debate between 'maximalists' and 'minimalists' Greece sided unequivocally with the former, submitting institutional proposals for the creation of a federal European entity (den Hartog, 1992). Even on the question of forgoing the national veto on questions of common foreign policy and security, Athens seemed to be prepared to relinquish this right. To be sure, this appeared to be a remarkable volte-face, compared to PASOK's earlier hard line stance. Yet Athens' enthusiasm for undiluted federalism did not last long. Greek commitment to a federal structure stemmed from the assumption that such an entity would contain an autochthonous security structure, with its own military capabilities, which presumably would guarantee Greece's territorial integrity and act as a deterrent against a putative aggression, especially by Turkey. However, as such a feat proved to be beyond the Twelve's reach, Athens soon had to trim its sails and accept the new geopolitical realities in Europe, and especially in the Balkans. For example, Greek eagerness to accede to the WEU, mainly due to the provisions of the Treaty of Brussels, especially of Article 5, which calls for automatic and unconditional military support in case one of its members faces aggression from a third party, was toned down, as this particular article of the WEU Treaty was not to be applicable when it involved a conflict between Greece and Turkey.

The outbreak of a violent conflict in the former Yugoslavia and its ensuing disintegration had had profound effects on Greece. What was at stake in the Balkans was nothing less than the unravelling of the status quo in the region, which had been held since the end of the Second World War. Greek sympathies for Serbia, and the dispute with the Former Yugoslav Republic of Macedonia (FYROM) over its name and its symbols, caused a severe strain between Greece and her EU partners. This contributed to a further questioning of the virtues of a federal Europe and in particular an appreciation of the value of the national veto on questions of vital importance. The cumulative effects of the Balkan crisis were to dampen earlier Greek enthusiasm for a federal European entity and a realization that, in the convoluted Balkans, the Twelve were far from sharing a common geopolitical perspective.

By 1993 a new outlook had emerged in Greece. This coincided with the return to power of PASOK, under the ailing Andreas Papandreou. PASOK's return to power, after a three-year Interregnum, far from marking a return to the past, signified the initiation of a new European strategy, which has been pursued, with minor adjustments, over the last ten years. Its main contours were a determined effort for economic convergence with her EU partners, a prerequisite for her accession to the EMU; a maximization of the benefits from the various Community funds, not least of the so-called 'Delors packages'; and the strengthening of Greece's position in the Balkan region by utilizing her EU membership. Thus after a critical initial phase in the late 1993-94, during which Greece's relations with her partners were strained to their limits, mainly due to the imposition of a trade embargo on the FYROM, there has been a remarkable improvement. In a sense the trade embargo on FYROM was a symbolic move. In spite of appearances it was evident by public statements, including those by the then Foreign Minister, Theodoros Pangalos, that Greece could not afford to 'Balkanize' her European policy. What he meant was that what was at stake in the EU was far too important for Greece to reduce this through the lenses of her dispute with a weak and precarious new Balkan state.

Hence, since 1994 a marked 'de-politicization' of Greece's Balkan policy has been in evidence. The ascendancy of the United States in the Balkans, as a result of the EU's inability to translate words into action in the region, made it imperative for the Papandreou Government to forge close links with the Clinton administration, and in effect, to acknowledge American primacy in the settlement of Balkan issues, including Greece's dispute with FYROM (Tsakaloyannis, 1996). The transfer of this issue to the Cyrus Vance Commission, under the auspices of the UN, in 1994, in combination with mutual concessions by Athens and Skopie, helped to defuse tensions and, in effect, to diminish the significance of this issue.

The relegation of this problem, which had reached a dead end and led to Greece's isolation from her EU partners, enabled Athens to focus on another issue which appeared to offer more promising ground, namely the promotion of Cyprus's accession to the EU. It should be recalled that the 'Enlargement Agenda' was initiated with the 'Copenhagen criteria' in December 1993. During Greece's Presidency, in the first half of 1994, Athens managed, in the Corfu European Council, to extract a pledge from its partners, for the inclusion of Cyprus, among the prospective candidates. Of course some crucial caveats were attached to this pledge, not least the normalization of Greece's (and by extension of the EU's) relations with Turkey and the finding of a lasting solution to the Cyprus problem. For the remaining of the 1990s Greek efforts concentrated, almost exclusively, on the promotion of this objective. In March 1995 the Council of Ministers of the EU agreed upon opening up accession negotiations with Cyprus six months after the end of the 1996 IGC, on the condition that her membership would not be detrimental to the interests of the Turkish-Cypriot Community, or to its security concerns. In return Greece lifted her long-standing objection to the conclusion of the EU-Turkish customs union.

This compromise opened the way for Cyprus's accession to the EU. Yet the caveats attached to it in March 1995, plus the reservations by some member states to Cyprus's accession, before a solution to the political problem was found, made it crystal clear that the attainment of this objective would be an uphill struggle. The crisis of January 1996 between Greece and Turkey over the islet of Imia, which brought the countries to the brink of armed confrontation, highlighted the utmost importance of smoothing over relations with Turkey as a prerequisite for easing Cyprus's accession to the EU. For the prolongation of tensions with Turkey not only hindered Greek attempts at coming closer to the mainstream of the EU but also it was a stumbling block to Cyprus's accession. The 'Imia crisis', arguably the most serious incident since 1974, also highlighted the importance of the United States in security issues. The virtual absence of the EU, and its being overshadowed by the US, helped reinforce the conviction in Athens that when the chips were down, the only power that mattered was the US. As Richard Holbrook, the US Under-Secretary of State, who brokered a climb down by both sides, observed with undisguished glee, the EU 'was caught napping' during the night of the crisis. This view was shared also by the Greek Foreign Minister, Theodoros Pangalos, who lamented the cumbersome, frustrating and time-consuming mechanisms of the EU, in responding to a crisis like that of Imia.

In a sense, however, the Imia incident acted as a blessing in disguise for Costas Simitis, the new Prime Minister who had just assumed office, replacing the ailing Andreas Papandreou. The accession of Simitis, in January 1996, marks a transition from the 'old' to the 'new' PASOK. The chief characteristic of the new PASOK was an attempt to shed the Party's populist-cum-nationalist image. Instead the new message was 'modernization' and full integration into the EU, not least into the Economic and especially the Monetary Union, which by 1996 was gathering momentum. Hence the Simitis premiership marks a clear shift from 'high' to 'low' politics. As mentioned above, the urgency of addressing Greece's economic problems was evident since 1990. Yet the unfolding crises in the Balkans, in conjunction with the vehement opposition to economic reforms by vested interests, deflected this objective. Papandreou endorsed the urgency of economic reform, when he returned to power, in October 1993. Yet his poor health and party bickering, stemming from the problem of overcoming its populist legacy, slowed down the economic reforms. The accession of Simitis marks a change of gear and a clear, if not singular, preoccupation with this objective. 'Meeting the Maastricht criteria', a prerequisite for admission to the Monetary Union, became the new 'vision' of the nation. By contrast, contentious political or security issues had to be downplayed. From this point of view the crisis in Imia, in January 1996, marked a further 'cooling-down' of Greece's political expectations from the EU. This became evident at the 'Amsterdam' IGC in 1996-97 (Papadopoulos, 2002). At the same time, Imia signified Greece's almost complete military-cum-security reliance on Washington. Thus, while Greece was vigorously pursuing her economic-monetary integration into the EU in the political and the security field, she was relying more and more on the United States. This reliance on Washington for vital political and especially security concerns was not automatic and not without profound effects for the governing Party. Between 1996-99 the 'old hands' of PASOK's foreign policy, associated with the 'traditional' PASOK of the 1980s, not least the Foreign Minister Theodoros Pangalos and the charismatic Giannos Kranidiotis, Minister of European Affairs and a Cypriot by birth, were out of office, the first a casualty of the 'Ochalan affair' and the second meeting a tragic death, in September 1999, in an air-plane accident. The net effect of these developments was that by the late 1990s, Greece's European and foreign policy had been transformed almost beyond recognition compared to the 1980s. Under the overall heading of 'modernization', which was, intentionally or not, juxtaposed to the 'populist' era of Andreas Papandreou, a more pragmatic, business-like and non-nationalistic outlook took shape. Its main features were a more accommodating foreign policy vis-à-vis Greece's northern neighbours, and with Turkey. Greece has participated in a number of peace-keeping operations in the Balkans, such as in 'operation Alba', for restoring law and order in Albania, in 1997, in the peace-keeping force in Kosovo, as well as in the Former Yugoslav Republic of Macedonia (FYROM). At the same time Greece has focused on strengthening her economic, trade and political-institutional links with her northern neighbours. The overall objective in Greece's Balkan policy has been to utilize her considerable political assets, not least her membership of the EU and NATO, as well as her economic weight, as compared to her impoverished Balkan neighbours, to enhance her presence in the region and to forge economic and political links.

A similar businesslike attitude has been discernible in relations with Turkey. After a bumpy start, due to the Imia crisis, the Simitis Government adopted a conciliatory, 'step by step' line towards Ankara. The objective was to de-escalate tensions and to create a positive environment for addressing the issues dividing the two sides. This line was deemed appropriate for three major considerations. First, because of US promptings on Athens and Ankara to work for a modus vivendi so that they could both contribute to strengthening security in the Balkans and in Eastern Mediterranean. Second, because an improvement in relations with Turkey could ease the reservations of some EU member states to Cyprus's accession. Cyprus's so-called political problem, in effect, was part and parcel of a wider problem of Greek-

Turkish antagonism, which had detrimental effects for the EC/EU, especially since Greece's accession in 1981. Third, because an improvement in relations with Turkey could contribute to Greece's effort to reduce its budget deficit—a prerequisite for acceding to monetary union—by cutting her hefty military expenditure. The devastating earthquakes in Greece, and especially in Turkey, in the autumn of 1999, provided another opportunity for forging a sense of 'common destiny' between the two neighbouring peoples, inflicted by natural disaster.

By the European Council meeting in Helsinki, in December 1999, the groundwork had been laid for an overall compromise. The European Council in Helsinki reiterated its pledge to Cyprus's accession to the EU, subject to the political caveats, and Greece lifted her objections to Turkey's inclusion among the perspective candidates for EU enlargement. Hence, by the time the IGC of Nice was under way Athens could focus on the more mundane issues to be discussed there, as well as on its major objective, namely her accession to the EURO-zone, as the single currency was baptised.

The Discussion about the Nice Agenda

The agenda of the 2000 IGC was already defined to a large extent in the institutional protocol which was attached to the Amsterdam Treaty. This protocol highlighted the failure of the Treaty to settle institutional questions of crucial significance for the smooth functioning of an enlarged European Union. These questions were basically related to the size of the Commission and the re-weighting of votes in the Council of Ministers. Furthermore, the common declaration by Belgium, France, and Italy brought in the foreground the issue of the further extension of the use of qualified majority voting (QMV) and, hence, this issue became inevitably also part of the future agenda of institutional reform. Therefore, already in the documents attached to the Amsterdam Treaty, there was an explicit call for a future Intergovernmental Conference as well as a reference to the main issues to be tackled. The timing of the next IGC was crucial given that institutional reform was largely seen as a can of worms that would be opened in due time when conditions were more conducive to reforms.

Developments in the EU between 1997 and 2000 showed that institutional reform could no longer be delayed. The initiation of accession negotiations with the first group of candidate countries in March 1998 made enlargement more imminent than ever and cast away doubts about the real commitment of the EU. The institutional crisis and the critical condition of the Commission status following the resignation of the Santer Commission in February 1999 were additional indications of the need to push forward institutional reform. Finally, the successful conclusion of negotiations for the multi-annual budgetary framework in the European Council in Berlin in April 1999 settled the pending financial issues and paved the way for enlargement.

In the pre-IGC period, the hovering, main unanswered question was whether the next IGC should focus exclusively on what was dubbed the 'Amsterdam leftovers', or whether a broader agenda should be put forward, reconsidering the whole EU institutional framework and a number of additional issues. In the European Councils of Cologne in June 1999 and Helsinki in December 1999, Greece, together with the European Parliament, Belgium, Italy and the Netherlands, supported the latter view for a more extended agenda. According to the Greek government, "...the revision of the Treaties provides an opportunity to respond to certain concerns and demands expressed by European citizens and the European society", tackling the problem of democratic legitimacy. In that respect, "...the Union needs to enhance, inter alia, its ability to contribute to alleviating the European citizen's and society's every-day problems."[1] Hence, additional topics that should be included in the agenda, according to the Greek position, ranged from the reform of other bodies of the EU (such as the European Court of Justice, the Court of Auditors, the Committee of Regions, and the Economic and Social Committee) to aspects of the European Security and Defence Policy (ESDP), and from the incorporation of the Charter of Fundamental Rights in the Treaty to other issues of great interest to the public (like sports, consumer protection and food safety, protection from natural disasters, enhanced provisions for employment, etc).[2] However, such a broad and ambitious agenda was not acceptable to other EU members, which finally led to the adoption of a much more restricted one.[3]

---

[1] *Memorandum from the Greek Government to the Intergovernmental Conference on Institutional Reform of the European Union*, CONFER 4719/00. The Memorandum was produced by a task force in the Ministry of Foreign Affairs founded in July 1999 by the late Y. Kranidiotis, then Alternate Minister of Foreign Affairs responsible for European affairs. The role of the coordinator of the working group was assigned to P.A. Ioakimidis, who also acted as Greek representative during the negotiations. The Greek delegation submitted also a second Memorandum containing the position of the Greek government on the reforms of the judicial system of the EU; CONFER 4730/00.

[2] *Memorandum from the Greek Government,* CONFER 4719/00. See also P.K. Ioakimidis, 2001.

[3] See in particular the *Presidency Conclusions* of the two most relevant European Councils in Cologne and Helsinki, SN 150/99 and 300/99.

THE AMSTERDAM 'LEFT-OVERS' AND BEYOND

In general, the starting point of Greek views on the institutional reform debate was that any reform initiative should not evolve into an attempt to upset fundamental and historically justified interinstitutional balances, which have ensured and guaranteed to a large extent the continuing success of the European system.

As regards the composition of the Commission, Greece supported the principle of 'one Member-State, one Commissioner' and expressed its willingness to examine an increased role for the President and a more precise definition of the individual responsibilities of each Commissioner. Furthermore, the suggestion put forward for a maximum overall number of Commissioners was critically received, since it was considered that it would transmit a negative message to candidate countries about their future representation in this body.[4]

As far as the re-weighting of votes in the Council was concerned, Greece argued that thc expansion of the present system without re-weighting was feasible, at least up to the point of 21 member states. The chosen threshold of 'system adequacy' as perceived by the Greek, suggests that even after the Helsinki decision on enlargement to open up negotiations with all candidate countries, Greece remained convinced that the enlargement of the EU would take place in successive waves. Hence, membership was considered by Greece to be imminent only for the six, most advanced candidate countries that were indicated in the '5+1 Luxembourg formula'. Therefore, Greece actually argued that the current system was capable of accommodating what was still—in Greece at least—perceived at that time as the 'first wave' of enlargement and any substantial discussion on institutional reform could be further postponed.

Nevertheless, sensing in which direction the wind was blowing, Greece made sure to enter the negotiations with a fallback position, according to which if change was inevitable, Greece would only consider a system of 'dual majority' of Member States and population. In that system Greece was an ardent supporter of relatively high thresholds for the use of Qualified Majority Voting (QMV) requiring 60% of Member States representing at least 60% of the European Union's total population.[5] These views were shared by the Commission, the European Parliament, Ireland, Portugal,

---

[4] *Memorandum from the Greek Government*, CONFER 4719/00, op.cit.

[5] Ibid.

Belgium and Germany although there was a divergence as regards the exact threshold that should apply to decision making (50%-50% or 60%-60%). The justification of this approach was based on the grounds that such a system would provide the necessary 'double legitimisation' of both countries and peoples. Fur-thermore, it was a transparent system away from the communitarian jargon, easily comprehended by the public and self-adjustable to future enlargements.[6]

In the convoluted negotiations that followed during the IGC, Greece ended up with 12 votes in the Council together with the Czech Republic, Belgium, Hungary, and Portugal. During the concluding stage of the negotiations in Nice, the French Presidency tried to appease strong Belgian reactions to the proposed changes by positively differentiating Belgium from Greece, despite Greece's larger population. The proposal put forward granted Belgium an extra vote in the Council (12 against 11 for Greece) and two extra seats in the European Parliament (22 against 20). Such a development was met with a vehement reaction by the Greek Prime Minister, who threatened to block the whole deal, if institutional parity between the two countries was not restored (Ioakimidis, 2001).

The issue of the extension of QMV to new areas of EU competence turned out to be equally controversial. Greece argued that these new areas should by no means include the constitutional and institutional structures of the EU, the association and accession of new states as well as matters which were subject to ratification by the Member States or were of intergovernmental nature.[7] Having explicitly stressed these points, the extension of QMV could then be examined on a case-by-case basis. This stance was very much similar to the one adopted in the 1996-97 IGC negotiations showing in that respect a great deal of continuity (Papadopoulos, 2002).

During the Nice negotiations, Greece showed a willingness to accept the extension of QMV to almost all of the approximately 50 cases that were put on the table with three notable exceptions. To be more specific, Greece fought for and finally achieved the preservation of the unanimity principle in the fields of maritime transportation, financial assistance to associate and candidate countries as well as the structural policy of the EU. The exception of maritime transportation from the use of QMV reflected the considerable Greek interest in the sector and was indicative of the strong influence of the Greek shipowners' lobby in the domestic policy-making procedure. In this

---

[6] See in particular the interview of P.K. Ioakimidis in *Vima*, 28/10/00 as well as P.K. Ioakimidis, 2001.

[7] *Memorandum from the Greek Government*, CONFER 4719/00 op. cit.

case, Greece found a very useful ally in the face of Denmark which also expressed strong reservations. As regards financial assistance to associate and candidate countries, Greece wanted to preserve the capacity of control over the allocation of funds and the cash flows to third countries, having undoubtedly in the back of the mind the case of Turkey. On this issue, Greece found no sympathetic ears by her EU partners and had to fight a lonely battle. Finally, the structural policy of the EU was a particularly thorny issue, which was resolved only after the three main demandeurs (Spain, Portugal and Greece) agreed to the extended of use of QMV after the conclusion of negotiations for the next multi-annual EU budgetary framework.[8] In the end, despite a rather weak negotiating position resulting from the relative isolation on these issues, Greece making good use of the existing alliances succeeded in having these three domains exempted from the final list of areas that were transferred to the QMV decision-making regime (Ioakimidis, 2001).

Directly linked to the question of the QMV extension was the role of the EP in the decision making process. As a general principle, Greece considered that qualified majority voting should be accompanied by the 'co-decision procedure' for all acts of legislative nature. This principle was in line with Greece's broader vision for the EP as an equal player in European integration with a much more active role in the new institutional environment. Beyond the extension of co-decision, this enhancement of the role of the EP could be realised with the more effective use of the 'consultation procedure' in some acts adopted under unanimity and, furthermore, with the application of the 'assent procedure' to Art. 308 of the Treaty as well as to the process of Treaty amendments. In general, as in the two previous IGCs, Greece was one of the most ardent supporters of the EP claims during the preparatory and bargaining stage of the Nice Treaty.[9] An important parameter of this closer cooperation and the deriving synergistic linkages was the fact that two Greek MEPs were directly involved in the Nice reform process on behalf of the EP. G. Dimitrakopoulos was involved in the drafting of the paper highlighting the EP's views on the reform debate (Dimitrakopoulos and Leinen, 1999), and D. Tsatsos represented the EP in

[8] Greece together with Spain and Portugal made clear in a common declaration that to their understanding the length of the multi-annual financial framework agreements would not be altered. That meant practically that structural policy would remain under unanimity rule until well in the first decade of the new century. The immediate reaction by four countries was to put forward another declaration stressing that the agreement should not preclude the right of initiative of the Commission to ask for shorter financial frameworks. With that movement, Germany, Denmark, Austria and the Netherlands tried to keep open some kind of back door undermining the value of the reached agreement.

[9] D. Tsatsos, *Europe and Greece after the Nice Treaty*, TA NEA, 19/12/00 [in Greek].

the Nice IGC,[10] working in close co- operation with the Greek representative in the negotiations, P. Ioakimidis (see in particular the account of the negotiations by Papagiannidis, 2001).

The Gordian Knot of 'Enhanced Cooperation'

To the core of the institutional reform debate belonged the question of 'enhanced cooperation' and the modality of enabling such cooperation schemes without endangering the overall cohesion of the EU. The topic did not feature in the initial agenda of the IGC and was added only after the Feira European Council in June 2000. This was an all but new issue, which had emerged as one of the most controversial areas already in the 1996 IGC, at least judged from the Greek perspective. The concepts of 'variable geometry' and 'structural flexibility' go of course a long way back and have in general generated a great deal of discussion. They were put forward more prominently in the controversial Schäuble/Lamers CDU/CSU document of 1994 on the future of the EU as a means to promote further integration among members of a hard core of 'capable and willing'.[11] However, in the early stages of the debate, flexibility was met with deep concern and suspicion by many Member States, which saw in it an attempt to bypass national sensitivities. As far as Greece was concerned, in particular it was feared that schemes of enhanced cooperation would leave behind not only the intentional laggards but also those incapable of riding the 'train of European integration'. Belonging in the latter category, and with only the most speculative of views in mind about the possible areas of implementation of the flexibility principle,[12] Greece adopted in Amsterdam a cautious if not negative approach to the issue. Hence, the Greek delegation reminded her partners at that time of the virtues of the long tested method of 'transitional periods' as an alternative to 'flexibility' and tried to bring the

[10] D. Tsatsos, professor of Constitutional Law in Greece, had also played an active role in the Amsterdam IGC as *rapporteur* for the European Parliament. See I. Mendez De Vigo and D. Tsatsos, *Report on the Treaty of Amsterdam*, A4-0347/97, 05 November 1997.

[11] 'Reflections on European Policy', text in *Europe*, Documents, No. 1895/96, 7 September 1994.

[12] Some analysts considered the EMU chapter and Social Protocol of the Maastricht Treaty as the first cases of applied flexibility, which actually triggered the opening of the debate. However, there was a crucial difference between the consensual admittance of the British and Danish 'opt-outs' from these provisions in order to save the Maastricht deal and the discussions at the 1996-97 IGC, during which unanimity on decisions about 'enhanced cooperation' was to be replaced with QMV.

flexibility principle as much as possible in concordance with the Community 'orthodoxy'.[13] From the Greek point of view, the third pillar and the EMU project looked like the most prominent candidate areas to introduce and test variable geometry. Flexibility was difficult to conceive in the first and second pillar, given the Single Market constraints and the exclusivity of Community competence in the first pillar as well as national sensitivities in foreign policy issues (Papadopoulos, 2002). In a nutshell, Greece's main intentions during the Amsterdam IGC were to avoid the undermining and rupture of the cohesiveness of the EU institutional structures and facilitate the accession of those Member States left behind in any scheme of enhanced cooperation.

In the post Amsterdam era Greece's position changed dramatically. Economic improvement highlighted by the accession to the EMU together with a more pragmatic and constructive foreign policy signalled the culmination of a long process of 'normalisation' (Featherstone, 1998; Mitsos, 2000). These developments helped Greece to shed her 'footnote' image that the country had acquired in the past. They generated also a great deal of optimism for the country's future in the EU and ambitions of belonging to the vanguard of European integration. This self-classification to the core of European integration facilitated the broadening of the domestic political debate on Europe with topics previously considered taboo and led to a more constructive participation in the ongoing discussion on the future of Europe (Simitis, 2000; Dalis, 2001; Ioakimidis, 2002).[14]

Hence, in the Nice IGC, Greece sided with the most integrationist group of member states in an attempt to further exhibit the European credentials and solidify the newly acquired position. In that respect, Greece appeared in principle much more positive to a wider implementation of enhanced cooperation in all three pillars under particular conditions that would safeguard national interests and the acquis (Papandreou, 2000). Although there was no illusion that enhanced cooperation would be the panacea to all problems and rigidities, it was still seen as a positive step towards further integration.

Nevertheless, the embracing of 'enhanced cooperation' was not unconditional. It is worth noting the initial scepticism with which Greece faced the renegotiation of this particular chapter of the Amsterdam Treaty, especially given the fact that it had not been tested empirically and could potentially send the wrong message to candidate countries. Greece's point of

---

[13] *Memorandum of the Greek Government to the 1996 Intergovernmental Conference*, CONFER 3866/97.

[14] P.K. Ioakimidis, 2001, The Treaty of Nice and the Future of Europe, op.cit.

view on the subject was that any form of enhanced cooperation should involve at least the majority of EU member states and that a solidarity clause should be incorporated. Keeping in mind the past experience of exclusion, despite the recent change in the country's status, this solidarity clause was meant to provide support and guarantees for future participation to those member states that, although willing, could not take part in various schemes of enhanced cooperation. This clause was deemed indispensable in particular if the existing clause, which catered for the invocation of important and declared national policy reasons to stop an initiative of enhanced cooperation, was to be reexamined.[15]

In the last meeting of the Ministers of Foreign Affairs of the EU-15 before the summer break in July 2000, the French Presidency produced a questionnaire covering both the form and the scope of 'enhanced cooperation'. Some of the questions raised grave concern among countries about the dilution of the EU acquis. In particular those questions about the value of cooperation schemes outside the current institutional framework and the exact nature of the links of such schemes with the EU structures made may bells ring in the European capitals. Naturally, Greece opposed any consideration of enhanced cooperation outside the Treaties.[16]

The direction of the discussion, especially in view of the danger of extra-institutional arrangements, and the intention to confirm the recently restored European credentials of the country, led the Greek side to consent to the gradual scaling down of the original conditions set for enhanced cooperation (Ioakimidis, 2001). In that respect, Greece finally accepted the abolition of the right of an individual member-state to block decisions for the launching of enhanced cooperation schemes (veto right) in the first and the third pillar. Accordingly, Greece had to reconcile its views as regards the prerequisite number of countries necessary to take part in any similar initiative and accept that enhanced cooperation could go forward with a minimum of eight countries instead of the majority of member states previously required. Whilst this clause makes no difference for the EU-15, it is obviously of great importance once the enlargement process is completed. Finally, after persistent Greek, Spanish and Portuguese demands, an explicit reference was incorporated in the relevant article of the Treaty, according to which any enhanced cooperation initiative should not jeopardise neither the common market—which was the original reference—nor the economic and social cohesion of the Union.

---

[15] *Memorandum from the Greek Government*, CONFER 4719/00, op.cit.

[16] *Kathimerini*, 25/07/00.

Common Foreign and Security Policy

The debate on schemes of enhanced cooperation had an inevitable spillover to the second pillar of the Union, which is apparently a field where such schemes can be applied. In that respect, and given the special nature of the field, the discussions about the use of enhanced cooperation schemes were particularly intense. During the negotiations, the majority of member states, including Greece, backed a proposal to make the second pillar eligible for some degree of flexibility, too.[17] Throughout the 1990s, the Common Foreign and Security Policy has been perhaps the most telling example of Greek ambivalent—almost Janus-headed—relationship with the EU. Due to Greece's particular geographic position and the general insecurity caused by the geopolitical fluidity of the Balkan region, after the end of the Cold War, Greece has been found several times in a 'Catch 22' situation. On the one hand, there were strong aspirations to European political and defence integration, which were considered as a means to enhance national security, while on the other hand, Greece fought doggedly to preserve the veto option in order to be able to block EU decisions, which might be detrimental to Greece's vital national interests.

Therefore, the Greek emphasis during the Nice negotiations on the necessary existence of 'emergency brakes' in the process comes as no surprise. Greece agreed with the proposal to use qualified majority voting for the launch of enhanced cooperation schemes in the field of foreign and security policy but preserve the right of a country to refer the issue to the European Council, where the final decision will be reached under the unanimity rule. In addition to that, Greece together with Germany, Portugal, and France supported the Italian proposal to implement enhanced cooperation arrangements in the defence field as well. In that respect, Greece and Italy tried to broaden the scope of the defence initiatives of the Union, calling for an extension of the Union's authority beyond crisis management and the Petersberg tasks, agreed in the Cologne and Helsinki European Councils as the tasks of the emerging common force. Naturally, such proposals were anathema to some other member states, not least Britain, and therefore, had to be abandoned.

CONCLUSIONS

[17] The countries opposing such a development included Sweden, Finland, Denmark and the UK.

Greece's positions in the Nice IGC reflected the country's upgraded status in the EU and its desire to play a more active role in the process of European integration. Hence, in the core issue of 'enhanced cooperation', Greece made a U-turn in comparison to the previous IGCs and supported under certain conditions the emergence of such ventures, aspiring to membership in the 'hard core' of European integration. As regards representation in the institutional bodies of the EU and the system of decision-making, Greece tried to safeguard the existing balance by preserving the parity principle inside the group of middle-sized countries and by not conceding to the increase of power of the 'big beasts in the jungle' of the EU. In that respect Greece was by no means the 'odd man out' in the IGC as similar concerns were shared by virtually all small and medium sized member states of the EU. Actually some of them, like Belgium, took an even more assertive stance in the course of the negotiations. Furthermore, Greece supported the extension of QMV and succeeded during the negotiations in preserving the unanimity principle in three sensitive areas considered of vital national interest. In general, Greece's strategy in Nice's IGC was to keep a low profile and make alliances with other small and medium-sized member states, while safeguarding her own particular national interests.

With the conclusion of the Nice IGC, Greece's accession to the EURO, and the discharging of the Presidency of the EU in the first half of 2003, the Greek Government seems to be in search for another major European goal, which could stimulate further domestic reform. For Greece this is an important consideration as the Greek people, especially the growing number of underprivileged, are still waiting to reap some benefits from the sacrifices they were called upon to pay for the attainment of the Government's European objectives, especially accession to the EURO-zone. At the same time, the EU's enlargement to 25 means that the course of European integration may follow a somewhat different, more convoluted course to the one it followed in the past fifty years. The crisis among the EU members on the recent war on Iraq, perhaps was just the writing on the wall. While it is too early to see how these historic developments will affect Greece's European policy, it is almost certain that she is in need of time to process them.

BIBLIOGRAPHY

Dalis, S., ed. (2001), From Amsterdam to Nice: Europe and Greece in a New Era. Athens: Kritikh [in Greek].

Dimitrakopoulos, G. and J. Leinen (1999), Report on the Preparation of the Reform of the Treaties and the Next Intergovernmental Conference, A5-0058/1999, 10 November.

Featherstone, K. (1998), "Europeanization and the Centre Periphery: the Case of Greece in the 1990s," South European Society and Politics, vol. 3, no. 1, pp. 23-29.

Hartog, A. den (1992), "Greece and European political union," in F. Laursen and S. Vanhoonacker (eds.), The Intergovernmental Conference on Political Union. Maastricht: EIPA.

Ioakimidis, P.K., ed. (2002), The Future of Europe and Greece. Athens: Sakkoulas [in Greek].

—— (2001), The Treaty of Nice and the Future of Europe. Athens: Themelio and EKEM [in Greek].

—— (2001), "Content and Evaluation of the Nice Treaty", in S. Dalis (ed.), From Amsterdam to Nice: Europe and Greece in a New Era. Athens: Kritiki [in Greek].

Ministry of Foreign Affairs (2000), Memorandum from the Greek Government to the Intergovernmental Conference on Insti-tutional Reform of the European Union, CONFER 4719/00.

Mitsos, A. (2000), "Maximising Contribution to the European Integration Process as a Prerequisite for the Maximization of Gains", in A. Mitsos and E. Mossialos (eds.), Contemporary Greece and Europe. Aldershot: Ashgate.

Papadopoulos, C.A. (2002), "Greece: the Difficult Road from Orthodoxy to Neo-Orthodoxy," in F. Laursen (ed.), The Amsterdam Treaty: National Preference Formation, Interstate Bargaining and Outcome. Odense: Odense University Press.

Papagiannidis, A. (2001), "In Quest of the Greek Position in the Discussion about the Reform of the Treaties," in S. Dalis (ed.), From Amsterdam to Nice: Europe and Greece in a New Era. Athens: Kritiki [in Greek].

Papandreou, G.A. The European Integration in the New Conditions of Globalization, VIMA, 18/06/00 [in Greek].

Tsakaloyannis, P. (1996), "The Limits of Convergence," in C. Hill (ed.), The Actors in Europe's Foreign Policy. London: Routledge.

Simitis, C. (2000), Greece in the EMU: the Beginning of a New Challenge. Speech at Zappeio, 15 June [in Greek]. Regarding the domestic discussion on the future of Europe.

CHAPTER 9

IRELAND: A TALE OF TWO REFERENDA

Introduction

Ireland's approach to the IGC 2000 was consistent with the pragmatic tradition of Irish policy towards the European Union. However, it took place within a new context marked by socio-economic confidence and the beginning of a more ideological debate on Europe in Ireland.

The pragmatic tradition of Irish policy towards the EU was exemplified in an early speech of the Taoiseach (Prime Minister), Bertie Ahern. Remarking on the opening of the IGC in February 2000, the Taoiseach emphasised its historic significance as providing for enlargement of the Union towards Central and Eastern Europe but then immediately proceeded to underscore his position that it was also necessary to "ensure that the wonderfully innovative institutional structures, and the balances which they represent, are passed on to future generations" (*The Irish Times,* 25 March 2000). This defensive position was to characterise much of the Irish contribution to the IGC.

While the strategy of the Irish government remained much the same, the context within which it operated had fundamentally changed, provoking minor political storms of controversy and debate. Ireland was a remarkably different state in socio-economic terms in the year 2000 than it had been even during the negotiation of the Amsterdam Treaty just a few years earlier. The Irish economic miracle had by now been running for nearly a decade, Irish growth rates were consistently in double digits, the budget was in healthy surplus, unemployment had been eliminated to such an extent that Ireland was now becoming a destination of foreign economic migrants, and there were declared labour shortages in key economic sectors. Together, these aspects had a huge psychological impact on political elites in Ireland and on the general public—especially as Irish per capita income in 2000 surpassed that of the United Kingdom, and Ireland had become one of the wealthiest states in the Union.

This new socio-economic situation brought its own challenges beyond that of net immigration. The Irish state as a whole could no longer qualify for Objective 1 status in cohesion and regional funding, while commentators began to calculate the date at which Ireland would become a net contributor to the EU budget. The political consequences of this seismic shift in Ireland's place within the Union and its self-perceptions soon made themselves felt.

On 21 July 2000, speaking at a meeting of the American Bar Association in Boston, the Tánaiste (Deputy Prime Minister), Minister for Enterprise and Industry and leader of the Progressive Democrats, Mary Harney, declared herself to be fully in favour of EU enlargement and a widening of the Union but expressed the hope that this might ultimately lead to a looser association of sovereign nation states in the Union rather than any federal-type development. In what came to be the label for a number of political debates and media interviews, the Tánaiste declared that based on its history and its interests, Ireland was spiritually, politically and economically "a lot closer to Boston than Berlin" (*The Irish Times,* 22 July 2000).

While that speech generated considerable debate, it was initially seen by many as the efforts of a small coalition partner anxious to define and clarify its ideological position. Within a matter of weeks, however, it appeared that Mary Harney's vision was shared not only by some outside her own party but also by other members of the Government. Síle de Valera – granddaughter of one of the state's founding figures and herself a Fianna Fáil Minister for Arts, Heritage, Gaeltacht and the Islands in the coalition government, spoke at Boston College in September, again on the theme of Irish, European and U.S. relations. Her speech went significantly further than that of Harney in its overt criticism of ways in which, she claimed, "the directives and regulations agreed in Brussels can often seriously impinge on our identity, culture and traditions" (*The Irish Times,* 20 September 2000). She went on to complain that "as we embraced Europe, we seemed at times to forget our close and very important ties with the United States of America"—reinforcing the Boston versus Berlin equation. She concluded by looking forward "to a future in which Ireland will exercise a more questioning attitude to the EU" (Ibid) and oppose pressures for ever greater integration.

While the merits of these respective arguments were thrashed out in various newspaper columns and television interviews, one main point of agreement between all of the interlocutors was that these speeches would simply never have been made as recently as five years ago. They represented not so much a maturity in the Irish debate but perhaps a new honesty coming from the body politic.

Bearing the aforementioned in mind, it is therefore more possible than in previous case studies of Irish approaches to the Union's evolution to accede to the demands of Moravcsik (1993, 1998) that economic interests predominantly determined the government's preferences. As will be illustrated below, Ireland's position towards the IGC was one which respected previous pragmatism but which now had a more ideological edge regarding Ireland's socio-economic interests. These interests were not so much imposed or lobbied by powerful sectoral interest groups—instead they are to be found in a comparatively new neoliberal orthodoxy espoused by leading figures within the coalition government. These figures insisted, for example, that national rights to determine taxation levels had to be retained so as to support an economic policy driven by low-taxation of capital and income, attraction of investment (especially from the U.S.) and the avoidance of regulatory frameworks that imposed additional costs on business.

THE IGC PROCESS AND NEGOTIATIONS

At the Cologne European Council of June 1999, the Member State governments agreed to convene an intergovernmental conference in the year 2000 to deal with the so-called 'left-overs' from the Treaty of Amsterdam (1997). These left-overs referred specifically to institutional and decision-making reforms perceived to be necessary to the Union's enlargement. They included the extension of qualified majority voting (QMV) to new policy areas, greater proportionality in the distribution of votes within the Council of Ministers and a more effective Commission—defined frequently in terms of a smaller membership and/or structural improvements (Dooge and Keatinge, 2001).

The Irish delegation to the IGC was led at official level by Noel Dorr, a former Secretary General of the Department of Foreign Affairs, who had successfully steered the last IGC through the Irish presidency in 1996. Dorr's team had won plaudits for their iteration of a draft treaty, which ultimately evolved into the Amsterdam Treaty.

Throughout the 2000 IGC, Irish ministers and officials re-iterated their support in principle and in practice for the accession of applicant states to the European Union. They also acknowledged the necessary costs that this would entail for some traditional Irish interests, such as agriculture. At the same time, they pointed towards the business and investment opportunities represented by enlargement and the opportunities generated by an enlarged market of consumers who, with the prosperity brought by enlargement, would eventually become valuable customers for Irish goods and services. The Taoiseach, for example, pointed out that "a large single market of 500 million people will create fresh opportunities for trade and investment, and indeed our business interests in Central and Eastern Europe are already expanding significantly" (*The Irish Times* 9 December 2000).

The moral and historic arguments were also deployed in as much as the Taoiseach strongly affirmed that "the enlargement of the EU is fundamentally about the further consolidation of freedom, democracy and human rights across our once-divided continent" (*The Irish Times* 7 November 2000).

He went on to argue that "it is profoundly in Europe's interest, and it is in our national interest too. Not to support it wholeheartedly would be hypocritical, short-sighted and ungenerous" (Ibid.)

In fulfilment of that over-riding objective, the government insisted that it supported a proportional division of votes in the Council to reassure larger states that their interests would be defended within a Union of many smaller states. The government also insisted that it had an open mind on extending QMV into a number of policy areas and expressed its support for the institutional changes that were necessitated by enlargement. On two issues, however, the government entered its strongest reservations: it would not support the extension of QMV into taxation matters, and it would not support an institutional package in which each state did not have a right to nominate a member of the College of Commissioners.

Over the course of nearly a year, leading up to the December 2000 Nice European Council the Irish stance was essentially defensive—allowing for only minor openings in its position. Overall, the government appeared to be concerned primarily with safeguarding its veto on taxation policy. This policy had come under sustained attack from Germany, France, and Belgium, which viewed the use of taxation as a tool of attracting overseas Foreign Direct Investment as a distortion of the single market. The focus for this debate was over Ireland's traditionally low corporate tax rates.

Over the course of what have been called the most secretive negotiations in our EU history the Irish Government, in 1996, agreed with the Commission that Ireland's corporate taxation rate would be brought down to 12.5 per cent for all companies from 1 January 2003. These negotiations were exceptionally difficult and were surrounded by very heavy lobbying by and on behalf of U.S. companies already based in Ireland. For the Minister of Foreign Affairs, Brian Cowan, "some larger states with more regulated economies with higher taxes would like others to be more in line with them in order to deal with their own domestic difficulties." This, however, was unacceptable and therefore, "For cogent reasons of national interest, we do not see this as an issue on which we can compromise at this time" (*The Irish Times* 7 November 2000).

This position extended to a number of other taxation issues upon which Ireland—alongside the United Kingdom, Sweden and others—fought to retain unanimity on issues such as: value added tax, excise rates, the fight against fraud, and double taxation. The perceived danger in these fields was, according to the Taoiseach that "Experience shows that all aspects of a tax code are, in the real world, interlinked. Changes in one area can have unpredictable knock-on effects. Moreover, there is a danger that a seemingly innocuous precedent could be seized on and used as a bridgehead for wider change" (*The Irish Times* 6 November 2000).

The second Irish reservation concerned the Commission. Early in the negotiations, Foreign Minister Cowan declared it to be "a fundamental objective" (*The Irish Times* 15 February 2000) during the IGC negotiations that Ireland would not lose its right to nominate a member of the Commission. He added that the same principle had to apply to the applicant states. While this remained the public face of the negotiations, active consideration was being given behind the scenes to 'best worst case scenarios.'[1] Internal debates suggested that there were very real problems of efficiency and credibility that would arise in a Commission of 25+ members. There was even greater danger in an enlarged Commission of a formalised hierarchy of Commissioners. If such a hierarchy were to emerge either formally or informally, the Commissioners coming from smaller states would inevitably lose out. Towards the end of the negotiations, therefore, the Minister's position appears to have softened somewhat. He insisted simply that Ireland would continue to resist suggestions that small states alone might lose their automatic right to nominate a member of the EU Commission. Therefore, he argued, "We should allow the position of one Commissioner per state to prevail" (*The Irish Times* 6 November 2000).

The Irish position on other issues was more open to evolution. It soon became clear, for example, that Ireland's veto on QMV's extension to decision-making on structural funds would not be defended—despite Spanish calls for support from its erstwhile ally. Irish officials and ministers also sought to ensure that Ireland's share of votes in the Council of Ministers would not be too drastically affected by the re-weighting in favour of larger states and similarly, that they might minimise the reduction in Irish seats at the European Parliament. Irish

[1] Author's interview with Irish officials.

trade-offs, in the pursuit of greater efficiency in an enlarged Union was to endorse plans for increased powers for the President of Commission.

While defence and security issues did not impinge upon the negotiations of the IGC itself, a parallel process of negotiations concluding under the French Presidency produced issues which would later impinge on Irish ratification. The first, and apparently minor issue, was the provision for the new Political and Security Committee of a treaty base for its operation. Even though the Council had legally established the Committee, the legal services argued that it should be provided with an explicit place in the treaties. The second issue—and a rather more substantive debate—surrounded the application of revised rules on 'flexibility' or 'enhanced cooperation' to operate in the field of security and/or defence.

The concept and mechanics of 'enhanced co-operation' or 'flexibility' had been introduced in the Amsterdam Treaty as a means to address fears of policy gridlock in an enlarged Union. These mechanisms would allow for the creation—on a case by case basis—of a policy vanguard where a substantial minority of states wished to move further and faster on the road of integration—without waiting for consensus among the full membership. EMU, the Schengen system and—during Margaret Thatcher's period as British Prime Minister—EU social policy, were all cited as positive precedents for such a system. Ireland—in common with many other states, had insisted on a number of safeguards to the operation of such a system (including Commission initiation, the principle of 'open to all' participation, the maintenance of a single legal framework and a bar to its operation where it would undermine the single market or in the field of security and defence). Several Member States had returned to this issue during the 2000 IGC with a view to loosening the strings on its operation. Ireland, however, worked alongside other Member States to block these provisions from applying in the fields of foreign policy and security and defence co-operation.

The Government was determined to maintain its pledge that any actions undertaken by the EU in the military field were tightly circumscribed by the Treaty and limited to peacekeeping and humanitarian missions.

Nice Summit and Treaty

The negotiating agenda at the European Council at Nice in December 2000 has been acknowledged as having been narrow but deep. This made it very difficult—according to the negotiators themselves—for certain traditional compromises to be facilitated through side-payments in the classical style of EU bargaining. Moreover, there was significant criticism at the time over the style and management of the summit by the French Presidency. Irish press and media reported that the Nice conference itself was badly prepared—alongside complaints that President Chirac had failed to act as an honest broker during the negotiations. The French were accused of bullying tactics matched with an absence of overall strategy, all of which simply served to exacerbate tensions and splits between the Member States (*The Irish Times* 16 December 2000).

The summit itself ended at 4:23 a.m. on the morning of the final day of the summit. Even so, the attending confusion over what had exactly been traded for what in those final hectic hours meant that the legal services had to work for several weeks to produce an agreed treaty text—and even then had to face down complaints from a few Member States that this text did not reflect their understanding of what had actually been agreed.

In the final agreement, more than 30 policy areas were transferred to QMV—although not matters related to taxation. The Commission's membership was capped—with a requirement for a cut in numbers (i.e. below the threshold of one Commissioner per Member State) linked to unanimous agreement on a means for equal rotation of nominations among the Member States. The concerns of larger states in the Council were met by increasing the percentage of votes needed for a qualified majority vote in an enlarged Community from 71.3 per cent to 73.4 per cent of the total, and this was then linked to a threshold to ensure that those votes represented at least 62 per cent of the population of the member-states. An increased vote weighting was also given to larger states, with the voting power of the six largest states in an enlarged Community being increased to 49 per cent, from a figure that would otherwise have fallen to less than 42 per cent.

On signing the treaty text Ireland's Minister for Foreign Affairs, Brian Cowan, expressed himself as being well pleased:

> "The overall outcome of the Treaty negotiations is satisfactory from Ireland's viewpoint. We are particularly pleased that, in relation to a major negotiating priority, it was possible to maintain the requirement for unanimity on taxation (…). As regards the institutional changes (…) Ireland's interests were well-protected in the outcome (…). Most importantly, it was agreed that all Member States, big and small, must be treated on the basis of strict equality" (Department of Foreign Affairs, Press Release, 26 February 2000).

Referring to ratification of the Treaty, the Minister then said:

> "The Treaty, of course, will only come into effect if ratified by all 15 Member States. To avoid delaying the enlargement process, the Member States have undertaken to seek to do so by the end of 2002. The question of whether a referendum will be required in this jurisdiction will be decided in the light of the advice of the Attorney General. However, the Government have instructed that the necessary preparations should already be put in hand on a contingency basis. It is likely that ratification in other Member States will be on the basis of approval by national Parliaments" (Ibid).

IRELAND AND THE NICE TREATY – ROUND ONE

EU treaty amendments must be ratified by each Member State according to that state's own constitutional requirements. Under the terms of the Irish Supreme Court's 1986 ruling on the Single European Act, if such amendments go beyond measures "necessitated by the obligations of membership" then the Irish constitution (Bunreacht na hÉireann) must be amended to provide for the ratification of such a treaty. Both before and after the conclusion of the Nice negotiations, members of the Government, including the Minister for Foreign Affairs, suggested that the proposed treaty amendments were so modest that they might not require constitutional amendment—in effect that they might indeed be judged to be "necessitated by the obligations of membership." However, the Attorney General judged that unspecified elements might be open to a successful court challenge, and it was judged necessary to propose a constitutional amendment.

The Nice Referendum was just the second taking place under the terms of the Referendum Act (1998) and in conformity with a 1998 High Court ruling on the allocation of broadcast airtime to the two sides in referendum campaigns. The Referendum Act had established a Referendum Commission to "explain to the people the subject matter of the referendum" as well as "ensuring that the arguments of those in favour and those against the proposed amendment to the Constitution are put forward in a manner that is fair to all interest concerned" (Referendum Commission, 2001). Previous Court rulings had prevented the Government from spending public monies in support of a particular result in a referendum campaign. Rather than allocate public monies to various campaigning groups, the Government, through the Referendum Commission, committed itself to spending public money first to publicise the referendum and also to disseminate pro and anti arguments. Pro-Nice campaigners were additionally constrained by the fact that a separate court ruling had found that the national broadcaster, RTE, had acted unfairly in allocating airtime in a previous referendum campaign. It had divided free broadcasts and apportioned news and editorial coverage according to the relative strengths of parties in the parliament as well as allocating a small additional share to pro and anti campaign groups. The court held that this arrangement would skew coverage in circumstances—such as that in European debates—where the 'opinion' in parliament was distributed in anything other than a 50/50 split.

It was within these new and largely untested rules that the Nice Referendum was conducted. The Referendum Commission was given a budget of € 3,175,000. The Commission then set about publicising the date of the referendum and inviting submissions from groups on both sides of the debate. These submissions were then synthesised and presented to the public in a series of print and broadcast commercials, booklets and on the internet (*The Irish Times,* 28 December 2000).

Among the political parties a familiar constellation of forces swiftly emerged. The mainstream political parties (Fianna Fáil, Progressive Democrats, Fine Gael and Labour) supported a 'Yes' vote—each with their own campaign, while a number of smaller parties (Sinn Fein, The Green Party, The Socialist Party) together with several dedicated campaign groups were to campaign against.

For the 'Yes' campaigners, the case in favour of the Treaty was presented as being fundamentally about EU enlargement and more broadly about Ireland's place in Europe and the benefits that would accrue to Ireland as a result of enlargement. A crucial subtext for the 'Yes' side was that many of the applicant countries were seeking to emulate Ireland's European experience, and that Ireland had a special moral and historic duty to welcome these Europeans into the Union's family of states.

On the 'No' side of the campaign, the themes were equally familiar, although the actors were slightly different. The themes of the 'No' campaign centred upon the loss of Irish sovereignty implied by any extension of QMV, the adverse impact on Irish representation in the core institutions, implied by a loss of seats in the European Parliament, a lost right to nominate a member of the Commission and the rebalancing of votes in the Council. Although the Nice treaty made no substantive changes to the Union's Common Foreign and Security Policy (CFSP) the treaty's provision of a legal base for the Political and Security Committee as well as the Nice Summit's conclusions related to security and defence were additional hooks upon which activists placed their opposition to Nice—and their claims that the treaty would further undermine Irish neutrality. A key slogan for some of these campaigners was 'No to NATO, No to Nice'.

The Nice Treaty campaign witnessed veteran anti-EU campaigners re-united and joined by a significant new group. Hence, the Green, Sinn Fein, and Socialist parties were joined by campaign groups such as The National Platform, the Peace and Neutrality Alliance (PANA)) and Action from Ireland (AfrI). Crucially, they were joined by a new organisation which styled itself simply as the 'No to Nice Campaign.' This organisation was constructed from an activist core with a passionate opposition to abortion. In political terms coming from the conservative Catholic right, the main protagonists of this organisation had already fallen out with the Church hierarchy and mainstream 'pro-life' groups as a result of their uncompromising position on abortion. They argued that the European project in general and the Nice Treaty in particular was forcing an unwelcome liberalisation on Irish society and that there was an immediate danger of European law being used to introduce a liberal abortion regime. This group used the same shock' tactics that they had employed in earlier referendum battles on divorce and abortion. In the case of Nice, these tactics employed the use of start black, red and white posters declaring that if Nice passed 'You will lose money, power and influence.'

The campaign itself was comparatively short and desultory. Pro Nice political parties were conspicuous by their absence from the doorsteps, while the smaller 'No' parties appeared to generate more passion in motivating their activists to campaign. The Referendum Commission's efforts to fulfil its mandate was criticised heavily first because in its TV, radio and print media ads, disembodied voices offered wholly contradictory messages about the treaty and its consequences. While this was consistent with its mandate to offer both pro and anti-arguments, it served more often to confuse voters than to illuminate issues. The 'Yes' side, however, were especially critical, seeing the ads as disseminating fundamentally untrue allegations

Early opinion polls suggested that the referendum would pass: three weeks prior to the poll, 52 per cent of respondents said that they would vote 'Yes', while 21 per cent would vote 'No' and 27 per cent did not know (*The Irish Times,* 19 May 2001).[2] Two weeks later—and just as the Referendum Commission's media campaign was launched—polls showed a much smaller margin, with 45 per cent declaring their support for the referendum proposal, 28 per cent opposing it and a significant 27 per cent unable or unwilling to declare their intentions (*The Irish Times,* 2 June 2001).

---

[2] The question posed was: "Are you likely to vote yes or no to the Nice Treaty which provides, among other things, for enlargement of the number of countries in the European Union?"

RESULTS

The result saw 34.79 per cent of eligible voters turning out to cast their ballots. This represented the smallest ever turnout in a referendum contest. Of those voters, 46.13 per cent supported ratification of the Nice Treaty while 53.87 per cent opposed it. In 39 of the 41 constituencies, there was a 'No' majority, while the two constituencies with an overall 'Yes' majority were both in the staunchly middle class south Dublin area with traditionally strong liberal voting traditions.

Initial comments on the result noted the fact of the exceptionally low turnout but differed in interpreting its impact. It was noted, however, that fewer voters had said 'No' to Nice than had said 'No' to the Amsterdam treaty.

REFERENDUM FALL-OUT

A subsequent study sponsored by the European Commission office in Ireland found evidence to suggest that potential 'No' voters voted in disproportionate numbers compared with potential 'Yes' voters—in other words, more 'Yes' voters stayed home on the voting day—illustrating a failure in the 'Yes' campaign to sufficiently motivate their electorate (Sinnott, 2001).

Another focus of post-referendum analysis was the role played by the Referendum Commission. 'Yes' campaigners bitterly criticised the nature of the Commission's advertising, and the fact that its media campaign started so comparatively late. This segued into a broader criticism of the political parties, who had, by and large, failed to put their hands in their own pockets to promote a 'Yes' message, leaving the field largely to 'No' campaigners—one of whose late and successful slogans had been 'If you don't know, vote no.'

Substantively, the Government's options in the immediate wake of the referendum defeat were few and far between. Politically, it judged that it was not realistic for it to demand a reopening of the Nice Treaty. With precisely the same political actors, arguments and issues, there was little expectation that the result of intergovernmental bargaining could throw up a substantially different result. Moreover, the Government was genuinely uncertain as to precisely what elements of the Nice Treaty had provoked a 'No' vote in such a low turnout. With such disparate campaign messages on the 'No' side—ranging from opposition to abortion, through neutrality to opposition to Irish membership of the Union, it was simply not possible to construct the kind of 'national compromise' that had resolved the Danish 'No' to Maastricht a decade earlier.

The Government had to face the Göteborg Council a week after the referendum with some concern. At that summit, the Swedish Presidency and Ireland's other 13 EU partners made sympathetic noises but also sent a clear message that the Nice package—so painstakingly crafted—could not be tampered with and renegotiated. The reverberations of the Treaty's defeat also rippled through the political establishment at home, with the Minister for Finance declaring that the result was good for Irish democracy and a "remarkably healthy development" (*Sunday Business Post,* 17 June 2001) while a junior cabinet minister revealed that while he had campaigned for a 'Yes' vote, he had himself voted 'No'. The Attorney General—who had made the legal case to the Government for a referendum—also weighed in, declaring that the Irish people would ultimately reject a federalist future for the EU and that while he supported the Nice Treaty for its enabling of enlargement, he felt that the Irish 'No' vote represented popular opposition to a European superstate (*The Irish Times,* 19 June 2001).

In an attempt to buy some time while the Government considered its options, the Taoiseach announced the establishment of a National Forum on Europe, to consist of the political parties and the social partners and which would be tasked with analysing Ireland's role in Europe.

Nice Referendum Mark II

The second Nice Treaty referendum campaign was markedly different from the first and was widely billed as Ireland's date with European history. To begin with, the Government's and the Taoiseach's credibility was more directly invested in the outcome than in 2001. This time round, the 'Yes' campaign mobilized far more effectively in a veritable army of interest groups, citizen organizations and others taking on the responsibility of campaigning. The 'No' campaign, with a successful campaign behind them, had something of a head start and initial momentum, but also rallied its own wide and sometimes disparate range of groups to launch an intense and energetic campaign. The Government's deadline for a second referendum was late autumn—following the summer General Election—with the precise date left for the Taoiseach to decide. As August 2002 drew to a close, the campaign kicked of with a bevy of press conferences.

CONTEXT

The context of the referendum had certainly changed from the last occasion. Since the first referendum, the National Forum on Europe had been established to broaden and deepen public understanding of Ireland's membership of the European Union. In addition, new measures had been introduced to increase parliamentary scrutiny of EU legislation and thus to improve democratic oversight. Finally, the Government had sought and obtained a formal declaration from Ireland's EU partners—the Seville Declaration—that underlined Irish neutrality. At the same time, however, those campaigning for a 'Yes' vote had to overcome considerable public antipathy. Following the General Election and in reaction to an emerging recession, a series of government cutbacks undermined confidence in both Government parties. Public cynicism was further fuelled by the publication of a report on political corruption that forced the resignation of the Fianna Fáil referendum campaign director.

The core message of the 'Yes' campaign was that the long term peace and prosperity of the whole of Europe depended on enlargement and enlargement depended upon the Nice Treaty. Thus, the 'reunification of Europe' became a key campaign message for the 'Yes' campaign. The 'No' campaign focused on fears of a small nation being swamped by a larger EU, with the emphasis on loss of sovereignty, the democratic deficit and the overall direction of the EU as a political project.

Significant in this referendum campaign was the emergence of civil society as a political actor. While the major parties and interest groups each had their own campaigns, some entirely voluntary organizations were formed solely for the 'Yes' campaign. One such organisation was the 'Irish Alliance for Europe' described by its leader, Professor Brigid Laffan, as a "coalition of the willing."[3] Otherwise there was an extraordinary cross-party and multi-interest cooperative effort among all of the main political parties and the social partners—including business groups, trade unions, farming organisations and other special interest groups. As well as their political mobilisation, these groups outspent the 'No' campaign by a factor estimated to be about 8-1.

The main 'No' campaigners again included The Green Party, Sinn Fein, the Socialist Party, a relaunched 'No to Nice' campaign led by anti-abortion campaigner Justin Barrett, and several other interest groups including the National

[3] (http://www.allianceforeurope.org/info.asp)

Platform, the Peace and Neutrality Alliance, the Irish Immigration Control Group and Action From Ireland (AfrI).

THE ISSUES

To some extent, many of the campaign issues were the same as the previous year, with an emphasis emerging on enlargement, the economy and neutrality. However, there were also some surprises, with immigration providing a new focus of opposition for some of the anti-Nice campaigners. Anti-treaty campaigners highlighted the scope for immigration from new Member States following accession. They placed particular emphasis on a letter addressed by the Irish Minister for Foreign Affairs to his accession state counterparts, assuring them that he had no intention of applying for unilateral transition measures on free movement that were to be provided under the terms of the accession treaties. This tactic provoked something of a split in the anti-treaty forces, with Green and self-declared left-wing parties rejecting the 'scare' tactics of those raising the immigration issue. This split between 'right' and 'left' was further exacerbated with the revelation that the leader of the 'No to Nice' campaign, Justin Barrett, had attended meetings and at least one public rally of a German party which employed neo-Nazi slogans and images.

Another important plank in the 'No' campaign's argument was the very fact of a second referendum. Campaigners insisted that the first referendum result was as valid as any electoral result and as valid as any previous referendum. The attempt to re-run the campaign was therefore characterised as an attack on democracy—with the well-sharpened quip that the Irish would simply have to keep voting until they provided the right answer. It moreover illustrated to those so-minded, the undemocratic nature of the Union since it would not accept Ireland's right to say 'No'. It also illustrated the unbalanced nature of the Union, with the allegation that had the French or the Germans delivered an earlier 'No', their governments would not have allowed themselves to be browbeaten into re-running the debate.

For those on the other side of the debate, the holding of a second Irish referendum was to prove one of the most difficult issues to address. Their answer was twofold: First, that on an issue of such importance not just to Ireland but to the rest of the continent of Europe, it was reasonable, in light of the poor turnout in the first referendum, to ask for reconsideration. Second, it was argued that the context of this referendum was different to the first in the light of legislative and other changes—including the Seville Declaration—which illustrated that the Government had responded to the first 'No' and was now entitled to seek a reconsideration of the main question.

A broad range of issues was presented over the course of the second campaign—with, it must be said, a clear pattern emerging. For the 'Yes' side, the focus was maintained on enlargement. Despite some early and contradictory statements from Commission President Prodi—which the 'No' campaign used to good effect—the 'Yes' campaign largely succeeded in presenting their case as being one of 'Nice equals Enlargement'. This was not without its dangers, since for some key constituencies, enlargement could be a difficult issue. It implied less money for Ireland through EU transfers and the Common Agricultural Policy as well as the prospect of immigration from new Member States. Nonetheless, on balance, keeping the focus on the issue of enlargement was crucial to the success of the 'Yes' campaign. A subsidiary but also key issue was also that of 'Ireland in Europe' and the loss to Ireland's position, strength and reputation within the Union that would arise from another and final 'No'. Again, this was a tough issue for 'Yes' campaigners—since it could, and was presented by those on the other side, as an implied threat of blackmail.[4] Again, however, skilful campaigning managed to get across the idea of negative consequences arising from a 'No' vote without raising persuasive counter allegations of bullying.

For the 'No' campaigners, a simple strategy emerged. They raised a barrage of criticism across a wide field of issues, making claims about the treaty's impact in areas that none of the treaty's drafters might have envisaged. The extension of QMV in certain areas related to trade in goods and services was highlighted by 'No' campaigners as presaging the privatisation of water supplies in Ireland, the introduction of water charges and the wide spread sale of state assets—implying a loss of jobs for public sector employees. Mention of the Charter of Fundamental Rights and Human Freedoms within the Nice Treaty, was presented by some 'No' campaigners as the first step toward the introduction of a liberal abortion regime into Ireland. Similarly, providing the Political and Security committee with a treaty base was represented in one set of posters as entailing a message of 'Hello NATO, Goodbye UN'.

Foreign commentators on the campaign often expressed their own confusion as to how such chimeras could be created from the dust of the Nice Treaty. They

---

[4] On this, the 'shock' tactics of the 'No to Nice Campaign' failed. They produced an iconic poster in their trademark red, black and white that showed a clearly frightened young man with a gun pointed at his head and a tag line that read 'Don't be Bullied'. The poster was condemned widely as being emotive and dangerous.

had frequently to be reminded that this was not a uniquely Irish phenomenon, since in almost all cases Irish campaigners presented MEPs, national parliamentarians, lawyers and NGO activists from other EU Member States in justification of the claims being made about the Nice Treaty.

The Results

As polling day arrived on 19 October 2002, much was made of the possible scale of the turnout. In the event, there was a significantly higher turnout—increasing from 32.7 per cent to 49.47 per cent. Holding the referendum on a Saturday with comparatively long polling hours facilitated this. For the first time, electronic voting on a large scale was used, which also gave much quicker results. As soon as the six large Dublin constituencies had reported their massive swings towards the 'Yes' side—of between 11 and 20 percentage points—on the night of 19 October, senior 'No' campaigners were already conceding defeat before the traditional ballot boxes had even been opened.

The resounding nature of the 63 per cent 'Yes' vote was very important to the pro-treaty campaigners. There was a 'Yes' in every constituency. It was also noted that there was a positive correlation between the turnout and the 'Yes' vote. In Dun Laoighaire, for example, a poll-topping 73.3 per cent 'Yes' vote came in a turnout of 56.56 per cent while Donegal North-East could manage only a 52 per cent 'Yes' on a turnout of just 39.28 percent.

The scale of the victory was important to several leading 'Yes' campaigners who argued that the substantially higher turnout coupled with the emphatic 'Yes' victory validated their claims on the legitimacy of having asked the same question a second time. For 'No' campaigners, the loss represented the inevitable outcome of a second referendum in which the political elites were determined to mobilise and employ their resources in pursuit of their desired outcome.

Conclusion

The Nice experience has proven to be traumatic to the Irish political system and was a very sharp lesson to those planning for the ratification of the Union's Constitutional Treaty, arising from the Convention on the Future of Europe. These lessons revolve around the fundamental consideration that electorates must never be overlooked. Moreover, the case for major constitutional change is much more difficult to make than the case for the status quo. Electorates must be convinced that change is necessary and only then will they be open to a debate about the kind of change that is then proposed. The nature of the European political system is also one that remains largely a mystery to national publics. One symptom of this is the ease with which issues—having little or nothing to do with the substance of the Nice treaty—still managed to galvanise debates during the two referenda campaigns. The public was unable to dismiss outlandish claims for or against the treaty because they felt themselves unable to judge just what the treaty entailed—and this despite an extensive and expensive information campaign.

Nevertheless, the experience also leaves us with some positive lessons. It certainly underscores the need to simplify the message and understanding of what the Union does. It also underlines the importance of testing the Union's constitutional foundations against the stresses of democratic accountability and legitimacy. Such tests are far from tranquil experiences, but the Union's foundations will undoubtedly be stronger as a result.

As regards the interests of the Irish government going into the negotiations, the process of negotiation itself and the resulting treaty, there are three conclusions. First, it is certainly true that in this instance, Ireland's position within the IGC was indeed driven by economic interest. Ireland has never had an ideological approach to EU membership—except to defend the Union's institutional infrastructure—but on this occasion certainly, the government's position on QMV and taxation was undoubtedly the central line of policy defence. Second, it is again remarkable to note the defensive nature of the Irish strategy. While newer Member States—such as Sweden, Finland and Austria—delivered of themselves a variety of initiatives and proposals designed to address common problems and interests, the Irish maintained a 'heads-down' posture throughout—determined in the final analysis to defend declared national interests with their powder still dry. Finally, it is important to question the model of the Union that divides it between larger and smaller states. Even at Nice with its narrow agenda and unwavering focus on issues which struck at the heart of institutional and state balances, there was considerable movement across lines among both smaller and larger states in terms of cross cutting issues, ideological predispositions and national strategies—all conspired still to ensure that while the small state/large state fissure was exposed as never before, it never became a critical fautline.

BIBLIOGRAPHY

Cowan, B. (2001), *Press Section.* Dublin: Department of Foreign Affairs.

Dooge, J., Keatinge P., eds. (2001), *What the Treaty of Nice Means*. Dublin: Institute of European Affairs.

Gilland, K. (1999), Referenda in the Republic of Ireland. Electoral Studies (18). *Irish Times*.

Moravcsik, Andrew (1993), "Preferences and Power in the European Community: A Liberal Intergovernmentalist Approach," *Journal of Common Market Studies*, vol. 31, no. 4, pp. 473-524.

—— (1998), *The Choice for Europe*. Ithaca, NY: Cornell University Press.

Referendum Commission (2001), *Your Voice, Your Choice: Treaty of Nice 2001*. Referendum Commission, Dublin. *Sunday Business Post.*

Sinnott, R. (2001), *The Nice Treaty Referendum: Results Analysis*. Dublin: Commission of the European Union.

CHAPTER 10

ITALY: WHEN INDIVIDUAL ACTORS MAKE THE DIFFERENCE

INTRODUCTION: MORAVCSIK'S PROBLEM WITH ITALY

According to Moravcsik, the great choices of the EU are due to the coincidence of interests of the major European States (Moravcsik, 1991, p. 41-84; 1998, p. 59-85): "From its inception, the EC has been based on interstate bargains between its leading Member States. ¨[...] Small States can be bought off with side-payments, but larger States exercise a *de facto* veto over fundamental changes in the scope or rules of the core element of the EC, which remains economic liberalization. Thus, bargaining tends to converge toward the minimum common denominator of large State interests" (Moravcsik, 1991, p. 47). If it is Larger States defining EU high politics, why is Italy not mentioned in Moravcsik's work? True, Italy has been defined by some as a 'medium-size power' (Santoro, 1989); yet from a formal point of view, Italy is a 'big' EU country. Also, though it is undeniable that in *low politics* (Hoffmann, 1966, pp. 862-915; 1982)[1] Italy's role has traditionally been poor (Bindi, 2001; Bindi & Cisci, 2004),[2] the case with high politics is different, which is both Moravcsik's and this work's focus.

One may for instance recall Italy's masterpiece in calling the IGC leading to the Single Act in June 1984. Yet in his article, 'Negotiating the Single European Act' (Moravcsik, 1991, pp. 41-84), Andrew Moravcsik affirms that the precondition for the SEA reform was the convergence of the economic policies of France, Britain and Germany. It was negotiations between France and Germany that mattered, coupled with the "negotiating leverage that France and Germany gained by exploiting the threat to create a 'two-track' Europe and excluding Britain from it" (ibid. p. 42). [...] "The importance of interstate bargains in the SEA negotiations is consistent with the broader experience of the EC since the mid-1960s. [...] The result represents the convergence of domestic policy preferences in the largest member States" (Moravcsik, 1991, pp. 67-68). The unprecedented Italian decision to ask for a vote (Stirk, 1996, p. 210), thus forcing the recalcitrant States (UK,

---

[1] The definition is Hoffmann's. With low politics it concerns technical or administrative matters, in contrast with high politics (state security, vital resources, etc.).

[2] For a more detailed description see Bindi (forthcoming 2005).

Denmark and Greece) and the political and diplomatic work undertaken by Italy, France and Germany is not even considered by Moravcsik. While this is not the place to discuss the SEA further, the above-mentioned suggests that Moravcsik's work does not appear to be consistent with the Italian case. The objective of this chapter is, thus, to test Moravcsik's theory in the light of the Nice Treaty negotiations. Our research suggests that in the case of the Nice Treaty, Moravcsik's work cannot fully be used to explain the behavior of the actors and the outcome of the negotiations.

Parties and Public Opinion

Support for EU is widespread in Italy. However, such Europhilia appears to have corresponded to a lack of confidence in the Italian institutional and political system;[3] as the Italian system was deteriorating, the EC began to be perceived as the only possibility of bringing order into the national system, thus, the demand for supranational structures corresponded to a demand for repairing the inefficiencies of the Italian system. On the other hand, the EC has at times been used by Italian politicians to legitimise their own actions, or to justify unpopular policies, like fiscal and monetary measures, as the headings of leading Italian newspapers show: "The Twelve ask for tears and blood" (*La Repubblica*, 5 May 1992); "Privatisation? It is imposed by the EC" (*Corriere della Sera*, 3 August 1992).

The attitude of Italian political parties vis-à-vis integration has generally been that of supporters of European integration. To the Christian-Democrats (DC) pro-Europe and pro-US values were the basis of foreign politics. Socialists (PSI) and Communists (PCI), initially against the EC, changed their positions over the years. The invasion of Hungary in 1954 marked the change for PSI, hence its abstention on the EEC and its vote in favour of EURATOM.[4] PCI remained against the EEC until the end of the 1960s,[5] and started to change its perspective when the first Communists were appointed

---

[3] See the Eurobarometre polls. Such perspective has been reaffirmed also in the 2002 poll, N. 57/2002 - *Report on Italy*.

[4] Telò, M. 1996: 197-200. The Socialist changed to being 'neutral' and then to being supporters of the integration process following the invasion of Hungry in 1954: already in 1955 the leader, Pietro Nenni, became member of Jean Monnet's *Comitè d'Action*). PSI then joined the majority supporting the Government in 1958, to enter the Government in 1963.

[5] The turning point was represented by the publication of the *Memoriale di Yalta* after Togliatti's death in 1964. In the *Memoriale,* Togliatti criticised the USSR. It is interesting to note that only in 1985 with Gorbachev did the USSR officially recognise the EEC as a legal entity.

to the European Parliament (1969) and embraced pro-European values by the time of the first direct elections to the European Parliament (1979). As a result, the EC gradually became a non-issue in the Italian political arena; in Giulio Andreotti's words: "[the EC] is a great tradition...of both cultural and political families of the [Italian] Nation" (*Dossier Europa,* 6.90, p. 8).

Policy Making Mechanisms[6]

In Italy, the assimilation of the newborn ECSC and then EEC to classical international organisations led to the attribution of the main role in dealing with European affairs to the Government and, within it, to the *Ministry of Foreign Affairs* (MAE)—also known as *Farnesina.* The Ministry of Foreign Affairs is subdivided into five geographical and seven thematic sections, 'Direction General' (DGs), among which one finds a DG 'European Countries' (DGEC), as well as a DG 'European Integration' (DGEI). While DGEC deals with bilateral issues, DGEI handles multilateral European questions (*in primis,* but not exclusively, the European Union). DGEI is also charged with the spreading of information coming from the COREPER and the Commission to the various branches of the Italian Public Administration. The duties of the Minister of Foreign Affairs in relation to the EU are multiple: to follow CSFP, the political and economic external relations of the EU, as well as eventual EU treaties negotiations. The Farnesina is very jealous of its role in EU affairs; when the Minister for EC Politics, Enrico Letta, scheduled a debate on the Nice IGC negotiations in the Parliament's Commission for EU Affairs, he received a sharp letter from the Minister of Foreign Affairs, Lamberto Dini, reminding him that Treaty negotiations were part of the Farnesina's competencies. Dini, thus, invited Minister Letta to be joined at the debate by the Undersecretary of State, Umberto Ranieri, and to never deal with such an issue again.[7] However, since 1999, the Presidency of the Council is also responsible for the "participation of the Italian State in the EU" and for the "implementation of EU policies."[8] Acting in co-ordination, the Presidency of the Council and the Foreign Ministry should thus ensure the promotion of the Italian positions within the European Institutions. In do-

---

[6] This part draws heavily on Bindi & Cisci (2004).

[7] Participant observation. The letter was in the hands of Letta's Chief de Cabinet when we had access to it.

[8] Art. 12, DL n. 300 del 30 luglio 1999 (*Decreto legislativo concernente riforma dell'organizzazione di governo ai sensi degli articoli 11, comma 1, lettera a) e 12 della legge 15 marzo 1997, N.59.*

ing so, they are supported respectively by the Undersecretary of State for Foreign Affairs charged with European Affairs and by the Minister for EC Policies. This, however, at times causes problems.

The Undersecretary of State for Foreign Affairs charged with European Affairs (*Sottosegretario agli Esteri con delega per gli Affari Europei*) has, on paper, wide tasks. S/he is in fact charged with the following of European bilateral relations and with the participation in the EU, in the OECD and in the Council of Europe. The Undersecretary is part of the delegation attending the General Affairs Council and the European Councils. However, s/he cannot act independently from the Minister, nor relate directly to the President of the Council.

Another actor in European affairs is the *Ministry for the Co-ordination of EC Policies* which was created in 1980 within the Presidency of the Council. Its lack of resources was such that it was once defined by Grottanelli de Santi as the *Cinderella* of the Italian Ministries (Grottanelli de Santi, 1992, p. 186). Thus, in 1995, it was suppressed and its tasks assigned to the Undersecretary of State for Economics; in 1996, the tasks were further divided between the Undersecretary of State at the Presidency of the Council and the Undersecretary of State for Foreign Affairs charged with European Affairs. In 1998, the re-named *Minister for Community Policies* was finally reintroduced and given enhanced powers and a political role. Yet, from a formal point of view, the Minister's tasks were not changed over the years. They concern above all the transposition of EC directives into national law. In addition, the Minister will deal with the ECJ cases concerning issues of national interest; promote the professional training of public officials in EU affairs; spread information on the EU; promote Italian citizens in the EU institutions; represent Italy in the Council for the Internal Market; co-ordinate *with* the different sectors of Public Administration and Social Partners on EU policies. This task would in particular be fulfilled by the means of an ad hoc meeting of the State-Region Conference (*Sessione Comunitaria della Conferenza Stato-Regioni*). However, the use of the word 'with' is not casual, since the Ministry never really had the authority to coordinate other Ministers. In addition, the Minister is neither part of the delegations attending the General Affairs Council, nor of the European Council, a fact that at times has undermined his role both domestically and at the European level.

As a non-departmental Ministry, the Ministry for Community Policies heads one of the Presidencies of the Council's Administrative Departments, the *Department for Community Policies*. The fortunes of the Department have been following the alternate phases of the Ministry for EC Policies itself; introduced in 1987 by the Fabbri Law, reformed and operative as from

June 1990,[9] it is only since 1998 that it was given substantial new means and resources.

In Italy there is no permanent body charged with the inter-ministerial co-ordination on European affairs, such as they exist in Portugal with the *Comissão Interministerial para os Assuntos Comunitários*, or in France with the *Secrétariat général du Comité Interministériel pour les questions de coopération économique européenne* (S.G.C.I.). Intra and inter-ministerial coordination is in fact the unsolved problem of the Italian Government in relation to EU politics. In the vertical Ministries, the level of *intra-ministerial co-ordination* on European affairs varies from no co-ordination at all (i.e. the Ministry of Environment), to little co-ordination (i.e. Ministries for Telecom, Health, Treasury and Transports), to the only example of effective co-ordination, the Ministry of Finances and Treasury, where a 'Unità di indirizzo' was set up in 1999 at the Director General's level to coordinate EU and international issues. EU and international affairs are thus generally considered issues to be dealt with by the Minister's Cabinet. Coupled together, the lack of intra-ministerial co-ordination and the high inter-ministerial rivalry have resulted in the absence of any attempt to create a body entrusted with inter-ministerial coordination on European affairs.

Governments in Power During the Nice Negotiations

During the year 2000, Italy had two governments, both supported by the Olive Tree Coalition: one led by Massimo D'Alema[10] and one by Giuliano Amato,[11] who was also present at the European Council in Nice. The two leaders are quite different, as regards their political and professional background. Massimo D'Alema, a former Communist and then PDS leader was in government for his first time ever, though he had long served in the Parliament. Thus, his experience in International Relations was mainly linked to

[9] Reformed by Law 139/90. For the use of EC funds Law 183/87 also established a *Fondo di Rotazione* charged to collect and re-distribute all EC subventions to Italy. However, as the experiment was not successful a new inter ministerial *task-force* (formed by the Ministers for Industry, Budget, EC Politics) was created and charged with the co-ordination of EU founds. Since this solution was inefficient, a new *Cabina di Regia* was thus created. The *Cabina* is now under the *Ministro del Bilancio* and works in cooperation with the regional *Cabine di Regia.*

[10] D'Alema I Government: 21 October 1998 - 22 December 1999; D'Alema II Government: 22 December 1999-25 April 2000 (http://www.palazzochigi.it/Governo/Governi/governi.html)

[11] Amato II Government: 25 April 2000- 11 June 2001 (http://www.palazzochigi.it/Governo/Governi/governi.html)

the relations within the Socialist International. As other European and international leaders of his generation for the first time in government, he at times felt the need to build good personal relations with other 'fellow' Prime-Ministers, in particular Socialist ones.[12] This proved successful to the extent that most governments—during the Nice IGC—were socialist-led, yet it can at times be dangerous if pushed to the limit of *personalisme*.

Giuliano Amato, a well known Professor of Constitutional Law, had a long career both in politics and in academics. He had been State Secretary, a Minister and Prime Minister. After a period at the European University Institute in Florence—where he lead the team that worked on the simplification of EU Treaties—he was at the Head of the Italian Antitrust Agency and then called to join the D'Alema Government as Minister for Institutional Reforms. He overtook the Presidency when – following the bad results in the regional elections—D'Alema resigned. His perfect command of English, his vast experience in politics and thorough knowledge of EU issues were certainly an asset during the negotiations.

All the same, the change of Head of Government has not really meant a change of Government, as most of the Ministers remained. The Minister of Foreign Affairs, Lamberto Dini, spent for instance the whole XIII legislature in such a post[13], while the post of Under Secretary of State for European Integration was first in Piero Fassino's[14] hands and then in Umberto Ranieri's.[15] Within the Ministry of Foreign Affairs, some of the most experienced diplomats held key posts related to the IGC; Rocco Cangelosi as Director General of the DG European Integration (DGEI), Ferdinando Nelli Feroci as his Deputy, Faggiolo as Permanent Representative in Bruxelles and Umberto Vattani as Secretary General of the Farnesina, just to mention the top posts. In Lisbon, the Ambassador was Michele Cosentino, previous Advisor to the President of the Republic Oscar Luigi Scalfaro. All in all, a very dynamic, experienced and knowledgeable team, whose members have negotiated most of the IGCs.

---

[12] When he left the government he is reported to have expressed the desire to go on a "tour des capitales" to bid farewell to his 'Colleagues'. His advisor restrained him from doing so (interviews).

[13] 9 March 1996 - 11 June 2001
(http://www.palazzochigi.it/Governo/Governi/governi.html)

[14] During the Prodi Goverment (17 May 1996 - 21 October 1998)
(http://www.palazzochigi.it/Governo/Governi/governi.html)

[15] From the D'Alema I Government to the end of the Legislature (ie. 21 October 1998 - 11 June 2001).

ITALY AND THE NEGOTIATIONS: THE DEFINITION OF THE NATIONAL POSITION

Italy's activities prior to the Nice IGC can be divided into two types—the domestic process of defining a national position and the negotiations with the other Member States. Besides the scheduled meetings for the IGC, an intensive parallel activity of political diplomacy and traditional diplomacy took in fact place. We will first examine the domestic policy-making for Nice and then, in the next paragraph, Italy's negotiating stance.

At the domestic level, the reflection on the Nice Treaty started in 1999 both at the Government and the Parliament levels. In the Parliament, on the 30th of September 1999, the Secretary of State for European Affairs appeared before the *Giunta per gli Affari Comunitari* to discuss the forthcoming IGC. Among other things, Ranieri affirmed that the IGC should be 'more ambitious' than discussing only the three Amsterdam left-overs. On the 2nd of December 1999, the *Giunta* approved a document asking the Government to request the European Council in Helsinki to adopt an agenda foreseeing a global and coherent revision of the EU institutional framework; a reinforcement of the Second and Third Pillar, with the view of abandoning the difference between inter-governmental and community policies; the reinforcement of the common policies; the revision of the EU financial system, with the introduction of real own resources; the fusion of the Treaties into one single text, the first part of which to have Constitutional status and including a list of fundamental rights. The *Giunta* also asked the Government to approve the new Treaty only after a positive opinion of the European Parliament and to regularly inform the Italian Parliament about the status of negotiations.[16] Also, the Giunta asked for an inclusion of the Charter of Fundamental Rights into the IGC agenda and into the Treaty.[17] A similar, maximalist position was taken on the 4th of February by the Committee for Foreign Affairs and the Committee for EU affairs in the Chamber of Deputies. Like the Senate, the Chamber also asked for a "global and coherent reform of the institutional framework", "a reinforcement of the democratic character of the Commission", the generalization of the QMV and of co-decision, the comunitarization of CFSP, ESDP and JHA.[18] Finally, a few weeks before the Nice European Council, after the President of the Council Giuliano Amato's interven-

[16] Senato della repubblica, Giunta per gli Affari Comunitari: *Relazione su il Consiglio Europeo di Helsinki e la CIG sulle Riforme Istituzionali*, Doc XVI, no. 12.

[17] Giunta per gli Affari Comunitari, 9 March 2000.

[18] Camera dei Deputati, XIII Legislatura, allegato B ai resoconti, Seduta del 4 February 2000, Risoluzione no. 7-00867.

tion in the Chamber of Deputies, both the governmental majority and the minority approved a motion supporting the government's action in the European Council to come.[19]

As concerns the Government, by all means the main actor in the negotiations, the official Italian position for the IGC was issued on the 27th of January, 2000 by the Minister of Foreign Affairs.[20] Consistent with the Italian tradition in EU politics, the position of the Government was also a 'maximalist' one. Italy held that, besides the 'left-overs' from Amsterdam and related questions, the Intergovernmental Conference should also address other issues (e.g. the questions of security and defence, the inclusion of the Charter of Fundamental Rights into the Treaties, and the reorganisation and simplification of the Treaties); yet it considered the most important issues of the IGC to be the extension of qualified majority voting and reinforced cooperation (or flexibility). The following points are the main positions held by the Italian Government.

The Composition of the Commission

Italy was prepared to give up its second Commissioner in exchange for compensation in terms of votes in the Council. The Government was also prepared to accept the principle of an executive composed by fewer members than the total number of Member States, considering that, as indicated by the first point of Art. 213 TEC, Commissioners are chosen on the basis of their general competences and must guarantee their independence. Should the Commission be composed by one Commissioner per Member State, this would have to be accompanied by an internal reorganisation of its structure to enable its effectiveness and efficacy. With regard to the question of the Commissioners' individual responsibilities, the Italian Government wished for a specific treaty disposition going beyond Art. 216 TEC (on the basis of which the Court of Justice can declare a member of the Commission dismissed). However, the Government excluded the European Parliament from the possibility of exerting individual censorship, opting instead for the idea of attributing further political coordination and directing powers to the President, including the ability to remove a Commissioner.

---

[19] Camera dei Deputati, Seduta no. 815 del 28 November 2000.

[20] Ministero degli Affair Esteri, DGIE, 27 January 2000: *La CIG sulla Revisione dei Trattati: la posizione dell'Italia.*

Reweighting the Votes in the Council

It had been argued in Amsterdam that some compensation should be given to the 'big' States in exchange for their second Commissioner. Enlargement signified a larger number of 'small' or 'medium' States, thus reducing the relative weight of the 'big' Member States, with consequences for the democratic legitimacy of the Union itself. Hence a modification of the decision-making process was needed, in particular for the Italian Government, in order to guarantee that the real threshold for adopting decisions by qualified majority - in terms of the votes of the population - would be maintained (in EU-15 one decision was valid with 71,26% of the votes, reflecting 58% of the European population). According to the Italian Government, there were two technical options that could be followed: a reweighting of the votes (the more preferable of the two for Italy), or the introduction, besides the majority of the votes, of a second majority based on the population.

The Extension of Qualified Majority Voting

For Italy, this represented the necessary conditions for guaranteeing the decision-making capacity of the European Union after future enlargements. In Amsterdam, there were some steps taken, even though it had not been possible to extend qualified majority voting to areas such as culture (Art. 151 TEC), the right to move and reside freely (Art.18 TEC), the social security as related to the free movement of workers (Art. 42 TEC), taking-up and pursuit of activities as self-employed persons (Art. 47, point 2 TEC), the social protection of workers (Art.137, point c TEC). According to the Italian Government, the IGC should have examined the whole question relating to one principle, that qualified majority voting should represent the general rule and unanimity the exception to be demonstrated on an ad hoc basis. Furthermore, the Italian Government held that for all types of legislation for which qualified majority voting is foreseen, co-decision with the European Parliament should be applied. For example, even after Amsterdam, co-decision was excluded from matters pertaining to agriculture and fiscal issues. The Government, in addition, supported a reflection on the second pillar and the communitarized part of the third pillar.

Enhanced Cooperation (Flexibility)

Together with the extension of qualified majority voting, enhanced cooperation was, for the Italian Government, a fundamental issue of the IGC, due to the fact that it represented the means to conjugate enlargement with the safeguarding of the EU's basic values—allowing States to proceed if they wished to do so, with respect to community methods. Among the examples that were presented by the Italian Government one finds the constitution of a European Intervention Force to execute the Petersburg tasks; common actions in the field of CFSP; the correct functioning of the Economic and Monetary Union; the constitution of an Area of Security, Freedom and Justice; social and environmental growth. The provisions of Amsterdam on closer cooperation did in fact appear insufficient to the Italian Government in the light of an enlarged Europe. Moreover, nothing was foreseen for the second pillar. In the First and Third Pillar, closer cooperation was foreseen by the Treaties, but the actual mechanism seemed extremely complex and difficult to apply. A certain perplexity arose among the Italians on account of the provision under which closer cooperation should only be used as a last resort. Furthermore, it was deemed necessary to foresee a minimum number of states, or else to refer the votes to the majority, and that the States that would not participate in closer cooperation would have to accept those actions as attributable to the EU.

The European Parliament

Besides the above-mentioned extension of the co-decision procedure and of the question of the individual responsibilities of the Commissioners, the Italian government was concerned about the problem of the so-called institutional equilibrium between the Parliament and the Commission (essentially, the former could approve a motion to censure the latter or constrain the other's resignation; however, an authority with the power to dissolve the Parliament or call for new elections does not exist). For the Italians, in the event of Parliament's lack of confidence in the Commission, the Parliament should automatically be dissolved and new elections called. With regard to the distribution of seats, it was considered necessary to find a way to proportionally reduce the number of seats for the actual Member States, with the possibility of ensuring a transition period between the accession of the candidates and the end of the current Parliament's mandate.

The Court of Justice

With the Treaty of Amsterdam, the jurisdiction of the Court of Justice was expanded to questions regarding asylum, immigration and visas. The jurisdiction of the Court should also be evoked in the area of the third pillar, in relation to a number of Conventions. The length of ECJ rulings (almost two years to produce a preliminary ruling) remained a problem, an issue destined to aggravate with enlargement. According to the Italian Government, the IGC was to reflect on possible modifications to the Treaties allowing for a more efficient functioning of the EU's judicial system. Two points of the current system were to be maintained—the representation of the Court of Justice and Court of First Instance, and the principle of unity of the acquis communautaire.[21] The main issues for Italy were therefore a revision of the mechanisms of revising the rules and procedures of the Court of Justice and Court of First Instance (i.e. either to foresee QMV in the Council on Court related issues or to give the Courts the power to modify their regulations).

The Court of Auditors

In the light of enlargement, the role of the Court of Auditors should grow in assisting EU budget authorities. Also, an increase in the number of the Court's members should suggest a reinforcement of the role of the Court's President and a better division of tasks. The Italian Government also believed it necessary for the Court to be able to appeal to the European Court of Justice, not only for "safeguarding its own prerogatives" (Art. 230, 3 TEC), but also whenever a Member State did not correctly fulfil an information request.

European Security and Defence Policies

Following the Conclusions of the European Council of Cologne, and the objectives defined at Helsinki in the field of military capacity for the management of the Petersberg tasks, it was deemed necessary to institute new organs and structures into the Council, both political and military in nature, in order to guarantee the Union the necessary political and strategic leadership, with respect to a single institutional framework.

---

[21] *Unicità del diritto comuntario* in the Italian text.

The Charter of Fundamental Rights of the European Union

For Italy, the Charter was to highlight fundamental rights and to define their nature (indivisibility, inviolability, justiceability) and, even if the Charter was not part of the agenda of the IGC, Italy wished it to be legally binding in nature. As a first step, the Charter should be included in the Treaties as an annexed protocol, with the idea that later it would become the core of the future European Constitution.

The Re-Organisation of the Treaties

The Italian government's idea was that of dividing the Treaties into two parts – a first part of constitutional and institutional nature, the other relating to common policies. The aim was to draw a systematic framework of the organs, of the division of the powers, of the decision-making process, of the hierarchy of the rules and of their content. A division of the Treaty would also allow for two different modes of revision, with the inter-governmental procedure remaining necessary only for amending the first part, while the second part of the Treaty would just require the approval of the Council and assent from the Parliament.

What is interesting to note is that the position of the Government was issued *before* an ad hoc (and only) *Meeting of the Director Generals of European Affairs and of Diplomatic Advisors* was held on the 31st of January 2000. On that occasion, Foreign Minister Lamberto Dini—joined by the State Secretary for European Affairs Umberto Ranieri and the Minister for EC Policies Patrizia Toia—introduced the paper outlining the Italian position. The paper was not changed afterwards, although later further papers and proposal were added (cf. infra). In any event, to our knowledge, only the Minister for Finance, Visco, felt the need to formally express his views on the IGC in the area that concerned him; in a letter to the Foreign Minister, Dini, he actually supported the idea of abolishing unanimity in favour of QMV and co-decision on fiscal issues.[22]

A couple of other ex-post consultative meetings took place during the following weeks, one reassembling a mix of policy makers, diplomats, advisors and scholars was held at the beginning of February,[23] while another consulta-

[22] See Letter from the Minister for Finances Vincenzo Visco to the Foreign Minister Lamberto Dini, dated 11 February 2000.

[23] The meeting took place on the 7th of February 2000 at the Farnesina (Sala Gaja) (participant observation). Some, like IAI, represented by its Director Gianni Bonvicini, then issued a note on the Italian position stating that the most important points for the IGC and for Italy

tion was organized by the Deputy Director of DGIE with Yves Meny, Director of the Schuman Center of the European University Institute who was leading a project on the simplification of the Treaties (co-led by Giuliano Amato).[24]

In sum, only the Ministry for Foreign Affairs was really involved in the making of the Italian position for the IGC. This can be explained in two ways. First, as mentioned above there is, no inter-ministerial co-ordination on EU affairs in the Italian Government, as opposed to other Member States, with the Ministry of Foreign Affairs (MAE) playing the pivotal role. Indeed, it is the *Farnesina* which is formally charged with intergovernmental issues related to the EU (and not the Minister for EC policies, as the very name is telling). Secondly, as mentioned, there is in Italy (or at least there was until more recent years) a broad consensus among political forces about the process of European integration, which makes it 'useless' for debate. The Italian position in Nice was in fact completely consistent with the positions Italy has had in the past ICG negotiations.

A confirmation of the Farnesina's leadership role in the IGC, prevailing over the Presidency of the Council (at least until Giuliano Amato's arrival) is the letter sent by Minister Dini to Prime Minister D'Alema on the 1st of February 2000. In it, Minister Dini *informs* D'Alema about the Italian position and about how things will work, including at the domestic level. The letter states, "At the end of the consultation work not only with Palazzo Chigi [the Presidency of the Council] but also with the other administrations, the Parliament, representatives of the civil society, of business and of trade unions, we have drafted a scheme of position. [...] I could distribute it and briefly present it in the next Council of Ministers and to the Senate's Foreign Affairs Committee."[25] Dini, besides *informing* the Premier about who were to be the major Italian actors in the IGC (himself, the State Secretary Ranieri and Ambassador Cangelosi in Rome and Ambassador Faggiolo in Bruxelles, see section 4), he outlined the conduct to be taken in the negotiations; the need to create a coalition with those Member States sharing a similar vision of the EU, as well as with the Commission and the Parliament. He also mentioned the risks coming from the internal difficulties in the German CDU, in Britain and in Austria. The letter also marks a sharp difference from the past: first, Dini expresses concerns about the CDU—a former good ally of Italy

---

were the reweighting of votes in the Council, the extension of QMV, and reinforced cooperation.

[24] Note of DGIE to the Minister on 22 February 2000.

[25] Letter from Minister Dini to President of the Council D'Alema, Gabinetto del Ministro reg. no. 5930, 001/0162, Rome, 1 February 2000.

until the beginning of the 1990s, but for the first time most of all the need to "safeguard the national interest" is clearly mentioned as the first criteria to define the Italian position. Indeed a 'Copernican revolution,' as in Italy mentioning national interests was for a long time considered 'politically incorrect'; among the issues related to national interests one thus finds "the need to reinforce the position of Italy in the Council". Such a need to primarily safeguard the Italian interests was, however, coupled with the need to ensure "the efficient functioning of the Union" and to "complete the democratic dimension of the Union". Hence, in Nice as in the past, the Italian national interest was in the last resort identified with the European interest and with the need to proceed further in the process of European Integration. For instance, a considerable convergence between the Italian position and the Opinion on the IGC issued by the Commission is found,[26] especially concerning the need to deeply modify the EU institutional framework before enlarging the Union to new members.[27]

Finally, among the political forces, debates on the IGC were scarce, even in those parties traditionally more pro-active in European Affairs such as the inheritors of the Christian Democrats. The *Democrats of the Left* (DS) organized a meeting on the 10th of March at Palazzo Sammacuto. Among the interventions, is it possibly worth noting the Secretary of State Ranieri's speech as he explained how Italy first opposed the notion of a Europe *à la carte* but was now supporting the idea of flexible cooperation and namely of its simplification and extension to all pillars of the EU.[28]

ITALY AND THE NEGOTIATIONS: POLITICAL DIPLOMACY AND TRADITIONAL DIPLOMACY

Concerning what can be defined as Italian EU political diplomacy, we can first of all report the role played by the Ambassadors stationed in the other Member States. They in fact initiated an intense activity of monitoring and lobbying Member States' governments on issues related to the IGC.[29] Particularly intensive was the activity of the Embassy in Lisbon, led by Michele Cosentino. He managed to keep very good relations with members of the Portuguese Government, who held the EU Presidency during the first half of

[26] Such an opinion was issued by the Commission on the 10 november 1999.

[27] See DGIE Note to the Minister of 2 February 2000.

[28] Intervento dell'On. Ranieri, Sottosegretario di Stato agli Esteri all'Incontro "La Conferenza Intergovernativa ed il Futuro dell'Europa", 10 March 2000).

[29] See the telegrams from the Italian Embassies in the EU member States.

2000, thus sending important information back to Rome.[30] The Permanent Representative in Brussels was also, and naturally so, a major actor: on behalf of Italy, Ambassador Faggiolo, also member of the IGC Preparatory Group,[31] was especially chosen to go to Brussels because of his vast EU experience. Besides being part of the preparatory group, Faggiolo also held regular meetings with his counterparts, as well as with relevant personalities within the Commission. As the conference proceeded, within the Preparatory group, the differences between the States willing to advance and the States unwilling to give up any further portion of national sovereignty became evident.[32] Italy was clearly among those willing to integrate further. For instance it held that the extension of QMV was one of its major objectives, together with the extension of co-decision.

The Director General of the DG European Integration (DGEI) Rocco Cangelosi and his Deputy, Ferdinando Nelli Feroci, were also major actors during the IGC. Among the meetings they organized, or took part in, it is worth mentioning the Meetings of Director Generals of European Affairs of the Foreign Ministries of Italy, France, UK and Germany.[33] In such meetings, the re-weighting of votes clearly constituted a matter of debate, with the Big Four divided due to the German desire to have its 'Bigger among the Big' status recognized.[34] On the other hand, the 'small' member States were starting to get anxious about the ambition of the 'big' ones for dominance, a fear stressed in particular by the Portuguese Secretary of State, Seixas da Costa who, with the active support of the Prime Minister Antonio Gutierres, became the leader and organizer of the Small States once the Portuguese EU Presidency was over.[35] Lisbon was also a strong supporter of the idea of reforming and extending the possibility of using the instrument of reinforced cooperation. Italy, as mentioned, initially against it, gradually came to change its position in the acknowledgement that in the absence of a mecha-

---

[30] Participant observation, interviews. Cf the telegrams such as on 7 January 2000; 21 January 2000; 24 January 2000; 27 January 2000; etc.

[31] See for example the telegrams of 25 February 2000, 8 March 2000.

[32] See Fagiolo reports on the works of the Preparatory group.

[33] Held on the 27th of January, on the 16th of March, 18th of May 2000, etc. See Reports of the DGEI to the Minister.

[34] Giuliano Amato was personally in favour of such an option, but was let down due to Chirac's opposition to it (*Il Sole 24 Ore*, 10 October 2004).

[35] See the Telex from the Italian Embassy in Lisbon as well as Seixas da Costa F.M. (2002): *Diplomacia Europeia,* Dom Quixote, Lisboa.

nism allowing for flexibility, there was a risk it would take place outside the Treaties.[36]

Other periodical meetings at the Director General/Ambassadorial level took place between representatives of the Founding States,[37] as well as bilateral meetings with the British.[38] To sum up Cangelosi, Nelli Feroci and Faggiolo, as well as the Head of Cabinet Ambassador Vattani, appear to have been the main negotiators of the Nice Treaty, suggesting to Minister Dini what moves to take. The Minister himself, as we will see, was a major actor during the Nice negotiations, but did not take a leadership role during the IGC process. Likewise, no meetings with the DGEI and the Secretariat of the Undersecretary of State for European Affairs were organized to discuss the IGC. As for the Undersecretary of State, Umberto Ranieri, he called for a couple of informal exchanges of views, but for the most part, he too leaned towards following the advice of the DGIE and leaving the whole issue in their hands. In sum, neither the Minister, the Undersecretary of State nor the President of the Council D'Alema, showed a great deal of activism or initiative; therefore the IGC issue was kept almost completely in the hands of their diplomats. If this could eventually be discussed under the point of view of democratization of Italian institutions, and under a procedural and effectiveness point of view, such a choice (or non-choice) was the most rational behaviour to opt for. Not only are the Farnesina Diplomats the elite body of the Italian Public Administration, but they are well know for their pro-European stance, completely consistent, as seen, with the views of the Parliament and the Government.

Things appear to have partially changed—yet with DGEI and the Permanent Representative still playing a major role—with the arrival of Professor Giuliano Amato to the Presidency of the Council. One of the leaders—of the project on the simplification of the Treaties undertaken at the EUI—took a much more active stance and direct role in the IGC business than his predecessor. For instance, he meet with Aznar on the 9th of June in Naples, just before the Feira European Council, to establish cooperation wherever possible (for instance on the need to include reinforced cooperation on the agenda). Amato also lobbied his counterpart on the issue of extending QMV,

---

[36] DGEI Reports, ex in occasion of the Meeting of the Personal Representatives of the 6th June.

[37] Especially the one organized in Paris on the 28-29th of April 2000, see note from DGEI to the Minister.

[38] For example on the 28th April: Cangelosi-Sheinwald (of the Foreign Office), see note to the Minister from the DGEI on 12 May 2000.

an issue about which Spain was rather cold.[39] A few days before the European Council in Nice, Amato and Aznar also sent a joint letter to Chirac regarding the need for an EU policy for immigration. In addition, a German-Italian Non-Paper was drafted asking for "a more precise delimitation of competences between the EU and the Member States; the further treatment of the Charter of Fundamental Rights; a better separation of powers between the institutions of the EU; a simplification of the Treaties."[40] The text was then approved by the European Council as a Declaration.

Finally, a novelty was introduced by the Nice IGC, also reproduced during the work leading to the new European Constitution, namely the activism of the President of the Republic Carlo Azelio Ciampi. The President in Italy is more of an honorary figure and a symbol of Italian unity than a concrete policymaker (Baldassare, 1997, pp. 219-269). Nevertheless, President Ciampi intervened several times in Italy and abroad about the theme of the IGC; for instance he gave a major speech at the University of Bologna on the 8th of February where he affirmed the need to reform and deepen the Union before enlarging it, and claimed the need for a European Federation of Democratic nations.[41]

Not only did President Ciampi publicly intervene on the theme of the ICG, but he also extensively 'lobbied' his European counterparts on the issue, marking another Copernican revolution for the Italian Constitutional and political custom. For instance, in a letter dated of 4th February 2000, Ciampi wrote to President Chirac reminding him how "there is an historical responsibility to keep faithful[42] with the original political project that brought together France, Germany, Italy an the other founding States" and asking him (as well as the German President) to act positively towards such a goal, by "following the IGC closely and in a visible way, and using institutional occasions as well as encounters with relevant personalities" to talk about the IGC.

Aproaching Nice, the Italian EU political diplomatic efforts mounted; for instance, most of the documents circulated in those last and preceding hours

---

[39] See note of the DGEI.

[40] See *German-Italian Non-Paper on the Post-Nice Treaty*.

[41] Segretariato Generale della Presidenza della Repubblica, Ufficio per la Stampa e l'Informazione: I discorsi del Presidente della Repubblica Italiana Carlo Azelio Ciampi." Intervento in occasione della Consegna al Capo dello Stato del 'Sigillo' dell'Università degli Studi di Bologna, Bologna-Uniersità, 8 February 2000.

[42] In the original version: 'mantenere la fedeltà'.

had an Italian signature.[43] In December, given the sharp contrasts among some of the Member States and the consequent risk of total failure, Italy's priority had become to actually achieve an agreement. Reduced to a wheel-chair because of back-pain, Amato as mentioned arrived in Nice with a strong mandate from the Parliament, as all political forces, except *Rifondazione Comunista,* had approved a motion supporting the Government's action. In addition, the Italian delegation could count on an authoritative Foreign Minister. Dini had in fact given his Diplomats a free hand in the previous months, but his past as Prime Minister, coupled with Amato's authority and negotiating skills gave the Italian Delegation a special status,[44] similar to the one that it used to have until the beginning of the 1990s, when authoritative and skilled politicians like Andreotti would either be President of the Council, or Foreign Minister[45]. In addition, as mentioned, the Italian delegation also included the most skilled Farnesina EU *sherpas*;[46] as a consequence, the Italian delegation's role as a mediator was praised in Nice by Chirac, Jaime Gama and Pierre Moscovici among others (*Il Sole 24 Ore,* 10 December 2000; *La Stampa* 8 December 2000). According to Moravcsik, high politics deals take place when the interests of the large EU States coincide; in this case, the Italian interests' were considered to be the European ones. As Umberto Ranieri put it, "The Italian interests are defended by promoting the European interest" (*Il Sole 24 Ore,* 10 December 2000). As the Italian President of the Council would comment at the end of the European Council, "We passed through a narrow road[47] [...] on the QMV we could have done better; still, in Nice, the possibilities for the future opened again" (*Il Sole 24 Ore* of 12 December 2000). a remark similar to Prodi's "I can not hide a cer-

[43] For instance the one on the re-weighting of the votes in the Council after enlargement and the one on the Post-Nice agenda (*Il Giornale*, 10 December 2000).

[44] Because of his negotiating skills Amato had been renamed Dr. Sottile or Eta-Beta (from the Disney cartoons). Of the praises from the other leaders, the best quote comes from the leading newspaper of the Italian opposition, usually not nice to Amato, considering it had joked about the wheel-chair issue: "All clapping hands for the Amato-Dini pair" (*Il Giornale*, 10 December 2000).

[45] At the calling of the IGC for the SEA, Milan 1985: Andreotti Foreign Minister, Craxi Premier; during the prenegotiations and negotiations for the TUE Andreotti Premier De Michelis Foreign Minister. On Andreotti's role in the IGC, cf. Margaret Thatcher's Memories (1993).

[46] On this point, see *Il Giornale*, 12 December 2000, the newspaper owned by the Berlusconi family and usually a severe critic of the centre-left.

[47] On the 20th of November, at EUI he said: "In Nice we will have to pass through a narrow road." Cf. *Il Sole 24 Ore* of 21 November 2000.

tain regret for not having achieved more in the extension of QMV" (*Il Sole 24 Ore* of 12 December 2000).

CONCLUSIONS

At the end of the Nice European Council, the President of the Council Amato affirmed, "I am now expecting a non-enthusiastic approval of the Treaty from the Italian Parliament" (*Il Sole 24 Ore* of 13 December 2000). The law ratifying the Nice Treaty landed at the Parliament on the 17th September of 2001. It was approved in the Chamber on the 26th of March 2002, with 298 votes in favour, 7 against and 6 abstentions.[48] In the Senate the discussion took place on the 7th of May and also concluded with a positive vote.[49] Though the Italian political forces had expected more from the IGC, they, nevertheless, supported the Treaty. What can be drawn, then, as a conclusion?

Italy is (or at least, it was until recently) a country where the political forces have long and overwhelmingly been in favour of European integration. Nice was no exception. The Nice case also confirms that despite this, Europe is considered a technical issue to be left to the expert and skilled Diplomats in the Farnesina. According to one of them, the now retired Ambassador Sergio Romano, "Italians are pro-European in the same way they are catholic—Europe has become a sort of religious icon in front of which politicians briefly kneel before talking about other things" (Romano, 1994). As several authors have pointed out (Blondel and Muller-Rommel, 1991; Blondel and Thiébault, 1991), Italian politicians are rather locally minded in their actions. Diplomats are therefore the back-bone of Italian EU high politics and try to act as default in EU low politics. Clearly, with the multiplication of EU policies, this role is far better achieved at the high politics level than at the low level, daily policy-making. In other words, domestic politics and the domestic political culture determine the way a country negotiates.

Yet, the Nice case also suggests that the individual actors make a difference; Amato, far more internationally minded that any other Italian politician and technically skilled in EU affairs, took a strong, personal role in the negotiations and was acknowledged by the other EU leaders. But also the Foreign Minister Dini, though he left the daily negotiations to his diplomats, played a major role when he was to negotiate. Finally, the Nice case shows that Italy

---

[48] In favour: Alleanza Nazionale, Democratici di Sinistra, Forza Italia, Lega, Margherita, UDC. Against: Rifondazione Comunista and part of the Mixed Group. www.banchedati.camera.it

[49] Legge n. 102 del 11 Maggio 2002, G.U. n. 126 del 31 Maggio 2002.

played a major role and that national interests were seen as coinciding with the European ones.

In sum, therefore, the Italian case in the Nice negotiations is not consistent with Moravcsik's assumptions, as it clearly shows how it is domestic politics and political culture, as well as the political leaders' personal input, that matter.

BIBLIOGRAPHY

Baldassare, A. (1997), "Il Capo dello Stato", in G. Amato and A. Barbera, *Manuale di Diritto Pubblico. II L'organizzazione costituzionale,* 5a ed. Bologna: Il Mulino.

Bindi, F. (2001), "L'Italia e l'attuazione delle politiche europee," in P. Cacace, and G. Mammarella (eds.), *L'Unione Europea nel 2000.* Firenze: Le Lettere.

— and M. Cisci (2004), "Italy, Spain and the EU: a Comparative analysis", in S. Bulmer and C. Lequesne (eds.), *Member States and the European Union.* Oxford: Oxford University Press.

— (2000), "L'influenza italiana nei processi decisionali UE," *Europa-Europe,* Anno VIII, N. 3, Roma.

— (forthcoming 2005), *L'Italia e l'Unione Europea.*

Blondel, J. and F. Muller-Rommel, eds. (1991), *Cabinets in Western Europe.* London: Houndsmills, Basingstoke and Macmillan.

— and J.-L. Thiébault, eds. (1991), *The Profession of Government Minister in Western Europe,* London: MacMillan.

Grottanelli de Santi, G. (1992), "The impact of EC integration on the Italian form of governament," in Francioni, F. (ed.), *Italy and EC membership evaluated.* London: Pinter Publishers.

Hoffmann, S. (1966), *Obstinate or Obsolete? The Fate of the Nation-State and the Case of Western Europe? DAEDALUS*, Summer, pp. 862-915.

— (1982), "Reflections on the Nation-State in Western Europe today," *Journal of Common Market Studies*, Vol. 21.

Moravcsik, A. (1991), "Negotiating the Single European Act", in R.O. Keohane and S. Hoffmann (eds.), *The New European Community. Decisionmaking and Institutional Change*. Oxford: Westview Press.

— (1998), *The Choice for Europe: Social purpose and state power from Messina to Maastricht*. Ithaca, N.Y.: Cornell University Press.

— and K. Nicolaidis (1999), "Explaining the Treaty of Amsterdam: Interests, Influence, Institutions," *Journal of Common Market Studies*, Vol. 37, No. 1, pp. 59-85.

Romano, S. (1994), *L'Italia scappata di mano.* Milano: Longanesi.

Santoro, C. M.(1989), *La politica estera di una media potenza. L'Italia dall'Unita' ad oggi.* Bologna: Il Mulino.

Stirk, M.R. (1996), *A History of European Integration since 1914*. London: Pinter.

Thatcher, M. (1993), *The Downing Street Years.* London: Harper Collins.

CHAPTER 11

LUXEMBOURG: BALANCING EU AND NATIONAL INTERESTS

Issues relating to European integration have never really given rise to heated debates between the main political parties in Luxembourg. Traditionally they share a pro-integrationist approach and do not oppose each other on questions relating to European integration. Thus, the positions of Luxembourg did not fundamentally change after the general elections held in June 1999 when as a result of which, the Socialist party was replaced, after 15 years of uninterrupted government membership, by the Liberal party as junior partner of the Christian Democrats in the coalition forming the new government.

The debates in Parliament on the ratification bill bear witness to this general consensus on European matters. The fact that the bill ratifying the Treaty was approved by 57 out of the 60 members of the 'Chambre des Députés', with two abstentions and a single vote in the negative by a communist member of parliament—who did so considering the Treaty did not go far enough on the substance—is further proof of this fact of political life in Luxembourg. From a national perspective, the main parties expressed great satisfaction with the more specific results of the negotiations as the Treaty retained those elements which had been identified as important for Luxembourg. From a more European point of view, the disappointment was tempered by the prospect of the larger debate on the future of Europe which was to be launched in the aftermath of the Summit.

This contribution aims to set out the positions which the Luxembourg government took during the course of the negotiations either individually or as a member of the Benelux. The government issued two memoranda of its own, the first in November 1999 and the second in September 2000, and also contributed to two Benelux memoranda dated December 1999 and September 2000.

For the purpose of this contribution, we shall first address the so-called Amsterdam left-overs before turning to some other topics which were of particular interest to Luxembourg in the course of these negotiations.

THE AMSTERDAM LEFT-OVERS

Size and Composition of the European Commission

Luxembourg's position on the question of size and composition of the Commission was particularly clear-cut. In its first memorandum, Luxembourg stated that it would insist on maintaining the right for every Member State to appoint a Commissioner who would have a full voting right in a Commission deciding by simple majority. It went on rejecting, on account of the legitimacy and acceptability of the institution in the eyes of the public, the idea of creating 'junior' and 'senior' commissioners or commissioners without portfolio.

In its second memorandum, issued in view of the Biarritz informal summit, it amplified its explanation as to why it considers it necessary for every country to be able to appoint a commissioner: in order to be able to express the common interest. By this point, Luxembourg's insistence was not only meant as a defence of its 'own' Commissioner but stemmed from a perception that a Commission in which for instance one of the large countries was not 'represented' would inevitably be a weak Commission and this could not be in Luxembourg's interest.

However, this dispute having been summarized by the French Minister for European Affairs, Mr. Pierre Moscovici, as a clear choice between 'dessert ou fromage'[1], Luxembourg was not ready to enter into this dietary logic. It did accept a more efficient organisation of the Commission but it argued that this power should be left to the President of the Commission, thereby enhancing his status. In order to preserve the necessary flexibility, Luxembourg believed any new form of organisation should not be laid down in the treaty.

The question of equality between Member States became thus the central issue and one about which Luxembourg, as others, could not negotiate. In the September 2000 Benelux Memorandum, the three countries reiterated their objection to the introduction of any sort of hierarchy among the members of the Commission and insisted vigorously on maintaining equality between Commissioners. On the same occasion they refused any distinction relating to the nomination procedure of the members of the Commission.

Even though in the end certain apprehensions remained about the agreed solution, the formula developed in the course of the Nice Summit provided

[1] The choice being between a reduced Commission or a large Commission with a degree of hierarchy between its members.

an equal rotation between members of the Commission and, thus, covered what had become the main point of the discussions. The importance of this guaranteed equality was also underlined in all the parliamentary documents issued in the course of the ratification procedure[2] as well as during the debates in Parliament.

Luxembourg was also satisfied with the new Article 217, para 2, which granted the President of the Commission additional powers in structuring and organizing the work of the Commission and thus providing the tools for the required flexibility of an efficient institution. In general, the government considered the new status of the President of the Commission a major improvement.

The Reweighting of Votes in the Council

The Amsterdam Protocol on Enlargement established a link between the large countries' loss of their right to appoint a second Commissioner and the question of a reweighting of their share in the votes. Luxembourg obviously did not contest this linkage. However, already in its first memorandum in December 1999 it set certain limits to an excessive reweighting by arguing that other linkages exist which should be taken into account in the context of this discussion.

For instance, according to the wording of Article 189 TEC, the continued strengthening of the powers and the role of the European Parliament would eventually increase the weight of the representatives of the peoples of the States brought together in the Community. The demographic factor is thus already reflected in the composition of the European Parliament and the Treaty itself clearly establishes a linkage between its members and the States they represent.

Of the two formulas suggested by the Protocol, Luxembourg clearly favoured the second, i.e. the double majority system and more particularly the simple double majority where a decision is adopted when it is carried by a majority of States representing a majority of the population. Such a system would have the advantage of being objective, simple and durable in the sense that, with each accession, the number of votes for each new Member State is determined automatically and would not give rise to difficult negotiations.

Furthermore, Luxembourg considered that a system based on such a double majority would reflect the dual nature of the Union: a union of Member States and of peoples. In its memorandum dated September 2000, the Government wrote for instance that demography should not represent the only

---

[2] Documents parlementaires 4783.

criterion by which the legitimacy of decisions within the European Union could be judged.

The reweighting that was eventually decided upon at Nice does take this duality into account although it complicates matters substantially: in effect, it introduces the two steps of decision-making from the double majority by providing that a decision shall be adopted if it gathers 169 votes representing a majority of Member States. To establish whether a decision can be adopted, it will first be checked whether a majority of Member States will approve the decision and then it will be tested against the criterion of numbers of votes. The third criterion, the demographic threshold of 62% does not fundamentally affect the position of a country like Luxembourg, except maybe in that it adds a hurdle to the decision-making process and, thus, makes it less efficient. Even that critique is tempered by the fact that in the Union of 12 Member States, the demographic level minimally represented by a qualified majority was 63.2%.

The fundamental point for Luxembourg was the need to have the majority of Member States as part of the voting formula which, with the weighting applicable at that time de facto always guaranteed, and as this provision was included at the last moment, the proposal seemed acceptable, given all the constraints with which the negotiators had to deal.

The fact that Luxembourg was granted four votes, which puts it within the group of countries with a population far larger than its own, was obviously an element that helped Luxembourg accept a withdrawal from its position as regards claiming simple double majority. However, it should be pointed out, as did the French Presidency's first proposal in Nice, that granting Luxembourg only three votes would not have been fair as all other countries either doubled or tripled their existing votes whereas Luxembourg's vote would have gone only from two to three.

Extension of Qualified Majority

This question was added to the agenda as a consequence of a joint declaration made by Belgium, France and Italy at the time of the Amsterdam Summit. It was to be one of the few points on which the position of Luxembourg would be less adamant, although in the end Luxembourg did agree and even suggested a whole series of moves towards decision-making by qualified majority vote. Among these should figure most prominently the suggestion made by Prime Minister Juncker in the final round at Nice to have the President of the Commission appointed by qualified majority, as well as most other high level appointments within the European institutions, such as the High Representative/Secretary General of the Council. Also as a positive contribution to this debate, it should be recalled that the Benelux countries in their second Memorandum pleaded for the extension of qualified majority voting to at least the following areas: free movement of people as regards asylum and immigration, environment policy, common commercial policy and social policy (taking into consideration the different national systems).

During the whole IGC, the Luxembourg Government did not hide its opposition to a generalized move towards qualified majority and kept pleading the more realistic case by case approach, clearly drawing a line where decisions would imply parliamentary sovereignty on topics such as taxation, social security or on questions implying military deployments. In both of its contributions, Luxembourg also insisted on unanimity for decisions regarding the Union's own resources. The government also excluded from the field of application of qualified majority voting questions of a constitutional nature, such as modifications to the Treaties, accession of new Member States and some institutional aspects. Among the latter, one would have expected Luxembourg to oppose any attempt to move to qualified majority on Article 289 TEC regarding the seats of the institutions.

Finally, ever the faithful defendant of the Commission, Luxembourg insisted on maintaining unanimity as regards article 250, i.e. to allow the Council to modify a Commission proposal.

Luxembourg argued, individually and with its Benelux partners, for the extension of the codecision procedure in all legislative fields to which qualified majority voting would apply.

Other Issues Relevant to Luxembourg

European Parliament Seats

The Amsterdam Treaty set the threshold of members of the European Parliament at 700. In view of enlargement this obviously meant that every Member State would lose a certain number of seats presently held by a Member State in order to accommodate the new Member States' representatives. At the time of the Amsterdam negotiations, however, a sentence was added on the initiative of the Luxembourg negotiators at the end of Article 190 para 2 which states that in case of amendment to the allocation of seats per Member State, the number of representatives from each Member State shall ensure an appropriate representation of the peoples brought together in the Community.

Having only six MEPs, Luxembourg considered that this number was an absolute minimum and could not envisage losing even one seat. It argued that the democratic process of the European Parliament elections would be rendered meaningless if the number of seats allocated to the country was smaller than six. The spectrum of national political parties needs to be represented on the European sphere in order to keep interest in these elections alive.

Another argument advanced by Luxembourg is the fact that with six MEPs a significant participation of a nation's representatives in the parliamentary committees and bodies is already illusory but with anything less than six it becomes meaningless.

At the end of the day, Luxembourg and Germany were the only countries whose number of representatives in the Parliament was not reduced as a result of the whole negotiation.

This fact was underlined, and rightly so, as a major achievement of the Luxembourg negotiators at Nice. All political parties stressed the importance of this point and expressed their appreciation of the result.

Enhanced Cooperation

Although the provisions regarding the closer cooperation mechanism introduced by the Treaty of Amsterdam had never been used as such, Luxembourg was among those countries advocating changes to them. In its various contributions, Luxembourg always insisted on the need for a few countries to be able to push ahead within the existing institutional framework and without thereby creating a two-speed Europe or, worse, a Europe *à-la-carte*. It also stressed that this mechanism should not be seen by those who were not going to be able to participate as a means of setting up a second category of Member States. Consequently, it underlined the inclusive character of the enhanced cooperation mechanism.

Foremost, the Amsterdam mechanism was considered too rigid as, on the one hand, it allowed a country to veto the use of it and, on the other hand, it required the participation of at least half the Member States. Luxembourg thus argued that the veto right should be abolished and that the minimum number of participants should be reduced to eight, independently of the future number of Member States. In its view, the central role of the Commission in the reinforced cooperation mechanism should be seen as sufficient guarantee for the preservation of the common good. This position was also expressed collectively with its Benelux partners in their October 2000 Memorandum.

In its second memorandum, dated September 2000, it introduced a nuance as regards reinforced cooperation within the ambit of the second pillar. In view of preserving the unitary character and the coherence of the Common

Foreign and Security Policy, decisions defining common strategies should be carried unanimously. This was a question of the credibility of Europe's external action. Enhanced cooperation could nevertheless prove to be a useful tool at the stage of implementation of common strategies.

The Judicial Architecture

As host country of the judicial institutions of the European Union, Luxembourg starts any discussion on the architecture of the judicial system with a credibility handicap as it is often perceived as defending the interests of the seat aspect. While it may be true in many institutional discussions that seat aspects tamper with principles, the positions Luxembourg expressed during the course of the Nice IGC on the question of the judicial system were motivated by a conviction that the Court is one of the most important institutions for a small country like Luxembourg whose fundamental interest lies in the equal application of the law to all Member States.

The positions put forward during the discussions on the Friends of the Presidency group thus tried to contribute to a real strengthening of the judicial institutions by helping to find long-term solutions to structural problems.

In both its national memoranda, Luxembourg repeatedly insisted on the necessity of preserving the unitary character of the judicial institutions, objecting thus to certain ideas brought forward in a proposal by the Commission whereby a separate jurisdiction on intellectual property should be established—albeit in Luxembourg, according to Commissioner Bolkestein.

CHAPTER 12

THE NETHERLANDS: FROM PRINCIPLES TO PRAGMATISM

INTRODUCTION[1]

The 1990s were the decade of pragmatism in Dutch EU policies. A businesslike approach, with a keen eye for the huge commercial interests of the trade and agricultural sectors in The Netherlands, has always been the hallmark of the Dutch attitude, whatever its idealistic overtones, but in recent years a lot of 'realism' has gradually gained the upper hand.

On a number of important points the Dutch have smoothly adapted themselves to the reality of European politics, and softened, or dropped long-cherished principles. They have accepted, for instance, a predominant role for the European Council in setting the priorities for the Union; the EU's responsibilities in the areas of security and defence; and the need for flexibility and closer cooperation among a limited number of countries. In addition, they are increasingly in favour of using informal cooperation techniques, such as 'benchmarking,' 'open coordination,' and 'peer pressure' in certain economic areas (like the Lisbon process). Moreover, in addition to the proper Community channels, The Hague is rapidly building up networks of bilateral cooperation. Finally, the 'national interest' is, whenever deemed necessary, openly invoked today. Most of these points would have been unheard of a quarter of a century ago.

A pragmatic, middle-of-the-road position has been taken as well during the preparations of the Treaties of Amsterdam and of Nice.[2] Although the Dutch government considered enlargement to be an essential precondition for the stability and the prosperity of the continent, at the IGCs it tried very hard, as the largest of the smaller and medium-sized member states, to defend its institutional 'rights' in a much wider Union. At the same time, any 'federalist' reference, still fatefully promoted in Maastricht, was quietly relegated into the background.

In this chapter we shall first give an outline of the Dutch approach to the IGC2000, as regards both internal organization, international orientation, and tactics for agenda-setting. Then we discuss in more detail the Dutch preferences for the principal points on the IGC-agenda, followed by an

---

[1] The Introduction is partly based on Pijpers (2001).

[2] See for the Dutch approach to the Treaty of Amsterdam: Langendoen and Pijpers (2002).

impression of the endgame in Nice itself. Thereupon the reactions to Nice in the Dutch Parliament are reviewed, and this section is followed by some concluding paragraphs about the Dutch preferences for the post-Nice agenda.

THE DUTCH APPROACH TO THE IGC2000

The run-up to Nice was conducted by the second 'purple' coalition (1998-2002), consisting of the Labour party (PvdA), the (conservative) Liberal party (VVD), and the smaller (social) Liberal party (D66). The government was headed by prime minister Wim Kok (Labour), one of the architects of EMU (he was the minister of finance during the Dutch Presidency in the months preceding Maastricht), and an outspoken, though unassuming, Europeanist.

Kok had a close relationship with his state secretary (junior minister) for European Affairs in the Foreign Ministry, Dick Benschop (also Labour). Benschop was a busy and, to Dutch standards, unorthodox European networker with excellent negotiation skills. He played an important role during the tough negotiations for the EU's Financial Perspectives (2000-2006) in Berlin, March 1999, which were highly succesful from a Dutch viewpoint. Benschop was widely considered as the eyes and ears of Prime Minister Kok, and took a large share in the preparations for Nice. His ambitions, however, were partly circumscribed by his formal boss, foreign minister Jozias van Aartsen (VVD). Van Aartsen was an appointee of his former party leader Frits Bolkestein, who counted as the foremost Dutch eurosceptic (still very moderate as compared to Danish or British standards) before he was called for service to the European Commission. Though Van Aartsen lacked the intellectual and polemic drive of his eurosceptic godfather, he shared the pragmatic, business-like, and non-ideological approach to the European Union, which has gradually become mainstream thinking in the VVD-party over the past decade (with some notable individual exceptions). The minister of finance Gerrit Zalm (VVD), who increasingly gained influence on European affairs, was built from the same material. From a Dutch viewpoint, shared among a broad party-spectre, the internal market and the EMU should remain the core of the European integration process, founded in a community legal order with certain necessary common institutions and some flanking policies to run them properly, but without a strong political dimension, let alone a federal Political Union.

'Nice' was, like the previous rounds for treaty reform, thoroughly prepared by the Dutch government. The government issued four substantial position papers,[3] in addition to the position documents drafted in collaboration with its Benelux partners.[4] The Parliament was properly briefed from the beginning, but debates there were muffled, while the public at large remained practically silent throughout the preparatory proceedings, as was the case with the previous occasions.

The laborious task of interdepartmental coordination was conducted by an IGC task force set-up in early 1999 at the Ministry of Foreign Affairs, and chaired by state secretary Dick Benschop. One of his principal tasks was to square the viewpoints of ministries, like Justice and Home Affairs, who were keen on preserving their national veto in a predominantly intergovernmental setting, with those of the Foreign Ministry, which is in principle favouring QMV across the board. Internationally the government tried to build coalitions with a wide range of member states, both large and small. Here Benschop's favourite concept of 'network Europe' was put to good use. The principal Dutch institutional preferences were coordinated within the Benelux-framework. The Benelux had regained in this repect a new function since the mid-1990s, but political coordination between the three founding EC members remained shaky, even in formulating their joint interest in a proper institutional representation for the smaller member states. Already in Amsterdam, this had led to a serious dispute between Belgium and the Netherlands, only to be repeated in Nice.

Agenda

The position of the Dutch government, as in any other member state, was the simple fact that the Treaty of Amsterdam had failed in its most essential objective: preparing for enlargement. The heads of state and government proved not to be able to reach agreement on the size and composition of the Commission and the re-weighting of votes in the Council. They did, however, reach agreement on an Institutional Protocol, comprehending that the institutional provisions be reviewed before the first coming enlargement.[5] If the enlargement would be limited to five new members, the protocol envisioned a modest reform of only the Commission and the re-

---

[3] Tweede Kamer, vergaderjaar 1998-1999, 26 559, no. 1; Tweede Kamer, vergaderjaar 1999-2000, 21 501-20, no. 101; Tweede Kamer, vergaderjaar 1999-2000, 26 559, no. 2; Tweede Kamer, vergaderjaar 2000-2001, 26 559, no. 4.

[4] Memorandum from Benelux, Brussels, 7 March 2000, CONFER 4721/00; Memorandum from Benelux, Brussels, 19 October 2000, CONFER 4787/00.

[5] "Protocol on the institutions with the prospect of enlargement of the European Union."

weighting of votes (Article one), whereas if the enlargement would lead to an EU of more than twenty member states, it envisioned a 'comprehensive review' of the institutional provisions, carried out by another IGC (Article two). In addition to the Institutional Protocol, Belgium, France and Italy declared in Amsterdam that a significant extension of qualified majority voting (QMV), as part of reinforcing the institutions, was also indispensable for the EU to be prepared for enlargement.[6] The size and composition of the Commission, the re-weighting of votes, and the extension of QMV—the so-called institutional 'leftovers' of Amsterdam—would in any case be part of the agenda for the IGC 2000. Indeed, the Cologne European Council (3-4 June 1999) confirmed that the IGC should be about the three leftovers, though it could also discuss "other necessary amendments to the Treaties arising as regards the European institutions in connection with the above issues and in implementing the Treaty of Amsterdam."[7]

Initially, most member states believed that the agenda should be confined to the three leftovers (a 'quick fix'). From the outset, however, the Dutch government advocated a much broader agenda, in line with article two of the Institutional Protocol, because several developments since Amsterdam necessitated a 'comprehensive review.'[8] Most notably, as in the meantime accession negotiations had been started or were being prepared with twelve candidate countries, probably leading within a few years to an EU of more than twenty member states. A broad agenda should guarantee that the institutions were reformed to such an extent so as to enable the union to function well after enlargement and to avoid that another IGC had to be convened halfway through the enlargement process, which would delay this process. At the same time, the Dutch government realized the contentiousness of the leftovers and that the agenda should not become unmanageable. After all, the IGC had to be concluded before the end of 2000—again, to avoid a delay in the enlargement process.

So what should the agenda for the IGC, according to the Dutch government, look like? In its second position paper, presented to the Second Chamber on 15 November 1999 and issued to the Conference on 5 March 2000, the Dutch government suggested the following agenda:

---

[6] "Declaration 6 by Belgium, France and Italy on the Protocol on the institutions with the prospect of enlargement of the European Union."

[7] "Presidency conclusions Cologne European Council, 3 and 4 June 1999."

[8] Tweede Kamer, vergaderjaar 1998-1999, 26 559, no. 1; Tweede Kamer, vergaderjaar 2000-2001, 21 501-20, no. 101. The latter contribution was issued to the Conference as CONFER 4720/00 on 6 March 2000: "The IGC 2000: An agenda for internal reforms in the European Union."

- the three leftovers;
- topics related to these issues, such as co-decision and the individual responsibility of Commissioners;
- issues crucial to the proper functioning of the Union in the light of the Treaty of Amsterdam, such as the division of labour in the Court of Justice and sound financial control and management;
- conditions on differentiated cooperation between member states within the framework of the European Union; and
- the institutional and legal provisions related to the European Security and Defence Policy (ESDP) (CONFER 4720/00)

The Dutch government had to try very hard to gather support for its idea of a broad agenda and for the specific issues it wanted to be put on this agenda. The Dutch government already pleaded for a broad agenda in its first position paper of May 1999. Initially, only the Commission and a few member states, among which the Benelux partners and Italy, supported the Dutch government. In realizing its preference, the Commission had insisted on the formation of a group of wise men, in preparation of the IGC, whose report confirmed the Commission's preference on the size and content of the agenda (Gray and Stubb, 2001, 9); the Benelux countries expressed their common preference on the size and content of the agenda in the first Benelux memorandum, originally presented at 6 December 1999.

In the course of the IGC, however, support was gradually growing. Shortly before the European Council of Helsinki (10-11 December 1999), a report of the Finnish Presidency suggested that "other necessary amendments" concerned the following issues: the individual responsibility of Commissioners; the European Parliament (allocation of seats and the extension of the co-decision procedure); the European Court of Justice and the Court of First Instance; and other institutions and bodies (the Court of Auditors in particular).[9] The Finnish report also indicated that there was insufficient support for putting the issue of closer cooperation on the agenda, but the Helsinki European Council stated that the incoming Portuguese Presidency "may propose additional issues to be placed on the agenda of the Conference."[10] The agenda thus remained open, due to the insistence of the Benelux countries, Italy and the Commission (Gray and Stubb, 2001, 9). Indeed, in its report to the Feira European Council (19-20 June 2000), the Portuguese Presidency officially proposed to add the issue of closer cooperation to the agenda, and in Feira the heads of state and government explicitly agreed on placing this issue on the agenda. Though the Presidency had indicated that it would possibly make a similar proposal as regards the

[9] "Efficient institutions after enlargement. Options for the Intergovernmental Conference."

[10] "Presidency conclusions Helsinki European Council, 10 and 11 December 1999."

ESDP, this issue was examined in a process parallel to the IGC until, in the end, the Biarritz European Council of 13 and 14 October 2000. Meanwhile, the size and content of the agenda were now, for the greater part, in line with the Dutch preference.

The Dutch Preferences and Bargaining in the Run-Up to Nice

In the light of unprecedented enlargement, the Dutch government formulated two interests the IGC had to safeguard.[11] First, the EU institutions should be strengthened, preventing a too dominant role of individual member states. Second, the Dutch influence in an enlarged union should be maintained, considering that the Netherlands deserved a strong position because of its demographic and economic weight. These two interests were reflected in the Dutch preferences on the respective issues of the agenda. Let us now take a closer look at these preferences and how the Dutch government tried to realize them during the negotiations.[12] What is striking again is that the Dutch preferences on the issues, just as on the size and content of the agenda, largely corresponded with the preferences of the Benelux partners and the Commission.

The Commission

During the IGC negotiations, two options came up to reform the size of the Commission (the first leftover): a Commission made up of one national from each member state, or a Commission composed of fewer member states than the future number of member states. Initially, the Dutch government adhered to the first option, combined with a strengthening of the internal functioning of the Commission, in particular of the position of the President. In the course of the negotiations, however, it became clear that the negotiators could not avoid discussing a possible future ceiling of the number of Commissioners. A meeting between Kok and Chirac in the context of the Biarritz European Council partly changed the Dutch position on this issue.

[11] Tweede Kamer, vergaderjaar 1998-1999, 26 559, no. 1, p. 4; Tweede Kamer, vergaderjaar 1999-2000, 21 501-20, no. 101, p. 16.

[12] In presenting the Dutch preferences we confine ourselves to the agenda proposed by the Dutch government itself in its second position paper and outlined in the foregoing; though there were some other issues on the agenda, the issues discussed here were the most important. The Dutch preferences are derived from the second, third and fourth position papers: Tweede Kamer, vergaderjaar 1999-2000, 21 501-20, no. 101; Tweede Kamer, vergaderjaar 1999-2000, 26 559, no. 2; Tweede Kamer, vergaderjaar 2000-2001, 26 559, no. 4.

At that meeting, Chirac presented to Kok the possibility of a reduced Commission *in combination with* a rotation system between the member states based on strict equality. Knowing that a reduction of the Commission was probably inevitable in the future, Kok realized that he should seize this opportunity. Up to the end summit in Nice, the Dutch still preferred and propagated one Commissioner per member state, but they could now accept, if combined with a strictly equal rotation system, a future reduction of the Commission.

In the light of the recent crisis of confidence between the European Parliament and the Commission, resulting in the resignation of the Santer Commission in 1999, the Dutch government took the view that the individual responsibility of Commissioners should be established in the Treaty. The President of the Commission should be granted the right, possibly after a vote of no confidence by the Parliament, to dismiss an individual Commissioner.

Re-Weighting of Votes in the Council

To compensate the large member states for the future loss of their second Commissioner, the Institutional Protocol envisaged a modification of the weighting of votes in the Council, either by a re-weighting of the votes or by the introduction of some kind of double majority. The Dutch government preferred a re-weighting of the votes, taking more explicitly into account the differences in population size of the member states, but it did not want to preclude the possibility of a double majority system. The Dutch government had formulated two criteria for the negotiations on this issue: the balance between the large and the small member states should be preserved; and, considering its population size in an enlarged union, the Netherlands should get a relatively greater weight.

Extension of Qualified Majority Voting (in Combination with Co-Decision)

The Dutch government did take the view that, as a general rule, decision-making by unanimity should make way for qualified majority voting, but that certain exceptions could be made to this rule. It especially wanted to extend decision-making by qualified majority voting with regard to the free movement of persons, common trade policy, environmental policy, and certain aspects of social and fiscal policy. Interestingly, what was presented as the 'Dutch interest'—a maximum extension of QMV—was in fact merely the interest of the Foreign and General Ministries, clashing tremendously with the interests of the other ministries – no extension of QMV. A lot of fine-tuning took place on this issue, resulting in a preference that was more extreme than the 'real' preference. In general, the other ministries could accept this relatively extreme preference, because they knew the end result would be less extreme. Related to this issue, the Dutch government was of the opinion that, whenever the Council decides by QMV on legislative acts, the Parliament should have the right of co-decision.

Closer Cooperation

Apart from the three leftovers, probably the highest Dutch priority for Nice was the issue of closer cooperation, or flexibility. The government believed that the provisions on flexibility introduced by the Amsterdam Treaty in fact provided too little flexibility. Already in 1999 the Dutch devised that this issue should be put on the agenda and that the negotiations should result in a relaxation of the conditions for closer cooperation. This relaxation had to consist of mainly two points. Firstly, the requirement that a least a majority of member states must take part in a closer cooperation should be replaced by a minimum of eight member states. Secondly, the possibility for a member state of appealing to the European Council, providing it with a *de facto* veto, should be abolished. The Dutch government did its best to gather support for putting the issue on the agenda. The issue already appeared in its second position paper of November 1999 and it was also part of the first Benelux memorandum. In the course of spring 2000, support for putting the issue on the agenda gradually increased, and the European Council of Feira (19-20 June 2000) officially added it to the agenda. Support was also growing for relaxing the two conditions mentioned, consistent with the Dutch preference. At Biarritz, where the main political agreement was reached, the Dutch government did indeed get what it wanted.

The European Court of Justice and the Court of First Instance

Another important issue, according to the Dutch government, concerned the reform of the organisation of the European Court of Justice and the Court of First Instance, and of the division of labour between these two institutions. The Dutch government deemed this reform necessary in the light of the already existing heavy workload, which had been further increased as a result of the extended competences of the Court of Justice, settled in the Amsterdam Treaty, and which would increase even further after the coming enlargement. The reform of the organisation should particularly consist of the introduction of specialized chambers, and the reform of the division of labour should result in an extension of the responsibilities of the Court of First Instance combined with an diminution of the responsibilities of the European Court of Justice. The Dutch government managed to optimally realize its preference on this issue, which was one of the few reforms settled before the Nice summit, but at the same time one of the most significant reforms agreed upon at the IGC (Gray and Stubb, 2001, 17-18).

The Court of Auditors

Another Dutch priority concerned sound financial control and management in the EU, particularly involving the Court of Auditors. To guarantee sound financial control in an enlarged union, the Court of Auditors should be reformed, consisting of a reduction of its size, a strengthening of its position and internal functioning, and a better cooperation between the Court of Auditors and the national audit institutions. On this issue, the Dutch government did not really get what it wanted. As to size, the principle of one member from each member state was maintained; apart from the possibility for the Court of introducing internal chambers, no real strengthening of the institution took place; and on improving cooperation, only a declaration was adopted.

European Security and Defence Policy

Finally, a high priority for the Dutch government was the development of a European Security and Defence Policy (ESDP). As stated before, this issue, just like the issue of the Charter of Fundamental Rights, was examined during a process parallel to the IGC, and could be added to the agenda later on if amendments to the Treaties were deemed necessary. From the start, the Dutch government took the view that the institutional and legal aspects of the ESDP should be discussed at the IGC, which for certain had to result in amendments to the Treaties. The Dutch interest on this issue was twofold. First, to prevent the formation of informal directories, the ESDP should be embedded in the Treaty. Second, the Treaty should clearly establish the relation between the ESDP and NATO. The government, especially Foreign Minister Van Aartsen, had tried very hard to convince the other member states of its perspective. Ultimately, in the margins of the European Council of Biarritz (13-14 October 2000), a coalition of Italy and the Benelux countries reached agreement on a draft proposal on amendments to articles 17 and 25 TEU, and subsequently presented this to the Conference.

THE DUTCH PREFERENCES AND THE END GAME IN NICE

At the start of the Nice European Council, 7 December 2000, many issues were still on the table and had to be decided on. How can the results of the Nice summit be evaluated as compared to the Dutch preferences? As to the size of the Commission, the heads of state and government decided to have one Commissioner per member state until the EU reaches 27 members, followed by the introduction of a rotation system based on strict equality. Though not completely in line with the original Dutch preference, the result was acceptable for the Dutch government, notably because the strictly equal rotation system—presented to Kok in his meeting with Chirac—was warranted.

The most difficult issue, taking most of the time in Nice, was the re-weighting of votes in the Council. From the start of the discussion on Saturday until its conclusion in the early Monday morning, many proposals were tabled and discussed. From a Dutch perspective, the outcome changed in the course of the negotiations into becoming more in line with the two criteria it had formulated: the balance between the large and the small member states had been improved, and the Netherlands had got one vote more (13) than Belgium (12). As is well known, the latter issue resulted in a major clash with Belgium. In the run-up to Nice, however, the Netherlands and Belgium had discussed two points concerning this issue. First, if Germany would get more votes than France, Belgium would not object to the Netherlands getting more votes than Belgium. Second, irrespective of the result on the first point, the Netherlands would strive for more votes than Belgium. Though Belgium did not agree with the second point, it did know about it. In the end, the extra vote was not disputed any more, due to the reasonableness of the Dutch argument about population size and, presumably, the authority of Kok. With hindsight, the Dutch government had in fact wanted to get 14 votes—Kok discussed this bilaterally with Chirac, considering the roughly equal population size of Romania and the Netherlands—but in the end this proved to be unattainable.

The issue of the allocation of seats for the European Parliament was clearly treated as part of the final compromise on the re-weighting of votes. Thus, besides the fact that the Dutch government did not get what it wanted as to the total amount of seats—it preferred not to break the ceiling of 700 MEPs—it had to accept a relatively big decline of its number of seats (from 31 to 25).

With regard to the extension of QMV, the expectation of the different sectoral ministries came true that the final result was less extreme than the Dutch government, i.e. the Foreign Ministry, had wanted. Though in numerical terms considerable progression was certainly made, on the more sensitive, but Dutch priority issues no agreement was reached (taxation, environment), or only partly (free movement of persons, social security).

Likewise contrary to the Dutch preference, the extension of QMV was only partly coupled with an extension of the co-decision procedure, and no extension was agreed upon as to provisions for which QMV already applied, but the co-decision procedure did not.

In addition to the agreement on closer cooperation reached at Biarritz, Nice decided, in line with the Dutch preference, that closer cooperation within the second pillar be confined to the implementation of joint actions and common positions, and not applied to defence.

As to the ESDP, after having deliberated bilaterally with the Irish delegation, the Dutch government in particular pushed, with success, the tabling of the amendments once again in Nice, which for a considerable part accepted them (Galloway, 2001, 156). However, an amendment to Article 17 TEU concerning the relation with the NATO, in accordance with the Dutch interest mentioned above, did not make it into the final act.

THE DUTCH RECEPTION OF 'NICE'

After the conclusion of the Nice summit, in the early morning of 11 December 2000, Kok described the result as 'a modest step forward.' The Dutch newspapers, however, were considerably less enthusiastic about the result.[13] They doubted the effectiveness of the compromises made and noted that the summit had resulted in a real struggle for power between the different member states. They concluded that, instead of the common European interest, mere self-interest had dominated the negotiations. A clear example of this was the fight of the Dutch delegation to get one vote more than Belgium in the Council. The extra vote was depicted as mere 'symbolic' and the 'victory' as a Pyrrhic victory. In reality, the small member states, not the least the Netherlands, were the losers of the Nice summit, and the big member states, especially Germany, the real winners. More generally, Nice had shown that there were limits to the deepening of the integration process. Without a substantial deepening, however, a widening of the EU after the next enlargement would threaten the cohesion of the union: a Europe 'à la carte' and 'multi-speed' would be inevitable in the future.

The Dutch government did send a report of the Nice summit to the Second Chamber on 12 December 2000. It stated that the institutional adaptations, as agreed upon in Nice, should be sufficient to prepare the EU for enlargement.[14]

---

[13] E.g. "Gestrand in Nice," in: *NRC Handelsblad*, 11 December 2000, p. 7; "Europa na Nice," in: *de Volkskrant*, 12 December 2000, p. 9.

[14] Tweede Kamer, vergaderjaar 2000-2001, 21 501-20, no. 146.

Although on certain issues the Dutch preferences were not fully realized, the Treaty as a whole should be considered as 'a meaningful step forwards'—a slightly different comment than the one given by Kok the day before. The government assessed particularly positively the results on the European Court of Justice and the Court of First Instance, closer (or enhanced) cooperation, ESDP, and the re-weighting of votes in the Council. As regards the future reduction of the Commission, the government indicated that it was partly on the insistence of the Netherlands and Belgium that a rotation system based on strict equality had been warranted. Concerning the extension of QMV, the government admitted that only modest progress had been made.

A plenary debate about the Nice summit took place in the Second Chamber only one day later, on 13 December 2000.[15] Most parties were disappointed about the result of the summit and assessed the new Treaty quite negatively. Although the Treaty formally prepared the union for enlargement, they questioned whether this was also the case in practice. Some parties noticed that Nice, just as Amsterdam, had also created leftovers, to be dealt with at the next IGC of 2004. Many parties stated that the method of Treaty reform had failed—such a meagre result after the longest summit in the history of the EU—and should be changed for the next IGC of 2004. For some eurosceptical parties, SP and SGP, the meagre result of the Nice summit supported their view that the limits to the European integration process had been reached.

For many parties, especially the result on the extension of QMV was disappointing. As regards the re-weighting of votes in the Council, several parties criticized the harsh position taken up by the Dutch government seeking for one vote more than Belgium. They questioned the value of one extra vote and pointed at the sacrifices the Dutch government had made in exchange, such as the considerable reduction of the number of Dutch MEPs. With respect to the size and composition of the Commission, most parties were happy about maintaining of the Dutch Commissioner for the time being and with the safeguarding of an equal rotation system for the EU-27. Concerning other issues, most parties judged positively about the result on closer cooperation and the ESDP. Some parties, on the other hand, regretted the limited extension of the co-decision procedure (as compared with the extension of QMV).

In his answer to the Second Chamber, Kok stated that in many fields the Dutch preferences were realized, though the result on QMV was not as good as the government had wanted. Kok was somewhat amazed about the reaction of the Second Chamber to the extra vote won vis-à-vis Belgium, since the parliament was familiar with the position of the government at this point and had not protested during the deliberation prior to the summit. Kok mentioned

[15] Handelingen 2000-2001, no. 35, Tweede Kamer, pp. 2898-2930.

that he and the Belgian prime minister Verhofstadt had declared after the summit that the incident should not impair the Benelux cooperation and stressed that the cooperation should even be strengthened, since in the future the Benelux countries together would have as many votes (29) as a big member state. Despite this, the Parliament adopted a motion asking the government to strengthen the Benelux cooperation and to develop a strategy accordingly.[16] Kok, together with junior minister Benschop for European Affairs, once again emphasized that the Nice Treaty sufficiently prepared the EU for enlargement. No new leftovers had been created, which otherwise had to be dealt with at the IGC of 2004, delaying the enlargement process. In accordance with this line of reasoning, but contradictory to the criticism expressed earlier in the debate, the parliament rejected a motion requesting the government to try to put the issue of QMV on the agenda of the IGC 2004.[17] It did, however, adopt a motion, though the government dissuaded it from doing so, which stated that that the Nice Treaty did not contain "all desirable institutional reforms" and asked for a governmental report about the coming IGC, paying special attention to the reduction of the democratic deficit.[18] Finally, it was striking that after all the criticism of the IGC method, the parliament rejected a motion requesting the government to look for improvements.[19]

The Treaty of Nice was officially signed on 26 February 2001. On 18 June 2001, the government presented to the Second Chamber the bill authorising the Nice Treaty.[20] In a clarification of the bill, the government called the result on QMV 'meagre.'[21] In addition to its assessment in the report of the Nice summit (see above), the government stated that the Dutch wish to strengthen the European Parliament, particularly by the extension of the co-decision procedure, had only partly been realized. The government was satisfied with the further strengthening of the position of the President of the Commission. Yet a Dutch proposal to give the European Parliament the right to dismiss individual Commissioners had not been successful. Likewise contrary to the Dutch preference was the future extension of the overall size of the European Parliament.

---

[16] Tweede Kamer, vergaderjaar 2000-2001, 21 501-20, no. 151.

[17] Tweede Kamer, vergaderjaar 2000-2001, 21 501-20, no. 148.

[18] Tweede Kamer, vergaderjaar 2000-2001, 21 501-20, no. 150.

[19] Tweede Kamer, vergaderjaar 2000-2001, 21 501-20, no. 149.

[20] Tweede Kamer, vergaderjaar 2000-2001, 27 818 (R 1692), no. 1 and 2.

[21] Tweede Kamer, vergaderjaar 2000-2001, 27 818 (R 1692), no. 3.

The general commission of European Affairs had to deal with the bill first. A report was produced, presenting the general opinion of the different parties and submitting many questions to the government.[22] In another voluminous report, the government in turn gave an answer to these questions.[23] The commission discussed the Treaty of Nice more technically in a deliberation with junior minister Benschop on 12 November 2001.[24] Once again the different parties agreed that the Nicc Treaty formally prepared the union for enlargement, but otherwise it was a meagre Treaty. They questioned the long-term effectiveness of the negotiated reforms, stating that the adoption of Declaration 23 on the future of the EU and a new Treaty reform supported their view. Some parties attributed the meagre result to the selfishness of the different member states. More specifically, attention was paid to the Irish rejection of the Nice Treaty and the possible implications of this for the ratification process.

During the concluding plenary debate on the ratification of the Nice Treaty, on 21 November 2001, the importance parties attached to enlargement became even more visible.[25] In fact, an important, if not decisive, reason for all parties to approve the Nice Treaty was that rejection would probably postpone the enlargement process. This argument especially applied for the Green Left and the eurosceptical, orthodox-protestant parties Christian Union and SGP, who had all voted against the Amsterdam Treaty. For the Christian Union and SGP, another argument was that in their view the Nice Treaty, as compared to the Maastricht and Amsterdam Treaties, did not significantly deepen the integration process. Several parties regretted that the re-weighting of votes had resulted in a more complex decision-making process. Most parties looked upon the post-Nice process and the IGC of 2004 as a new opportunity to reform the union more radically after all. Related to this, a motion was adopted requesting the government to try to put the issue of QMV in combination with co-decision on the agenda of the coming IGC.[26] This was striking, because a large majority had rejected a similar motion during the debate on the Nice summit. At that time, the government explicitly interpreted the issue as creating a new leftover, which would probably delay the enlargement process; now the issue was not

[22] Tweede Kamer, vergaderjaar 2000-2001, 27 818 (R 1692), no. 4.

[23] Tweede Kamer, vergaderjaar 2000-2001, 27 818 (R 1692), no. 5.

[24] Tweede Kamer, vergaderjaar 2000-2001, 27 818 (R 1692), no. 6.

[25] Handelingen 2000-2001, no. 26, Tweede Kamer, pp. 1862-1891.

[26] Tweede Kamer, vergaderjaar 2000-2001, 27 818 (R 1692), no. 10.

interpreted in that way. Besides, two other motions were adopted aimed at diminishing the workload of the European Court of Justice.[27] Furthermore, a motion of the SGP and Christian Union was adopted, calling for a more precise delimitation of powers between the EU and its member states to be made in the future. It asked the government to put forward some proposals making the principle of subsidiarity more concrete.[28] For the SGP, a vote in favor of the Treaty was more or less conditional upon the adoption of this motion. Finally, all parties except the SP ratified the Nice Treaty—the greatest majority in the history of Treaty reforms as far as the Second Chamber is concerned. The SP criticized the elite driven process of European integration, and voted against the Nice Treaty because the party considered it a next step on the road to a federal union, which it opposed.

THE HAGUE AND THE POST-NICE AGENDA[29]

Though the principal business at Nice was about the left-overs (plus closer cooperation, and partly, defence), the heads of government and state turned their minds also to other issues, in particular those related to the follow-up agenda in the process of EU-treaty reform. In a 'Declaration on the Future of the Union,' annexed to the Treaty of Nice, the Fifteen call for a "deeper and wider debate about the future development of the European Union." This debate, which started already in early 2001, should involve, apart from the Community institutions themselves, "representatives of national Parliaments and all those reflecting public opinion; political, economic and university circles, representatives of civil society, etc." The idea was to adopt, following a report by the Swedish Presidency to Gothenburg (15/16 June 2001), a common declaration on the future of the Union in Laeken in December 2001 (under the Belgian Presidency). The debate should address, *inter alia*, the following questions: a more precise delimitation of powers between the Union and the member states; the status of the Charter of fundamental Rights of the EU; simplification of the Treaties ('without changing their meaning'); the role of national Parliaments in the European system.

Though this is not a mandate for a full-fledged debate on the celebrated *finalité politique* of the Union, the future-oriented flavour of the post-Nice

---

[27] Tweede Kamer, vergaderjaar 2000-2001, 27 818 (R 1692), no. 8 and 9.

[28] Tweede Kamer, vergaderjaar 2000-2001, 27 818 (R 1692), no. 11.

[29] This paragraph is largely based on Pijpers (2001).

agenda nevertheless echoes the federalist calls of Joschka Fischer and others over the past year, and it forces the Dutch government to think about certain European matters which she would rather eschew.

As we have seen, the Netherlands have always favoured economic integration based upon strong Community institutions rooted in a firm Community legal order. The Dutch preference for supranational arrangements was and still is mainly restricted to the internal market and some closely related fields, like monetary affairs, the environment, or certain social policies. But the Dutch government has always resisted moves for a stronger *political* union, particularly in the areas of foreign policy and defence, and it has never clearly spelled out the outlines of a European political union. A European Union was useful so long as the concept remained vague and ill-defined.

To the present day this basic attitude has remained by and large the same, and it was, therefore, not surprising that the Dutch reaction to the relaunch of the *finalité*-debate last year was very cool. Foreign minister Van Aartsen thought the May 2000 Berlin-speech of Joschka Fischer unrealistic. He considered a debate on the *finalité politique* not very helpful for the IGC, nor for a better understanding of the European Union by its citizens. After Nice Van Aartsen has repeated this viewpoint. In a speech for the Dutch Society of International Affairs in The Hague on 13 March 2001, he contended that a wide-ranging debate about the future of the Union should not focus on "abstract concepts and remote vistas," but on "bread-and-butter issues" such as food safety, livelihoods, and security in the streets. "I venture to doubt," he said, "whether Brussels will ever see demonstrations for or against a federalist vision of the future, or for or against the European Political Area [*sic*]. Quite simply because that is not uppermost in the minds of most EU citizens."[30] The Dutch State Secretary for European Affairs, Dick Benschop, has, in a similar mood, called a discussion about the final political structure of the Union 'absurd' (*NRC Handelsblad*, 20 March 2001). Many feel that European integration has become so succesful because progress was planned and made step-by-step in concrete projects, without bothering about the final status of the process.

This is not to say, however, that the Dutch government has no ideas at all about the future shape of the Union, or about the desirability of a thorough European debate. But instead of a federal blueprint or a complete catalogue of competences, it prefers progress along charted routes, an 'evolutionary approach.'[31] A number of features stand out.

---

[30] Speech by Jozias van Aartsen, The Hague, 13 March 2001.

[31] *State of the European Union* 2001, p. 15.

Firstly, the present Dutch government considers the national state as the primary framework and reference-point for the organization of political life, particularly for the conduct of democracy. It declares very clearly that the "Member States remain the foundation of the European Union now and in the future."[32]

Secondly, the 'unique' institutional structure of the Union, with its mix of intergovernmental and supranational elements, should essentially remain the same. Changes in the balance between the institutions, and/or between the institutions and the member states may be necessary, but these in themselves should not disrupt the set-up as such. "The succesful Community method continues to be of the greatest importance to the process of European integration."[33] A traditional Dutch preference, this last point, but today it sits slightly uneasily along the open belief in the merits of the nation-state. A similar tension may be perceived between the community orthodoxy and the liberal allowance of bilateral networking and informal integration techniques.

This rather reticent view on the future of the European Union has also trickled down into the Dutch approach to the individual items on the post-Nice agenda, particularly regarding the *Kompetenzkatalog*, the status of the Charter of Fundamental Rights, and the possibility of creating some sort of Senate.

The Hague is not very happy with the idea of drawing up a *Kompetenzkatalog*, which is pressed upon the Fifteen by the German Länder, concerned about the loss of power at each successive round of EU-treaty reform. It is feared that the exercise could lead to endless squabbling, and eventually to an unduly rigid division of power between the Union and the member states, which could paralyse the integration process. Moreover, the government is not in favour of a significant further transfer of competences to the European level, either in the existing or in any new policy sector. If new policies are called for, these should be dealt with primarily in a national context, using the European Union only as a means for coordinating national positions and for setting broad guide-lines. However, a sound and clear division of responsibilities between the Union and its member states, based upon the principles of subsidiarity and proportionality, may enhance the transparancy of the European institutions, and contribute to their legitimacy. As such it will also help to simplify the treaties.

The Dutch government opposed on the eve of Nice the call to give the Charter of Fundamental Rights a legal basis. However, it is prepared to

---

[32] *State of the European Union*, p. 14.

[33] *State of the European Union*, p. 8.

discuss the legal status of this charter as part of a possible further process of constitutionalization of the European Union. It does not reject a European Constitution out of hand, but considers such an instrument much more as a refined codification of the existing treaties, which "would have the benefit of conferring visible legitimacy on the activities by the Union and its institutions in the eyes of Europe's citizens," than as a new political and legal source for the generation of European legislation.[34] The Dutch government uses the concept of a 'constitution,' therefore, in a completely different way than Fischer did.

A similar remark can be made on the proposals for a European Senate. Here we see in the current European debate widely different meanings attached to the same label. Some consider the present Council as a senate-in-being; others use the term for a second chamber of the European Parliament. The Dutch have mixed feelings. On the one hand it is felt that a European Parliament with two chambers, one consisting of the directly elected representatives of the people, and the other (the Senate) of representatives of the member states, could enhance the democratic process in Europe. A Senate might serve as a "balance in the institutional field by countering any unduly centralizing tendencies."[35] On the other hand it is realized that in a field already flooded with representative bodies (Council, European Parliament, Committee of the Regions, comitology), an additional chamber is not very helpful for the transparency of decisionmaking. In the Second Chamber of the Dutch Parliament the idea of a Senate is seen as a possibility to better control the developments in the intergovernmental second and third pillars. But the Dutch Members of the European Parliament strongly oppose the construction, which, indeed, still leaves more questions open than it can answer. Can anybody conceive a European Senate with, for instance, effective powers in defence, a field where even the national parliaments in London or Paris have a subdued role?

Whether the post-Nice agenda will really trigger a 'deeper and wider debate' on the future of the European Union in The Netherlands is highly doubtful. European economic integration, and the legislation this entails, is since the beginning taken for granted by broad sections of the population to such an extent that a debate on the core business of the European Union has never emerged. Only a few academics doubt the blessings of the EMU, and criticism arises from time to time in areas where the Dutch cherish some national habits, like police cooperation in criminal matters. More recently objections are raised as well against the ways the Common Agricultural

[34] *State of the European Union*, p. 14.

[35] *State of the European Union*, p. 15.

Policy is being conducted, particularly its implications for food safety and animal welfare. But generally speaking, a truly European debate is non-existent in Dutch society. As such the Dutch experience differs widely from, for instance, the British record. Even the process of enlargement is hardly discussed (to the regret of the Foreign Ministry), let alone the remote vistas opened in Nice.

BIBLIOGRAPHY

Galloway, D. (2001), *The Treaty of Nice and Beyond. Realities and Illusions of Power in the EU.* Sheffield: Sheffield Academic Press.

Gray, M. and A. Stubb (2001), "Keynote Article: The Treaty of Nice – Negotiating a Poisoned Chalice?", *Journal of Common Market Studies*, Vol. 39, Annual Review, pp. 5-23.

Langendoen, M. and A. Pijpers (2002), "The Netherlands: The Mixed Fruits of Pragmatism," in F. Laursen (ed.), *The Treaty of Amsterdam. National Preference Formation, Interstate Bargaining and Outcome.* Odense: Odense University Press, pp. 267-289.

Pijpers, A. (2001), "Evolution or Constitution? Dutch Pragmatism and the Debate on the Future," in M. Bond and K. Feus (eds.), *The Treaty of Nice Explained.* London: Federal Trust, pp. 187-199.

CHAPTER 13

PORTUGAL: THE FIGHT AGAINST THE 'BIG' ONES

INTRODUCTION

The main purpose of this paper is to analyse the positions that Portugal took before and throughout the negotiation of the Treaty of Nice. It then focuses on the internal ratification process of the Treaty, and concludes with a discussion of the Treaty's implications for Portugal and the debate about the future of Europe.

In order to clarify the present situation, we are briefly delineating the background of Portugal's participation in the process of European integration from adhesion to the Treaty of Amsterdam.

BACKGROUND

After eight years of hard negotiations, begun in March 1977, Portugal finally signed the Accession Treaty to the European Communities in June 1985, at Mosteiro dos Jerónimos. The Treaty came into effect on the 1st January 1986, and Portugal became the eleventh member of the European Communities. Consequently, Portugal could already sign the Single European Act, in February 1986, as a full Member State.

Since entering the EU a large consensus had been formed in the political arena about the participation of Portugal in the European Communities. The two major parties (the Socialist Party and the Social Democratic Party) that altogether had more than two-thirds of members of Parliament (*Assembleia da República*) have always been in favour of European integration, and this was also the case with some minor parties represented in Parliament. The sole discordant voice came from the Communist Party.

As an example, the Accession Treaty was ratified—the Communists being the only exception—by all the members of Parliament (Socialists, Social Democrats, Christian Democrats, and by members of two smaller parties—UEDS (*União de Esquerda Democrática e Socialista*) and ASDI (*Associação Social Democrata Independente*).[1] The same near-unanimity occurred

[1] See the debate and the voting *in Diário da Assembleia da República*, I Série, nos. 105 and 106 of 10 and 11 July 1985.

with the Single European Act.[2] Likewise, all Portuguese governments, whatever their political colour, had considered European integration as a priority.

The strong will of belonging to the European Communities can be illustrated with the first revision of the Constitution as well. In 1982, i.e. three years before the adhesion, Portugal anticipated the reform of its 1976 Constitution,[3] with the aim of eliminating the provisions incompatible with the EC Treaties and introducing some new articles considered necessary for the accession.[4] Indeed, Portugal wanted to make the Constitution agree with the European Treaties, even before the accession.[5]

However, the debate about European integration within Portuguese civil society had been very unclear and poorly informed.

The subsequent revisions of the European Treaties, especially the Treaty of Maastricht, provoked a more enthusiastic discussion, since the amendments had been deeper and wider, not only on economic matters, but also regarding the political issues. Concerning the Treaty of Maastricht, some politicians had defended holding a referendum about the participation of Portugal in the European Union, based on the fact that the Treaty would impose such a significant transfer of sovereignty from the Member States to the Union that the people should have the opportunity to pronounce themselves in favour or not. Nevertheless, by that time the Portuguese Constitution did not permit a referendum when the ratification of a treaty was in question.[6] So instead of a referendum the politicians concentrated their efforts on the revision of the Constitution. In order to be ratified, the Treaty of Maastricht in fact imposed another reform of the Portuguese Constitution[7] (the third), since some provisions of the Treaty were inconsistent with the Portuguese Constitution (see Miranda, 1996, and Duarte, 1993).

Since the Communist party was completely against the Treaty, it tried to prevent its ratification by blocking the revision of the Constitution, which it did not achieve.

---

[2] See the debate and the voting *in Diário da Assembleia da República*, I Série, n. 23, of 18 December 1986.

[3] Constitutional Law no. 1/82 of 30.9.82.

[4] On this reform of the Portuguese Constitution see Gomes Canotilho, 1999, and Miranda, 1997b.

[5] For the implications of European integration in our Constitution see Mota de Campos, 1985, Vitorino, 1984, Jalles, 1981, and Jalles, 1980.

[6] Article 118, currently 115

[7] Constitutional Law no. 1/92 of 25.11.92.

Only after that revision (see Gomes Canotilho, 1999, and Miranda, 1997b) did *Assembleia da República* ratify the Treaty by an overwhelming 200-21 majority. The Treaty was favourably voted for by members of the Socialist Party, the Social Democratic Party and the independent Diogo Freitas do Amaral.[8]

The subsequent revision of the Treaty—the Treaty of Amsterdam—could have been ratified without a constitutional reform, as observed by Miranda (1997a, 151), since no amendment came into conflict with our Constitution. However, *Assembleia da República* assumed extraordinary powers of revision in 1996 and approved the fourth constitutional revision in 1997.[9]

One of the amendments introduced accepted the holding of a referendum on the treaties (currently Article 115, no. 5).

In the process of that amendment a rather strong movement appeared in favour of asking the people whether or not the Treaty of Amsterdam should be ratified. After a generalised discussion, where the arguments for and against the treaty had been exhaustively enunciated, the Portuguese Parliament decided for the approval of a referendum resolution.[10] Voters would be asked to take a position on the following question:

> Do you agree with the continuation of Portugal's participation in the construction of the European Union in the framework of the Treaty of Amsterdam?

Under the Portuguese constitution, a referendum proposal must be submitted to the Constitutional Court in order to assess its constitutionality.[11] In this case, the Constitutional Court decided the question was not objective enough, concluding that the referendum was unconstitutional.[12]

As a result, the Treaty of Amsterdam was subject solely to the approval of the national Parliament[13] followed by ratification by the President of the Republic.[14] Once again, the Treaty was approved with the votes of the Socialist Party, the Social Democratic Party and some of the Social Democratic Centre (now named Popular Party). Opposing the Treaty were MPs from the

---

[8] See the debate and voting *in Diário da Assembleia da República*, I Série, n. 18 and 19 of 10 and 11/12/92.

[9] Constitutional Law n. 1/97 of 20.9.97.

[10] Resolution n. 36-A/98 of 30.6.98.

[11] Article 115, n. 8 Constitution.

[12] Sentence n. 531/98 of 30-7-98. For a commentary of this sentence see Duarte, 2000.

[13] Resolution n. 7/99 of 6.1.99.

[14] Decree nº 65/99 of 19.2.99.

Communist Party, the Greens and some MPs from the Social Democratic Centre.[15]

To conclude, we would like to point out that whereas the Treaty of Maastricht had been negotiated by the 12th Government, which was a Government of the Social Democratic Party, the negotiation of the Treaty of Amsterdam occurred during the end of the mandate of that Government and the beginning of the 13th Government. In 1995 the Socialist Party won the elections and as a consequence formed a Government.

The Socialist Party has traditionally been much more open to European integration and to international affairs in general than the Social Democratic Party. This had clear consequences in the negotiation strategy of the treaties of Amsterdam and Nice.

In the case of the Treaty of Amsterdam, whose negotiation had already begun when the Socialist Party came into the Government, the negotiation process went on with neither breaks nor major changes in positions because, as we have already stressed, there existed (and still exists) a general consensus between these two parties concerning the process of European integration.

The negotiation of the Treaty of Nice occurred during the mandate of the 14th Government, which was a Government of the Socialist Party.

The Negotiation of the Treaty of Nice

Initially, we should point out that because Portugal took over the Presidency of the Union in the first half of the year 2000, it is rather difficult to draw a clear line between the position of the country as a Member State and the work of the Presidency as such, which was supposed to be neutral.

The Role of Portugal during the Portuguese Presidency

Before enunciating Portugal's positions regarding each issue, we should mention that Portugal considered the current institutional balance quite satisfactory, despite the acceptance of the generalised idea that future enlargement would impose some institutional modifications. Moreover, it is also important to underline that on the most relevant matters, Portugal has advocated the same positions about the Union since its accession. Hence, Portugal's position throughout the IGC 2000 did not substantially differ from po-

---

[15] See the debate and voting in *Diário da Assembleia da República*, I Série, n. 31, of 7/1/1999.

sitions taken during the previous IGC 1996,[16] which does not necessarily mean that the evolution of the negotiation and the general changes in the world situation have not led to any detour from the initial framework.

As a matter of fact, the Government of the Socialist Party assumed a more positive perspective, accepting the idea of more Europe. As Seixas da Costa points out (2001), by the beginning of the negotiation, Portugal was supporting the following positions:

First, Portugal agreed that unanimity should be reserved only to the provisions concerning taxation, social issues, justice and home affairs and economic and social cohesion matters, which means that Portugal was not against the extension of qualified majority voting. In view of Portugal's size, this position could be seen as a position of weakness and even somewhat contradictory. However, it could be explained by the fact that Portugal also represented a part of the common interest of the Union. In addition, for a small country, it is rather hard to exercise the right of veto in practice.

Second, Portugal defended the review of the enhanced cooperation mechanisms. That could be understandable, taking into account our permanent desire to remain in the core of the EU (see, for instance, the cases of Schengen and the monetary union). In other words, Portugal was terribly afraid of being excluded. In reality, a small country would rather settle for some clear rules in the Treaty about the differentiated integration than act without knowing the rules, risking exclusion.

Third, Portugal focused on the sphere of the two main sources of power and influence in the Union: the Commission and the Council. Portugal has always struggled for the preservation and even the reinforcement of the Commission's role in the context of the Community's institutional framework. On the one hand, Portugal considered that the powers of the President should be increased. On the other hand, Portugal belonged to the group of States that were against the drastic reduction in the number of Commissioners, since this should reflect the diversity of cultures and interests existing in the Union. Furthermore, Portugal affirmed the principle of one state, one member. Finally, the loss of the second member of the Commission by the big Member States would necessarily have consequences concerning the weighting of votes in the Council. For Portugal, the priority was to ensure its relative weight in this institution. Otherwise, Portugal defended the position that the EU Charter of Fundamental Rights should be binding.

---

[16] For the position of Portugal during the IGC 1996 see *Portugal e a Conferência Intergovernamental para a Revisão do Tratado da União Europeia*, MNE, 1996.

The Work of the Portuguese Presidency

Apart from Portugal's point of view as a Member State which should express and support Portuguese national interests, the Portuguese presidency, during the first semester of 2000, tried to conciliate the different national positions in a neutral way.

The tasks of the Portuguese Presidency were essentially two: (1) the finalizing of the ICG 2000 agenda, since Portugal had been mandated by the Helsinki European Council to introduce new issues into it, and (2) the preparation of the final decision, although it had been agreed since the beginning that the Treaty would be signed under the French Presidency. In that context, it was important to define the different options in each field, while maintaining during discussions those that were relevant to Portugal as a Member State.

During its Presidency, Portugal always showed itself to be open-minded. Proof of this can be seen in the proposals of the enlargement of the Helsinki agenda and the major involvement of the candidate countries in the institutional reform.

The first proposal was crucial to obtaining the favourable opinion of the European Parliament.[17] Notwithstanding, the preference of the majority of delegations was for a narrower agenda. As a result, the Portuguese Presidency concentrated its efforts on including the enhanced cooperation in the agenda.

The second proposal was founded not only in a spirit of fairness, but also in the hope that the candidate countries would support our positions, which had been confirmed in the negotiation.

During the Portuguese Presidency there were ten meetings of Government representatives and five at the ministerial level. The first discussions were based on the documents of the Presidency and concerned the following issues: the extension of qualified majority voting, the composition, the mandate and the working method of the institutions, the reform of the jurisdictional system and Article 7 TEV.

On 14th and 15th April, an informal meeting was held in Sintra, where the Portuguese Presidency proposed the introduction of enhanced cooperation on the agenda.

Finally, the Presidency reported to the European Council of Santa Maria da Feira, which took place on 19th and 20th June, indicating developments in the main trends of the negotiations and the main options on the table.[18]

---

[17] The Parliament delivered its opinion on 3 February 2000.

[18] CONFER 4750/00.

The principal feature of that report was its neutrality. This could be explained by the early stage of the negotiations.

The two more complicated questions related to the number of Commissioners and the weighting of votes in the Council. Concerning the former, the Portuguese Presidency supported the proposal of one State, one Commissioner, which should have implications for the weighting of votes. According to Portugal, the votes in the Council should be duplicated for every Member State, and the states that would have lost a Commissioner should have five more votes, which mean 25 votes for countries such as Germany and 10 votes for countries which have ten million inhabitants, which would include Portugal.

As we shall see below, the final proposal that was approved in Nice, after an extremely hard round of bargaining, was slightly more favourable to the medium-sized states than the proposal advanced by Portugal.

These issues reflected the most sensitive question inside the European Union: the sharing of power among the Member States.

In that context, the divergences among the Member States were so accentuated that the achievement of an agreement was by then quite impossible. The Member States reserved their last word for a later moment, closer to the end of the negotiations, and they did not reveal their negotiation strategy.[19]

The Position of Portugal during the French Presidency

The French Presidency, which led the ICG from July to December, was characterised by fierce opposition between the small and the medium-sized Member States versus the big ones (see Seixas da Costa, 2001, 55). To illustrate this point, it should be mentioned that the Presidency often presented unbalanced documents, clearly favourable to the large Member States, but which could not be supported by a majority of states, including Portugal.

The main divergences occurred on the issues of enhanced cooperation, the Commission's size and the Council's voting. By September/October the debate was proceeding along such a dangerous track for the small and medium-sized Member States (see again Seixas da Costa, 2001, 56) that some observers feared a widespread confrontation between small and big states that could only lead to the failure of the ICG.

Due to that situation, Portugal began a real diplomatic and media 'war' by exploiting the contradiction between big and small and the lack of neutrality

[19] For the negotiation during the IGC 2000 and its difficulties see Guerra Martins, 2002a, Gutiérrez Espada, 2001, Yataganas, 2001, Van Nuffel, 2001, Wiedmann, 2001.

of the Presidency. Portugal sought to share its concerns with the public opinions and the national parliaments of the similarly-sized Member States.

The peak of disagreement between small and big Member States was achieved at the informal European Council in Biarritz in October 2000. Indeed, the inflexibility of the Presidency led to a point of no return and the tension inside the ICG could not be hidden any more.

Apparently, the debate went on until the Summit of Nice in December without any relevant progress and, honestly speaking, no one was expecting it. Only in Nice did the Presidency introduce a quantified proposal about the votes in the Council and the number of Commissioners (see Seixas da Costa, 2001, 61).

The Presidency proposed for the Council a scale from three to thirty votes (ten votes for Portugal). The total number of votes would be 321. The qualified majority was fixed at 231 votes (71.9% of the votes). The proposal further included the rule that there could be no qualified majority if a simple majority of Member States votes against.

For the Commission the proposal fixed the number of Commissioners at twenty in 2010 with an automatic rotation system among nationals from all Member States, placing all of them on an equal footing.

The share of seats among the Member States in the European Parliament without doubt favoured the big Member States, although it still respected the ceiling of 700 seats.

Portugal rejected all those proposals, with the Portuguese Prime Minister even having used the expression 'institutional coup d'État' by the big Member States to qualify the proposals contained in that document. After the first *tour de table*, the Presidency's proposals could only obtain a strict minority support.

Later on, during the afternoon session, the Presidency appeared with a new proposal which maintained the same principles as regards the Council and the European Parliament. Surprisingly, the Commission proposal had been changed in a way absolutely acceptable to Portugal.

The consensus about the Commission having been achieved, the IGC now concentrated its efforts on the Council and the European Parliament, where the divergences were so deep that they jeopardised the success of the Summit. Actually, since some Member States considered the size of the Commission to be a crucial question, France made a blunder when it decided to separate the negotiation of the size of the Commission from the issue of the number of votes in the Council.

The small and medium-sized Member States had some informal meetings at the initiative of Portugal, and despite their disagreements regarding the models of weighting of votes, they agreed with the system of 'dual majority' as a starting point, which implies the majority of population and the majority of states.

On Sunday, December 10th, the Presidency introduced another working document containing some changes relating to the Council. In addition, the ceiling of 700 seats in the Parliament was for the first time overcome, in clear violation of the material limits of revision imposed by the Treaty itself (see Guerra Martins, 2000, 562).

Of course, that new scenario continued to be slightly favourable to the big Member States, and, consequently, Portugal pronounced itself once again against the proposal. The Prime Minister communicated to his French counterpart that Portugal wanted at least twelve votes in the Council, fewer votes for the large Member States and a majority of states when determining the majority of votes.

In the afternoon session, the ICG finally achieved consensus about the final version of the enhanced cooperation clauses and about Article 17 TEU concerning the European Security and Defence Policy (ESDP) in a form acceptable to Portugal. Yet the votes question remained, and with it the visible isolation of Portugal and Belgium. The two countries even threatened to exercise the right of veto.

The Portuguese Delegation was so prepared for the eventuality of not approving the final agreement of the Summit that it had even drafted an explanatory declaration. Such an act would have had serious consequences for Portugal, but also for the Nice Summit and for the future of Europe in general. No one was prepared to accept the failure of the Nice IGC and, even less, to assume the inherent responsibility for any failure.

After long and painful negotiations, Portugal finally acquired its sought after twelve votes on the Council, the big Member States unexpectedly reduced their number of votes from 30 to 29, and the system of majority included in the Treaty did not significantly differ from the version originally supported by Portugal.

As a matter of fact, that agreement was more favourable for Portugal than the Portuguese proposal during its Presidency (25-10) and during the Nice Summit (30-12). For Portugal, this was the most favourable proposal ever presented (including in Amsterdam).

Naturally, this agreement was neither the most perfect for Europe nor the most desirable for Portugal, but in view of the circumstances, it presented the unique possibility of saving the face of the Portuguese Prime Minister and his Government.

Once the negotiation and signature of the Treaty were concluded, the Member States had obtained the conditions to promote the internal procedures of ratification, which, it must be said, was far from easy. The case of Ireland illustrates rather well the difficulties of ratification.

The Portuguese Ratification Procedure

Under Portuguese constitutional law, a treaty comes into force and becomes binding in Portugal after having been subjected to the following measures: According to Article 161, al. i) of the Constitution, the Portuguese Parliament shall approve it with a simple majority of its members. The act of approval is termed 'resolution'.[20]

Subsequently, the treaty shall be sent to the President of the Republic, who can either submit the treaty to the control of the Constitutional Court or ratify it.[21]

In the case of control of constitutionality, if the Constitutional Court determines that the treaty is unconstitutional, it is again sent back to Parliament, which is competent to reapprove it by a majority of 2/3 of its present members, if the number is superior to the majority of the members in general.[22]

The Participation of the Portuguese Parliament

The *Assembleia da República* is one of the most activist national organs concerning the debate about European integration, although this is not evident to the public. As with the previous revisions of the European Treaties,[23] the Portuguese Parliament, especially the European Affairs' Committee, followed the negotiation of the Treaty of Nice through the organisation of regular meetings between the members of the Government involved in the IGC and some members of Parliament. The Plenary of the Parliament debated the IGC several times (on 31 May in the presence of the Prime Minister and on 22 June with the participation of the Minister of Foreign Affairs). Otherwise, before the meetings of the European Council, the Prime Minister had heard the leaders of each party represented in Parliament.[24]

---

[20] Article 166, no. 5, Constitution.

[21] Article 278 no. 1 and Article 135, al. b) Constitution.

[22] Article 279, no. 4, Constitution. For this procedure, see Miranda 2002, Miranda, 2000, Loureiro Bastos, 1998, Gonçalves Pereira and Quadros, 1993, Barbosa Rodrigues, 1991.

[23] See *Acompanhamento parlamentar da revisão do Tratado da União Europeia na Conferência intergovernamental de 1996,* 2 vols., published by the Assembleia da República, Comissão dos Assuntos Europeus, Lisbon, 1995.

[24] See the reports and opinions of the Foreign Affairs Commission and the European Affairs Commis-sion in *Diário da Assembleia da República,* II Série A - n. 10.

The European Affairs Committee organised meetings with the European Affairs' Secretary, the Minister of Foreign Affairs and other ministers.

On 29 and 30 May, the 22nd COSAC meeting took place in Lisbon, where the Portuguese Presidency, the Charter of Fundamental Rights and the relationship between members of the European Parliament and the members of the national parliaments were discussed.

Throughout the year 2000, the Parliament's European Affairs Committee often received delegations from the other Member States and from candidate countries with the objective of discussing the ICG 2000 and the enlargement.

After the signing of the Treaty, the Portuguese Parliament organised meetings with members of the European Parliament. On 4 July, the European Affairs' Committee invited some former Foreign Ministers to a round table about the Treaty of Nice. In the meantime, the Parliament asked for opinions from the universities[25] and from civil society, culminating in a public hearing on 26 September.[26]

Furthermore, two members of Parliament participated in the Convention which prepared the Charter of Fundamental Rights.[27] Concluding, the Treaty was approved by the Parliament on 25 October 2001.[28]

The Ratification

The next step of the Portuguese ratification procedure is ratification by the President of the Republic. This occurred on 18 December 2001.[29]

In the case of the Treaty of Nice, as in all former revisions of the European Treaties, the President proceeded with the ratification without submitting the Treaty to the Constitutional Court, since he had no doubt as to its constitutionality.

---

[25] See, for example, Poiares Maduro, 2001, Botelho Moniz, 2001, Gonçalves, 2001.

[26] The author of this paper participated in that public discussion.

[27] José de Barros Moura (PS) and Maria Eduarda Azevedo (PSD).

[28] Resolution n. 79/2001 of 25/10/2001, *in Diário da República,* Série I A, n. 291 of 18/12/2001.

[29] Decree of the President of the Republic n. 61/2001 of 18/12/2001, *in Diário da República,* Série I A, n. 291 of 18/12/2001.

THE IMPLICATIONS FOR PORTUGAL

Ratification of the Nice Treaty has had several implications for Portugal. First, it is important to emphasise that the assessment of the Treaty might not strictly consist of a mere accounting of loss and gains in the institutional framework. The enlargement pushed the debate of the future of Europe in such a way that the failure of Nice would have been a political catastrophe not only for enlargement, but for the Union as a whole.

Second, the implications of the Treaty must be evaluated taking into account the scenario of the negotiation. The limited character of the Nice agenda did not favour the small and less developed Member States. On the contrary, the final arrangement both in the Council and in the European Parliament clearly favours the more populous Member States. In spite of this, if one compares the final text of the Treaty with some proposals that had been on the table throughout the negotiations, we must admit that in the final analysis, the fundamental interests of Portugal were hardly threatened.

Third, Portugal actually made some gains out of Nice. As an example, we can mention the case of the amendments introduced in the provisions of the enhanced cooperation. As we have already underlined, for a small, or a medium-sized country, like Portugal, clarification of the rules of flexibility assures the fairness and the transparency of its participation.

THE DEBATE ABOUT THE FUTURE OF EUROPE

As has already been pointed out, the Treaty of Nice does not represent major progress in the evolution of the European Union's structure and its institutional framework (Dehousse, 2001, 413; Favret, 2001, 303 and Bradley, 2001). To quote Michel Petite (2001, 887), 'the charm of the Treaty is to open a debate about the future of Europe.' Indeed, the Treaty itself points towards its unfinished character, by adopting the Declaration no. 23 (see Witte, 2001).

In Portugal, the national institutions, especially the Parliament and the Presidency of the Republic, are making a considerable effort to attain participation of the common citizens in this debate. In June 2003, for example, the Presidency of the Republic organised a meeting of some forty former members of Government, former and current members of European institutions and academics to discuss the political model for Europe in the 21st century.

Conversely, the Government seems too concerned with the Union's internal governance, and not very interested in the debate about the future of Europe. However, our Prime Minister accepted an invitation to speak in the inaugural session of the Summer Course at the Faculty of Law, in Lisbon, in July 2002 precisely on this issue. After outlining some well-known positions, he compared the European Union to a Boeing aircraft without a pilot, and was harshly criticised by all the sectors of Portuguese society and by public opinion in general for not showing a greater interest.

BIBLIOGRAPHY

Acompanhamento parlamentar da revisão do Tratado da União Europeia na Conferência intergovernamental de 1996 (1995), 2 vols., Comissão dos Assuntos Europeus. Lisbon: Assembleia da República.

Barbosa Rodrigues, Luís (1991), *O processo de conclusão de convenções internacionais após a revisão constitucional de 1989.* Lisbon: AAFDL.

Botelho Moniz, Carlos (coord.), (2001), *O Tratado de Nice e o futuro da União – estudo elaborado a solicitação da Assembleia da Républic.* Lisbon: unpublished.

Bradley, Kieran St C. (2001). 'Institutional Design in the Treaty of Nice', *Common Market Law Review*, Vol. 38, No. 5, pp. 1095-1124.

Dehousse, Franklin (2001), "Le Traité de Nice: un tournant fondamental dans l'histoire de l'intégration européenne", *Journal des Tribunaux*, pp. 409-413.

Duarte, Maria Luísa (1993), "Portugal", in Jean-Claude Masclet, Didier Maus (eds.), *Les Constitutions nationales à l'épreuve de l'Europe.* Paris: La documentation française, pp. 207-214.

— (2000), "União Europeia e consulta referendária. A propósito do acórdão nº 531/98 do Tribunal Constitutional", *Estudos de Direito da União e das Comunidades europeias*, pp. 137-178.

Favret, Jean-Marc (2001), "Le Traité de Nice du 26 février 2001: vers un affaiblissement irréversible de la capacité d'action de l'Union européenne?", *Revue Trimestrielle de Droit Européen*, pp. 271-304.

Gomes Canotilho, J. J. (1999), *Direito Constitucional e Teoria da Constituição*, 3rd ed. Coimbra: Almedina.

Gonçalves Pereira, André & de Quadros, Fausto (1993), *Manual de Direito Internacional Público*, 3rd. ed. Coimbra: Almedina.

—, Maria Eduarda, Simão José, Pedro Quartin Graça & Gomes, João Salis (2001), *O Tratado de Nice e o futuro da Europa.* Lisbon: Áreas Editora.

Gorjão-Henriques, Miguel (2002), "Novas Reflexões sobre o Sistema Institucional Comunitário Antes e Depois de Nice", *Temas de Integração*, pp. 145-171.

Guerra Martins, Ana Maria (2000), *A natureza jurídica da revisão do Tratado da União Europeia.* Lisbon: Lex.

— (2002a), "O Tratado de Nice – a reforma institucional e o futuro da Europa", in Moura Ramos, Rui Manuel e.a. (eds.), *Estudos em homenagem à Professora Doutora Isabel de Magalhães Collaço.* Coimbra: Almedina, pp. 779-815.

— (2002b), "Alguns tópicos de reflexão sobre a constituição europeia", *Política Internacional*, No. 25, pp. 249-264.

Gutiérrez Espada, Cesáreo (2001), "Una reforma 'difícil pero productiva': la revision institucional en el Tratado de Niza", *Revista de Derecho Comunitario Europeo*, pp. 27-75.

Jalles, Maria Isabel (1980), "Primado do Direito Comunitário sobre o Direito nacional dos Estados membros", *Documentação e Direito Comparado*, separata.

— (1981), *Implications juridico-constitutionnelles de l'adhésion aux Communautés européennes – Le cas du Portugal.* Brussels: Bruylant.

Leitão, Augusto Rogério (2002), "A Personalidade Jurídica da União Europeia", *Temas de Integração*, pp. 69-75.

— (2002), "O Tratado de Nice: Um Novo Modelo de Governação para a União Europeia?", *Temas de Integração*, pp. 131-144.

Loureiro Bastos, Fernando (1998), "O procedimento de vinculação internacional do Estado português após a revisão constitucional de 1997", *Revista da Faculdade de Direito da Universidade de Lisboa*, pp. 17-64.

Miranda, Jorge (1996), "O Tratado de Maastricht e a Constituição Portuguesa", *A União Europeia na encruzilhada.* Coimbra: Almedina, pp. 45-62.

— (1997a), "A integração comunitária e a presente revisão constitucional", in *Em torno da revisão do Tratado da União Europeia.* Coimbra: Almedina, pp. 145-160.

—— (1997b), *Manual de Direito Constitucional*, vol. 1, 6th ed. Coimbra: Coimbra Editora.
—— (2000), *Direito Internacional Público – substituições e aditamentos*. Lisbon: AAFDL
—— (2002), *Curso de Direito Internacional Público*. Lisbon: Principia.
Mota de Campos, João (1985), *As Relações da Ordem jurídica Portuguesa com o Direito Internacional e o Direito Comunitário à Luz da Revisão de 1982*. Lisbon: Instituto Superior de Ciências Sociais e Políticas.
Moura Ramos, Rui Manuel (2002), "O Tratado de Nice e a Reforma do Sistema Jurisdicional Comunitário", *Temas de Integração*, pp. 77-104.
Petite, Michel (2001), "Nice, traité existentiel, non essentiel," *Revue de Droit de l'Union Européenne*, pp. 887-903.
Poiares Maduro, Miguel (2001), *O Tratado de Nice e o futuro da Europa, opinion delivered at the Assembleia da República*, Lisbon: unpublished.
Portugal e a Conferência Intergovernamental para a Revisão do Tratado da União Europeia, MNE, 1996.
Seixas da Costa, Francisco (2001), "Portugal e o Tratado de Nice – Notas sobre a estratégia negocial portuguesa", *Negócios Estrangeiros*, no. 1, pp. 40-70.
Van Nuffel, Pieter (2001), "Le traité de Nice – un commentaire", *Revue de Droit de l'Union européenne*, No. 2, pp. 329-387.
Vila Maior, Paulo & Castro Marques, Nuno (2002), "O Tratado de Nice: um "Nice Treaty"? Para que Estados Membros?", *Temas de Integração*, pp.173-198.
Vitorino, António (1984), "A adesão de Portugal às Comunidades Europeias", *Estudos de Direito Público*, No. 3, pp. 1-65.
Wiedmann, Thomas (2001), "Der Vertrag von Nizza – Genesis einer Reform," *Europarecht*, Vol. 36, No. 2, pp. 185-215.
Witte, Bruno de (2001), "The Nice Declaration: Time for a Constitutional Treaty of the European Union", *The International Spectator*, Vol. 36, No. 1, pp. 21-30.
Yataganas, Xenophon A. (2001), "The Treaty of Nice: The Sharing of Power and the Institutional Balance in the European Union – A Continental Perspective," *European Law Journal*, vol. 7, Issue 3, pp. 242-291.

CHAPTER 14

SPAIN: THE NEED TO SELL A VICTORY

INTRODUCTION

The attitudes and strategies followed by the Spanish political establishment vis-à-vis the Intergovernmental Conference (IGC) 2000 could be consistently defined—similar to the trends already ascertained throughout the Amsterdam negotiations—as of "change within fundamental continuity" (Basabe, 2002a). On the whole, it could be stated that the main and crucial feature of the Nice process for Spain was the fact that the Spanish positions, negotiation strategies and outputs were a direct consequence of the results and experiences of the Amsterdam negotiations.

We can speak about 'fundamental continuity' of the Spanish positions and strategies insofar as the opinion trends vis-à-vis the process of European integration on the part of political parties and their internal fractions (Catalan Socialists, Liberal Conservatives), as well as of the Spanish public opinion and the political establishment have remained stable throughout the process: broad pro-integrationist consensus, lack of in-depth public debate, continuous reference to the issue of structural and cohesion funds (Elorza, 1997; Newton and Donaghy, 1997).

Spain has also continued, as it did in the Amsterdam negotiations, with the search for new negotiation allies, especially among the 'small' Member States and 'non-traditional friends', such as the United Kingdom, the Nordic countries or Austria. Nonetheless, the reinforcement of contacts and common action with traditional partners, such as Portugal, the 'cohesion' countries and, more particularly, the Franco-German axis, remained the basis of the Spanish negotiation strategy (Roldán, 2001).

Similarly to the previous IGC, Spain did not take a proactive attitude during the negotiation phase—presentation of proposals, negotiation brokerage, but reinforced its tough negotiating style with less and less of its traditional fear of political isolation. At all stages of the negotiation process, the Spanish Government has made clear its express desire to be considered among the group of large Member States and has thus adopted negotiation lines in the institutional chapter alongside them (Barbé,1999).

Finally, the above mentioned broad consensus among political forces on EU matters has been again the main reason both for the irrelevance of the *a posteriori* parliamentary debate and political control of negotiations and of the lack of problems during the parliamentary ratification procedure, except for the traditional complaints and institutional requirements from nationalist parties (PNV, *Partido Nacionalista Vasco;* CiU, *Convergencia i Unió*).

On the other hand, we can speak about 'change'—more formal than substantial—regarding the Spanish attitudes and positions in the Nice IGC, insofar as the Conservative Popular Party (*Partido Popular*) for the first time has been in Government from the beginning to the end of an IGC and has thus been 'obliged' to clearly apply its not so well defined 'European policy.' The results of the March 2000 parliamentary elections brought along a surprising absolute majority for the Popular Party, which granted Aznar time and political *marge de manoeuvre* to be devoted to international and European matters, as well as mid-term internal dossiers.[1]

In contrast to the 1996-2000 legislative period, the Popular Party did not feel the pressure or need of political support by the 'nationalist' political parties at the internal level and the Socialist Party (PSOE) was left undergoing a painful internal 'reconstruction process' that led to the election of José Luis Rodríguez Zapatero as new Secretary General.

During the Nice process, the traditional Spanish negotiation structures and institutional mechanisms (EU Permanent Representation, Secretariat of State for European Affairs, Ministry of Foreign Affairs, Interministerial Coordination Commission for European Affairs) were overshadowed by the role directly played by the Cabinet of the Prime Minister. A direct consequence of this was the weak role played by the Ministry of Foreign Affairs under non-diplomat Minister Josep Piqué.

A major new element in this IGC—not to be undervalued—is the fact that in the Spanish public opinion what was at stake during the Nice negotiations was the personal 'international dimension' of Aznar and his negotiation abilities, always with regard to Gonzalez's reputation as an international statesman.[2] The Nice European Council had something as a 'personal plebiscite' of the pragmatic political attitude of Aznar at all levels and its rejection of theoretical approaches and concepts, especially with regard to international issues (Bonet, 2002). In recent times, the Spanish Government has clearly favoured a new style of external policy, based on Aznar's 'proatlanticism' and his personalised foreign contacts with Blair, Berlusconi or Durao Barroso within the EU (Powell, 2001).

As a direct consequence of the previous point, there was for the first time

[1] Such as: the so-called Basque 'peace process', linked with the fight against ETA and the illegalisation of its political branch, Batasuna; immigration regulation and police measures in Andalusia and Canary Islands; market liberalisation in the energy, post, telephone and airline sectors; and an active employment policy.

[2] See Gonzalez's article in El Pais (15 June 2001) after the Göteborg European Council.

after an IGC negotiation an active information and media policy on the part of the Spanish Public Administration (Ministry of Foreign Affairs, Parliament), protagonised by Aznar, which focused on the results of the negotiation for the country, prompting continuous comparison with Gonzalez and the Edinburgh and Amsterdam negotiations. An extreme contrast can be noted between the rigorous secrecy and lack or avoidance of a public debate during the pre- and actual phases of the negotiation process and the active promotion of information and discussion of the post-Nice era.

On the other hand, for the first time in an IGC, Spain has had to face critics making repeated reference to its 'anti-integrationist' approach to the negotiations. The official line of the Ministry of Foreign Affairs was the defence of a double information strategy, which presented the Spanish positions as seeking the legitimate preservation of the 'orthodoxy' of the process of European integration,[3] while making continuous links and reference to the agreements and lessons learnt from Amsterdam (Declaration 50 acknowledging the existence of a 'Spanish problem', political asylum protocol, enhanced cooperation) (Powell, 2001).

The Political Context: Aznar's Efforts to Develop His Own European Policy (1996-2000)

Very little was known about the type of European policy that Jose María Aznar would favour before he was nominated Prime Minister in the spring of 1996. In opposition, the Conservative leader had been critical of what he described as Gonzalez's failure to defend Spanish national interest in Europe, but without clarifying how he would assume this task himself. Similarly, the Socialist former Prime Minister had come under attack for accepting Franco-German initiatives unquestioningly, but alternative alliances were not explicitly suggested.

At a more ideological level, neoliberals within the Popular Party argued that under PSOE rule Spaniards had become accustomed to a bewildering range of public subsidies, many of them results of Gonzalez's European policy—which would ultimately prove counter-productive and incompatible with genuine socio-economic modernisation. On a more personal level, Aznar himself was unusually anglophile for a Spanish politician, and some sections of his party, strongly under the influence of their British Conservative colleagues, had openly embraced a Spanish variety of Euroscepticism.

[3] This might also explain Aznar's unusually harsh reaction to the press (11 June 2001), proclaiming his "honest and original defence of Nice" and "other's tactical hipocrisy" accompanied by direct attacks on Schröder, Chirac, Prodi and the European Parliament (Egurbide, 2001).

Since Gonzalez's solution to Spain's ills had traditionally been 'more Europe', even those who did not share such a radical position felt that their own recipe would have to be somewhat different, perhaps something along the lines of 'more Europe and more Spain'.

While admitting that Aznar's European policy represents a departure from that of his predecessor, some authors (Barbé, 1999; Powell, 2001) have argued that it is best explained in generational, rather than strictly ideological, terms. While Gonzalez belonged to the 1960s generation which had experienced the isolation endured by Spain under Franco and later played a role in the transition to democracy, Aznar and his Ministers were members of a new political generation, which had come of age politically in a fully democratic, European context. By comparison with his predecessor, therefore, Aznar favoured a far less traumatic view of Spanish recent history, one which explained the country's evolving role in Europe in less 'heroic' terms, and which tended to see integration in Europe largely as a consequence of the remarkable socio-economic changes experienced in Spain in the late 1950s to early 1960s. Hence, while González considered Spain's presence in Europe as something exceptional, Aznar could begin to take it for granted (Powell, 2001).

Overall, by comparison with that of his predecessor, Aznar's European policy since 1996 had introduced a number of interesting changes without questioning the fundamentals of Gonzalez's legacy, and may therefore be seen—as stated above—as a combination of change and continuity, with the emphasis on the latter.

Some of these changes had already become apparent in the debates and negotiations leading up to the Amsterdam Treaty, in the course of which Spain advocated institutional reforms which would pave the way for enlargement while strongly resisting attempts by certain Member States to undermine the status quo (Basabe, 2002a). More specifically, Madrid rejected the notion of a 'two-speed' Europe advanced by Paris, out of fear of being pushed to the margins of EU affairs on account of its economic vulnerability. The Aznar Government was also sceptical about the slightly different notion of 'enhanced co-operation', perceiving in it the danger that some states might be excluded from deeper co-operation against their will. At the institutional level, Spain struggled to retain what it had won at Ioannina, namely its right to be considered one of the 'big five'. This required Aznar to put up a solitary struggle well into the last night of the Amsterdam Council of June 1997, forcing the Dutch presidency to acknowledge the existence of a 'Spanish problem', which could only be solved by compensating Madrid with more votes in the Council of Ministers in return for the future loss of one of the two Spanish Commissioners.

In spite of these continuities, a comparison between the Maastricht and

Amsterdam IGCs already reveals certain changes in emphasis (Powell, 2001). At Amsterdam the Aznar government devoted considerable attention to third pillar issues, most notably by rejecting the very notion of political asylum for EU nationals in other Member States, a concern largely dictated by its determination to develop EU procedures and institutions (such as Europol and Eurojust) capable of proving effective in the on-going struggle against ETA. Some of these concerns were later given even greater relevance at the Tampere Council in October 1999, at which meeting Spain advocated the development of the EU as an Area of Freedom, Security and Justice (Various authors, 1998). With regard to the CFSP, Madrid's position remained prudent, advocating the establishment of a permanent body for planning and analysis, its centralisation in the figure of the Secretary General of the Council, and the maintenance of unanimity for decision-making while allowing for the introduction of constructive abstention. Overall, during the 1996-97 IGC the Government clearly attached less importance to second pillar reforms than to issues relating to the first (such as the weighting of voting in the Council) or third (terrorism and political asylum) pillars, and the CFSP was far less prominent on the Spanish agenda than it had been in the 1990 IGC. It should be noted, however, that this trend was already evident during the final months of the Gonzalez Administration: when the latter listed Spain's future priorities during his farewell speech at the Turin European Council in March 1996, he discussed EMU and the challenges of enlargement, forgetting to mention the CFSP altogether. All of this suggests that as far as Madrid was concerned the debate on the CFSP was by then a question of instruments rather than essence, and that Spain was largely content with the existing mechanisms (González Vega, 2001).

During his first years in office, Aznar was driven by an almost obsessive determination to ensure that Spain would be in a position to join the single currency and take full advantage of Economic and Monetary Union. By then the Spanish economy was beginning to show signs of recovery, and the Maastricht criteria no longer seemed as remote as they had during the past economic recession. Nevertheless, Aznar could have succumbed to the temptation of seeking a political solution to the nation's economic shortcomings. However, in September 1996 Aznar turned down Romano Prodi's suggestion that Spain and Italy should reach an agreement which would make it difficult—if not impossible—for Germany and France to introduce the single currency without them, making it clear that he intended to meet the Maastricht criteria whatever the cost.

This exchange had two immediate consequences: on the one hand, it forced Prodi to abandon his internal plans to delay structural reforms necessary to enable Italy to meet the criteria; more importantly, it won Aznar the respect of other European leaders, giving Spain the opportunity to enhance its image almost overnight. The Spanish Government reminded the public opinion time and again that, for the first time in its history, Spain would be taking part in a key aspect of European integration from its inception. In his determination to neutralise Spanish fears of exclusion from the EU's hard core, Aznar was thus following firmly in Gonzalez's footsteps (Powell, 2001).

This fundamental continuity was also evident in the government's efforts to defend the principle of socio-economic cohesion. Ironically, the impressive performance of the Spanish economy in the late 1990s made it increasingly difficult to defend this principle in the face of growing opposition from other net contributors, most notably Germany. Having met the Maastricht criteria, with average annual growth rates of 4% and GDP levels at 78% of the EU average, it was not easy to demand special treatment for Spain. Additionally, having criticised Gonzalez in 1992 for the supposedly undignified manner in which he had secured the Cohesion Fund, Aznar was under considerable pressure to outdo his predecessor. This no doubt explains his tough, somewhat abrasive attitude at the Berlin Council held in March 1999, at which Spain was promised an enormous amount for the years 2000-06 from the structural and cohesion funds. Thus, if Edinburgh was the price Member States paid to keep Spain sweet on the EFTA enlargement, Berlin could be seen as the concession necessary to ensure that Madrid would not obstruct the forthcoming Eastern enlargement.

It is probably with regard to the defence-related aspects of Spanish European policy that Aznar more obviously left the path frequented by Gonzalez (Barbé, 2000). This was largely due to the fact that in the post-cold war era, the Atlanticist-Europeanist fracture, which had long divided Member States over relations with the US, and questions of security and defence lost much of their relevance. More specifically, this paved the way for Spain's full incorporation into NATO's military structure at the Atlantic Council held in Madrid in July 1997, thereby suppressing the constraints imposed by the terms of the 1986 referendum. By the late 1990s, Madrid thus formed part of the hard core of the EU in matters of defence and security thanks to its new role in NATO and its by now traditional support for the WEU. Unexpectedly, however, this did not lead to greater Spanish presence in defence-related initiatives. In 1998 the 'big four' embarked on a political dialogue which led to the decision to establish military forces for the prevention of conflict and crisis management adopted at the Helsinki Council in December 1999. Although Spain subsequently supported the birth of a Common European Security and Defence Policy (ESDP), it was not one of the promoters of the project. This represented a departure from what had occurred during the negotiations leading to the Maastricht Treaty, in which, as we saw, Spain had played the role of a major player with regard to the birth of the CFSP.

Paradoxically, this had been attributed to the replacement of the traditional Franco-German axis by a British 'motor', which in theory should have benefited Madrid given Aznar's 'special relationship' with Tony Blair. Be that as it may, in Barbé's view "the effects on Spain are fairly clear: Spain has joined the hard core, but without having performed the function of political motor, the traditional function of major players" (Barbé, 2000).

Aznar's attitude towards the future of ESDP may have been coloured by his Atlanticist bias. Although Gonzalez's early relations with the US were difficult, by the time he left office they could hardly have been improved. The novelty, however, lies in the fact that Aznar not only accepted and welcomed US leadership, as his predecessor had done, but often appeared to be closer to Washington than Brussels. Since 1996, at times of Europeanist-Atlanticist friction Spain has tended to side with the US and Britain, a good example of this being Aznar's reaction to the Anglo-American bombing of Iraq in 1998. This alignment with the US and Britain represents a departure from the behaviour of PSOE Governments, which almost invariably sided with the Franco-German axis in times of international crisis. The Spanish Prime Minister's response to the terrorist attacks of 11 September 2001 would also appear to confirm this trend. Indeed Aznar is of the opinion that some EU Member States have not been strict enough in their response to the terrorist threat, a perception which would draw him even closer to Washington and London in the future.

This latter point leads us to the question of the importance of alliances between Member States in the promotion of national interests. As leader of the opposition, Aznar had been highly critical of Gonzalez's subservience to the Franco-German axis, and was therefore unlikely to follow his lead in this respect. More importantly, however, the Franco-German axis was far less relevant in the late 1990s than it had been a decade earlier. Similarly, Aznar could no longer benefit from the existence of a strong Commission, though he did his best to support Jacques Santer in the face of European Parliament criticism (Basabe, 2000).

During the final years of the Gonzalez administration, Spanish representatives had increasingly found themselves in the same camp as the British, a trend which became more apparent under Aznar. In an ideologically hostile European Council, it is understandable that the Spanish Prime Minister should have found solace in Blair's political positions. However, the existence of a Madrid-London axis as such should not be taken too literally. Spain's decision to veto Britain's accession to the Schengen group in 1999 confirms that Gibraltar remains a significant obstacle. More importantly, perhaps, as the Lisbon and Stockholm European Councils showed, when it comes to major economic issues, both Britain and Spain find it difficult to promote their own national interests: the former because of its attitude to

EMU, the latter because of its high rate of unemployment and its poor performance in areas such as R&D. Under such conditions, it is no easy task to lead by example.

THE SPANISH GOVERNMENT'S MAIN PRIORITIES VIS-À-VIS THE IGC 2000

Contrary to the Amsterdam negotiations, there was no official document issued by the Spanish Government or even from the Ministry of Foreign Affairs during the whole negotiation process which could explain and justify the Government's positions. Official declarations were scarce, exclusively in favour of the maintenance of an IGC 'limited agenda'. In fact, most of the political debate and its subsequent reflection in the press took place in informal contexts or during the interpellations before the Joint Congress-Senate Committee for the EU (Fonseca, 2001).

The Spanish Government's priorities were initially focused on the 'institutional chapter', on the basis of continuous references to the literal terms of the Amsterdam agreements; it always intended to stress its alignment to the positions of the 'big four' and the efforts of the successive Presidencies. The No. 1 and almost exclusive priority was the so-called Spanish problem', according to the wording of Declaration 50 of the Amsterdam Treaty: the reweighting of votes within the Council as part of the compensation for the Spanish accession agreements' institutional clause. Spain was to be considered as a 'large' Member State within the Council, which ultimately implied blocking power similar to the 'big ones', once it was officially accepted that a similar number of votes was impossible and unrealistic. This was the further development of the so-called 'equality concept', frequently referred to in the Spanish press.

The size of the Commission was at all times a subsidiary issue for the Spanish official negotiators, always subject to the final solution agreed for the former issue. The lack of a clear official doctrine at all stages of the negotiations vis-à-vis the Commission's powers and the legal status of the Charter of Fundamental Rights clearly led to *de facto* contradictions between the political positions expressed by members of PP's Parliamentary Group in the Congress and the Government's Spokesman. The opposition used these inconsistencies to undermine the Government's exigence not to weaken the national negotiations strategy, what at a certain stage led to a punctual parliamentary crisis with the Catalan nationalists. No official declaration whatsoever was issued on the question of the number of seats in the European Parliament before or during the negotiations (Elorza, 2001b).

Enlargement was not used at any time by the Government as an official, key national objective in the negotiations. The mere rethorical declarations by the Spanish Prime Minister in this respect show to what extent Spain missed an excellent opportunity to start developing common strategies with Poland, the future Member State in the same uncomfortable position within the EU institutional framework. Another sign which shows the low relevance given to the enlargement issue is the fact that the Treaty of Nice was later simply not sold in terms of facilitation of the latter, which by the Spanish public opinion is generally perceived as a threat (Guardans, 2001; De Miguel, 2002).

The Spanish Government permanently refused to extend the IGC agenda scope for tactical and global strategic reasons, basically not to weaken its institutional claims. The rejection to enter the debate on the easening of the flexibility clauses should also be interpreted as a move to avoid the Amsterdam experience with the unexpectedly harsh side-negotiations on the political asylum protocol. This reluctancy towards the introduction of new issues in the agenda for fear of losing negotiation weapons was a clear-cut strategy streamlined from Moncloa, the Prime Minister's Cabinet (Taibo, 2001).

Spain's final 'yes' to the extension of QMV was only to be granted on the condition of not harming the Berlin 1999 agreements on structural and cohesion funds. Nevertheless, the Spanish Government would really be ready to fight to maintain unanimity voting on specific issues, such as external borders—because of the Gibraltar problem—taxation policy (with regard to company tax), social security, water resources and other sensitive environmental matters.

The initial 'no' to the re-opening of the debate on enhanced cooperation, besides the tactical reasons outlined above, is to be understood on the basis of the traditional Spanish fear of institutional mechanisms which might prompt exclusion from the EU's hard core. The change at a certain stage of the negotiations was later justified on grounds of 'orthodoxy' and commonly accepted as a sign of cooperation both with the Portuguese and French Presidencies. Spain defended the preservation of the national veto at least in first pillar issues, what was paradoxically supported with a last-minute tactical proposal to extend QMV to the second pillar (Elorza, 2001a, 2001b).

Spain and the IGC 2000 Negotiations

Many of the continuities between Gonzalez' and Aznar's European policy outlined above were again in evidence in the very negotiations leading up to the Nice European Council of December 2000. Broadly speaking, Spain had strictly favoured a minimalist IGC; in other words, one which would merely allow the EU to strike the institutional bargains 'necessary for enlargement'. Madrid was also anxious to prevent the adoption of qualified majority voting as a general rule, essentially so as to retain veto powers over the cohesion and structural funds, but was happy to see it extended to the second pillar, as long as this did not include military operations as such (González Vega, 2001; Solana, 2001).

After lengthy discussions, Spain succeeded in retaining its ability to veto decisions on both cohesion and structural funds during the period of 2007 to 2013, which was hailed as a major political triumph. More generally, Spanish representatives argued that enhanced co-operation should not apply to the 'heart' of European integration, namely the single market and the principle of social and economic cohesion, one of several battles they would lose.

Overall, however, the Government's top priority was to fight attempts to use enlargement as an excuse to alter the institutional settlement reached during accession negotiations. The official view was that in 1985 Spain had been given 'large' power status in the Commission (with two Commissioners, similarly to the 'big four') and 'medium-sized' power status in the Council of Ministers (with 8 votes as opposed to the 10 held by the 'big four'). Consequently, if Spain was to lose 'large' power status in the Commission as a result of enlargement, it was entitled to 'large' power status in the Council by way of compensation. This goal was largely achieved when Spain—actively supported by France, which no doubt felt it could do better with a large Southern ally in an enlarged EU—was allocated 27 votes in the future Council, only two short of the 29 awarded to the 'big four', even though this meant losing more MEPs—fourteen (14)—than any other Member State.

The Nice Council also agreed that yet another IGC would have to be convened by 2004 in order to continue shaping the process of European integration. True to his pragmatism and his 'deeds, not words' approach to politics, Aznar has always been somewhat reluctant to take part in the debate about the future European 'architecture,' and believes "it is somewhat irresponsible, indeed frivolous, to talk of a future federal Europe when the current EU budget cannot exceed 1.27% of the combined GDP of its Member States." The Spanish Prime Minister is similarly wary of the notion that Europe's political problems—most notably its legitimacy deficit—will be solved by adopting a formal Constitution, and harbours grave doubts as to the opportunity of seeking to impose Germany's constitutional model on the EU as a whole (Elorza, 2001a; Basabe, 2002b; Gallego-Díaz, 2002).

Coming down to detail with the actual strategies followed by the Spanish representatives during the negotiations, it should be noted that Spain tended to co-operate closely both with the Portuguese and, in particular, the French Presidency. The level of understanding and concerted action at bilateral level with the latter was by far the most effective in the very final results of the Nice European Council, though the Spanish chief negotiators admitted having a constant fear during the negotiations that the French Presidency would not keep its compromises and would end up selling the Spanish support for the defence of its own national objectives. In any case, the French Presidency always held a clear position towards Spain and its 'institutional claims' throughout the negotiations: to avoid problems arising from a 'difficult' negotiating partner and to ensure winning a powerful, solid Southern ally in its need to concentrate diplomatic efforts and to eventually receive last-minute help in the Franco-German battle. Some authors have defined this negotiating behaviour very expressively when they state that "the best representative for the Spanish national interest was indeed France" (Barón, 2001).

The Spanish delegation kept throughout the negotiations a low public profile and its attitude was not at any time proactive. There were no frequent public interventions by the Spanish negotiators, except at initial stages with regard to the issue of 'agenda-limiting' and to rhetorically express its alignment with the 'big four. Once again, the Spanish attitude in a crucial EU negotiation reflected the paradox of claiming to be a 'large' Member State and not acting as such (Barbé, 1999; Powell, 2001).

With regard to the setting up of negotiation alliances with other Member States, Spain was quite successful in its efforts to minimise the simplification of 'enhanced cooperation' procedures, together with a whole range of 'non-traditional' allies. This trend was even more ascertainable on the issue of extension of QMV: on the one hand, on matters such as water resources or tax policy, Spain joined efforts with Austria or the United Kingdom; on the other, on the crucial chapter of structural and cohesion funds, Spain fought alongside its classical Southern and cohesion allies, basically not to reopen the Berlin agreements and to clarify the financial costs of enlargement.

The internal cohesion within the Spanish delegation was about to break apart with regard to two relatively 'side' chapters: the role and new internal architecture of the European Court of Justice (Ruiz-Jarabo, 2001) and the legal nature of the Charter of Fundamental Rights (Laso, 2001). In the former case, clear and detailed proposals arising from sectorial Ministries (Justice and Foreign Affairs, but also the Legal Counselling of the Permanent Representation) were in practice silenced during the actual negotiations by the Prime Minister's Cabinet; in the latter, more than in any other negotiation issue, the rethorics at domestic level and at the negotiation table were extremely differentiated. The Spanish negotiators later referred to the case as 'pure tactics': knowing the introduction of the Charter would not be agreed, there was simply no need to lose negotiation tools in this battle (Elorza, 2001b).

All in all, the negotiation strategy, designed by Aznar and followed by the Spanish delegation at all levels, more than in any previous IGC, revealed an extremely pragmatic approach: to limit the extension of reforms and agenda scope as much as possible, and to try to avoid any obstacle that might dilute the institutional debate and the 'legitimate' reference to the Amsterdam agreements.

During the actual negotiation at the Nice European Council, a strong role was personally played by Aznar, who hid well behind the front-line defended by the French Presidency. Newspapers later attached great importance to the 'bilateral conflict' with Portugal caused by the interventions of Guterres on behalf of the 'small' Member States, making direct reference to the Spanish-Portuguese relationship. At the same time, the scandalous leak of the European Council proceedings to the press later dismantled the official version given by the Spanish Government on supposed concerted action with Polish Prime Minister Buzek on the equality of votes and the number of EP seats for Poland and Spain. The self-proclaimed role of Aznar as leader of the 'ideologically Conservative faction' within the European Council was clearly overestimated on account of the actual terms of the negotiations.

In any case, there was no clear interference from the domestic political arena at the moment of the very negotiations. Not having experienced a real public debate in Spain—apart from the institutional issues—the Government had nothing to fear from the national base of support. Only at the final stage of the negotiations, the sudden reappearance of the key domestic issue of the structural and cohesion funds required the immediate official denial that this could be the price to pay for acceptance of the Spanish positions in the institutional chapter.

The Reception of the Results of the Nice Negotiations in Spain and the Subsequent Ratification Debate

The results of the Nice European Council were proclaimed by the Spanish Government's Spokesman right after the closure of the negotiations and were later received by the national press with grand official declarations: "the Government is happy to have overcome the problems;" "nothing in the end happened that changed our constant strategy;" "Spain is to be regarded as a clear winner of the Nice negotiations." All official comments insisted on a personalised attribution of the success in the negotiations to Aznar's intervention. This triumphant reaction was especially reinforced by a biased and interested reading of the Commission internal report on the negotiation results, which the Government exhibited as a proof of success.

In opposition to this extremely early announcement from official quarters that Spain had been granted 'large' power status within the EU decision structure, the Spanish press indulged during the following days in what the

Government called the 'calculator debate' (Medina, 2001). Angry headlines in the pro-opposition press denied the 'triumph' alleged by the Government on statistical grounds and most of the media prompted a debate focused on to what extent Spain had lost its opportunity in the negotiations to become a real 'large' EU Member State. Nevertheless, the issue of the number of seats attributed to Spain in the European Parliament seemed to be forgotten in the post-Nice debate both by the press and political parties in opposition, with the exception of some 'nationalist' spokespersons (CiU) (Taibo, 2001). The Government actually managed to concentrate the debate on the issue of the real blocking capacity acquired by Spain within the Council.

This intense exchange of information between the Government itself and the press is at the basis of the immediate and unusual reaction by the Ministry of Foreign Affairs to design and implement an information strategy addressed to the Spanish public opinion on the results of the IGC 2000 negotiations and the contents of the Treaty of Nice. The information campaign was devised both on the lines of selling a 'national victory', as well as justifying it with the facilitation of enlargement: "Spain not only remains treated as one of the large EU Member States, but even more, has regained and improved its institutional status".[4] In any case, the slight gap between the official 'integrationist rhetoric' of the Ministry of Foreign Affairs—pro-enlargement and pro-reinforcement of CFSP—and the information line followed by the Government's Spokesman could be attributed to the reasons outlined above.

The parliamentary debate which followed the presentation of the results of the Nice European Council by the Prime Minister before the Plenary Session of the Congress lacked political relevance, because of its exclusively informative nature and the absolute majority of seats held by the Popular Party in Parliament, which ensured no political problems at the domestic level. The political parties in opposition focused their criticism on those aspects traditionally thrown upon the Government's attitude in European negotiations: secrecy in the formation and definition of national positions and rejection of a concerted strategy with other political actors; lack of an EU overall model and of a coherent and consistent European policy on the part of the Popular Party; the simple arrogant defence of national interests as the only short-term approach implemented by Aznar; no defence of what the Spanish people and political actors actually want and need from the process of European integration. No matter the level of internal criticism shown by the opposition parties, the Government managed to transmit a clear message to the Spanish public: the satisfactory results obtained by the Spanish delegation in the Nice negotiations were the direct consequence of a firm and well-

---

[4] Spain, Ministry of Foreign Affairs (2001), *Tratado de Niza (Memoria justificativa para el expediente de ratificación del Tratado de Niza)*, Madrid: O.I.D.

planned negotiation strategy at the European level, which started to render interesting fruits both in economic and political terms.

The use of an 'urgent parliamentary procedure' for the formal ratification of the Treaty of Nice[5], which actually reduced the political debate to a minimum, was justified on grounds of the need to finish all formal stages of ratification at any price before the beginning of the Spanish Presidency, to be held in the first semester of 2002.[6]

Though the formal aspects might give a poor impression, an in-depth analysis of the substantial contents of the post-Nice Spanish domestic political discussion well shows the first signs of a more mature general debate on the evolution of the European Union than on any other previous post-IGC occasion. While the 'nationalist' parties interpreted Nice with a view—and a continuous reference—to the IGC 2004 and the issue of the 'list of competences', the Socialist Party insisted on the incoherence of Aznar's positions and the Government's later official explanations about the legal status finally granted to the European Charter of Fundamental Rights and the decision mechanisms vis-à-vis the structural and cohesion funds.

On the other hand, and surprisingly enough, all parliamentary forces easily reached a common agreement during the debates on the issue of the 'role of national Parliaments'. Its first practical consequence was the setting-up of an independent 'Sub-Committee to follow up the IGC 2004 debate' within the Joint Committee Congress-Senate for the European Union, as well as the revitalisation of the 'Sub-Committee to follow up the EU enlargement process' created some years before (Basabe & González-Escudero, 2002c).

The simplicity of the parliamentary procedure to pass the Organic Law approving the ratification of the Treaty of Nice was reinforced by the double fact that on this occasion no legal complaints whatsoever were raised by any parliamentary group and that the respective amendments proposed by the Basque and Galician 'nationalists' were merely nominal. Curiously enough, a substantially external topic of European dimension, though with direct domestic repercussions on the international struggle against E.T.A.—the

---

[5] Spain, Cortes Generales, *Boletín Oficial de las Cortes Generales* (BOCG. Congreso de los Diputados), serie A, No. 39-1, 15 June 2001 (Número de expediente 121/000039), Proyecto de Ley Orgánica 3/2001, de 6 de noviembre, por la que se autoriza la ratificación por España del Tratado de Niza por el que se modifican el Tratado de la Unión Europea, los Tratados Constitutivos de las Comunidades Europeas y determinados actos conexos, firmado en Niza el día 26 de febrero 2001.

[6] Spain, Cortes Generales, Ley Orgánica 3/2001, de 6 de noviembre, por la que se autoriza la ratificación por España del Tratado de Niza por el que se modifican el Tratado de la Unión Europea, los Tratados Constitutivos de las Comunidades Europeas y determinados actos conexos, firmado en Niza el día 26 de febrero de 2001 (*Boletín Oficial del Estado* No. 267, 7 November 2001).

'European arrest warrant'—interfered with the ratification process and in particular the plenary debate, and filled the headlines and declarations by most politicians to the press.[7]

Finally, another sign of this Government's new attitude and its rapid reaction to critics connected with the European debate, partly due to the beginning of the Spanish 2002 Presidency—was again the setting up of a consultative body, the 'National Council for the Debate on the Future of the European Union' (*Consejo Nacional para el Debate sobre el Futuro de la Unión Europea*), which was to foster the exchange of ideas on European matters among societal, economic and political actors.[8]

THE POST-NICE SITUATION IN THE SPANISH POLITICAL DEBATE

The post-Nice era in the Spanish public sphere has witnessed extremely interesting developments both in political and academic terms concerning the debate on the future of the process of European integration. Indeed, most commentators agree that there is much more to understand from the post-Nice than from the pre-Nice scenario about the positions and strategies followed by Spain during the actual Nice negotiations (Powell, 2001; Fonseca, 2001; Pérez Tremps, 2001).

All Spanish political forces at once were soon aware of the risks and opportunities involved in the IGC 2004 negotiations and of the domestic political relevance of certain chapters on the agenda. The debate unavoidably seemed at the time to focus on the issue of the EU/Member States' 'list of competences'. Both the 'nationalist' political parties and the regional institutions (Governments, Parliaments, Universities), as well as the Spanish Government and the different bodies of the central public administration have envisaged the post-Nice debate as the framework within which the on-going process of internal power distribution foreseen in the 1978 Constitution could have an end.

This was the initial conceptual scenario in the spring/summer of 2001 surrounding the Spanish debate on the different models for the future of the European Union. Though Aznar, loyal to his pragmatic approach, initially refused to enter any theoretical discussion, the proposal of 7 June 2001 on

[7] Spain, Cortes Generales, *Diario de Sesiones del Congreso de los Diputados*, VII Legislatura, No. 102, Debate de totalidad de iniciativas legislativas (Proyecto de ley orgánica de ratificación del Tratado de Niza)", 13 September 2001, pp. 4949-4968.

[8] So far the works and procedures of this body have not excelled in public impact and only produced scarce results; a certain political controversy arose on grounds of the nomination of its members instead.

the future of Europe made public by José Luis Rodríguez Zapatero, the new leader of the Socialist Party,[9] and the press articles on the issue by former Prime Minister González (González Márquez, 2001) forced a counterintervention on the part of the Popular Party. Aznar reluctantly accepted to propose his own model—in fact, a diffuse mixture of liberal and pro-integrationist recipes—for the future of the process of European integration in his 'Oxford speech'.

This external deliberation and definition process on European issues has been accompanied by a parallel internal one. The Spanish institutional structures and foreign policy mechanisms have during the years 2001-2002 undergone a general transformation process, due to the urgent need of *aggiornamento* of the Foreign Services and the adoption of new choices in foreign policy directly agreed at the Prime Minister's Office. Examples of such transformation, together with the redefinition of new priority areas for the Spanish foreign policy (Central and Eastern European countries, Asia) have been the massive reshuffling of ambassadors appointed to crucial destinations, the internal re-organization of the EU Permanent Representation, the reinforcement of the 'Agency for International Cooperation' (AECI) or the creation of new bodies, such as the Elcano Royal Institute on International Affairs and the State Society for External Cultural Action (SEACEX).

The abovementioned lively initial debate on the IGC 2004 negotiations has mostly taken place in the press; so far not much has happened at the level of the public opinion or within Parliament, with the exception of the high level discussions and proposals put on the table on the issue of the role of national Parliaments in the European Union institutional framework.[10]

It should finally be noted with regard to the initial work undertaken so far by the Convention that both the selection of the members appointed to represent Spain in it—what prompted a major political row with the 'nationalist' political parties and provoked the parallel creation of a so-called 'Basque Convention on the Future of the EU'—and the lack of clearly defined national positions with regard to the institutional issues have so far strongly reduced its day-to-day impact on the Spanish political arena.

Conclusions

It seems quite difficult to give a thorough and clear-cut explanation of the actual negotiation strategies and expected outcomes for Spain in the Nice

[9] P.S.O.E., Documento "Las propuesta del PSOE sobre el futuro de Europa", 7 June 2001.

[10] See Inauguratory Speech by Mrs. L.F.Rudi, President of the Spanish Congress, at Madrid COSAC (2002), with a realistic approach to the issue on safe legal grounds.

IGC, without just focusing on the 'institutional chapter'; many aspects of and reasons for the definition process of the Spanish national positions and of the very negotiations remain unclear because of the lack of specialised literature with an insider's view—which was not the case in previous IGCs—, together with the existence of an official 'version of facts' which tends to ignore external variables.

When explaining the issue of national preference in Nice, the 'economic interests' traditionally underlying the Spanish positions in EU negotiations (social and economic cohesion, real economic convergence, immigration) were this time overshadowed by specifically clear 'geopolitical interests', particularly the institutional 'relative weight' in the Council.

On the other hand, regarding interstate bargaining, there was an obvious presence of asymmetrical interdependence, insofar as Spain had clearly identifiable institutional aims, the reweighting of votes in the Council, without a special wish or need to support the enlargement towards the Central and Eastern European countries, together with its traditional fear of exclusion from the 'hard core' of the EU. The latter is fully applicable to the initial postion and later change of strategy in the dossiers of 'enhanced cooperation' and extension of QMV. More perhaps than in previous IGCs, the domestic implications of the negotiations' outcome and questions of 'national prestige' acted as major constraints in the definition and adoption of specific negotiation priorities.

As expected in an international negotiation where direct national interests were at stake, Spain did not expressly support a clear institutional choice in Nice, apart from its agreement to centralized technocratic management in fields like CFSP or ESDP, not least with a view to more credible commitment vis-à-vis its EU partners.

With reference to relative gains, the Spanish behaviour in the Nice negotiations says a great deal about the asymmetric importance of the Council against the European Parliament and the real underlying objective of being aligned with the group of 'large' EU Member States. Spain has virtually fallen to the obsessive dynamics of subordinating its whole negotiation aims to the objective of being treated in decision-making mechanisms as a 'large' Member State both for economic and strictly political reasons.

Let us illustrate historically the previous statements both on institutional choice and relative gains in the Spanish case. Since its accession in 1986, Spain has sought to establish itself as one of the 'hard core' members of the EU while recognising the constraints imposed by its size, its comparatively low level of economic development, its consistently high levels of unemployment and its status as a 'cohesion country'. Over the past fifteen years it has attempted to do this in a number of different ways. In the first place, it has taken full advantage of EU policies in order to advance along the road to real—as opposed to merely nominal—convergence with the more economically developed Member States. Secondly, and fully in keeping with the principle that EU membership is about sharing rather than losing sovereignty, and hence about sharing rather than losing influence, Spain has been a consistent advocate of a 'deepening' of the EU, as its attitude to EMU, amongst many other major projects, reveals. Thirdly, it has also consistently favoured the EU's ability to play a leading role in world affairs, largely so as to overcome its own shortcomings in this sphere prior to accession. Finally, in order to guarantee all of the above, Madrid has necessarily done its best to fight hard to retain its institutional status within the EU and reach fruitful alliances with other Member States.

The forthcoming Eastern enlargement may significantly modify Spain's current weight and role within the EU as a whole. Indeed Spain is facing the prospect of ceasing to be a major recipient of EU funds and instead becoming a potential donor, and moving from a context in which Spanish democracy had been bolstered by other EU members to one in which Spain will be expected to contribute to strengthening the new democracies of Central and Eastern Europe.

This challenge no doubt offers fresh opportunities for Spain, but it is by no means certain that it will be able to take advantage of them unless it undertakes certain reforms, both economic and institutional, at domestic level. Some of these will require substantial changes in the Spanish economic structures—most significantly with regard to the labour market and public decisions at local level—and cannot be expected to take place overnight. Others, however, could be tackled with relative ease.

A simple example of the institutional reforms required is that of the proportion of the budget devoted to the Foreign Ministry, which will have to be increased significantly in the future given that the system will be even more over-stretched than it is at present.[11] Similarly, for many years now defence expenditure has remained one of the lowest in Europe, a trend which has slowed down the transition from a conscript to a professional army currently almost implemented, thereby undermining the credibility of Spain's commitment to international military projects, such as the European Rapid Reaction Force, among others. These and other considerations might give credence to the view that in recent years Spain has been living beyond its means in the EU, or 'punching above its weight', in substantial contrast to the official positions defended during the Treaty of Nice negotiations (Powell, 2001).

[11] In this respect it is very telling that five future accession countries do not yet have a Spanish diplomatic representation.

No doubt it can be summed up that Spain managed to develop a clear and successful strategy along the Nice IGC negotiations with its exclusive focus on institutional issues. This strategy was not least reinforced and sustained by the need for the Spanish Government, the Popular Party and Aznar himself to sell a victory domestically. In this respect, the practical strategies to handle the negotiations were directly influenced by the new solid parliamentary political situation of the Popular Party, as well as restricted by the personal needs and objectives of the Spanish Prime Minister. The Spanish negotiating team clearly learned and applied the lessons learnt from Amsterdam, and used them both in a tactical and substantial way to support its claims.

Nevertheless, Spain has once again suffered from the traditional paradox and incoherences of its position with regard to European policy, that is, trying to be simultaneously a 'large', but 'poor' Member State. The maintenance of the paradox does not allow the Spanish Government to develop a mid- or long-term policy strategy; in fact, Spain is thus forced to envisage the successive intergovernmental negotiations at European level as an on-going series of 'individual battles' instead of a linear process along which Spain would be progressively defining its role at all levels (economic, political, military...).

The reception of the results of the Nice negotiations has resulted in the first signs of a substantial and mature political debate on European issues by most Spanish political parties and various societal, economic and political actors. We hope that the post-Nice political developments help us explain and interpret to what extent the actual behaviour during the IGC negotiations paved the way for a far-reaching Spanish strategy with regard to its active and fruitful membership of the European Union.

BIBLIOGRAPHY

Aldecoa Luzarraga, Francisco (2001), "La apertura del proceso constituyente," *Boletín Europeo de la Universidad de La Rioja*, No. 7-8, March (Especial Monográfico Tratado de Niza), pp. 7-14.

Almarcha Barbado, Amparo (ed.) (1993), *Spain and EC membership evaluated.* London: Pinter Publishers.

Ama, Carlos del (2001), "Misión de España en Europa y la agenda de la Presidencia española," paper presented at the TEPSA Seminar *La Presidencia española de la Unión Europea.* Madrid, Fundación Ortega y Gasset, 23 November.

Andrés, María (2001), "L'après Nice," *Nueva Revista de Política, Cultura y Arte,* Vol. II, No. 5.

Areilza Carvajal, José María (2001), "La reforma de Niza: ¿hacia qué Unión Europea?", *Política Exterior*, Vol. XV, no. 79, pp. 104-119.

— José María (2002), "La Unión Europea de 2004 y la piedra filosofal," *Política Exterior*, Vol. XVI, no. 85, pp. 57-68.

Aznar López, José María, Speech at the European Merit Awards' Ceremony, Brussels, 9 October 2001.

—, Speech at the Seminar "Europe without Borders," organised by the Bertelsmann Foundation, Berlin, 19 January 2002.

Barbé, Esther (1999), *La política europea de España.* Barcelona: Ariel.

Barón Crespo, Enrique, "Post Niza," *El País*, 1 March 2001.

—, "Post-Niza, diez tesis para el debate," *El País*, 26 June 2001.

Basabe Lloréns, Felipe (2000), "Spain: new allies?", in A. Pijpers (ed.), *On cores and coalitions in the European Union.* The Hague, Clingendael Series.

— (2001), "The Parliament of Spain: Slowly Moving onto the European Direction?" in Andreas Maurer and Wolfgang Wessels (eds.), *National Parliaments on their Ways to Europe: Losers or Latecomers*, Schriften des Zentrum für Europäische Integrationsforschung (ZEI). Baden-Baden: Nomos, pp. 199-223.

— (2002a), "Spain and the Negotiations of the Amsterdam Treaty: The Arising of a 'difficult' EU Negotiation Partner?", in F. Laursen and S. Vanhoonacker (eds.), *The Amsterdam Treaty: National Preference Formation, Interstate Bargaining, Outcome and Ratification.* Odense: Odense University Press, pp. 311-340.

— (2002b), "European Constitution-Making from a Spanish Perspective", in P. Cullen and P. Zervakis (eds.), *The Post-Nice Process: Towards a European Constitution?* Baden-Baden: Nomos, pp. 153-172.

— and González Escudero, Mª Teresa (2002c), "Papel del Parlamento español en la estructura europea después de Niza," *Revista Parlamentaria de la Asamblea de Madrid*, No. 6 – June 2002, pp. 95-114.

— (2003), "Spain: the Emergence of a new major actor in the European Arena?", in Wolfgang Wessels, A. Maurer and J. Mittag (eds.), *Fifteen into One? The European Union and the Member States.* Manchester: Manchester University Press, pp. 184-215.

Bassols, Raimundo (1995), *España en Europa. Historia de la adhesión a la CE (1957-85).* Madrid: Política Exterior.

Best, Edward (2001), "The Treaty of Nice: Not Beautiful but It'll Do," *EIPASCOPE*, No. 1, pp. 2-10.

Bonet, Pilar, "Aznar alerta contra el federalismo en la construcción europea," *El País*, 20 Jan 2002.

Burgorgue-Larsen, Laurence (1995), *L'Espagne et la Communauté Européenne.* Bruxelles: ULB.

— (1997), "Espagne," in Joël Rideau (ed.), *Les Etats membres de l'Union Européenne: adaptations, mutations, résistances*. Paris: LGDJ.

C.E.O.E. (1996), *Diez años de España en la Unión Europea.* Madrid: Publics. C.E.O.E.

Cienfuegos Mateo, Manuel (1997), "La Comisión Mixta para la Unión Europea: Análisis y balance de una década de actividad en el seguimiento de los asuntos comunitarios," *Gaceta Jurídica de la CE*, Serie D, No. 27, pp. 7-69.

De Miguel y Egea, Ramón (2002), "La presidencia española y el futuro del proyecto europeo," *Política Exterior*, Vol. XVI, no. 85, pp. 43-56.

Dehousse, Franklin (2001), *Le Traité de Nice et la déclaration de Laeken*, Courrier Hebdomadaire, No. 1735. Brussels: C.R.I.S.P.

Egurbide, Peru, "Aznar califica el proyecto europeo de Zapatero de simple ocurrencia," *El País*, 8 June 2001.

—— "Aznar se postula como defensor del tratado de Niza y critica a los que han puesto dificultades a la ampliación," *El País*, 17 June 2001.

Elorza Cavengt, Javier (1997), "*Reflexiones y balance de diez años de España en la Unión Europea,*" Información Comercial Española, No. 766, pp.15-29.

—— (2001a), "La UE después de Niza," *Política Exterior*, Vol. XV, n.79, pp. 84-103.

—— (2001b), "La batalla de Niza," http://www.esi2.us.es/pdffiles/elorza.pdf

Estella de Noriega, Antonio, "Berlín 2004 y las competencias de la Unión," *El País*, 11 April 2001.

Fonseca Morillo, Francisco J. (2001), "De Berlín a Niza: Panorama y lecciones," *Boletín Europeo de la Universidad de La Rioja*, No. 7-8, March 2001 (Monográfico Tratado de Niza), pp. 2-7.

Fuentes García, Josefa (2001), "Datos y fuentes documentales para el estudio del Tratado de Niza y del proceso post-Niza," in Ricardo Alonso García and Pablo Pérez Tremps (eds.), *Retos constitucionales de la Unión Europea Constitución e integración después del Tratado de Niza*, Cuadernos de Derecho Público, No. 13. Madrid: Publicaciones del INAP, pp. 295-310.

Fundación Carlos de Amberes (2000a), "La Reforma Institucional," *Jornadas sobre la Conferencia Interguberna-mental*, Primera Jornada, 12 May, pp. 5-46.

—— (2000b), "La Conferencia Intergubernamental después del Consejo Europeo de Feira", *Jornadas sobre la Conferencia Intergubernamental*, Segunda Jornada, 7 July, pp. 9-45.

—— (2001), "La Construcción de Europa," *Jornadas sobre la Conferencia Intergubernamental*, Tercera Jornada, 9 February, pp.5-47.

Gallego-Díaz, Soledad, "Las trampas de los modelos europeos," *El País*, 3 June 2001.

Galloway, David (2001), *The Treaty of Nice and Beyond. Realities and Illusions of Pow-er in the EU.* Sheffield: Sheffield Academic Press

Gillespie, Richard et al. (1995), *Las relaciones exteriores de la España democrática.* Madrid: Alianza.

González Márquez, Felipe, "De Niza a Berlín: oportunidades y riesgos," *El País*, 15 June 2001.

González Vega, Javier A. (2001), "Los acuerdos de Niza, la PESC y la arquitectura europea de seguridad y defensa," *Boletín Europeo de la Universidad de La Rioja*, No. 9, Dec. 2001, pp. 11-28.

Guardans Cambó, Ignasi (2001), "Construcción europea y ampliación: Las repercusiones para España e Italia," *CIDOB, II Foro de Diálogo Hispano-Italiano "España-Italia 2001: cuestiones a debate*" (Barcelona, 15-16 December 2000).

Jones, Rachel (1997), "Regional Participation in Spanish European Policy: Implications for the Level of State Autonomy," *Estudios* No. 0197, Instituto Universitario Ortega y Gasset.

Laso Pérez, Javier (2001), "La intervención democrática en la Unión Europea después del asunto austríaco y la reforma del Tratado de Niza," *Boletín Europeo de la Universidad de La Rioja*, No. 7-8, March (Especial Monográfico Tratado de Niza), pp. 45-60.

Lirola Delgado, Isabel (2001), "El espacio de libertad, seguridad y justicia en el Tratado de Niza: ¿una cuestión meramente incidental?", *Boletín Europeo de la Universidad de La Rioja*, No. 9, December, pp. 29-36.

Matutes, Abel et al. (1999), *Spanien und Deutschland als EU-Partner*, Schriften des Zentrum für Europäische Integrationsforschung. Baden-Baden: Nomos.

Medina, Manuel (2001), "La Cumbre de Niza y la calculadora," http://www.psoe-pe.org

Ministry of Foreign Affairs (1995), *Reflexiones sobre la Conferencia Intergubema-mental 1996*. Madrid: Publicaciones del Ministerio de Asuntos Exteriores.

— (2001), *Tratado de Niza (Memoria justificativa para el expediente de ratificación del Tratado de Niza)*. Madrid: O.I.D.

Ministry of Home Affairs (1997), *El tercer pilar de la Unión Europea. La cooperación en asuntos de justicia e interior*. Madrid: Publicaciones del Ministerio del Interior.

— (1999), *El espacio europeo de libertad, seguridad y justicia*. Madrid: Publicaciones del Ministerio del Interior.

Molina del Pozo, Carlos F. (1996), *España en la Europa comunitaria: balance de diez años*. Madrid: CEURA.

Morata, Francesco (1998), "Spain," in Klaus Hanf and Ben Soetendorp (eds.), *Adapting to European Integration*. London: Longman, pp. 100-115.

Moreno Juste, Antonio (1998), *España y el proceso de construcción europea*. Barcelona: Ariel.

Newton, Michael T. and Peter J. Donaghy (1997), *Institutions of modern Spain: A political and economic guide*. Cambridge: Cambridge University Press.

Olesti Rayo, Andreu (2001), "Las modificaciones institucionales en el Tratado de Niza," *Boletín Europeo de la Universidad de La Rioja*, No. 7-8, March (Especial Monográfico Tratado de Niza), pp. 14-27.

Ortega, Andrés, "Amistades peligrosas," *El País*, 26 February 2001.

Pérez Tremps, Pablo (2001), "La Constitución española antes y después de Niza," in Ricardo Alonso García and Pablo Pérez Tremps (eds.), *Retos constitucionales de la Unión Europea Constitución e integración después del Tratado de Niza*," Cuadernos de Derecho Público, No. 13. Madrid: Publicaciones del INAP, pp. 267-292.

Piqué, Josep (2001), "Nuevas fronteras de la política exterior de España," *Política Exterior*, Vol. XV, no. 79, pp. 57-72.

Powell, Charles T. (2000), Cambio de Régimen y Política Exterior: España 1975-1989, *Cuadernos de Política Exterior* No. 8, Madrid: INCIPE-CERI.

— (2001), *Fifteen years on: Spanish membership of the European Union revisited*, paper presented at the Conference "From Isolation ot Integration: 15 Years of Spanish and Portuguese Membership in Europe," Minda de Gunzburg Center for European Studies, Harvard University, 2-3 November. Kindly provided by the author.

P.S.O.E., Documento "Las propuesta del PSOE sobre el futuro de Europa," 7 June 2001.

Ramírez Jiménez, Manuel (1996), *Europa en la conciencia española y otros estudios*. Madrid: Trotta.

Roldán Barbero, Javier (2001), Las relaciones exteriores de España. Madrid: Dykinson.

Ruiz-Jarabo Colomer, Dámaso (2001), "La reforma de la arquitectura judicial europea: un emplo del grial falto de inspiración," in Ricardo Alonso García and Pablo Pérez Tremps (eds.), *Retos constitucionales de la Unión Europea Constitución e integración después del Tratado de Niza*, Cuadernos de Derecho Público, No. 13. Madrid: Publicaciones del INAP, pp. 125-152.

Solana Madariaga, Javier (2001), "Desafíos de la defensa europea," *Política Exterior*, Vol. XV, no. 79, pp. 73-83.

Spain, Cortes Generales, *Boletín Oficial de las Cortes Generales* (BOCG. Congreso de los Diputados), serie A, No. 39-1, 15 June 2001 (Número de expediente 121/000039), Proyecto de Ley Orgánica 3/2001, de 6 de noviembre, por la que se autoriza la ratificación por España del Tratado de Niza por el que se modifican el Tratado de la Unión Europea, los Tratados Constitutivos de las Comunidades Europeas y determinados actos conexos, firmado en Niza el día 26 de febrero 2001.

—— *Diario de Sesiones del Congreso de los Diputados*, VII Legislatura, No. 102, Debate de totalidad de iniciativas legislativas (Proyecto de ley orgánica de ratificación del Tratado de Niza)", 13 September 2001, pp. 4949-4968.

——, Ley Orgánica 3/2001, de 6 de noviembre, por la que se autoriza la ratificación por España del Tratado de Niza por el que se modifican el Tratado de la Unión Europea, los Tratados Constitutivos de las Comunidades Europeas y determinados actos conexos, firmado en Niza el día 26 de febrero de 2001 (*Boletín Oficial del Estado* No. 267, 7 November 2001)

—— (2002), Speech by Mrs. Luisa F. Rudi, President of the Congreso de los Diputados to the Conference of Presidents of European Parliaments (Madrid, 8 June). Kindly provided by the Interparliamentary Relations' Unit of the Senado.

Taibo, Carlos, "Los silencios de Niza," *El País*, 2 March 2001.

Vidal-Folch, Xavier (2002), "La Europa que viene: retos políticos y económicos," *Política Exterior*, Vol. XVI, no. 85, pp. 94-110.

Various authors (1998), *España y la negociación del Tratado de Amsterdam*. Madrid: Política Exterior

Yárnoz, Carlos, "Zapatero busca el equilibrio entre Schröder y Jospin," *El País*, 11 June 2001.

—— "Aznar se abre paso en Europa," *El País*, 9 June 2002.

CHAPTER 15

SWEDEN: IN THE SHADOW OF ENLARGEMENT?

INTRODUCTION

In a speech delivered on 14 December 2000, Prime Minister Göran Persson informed the Swedish parliament about the content of the Nice agreement. The Prime Minister emphasised that the agreement reached in Nice was an important and necessary step on the road towards a successful enlargement of the Union (Speech by Göran Persson, 14 December 2000).

The fact that Persson declared the conference a success because the treaty provided the necessary conditions for enlargement might seem perfectly natural. After all, the overriding purpose of the Intergovernmental Conference (IGC) was to reform the institutions in order to prepare the Union for the accession of new Member States. However, during an IGC, each Member State faces the double task of contributing to the promotion of the common interest and pursuing its own national goals. Accordingly, whether a treaty agreement is to be deemed a success or a failure can be determined in each Member State either by the contribution made to promoting the common interest, or by the degree to which national goals have been furthered.

Judging from Prime Minister Persson's speech, one is tempted to argue that the Swedish preparations and negotiations took place in the *shadow of enlargement*. During the stages of national preference formation and interstate bargaining (Moravcsik, 1993, 1998), Sweden's behaviour should then have been determined primarily by concerns for contributing to a successful enlargement. Is this picture correct or were there other concerns that were equally or even more important?

The Amsterdam treaty had left unresolved some pressing institutional issues, and Member States were in agreement on the need of future institutional reform. In order to perform efficiently, an enlarged Community required a reformed institutional framework. However, as the opening of IGC 2000 drew closer, it became apparent that there were differing opinions regarding the elements of reform considered necessary for enlargement. Some argued that now was the time for comprehensive reform and that there might be no better opportunity in the future to agree on a new institutional framework, suitable for a community of 25-30 Member States. The report delivered by Jean-Luc Dehaene, David Simon and Richard von Weizsäcker on 18 October 1999 was typical of this ambitious approach.

Referring to the protocol on enlargement and institutional reform, agreed upon in Amsterdam, they argued that "an effort at comprehensive reform should be undertaken right now" (Dehaene et al., 1999). The Amsterdam protocol stated that a comprehensive reform should be made before the number of Member States exceeded twenty. Given the pace of the negotiation process, it was argued that the first enlargement could bring the number of Member States beyond twenty. Thus, in order to uphold "the spirit of the Amsterdam protocol" (ibid.) comprehensive reform was required sooner rather than later. In their report, Dehaene, Simon and Weizsäcker offered a number of ambitious proposals for institutional reform. The proposed reform package was clearly more ambitious than the preliminary agenda laid down by the Cologne European Council, which had simply reaffirmed the need to resolve the institutional issues left open in Amsterdam (European Council, 1999a). The report now advocated that the agenda of the IGC, besides the Amsterdam left–overs, should include flexibility, defence issues and a reorganisation of the treaty texts (Dehaene et al., 1999).

On the other hand, there were those who favoured a far less ambitious approach to institutional reform. In light of previous experiences, where IGCs had tended to promote overambitious goals which could not be fulfilled, it was argued that the agenda should be restricted to a minimum of reform issues in order to ensure the signing of a new treaty before the end of the year. Anxious not to delay the enlargement process by taking on a broad agenda, Sweden was clearly among those Member States that advocated a safe journey towards a limited reform package which could then be complemented by additional reforms at a later IGC, if necessary.

In this chapter, we will first of all describe in more detail the positions taken by Sweden on those issues that finally made it to the IGC agenda and the overriding concerns guiding Sweden's preparations. Is it fair to argue that Sweden's preparations took place in the shadow of enlargement? Or do concerns such as national interests and pressure from public opinion provide better ways to understand Swedish positions? Next we turn to the stage of interstate bargaining, analysing how the points of departure influenced Swedish negotiating tactics. Finally, we consider the ratification debate and the adoption of the Nice Treaty.

PREPARING FOR NICE—CAUTION AND CONTINUITY

Ever since Sweden joined the European Union in 1995, its citizens have been rather sceptical regarding the alleged benefits of membership. Data from the Eurobarometer presented in the table below reveal that the lowest levels of public support for the EU are found in Sweden, Austria and Great Britain, with the highest levels of support in Ireland, Luxembourg, Netherlands, Spain and Portugal. In 2000, as the IGC opened, only 35.9 per cent of the Swedish citizens believed that membership of the Union was a good thing, whereas 37.5 percent held it to be a bad thing. These figures compare with the 53.9 per cent of all EU citizens who believed that membership was a good thing and the 15.7 per cent who considered the EU negatively.

One would perhaps expect that these widespread negative attitudes towards the Union would lead to a heated public debate on EU issues, especially in times of important change. This has not been the case in Sweden, however. For a number of reasons, the public debate on EU issues has been rather restricted and cautious. This is first of all a consequence of the fact that the political, economic and administrative elite is not polarised in their attitudes about the EU in the same way as the citizenry. In Sweden, as in many other Member States, we find an extensive gap between attitudes held by citizens and those of elites. In the 'Top Decision-Makers Survey' from 1996, based on interviews with senior elected politicians, senior civil servants, business and trade union leaders and members of the media, 84 per cent of the Swedish respondents were of the opinion that EU membership was a good thing versus only 29 per cent of the citizens (Karlsson, 2001). Among the political parties, only the Left Party and the Green Party hold positions that conform to the negative attitudes harboured by the citizens.

Table 15.1: Public Support for the EU, 2000 (percentages)

Attitude	*Positive*	*Indifferent*	*Negative*	*Net support*
EU	*53.9*	*30.4*	*15.7*	*38.2*
Austria	36.4	35.8	27.8	8.6
Belgium	65.4	23.9	10.7	54.7
Denmark	54.9	20.3	24.8	30.1
Finland	42.2	35.8	22.0	20.2
France	52.4	32.9	14.8	37.6
Germany	43.7	40.5	15.8	27.9
Great Britain	32.8	37.6	29.6	3.2
Greece	66.6	25.7	7.7	58.9
Ireland	81.6	12.5	5.9	75.7
Italy	62.9	27.1	10.0	52.9
Luxembourg	78.4	14.9	6.7	71.7
Netherlands	76.7	16.8	6.5	70.2
Portugal	70.0	24.8	5.2	64.8
Spain	71.3	22.3	6.4	64.9
Sweden	35.9	26.6	37.5	- 1.6

Source: Eurobarometer 53. These results are calculated by using weighted data. The EU 15 weight included in the Eurobarometer has been utilised. This weight adjusts each national sample in proportion to its nation's share in the total population of the Member States.

Second, all the pro-EU parties—The Social Democratic Party, the Centre Party, the Liberal Party, the Christian Democratic Party and the Moderate Party—have experienced conflicts and intra-party fractionalism due to EU issues. This has been a difficult problem to handle, not least for the Social Democratic Party. In order to minimise internal conflicts, the parties have tended, for as long as possible, to avoid taking firm positions on controversial issues such as the EMU—to 'wait and see' was for a long time the position of the Social Democratic Party (Johansson & Raunio, 2001).

Third, EU issues have often been described as 'technical' and difficult to understand. Although these characteristics may have been exaggerated, this argument may be relevant for explaining the relative absence of a Swedish public debate on EU issues. Especially during the IGC 2000, the issues on the agenda were rather 'technical' and difficult to grasp. It is not easy to initiate widespread public debate on issues regarding different methods for the weighting of votes in the Council, or the size and composition of the Commission.

These factors have had an inhibiting effect on the Swedish public debate. The fact that Sweden has the most Eurosceptical public of all Member States is not reflected in a public discussion where different positions and arguments stand against each other on important EU issues. The waiting game played by many parties, most notably the Social Democrats, has contributed to the creation of a rather restricted and cautious public debate on European affairs. The widespread Eurosceptic sentiments among the Swedish citizenry have not been effectively voiced in public debate. This does not mean that public opinion is irrelevant. On the contrary, public opinion does matter and certainly provides a constraint on political elites and decision-makers. However, the political elites' and decision-makers' room for manoeuvre is more generous than would perhaps be expected in a country where a majority of citizens are negative or indifferent to European integration.

Public opinion was therefore not an important factor during the process of forming national positions. The government did not have to consider the impact of Eurosceptic and anti-federalist sentiments voiced in public debate, because such a debate was largely absent. The role played by interest organisations was also very limited during the preparations to IGC 2000. No great effort was made by the main interest organisations to influence the Swedish negotiating positions. The clear institutional focus of the IGC probably goes a long way toward explaining the limited interest displayed by interest organisations in making their voices heard during the preparations for IGC 2000. The interest organisations were actually more interested in the upcoming Swedish presidency.[1]

As the real preparations began and the opening of the IGC drew closer, the Swedish government was—in the absence of a critical public debate and organised interests trying to make their voiced heard—concerned mainly with having to inform and consult with the *Riksdag*. The main forum for consultations between the government and the parliament was the Advisory Committee on EU Affairs. At a meeting of the Committee on 11 February 2000, Prime Minister Göran Persson and chief negotiator Gunnar Lund gave an account of the Swedish position. It was, first of all, made clear by Persson and Lund that Sweden advocated a limited agenda for the IGC. The reason for wanting to keep the list of issues as short as possible was the risk of delaying the entire enlargement process (EU Advisory Committee, 11 February 2000). Being one of the strongest supporters of the enlargement project, it was natural that Sweden wanted to avoid unnecessary delays of the process. Already at the previous IGC, preparing for enlargement had been presented as a key Swedish

[1] Interview with Annika Söder, 8 November 2002.

priority (Swedish Government, 1995). The dedication to a successful and rapid enlargement of the EU was now reaffirmed.

The opening of the IGC 2000 coincided, for Sweden, with preparations for taking over the presidency from France in January 2001. At an early stage, it was decided that enlargement would be one of the priority issues during the Swedish presidency. Had the IGC failed to reach an agreement in Nice, it would have been more difficult for Sweden to reach the desired "breakthrough in the membership negotiations" (Speech by Göran Persson, 14 December 2000) during its presidency. It was imperative to maintain a clean slate for the incoming presidency, thus making it possible to give full priority to Swedish key issues. The prospect of a successful presidency focused on issues related to enlargement, employment and the environment certainly provided additional incentives for Sweden to support a limited agenda.

Besides missing out on the opportunity to place Swedish key issues on the EU agenda, failure to achieve an agreement in Nice would also mean that Sweden would have to assume responsibility for leading the negotiations to a successful conclusion. Representatives of the Swedish Government made it clear that having to take over responsibility for the IGC was not an appealing prospect (EU Advisory Committee, 11 February 2000; *Göteborgs-Posten,* 26 September 2000). To find new momentum in the negotiation process and reach a final agreement would have been a difficult task for even the most experienced of Member States, not to mention a newcomer to the presidency. Advocating a limited agenda would serve the purpose of maximising the opportunity to actually reach an agreement in Nice, thus freeing Sweden of the burden to take over responsibility for the making of a new treaty. The incoming presidency was thus an important factor as Swedish preparations for IGC 2000 continued.

Supporting a limited agenda was also consistent with Sweden's general ambition to avoid any further delegation of competencies to the EU (Interview with Annika Söder, 8 November 2002). Sweden has always been a firm believer in a Union based on a nation-state logic. The foundation of the integration project should be nation-states that choose to pool their sovereignty within certain policy fields. By aiming for a limited agenda, Sweden hoped to minimise the risk of further steps being taken on the road towards something like a United States of Europe.

Chief negotiator Gunnar Lund informed the committee on the Swedish positions regarding the specific issues on the agenda for the IGC—as laid down by the Helsinki European Council (European Council, 1999b)—emphasising that Sweden's opinions were the same as during IGC 96. Chief negotiator Lund thus described Swedish European policy as being characterised by continuity. The negotiating positions, he argued, were well known by all the political parties and had been supported by the *Riksdag* during IGC 96 (EU Advisory Committee, 11 February 2000).

As for the size and composition of the Commission, Sweden would, according to Gunnar Lund, fight for the continued right of each Member State to nominate one member of the Commission (EU Advisory Committee, 11 February 2000).

Chief negotiator Lund recognised the need for a re-weighting of votes in the Council. At the same time, he emphasised that Sweden did not accept the argument made by the larger Member States, that the successive additions of new members had led to an unacceptable overrepresentation of the smaller Member States that now had to be rectified (EU Advisory Committee, 11 February 2000). From the outset, the ambition of the government was to secure Sweden's relative power in the Council and, if possible, strengthen its position vis-à-vis other small and middle-sized Member States. The government pointed out that Sweden had fewer votes per capita than other middle-sized Member States (Swedish Government, 2001). Chief negotiator Lund also made it clear that Sweden rejected the introduction of a system of dual majority (EU Advisory Committee, 11 February 2000).

Regarding the possible extension of qualified majority voting (QMV) in the Council, Sweden firmly rejected ideas to the effect that QMV should "become the rule, apart from a very few exceptions" (The Commission, 2000). Instead, Sweden advocated that the issue should be dealt with on a case-by-case basis. Sweden was only willing to accept an extension of QMV on a number of issues within the fields of social policy, asylum policy and migration policy, as well as on those matters within the internal market that still required unanimity (Swedish Government, 2001).

The Government was able to find support for its negotiating positions in the Parliament. The greatest differences of opinion related to the issue of extended majority voting. Five of the parties in the *Riksdag* were in favour of an extension of qualified majority voting on certain taxation issues within the fields of energy and the environment. The Government, however, forcefully rejected any extension of majority voting on taxation issues and was backed by the Moderate Party. In fact, the Government and the Moderate Party were in agreement on all major issues during the Swedish preparations for IGC 2000,[2] thus forming a somewhat unusual alliance in Swedish politics.

Negotiations from a Swedish Point of View

The overall strategy pursued by Sweden, once the negotiations started, was to strive for a solution that could favour a quick conclusion and an open road towards enlargement. This point of departure can be said to have decided the course of action for the Swedish negotiators.

The Portuguese Presidency (Guerra Martins, contribution to this volume) sought rapid progress and to discuss all the leftovers thoroughly among the chief negotiators prior to the European Council meeting in Lisbon in March (*Europe,* 8 March 2000). These intentions were fully in line with Swedish desires for a short and limited IGC. Sweden supported all attempts to clear the table from unnecessary non-starters and unwanted surprises at the last minute. Sweden was therefore not keen on proposed additions such as Article 7 and the early warning system to prevent serious and persistent breaches of fundamental rights and freedoms (EU Advisory Committee, 15 June 2000).

The Swedish government could not altogether get its views across. Broadening the agenda was an issue from the very start of the negotiations (*Europe,* 17 February 2000) and even though no formal additions were made to the agenda at the European Council meeting in March, the agenda was not closed. Moreover, the discussions that had taken place clearly showed that the Presidency and several other Member States were positively disposed toward an extended agenda (*Europe,* 2-3 March 2000 and 8 March 2000). As weeks went by without much progress in the discussions on extension on qualified majority voting, the option of extending the agenda proved more and more tempting. It was a vehicle for presenting at least some results to the public (Holmlund, 2001; EU Advisory Committee, 6 October 2000). Furthermore, the issue of enhanced co-operation was an issue of great symbolic value for many states (EU advisory Committee, 15 June and 15 September 2000). The Swedish Government probably felt less convinced of the consequences of such a strategy, but was also loath to block a process desired by the majority. Somewhat reluctantly, therefore, Sweden in spring had to accept that enhanced co-operation or flexible integration was added to the agenda and that preparations for a Swedish position

[2] Interview with Lars Tobisson, 12 January 2003.

had to be accelerated (EU Advisory Committee, 11 February and 15 June 2000). Sweden thus had reason to worry that its strategy of limiting the agenda to the bare necessities was actually failing.

Discussions during the first half of the IGC can best be described as a preparatory phase, including tedious repetitions of previous positions from the Amsterdam negotiations (*Europe,* 8 March 2000 and 1 June 2000). During this stage of the process, however, Sweden started to plant its ideas and adopt firm stances on all institutional issues. Swedish positions were thus well known as negotiations intensified during the autumn.

This stood in sharp contrast to negotiation behaviour in the IGC 1996-97, when Sweden actually kept a rather low profile on institutional issues (Johansson & Svensson, 2002). This reversal of tactics can best be understood from the perspective of the fast approaching first Swedish presidency. The government obviously wanted to avoid having to fight overly much for its stance in the end negotiations.

The change in negotiating tactics was most apparent in the case of C*ouncil voting*. Securing a satisfactory result here, in terms of both an efficient, legitimate and long-term agreement, and a better position for Sweden, continued to be a top priority (Swedish Government, 2001). However, the differences between the positions of the larger and the smaller Member States were as clear as ever. Curiously, this could be argued to have opened up some scope for constructive and inventive proposals.

A new solution, according to Sweden, should build upon transparent and objective criteria, and have a permanent character so as to avoid reforms and the accompanying harrowing and time-consuming negotiations, in view of every new enlargement. Such a solution thus had to meet the demands of the larger Member States for a credible system, while at the same time ensuring that smaller states had sufficient influence (Swedish Government, 2001). The Swedish government clearly thought that it had found the solution in the very logical and, relatively intelligible square root model, where the votes were distributed in proportion to the square root of the population of the Member States. Several alternatives were possible, and later presented, depending on what limits were set for highest and lowest number of votes.[3] What worried Sweden here was that although the larger states seemed well co-ordinated in their views, the smaller states were split between those wanting a re-weighting

[3] Interview with Torbjörn Haak, 21 January 2003.

of votes, such as Sweden, and those that argued for some system of double majority (EU Advisory Committee, 1 December 2000).

The idea seemed to have been to present the Swedish square root model as an "objective" idea. To get the merits of its proposal across, Sweden had first had to disarm one of the arguments of the larger Member States. During spring and summer, Sweden argued forcefully against the larger Member States which claimed that they had lost proportionally more votes as a consequence of previous enlargements and that they should therefore be properly compensated. It was now time for the smaller Member States to give up one commissioner (Swedish Government, 2001; *Europe,* 13 September 2000). The compensatory argument put forward by some of the larger Member States (*Europe,* 19 April 2000, 14 July 2000 and 28 September 2000) was no doubt a manoeuvre intended to uphold pressure in the negotiations. The Swedish negotiators took on a special task here, trying to expose these arguments, as they did in the IGC 1996-97. Throughout the autumn, Sweden attempted to demonstrate that all Member States had lost equally much in influence in relative terms. This argument was never fully accepted by the larger states, but they nevertheless seemed to have taken less and less recourse to this argument (Moberg, 2002).

The battle was also fought on another, and more nationally oriented front, as Sweden presented figures showing that middle-sized Member States with a few million more inhabitants than Sweden actually had more votes per capita than Sweden. This was argued as being contrary to the principle of degressive proportionality underlying the whole system, thus undermining long run legitimacy for the system in Sweden.

The Swedish negotiators had calculated that the right moment for presentation of the square root model would be during the first half of the IGC. Seeing that the proposals for Council votes presented by the presidency did not meet the criteria actually stipulated also by the presidency (Portuguese Presidency, 2000a) that had been set out, Sweden took the opportunity to launch its own initiative (Moberg, 2002). Several Member States showed interest in the model, and it was agreed that it should be presented as one of several alternatives in the presidency report to the European Council in Feira at the end of June (Portuguese Presidency, 2000b).

The model was included in the discussion right up to the end of the conference (*Europe,* 27-28 November 2000) but by then Sweden, doubtlessly with a view to the upcoming presidency, decided to maintain a low profile on the issue. With such considerations hindered Swedish actions, there were really no partners to stand up for the proposal. The square root model could not quite capture the attention of all parties, appealing mostly to the smaller and middle-sized Member States, which as seen above were split between different re-weighting and double majority solutions. The main drawback of the model was that it was too frank on power relations in the Union. Several states thus argued that a new vote-weighting system ultimately had to take politics into account and that Council voting could not solely be treated as a technical issue.

Regarding another prioritised issue, the *composition of the Commission*, Swedish negotiators argued alongside colleagues from other smaller or middle-sized states that the legitimacy of the Union was at stake. Good decisions by the collegiate depended on knowledge of culture, history and political characteristics in each and every Member State (Swedish Government, 2001). It was argued that the solution to the problem had been laid out already in Amsterdam, where it was agreed that the larger Member States were to give up one of their commissioners in exchange for more votes in the Council (EU Advisory Committee, 6 October 2000 and 1 December 2000).

The issue of the composition of the Commission even more clearly pitted the smaller against the larger Member States (*Europe,* 20 September 2000). In contrast to the re-weighting of votes where interests differed and all states ultimately had to ensure their own votes, the issue of the composition of the Commission invited co-operation. The smaller states held frequent meetings and showed a unified front during most of the IGC.[4] It was underlined that compensation to the larger states could only be given once, through re-weighting of votes, and not additionally through reforms of the internal organisation of the Commission or other issues on the IGC agenda (EU Advisory Committee, 1 December 2000).

This co-operation did not show itself as joint statements or papers, but as a concert of voices all asking for the same thing.[5] At the informal meeting in Biarritz, however, this unity began to crumble when Finland suddenly announced that it could accept other arrangements.[6] This naturally put considerable pressure on the other smaller states. In an effort to extract the most from the re-weighting debate, Sweden withheld an acceptance of solutions that

---

[4] Interview with Torbjörn Haak, 21 January 2003.

[5] Interview with Torbjörn Haak, 21 January 2003.

[6] Interview with Torbjörn Haak, 21 January 2003.

provided for a smaller collegiate in a Union with more than 28 members until the final discussions in Nice (*Europe,* 27-28 November 2000).

In comparison, the provisions discussed in connection with the internal organisation of the commission were given much less attention by the Swedish Government.[7] It seems to have been mostly content to follow the debate at a distance while in general terms underlining the importance of equality and transparency. It was deemed more important to defend Swedish interests on other issues.

Qualified majority voting, on the other hand, needed constant attention. In this field, real discussions began right from the start of the IGC and progressed, if sometimes slowly, throughout the spring and autumn (Holmlund, 2001).

Sweden was in the middle position on most issues in the QMV discussion. There were, however, some notable exceptions concerning the articles on taxes and family law (Swedish Government, 2001). On the issue of taxes, Sweden especially pointed out that these issues were closely connected to national sovereignty and to the fact that taxes were often used as an important steering tool. Sweden did not think it possible to find proper definitions and delimitations of this use and therefore feared endless discussions about the legal basis and as a consequence, less efficient implementation (Swedish Government, 2001).

The same argument of closeness to national sovereignty was to underlie the Swedish position on family law. Here Sweden did not want to accept rules that could run contrary to fundamental Swedish values in this area. It was argued that family law, as opposed to civil law in general, is closely linked to a country's cultural, economic and social characteristics (Swedish Government, 2001). Behind this argument lay a fear that Sweden would be forced to adjust its rather progressive legislation to what it considered to be lower standards (EU Advisory Committee, 10 December 2000).

In other areas, Sweden showed more willingness for reform and argued for an extension of the use of QMV. This was especially true for the social area, which had always received special attention from the Swedish government, not least in the negotiations leading up to the Amsterdam Treaty (Svensson, 2000). In addition, Sweden worked for a transition to QMV concerning those articles on the internal market that still required unanimity, as well as for asylum and migration issues (Swedish Government, 2001).

---

[7] Interview with Torbjörn Haak, 21 January 2003.

The principles of fairness and equality also permeated Swedish positions on reforms on *other institutional issues*. Sweden thus argued for one representative per Member State in the Court of Auditors, the Committee of the Regions, and the Economic and Social Committee. The Government was not opposed to discussion on size and composition of these bodies, but was clearly negative regarding any other reforms, such as adding competencies (Swedish Government, 2001).

Neither did Sweden accept any discussion on added competencies of the European Parliament. Although the Government was open for discussion on the distribution of seats and size, it also argued that this issue had already been solved in Amsterdam, where a ceiling was set at 700 MEP. This slight ambiguity must be interpreted as an acknowledgement that some changes were necessary to be used as a pay-off in a final agreement.

Regarding court issues, Sweden wanted to concentrate on such changes that were necessary to directly increase flexibility and efficiency in the system and could eliminate hindrances for later reforms to be decided by the Council (Swedish Government, 2001).

As shown above, Sweden had initially hoped to avoid discussion on *enhanced co-operation*, but it turned out to be an issue that required a great deal of rethinking and political effort. Once it realised that the issue was irrevocably on the agenda, the Swedish Government put great weight on the points of departure for such action, i.e., the underlying criteria. Here several necessary provisions without which Sweden could not accept any changes had been identified: integration not segregation, open for all, role for the Commission, positive to common goals and used only as last resort. If these criteria were ensured, Sweden showed readiness to discuss the modalities (Swedish Government, 2001).

Once these underlying criteria were accepted as a basis for negotiation, enhanced co-operation in the first and third pillar turned out to be less of a problem for Sweden. What Sweden wanted above all was to avoid enhanced co-operation in the second pillar. Approval of an agreement could therefore not be given until it had been ensured that solution had been reached in that field which was acceptable to Sweden. The official Swedish argument here focused on the importance of Union cohesion at the international level. It was argued that it would be very worrying indeed to send the signal to the international community that the Union had already given up on the ambition of having a common foreign and security policy. In addition, it was pointed out that the treaty could already provide some flexibility in this area (EU Advisory Committee, 1 December 2000).

Behind this stance, of course, lay the Swedish policy of neutrality, which was feared to be compromised if some EU states would be allowed to initiate closer co-operation concerning, for instance, military crisis management. Even though Sweden would not join such a project, the government worried that this would not be altogether clear to international actors, who for simplicity's sake prefer to view the Union as one actor. Consequently, as a fall back position, Sweden could accept some sort of flexibility in the second pillar, as long as it did not touch upon defence policy or had any military consequences (Swedish Government, 2001). This was finally secured in Nice (EU Advisory Committee, 10 December 2000).

Judging the Outcome

On the face of it, the Swedish government had reason to be satisfied after Nice. If one views the Swedish goals as evolving around the three tiers of identification, legitimacy and efficiency, good results had, in principle, been achieved. This was also how it was presented in the national arena immediately after the Nice meeting (Speech by Göran Persson, 14 December 2000). On closer inspection, however, such a conclusion seems less accurate.

The Swedish Government was most successful in the discussion on QMV, where it was not overrun on taxes or family law and where progress was achieved in the areas supported by the Government. The result is less clear as regards the Commission, where the absolute principle of one commissioner per Member State had to be abandoned in the end. One could of course argue that this was a small price to pay for a country so committed to enlargement, and that the hard stance was only a posture to extract gains in the negotiation on Council votes. This might be true, but Sweden was not altogether successful in that case either. On the positive side, some of the imbalance negatively influencing Swedish votes was corrected and the Swedish portion of the votes will be only slightly reduced, from 2.99% of the total votes to 2.90% in a Union with 27 Member States. The Swedish government thus proudly announced that Sweden's relative strength was little affected by the final solution, and that other states had paid a heavier price for enlargement (Swedish Government, 2001).

The major failure was nevertheless the fact that the Swedish square root model was not accepted. It was a considerable loss of prestige when nothing came out of months of arguing and lobbying for a perceived technically superior 'product'. The disappointment was all the more significant since the end result really closely resembled some sort of double majority system that gave great weight to Germany and was from the outset seen as the worst alternative from a Swedish point of view. Given the fact that the Swedish proposal could actually have negatively affected the French Presidency's portion of the votes in comparison to Germany, this outcome was not a total surprise.

In sum, the enlargement deadline played into the hands of the Swedish government. The main goal of securing enlargement was reached, while responsibility for end-negations in the IGC was avoided. In this sense, Sweden was a winner and could take over the Presidency without a heavy package on this issue.

In one sense, however, the IGC spilled over into the Swedish presidency period as it was decided—in the declaration on the future of the Union—that the incoming Swedish and Belgian presidencies should start the debate and lay out the tracks for another IGC in 2004.

The Ratification Debate

A government bill on ratification of the Nice Treaty (Swedish Government, 2001) was tabled in September 2001 and adopted by the *Riksdag* on 6 December 2001. The ratification debate preceding the government bill and the parliamentary vote was not very intense, and the government had few problems finding the required support in the *Riksdag*.

Some critical voices heard immediately after the Nice agreement argued that the Swedish government had failed to effectively promote the national interest. The critique was focused on the agreement on Council votes. It was argued that Sweden should - and could - have gotten one additional vote in the Council had Prime Minister Persson not been so keen to compromise (*Göteborgs-Posten,* 12 December 2000). Some observers even argued that Sweden should have vetoed the agreement in Nice in order to secure a better deal (*Dagens Nyheter,* 31 December 2000). However, the argument that the Nice Treaty was a failure from a Swedish point of view never found widespread support. The public debate that followed in the aftermath of Nice was not very intense and did not present any serious problems for the government to handle.

The debate in the *Riksdag* was fairly predictable. In a report delivered by the Joint Committee on the Constitution and Foreign Affairs on the 22 November

2001 (Swedish Parliament, 2001a), the pro-EU parties recommended the Parliament to accept the government bill. The Green Party and the Left Party, on the other hand, were against ratification of the Nice Treaty. The agreement in Nice would, according to these parties, lead to further steps towards a federalisation of the Union. At the same time, no effort was made in the Nice Treaty to address the democratic deficit and the legitimacy problems plaguing the EU. As for enlargement, they argued that the Nice Treaty was not a necessary prerequisite to push negotiations along and accept new Member States. Issues such as the number of votes in the Council, seats in the Parliament, membership fees, and the like could just as well be defined in the accession treaties (Swedish Parliament, 2001a).

The pro-EU parties, for their part, emphasised the importance of the Nice Treaty in paving the way for a successful enlargement process. In the report, it is argued that the new treaty provides a solution to the Amsterdam leftovers which makes it possible to accept new Member States in the Union (Swedish Parliament, 2001a). The fact that not only the Social Democratic Party but also the Moderate Party, the Christian Democratic Party, the Liberal Party and the Centre Party recommended that the Parliament vote 'Yes' on the Government bill does not mean that these parties were fully satisfied with the Treaty from a Swedish point of view. For example, leading representatives of the Moderate Party were dissatisfied with the way the government had handled the negotiations regarding distribution of votes in the Council.[8] However, dissatisfaction with the content was not of such a magnitude that the right-wing parties considered the possibility to reject the Government's bill.

Just days before the scheduled vote, an attempt was made to disrupt the ratification of the Nice Treaty. In a joint declaration, six members of the Parliament—representing all parties except the Liberal Party—demanded that the vote should be postponed on the grounds that no Treaty existed, as the Irish people had already rejected it (*Göteborgs-Posten,* 6 December 2001). The demand to postpone the decision was rejected by Parliament and the debate and vote took place as planned on 6 December 2001. During the debate preceding the vote, it was argued by the authors of the joint declaration that the Parliament by going ahead with the ratification process, was participating in a "gigantic policy of extortion" with the purpose of putting the Irish people under pressure to accept the new treaty (Swedish Parliament, 2001b). The advocates of the Nice Treaty pointed out that only one-third of the Irish voters had participated in the

[8] Interview Lars Tobisson, 13 January 2003.

referendum and repeatedly emphasised the importance of the agreement made in Nice as a prerequisite to push forward with the enlargement process (Swedish Parliament, 2001b).

Demands for a Swedish referendum were also voiced towards the end of the debate but did not find support in Parliament. The Minister for Foreign Affairs, Anna Lindh, argued that the Nice Treaty would not entail a transfer of power to the EU level substantial enough to motivate the holding of a referendum (Swedish Parliament, 2001b). When the vote finally took place, the Government had no trouble securing the required support in the Parliament. The treaty was adopted by 249 votes to 51, with 4 abstentions and 45 members absent. Only the Green Party and the Left Party voted against ratification of the treaty (Swedish Parliament, 2001b).

In the Shadow of Enlargement – and Presidency

Sweden has from the outset been a keen supporter of the Enlargement project. For economic, security as well as ideological reasons, Sweden has argued that the accession of new Member States is a task of vital importance for the European Union. The overriding purpose of IGC 2000 was to reform the institutions in order to prepare the Union for enlargement. To agree on matters of institutional reform is a difficult task, since vital national interests are at stake for the Member States. Governments find themselves in pursuit of solutions to promote the common interest, but they also fight to safeguard and possibly increase the relative power and influence that they currently enjoy.

Accordingly, the conduct of each Member State during an IGC will be decided by the strength of its commitment to promote the common interest *and* its determination to pursue national goals. As we set out to analyse Sweden's role during IGC 2000, we asked whether it would be correct to argue that Sweden's preparations and negotiating behaviour took place in the shadow of enlargement. Now, there can be no doubt that the Swedish government was committed to the aim of rapid enlargement. Hence, it supported a limited agenda and sought to reach an agreement in Nice in order to avoid delays. But was Sweden's commitment to enlargement strong enough to provide sufficient incentives to accept an agreement that hardly could be deemed a success if measured by the yardstick of promoting national goals?

The fact that Sweden was willing to accept the Nice agreement cannot be ascribed exclusively to its commitment to contribute to the enlargement project.

We would argue that concerns for a successful presidency were equally important. Sweden wanted to reach an agreement in Nice in order to avoid having to assume responsibility for the difficult task of leading the IGC to a happy end. Having to take over responsibility for the negotiations would have disrupted Sweden's preparations for the presidency and make the upcoming task much more difficult. As a relative newcomer to the EU, it was important for Sweden to do a good job as president of the Union, thus becoming acknowledged as a Member State able to fulfil its obligations. Keeping the slate clean for the incoming presidency would also make it possible for Sweden to actually achieve some tangible results on its key priorities—enlargement, employment and the environment.

Sweden was certainly strongly committed to finding a solution to the common interest of promoting enlargement, but its behaviour was also determined by concerns over national objectives. Among these goals, specific solutions to institutional issues were not the highest priority. What mattered most were the prospects for making a success of the incoming presidency. Our conclusion, then, is that Sweden's preparations for IGC 2000 and its negotiating behaviour took place in the shadow of enlargement *and* presidency.

BIBLIOGRAPHY

Dagens Nyheter (2000), 'Pehr G. Gyllenhammars nyårshälsning till Göran Persson', 31 December.
Dehaene, Jean-Luc & David Simon, Richard von Weizsäcker (1999), *The Institutional Implications of Enlargement*. Brussels: Report to the European Commission.
European Commission (2000), *Adapting the Institutions to make a Success of Enlargement.* Brussels, Com 34.
European Council (1999a), "Conclusions of the Presidency," European Council in Cologne, 3-4 June. *Bulletin of the European Union* no. 6.
— 1999b, "Conclusions of the Presidency," European Council in Helsinki, 10-11 December. *Bulletin of the European Union* no. 12.
Göteborgs-Posten (2000), "Snart bestämmer Sverige", 26 September.
— (2000), "Vägrar rösta om Nicefördrag", 6 December.
— (2000), "Är Nicefördraget bra eller dåligt?", 12 December.
Holmlund, Staffan (2001), "Nicefördraget", *Europarättslig Tidskrift*, no. 2, vol. 4.
Johansson, Karl Magnus and Tapio Raunio (2001), "Partisan responses to Europe: Comparing Finnish and Swedish political parties." *European Journal of Political Research*, vol. 39, no. 2, pp. 225-249.
— and Anna-Carin Svensson (2002), "Sweden: constrained but con-structive?" in Finn Laursen (ed.) *The Amsterdam Treaty. National Preference Formation, Interstate Bargaining and Outcome.* Odense: Odense University Press.
Karlsson, Christer (2001), *Democracy, Legitimacy and the European Union.* Uppsala: Acta Universitatis Upsaliensis.
Moberg, Axel (2002), "The Nice Treaty and Voting Rules in the Council", *Journal of Common Market Studies*, vol. 40, no. 2, pp. 259-82.
Moravcsik, Andrew (1993), "Preferences and Power in the European Community: A Liberal Intergovernmentalist Approach", *Journal of Common Market Studies*, vol. 31, no. 4, pp. 473-524.
— (1998), *The Choice for Europe*. Ithaca, New York: Cornell University Press.
Portuguese Presidency (2000a), "Weightings of the votes in the Council," 24 May. CONFER 4745.
— (2000b), "Intergovernmental Conference on Institutional Reform". Presidency Report to the Feira European Council, 14 June. CONFER 4750.
Svensson, Anna-Carin (2000), *In the Service of the European Union. The role of the Presidency in Negotiating the Amsterdam Treaty 1995-97.* Uppsala: Acta Universitatis Upsaliensis.
Swedish Government (1995), "EU:s regeringskonferens 1996", Regeringens skrivelse 1995/96:30.
— (2001), "Nicefördraget", Prop. 2001/02:8.
Swedish Parliament (2001a), "Sammansatta konstitutions- och utrikesutskottets betänkande," 2001/02:KUU1.
— (2001b), "Debatt om Nicefördraget", Prot. 2001/02:42.

Speeches
Speech by Göran Persson to the Swedish Parliament, 14 December 2000.

Interviews
Torbjörn Haak, member of the Swedish negotiation team, 21 January 2003.
Annika Söder, Swedish deputy chief negotiator, 8 November 2002.
Lars Tobisson (the Moderate Party), former Member of the EU Advisory Committee in the Swedish Parliament, 12 January 2003.

Archives
EU Advisory Committee in the Swedish Parliament. Shorthand records of deliberations from the Committee's meetings with Swedish negotiators 2000. Stockholm.

Periodical Sources
Europe.

CHAPTER 16

THE UNITED KINGDOM: NEW APPROACH AND NEW INFLUENCE?

INTRODUCTION

In contrast to the other intergovernmental conferences that had taken place since the emergence of a new institutional dynamism in 1984, the Nice intergovernmental conference (IGC) in 2000 was negotiated by a Labour Government from beginning to end.[1]

The electoral success of the Labour Party meant that the 2000 IGC was negotiated by a government that had a different understanding of the position of the UK vis-à-vis the European construction. The Labour Government had conducted a more active and constructive EU policy since its coming to power in 1997. This policy was based on an understanding or *discourse* which saw a central and leading role for the UK in the EU as a necessity for a continued global political role for the UK. According to this discourse, European cooperation was essential for the UK, and it was worth paying a price for a fruitful relationship. A close and cooperative relationship was necessary in order to further national interests. Possible losses of sovereignty in some areas were considered insignificant in comparison with the possible gains for the UK. But sovereignty continued to be an important concern. This understanding can be called the *essential cooperation discourse.* Within the former Conservative Government, this discourse had also been present, but during the 1990s another understanding had gained ground within the Conservative Government, the Parliamentary Party and, indeed, the Party grassroots. According to this understanding, the EU should by its nature represent strict interstate cooperation. This discourse can be labelled the *interstate cooperation discourse.* The relationship to Europe was clearly 'we'/ 'they', and the issue of national sovereignty vs. Europe was presented as a zero-sum game. The dominance of this understanding within the Conservative Party in the 1990s (and the battles between the two understandings) had significantly contributed to an increasingly harsh and isolationistic tone in the Conservative Government's approach to the EU.

[1] A Labour Government had completed negotiations over the Amsterdam Treaty in June 1997, taking over after the Conservative Government's defeat in the General Election in May 1997.

Both discourses, however, shared a concern for national sovereignty, and co-operation in the EU or Europe was legitimised by the concrete national interests it could fulfil. They both legitimised relations with Europe within a broader instrumental discourse rather than in cultural terms (Larsen, 1997; Larsen, 1999), an important difference from many other Member States.

On a range of issues, the Labour Government, beginning in May 1997, attempted to move closer to the EU core and reactivated bilateral links within the EU. However, a central and leading role for the UK in the EU remained difficult to envisage as long as the UK was outside the Euro, which entered into force on 1 January 1999, and outside central parts of the third pillar. The British initiatives launching the St. Malo development within the field of defence from 1998 clearly took place on the background of the international strategic trends (in particular the increasing doubts about the continued willingness of the US to engage in European crisis management). However, the timing of the British change with regard to European defence could be seen as aimed at launching a dimension within the EU on which the UK would play a central role as the Euro, in which the UK did not take part, was entering into force. The new impetus in the field of defence within the EU has clearly meant that the UK is, to a large extent, setting the pace in a crucial part of the EU's new agenda. Although the timing of the British initiative can thus be considered as tactical, it must also be seen as taking place on the background of an increasing understanding within the dominant discourse of the EU, and British leadership within it, as an essential part of UK foreign policy.

In this chapter I will first briefly discuss the relevance of the theoretical framework of Andrew Moravcsik for analysing the British approach to the IGC 2000. I then go on to present and discuss the official British positions and proposals prior to the IGC. Following on from that, I discuss the issues of continuity and change from the approach to earlier conferences and changes in British positions during the conference. Finally, I present what could be seen as the balance sheet for Britain after the 2000 IGC followed by the conclusion. The chapter does not attempt to delineate in detail the British role in the 2000 IGC, but rather tries to analyse the broader questions relating to Britain's role at the IGC.

Moravcsik and the British Approach to the IGC 2000

The concern with decision-making procedures preparing for enlargement, rather than substance at the IGC 2000 has consequences for how Moravcsik can be used in relation to the formation of *preferences*. The procedural focus at the conference makes it difficult to argue, as does Moravcsik (1993, 1998), that economic interests, often constituted through pressures from national interest groups, predominantly determined the Government's preferences.[2] Rather, it lends credibility to the possibility—which Moravcsik brings up but does not support—that geopolitical interests or, indeed, ideological concerns, shaped preferences, and that these preferences emanated primarily from the political elites rather than interest groups (Moravcsik, 1993, 493-494). This can be expected to be the case when the objects of negotiation are broad institutional questions, foreign policy-related questions, or questions in the field of justice and home affairs rather than economic ones (ibid.). However, there might be specific issues at the conference where socio-economic interests may have played a role in defining preferences: on the issue of extension of the area for qualified majority voting (QMV), socio-economic interests can be expected to have played a role in forming the preferences at IGC (Laursen, introductory chapter in this volume).

The point of departure in this chapter, therefore, is that, with the exception of many of the provisions on QMV, the British preferences will be seen as emanating from broad, dominant geopolitical and ideological concerns within the political sphere rather than the results of pressures from socio-economic interest groups. These broadly-based understandings are conceptualised as discourses which shape the British Government's preferences. The focus is on these broad discourses as sources of governmental preferences and the way in which these discourses are expressed in public documents.[3]

The question of *interstate bargaining* in negotiations obtained through possible unilateral policy alternatives rather than agreement, possible alternative coalitions and possibilities for side-payments (Laursen, introductory chapter in this volume) must also be considered to be affected by the narrow decision-making agenda of the conference aimed at furthering enlargement. From the point of view of Liberal intergovernmentalism, the Member States which favoured speedy enlargement are arguably the weaker ones in determining the nature of the nature of treaty changes (Laursen, introductory chapter in this volume). The

---

[2] This is not the case, of course, if the push for enlargement is viewed primarily as driven by economic concerns, or if a well-functioning EU was predominantly supported for economic reasons. The argument here is that these concerns, although present, were so broad that they would not engage specific interest groups.

[3] For an example of the use of discourse analysis in the analysis of foreign policy, see Larsen (1997).

question of what determined British success or failure at the IGC on the background of *interstate bargaining* is dealt with in more detail below in the section 'the balance sheet'.

The Positions and Proposals of the Blair Government before the 2000 IGC

The dominance of the essential cooperation discourse within the Labour Government shaped the language used in relation to the general approach to the conference. The Labour Government's main issues of concern at the IGC were outlined in the White Paper *IGC: Reform for Enlargement—The British Approach to the European Union Intergovernmental Conference*, published in February and presented to the House of Commons by Foreign Secretary Robin Cook on 15 February 2000. Its style was the style of a pedagogical piece designed for persuasion. For Britain, the preparation of the enlargement was presented as the most important aim of the IGC. This was both legitimised on the basis of the value of entrenching stability, peace, free markets and democracy across the European continent, and because enlargement would bring 'huge economic opportunities to the UK' (*IGC: Reform for Enlargement,* 2000, 1). Although the conference was also presented as part of a wider reform and necessary agenda, the preparation of the enlargement was clearly the main focus and the reason why institutional reform was necessary. This was also reflected in the title of the Government's White Paper (*IGC: Reform for Enlargement,* 2000, 2).

On the so-called 'Amsterdam Issues', the UK did not have fundamentally different preferences from the ones of Germany, France and Italy, apart from the precise areas to which QMV should be extended.

Concerning reform of the Commission, the UK was willing to move to One Commissioner per Member State as part of a general streamlining of the Commission, provided that an appropriate modification of voting rights in the Council would take place at the same time (as stated in the protocol at Amsterdam on this issue). But the UK government also believed that further limitation of the size of the Commission could be considered as the number of Member States increased further. The White Paper was open on this issue, conceding that there were no easy solutions in this field. Suggestions were made for reform of the Commission regarding the designation of senior commissioners and flexibility with regard to the number of Vice Presidents (currently limited to two) (*IGC: Reform for Enlargement,* 2000, 17). The UK Government was against giving the

European Parliament the power to sack individual commissioners as a way of achieving greater accountability (*IGC: Reform for Enlargement,* 2000, 24).

As far as the reweighting of votes in the Council was concerned, the White Paper listed two possible approaches: either to maintain the existing system of weighted votes while changing the number of votes per Member State to give more weight to population, or to introduce a two-pronged system of a certain number of votes per Member State plus a pure population criterion. The UK was willing to consider either system, or a combination of both, although the simple reweighting was seen as having the advantage of being clearer. The Government's starting point was that votes should be reweighted in favour of the more populous Member States due to the impending loss of influence for the UK in an enlarged Union. The solution should strike the right balance between the ease with which legislation could be passed and the ease with which it could be blocked (*IGC: Reform for Enlargement,* 2000, 18-19).

The possible extension of Qualified Majority Voting was the third of the Amsterdam issues. The UK Government had no objection, in principle, to the inclusion of QMV on the agenda, as QMV was seen as having benefited the UK on many occasions. On issues such as Treaty change, accession, taxation, border controls, social security, defence and 'own resources' (the EU's revenue-raising mechanism), the UK insisted on retaining unanimity due to what it saw as national interests. But, in some areas, an extension of QMV was considered to be in the UK's interest and something the UK would promote at the conference. An example given of such an area in the White Paper was approval of European Court of Justice (ECJ) rules of procedure. UK flexibility was signalled in other areas (appointments to the Economic and Social Committee, the Committee of the Regions or transport). UK national interest was to be the guiding principle on a case-by-case basis (*IGC: Reform for Enlargement,* 2000, 20-21). Where QMV was recently extended to legislative articles, the extension of co-decision with the European Parliament was likely to be appropriate (*IGC: Reform for Enlargement,* 2000, 23).

With respect to the possible issues on the agenda which were not directly part of the 'Amsterdam issues', the UK White Paper presented the following British views:

- The UK wanted to make the Court of Justice and the European Court of Auditors more efficient not least with a view to enlargement (*IGC: Reform for Enlargement,* 2000, 22-23).
- Concerning the number of seats in the European Parliament after the enlargement, the UK would support the retention of the 700-seat ceiling. It did not pre-

sent a preference for any particular re-allocation of seats (*IGC: Reform for Enlargement,* 2000, 24).

- Flexibility was one of the issues on which UK disagreed the most with the other major states prior to the conference. The UK's view was that there was no reason to change the procedures on flexibility, which had been agreed in the Amsterdam Treaty only three years before and which had not been used. The UK stressed what it saw as the key features of the existing rules of flexibility in the Amsterdam Treaty and which remained important: that too much flexibility could undermine the Single Market, or could be used against the interests of a minority of Member States. Possible provisions on flexibility in the field of defence should not be simple replications of the provisions on closer cooperation, but should relate to the special character of this area (*IGC: Reform for Enlargement,* 2000, 25). Interestingly, possible reform of the defence dimension was not dealt with as a separate issue in the White Paper before the conference (only in relation to flexibility).
- The UK did not desire a restructuring of the treaties, including, for example, different ratification procedures for different parts of the treaties, to be part of the IGC (*IGC: Reform for Enlargement,* 2000, 26). Neither did the UK want the Charter on Fundamental Rights which had been prepared before the conference to have legal status (the latter was not mentioned in the White Paper).
- All in all, the UK's agenda for the IGC 2000 was relatively limited. There was a considerable overlap between the British concerns and the concerns of the other major powers in the EU. The British concerns differed from the French and German ones in relation to the nature of the areas that should be transferred to QMV, flexibility and the question of the legal status of the Charter of Fundamental Rights.

The UK and the Negotiations during the Conference

A significant feature of British participation during the negotiations was the absence of formal British proposals put forward at the Conference in any of the general institutional areas of the conference. There were thus no formal proposals put forward by the UK within the field of the Amsterdam leftovers, neither on its own nor with other countries. This distinguished the UK from France, Germany and Italy, who all put forward formal proposals in these fields and in other fields such as enhanced cooperation and defence.

However, the UK often supported these countries' proposals, as it generally supported the other large countries' views in relation to reform of the Commission and reweighting of votes. The level of informal UK involvement in the drafting of these proposals together with the other big countries is not known. In particular, we do not know the extent to which there was cooperation with France before and during the latter's presidency on the issue of the German 'weight' in a future reweighting of votes. It is striking, however, that the UK (together with Spain) was the only country which expressed its satisfaction with the French presidency's proposal for reweighting of votes at the beginning of the Nice meeting on 9 December 2000, which maintained German voting weight at the same level as the other big states while generally increasing the strength of the larger countries (*Bulletin Quotidien Europe,* 2000a, 1-4).

The level of British engagement and activity seemed highest in relation to preventing certain institutional developments. It was thus very active (and successful) in relation to preventing QMV in the fields of social security and taxation (in relation to the latter an informal paper was put forward) (*Bulletin Quotidien Europe,* 2000b, 3). The UK also actively attempted to shape the changes on enhanced cooperation and to prevent the incorporation of the charter, although no formal proposals were put forward.

The absence of British formal initiatives during the conference can be seen to be somewhat at odds with the Blair Government's stress on the need for the UK to play a leading role (and, indeed, that the UK was now playing such a role), although the absence of formal proposals does not exclude that the British profile in the form of presentation of informal proposals/non-papers might have been higher.

Change from and Continuity with the Previous Government and the Previous IGC

On many key issues, there was continuity not just with the Labour government, which was in power with the signing of the Amsterdam Treaty in 1997, but also the Conservative government which preceded it. These issues are as follows: scepticism towards a legal approach to the question of fundamental rights in the EU, a wish to strengthen the Court of Auditors, a wish for a reweighting of votes in the QMV system, a wish for a smaller Commission by leaving the principle of one Commissioner per Member State, maintaining the intergovernmental character of the CFSP, insistence on the right to maintain border controls (and therefore the continued opt-out of this aspect of Schengen), reticence about flexibility (Best, 2002, 362-268), and opposition to QMV on treaty change, taxation, border controls, social security and defence and the EU's 'own resources'.

The main difference was that compared to the Conservative Government which started the former intergovernmental conference, there was an openness towards the acceptance of QMV when this was in the British interest (a change which already took place when the Labour Government took over from the Conservative Government during the negotiations over the Amsterdam Treaty). Also, the Labour Government was willing to accept a merger of most parts of the WEU into the EU (which also constituted a change of its own position at the final part of the Amsterdam negotiations). More important than the concrete stances was that the Labour Government entered the conference using a different language from that of the Conservative Government four years earlier (Larsen, 1999). Although the UK as a result found itself in disagreement with other major countries on issues such as flexibility or the Charter on Fundamental Rights, the general language used was much more in line with the mainstream at the conference in its emphasis on the necessary institutional measures to ensure possible enlargement. The absence of presentation of concrete formal proposals in the more general areas at the conference, however, is somewhat surprising in this light (see also below).

THE BALANCE SHEET: THE RESULTS OF UK NEGOTIATIONS IN THE IGC

The evaluation of the results of the IGC from the perspective of the UK depends (as in all other cases) on the yardstick used. The standard used here will consist mainly of the priorities laid out in the British Government's White Paper before the conference as described above.[4] In the following, I deal only with the IGC agenda at Nice and not the other issues decided at the Nice European Council in December.[5]

Generally speaking, the UK was not as isolated in its stance towards the central items on the agenda of the IGC, the 'Amsterdam leftovers', which had been a tendency at the negotiations leading up to the Amsterdam Treaty (Best, 2000, 370-373). This in itself made it easier to obtain a result closer to British preferences. The absence of formal British proposals or formal co-sponsorship on re-

[4] One of the problems with this way of evaluating the results is that a government might present its aims in modest terms prior to a conference, so that they can be seen as successful after a conference.

[5] Although the British Government accounts do not distinguish clearly between the two, see for example Prime Minister Tony Blair's statement to the House of Commons, London, Monday 11 December 2000.

form of the Commission and reweighting of votes could be seen as a reflection of the degree of common ground with the other major countries. On these two issues as well, the UK had signalled in its White Paper significant flexibility towards different solutions. As long as the other large countries were behind it, the proposal was likely to be palatable to the UK also. On one of the most sensitive issues at the final meeting in Nice, the balance of votes between Germany and the rest of the Member States, France was, if anything, the outsider in its insistence on parity between Germany and France. Even if Britain shared France's concerns about the political weight of Germany, it could rely on France to conduct the political battle if necessary on her own.

For the UK, the result must be said to have been positive: a rebalancing of votes in favour of the four biggest countries, the commencement of reform of the Commission in line with UK wishes, and the extension of QMV in areas where the UK wanted it and its prevention in areas where it did not. The QMV extensions did not touch upon the areas of social security or taxation, which the UK opposed. But there was an extension into the areas relating to efficiency of economic management and the single market, which had traditionally been considered a British interest. The changes in the appointments or roles of procedure were beneficial to the UK or of no particular concern. The extensions in the areas concerning freedom of movement are areas where the UK has a possibility of an opt-out by virtue of a special agreement concerning justice and home affairs agreed at Amsterdam. However, it seems fair to suggest that the UK would rather have preferred the retention of unanimity.

On the so-called parallel agenda, the provisions in the treaty regarding the ESDP (Art. 17 and Art. 25) reflected the new institutional development in this field since St. Malo, where the UK had played a leading role. The public argument between Prime Minister Blair and President Chirac at the conference had nothing to do with the new provisions in the Treaty but was rather political statements relating in particular to protocols on defence which were also decided at the Nice European Council. Flexibility or enhanced cooperation, which was made easier by the Nice Treaty, was a prime candidate for being characterized as a major British defeat at the conference. The UK Government's White Paper before the conference had stated that there was no reason to change the rules in this field. The possibility of a veto on enhanced cooperation on issues relating to the internal marked had been removed. The Feira European Council, in March 2000, made clear that this would be part of the agenda of the conference, contrary to the wishes of the UK. However, the UK adapted its position to this item, and it became part of the agenda in autumn 2000. Prime Minister Blair, speaking in Warsaw on 6 October 2000, declared that "Efficient decision-making in an enlarged Union will also mean enhanced cooperation. I have no problem with (…) groups of Member States going forward together (...) but that must not lead to a hard core (...). Such groups must at every stage be open for others who wish to join." Apparently, this acceptance was confirmed at the EU summit in Biarritz, 6-7 October 2000 (Moore, 2000). The British change was (indirectly) legitimised both with reference to the needs of efficient enlargement, the UK's interest in being able to take part in the advance group, and on the maintenance of the political and legal safeguards on flexibility decided in Amsterdam (Blair, 2000).

Drawing on Moravcsik (Laursen, introductory chapter in this volume), this relatively good result could be seen as a reflection of the fact that although the UK was favourable towards the enlargement of the EU, the UK was not the strongest proponent of enlargement. Neither were there any great prospects of alternative coalitions leaving out the UK on the Amsterdam leftovers, although one could imagine that the new provisions on flexibility could be used for going ahead in policy areas where the UK prevented an extension of QMV. The lack of prospects for alternative coalitions aimed at bypassing the UK at the Nice negotiations were probably also affected by the UK's new central role in the field of defence. This must have increased the UK's influence generally and made it less vulnerable to the threat of alternative coalitions. In a much broader sense, the international context (which Moravcsik generally downplays) can explain why the defence dimension suddenly became so important in the EU and upgraded the UK's power. Could other countries, in particular France and Germany, use the threat of exclusion against the UK to the same extent as before when defence, an area in which the UK played a leading role, had become a prominent part of the EU's agenda?

The Moravcsik-inspired thesis, that a strong desire for provisions to secure the enlargement meant a weak hand at the negotiations, is difficult to evaluate. This is because most countries, including Britain, were in favour of the enlargement, and it is difficult to judge in precise terms which were more in favour than others. If Germany and the Scandinavian countries were the strongest proponents and the Southern countries much more lukewarm, it is not obvious where precisely the UK should be placed. From focusing on the Moravcsik-inspired thesis alone, it seems that the UK was not as vulnerable as Germany and the Nordic Countries, but had much less 'nuisance power' than the Southern countries because it fundamentally supported the enlargement in line with the EU mainstream.

More than anything else, the UK's relatively successful IGC can be seen as based on the comparatively narrow agenda of this IGC and the Labour Government's understanding of the role of the EU, an understanding more in line with that of the other Member States (if not identical with them) than that of the former Conservative Government. There was a large amount of common ground with Germany, France and Italy concerning the 'Amsterdam leftovers'. The UK was therefore under less pressure at this IGC than it had been at any IGC since the beginning of the new EC/EU dynamism in 1984. But the new developments within the EU defence dimension also increased the UK's political strength. The inclusion of new provisions on enhanced cooperation in the Treaty, however, can be seen as an expression of UK weakness, as the UK had argued prior to the conference against the need to change the provisions in the Amsterdam Treaty in this field.

MORE INFLUENCE UNDER NEW LABOUR?

The coming to power of Labour had clearly meant that relations with EU partners had become easier, as the language of the Labour Government was closer to the EU mainstream—also at the IGC. There was more leeway and more of an ear for Britain's case. The UK change on defence also meant that the UK was at the forefront on a key item of the EU's new agenda. Although there was continuity on many issues with the former government, Britain's greater willingness to consider concrete changes on their merits rather than being opposed on principle gave Britain more scope in the negotiations (i.e. their benefit for the enlargement and for UK interests). The clearest case of this was the expansion of the number of areas where decisions were to be made by QMV.

The fundamental British problem for setting the agenda in the EU, however, remained: the UK's difficulty in leading the EU while remaining outside the Euro and not having the same long-term political purpose as the original six Member States, including Germany and France. But the Labour Government's approach did draw on a language which brought it closer to the *Community of destiny,* often referred to by Germany and France as the grounds for the EU.[6] However, the UK's problem of leading and setting the agenda was arguably less pressing at the 2000 IGC than at any IGC before it, because the agenda was nar-

---

[6] See for example the Government's White Paper *IGC: Reform for Enlargement-The British Approach to the European Union Intergovernmental Conference 2000*, p. 1-2.

row and because there was a great overlap between the bigger countries about where to go.

The Domestic Factor: the Importance of Conflicts over Europe

Compared to the situation at the run-up to IGCs before, the UK Government was in a fundamentally different situation at the 2000 IGC. The Conservative Government had been constrained by a sizeable Euro-sceptic minority within its own Parliamentary Party which, in collaboration with the Labour Party, would have been able to threaten the adoption of the treaty in the UK. This situation, and the broader societal currents that it reflected, had shaped the Conservative Government's approach to the Amsterdam conference (Larsen, 1999). When the Labour Government had taken over from the Conservative Government during the last IGC in 1997, this had secured ratification of the treaty in the UK. The new Labour Government was based on a solid parliamentary majority whose dominant view was that the EU was an essential and useful tool for British policies. This fundamental basis provided a different context for the UK Government's approach to the conference in 2000 (as had been the case at the last part of the Amsterdam negotiations). The Labour Government was not likely to face subsequent parliamentary opposition to the ratification of the Nice Treaty or rather the parts of it which necessitated incorporation into British law.

However, it does not follow that the UK Government's approach to the IGC was not affected by domestic concerns in a broader sense. There was a significant, broad, and possibly rising, Euro-sceptical current in the UK (Baker, 2000). The way in which the UK's result at the negotiations could be presented (in particular, whether or not the Government could be accused of selling out British sovereignty) was clearly an important concern for the Government in light of the coming general election towards which the Government always had its eyes fixed. The domestic battle over the meaning of the Nice Treaty was, to a large extent, a battle along the lines of the two different discourses identified above. The Labour Government was engaging itself in a two-term project, an aim which greatly affected policies and their packaging! This made the Government very aware of the media coverage of the conference just as in other fields of Government policy. Before the Nice summit, a considerable effort was put into the framing of the British results (*BBC News* 5 December 2000). Part of the attempts to frame the issue in a way favourable to the Government was to stress that it was time to abandon the 'cliché' that the summit was about Britain against the rest, and that the aim of enlargement was shared with the other EU Members (ibid.). However, at the same time as the Government emphasized the central role of the EU and its enlargement and the defence and furthering of UK interests herein, drawing on the essential cooperation discourse, and part of the domestic debate towards the end of the conference shifted towards the question of whether the Government had sold out British interests or abrogated sovereignty. It seems likely that this affected the Government's approach to some of the issues at the conference in the direction of a cautious stance. The Conservative Party stated that it would not ratify the Treaty and wanted a referendum on it. They claimed, drawing on the interstate co-operation discourse, that the Nice summit was about further and deeper integration rather than about the necessary preconditions for enlargement (*BBC News* 11 September 2000).The press was also divided between these two interpretations which drew on the two different discourses identified above (*BBC News* 12 December 2000).

When the theme of Europe was brought up at the General election in June 2001, the Conservative opposition attacked what they saw as the Labour Government's willingness to abandon the Pound in contrast to the Conservatives who wanted to keep the Pound for reasons of principle, signalling a firm Conservative limit to European integration. The Labour Government emphasized the broader issues relating to what it saw as the benefits of the Government's constructive approach to European integration which had brought concrete and general benefits to Britain, contrary to what it saw as the Conservatives' negative and isolationist approach. These arguments could also be seen as reflecting the logic of interstate cooperation vs. the logic of essential cooperation. The Labour Government won the general election in 2001 and secured a huge majority comparable to the one obtained in 1997. A Guardian/ICM opinion poll concluded that the euro was the lowest on the list of eleven priorities, and that the Conservative Party was, if anything, losing by emphasizing Europe (Baker 2002, 321). We may suggest that the general Euro-sceptical mood mentioned (and the strong opposition to the euro registered in polls) did not greatly affect the British people's voting behaviour at the general election. The broad constraint on British policy at the IGC constituted by the assumed presence of a general Euro-sceptical mood may therefore have been overestimated by the Government. An alternative explanation is that Labour's arguments on Europe persuaded that part of sceptical public opinion that was interested in the European issues, at least on the occasion of the general election.

CONCLUSIONS

On many issues there was continuity in the British positions at the IGC 2000 both that of the Labour Government which concluded the Amsterdam IGC and the Conservative Government which preceded it. There was, however, an entirely new position on the issue of EU defence. Perhaps most importantly, the full participation of a new government meant that a new language framed and shaped the UK's approach.

Britain's results at the conference were close to the objectives outlined before the conference, although it had to adapt its position on the issue of flexibility/enhanced cooperation. The outcome can be seen as reflecting the overlap between the British preferences on the 'Amsterdam leftovers' and the preferences of the other major countries, including the importance attributed to preparing the enlargement. However, the new developments within the EU defence dimension also increased the UK's political strength. As for the possible bargaining weaknesses arising from the support of the enlargement along the lines of the Moravcsik argument, the UK can be said to have found itself in a middle position: between the enthusiastic Nordic countries and Germany and the less enthusiastic Southern countries, though closer to the enthusiasts than to the sceptics on this point. This could be expected to place the UK on a parallel scale in terms of influence. The UK was thus willing to compromise to some extent to achieve enlargement, but not as much as the most enthusiastic countries. The UK weakness on this point, however, does not seem to account for the inclusion of enhanced cooperation in the treaty against the UK's wishes, as those states supporting new provisions on enhanced cooperation were not the ones that were also sceptical towards the enlargement.

While it can be argued that the balance sheet for the UK at the conference was fairly good, an important decision was made against British wishes at the Nice Conference which may have wide and immediate implications for the institutional development of EU: A conference will be called in 2004 which will engage in a deeper and wider debate about the future development of the EU (Britain had not wanted a set date set for the next conference). The much broader agenda of a new IGC as soon as 2004 may mean larger problems ahead for a British Government than those generated by the 2000 IGC—both in Europe and at home. The 2004 IGC might lead to a more general treaty which consolidates the relationship between the Union and its parts in a qualitatively different way from the IGC 2000, which (from the British point of view) primarily adjusted British power within the EU as a consequence of enlargement.

There are signs that the British Government is preparing for this conference with the aim of putting forward constructive proposals and not distancing itself from the EU mainstream. After some initial scepticism about the term, the British Government has now put forward a proposal for a European constitution together with a proposal for a new subsidiarity watchdog (Straw, 2002). However, the focus is still on national political control of EU decision-making (Blair, 2000a).

The dominant essential cooperation discourse on which the Labour government now draws primarily legitimises the participation in the EU through Britain's self-interest. But it also presents the EU as an important and positive fact in many areas of life for UK society. It is seen as a central factor for peace, and a promoter of liberal values. So although the British approach is still instrumental, the instrumentality extends to so many areas that it is presented as a firm and necessary anchoring point for UK foreign policy and indeed for UK society. There are clearly also formulations in Government speeches that suggest a more mythological, organic view, such as 'Britain's destiny is in Europe'. But the language still does not have an organic tone which promotes European unity as a process in its own right. At the same time, within the Conservative opposition, the interstate cooperation discourse seems to have gained even more ground after the general election. Domestic political debate in relation to the 2004 IGC is likely to be more confrontational than was the case at the 2000 IGC.

BIBLIOGRAPHY

Baker, David (2001), "Britain and Europe: The Argument Continues", *Parliamentary Affairs,* Vol. 54:276-288.

— (2002), "Britain and Europe: More Blood on the Euro-Carpet", *Parliamentary Affairs,* Vol. 55:317-330.

BBC News, 11 September (2000), http://news.bbc.co.uk/2/hi/uk_politics/1065933.stm.

—, 5 December (2000) , http://news.bbc.co.uk/2/hi/uk_politics/talking_politics/1056026.stm.

—, 12 December (2000), http://news.bbc.co.uk/2/hi/uk/1065100.stm

Best, Edward (2002), "From Isolation towards influence?" in Finn Laursen (ed.), *The Amsterdam Treaty: National Preference Formation, Interstate Bargaining and Outcome.* Odense: Odense University Press.

Bulletin Quotidien Europe (2000a), No. 7860, 10 December 2000.

— (2000b), No. 7710, 5 May 2000.

Foreign Affairs Committee (2000), *Developments at the Intergovernmental Conference 2000. Response of the Secretary of State for Foreign Affairs.* Sixth Report from the Foreign Affairs Committee, Session 1999-2000.

Larsen, Henrik (1997), *Foreign Policy and Discourse Analysis: France, Britain and Europe.* London and New York: Routledge.

— (1999), "British and Danish Policies towards Europe in the 1990s: A Discourse Approach", *European Journal of International Relations*, 5(4).

More, Barry (2000), "EU Summit Outlook – UK Flexibility to Aid EU Progress on Decision-making", *AFX European Focus*, 10 October 2000.

Moravcsik, Andrew (1993), "Preferences and Power in the European Community: A Liberal Intergovernmentalist Approach", *Journal of Common Market Studies*, vol. 31, no. 4: 473-524.

— (1998), *The Choice for Europe*. Ithaca, NY: Cornell University Press.

White Paper *IGC: Reform for Enlargement – The British Approach to the European Union Intergovernmental Conference (2000),* Presented to Parliament by the Secretary of State for Foreign and Commonwealth Affairs by Command of Her Majesty, February 2000.

Speeches

Blair, Tony (2000a), *Speech by the Prime Minister, Tony Blair, to the Polish Stock Exchange, Warsaw, Friday 6 October 2000.*

— (2000b), *Statement by the Prime Minister, Tony Blair, to the House of Commons, London, Monday 11 December 2000.*

Cook, Robin (2000), "Britain's approach to the IGC", statement by the Foreign Secretary, Robin Cook, HoC, London, Tuesday 15 February 2000.

Straw, Jack (2002), *Strength in Europe Begins at Home*. Speech in Edinburgh 27 August 2002 on UK-wide tour to promote the benefits of EU membership.

CHAPTER 17

POLAND AND THE OTHER CANDIDATE COUNTRIES: INFLUENCING THE TREATY FROM THE SIDELINES

INTRODUCTION

For the very first time in the history of European integration, the countries from the Eastern part of Europe were directly concerned by European Treaty negotiations (Baun and Marek, 2001, 13). Although they contributed to integration of Europe a great deal already before and perhaps even more after the fall of the Berlin Wall (Wilga, 2002), they could do so in the framework of the negotiations on a European treaty, though still without voting rights. Nevertheless, December 2000, when the negotiations on the Nice Treaty went into the final game, was magic time for the applicant countries, symbolising that the process of overcoming Yalta and Potsdam was literally over (Wilga, 2001a, 3; Parzymies, 2002, 1). And this all the more so because, as one Polish dictum put it, decisions (taken in Europe and) with direct implications for Polish people should not and, in fact, are no longer taken without them.[1] In this very sense, even if those countries were not directly sitting at the negotiating tables, they all had an observer status and could therefore involve themselves in discussions with the Portuguese and French presidencies and other EU states.

During the 2000 Intergovernmental Conference (2000 IGC, henceforth), but long before the Nice summit, some of the candidate countries voiced their primary concerns. For example, in one of his speeches the Czech president Vaclav Havel articulated the necessity to fully overcome the division in Europe. The response to history cannot only be given through deepening. It must necessarily comprise the process of widening of the European Union. Only this route will eventually bring about a truly integrated Europe, and this will help to create a new post-cold-war pan-European political order, which is still in the making.

Contributing to the analysis of the Nice Treaty, this chapter examines the candidate countries from the Luxembourg group,[2] with Poland as an example in more focus. Albeit mostly concentrated on the latter, the following will also refer to the positions of other applicant states, in order to see their concerns about the issues of the Nice agenda as well. Firstly, the objectives

---

[1] Literally *nic o nas bez nas*, in translation *nothing about us without us*".

[2] To the 'Luxembourg group' of candidate countries belong Czech Republic, Estonia, Hungary, Poland, Slovenia and Cyprus. The Luxemburg EU presidency named during the European Council on 12 and 13 December 1997 six countries to formally open negotiations with on 30 March 1998.

of and issues on the agenda of the 2000 IGC are recalled. Secondly the positions of the candidate countries are presented and summarised. Their positions are then compared with the outcomes of the Nice Treaty bargain and finally, in order to complete the analysis of this volume, the utility and applicability of liberal intergovernmentalism is briefly addressed.

Why Poland?

There are several reasons to examine Poland in more focus. First, Poland is without doubt the biggest country among those aspiring to EU membership. It is in fact an exception (Laursen, 2002b, 2) since all other candidate countries are rather small. If they should have influenced the final outcome of the Nice Treaty negotiations, in whatever way, then obviously it would be due to Poland and its diplomatic efforts, whether in concert with other candidate countries, on its own, or with help of one or more EU member states.

Second, since the early years after the submission of its EU membership application, Poland has tried to build best relationship possible with the united Germany, knowing very well that its weight after unification has increased in the EU policy making, and, consequently, also in treaty amendment negotiations such as those taken place in Nice. One of the goals was therefore to use this relationship in the pre-accession negotiations and in the Nice bargain as well, in which Poland badly needed a reliable partner to represent and to support its concerns (Baun and Marek, 2001, 29, 32). Because of the new importance of the united Germany and its ongoing assurances to play an attorney role for Poland, this is another good reason to concentrate more on this candidate country.

Thirdly and finally, the decision was influenced by the availability of documents and personal affinity of the author. As to the first, it seems that Poland produced most extensive analysis and a number of the papers on the issues negotiated at the Nice summit (Baun and Marek, 2001, 32). Poland was also largely engaged and involved in the debate. Furthermore, given the fact that this is the only medium or, as some would prefer to put it, big country—among those that finalised their negotiations of the membership conditions in Copenhagen in December 2002—the stakes resulting thereof were accordingly higher. As to the second, the personal interest in this country played a role too, since Poland is the country of origin of the author. Due to language knowledge, an advantage for this article was of course the access to valuable media reports.

OBJECTIVES AND ISSUES ON 2000 IGC AGENDA

General Wishes of the Candidate Countries

Prior to the 2000 IGC, the candidate countries gathered and tried to specify the most important issues relevant for enlargement.[3] In the ninth meeting of the heads of negotiating teams, the candidate countries "exchanged views on the outcome of the Helsinki European Council and in particular on the issue of enlargement of the European Union which became an important part of the summit conclusions" (Ministry of Foreign Affairs, 1999). After this meeting, the negotiating teams were "pleased with the commitment that the Union should be in a position to welcome new member states from the end of 2002" (ibid.). Identifying the objectives in more general terms, the applicant countries underlined that the reforms to be undertaken in Nice should help to "improve the efficiency of functioning of the EU institutions through their internal reform and strengthening of the decision-making process" (Ministry of Foreign Affairs, 2000, 5). It should also "make the mechanisms of EU functioning more transparent, which would allow the citizens to understand better what the EU is about, what purposes it serves and how it achieves them" (ibid.). If seen in connection with the objective to simplify the Treaties by dividing them into two parts—first basic and second more technical—this issue was abandoned for reasons of feasibility. An additional expectation of the candidate countries was a Union based on solidarity, if it was to remain a collective pan-European project. The issue of solidarity seems, for obvious reasons, to be most important for Poland. Also economic stability and political security were named among the more general objectives to be achieved.

Additionally, the reforms were expected to "strengthen the protection of the citizens' fundamental rights" and to "define the principle of subsidiarity more clearly, so that the citizens may rest assured that the EU, having no intention of interfering with national affairs, intends, rather, to deal solidly with issues that are difficult to handle at the national level" (ibid.). Finally, yet importantly, the reforms would also have to consolidate the sense of shared responsibility in an enlarged Union, which is yet another expression of solidarity.

Curiously, the public debates in Poland on Europe and, to some extent, in other candidate countries were not so much concerned with the issues from the Nice negotiations agenda (Baun and Marek, 2001, 17). Rather, however

---

[3] On the conditions for enlargement from the viewpoint of the candidate countries see Wilga (1999).

irrelevant it might appear at first glance, the key question about the context of the European debate in Poland and other applicant countries were the membership negotiations. If we take the former as a case, since the very beginning, when it started negotiations with the European Commission, the debate has only been circulating around the points concerning membership, more or less determined bilaterally by the European Commission and the Polish negotiating team. If pitted against this background, the real issues seemed to be of domestic nature and the Nice Treaty negotiations with its 'left-overs' of Amsterdam appeared by far less important to the Polish people and Polish politicians. In fact, they were largely barred from the Polish domestic concerns and media coverage. Those issues became excluded for just one simple reason. They were assumed to be a prerequisite to be taken care of by the European Union. If one had to make a *revue-passé* of the institutional reform of the European Union and in particular to understand its meaning and effect on Poland, it would be exactly against this backdrop that one would have to conduct an analysis.

What follows from the above is that only a part of the Polish political establishment in power was really directly interested in, say, how many votes Poland would obtain in the future composition of the Council. Although the Nice negotiations agenda did not touch directly upon the concerns of the Polish people, one can nonetheless analyse the positions of the Republic of Poland since the issues referred to in Nice interested the Polish *raison d'état*.

Having the ambition to shape the European continent since the very beginning, successive Polish governments, the Polish presidents and other Polish officials were widely engaged in the debate either by virtue of the position held or, as it is the case with the current Polish president, voluntarily.[4] The foreign minister, Bronislaw Geremek,[5] as the key Polish official confirmed officially the general objectives mentioned above and issued a letter addressed to the Portuguese presidency, informing the Portuguese Prime Minister Jaine Gama that Poland was "interested in conclusion of the institu-

---

[4] Under an eminent title "We should not ask what Europe can do for us. We should ask what we can do for Europe," the Polish president pencilled his position on the relationship between Poland and European Union in one of Brussels' leading weeklies on European affairs (Kwaśniewski 2001). The Polish president also launched a series of round table discussions—*Reflection Group*—with all relevant and engaged Polish politicians, which are accompanied by an internet website directly linked with his presidential office;
see <http://www.prezydent.pl/bie/>. The content of the specific discussions is made only partly accessible to the wider public.

[5] Prof. Geremek was Polish foreign minister as long as the coalition between the liberal Freedom's Union (UW) and the Electoral Action 'Solidarność' (AWS) lasted. He was replaced by Prof. Bartoszewski, who was appointed to this position after the UW abandoned the centre-right coalition.

tional reform in the year 2000, so that the process of enlargement is not delayed" (Poland, 2000, 2). The Polish foreign minister argued that "thanks to the reform the Union will become more efficient, closer to its citizens and equipped with effective decision-making mechanisms. The agenda of the intergovernmental conference should be a function of the goal that the European Council in Helsinki put before the European Union: *attaining readiness for enlargement by the end of 2002*" (ibid. pp. 2, author's italics).

Another Polish foreign minister in office during the 2000 IGC, Władysław Bartoszewski, underlined in his position the role of the Union to play and to fulfil its obligations in international affairs (Bartoszewski, 2000). He also reminded that the Union must necessarily make sure that the new structures can well accommodate the peripheries within its borders to give those states the chance to catch up with the centre and to overcome the social and economic differences. Indispensable, according to him, would be furthermore an intensive cooperation in all those issues by which the candidate countries will be directly influenced after the adhesion, and this regardless of the outcomes in the 2000 IGC.

Finally, the Polish public was less concerned with anything European. In the last years we could even observe a diminishing interest and melting support of the Polish population for EU membership, let alone the negotiations in Nice.[6] Also the voices rejecting the idea of Polish membership in the European Union are less and less occasional. Some of the political groupings find such a move unjustified and others even immoral.[7]

Despite diverging attitudes towards European integration, the Polish government wished in general that after the reform the Union would emerge in a new shape allowing it to embrace new members, to emerge as a cohesive body capable of decisive and logical action, and proving necessary transparency for its citizens to understand its stakes, responsibilities and duties (Poland, 2000, 2).

---

[6] On reasons why the public support for European integration in Poland has diminished in recent years see Szczerbniak (2001). The support might be growing in the last months as a result of the official government's campaign *for* the Polish EU membership. In an opinion poll presented in the *TV Polonia*'s News 19.30, on 12th September 2002, the percentage of the 'Yes-votes' would go up to 74% by the frequency of 76 % of all entitled to do so.

[7] "Poland warns against 'immoral' price of joining Europe", *European Voice*, 1-7 July, 2001, pp. 14.

2000 IGC Agenda

Beside other relevant issues, the candidate countries were mainly interested in settling the principal questions not resolved in the 1996 IGC.[8] Those issues constituted for all candidate countries a range of conditions *since qua non* for enlargement to successfully take place. The three most urgent leftovers, which had to be tackled first, were specified by the EU Member States. To them belonged (1) the reform of the voting system in the Council of Ministers, (2) the question of qualified majority voting and (3) the composition of the European Commission. All those issues merit a particular consideration in this chapter, for to have them settled in the Nice Treaty negotiations was the most important preoccupation for all, not only the applicant states.

The above objectives were set out in the Cologne and Helsinki European Councils in 1999. In the presidency conclusion of the Cologne European summit we can read that "[i]n accordance with the Amsterdam Protocol on the institutions with the prospect of enlargement of the European Union and the declarations made with regard to it, the brief of the Intergovernmental Conference will cover the following topics: (1) size and composition of the Commission; (2) weighting of votes in the Council (re-weighting, introduction of a dual majority and threshold for qualified-majority decision-making); and (3) possible extension of qualified-majority voting in the Council."[9]

The same has been confirmed in the final conclusion of the Helsinki European Council, similarly declaring that "the conference should complete its work and agree the necessary amendments to the Treaties by December 2000".[10] Thus, as we can read in both presidency conclusions, it is these

[8] The conclusion of the European Council in Helsinki suggested that the agenda of the negotiations in the final round of the 2000 IGC could be expanded to such issues as e.g. closer cooperation, new arrangements in the area of the Common Foreign and Security Policy, the Charter of Fundamental Rights, and some others. The candidate counties were rather sceptical about this proposition, for it would make more likely—and that was their primary fear—that this would only unnecessarily prolong and possibly overload the agenda and put in danger issues screaming for settlement.

[9] Presidency conclusions, Cologne European Council, 3-4 June 1999.

[10] Presidency conclusions, Helsinki European Council, 10-11 December 1999; Press release: Brussels 11.12.1999, Nr. 00300/1/99, pp. 2. More specifically, the conference "will examine the size and composition of the Commission, the weighting of votes in the Council and the possible extension of qualified majority voting in the Council, as well as other necessary amendments to the Treaties rising as regards the European institutions" (ibid., pp. 3).

basic issues that were repeatedly named. It is also to these that the candidate countries formulated their positions,[11] to which we turn in the next section.

Positions of the Candidate Countries during the 2000 IGC

The foreign ministers from applicant countries were invited by the Portuguese presidency to present their positions on key issues of the reform. Like all his counterparts from candidate countries, the Polish foreign minister was asked to "convey to the Portuguese Presidency the Polish position regarding the agenda of the IGC as defined in the conclusions of the European Council in Helsinki" (Poland, 2000, 2). The respective responses to this enquiry constitute the basis out of which the following section will filter out the individual positions of the candidate countries, with the particular focus, as mentioned before, on Poland.

Before we go through the specific issues, one has to mention one point beforehand. The applicant countries basically agreed that all three leftovers had to be dealt with in the Nice summit by the EU Member States. Those questions seemed to be the most preoccupying ones for the applicant countries and it is to them that they were able to formulate their positions very early and present them subsequently to the Portuguese presidency. But one must not forget that this was just a prerequisite to the ultimate success of 'being in the club'. It is with this in mind that one can turn to the above-mentioned issues to explicitly see what were the exact (pro-)positions of Poland and other applicants.

Weighting of Votes in the Council

Perhaps the most important aspect for all candidate countries were the negotiations on the new voting system in the Council of Ministers, where the political power of every single Member State is literally translated into a given number of votes. The matter was for this reason very sensitive and highly contentious before and in particular during the end game in Nice. Despite this difficulty, the candidate countries tried and succeeded to make realistic propositions.

Considering itself a large, or at least, a medium-sized country, Poland made its argument clear right from the beginning. According to its official

[11] The above brings us to the conclusion that the candidate countries had to concentrate themselves on the issues just enumerated and because they had been for quite a time in the parlance of the European debate on institutional reform, those countries had to concentrate on them in producing their positions.

position, the influence of states with large populations systematically decreased with a growing number of the Member States with small populations. It is therefore not surprising that Poland, unlike all other applicant states except Turkey, wanted to take part in the camp of big states, for it would mean favouring and bettering their final weights of votes in the Council. The best option for Poland was just to plead for as high a number of votes for itself as for Spain, or nearly so, supporting at the same time the increase of votes for other big countries, like e.g. Germany.

To furthermore ensure the influence of big countries in the Union, it would be necessary, Poland argued, to correct the current power balance in the Union. If done otherwise, the enlargement would further lower both the qualified majority and blocking majority threshold, meaning that less and less small countries would be able to block the progress in integration.

Additionally, the demographic criterion was meant to be decisive in the reform of weighting of votes in the Council. This criterion "should remain the principle governing the distribution of votes" (Ministry of Foreign Affairs, 2000, 12) in the new heart of EU decision-making body, correcting in the first place the growing disproportions in the votes of big and small states respectively—a disproportion, which predominantly resulted from the growing number of states with smaller populations. Relevant was hereby also the fact that the change in the proportion of votes in the Council be accompanied either independently or by a parallel introduction of a double majority.[12]

Finally, according to Poland, the reform of the weighting of votes in the Council had to make sure that there was an adequate compensation being made to those big countries that would relinquish one member of the European Commission (Ministry of Foreign Affairs, 2000, 12). The issue of reforming the Commission, to which we turn later, and the reform of voting system had to be seen in this regard as linked issues.

To take another candidate country, Hungary for example was, plainly stated, interested in bringing about a simple, "consistent and transparent voting system, which would not require further amendments in the process of the gradual accession of new members" (Hungary, 2000, 3). More precisely, Hungary, like Poland, supported the weighting of votes in the Council of Minister reformed in the manner as to "better reflect population figures" (ibid.). The principle of demographic representation was called upon here once again. However, and this seems to correspond with the size of Hungary, out of which of course some of the Hungarian interests derived, this principle should be accompanied at the same time by "a relative overrepresentation of small Member States" (ibid.). In terms of numbers, Hungary

[12] Some scientists speak in this regard about 'triple majority requirements' for Council decisions (Tsebelis and Yataganas 2002, Baun and Marek 2001: 26).

expected, as its position paper stated, to grant a similar number of votes to countries with similar population figures. Here, the principle of equality was invoked again.

Qualified Majority Voting

A closely related aspect to the voting system in the Council was the extension of majority voting to areas covered so far by unanimity. The pair of 'qualified majority voting' and its counterpart 'unanimity' has almost always constituted the controversial relationship between supranationalism and intergovernmentalism in the European integration process. Whereas unanimity refers to pure intergovernmentalism, any single shift to qualified majority voting usually means a move to more supranationalism. In general, the candidate countries do not understand this reasoning differently and indeed it conditioned their political behaviour exactly in the same way as it did for the member countries. The positions of the applicants therefore uncover that they have been as careful about any extension of this principle as the current Member States themselves.

More specifically, according to the position of Poland, extended application of the qualified majority voting "should only be preceded by a thorough analysis of all articles in the treaties wherein the principle of unanimity still applies" (Poland, 2000, 3). Even if done so, unanimity should still pertain to all issues having special importance to the Member States and in particular to those of constitutive character, such as Treaty revisions or enlargement of the Union—both of which require a ratification of all EU members. What is more, nominations to different EU posts of high relevance as well as decisions on own resources of the Union should also remain subject of unanimity.

As to other candidate countries, the Czech minister for foreign affairs for instance endorsed the "endeavour for broader decision-making by a qualified majority" (Czech Republic, 2000, 3). Hungary, for its part, was also "in favour of widening the scope of qualified majority voting" (Hungary, 2000, 3). In the opinion of the latter, this would allow further strengthening of the process of integration in its incremental development as well as moving to a higher "degree of resolve and determination of Member States to move forward" (ibid.). Simultaneously though, as in the case of Poland, "in constitutional and sensitive issues, the principle of unanimity should be preserved" (ibid.).

Composition of the Commission

As far as the composition of the European Commission is concerned, basically two options were available. One was to support the limitation of the number of Commissioners to twenty regardless of the number of EU members. Here of course, not every single state would be represented and, as some would claim, democratic principle would be violated. The same principle however is not even fully respected in today's composition of the Commission, since the big Member States nominate two commissioners, and the small and medium states just one. Additionally, to adequately accommodate the appetites of the newcomers, the Member States would have to come up with supplementary, presumably very complicated mechanisms such as for instance 'rotation principle'.

The second option for the applicant states was to acknowledge the right to every single member to nominate one commissioner. This however would first and foremost harm the internal coherence and as a consequence also the working effectiveness of the Commission. A body comprising 27 and more members is just by nature harder to administer and it is more difficult for its members to reach unanimous decisions.

Understandably, the second option was more interesting for the candidate countries, for only in this way it would be ensured that from the adhesion onwards every single candidate would have a member in the European Commission. The answer to the question whether the first or second option is more preferable is a function of the extent to which the prestige to be represented in the Commission would be more relevant for the candidate countries than the ultimate effectiveness of this body.

As expected, we can read in Poland's position paper "that each Member State should retain the right to propose a candidate for a European Commission member" (Ministry of Foreign Affairs, 2000, 9). One of the reasons provided for this preference is the principle of democratic legitimisation of the Commission, being a necessary condition for the entire process of integration. The worries about the effectiveness of a Commission of 27 and more were 'overshadowed' by the arguments about (1) transparency, on which, in Poland's view, the working efficiency is primarily dependent and about (2) a clear-cut division of responsibilities among the respective commissioners (Poland, 2000, 2). It was argued that even the college of the Commission more "numerous than the present one will be comparable in terms of size to the cabinets of some Member States" (Ministry of Foreign Affairs, 2000, 9), which are still perfectly manageable.

The positions of other candidate countries are in this particular issue exactly the same. Hungary, for instance, as expressed by its minister of foreign affairs János Martonyi, pleaded that "every Member State should be represented by a Commissioner" (Hungary, 2000, 3). The principle of equal representation, to which Hungary attached the highest importance, should also be applied to all other institutions of the European Union (ibid.).

The Czech Republic for its part voiced the same desire, supporting the move to nominate one national to the Commission from every Member State. This would be the only way, according to the Czech foreign minister Jan Kavan, to guarantee the "Commission's neutral prestige vis-à-vis the Members States general public" (Czech Republic, 2000, 3).

In conjunction with the composition of the Commission, another issue, apparently more important to Poland than to other candidate countries, was the introduction of the Commissioners' individual responsibility. The collective character of the Commission should remain untouched, though. After the crisis of the Santer Commission it became clear enough that troubles with just one commissioner could bring down the entire college and thereby trigger a political crisis in Europe. Therefore, Poland pleaded for amending the article 213 or 215 of the Treaty, to avoid such a crisis in the future ,Ministry of Foreign Affairs, 2000, 9). It was an expression of support to the proposition to codify this principle made by the president of the European Commission Romano Prodi in September 1999 (ibid.).

Composition of the Parliament

The last issue of interest here is the composition of the European Parliament (EP). In general, as Poland noticed, the principle of 'degressive proportionality', which favoured so far small countries of the Union, ruled the distribution of seats in the EP. The limit of the seats should, according to Poland, remain at the level of 700 as defined in the 1997 IGC (Poland, 2000, 3).

Additionally, because Poland was more interested in having an effective EP, the maintenance of the upper limit of seats in the EP would require an elaboration of a new formula of seats' distribution (Ministry of Foreign Affairs, 2000, 13). After initially toying with four alternative solutions to remedy this situation,[13] Poland decided to prefer a modification of the 'degressive proportionality' principle "in favour (...) of balancing the interests of 'large', 'medium-sized' and 'small' States" (ibid., pp. 13).

[13] The four possible solutions were respectively (1) strict application of the proportionality principle applicable to population size; (2) modification of the present degressive proportionality; (3) linear reduction of the MEPs fixed according to the present principle and (4) introduction of a general European list to cover a certain number of MEPs (Ministry of Foreign Affairs 2000: 13).

What is of less importance here but still interesting is the fact that Poland supported the proposal to create EU-wide lists on which a certain number of MEPs could be elected into the EP (ibid., pp. 14).

As to other candidate countries, they expressed more or less resembling wishes, though supporting less the proposal to take hold more of current disproportionalities in the distribution of EP seats.

Before the Nice Summit: Some Observations

A number of interesting observations follow from the analysis just made. Whether weighting of votes in the Council, qualified majority voting or the composition of the European Parliament, none of the candidate countries dared quantify their specific wishes. In the case of weighting of votes, only the demographic criterion was proposed as a basis for the reform. No specific calculations for qualified majority were proposed either. The same can be observed with relation to the distribution of seats in the European Parliament.[14]

How can this be explained? Tentatively, at least two basic reasons may help. The first is the availability of relevant inside information; a fact about which some candidate countries were not directly complaining but certainly stressed, if not requested, a timely and quick provision of all relevant documents.[15] But they still lacked the necessary inside information, the absence of which might have become an impediment to a certain extent for some of the candidate countries to formulate their propositions more explicitly. Another option here could be that, despite assurances of the presidencies, it was a deliberate policy during the intergovernmental conference to create an information asymmetry, which could have disadvantaged the countries from Eastern Europe in formulating their requests.

The second reason seems to be negotiations intrinsic low predictability as to the possible outcomes of the reform. Basically, this resulted from a high number of options and possibilities for the reform, even in cases where the Treaties were very clear. For example, although the number of MEPs was

---

[14] According to the then minister of foreign affairs, Prof. Bronislaw Geremek, the 2000 IGC should also embark upon the allocation of seats in the European Parliament, trying to preserve the upper limit of 700 members (Poland, 2000: 3). This was in fact the only quantification made by the Polish officials and other applicant countries.

[15] Though in very diplomatic manner, the foreign ministry of the Czech Republic underlined the necessity to provide all the documents to the associated countries "to the same extent and at the same time as to the Member States" (Czech Republic 2000: 2, also Baun and Marek 2001: 16).

plainly specified in the Amsterdam Treaty (limited to 700), it was eventually changed in the Nice Treaty by increasing it to 732. The applicant countries could not have predicted this adjustment at all. Nor was it possibly feasible for the Member States themselves.

All in all, the positions of the candidate countries were clear and realistic. Despite the difficulties to quantify their wishes, all applicants showed both their outstanding knowledge about the issues under negotiations and about the issues relevant for the Union as well as their engagement in and commitment to European integration in general.

NICE TREATY OUTCOMES: A COMPARISON

In this section, the outcomes of the 2000 IGC and of the Nice Treaty itself are subject to examination. One can compare the end product of the 2000 IGC negotiations, as they are worded in the final version of the Nice Treaty,[16] with the positions formulated by the candidate countries prior to the final game.

The Nice Treaty had been negotiated in the time during the Portuguese and French presidencies, from 14 February until 11 December 2000. The most interesting time in the 2000 IGC were the negotiation days in the Nice summit. As we can learn from the Polish leading daily *Rzeczpospolita*, the heads of the candidate countries arrived in Nice to follow, observe and even, if necessary, to intervene in the negotiations, thus profiting directly from the presence and the observer status they were accorded.

Right after his arrival, the Polish Prime Minister, Jerzy Buzek, in a short statement voiced his expectation that the EU Member States will show necessary commitment to preparing the Union for enlargement and asked them to consider the efforts that the Polish society has been making in the last yeas.[17] This statement makes clear how important for Poland and for all candidate countries was only one issue, namely the ability of the Union to soon welcome new members. The specific subjects on the negotiation agenda were just a palliative step on the way to this ability and to the ultimate date of enlargement.[18] The Polish Prime Minister commented after the Nice summit that the Union "has never come so close towards the Polish and

[16] The references to the specific articles and/or pages are made throughout this section on the basis of the Nice Treaty version from 10 March 2001.

[17] "Niemcy na swoją miarę", *Rzeczpospolita*, 8 December 2000.

[18] *Rzeczpospolita*, 8 December 2000.

other candidate countries' requests"[19] in publicly determining the final date of widening the Union. In this sense, Nice was already a success for the countries from Eastern Europe, regardless of the specific reforms, upon which we will take a closer look in the following sections.

Weighting of Votes in the Council

Beyond the issues of less direct importance to candidate countries,[20] which cannot be discussed here, the Treaty of Nice changed first of all the numbers of votes allocated to individual Member State. After successful negotiations, the EU members agreed to a common position in determining the number of votes held by applicant countries after enlargement. As table 5 in Laursen's chapter on Re-weighting of votes in this volume shows, the results are not very much diverging from the initial positions of the candidate countries. In the final paper submitted to negotiations in the last day of the Nice summit, all EU Member States agreed that Poland should have the same number of votes as Spain, although the population number of Poland is slightly inferior. This alone, as Polish domestic media reported, was a great success.

However, the final outcome of negotiations did not come about as smoothly as one would expect or wish. On the contrary, the talks were extremely contentious, nearly leaving an impression that the negotiations would even break down altogether. These perturbations allowed us to follow the specific moves. In the night from Friday to Saturday, already after initial serious squabbles, the French presidency submitted a compromise paper that was rejected as well.[21]

Sunday morning, a second paper was submitted, in which Poland surprisingly received less votes in the Council than Spain. Swift reactions from other Member States and, as the Polish media reported, the famous telephone calls between the Polish Prime Minister Jerzy Buzek and the Spanish Prime Minister José Maria Aznar and the German chancellor Gerhard Schröder

---

[19] "Drzwi otwarte od 2003 roku", *Rzeczpospolita*, 9 December 2000, (author's translation).

[20] To them belonged in particular the fate of the Charter of Fundamental Rights, further development of the Common Foreign and Security Policy, European Security and Defence Policy, of which the latter two might be interesting for further integration of the candidate countries since the debates on their sovereignties, only recently regained, are still very much alive and cause sometimes deep concerns, producing for instance such claims that, as it is most obvious in Poland, the successive governments make themselves dependent yet again, only this time replacing Moscow for Brussels. This is a typical high politics issues, thus it is sensitive for all candidate countries.

[21] "Kulisy negocjacji", *Rzeczpospolita*, 11 December 2000.

respectively could alter the situation, assuring the Poles that this proposal would never be accepted.[22]

Finally, Monday morning, all big countries agreed to renounce one vote in the Council. For this reason Spain and Poland also lost one vote. Simultaneously, some small Member States won one vote respectively and this was also why some small candidate countries received one vote more in the Council[23] (see 2. in table 17.1).

Interestingly, as summarised in table 17.1, one can notice that the logic according to which the numbers of votes proposed and accorded to different candidate countries were intrinsic to negotiations.[24] With proposals subsequently tabled by the French presidency during the Nice summit, the votes were either (1.) constant all the time (Latvia, Estonia, Slovenia), (2.) steadily growing with subsequent days (Hungary, Czech Republic, Romania), or (3.) neither of them (Poland, Slovakia, Lithuania, Cyprus). As it seems, the logic of distribution of votes was therefore more political in nature (Laursen, 2002b, 6) than one would expect.

---

[22] As Polish media reported, surprised were also other Nice summit participants, e.g. the spoke person of the European Commission Jonathan Faull, the Polish negotiators and the heads of governments of Sweden and Denmark, of which both prime ministers promised to support the Polish concerns; "Zacięta walka o miejsce wśród wielkich", *Rzeczpospolita*, 11 December 2000.

[23] "Unia otwarta dla kandydatów", *Rzeczpospolita*, 12 December 2000.

[24] For one interesting perspective as to how the negotiations in the European Council make sense and condition the final outcome see Beach (2002).

Table 17.1: Candidate countries and different logics in weighting of votes in the Council during Nice summit negotiations.

Nice summit *Candidate country*	9 December	10 December	Final outcome
Poland	26	28	27
1. Countries with stable number of votes during the negotiations			
Latvia	4	4	4
Estonia	4	4	4
Slovenia	4	4	4
2. Countries with increasing number of votes during the negotiations			
Hungary	10	11	12
Czech Republic	10	11	12
Romania	12	13	14
3. Countries with other than 1. and 2.			
Slovakia	6	7	7
Lithuania	6	5	7
Cyprus	3	4	4

Source: Compiled by the author from table in Laursen's chapter on re-weighting of votes.

Tuesday, after the Nice summit, the Polish Prime Minister, Buzek, and Minister of Foreign affairs, Bartoszewski, "were not hiding their satisfaction that the Fifteen promised to finalise the negotiations with candidate countries in the year 2002."[25] Once again, if one forgets the incidents with the telephone calls, it becomes clear that not so much the individual issues under reform but rather the overall issue of the Union's ability to accommodate new members were really at stake for the candidate countries.

True or not, other Polish officials were also very much satisfied with the final outcome produced in Nice. Making his support for Spain laud and apparently assuming that what Spain gets Poland will get as well,[26] the then Polish chief negotiator Jan Kułakowski obviously cannot be unsatisfied. At the first day of Nice Treaty negotiations, he repeated that Poland "should keep its fingers crossed for Spain because due to nearly the same population numbers, what Madrid gains, will be given to us".[27] If one takes only those

[25] Ibid., (author's translation). As the Copenhagen summit last December showed (2002), the promise was kept.

[26] *Rzeczpospolita*, 08 December 2000.

[27] "Trzymamy kciuki za Hiszpanię", *Rzeczpospolita*, 09 December 2000 (author's translation).

two states as evaluative comparison, one can observe that the demographic criterion, including that of equality, were in fact applied.

The wishes and predictions of only one Polish official from the government were wrong. Following United Kingdom and Italy, the head of the UKIE,[28] Jacek Saryusz-Wolski, expressed his support for Germany and expected it to receive more votes in the Council of Ministers than France, arguing that the time has finally come to trust a Germany which is unquestionably pro-European.[29] But also Germany had to change its original position on this matter, probably giving in to France and because of the double majority favouring Germany in the Council without an explicitly higher number of votes (see hereto the chapter on Germany in this volume).

Qualified Majority Voting and Qualified Majority Threshold

The second issue that the heads of governments of EU states agreed to was the qualified majority voting—another leftover not resolved in Amsterdam. The Union's Member States decided that the system of decisions taken by qualified majority would be modified from 1 January 2005. In general, the 2000 IGC agreed that six articles relating to appointments, including the appointment of the president and members of the Commission, and eight other provisions relating to institutional questions, become subject to qualified majority voting. Here, the decision has been taken irrespective of the position of Poland, whose officials argued that all nominations of high relevance should remain subject to unanimity.

Moreover, the Treaty of Nice introduced qualified majority voting in some of the articles relating to Community policies.[30] The same has been decided to regulate and resolve situations where a Member State does not comply with the most basic provisions of the European Treaties.[31] As to the

[28] UKIE is an acronym standing for the 'Urząd Komitetu Integracji Europejskiej' (Office of the Committee for European Integration) responsible for coordination of the Polish membership negotiations and other issues relevant for European integration affairs.

[29] *Rzeczpospolita*, 08 December 2000.

[30] Here the "[a]rticles 13, 18, 65, 100, 123, 133, 157, 159, 279 and the new Article 181a EC" are concerned. In the case of a "further four articles the move to qualified-majority voting was deferred for all or part of the areas covered by the relevant provisions (Article 67 in conjunction with Articles 62, 63, 66 and Article 161 of the EC Treaty)"; cf. European Commission, <http://europa.eu.int/comm/archives/igc2000/>.

[31] Acting by a majority of four-fifths, the Council may suspend the rights of voting of a member state, if a serious breach of the Treaties or a potential risk thereof has been observed. The Art. 7 of the Nice Treaty states that "[o]n a reasoned proposal by one third of the member states, by the European parliament or by the Commission, the Council, acting by a majority of

threshold, it will evolve in step with the accessions. Once the twelve applicant countries have joined the Union, the qualified majority threshold will be set at 255 votes out of 345. If requested, a Member State may ask for verification that the qualified majority comprises at least 62% of the total EU population. In other words, is this not the case, the double majority does not exist and the decision will not be adopted.[32]

Finally, according to the wording of the declaration approved in the 2000 IGC and attached to the Nice Treaty, the precise decision to define the qualified majority threshold was left to the accession treaties,[33] since there is still an uncertainty as to the final number of new Member States, upon which the specific mathematical calculations for the qualified majority and its threshold are dependent.

Composition of the Commission

The size and composition of the Commission was the last leftover to be settled in Nice. The heads of governments of the EU Member States decided to postpone establishing a Commission with a number of its members inferior to the number of the EU members until the Union will comprise 27 states. What results thereof is that after enlargement, to be more precise, "on 1 January 2005 and with effect from when the first Commission following that date takes up its duties" (Art. 4, Treaty of Nice, 2001, 51), the Commission will consist of one commissioner per Member State. Should the number of the EU members go beyond twenty-seven in the future, so the number of commissioners will necessarily have to be inferior. The Council acting unanimously will then determine the exact number of commissioners as well as the rotation order. In the latter case, the members of the Commission will be selected on the basis "of a rotation system, based on the principle of equality" (ibid.: 52).

As the section 3(a) of the article 4 stipulates, the Member States "shall be treated on a strictly equal footing as regards the determination of the sequence of, and the time spent by, their nationals as Members of the Commission, consequently the difference between the total number of terms of office

---

four-fifths of its members after obtaining the assent of the European Parliament, may determine that there is a serious breach by a member state of principles mentioned in Article 6(1), and address appropriate recommendations to that State".

[32] Server of the European Commission, <http://europa.eu.int/comm/archives/igc2000/>; factsheets, weighting of votes.

[33] The accession treaties are to be signed during the Greek presidency in the first half of 2003.

held by nationals of any given pair of Member States may never be more than one“ (ibid.).

Here again, the expectations of the candidate countries are largely fulfilled. After the accession, all of them will be accorded a place for a commissioner, without greatly putting in danger the cohesion and the working efficiency of the college, although it will certainly become more difficult to produce meaningful decisions in contentious matters with 27 members than it has been the case with 15.

Regarding the individual responsibility of the commissioners, as Poland requested to introduce, the Treaty of Nice does not provide any far-reaching specification. Only modest reference has been made to this request by revising the Art. 214(2), the amended version of which provides that "[a] Member of the Commission shall resign if the President so requests, after obtaining the approval of the College" (Art. 217, Treaty of Nice, 2001, 22). However modest its form might appear, this materialises the Polish position and gives it an expression in the new Treaty.

Composition of the Parliament

Though not an explicit leftover from Amsterdam, the settlement of the distribution of seats in the EP was still an interesting issue for the candidate countries. Here, the 2000 IGC surprisingly decided to change the number of seats. The ceiling of 700 fixed in the Amsterdam Treaty was increased to and should not now exceed 732 seats. This number of course includes the MEPs from the future Member States. As in the case of weighting of votes in the Council, also here the number of MEPs accorded to Poland is exactly the same as that of Spain (see table 20.7 in Laursen's chapter on re-weighting of votes in this volume). Once again, the principle of equality with the demographic criterion was applied.

This, however, was not the case with for instance Hungary and the Czech Republic. One can notice in the same table 7 that although Hungary, Czech Republic, Belgium, Portugal and Greece all have nearly the same population numbers, the respective representations of the former two in the EP are lower, namely only 20 MEPs, than those of Belgium and Portugal having 22 MEPs. Whether this is a result of not being at the negotiating table or of other reasons is difficult to answer. But what is clear is that these countries did not have an option to credibly threaten to break down the negotiations. They could only protest against such decisions and express their dissatisfactions, as some of them did (Baun and Marek, 2001, 27, 28). Right after the final game in Nice, both the Czech and Hungarian officials announced that they would try to correct these unfortunate precedents within the accession negotiations and accession treaties (Szentiványi, 2001, 146). Ultimately, however, it was possible for all participating parties to accept the 'final deal'.

Provisionally, for the parliamentary term 2004-9, and after distribution of seats allocated to the current Member States and to the countries with which accession treaties are signed by the 1st January 2004, the number of EP members will, if necessary, be increased proportionally for each Member State up to the ceiling of 732. This means that any country that succeeds to join the Union during the current parliamentary term will also be able to elect their MEPs—as was for instance the case after the German unification, where the representatives from Eastern part of Germany could enter the European Parliament in the middle of the term.

All in all, there was no reason for Poland to argue and to be unsatisfied with the results of the 2000 IGC finalised in the Nice European Council. Not only the Union became able to enlarge itself to new countries, what was the most vital issue, but also many of the Polish positions materialised.

Liberal Intergovernmentalism: Candidate Countries and the Nice Treaty Bargain

An additional task to be addressed in this chapter is the assessment of the applicability and explanatory power of liberal intergovernmentalism (LI, henceforth) as confronted with the insights from the analysis of Poland and the Nice Treaty bargain (summarised in table 17.2, below). In fact, the main question in this volume is to gauge the extent to which LI can explain the 2000 IGC outcomes (Laursen, 2002a, 1-5; Laursen, 2002b, 11-13).

To briefly recall, the LI logic, which was most extensively outlined in *The Choice for Europe* (Moravcsik 1998: 18-85), singled out three specific phases: (1) national preference formation, (2) interstate bargaining and (3) institutional choice.

National Preference Formation

The national preference formation (first stage), as Moravcsik's analysis framework assumes, was in Poland rather scanty. This was also the case in other candidate countries (Baun and Marek, 2001, 17). As we learned in the lines above, the Polish political establishment has always, and this is still the case, been interested in the enlargement *per se*. The accession negotiations were more in focus than any other issue. All forces concentrated entirely on the agenda of accession negotiations, where the Polish officials have been involved and felt that they could actually exercise some influence over outcomes. In fact, this focal point dominated all others and, indeed, was debated domestically.

In contrast, the national preference formation process on the Nice summit agenda and the Nice Treaty negotiations did not follow Moravcsik's expectations. The Polish foreign ministry just pencilled the position papers, informed the Polish prime minister and the Polish *Sejm* (lower house in the national assembly), after which then the government simply submitted them to the respective EU presidencies. High consensus on the principal objective of integration (*enlargement*), which has been the highest priority of the Polish foreign policy since the fall of the Berlin Wall, made that nothing was really to debate about.

Such a pattern is not an exception. As some chapters in this volumes document, in many EU Member States the situation was similar. For example, like in Poland, Italian preference formation was reduced to the role of the Italian foreign ministry (see chapter on Italy, in this volume). Similarly, the Spanish prime minister, only sometimes in consultation with the members of the prime ministerial cabinet, defined Spanish national preferences only by himself (see the chapter on Spain, in this volume). The French case is also illustrative here. The so-called '*Conseil Restraint*', dominated by Jacques Chirac, Pierre Moscivici and Hubert Vedrine, thus by the very few from the national political elite, did exactly the same.

Another problem with LI is its assumption that preference formation is somehow based on national geopolitical or economic interests. However, it is very often the case that the causes for national interests lie outside the national political arena. Indeed, they can be found at the national level as well, but frequently they are also at the regional (European) and international level. Moravcsik himself allows for such a possibility when he argues that national interests can be "reflected in pressures from domestic constituents in response to international externalities" (Moravcsik and Nicoladïs, 1999, 61).

All the above makes that the first part of LI framework can certainly be applied as there are countries which confirm Moravcsik's assumption (e.g. Germany; federal government vs. Länder), but because the national preference formation neither did take place in many EU Member States nor in Poland and in other candidate countries, its explanatory power seems limited.

Interstate Bargaining

Another problem that diminishes the applicability of the LI framework arises in respect to both the end game of the Nice Treaty negotiations and to the 2000 IGC alike (second phase). Because the negotiations in the European Union are highly institutionalised and regulated as to when and who does have a say, Poland and other candidate countries as not-yet-EU-members were not *sensus stricto* directly involved at the negotiation tables. While the candidate countries could, at least partly, negotiate during the 2000 IGC, those countries could not intervene in the Nice European Council negotiations. As a result, they could not use a veto or credible threat option to break down the negotiations, as some of the EU members in fact did. Having only an observer status, the options left for them were e.g. bilateral deals, classical diplomatic instruments with some EU insiders, press statements or voice options, of which Poland made use after France tabled its second proposal.[34] It is however only difficult to assess to what extent the Polish 'phone calls' incident might have influenced the final outcome of negotiations.

In either case, Poland and other candidate countries were very dependent upon the outcome, which diminished their bargaining powers significantly. But the fact that Poland received as many votes in the Council and in the EP as Spain, although the latter had rather a strong bargaining position – not only because of its presence at the negotiation table but also because of its strong veto incentive to the reform of structural funds, perceived by many as being in danger because of enlargement—somehow refutes the outcome dependency assumption. Therefore, both the applicability and the explanatory power of LI in the case in focus are also of minor significance.

Table 17.2: LI and candidate countries in Nice Treaty bargain.

	1. National preference formation	2. Interstate bargaining	3. Institutional Choice
Applicability of the framework	high	low	non – low
Explanatory Power	non – low	low	non – low

Source: Compiled by the author.

[34] Baun and Marek write that "[t]he Polish government reacted with considerable alarm to the French presidency's initial proposal giving Poland one vote less than Spain, a country with a similar population (...). After phone calls to the leaders of Germany, France, Spain, Denmark, and Sweden to lobby against the French plan, and after issuing a press statement highly critical of the Nice proceedings and demanding equal treatment, Poland was able to gain parity with Spain at 27 votes apiece" (2001: 27).

Institutional Choice

As a result of the first and second stage, the ultimate impact of the candidate countries on the new institutional choice for the EU (third phase), although they seem very pleased with the results, has been low as well, if not near to nonexistent. Because the Union has finally been prepared to welcome new states, which was the highest priority of the candidate countries, the ultimate institutional choice was of minor importance. Again, this makes that the LI framework turns out in this very case to be of low general utility, applicability and explanatory power.

CONCLUDING REMARKS

In brief, the main task of this chapter was to overview the positions taken by the candidate countries on the EU institutional reform in the 2000 IGC negotiations. A comparison of what those countries anticipated and what the final outcomes looked like was made. For reasons provided at the beginning, the particular focus has been laid on Poland, though references has also been made to the positions of other candidate countries.

As regards the primary task of this chapter, the expectations of the states under consideration, as they have been defined in their positions papers, are, with only some minor exceptions, mirrored in the final outline of the Nice Treaty. Poland received 27 votes in the Council of Ministers, 50 seats for the Polish representatives in the European Parliament and one Commissioner. In all cases, the results are similar to those of Spain. Poland has even more reason to satisfaction when it compares itself with Germany. Here, it has only two votes less in the Council than Germany, while its population figure is half as big as that of the latter.

The secondary task, not only of this chapter, was to estimate the applicability and explanatory power of liberal intergovernmentalism when applied to the case of candidate countries. It became clear that there are several problems with LI and therefore the relevance of alternative approaches, as suggested in the introductory chapter (Laursen, 2002b, 13), either in conjunction or in competition to LI, would be to (re)consider.

BIBLIOGRAPHY

Bartoszewski, Władysław (2000), *Vision and Potential: For a new direction in European Integration*, speech of the Minister of Foreign Affairs of Poland at the Centre for European Studies, Brussels, 25 July.

Baun, Michael J. and Dan Marek (2001), "The Candidate States and the IGC," *Journal of International Relations and Development*, Vol. 4, No. 1, pp. 13-37.

Beach, Derek (2002), "The negotiation of the Amsterdam Treaty – when theory meets reality," in Finn Laursen (ed.), *The Amsterdam Treaty: National Preference Formation, Interstate Bargaining, Outcome and Ratification*. Odense: Odense University Press, pp. 593-637.

— (2002), *Bringing Negotiations Back – supranational actors and the negotiation of intergovernmental conferences in the EU*, Ph.D.-dissertation. Odense: Odense University Press.

Czech Republic (2000), Conference of the Representatives of the governments of the Member States, IGC 2000: Contribution from the Government of the Czech Republic, CONFER/VAR 3958/00, Brussels, 24 February.

Hennessy, Mark (2002), Government plans second Nice Treaty referendum for autumn, *Irish Times*, 2 April.

Hungary (2000), Conference of the Representatives of the governments of the Member States, IGC 2000: Contribution from the Government of Hungary, CONFER/VAR 3952/00, Brussels, 24 February.

Kwaśniewski, Aleksander (2001), "We should not ask what Europe can do for us. We should ask what we can do for Europe," *European Voice*, 11 January.

Laursen, Finn (2002a), *The Treaty of Nice: National Preference Formation, Interstate Bargaining, Outcome and Ratification*. Project Description. Odense: Department of Political Science, University of Southern Denmark.

— (2002b), *Introduction: Overview of the Intergovernmental Conference 2000 and the Treaty of Nice*. Paper prepared for Centre of European Studies, University of Southern Denmark, Odense, 6-7 September.

Ministry of Foreign Affairs (1999), *Joint statement of the Ninth meeting of the heads of negotiating teams of Cyprus, Czech Republic, Estonia, Hungary, Poland and Slovenia*, Bled 16-18 December, Warsaw.

— (2000), *Republic of Poland, Intergovernmental Conference 2000: The Polish Position*, 12 June, Warsaw.

Moravcsik, Andrew (1998), *The Choice for Europe. Social Purpose and State Power from Rome to Maastricht*. Ithaca: Cornell University Press.

— and Kalypso Nicolaïdis (1999), "Explaining the Treaty of Amsterdam: Interests, Influence, Institutions," *Journal of Common Market Studies*, Vol. 37, No. 1, pp. 59-85.

Parzymies, Stanisław (2002), *Poland negotiates EU accession*, Ministry of Foreign Affairs, <http://www.msz.gov.pl/english/unia/polandnegot.html>.

Poland (2000), Conference of the representatives of the governments of the Member State, IGC 2000: Contribution from the government of Poland, CONFER/VAR 3960/00, Brussels, 24 February.

Szczerbniak, Aleks (2001), "Polish Public Opinion: Explaining Declining Support for EU Membership," *Journal of Common Market Studies*, Vol. 39, No. 1, pp. 105-22.

Szentiványi, Gábor (2001), "Europe's Silent Revolution: No Blood, No tears, All Sweat," in Martyn Bond and Kim Feus (eds.), *The Treaty of Nice Explained*. London: The Federal Trust for Education and research, pp. 139-47.

Treaty of Nice (2001), "Amending the Treaty on the European Union, The Treaties establishing the European Communities and certain related acts," *Official Journal of the European Communities*, (2001/C 80/01), 10.03.2001.

Tsebelis, George and XenophonYataganas, (2002), "Veto Players and Decision-making in the EU After Nice: Policy Stability and Bureaucratic/Judicial Discretion," *Journal of Common Market Studies*, Vol. 40, No. 2, pp. 283-307.

Wilga, Maciej (1999), "Motywacje, warunki i niebezpieczeństwa rozszerzenia Unii Europejskiej" [Motivations, preconditions and dangers of the EU enlargement], *Sprawy Polityczne*, No. 1, pp. 17-30.

— (2001a), "Zagadnienia integracji europejskiej" [Issues of European integration], in Maciej Wilga (ed.), *Europa a regiony* [Europe and the regions], 2001 special edition of *Sprawy Polityczne* on European integration, pp. 3-16.

— (2001b), "Czy już wiadomo dokąd to z Europą?" [Do we know where to go with Europe?], *Sprawy Polityczne*, No. 4, pp. 94-105.

— (2002), *L'élargissement et la contribution de la Pologne à l'intégration du continent. Note de réflexion sur les éléments historiques et politiques de la Pologne et leur importance pour la construction européenne*, unpublished document.

Zielonka, Jan (2000), "Enlargement and the Finality of European integration," in Christian Joerges, Yves Mény and Joseph Weiler (eds.), *What Kind of Constitution for What King of Polity? Responses to Joschka Fischer.* Cambridge, MA: Robert Schuman Centre for Advanced Studies/European University Institute, The Jean Monnet Chair/Harvard Law School, pp. 151-162.

SECTION 2

INSTITUTIONAL ACTORS

CHAPTER 18

THE EUROPEAN PARLIAMENT AND THE EUROPEAN COMMISSION: 'YOU CAN'T ALWAYS GET WHAT YOU WANT'

INTRODUCTION

As is well known, the Treaty of Amsterdam, which entered into force on 1 May 1999, left a certain number of 'left-over' issues: changes in the size and composition of the Commission, re-weighting of votes in the Council, possible extension of qualified majority voting (QMV) as well as other necessary amendments to the Treaties arising in connection with the reform of the European institutions. It was admitted that these issues would have to be addressed before enlargement of the Union took place.

In this quest, the governments attached a "Protocol on the institutions with the prospect of enlargement of the European Union" to the Treaty. This protocol stated that by the time the first of the new Member States joined, the Commission should be made up of one national from each Member State (provided that by that date there should have been either a re-weighting of votes in the Council or a dual majority system in order to compensate the larger Member States for the loss of one commissioner). It further stated that at least one year before EU membership exceeds 20, a new Intergovernmental Conference (IGC) would be held "in order to carry out a comprehensive review of the provisions of the Treaties on the composition and functioning of the institutions" (OJ C 340 of 10 November 1997).[1]

The IGC was convened under the Portuguese Presidency of the Council on 14 February 2000. After 330 hours of formal discussion, the European Council concluded the negotiations and the Treaty of Nice was then eventually signed on 26 February 2001.

This paper sets out to analyse the role of two institutional actors at the IGC—the European Parliament (EP) and the Commission—before, during and after the Conference. After a short overview of the state of affairs within both institutions prior to Nice, the paper sets out to compare the formal role both institutions are prescribed to play at IGCs (by the Treaties) with the actual transposition of these provisions into the practical political process. The

---

[1] The Protocol can also be located at http://europa.eu.int/eur-lex/en/treaties/dat/amsterdam.html#0111010014.

paper concludes with an analysis of the implications of the results of the Conference for both institutions.

THE SITUATION PRIOR TO NICE

The fact that the European Parliament (EP) is now commonly seen as a co-legislator with the Council is a relatively new development. For more than three decades, the EP did not enjoy any effective rights of participation in the legislative process. It started out as an assembly with only two major powers: the power to pass a motion of censure against the High Authority[2] and the right to be consulted by the Council on selected legislative proposals. The opinions given in this classical consultation procedure were non-binding.

The 1987 Single European Act (SEA) represented a major step forward for the EP. It marked the beginning of a new triangular relationship between the Council, the Commission and the EP by introducing the co-operation procedure, which significantly improved inter-institutional dialogue, giving the EP the first opportunity to 'flex its legislative muscles' and to make use of its agenda-setting powers whenever possible.

Building on the positive experiences of the co-operation procedure, the EP's legislative competencies were extended by the Treaty on European Union, commonly known as the Maastricht Treaty (1993). Through the introduction of the co-decision procedure, the Members of the European Parliament (MEPs) were for the first time granted the power of veto in several policy areas.[3]

The Treaty of Amsterdam (1999) strengthened the EP's role considerably, especially as regards its involvement in the legislative process. The co-decision procedure has been extended from 15 to 38 Treaty areas or types of Community action and now applies to new areas within the fields of transport, environment, energy, development co-operation and certain aspects of social affairs. A significant new element in the Amsterdam Treaty is the streamlining of the co-decision procedure. Most importantly, a legislative act can now be adopted at the first reading if the EP fails to suggest amendments to the Commission proposal or the Council agrees to the changes suggested by the EP. The Treaty has also extended the scope of application of the as-

---

[2] The forerunner of the European Commission.

[3] Initially only 15 Treaty items were covered by the procedure: articles falling into the policy fields of the internal market, consumer protection, trans-European networks, cultural policy, public health and education.

sent procedure.[4] Another important post-Amsterdam innovation, which has been very topical, is that the EP now plays a role in the nomination procedure of the Commission President (Westlake, 1994; Maurer, 1999; Hix, 1999; Smith, 1999; Peterson and Bomberg, 1999; Shackleton, 1999; Corbett, Jacobs and Shackleton, 2000; Neuhold, 2000).

Contrary to the EP, the European Commission has suffered from a relative loss of importance in the 1990s. The 'motor of European integration' seemed to stall after the success of the internal market programme and the initiation of the Economic and Monetary Union (EMU). Several political and institutional factors lie behind this loss of impact.

A very important factor is the extended role of the European Council, which was not only responsible for strategic decisions influencing the further development of the European Union (for example in the context of EU-enlargement), but also for guidelines and detailed decisions in selected policy areas such as social policy or Justice and Home Affairs.

In the second half of the 1990s, the Commission's role was limited by the lack of a convincing integration project, with Member States increasingly protecting their national interests and problems resulting from internal inefficiency. The Commission's organisational problems resulted from a discrepancy between the extension of its competencies and somewhat antiquated structures and insufficient (personnel) resources. The crisis of the Commission in 1999, caused in part by deficiencies from the Delors Commission, has severely damaged the reputation of the 'watchdog of the Community' (Monar, 2001).

Overall, one can say at this point that while the EP was at its strongest position yet as it went into the Conference, the Commission was comparatively weak.

The Role of the EP and the Commission at the IGC 2000

It is important to note that once an IGC has been set on track, the institutions no longer have a formal role in the process of negotiation and adoption. Although the Conference is formally convened by that Member State exercising the Presidency of the Council, the Council itself plays no explicit institutional role. The negotiations take place among the governments of the Member States. The 'constituent power' for Treaty change is bundled with the Member States as contracting parties to the Treaties.

---

[4] The Treaty of Amsterdam extends the EP's right of assent to cases where the Council determines a breach of the Union's principles by a Member State (Article Fa TEU).

Nevertheless, both the EP and the Commission have tried (with varying degrees of success) to maximise their influence on the progress of the IGC negotiations. The strategies and the outcome of the Nice IGC will be analysed below.

The Role of the EP at the IGC

The Parliament's role at IGCs has been the subject of much controversy. The Treaty foresees no role for the EP in IGCs, either to put forward proposals or to attend Conference meetings; nor does the EP have any role to play at the end of the Conference, i.e. it does not have to ratify the Treaty (contrary to national parliaments).

Up to the IGC at Nice, the EP was not formally represented at any Conference sessions. The EP had already tried in the Amsterdam IGC to maximise its influence on Conference proceedings by being represented at the Conference but was met with opposition by some of the Member States (notably the UK and France). As a compromise, a rather complex arrangement was set up in the Amsterdam IGC, according to which two representatives of the EP had additional meetings with IGC representatives and a monthly (informal) dinner.

The EP went into the Nice IGC with elaborate demands ranging from the *constitutionalisation* of the Union to altering the procedure for the future revision of the Treaties by introducing a power of co-decision for the Council and the EP. Furthermore, it asked for "sufficiently ambitious institutional reforms", where for example QMV and co-decision should become the 'normal' legislative procedure.

The ceiling of 700 seats planned for the size of the EP was not to be breached but entailed, according to the EP that the number of seats per Member State was to be reviewed.

Moreover, the EP called for clarification of the existing Treaty provisions regarding the possibility of collective resignation of the Commission and asked to be given the same right as the Council to apply to the Court of Justice for the compulsory retirement of an individual Commissioner. The EP also demanded that the procedure whereby the President of the Commission may dismiss an individual Commissioner be written into the Treaty (European Parliament, 2000a).

For the negotiations at the IGC itself, the Helsinki Council foresaw that two 'observers' from the EP may attend meetings of the Preparatory Group, but the EP was excluded from formal meetings at ministerial level and meetings of Heads of State and Government. Prior to each formal ministerial session of the Conference, an exchange of views was carried out with the President of the EP, Nicole Fontaine. During the Conference, MEPs were also allowed to attend meetings of the Friends of the Presidency and informal ministerial conclaves. This gave the two parliamentary observers[5] the possibility to take the stand of the EP and to push for specific points of interest to the Parliament. These rather complex arrangements were far from what the EP had initially demanded (to be a full member of the Conference and to give its assent to the results) (Galloway, 2001, 38). According to an interview with an MEP, the representatives of the EP were very well informed, but not directly implicated into the proceedings: "We were very well briefed, by everyone: by the cleaners, by the Commission, by Member State etc. We were also very well prepared, but not involved."[6] Despite its increasing role in the legislative process, the EP was for the most part given only observer status and had no real means to influence the negotiations. The arrangements for its involvement were highly formal and rather futile. The reigns were still held by the Member State governments. This gives rise to fundamental questions of balance of power between the institutions and whether the intergovernmental method is adequate within a complex (multi-level) system such as the EU, where political power is not concentrated, but spread over territorial levels and decision-making arenas (Grande, 2000; Marks, Hooghe and Blank, 1996).

The Role of the Commission at the IGC

Even if the political reality of IGCs may be highly complex, in this case the title 'Intergovernmental Conferences' is somewhat programmatic. As the negotiations take place between the *governments* of the Member States, the Commission's role is accordingly, just like the EP, much more circumscribed than in the EC-related negotiations within the Council. Nevertheless, the Commission has in the past succeeded in influencing the negotiations by launching political initiatives and by taking over the role of conciliator.

The Commission's role within IGCs is based on its institutional role as 'watchdog of the Community', as guardian of the Treaties and on Article 48 TEU, which gives it the right to forward proposals for Treaty change to the Council. The Commission, by way of its very detailed opinion, formal and informal contributions and interventions in meetings, played a quite active role in the Conference. It was formally represented by Michel Barnier and by

[5] Elmar Brok, Germany, European People's Party and Dimitios Tsatos Greece, Party of European Socialists.

[6] Interview with MEP, June 2001.

its President Romano Prodi at meetings of the Heads of State and Government (European Commission, 2000; Galloway, 2001, 37)

Despite these facts, the Commission's actual influence on the outcome of the Conference seems to have been somewhat modest when compared to previous IGCs. Although the Commission has defended its traditional positions (for example as regards the extension of QMV) and defended its role in key-areas such as common trade policy, it does not appear to have succeeded in influencing the negotiations decisively. One reason for this relatively weak bargaining position of the Commission is the fact that the Prodi Commission was just appointed at a time (Autumn 1999 until February 2000) where the preparations for the Conference were already in full swing.

Due to the fact that the Commission was engrossed in its endeavours of internal reform, it had difficulties developing an all-encompassing position and defending it. Other reasons to be mentioned in this context are that although the President of the Commission is a sixteenth member of the European Council, the position of the Commission at meetings of Heads of State and Government is rather weak as it is not formally a part of the Conference (as it was not a Member State government). Another reason was that the Commission was at times defending politically difficult positions such as a significant extension of QMV on taxation, social security and social policy. Third, on issues concerning the Commission directly such as its composition, the Commission had no clear position. Instead, it put forward the following different options for reform:

- the Commission could either be composed of fewer Members than the future number of Member States. In this case the Treaty would provide a system of rotation that would treat all Members strictly equally on the basis of a pre-set order.
- the Commission could be made up of one national from each Member State, with its structure overhauled to increase its efficiency, for example by significantly increasing the President's power to allocate or not allocate portfolios to Members of the Commission and to increase the powers and number of the Vice Presidents (Commission, 2000,13f).

One also has to note that the agenda of the Nice IGC did not aim to strengthen the position of the Commission. Compared to other IGCs, the Commission was not only actor but at the same time target of the negotiations. The reform of the Commission was explicitly on the IGC's agenda. It had become evident that the Commission's structure needed to be overhauled well before enlargement. This implied that more was decided *about* the Commission than *with* the Commission itself (Galloway, 2001, 37; Monar, 2001, 115).

The Results of the Treaty for the EP and the Commission

The Effect of the Nice Treaty on the European Commission

The only specific agreement within the Treaty of Nice concerning the size and composition of the Commission is that the five largest countries will lose their right to a second Commissioner: as of 2005, the size of the European Commission will be one Commissioner per Member State, at least until the Union reaches 27 countries (TEC Article 213.1). Thereafter, not all Member States will always be able to nominate a Commissioner. At that point, the Council, acting unanimously without consulting either the Commission or the EP, will be able to choose the Members of the Commission according to a rotation system yet to be devised 'based on the principle of equality' and reflecting demography and geography. The practical details of this rotation seem complicated, but they have been postponed to be decided upon at a later date.

For the next Commission (and most probably also for the one after that) the principle of one Commissioner per Member State will apply. At least from a short- to medium-term perspective, one can therefore conclude that the smaller countries were successful in defending their position, as they do not have to give up 'their' Commissioner immediately. The representation of one national per Member State is advantageous insofar as it is felt to increase the public acceptance of the institutions. On the other hand, the citizens and governments might still (as was sometimes the case in the past) regard Commissioners as 'our' man/woman in Brussels (Best, 2001, 3). This gives rise to more fundamental questions which cannot be resolved by a mere reshuffling of numbers. The Commission must (continue to) act independently as a collegial organ and not as vehicle for (Member State) interests.

Article 214 TEC contains a fundamental innovation as regards the nomination procedure of Commissioners. The Council, meeting in the composition of Heads of State or Government, now has to nominate the candidate it intends to appoint as President of the Commission with a *qualified majority*. After the Council has received the assent of the EP[7] it shall, again acting by qualified majority and by common accord with the nominee for President, adopt the list of persons to be appointed as Members of the Commission.[8] In the third phase of the nomination procedure, the EP must give its assent to the President of the Commission and the other

[7] The approval by the EP is foreseen by the Treaty of Amsterdam.

[8] This list is drawn up in accordance with the proposals made by each Member State.

Members of the Commission. An innovation in this context is the fact that after the EP's approval, the Council will appoint the President and the other Members of the Commission by qualified majority and not unanimously, as was formerly the case.

Thus, in all phases of the nomination procedure of the Commission, qualified majority has to be applied. This reform is important insofar as it breaks with the tradition of unanimity when nominating the Commission President and introduces the 'community method' into the intergovernmental character of decision-making among the Heads of State and Government. It is almost without doubt that this new provision will bring new dynamics into the institutional conglomerate. Even if decisions are taken with unanimity, the very possibility of qualified majority will most probably increase the willingness to compromise.

In the practical political process, this might be the end of solutions at the level of the lowest common denominator, which in the past has often led to the appointment of weaker candidates for the office of Commission President. However, one should not overestimate the implications for the practical political process. The Heads of State and Government are not forced to vote with qualified majority, of course. In fact, they will more likely try to take a consensual decision to avoid conflicts at the political level and to present the image of unity to the public.

Since a Commission of 20 to 27 Members clearly requires an improved and stronger organisation, one of the objectives (before the backdrop of the crisis of the Santer Commission) was the strengthening of the role of Commission President. One of the most important innovations in this context (as demanded inter alia by the EP) is surely the possibility for the Commission President to ask a Member of the Commission to resign. This implies not only a strengthening of the position of President but of the institution as a whole, as a Commissioner suspected of incompetence or inappropriate conduct can be asked to step down. The only, but significant, hurdle in this context is that the President needs the collective approval of the Commission. This provision might, however, contribute to a Commission which is based on the principle of equality and with a President who is not overly powerful. The Commission President can also appoint Vice-Presidents, but only after obtaining the collective approval of the Commission (Best, 2001, 3).

It is important to note that if a Member of the Commission is asked to resign, he or she is to be replaced on the basis of a qualified majority vote in the Council, but there seems to be a certain inconsistency within the Treaty, as the EP has no role to play in this process (contrary to its important role in the process of appointing the Commission).

Another new development is that the powers of the Commission President are now laid down with more precision. The political guidance of the Commission President is seen to exist in the attainment of consistency, efficiency and collective responsibility. The former Commission has been characterised by weakness in all three areas. This is to be alleviated by strengthening the Commission President. Along the same lines, another provision foresees that the President may allocate and reshuffle responsibilities among its Members (Monar, 2001, 120).[9]

The situation is rather bleak as regards the role of the Commission in selected policy areas. In the two policy areas of Common Foreign and Security Policy and Justice and Home Affairs, its role was not strengthened or strengthened to only a very limited extent. The Member States did not undertake any steps to counterbalance the marginal position of the Commission as regards the establishment of a Common Security and Defence Policy. In the area of Justice and Home Affairs, the sole right of initiative of the Commission is extended only to judicial co-operation in civil matters, with the exception of family law.[10]

Although the Commission will (according to the Treaty of Amsterdam) have a sole right of initiative in all communitarised areas of Justice and Home Affairs as of 1 May 2004, it is highly probable that very important decisions will have been taken until then, especially as regards asylum and immigration policy. The Commission also suffered from setbacks in areas where it traditionally had a very strong role, such as Common Commercial Policy. An example would be the fact that unanimity in the Council is maintained in certain areas of Common Commercial Policy, significantly reducing the room for manoeuvre of the Commission when negotiating international agreements.[11]

Overall, one can conclude that the reforms introduced at Nice are a good compromise between the necessity of strengthening the Commission President and retaining the principle of collegiality. The fact that the Conference agreed to reduce the size of the Commission, even at a later date, was a far more ambitious result than could have been foreseen at the outset or even halfway through the negotiations. On the other hand, it should be pointed out that the Treaty has done little to alleviate the gradual loss of importance of the European Commission. Its role in decision-making procedures and policy areas is not only strengthened but one can even

[9] Article 217 TEC.

[10] Article 65 TEC.

[11] Article 133 TEC.

observe a tendency of weakening the Commission in selected areas. Whether the Commission President can put an end to this rather negative trend depends to a great extent on his/her political and personal capabilities. This is not sufficient in itself, however. The current institutional set-up within the European system of governance is also in need of a strong Commission, especially in view of the impending enlargement. Within a larger Union, it is especially necessary that the Commission work efficiently and effectively. This cannot only be tackled within IGCs but also implies internal reform of the Commission, a process which has been of special importance within the Prodi Commission.

Reform of the European Parliament – Breaching Treaty stipulations

The EP currently has 626 Members,[12] where a ceiling of 700 Members was enshrined in the Treaty of Amsterdam. The number of seats allocated to each Member State in the EP was an issue of political significance at the IGC for two reasons. First, the EP has great influence on the legislative process as co-legislator and as one arm of the budgetary power it exerts influence over the budget of the EU.[13] Second, the view prevailed that a 'real' political link existed between the weighting of votes in the Council and the allocation of seats in the EP. Although MEPs do not represent governments, but are directly elected, there are some issues where national divisions are rather strong.[14] Hence, "[the] allocation between Member States should take account of the dual nature of the Union—both a Union of States and a Union of peoples" (Conference of the Representatives of the Governments of the Member States, 2000, 33).

Two main options were put forward at the Conference:

- One based on the extrapolation of the current system and a reduction in a linear fashion to remain within the threshold of 700, with a correction to ensure a minimum level of representation for the States with the smallest populations (put forward by the Portuguese Presidency) (Conference of the Representatives of the Governments of the Member States 2000, 34).

---

[12] Article 190(2) TEC.

[13] The co-decision procedure is—according to the Treaty of Amsterdam—applicable to 38 Treaty areas or types of Community action. The EP has a right to decide on non-compulsory expenditures (i.e. has a say over the allocation of structural funds but not over agricultural expenditures.

[14] Such issues include, for example, the directive on broadcasting or the directive on migrant workers.

- An EP proposal allocating each of the Member States a minimum of four seats and distributing the remaining seats according to a scale directly proportional to the population of each Member State (EP, 2000b).

Both options were the subject of much controversy at the Conference, where neither one was likely to achieve consensus. The Presidency tried at first to bridge the gap by putting forward a compromise solution that was based to a greater extent on the proportionality of population (as compared to the present system), but not going as far the EPs proposal. This was rejected by a majority of the Member States as insufficient (Galloway, 2001, 119). The solution found went against what the EP had stipulated but was rather simple: the ceiling of 700 seats in the EP has been breached: with 27 Member States there will now be 732 MEPs. According to the revised Article 190(2) TEC, seats in the Parliament are to be reallocated as follows: Germany: 99; UK, France & Italy: 72 each; Spain: 50; Netherlands: 25; Greece, Belgium & Portugal: 22 each; Sweden: 18; Austria: 17; Denmark & Finland: 13 each; Ireland: 12; Luxembourg: 6.

This is, supposedly, a good result for both Germany and Luxembourg, which have had no reductions in their representation. It is less advantageous to the Parliament, which will be blamed for being too big and might have difficulties working effectively. The number of seats for the accession states will be as follows: Poland: 50; Romania: 33; Czech Republic & Hungary: 20 each; Bulgaria: 17; Slovakia: 13; Lithuania: 12; Latvia: 8; Slovenia: 7; Estonia & Cyprus: 6 each; Malta: 5.

This allocation of MEPs breaks with the convention that representation in the Parliament should be broadly proportionate to the size of population. For example, Hungary and the Czech Republic, which have larger populations than Portugal or Belgium, have fewer seats. Why this should be accepted by the two accession countries is unclear. The new arrangements are supposed to come into force in time for the next elections to the EP in June 2004. New Member States will have had to have signed their accession treaties by 1 January that year in order to participate in the elections. The 2004-09 Parliament will have 732 MEPs, with current Member States having an inflated number of seats in the case where not all the 12 accession countries have concluded their negotiations (Duff, 2001).[15]

Following in the 'footsteps' of Maastricht and Amsterdam, the extension of co-decision was also on the agenda of this IGC. The Commission took the side of the EP in agreeing that the bulk of legislative work, including Common Agricultural Policy, should be subject to co-decision. A majority

[15] In practice, this means that only Poland, the Czech Republic, Hungary, Slovakia and any one other candidate country need to have signed their accession treaties by 1 January 2004 for the new system to be entirely operational. MEPs from new Member States joining between 2004 and 2009 would simply be added to the total of 732 ad interim.

of the Member States opposed an automatic link between the use of co-decision and the use of QMV. At the end of the day, the extension of QMV was immediately matched by the extension of co-decision in only six areas, thereby defying the demands of the EP:

- Incentive measures to promote non-discrimination: *QMV + co-decision* (Article 13.2 TEC).
- To facilitate citizens to exercise their rights to move freely, with the notable exception of provisions on passports etc and social security: *QMV + co-decision* (Article 18.2 TEC).
- Judicial co-operation in civil matters with the exception of family law: *QMV + co-decision* (Article 65 TEC).
- Specific measures in support of actions in the field of industrial policy: *QMV + co-decision* (Article 157 TEC).
- Specific action to achieve economic and social cohesion outside structural funds: *QMV + co-decision* (Article 159 TEC).
- Political parties' statute: *QMV + co-decision* (Article 191 TEC).

Apart from this extension of co-decision, there are three other important additions to the powers of the Parliament. The standing of the EP before the European Court of Justice was improved in two significant ways:

- Parliament was given equal status with the Council, Commission and the Member States to challenge the legality of an act before the Court of Justice. The EP will be entitled to bring actions on grounds of lack of competence, infringement of an essential procedural requirement, infringement of the Treaty or of any rule of law relating to its application or the misuse of powers before the Court (Article 230 TEC).
- Parliament also has equal status with the Council and Commission in seeking an opinion from the Court of Justice about the validity of international agreements (Article 300(6) TEC).
- Furthermore, the Parliament's right of initiative was extended. The Parliament may now take the initiative in charging a Member State with a breach of fundamental rights (by two-thirds of a majority) (Article 7.1 TEU).

Overall, one can say that for the EP, which put forward far-reaching demands for the Nice IGC, the outcome was less spectacular than at previous conferences. The only main demand of the EP regarding institutional reform that was actually enshrined in the (draft) Treaty was the introduction of the so-called 'Prodi procedure', whereby the President of the Commission may dismiss an individual Commissioner. Other demands directly concerning the EP, such as co-decision and QMV becoming the 'normal' procedures for decision making and reviewing the composition of the EP, while not breaching the ceiling of 700, have not been met.

One must note, however, that the chapter of institutional reform was far from being closed. At its meeting in Laeken in December 2001, the European Council convened a Convention on the future of the European Union. The task of the Convention is "to pave the way for the next Intergovernmental Conference as broadly and openly as possible."[16] Some of the following key issues arising for the Union's future development are on its agenda: what do European citizens expect from the Union? How is the division of competence between the Union and the Member States to be organised? And within the Union, how is the division of competence between the institutions to be organised? How can the efficiency and coherence of the Union's external action be ensured? How can the Union's democratic legitimacy be ensured?

The Convention opened its proceedings with a period of 'listening' in order to find out what people wanted and expected from the European Union. The second stage entailed a period of analysis for comparing the pros and cons of the proposals put forward for organising the European Union. The third phase will draw together the different proposals and draft recommendations. It remains to be seen regarding the extent to which the Convention will contribute to institutional reform as regards the Commission and the EP.

Concluding Remarks

The starting positions of the Commission and the EP differed greatly within this IGC. The EP had been hailed as a winner of previous IGCs: it was, for example, placed on an (almost) equal footing with the Council as co-legislator by the Treaty of Maastricht, and at Amsterdam the procedure was streamlined and significantly extended.

On the other hand, the Commission was significantly weakened prior to the Nice IGC. The downfall of the entire Commission in 1999 was only a symptom of a larger malaise: with somewhat antiquated structures and limited personal resources, it was facing difficulties dealing with an ever-increasing catalogue of competencies.

The *formal* role of both institutions at IGCs differs: whereas the Commission is entitled to put forward proposals, the Treaty foresees no role for the EP. The EP, however, has tried to strengthen its role at the IGCs in order to go beyond Treaty provisions. At Amsterdam, MEPs had meetings with IGC representatives, and at Nice the EP delegated two 'observers' to attend meetings of the Preparatory Group. When comparing formal provisions and their implementation into the practical process, one can say that during the Nice IGC, the EP tried to make 'something out of nothing', whereas the Commission failed to maximise its possibilities possessed according to Treaty provisions. It seems that it did not succeed at any point

---

[16] The Laeken Declaration can be located at http://europa.eu.int/futurum/documents/offtext/doc151201_en.htm.

to decisively influence the negotiations. Its position was further weakened as it failed to put forward a cohesive and uniform proposal concerning its size and composition.

For both institutions, the Conference produced mixed results. The Commission's organisational structure was strengthened, where, for example, the President now has enhanced powers. On the other hand, the Treaty of Nice has done little to counterbalance the general loss of importance of the Commission.

As regards the results of the Conference for the EP, one has to say that the expectations were not high: "We did not expect much and not a lot has happened, but we undersold ourselves at Nice, the EP should have pressed more for the extension of co-decision."[17]

The EP was highly critical as regards the outcome of the IGC, as *inter alia* reflected in its May 2001 resolution on the Treaty of Nice and the future of the European Union. With regard to the proposed make-up of the Parliament, the EP states *inter alia* that it deplores the fact that this does not follow any clear logic. It expresses its surprise at the decision to exceed the limit of 700 Members laid down at Amsterdam. Moreover, the EP hopes that the deficits and shortcomings with regard to the establishment of an effective and democratic European Union can be dealt with during the post-Nice process. The EP also emphasises the point that decision-making within the EU has become more confused and less transparent, and that there is no automatic link between QMV in the Council and co-decision.

The EP heavily criticises the negotiation modi of the IGC, believing that the unsatisfactory outcome of the last IGC served to underline the limits of the purely intergovernmental method. It therefore demands that the IGC in 2004 will be based on a radically different process, one which is transparent and open. Accordingly, the EP *inter alia* supported the opening of the Convention at the start of 2002, composed of Members of the EP, national parliaments and the governments of the Member States to prepare for the IGC. This Convention is currently at work with the task of preparing the next Intergovernmental Conference as openly as possible. MEPs are represented at the Convention. To what extent their demands will become part of the final document of the Convention and what is going to be agreed in the next ICC remains to be seen.

The IGC at Nice might have been the last of its kind with Heads of State and Government meeting behind closed doors and Commission and EP playing the minor parts. Opening the doors of the next IGC to a broader audience and not principally to the Member State governments might not

[17] Interview with MEP, June 2001.

only increase the transparency of the proceedings but also the legitimacy of decisions.

The ratification process by national parliaments could be drastically improved by involving these actors directly in the Treaty negotiations. Furthermore, the support of the institutional actors such as the Commission and the EP would increase if they were directly implicated in the process of Treaty reform. The intergovernmental method does not adequately reflect a Union where decisions are taken by and affect a plethora of actors, not solely Member State governments.

The Convention is one step in the right direction, in the sense that a wide range of actors are involved in the 'preparatory phase' of the next IGC. Whether, and to what extent their voice will be taken into account can only be evaluated at a later stage.

BIBLIOGRAPHY

Best, Edward (2001), "The Treaty of Nice: Not Beautiful but It'll Do", *EIPASCOPE* 2001/1, p. 2-9.

—, Mark Gray and Alexander Stubb, eds. (2001), *Rethinking the European Union. IGC 2000 and Beyond.* Maastricht: European Institute of Public Administration.

Brok, Elmar (2001), "Die Ergebnisse von Nizza. Eine Sichtweise aus dem Europäischen Parlament," *Integration* 2/01, pp. 86-93.

Conference of the Representatives of the Governments of the Member States (2000), Intergovernmental Conference on Institutional Reform. Brussels: Presidency Report to the Feira European Council, 14 June.

Committee of Independent Experts (1999), First report on Allegations Regarding Fraud, Mismanagement and Nepotism in the European Commission, 15 March.

Corbett, Richard, Francis Jacobs and Michael Shackleton (2000), *The European Parliament*, Fourth edition. London: John Harper Publishing,.

Duff, Andrew (2001), The Treaty of Nice: from left-overs to hangovers. A briefing on the outcome of the Intergovernmental Conference and European Council of Nice, 7-11 December 2000.

Edwards, Geoffrey and David Spence, eds. (1997), *The European Commission.* London: Cartermill Publishing.

European Commission (2000), Adapting the institutions to make a success of enlargement. Commission opinion in accordance with Article 48 of the Treaty on European Union on the calling of a Conference of representatives of the governments of the Member States to amend the Treaties.

European Parliament (2000a), Report on the European Parliament's proposals for the Intergovernmental Conference (14094/1999–C5–0341/1999–1999/0825 (CNS)), Committee on Constitutional Affairs, Rapporteurs: Giorgos Dimitrakopoulos and Jo Leinen, PE 232.758/fin./Part 1.

— (2000b), European Parliament resolution on the European Parliament's proposal for the Intergovernmental Conference, A5-0086/2000, 13 April 2000.

— (2000c), Resolution on the outcome of the European Council on 7-11 December 2000 in Nice, R5-0579/2000.

— (2000d), The Treaty of Nice and the future of the European Union, PE R5-0301/2001, 31 May 2001.

Galloway, David (2000), *The Treaty of Nice and Beyond: Realities and Illusions of Power in the EU.* Sheffield: Sheffield Academic Press.

Grande, Edgar (2000a), Interest Groups in the European System of Multi-Level Governance, Paper prepared for the workshop "Instituciones y Politicas Públicas en la Unión Europea," El Colegio de México, Centro de Estudios Internacionales, November 30, 2000, Mexico.

Hix, Simon (1999), *The Political System of the European Union.* Houndmills, Basingstoke, Hampshire and London: Macmillan Press.

Marks, Gary, Liesbet Hooghe and Kermit Blank (1996), "European Integration from the 1980s: State-Centric vs. Multi-Level Governance," *Journal of Common Market Studies*, Vol. 34, No. 3, pp. 341-378.

Maurer, Andreas (1999), "(Co-)Governing after Maastricht: The European Parliament's institutional performance 1994-1999. Lessons for the implementation of the Treaty of Amsterdam", European Parliament, Directorate General for Research, Political Series, POL 104/rev. EN, 10/99.

Monar, Jörg (2001), "Die Kommission nach dem Vertrag von Nizza ein gestärkter Präsident und ein geschwächtes Organ", *Integration* 2/01, pp. 114-123.

Nentwich, Michael and Gerda Falkner (1997), "The Treaty of Amsterdam: Towards a New Institutional Balance," *European Integration online Papers* (EIoP) Vol. 1, No. 015; http://eiop.or.at/eiop/texte/1997-015a.htm.

Neuhold, Christine (2000), Into the new millennium: the evolution of the European Parliament from consultative assembly to co-legislator, *EIPASCOPE*, European Institute of Public Administration, No. 2000/1.

Nugent, Neill (1995), "The leadership capacity of the European Commission", *Journal of European Public Policy*, Vol. 2, No. 4 (December), pp. 603-623.

Peterson, John and Elisabeth Bomberg (1999), *Decision-making in the European Union*, The European Union Series, Macmillan Press LTD.

Shackleton, Michael (1999), "The Politics of Codecision", *Journal of Common Market Studies*, Vol. 38, No. 2, pp. 325-42.

Smith, Julie (1999), *Europe's Elected Parliament,* Sheffield Academic Press, Sheffield.

Westlake, Michael (1994), *A Modern Guide to the European Parliament.* London and New York: Pinter Publishers.

CHAPTER 19

THE COMMISSION AND THE COUNCIL SECRETARIAT: HOW THEY GAINED SOME INFLUENCE

INTRODUCTION

The 2000 IGC was an almost exclusively intergovernmental affair. French President Chirac went so far as to politely remind Commission President Prodi in the Nice Summit that "it is up to the Member States to decide these matters."[1] In the crucial negotiations in the IGC end-game, the French Presidency attempted to undertake all of the entrepreneurial and brokerage functions itself—with somewhat predictable results.

The 2000 IGC contrasts with the negotiation of previous major IGCs, where both the Commission and Council Secretariat have played central roles, enabling them in the process to gain significant influence upon outcomes (Beach, 2004; Christiansen, 2002). Especially the Secretariat's role of drafting treaty texts in the IGC for the Presidency—for the most overlooked in the literature—is significant. For example, in negotiating the Treaty of Amsterdam, the Secretariat was highly influential in salient issues such as flexibility, legal personality for the Union, and the extension of qualified majority voting (QMV) (Beach, 2004; Christiansen, 2002).

This chapter investigates 'what went wrong' for the two institutions in the 2000 IGC, and how these institutions, nevertheless, were able to gain some influence on the margins. A theoretical framework is first put forward that details how supranational influence is contingent upon both the context and actual strategies employed by supranational actors[2] in an IGC. Following this, the chapter will first review the preferences of the two supranational actors in the 2000 IGC, showing that they do not always reflect Member State government preferences. Thereafter, the chapter looks at the bargaining resources that the Commission and the Secretariat had in the 2000 IGC

[1] Interview with member of the UK negotiating team in the 2000 IGC, London, 22 February 2002.

[2] The Secretariat is understood here as a supranational institution. While this can be debated, given that the Secretariat plays an increasingly important role as a "co-guardian" of the Treaties alongside the Commission in both the day-to-day work in the EU and in IGCs (Stubb 1998:282; Westlake 1999:317-318), and given that it possesses distinct institutional preferences that are not a mere aggregation of Member State preferences (see below), the term "supranational" will be used. For another discussion of the issue that reaches a similar conclusion, see Christiansen 2002.

which could potentially be translated into influence through the negotiation process. Next, the analysis will investigate the context of the IGCs, showing the contextual factors which limited the range of opportunities available to the two actors. Finally, the empirical analysis details the actual strategies used by the two actors in their relatively unsuccessful attempts to gain influence upon the final result. The sources used for this analysis include a series of interviews with high-level civil servants in the two institutions, and with civil servants in both the United Kingdom and Denmark, along with relevant primary and secondary literature.

In the conclusion, these results are compared against the relative influence of the two institutions in other IGCs, and with the parallel negotiation of the EU Charter of Fundamental Rights.

A Contingency Model of Supranational Influence in IGC Negotiations

This section develops a theoretical framework for how negotiations affect the ability of supranational actors to gain influence over IGC outcomes. As suggested by the literature on supranational entrepreneurship, multilateral negotiations, and the general critique of rationalist decision-making in political science, it is by no means certain that the parties involved in complex, multi-party negotiations such as IGCs will be able to first find a zone of possible agreements, and then subsequently agree upon an outcome within this zone (Sebenius, 1992, 338; Sandholtz, 1992, 20-28; Melchior, 1998; Young, 1991, 1999; Bercovitch, 1996a, 1996b; Hampson with Hart, 1995; Raiffa, 1982; Tallberg, 2002).[3] While bilateral negotiations tend to be well-defined bargaining situations in which the parties make concessions until they converge at a mutually acceptable agreement, multilateral and multi-issue negotiations generally have much higher bargaining costs (Hopmann, 1996, 258; Sebenius, 1983, 1984, 1992; Pfetsch, 1999, 198-199). In such a complex, multilateral negotiating situation, third party intervention can be necessary in order to help the parties find a mutually acceptable agreement (Hampson with Hart, 1995; Hopmann, 1996; Raiffa, 1982; Young, 1991, 1999). Third parties can bring either material resources (great power intervention), or informational resources, such as substantive expertise on the issues at stake (Wall and Lynn, 1993). By intervening in the negotiating process, however, the third party also gains opportunities to influence the final outcome for private gain (Young, 1991, 296), by, for example, shifting the final agree-

[3] For more general critiques of the low bargaining cost model in political science, see Kingdon, 1984; Lindblom 1979; Simon 1997.

ment closer to its own preferred outcome. This can take the form of a relatively moderate form of influence, where outcomes are skewed closer to the third party's ideal point *within* an existing zone of possible agreements, or it can take the form of a stronger form of influence where the third party succeeds in shifting the actual zone itself so that its ideal point is included within the new zone of possible agreements.

In the following, the theoretical significance of asymmetrically distributed informational resources and the perceived acceptability of supranational actors are first discussed (see figure 19.1). Thereafter two categories of intervening variables that can affect how these bargaining resources are translated into influence will be put forward. In the first category are three contextual variables relating to the nature of the particular IGC negotiations. Contextual factors that are constant across all IGC negotiations, such as the impact of unanimous decision-making in IGCs, will not be investigated. These contextual variables define the range of intervening strategies available to supranational actors during the negotiation process. In the second category of intervening variables are two forms of actor strategies that can be used during the actual negotiation process, looking at the ability of supranational actors to either shape the IGC agenda, or to play a brokering and mediating role in the negotiations.

The Independent Variables – Bargaining Resources

Complex, multilateral bargaining situations such as IGCs are, despite extensive preparation at both national and EU levels, often poorly defined negotiating situations. National representatives in such situations tend to possess imperfect knowledge of the many complex issues on the agenda, and about their own and the preferences of other actors (Stubb, 2002; Pollack, 1997; Midgaard and Underdal 1977; Hampson with Hart 1995; Hopmann 1996).[4] As one well-informed EU insider puts it, "Governments and their negotiators do not always know what they want, and the situation changes unpredictably with the dynamics of the negotiations, where written and oral proposals are floated around the table by all the participants at frequent intervals" (Stubb, 2002, 27). Actors in IGCs have only 'bounded rationality' (Simon, 1997, 94).

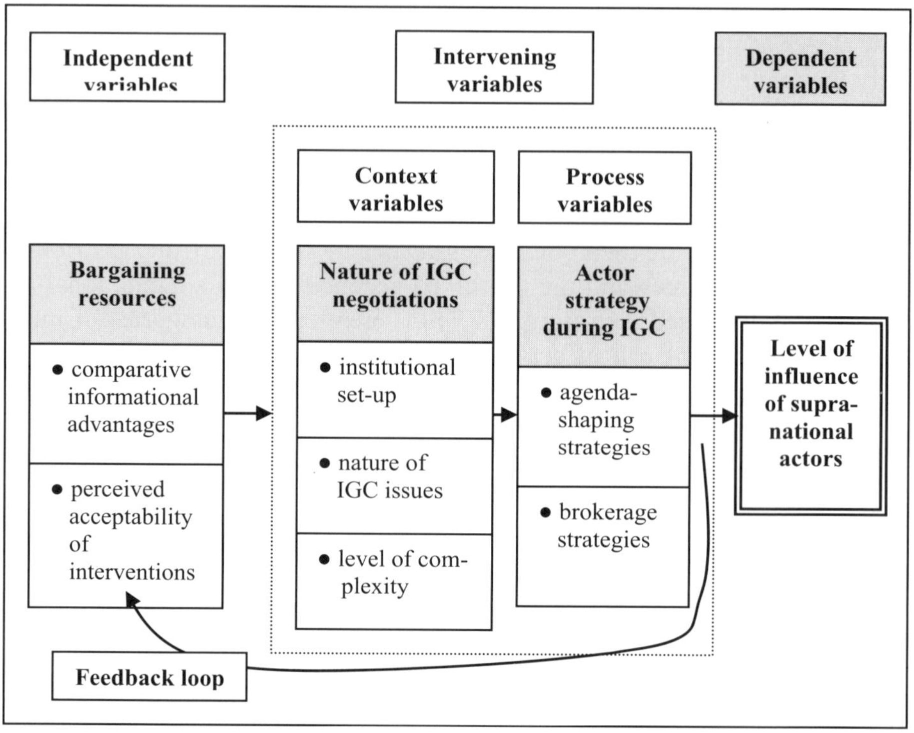

Figure 19.1: Causal model of the importance of the IGC negotiation process.

In such circumstances, asymmetrically distributed informational resources can potentially be translated into influence through persuasion by offering the negotiating parties, "good reasons for doing something [which] may sway his or her decisions, and a wide variety of reasons can have this effect, from advice grounded in technical knowledge to moral admonition" (Malnes, 1995, 96).

Why would information ever be asymmetrically distributed among the actors in an IGC? First, not all actors possess equal levels of substantive knowledge of the issues under discussion (content expertise), analytical skills (process expertise), or knowledge of the state-of-play of the negotiations (Wall and Lynn, 1993; Sandholtz, 1992, 27-28; Cox and Jacobson, 1973, 20; Finnemore and Sikkink, 1998, 899-900). Regarding content expertise, technical and legal knowledge are most relevant in IGCs. Technical expertise relates to detailed and qualified knowledge of how a certain treaty provision works at present and/or the anticipated consequences of the

---

[4] See Stubb, 2002 on IGC negotiations. See Pollack, 1997 for more on daily EU policy-making negotiations. For more on international multilateral negotiations more generally, see Midgaard and Underdal, 1977; Hampson with Hart, 1995; Hopmann, 1996.

changes under consideration. Legal expertise is the possession of extensive knowledge of the body of EU law that can be used to estimate the potential impact and legality of changes in the EU Treaties.

Looking at process expertise, not all national delegations in an IGC possess the analytical skills to be able to digest the hundreds of often very complicated and technical proposals on the many different issues under discussion. This prevents them from entering into an efficient joint problem-solving effort aimed at finding a mutually-acceptable outcome. Compared to the national delegations, the Council Secretariat, with its' extensive experience in brokering compromises in day-to-day EU politics, often has significant advantages in finding acceptable compromises.

Finally, turning to the importance of information on actor preferences and the state-of-play of negotiations, there are two reasons why national delegations in IGC negotiations often do not have detailed information on the nature and intensity of the preferences of other actors on the myriad of issues under discussion. First and related to the above on analytical skills, it is often difficult for national delegates in an IGC to keep track of different actor preferences on the large number of very detailed issues under discussion, especially given the absence of across-the-board cleavages.

Second, many delegations, despite publishing opinions prior to the IGC and presenting arguments and proposals during the IGC, are reluctant to reveal their 'true' preferences during an IGC negotiation (Metcalfe, 1998, 425; Stenelo, 1972, 54; Moravcsik, 1999a, 279).[5] Delegates may have strategic reasons for holding their cards, waiting to see how an issue plays out before revealing their hand (Underdal, 2002, 115). In such a situation, a trusted third party such as the Council Secretariat can discuss with each party the nature and intensity of their preference in an attempt to find a mutually acceptable, Pareto-efficient outcome (Scharpf, 1997, 145; Raiffa, 1982; Metcalfe, 1998, 424-425; Stenelo, 1972, 54). But by gaining private information about the zone of possible agreement, the intervening actor can also craft an agreement within this zone that is closest to its own preferred outcome (Lax and Sebenius, 1986).

A second type of resource that supranational actors can possess is the acceptability of their intervening role among the Member States. While both the Commission and the Council Secretariat are inside actors—being directly affected by the outcomes of an IGC—it is necessary that their interventions

[5] Metcalfe 1998, 425; Stenelo 1972, 54; Moravcsik 1999a, 279 make the point that actors that have incentives to withhold information from one another would also have incentives to withhold it from a supranational actor. However, as will be seen further below, as the Council Secretariat sits at the center of a web of communications, and given its reputation as a trusted insider, national governments often are more open with the Secretariat than they are with other national delegations.

are accepted by all the negotiating parties. This acceptance requires that the parties mutually recognize the utility of the intervening actor, and the legitimacy or reputation of the intervening role of the actor (Wehr and Lederach, 1996; Bercovitch and Houston, 1996, 25-27; Hampson, 1995, 18; Tallberg, 2003; Hopmann, 1996, 225; Kleibor, 1998). Acceptance can thus be based upon the recognition by the Member States of their dependence upon the informational resources of the supranational actor, or it can be ideologically based, with Member States seeing the supranational actor as acting in the common European interest as 'the champion of Europe,' thereby strengthening its ability to act as a trusted broker.

The reputation of the supranational actor can though be threatened if the actor is excessively partial either in the conduct of the IGC (procedural bias), or as regards promoting a particular outcome in its interventions (outcome bias) (Bercovitch, 1996b, 5).[6] If an intervening actor is perceived by the parties to be excessively pursuing its own interests, they may undermine their ability to assist the formal parties in achieving their common interests (Watkins and Winters, 1997, 138; Sebenius, 1992, 336; Raiffa, 1982). This is modelled in my theory as a feedback loop from actor strategies during the negotiations back into the perceived acceptability of supranational intervention (see figure 19.1, above). If a supranational actor chooses an excessively partial strategy, this will damage its reputation as a trusted insider, which then can lead governments to for example change the institutional set-up of the negotiations so as to weaken the role played by the supranational actor.

The Intervening Variables

Contextual Variables

Looking first at the structure of the negotiations, a widely held conjecture in negotiation theory holds that the structure of negotiations affects how actor power resources are translated into influence over outcomes (Zartman, 2002).[7] This is particularly evident when we are dealing with highly institutionalised, multilateral negotiations, such as those carried out during an IGC.

First, the institutional set-up of the negotiation can influence whether actors start with or gain a privileged position during a negotiation that can be exploited to influence outcomes. Examples of privileged institutional positions in an IGC include being in charge of the formal drafting process of

[6] Bercovitch, 1996b, 5. The distinction between perceived acceptability and excessive partiality is an invisible red-line, but the effects of crossing this are often very evident.

[7] Most prominently, Zartman, 2002.

treaty texts, or having control of the agenda for each individual negotiating session. These different institutional settings affect the opportunities and constraints upon actor strategies for gaining influence. Based upon general conjectures in the negotiation literature, we should expect that the ability of supranational actors to translate asymmetrically distributed informational resources into influence increases with the level of their involvement in the negotiation and drafting process.

The nature of the issues under negotiation can also have an impact upon the ability of supranational actors to translate informational power resources into influence. There are two dimensions to the nature of an issue: political saliency and complexity/technicality. First, while we can expect that very salient issues will be kept firmly under the control of national delegations, in less salient issues we would expect that supranational actors would have more discretion to shape the discussions and outcome. Second, if we assume that national delegates do not have perfect knowledge of the often very complex institutional and legal implications of the many issues under discussion in an IGC due to high information costs, then we would expect that in complex and/or technical issues, supranational actors could more successfully utilize their comparative informational advantages. Therefore, we should expect that the ability of supranational actors to translate asymmetrically distributed informational resources into influence varies inversely with the level of political salience of the issue, and influence would increase the higher the technicality and complexity of the issue-area.

Finally, the number of issues and parties to the negotiations, insofar as they increase the number of cleavages in a given negotiating situation, can also lead to an increase in the level of complexity of a negotiation (Midgaard and Underdal, 1977; Hampson, 1995, 28-29). In highly complex, multilateral IGC negotiations, with many cross-cutting cleavages, it is difficult for the parties to identify possible agreements, while meaningful communication between parties also becomes increasingly difficult (Hampson, 1995, 28-29; Raiffa, 1982; Midgaard and Underdal, 1977; Hopmann, 1996). In these types of complex situations, the possession of analytical skills and the knowledge of actor preferences is a strategic asset that enables intervening actors to help the parties find a mutually agreeable outcome and to influence the final outcome. Therefore, we should expect that the ability of supranational actors to translate asymmetrically distributed informational bargaining resources into influence increases with the number of issues and parties to a given negotiation.

Process Variables: Actor Strategy During the Negotiations

While the contextual variables described above define the available range of intervening strategies, supranational actors must successfully use their informational power resources and institutional position in order to gain actual influence over outcomes. In the following, two types of strategy are discussed: agenda-shaping and brokerage.

First, using an agenda-shaping strategy, supranational actors can attempt to set, manipulate or insert new issues onto the agenda of the conference. Agenda manipulation involves actions to emphasize, de-emphasize, remove, or exclude issues from the negotiating agenda. While formal control of an IGC agenda rests with the Member State holding the Presidency of the Council, the Presidency works in close co-operation with the Council Secretariat, and sometimes also the Commission. This gives supranational actors the possibility to informally manipulate the agenda, by for example emphasizing or removing certain issues in the briefs that they prepare for a specific IGC meeting.

Second, supranational actors can attempt to play a brokering or mediating role, utilizing their informational power resources to help the parties find a mutually acceptable outcome, but also gaining opportunities to influence outcomes in the process (Carnevale and Arad, 1996; Young, 1991; Kressel, 1989). While there are many different typologies of brokering and mediating strategies, it is most useful for present purposes to focus on the more active types that attempt to affect the actual content and substance of the negotiations. In an IGC context, the most relevant mediating strategies deal with putting forward compromise proposals and brokering support for certain positions. Crucial in this respect is the possession of extensive and reliable information on the nature and intensities of national preferences, and having a reputation as an honest broker.

THE PREFERENCES OF THE COUNCIL SECRETARIAT AND THE COMMISSION IN THE IGC

The Council Secretariat: Advocating the Upper-End of Realism

While the Secretariat does not publish written opinions prior to the IGC as do the Commission and other actors, and while it attempts to maintain the 'fiction' of its neutrality in the negotiations, it is evident that the Secretariat has aggregate institutional interests and that key officials also have personal preferences that they pursue during IGCs. It is therefore possible to construct a preference profile for the Secretariat using interviews with Secretariat officials and other IGC participants and articles published by Secretariat officials prior to the 2000 IGC.[8]

On an aggregate level, the institutional interests of the Secretariat in the 2000 IGC were primarily to strengthen the Council vis-à-vis the European Parliament and Commission. Additionally, as in previous IGC's, the Secretariat attempted to push for an outcome that was slightly more ambitious than that which the Member States would otherwise have agreed upon—what Noel Dorr has termed the 'upper end of realism' (McDonagh, 1998).

As in previous IGCs, the individual preferences of key officials in the Secretariat were very significant in determining which set of goals the Secretariat advocated. Participants in the IGC noted that the Secretariat had a 'big state' bias in many of the papers that they drafted, perhaps due to the fact that key IGC staff members all came from big Member States.[9]

Insiders also point out that newly appointed deputy Secretary-General de Boissieu has the aim both within the IGC and in daily policy-making of attempting to transform the Secretariat into the 'new Commission' in a more intergovernmental EU.[10] The head of the Secretariat's Legal Service, Piris, who also acted as the Legal Adviser to the IGC, had several issues for which he personally lobbied during the IGC. Piris wanted to clarify the status of inter-institutional agreements, which are political declarations between the Council, Commission, and European Parliament.[11] Piris had additionally gone on the record in his advocacy of several issues: the extension of the scope of Art. 133 EC to include services and intellectual property (Piris, 1999, 574), extension of QMV through the 'quasi-elimination' of unanimity (Piris, 1999, 582) and a re-weighting of Council votes skewed towards the large Member States (Piris, 1999, 582).

---

[8] Prior to the 2000 IGC, head of the Secretariat's Legal Service, Jean-Claude Piris, published an article in *European Law Review*, that quite clearly illustrated his preferences regarding the upcoming IGC's agenda. See Piris, 1999.

[9] If we look at the key Secretariat officials in the 2000 IGC, both deputy Secretary-General Boissieu, and head of the Secretariat's Legal Service, Piris, and Keller-Noëllet, from the private office of the Secretary-General are all French. Galloway, also from the private office of the Secretary-General, is British.

[10] Interview with member of the Finnish IGC negotiating team, Brussels, 8 May 2001 and 25 April 2002.

[11] Interview with member of the UK's IGC negotiating team, London, 22 February 2002. For more on Inter-institutional Agreements, see Galloway 2001, 159.

Table 19.1: The preferences of the European Commission in the 2000 IGC

Issue-area	Commission preferences
re-weighting of Council voting weights	• the Commission was somewhat uninterested in the question, as "re-weighting seems to us to have extremely undramatic effects" (Petite, 2000, 65); • advocated simple dual majority; • potentially lower the threshold for a majority;
size and reform of the Commission	• proposed two options: 20 with equal rotation or one member per Member State; • strengthened President and the individual accountability of Commissioners; •strengthen the Commission by amending the enforcement procedure in the EC Treaty along the lines of the ECSC Treaty, where the Commission has much stronger authority in deciding whether a Member State has failed to fulfil its Treaty obligations;
size of the European Parliament and the extension of co-decision	• EP: upper limit of 700 members, let the EP allocate seats, and consider EU-wide lists for electing MEPs; • the use of co-decision should be extended to all policies where QMV is used (including for CAP and fisheries policies);
the scope of EC competences	• extend the scope of Article 133 EC to all services, investment and intellectual property;
reforms of other institutions	• ECJ – set-up a reflection group on the future of the EU's justice system; the group reports to the IGC; – make the legal system more effective by transferring a portion of cases to lower courts; • establishment of European Public Prosecutor to combat fraud; • formation of Europe-wide political parties;
extension of QMV	• QMV should be the general rule, but allow for exceptions in five categories; • QMV should be extended to trade policy, social policy, asylum and integration, cohesion policy, and certain tax matters (*Agence Europe* no. 7833, 01.11.00);
flexibility	• keep strict conditions for the use of flexibility, while removing the veto option; • fix the minimum number of participants at one third of Member States; • extend flexibility to the 2nd pillar;
other questions	• amend the way in which the Treaties themselves are revised by creating a two-tier treaty split into a hard-core of constitutional provisions and implementing provisions, thereby enabling the less fundamental provisions to be amended by the Council of Ministers with the assent of the European Parliament (Commission, 1999, 7-8, 2000b; Petite, 2000; Europaudvalget, 2000).

The Commission – Towards a More Effective Enlarged Union

While the Commission's overall institutional interests are to strengthen the power and prestige of the Commission, the Commission had learned the lessons of the intergovernmental backlash of the mid-1990s. Hence, it attempted to play a lower profile public role, while also trying to gain support from the European Parliament for its advocacy of more ambitious but contentious points in the 2000 IGC.

The Commission's main aim was to ensure that the 2000 IGC prepared the EU for the upcoming enlargement. The Commission therefore advocated a more ambitious agenda in order to ensure the effective operation of the institutions in an EU-27, although some of its proposals were more aimed at setting the agenda for the next IGC that was already looming on the horizon (see e.g. Petite, 2000, 62). The two central priorities of the Commission in the 2000 IGC were the extension of QMV coupled with the extension of Commission competences in Article 133 EC. Table 19.1 shows Commission preferences across the main issues in the IGC, based upon the Commission's published opinions prior to the IGC (European Commission, 1999, 2000a, 2000b; Petite, 2000; Europaudvalget, 2000).

The Resources of the Council Secretariat and the Commission

The Informational Advantages of the Council Secretariat

If we first examine the staff of the Secretariat, the core of the staff had taken part in every IGC since 1985, giving them an institutional memory and experience unparalleled by any other actor in the IGC (Christiansen, 2002, 47; Galloway, 2001, 38-39). The extremely competent core of Secretariat officials, including Keller, Galloway and Piris, also has extensive experience from daily EU policy-making in finding the centre of gravity of Member State positions, and formulating acceptable compromises. However, the official directly responsible for Presidency-Secretariat relations was Deputy Secretary-General Pierre de Boissieu,[12] who had been appointed at the Cologne European Council Summit in June 1999. De Boissieu had some prior experience with IGC negotiations, having been the French Permanent Repre-

[12] While the Secretary-General had the overall responsibility for the IGC, as the post had been upgraded to also be the High Representative for CFSP in the Treaty of Amsterdam, the Council created the post of deputy Secretary-General, who then assumed primary responsibility for the IGC in the 2000 IGC.

sentative in the 1996-97 IGC, and had been closely involved with the 1990-91 IGC as a civil servant in the French Foreign Ministry.

The Informational Advantages of the Commission

Starting at the top of the institutional hierarchy, both of the top officials in the Commission that dealt with the 2000 IGC were relative novices. Newly appointed Commission President Prodi had no direct experience in IGC negotiations from the Commission side, although he had taken part in the European Council summits during the 1996-97 IGC as Italian Prime Minister. The Commissioner appointed to be responsible for the IGC was Michel Barnier, who had also taken part in the 1996-97 IGC at the political level as the French European Affairs Minister until June 1997. Both lacked familiarity with the lower-level, technical negotiations.

Examining trade policy, one of the areas central for the Commission, we find that Barnier had no direct policy experience with the EU's common trade policy; in contrast to Pascal Lamy, Commissioner for Trade. By appointing Barnier as Commissioner responsible for the IGC, it was then not formally or politically possible for Lamy to take over the negotiations in trade policy in IGC negotiations at either the Foreign Minister or Preparatory Group level.

At the lower level, the Commission's IGC team was also reduced from 10 members in the 1996-97 IGC to four members in the 2000 IGC, although the core of the group was the same as it had been in the 1996-97 IGC (Gray, 2001), ensuring a degree of consistency and expertise.

The Perceived Acceptability of the Secretariat

The perceived acceptability of the Secretariat had not changed since the previous IGC, with Member States in general viewing the utility of using the Council Secretariat as both a source of information and as an effective 'honest' broker. Additionally, key Secretariat officials such as Keller-Noëllet and Galloway had built up strong trust relationships with Member State representatives, both from their work in the daily EU policy-making process and in previous IGCs.[13] However, both Deputy Secretary-General de Boissieu

[13] Interviews with member of the UK negotiating team in the 2000 IGC, London, 22 February 2002; senior British civil servant, London, 29 April 2002.

and the head of the Secretariat's Legal Service Piris were widely perceived to be political actors with strong personal agendas in the IGC.[14]

The Perceived Acceptability of the Commission

The downfall of the Santer Commission in March 1999 left the Commission in a very weak position in the 2000 IGC. While Prodi attempted to rectify this situation by for example advocating the creation of a European Public Prosecutor in order to be seen as fighting fraud in the EU, the views of the Commission were widely seen as lying far outside of the zone of possible agreements. By advocating 'politically difficult positions' (Galloway, 2001, 37) in the 2000 IGC, the Commission was unable to play the role of an 'honest broker' in the IGC (Christiansen, 2002). This was particularly evident in issues such as the creation of a two-tiered treaty structure; an issue that, despite repeated Commission attempts to put on the agenda, was never seriously discussed in the IGC.

Another factor that crippled the acceptability of the Commission's interventions during the 2000 IGC were the French views of the Commission, given that the French held the Presidency of the EU in the second half of 2000. President Chirac had a traditional Gaullist view of the proper role of the Commission in the EU. While pro-Commission Member States such as the Netherlands have often let the Commission play a very important role in their Presidencies, Chirac was a strong advocate of the Gaullist vision of a *Europe des patries*. Hence, he went out of his way in the Nice Summit to remove the Commission from all influence.

A somewhat mitigating factor in this respect was Barnier's appointment as Commissioner in charge of the IGC, given his close relations with and influential position in Chirac's *RPR* party. Yet Barnier's close ties with *RPR* had the opposite effect during the Portuguese Presidency, with the Portuguese State Secretary for European Affairs seeing Barnier as 'singing Chirac's tune', a view widely shared by many other actors in the IGC.[15]

---

[14] Ibid.

[15] Interviews with member of the Commission's IGC Task Force, Brussels, 26 April 2002; senior member of the UK negotiating team in the 2000 IGC, London, 21 February 2002; MEP, Brussels, 25 April 2002.

The Impact of the Negotiation Context

The Level of Involvement of Supranational Actors in the IGC

The Council Secretariat's role in the 2000 IGC – a secretary and adviser to the IGC

As in previous IGCs, the official mandate of the Secretariat was to play a secretarial function for the IGC and the Presidencies in charge of the negotiations. In the 2000 IGC, the Secretariat supported the Presidencies by drafting most of the Presidency texts for the IGC, together with the agenda and minutes of meetings, though often under strong guidance by the Presidencies.[16] The Secretariat also provided assistance to the Presidencies by offering suggestions and ideas on how to reach acceptable agreements based upon its prior experience in IGCs and from daily EU policy-making, and from its close contacts with Member State delegates prior to and during the IGC.

Piris, as head of the Secretariat's Legal Service, acted as the official legal adviser to the 2000 IGC. As argued by Christiansen, this role gives the Secretariat a crucial position, in that "[...] in the absence of recourse to judicial review of individual aspects of the negotiation results, the 'legal advice' of the Council's legal service on proposals for draft articles is authoritative and can therefore constitute a constraint on the possibilities for treaty reform" (Christiansen, 2002, 47). This is very significant, for as seen above, Piris had strong preferences for certain outcomes that clearly did not reflect the centre of gravity of Member State preferences.

The Role of the Commission in the 2000 IGC – the 16th 'Member State'

The Commission had a much less privileged institutional position in relation to the Secretariat. Article 48 TEU gave the Commission the right to put forward proposals in the IGC and to participate at all levels of the IGC. While the Commission had no vote, it was utilised by the Presidency and individual delegations as a source of advice and information.

This relatively weak role of the Commission in the negotiation of most of the issues in the IGC can be contrasted with the Commission's role in the negotiation of the reform of the EU's judicial system. Through institutional politics, the Commission was able to set up the Working Party on the Future of the European Court of Justice in the spring of 1999, which consisted of former members of the ECJ and CFI (Due, 2000). The Commission provided

---

[16] Interviews with senior member of the UK negotiating team in the 2000 IGC, London, 21 February 2002; member of the Finnish IGC negotiating team, Brussels, 8 May 2001 and 25 April 2002.

the working party with a set of questions to discuss. By creating a relatively 'technical' group of experts—an 'epistemic community'—this cemented the importance of technical knowledge contra political power in the discussions on the reform of the judicial system. The effect was similar to the depoliticising effect of the Delors Committee prior to the 1990-91 IGC on EMU on many of the issues (Dyson and Featherstone, 1999, 774). The Commission was then able to convince Member States to conduct the negotiation of the issue in the IGC within a Friends of the Presidency Group, to be composed of national legal counsellors together with a representative of the Commission. This structure created a privileged institutional forum for Commission attempts to gain influence. Here the Commission played a central role, and the type of delegate chosen ensured that the actors had a common policy goal which was close to the Commission's own preferred outcome.

The Nature of the Issue Being Negotiated

Unlike previous IGCs, the agenda of the 2000 IGC was very limited. Additionally, many of the key issues were zero-sum or re-distributive, where one party's gain was another party's loss. Issues such as the re-weighting of Council votes pitted Member States directly against each other, with the increase in the voting power of one Member State decreasing the voting power of other Member States. Other issues, such as the number of Commissioners, touched on delicate matters of national power and prestige, with the appointment of a Commissioner being seen by smaller Member States as essential to ensure that their interests were protected in an EU increasingly dominated by the larger Member States (Galloway, 2001, 46; Schout and Vanhoonacker, contribution to this volume). In such issues, the potential for intervening actors to gain influence through clever drafting and brokerage is, at least in theory, lower. Participants in the IGC noted, for example, that national delegates scrutinised proposals and their implications on these core issues in much more detail than in previous IGCs.

While the institutional questions of the re-weighting of votes and the composition of the Commission were relatively clear-cut, there were also many more substantive issues on the IGC agenda that were highly technical and complex. For instance, revising Article 42 EC (social security coordination) and Article 133 EC (common trade policy) were legally complex, and national delegates were dependent upon Secretariat and/or Commission expertise in order to determine the existing legal status quo and the possible implications of different changes in the articles.

The Level of Complexity of the Negotiating Situation

The 2000 IGC was a relatively simple negotiating situation, with two primary cleavages (see figure 19.2). One of the cleavages was between small and larger Member States regarding the distribution of power in the EU as regards both voting weights in the Council of Ministers and the composition of the Commission.[17] The second cleavage was between those Member States desiring a strengthening of the powers of supranational institutions, primarily through the extension of QMV voting and co-decision, and those seeking to maintain the status quo. National delegates were therefore able to relatively easily discern the zone of possible agreements without the assistance of intervening actors like the Secretariat and the Commission. However, as will be discussed further below, the strong divergence in opinions created a demand for brokerage in order for the parties to reach a mutually acceptable agreement.

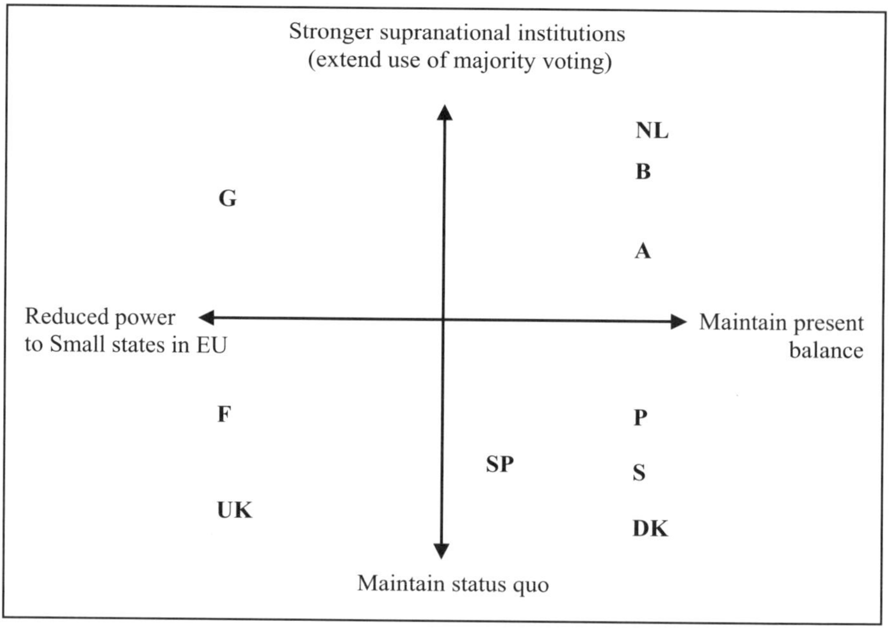

Figure 19.2: Major cleavages in the 2000 IGC negotiations.

[17] It must be noted, however, that there were cleavages within these two groupings between France and Germany, and between Belgium and the Netherlands regarding the parity of voting weights in the Council. See the national chapters in this volume.

Agenda-Shaping by Supranational Actors

The above makes it clear that in contrast to previous IGCs, the opportunities for supranational actors to gain influence through intervening behaviour were significantly lower in the 2000 IGC, both due to the roles that the two supranational actors were allowed to play, and the nature of the negotiating situation. But was the Secretariat or the Commission able to successfully exploit the limited instruments that they possessed in order to gain significant influence upon the Treaty of Nice? The following analysis will first examine the ability of supranational actors to gain influence through shaping the IGC agenda, and then turn to assess whether they were able to gain influence through brokering activities.

The Council Secretariat

The Secretariat attempted to use its institutional position to influence the IGC's agenda and outcome. During the Finnish Presidency that prepared the agenda of the IGC, the Secretariat drafted the Presidency's IGC report together with the Presidency. According to inside sources, Deputy Secretary-General de Boissieu was able to significantly modify the original Finnish report, which had originally been oriented towards small states and was somewhat close to the Commission's opinions. De Boissieu, for example, prevented the Finns from attempting to widen the IGC agenda along the lines advocated by the Commission.[18] The Secretariat put forward the first papers on flexibility, and suggested that it should be put on the official agenda, while other issues such as defence should be excluded from the agenda.[19]

The Secretariat had relatively poor relations with the Portuguese Presidency, preventing it from successfully playing the role of trusted adviser and confidante in the negotiations as in previous IGC's. One of the main problems was that Portuguese State Secretary for European Affairs de Costa perceived that de Boissieu was pursuing a pro-large state (read French) agenda, and made it clear that Portugal would not accept de Boissieu changing the Presidency's papers and drafts, as had been the case with the Finnish IGC report. De Costa even went so far as to exclude de Boissieu from co-

---

[18] Interviews with member of the Finnish IGC negotiating team, Brussels, 8 May 2001 and 25 April 2002; member of the Commission's IGC Task Force, Brussels, 26 April 2002; member of the UK negotiating team in the 2000 IGC, London, 22 February 2002.

[19] Interview with member of the Finnish IGC negotiating team, Brussels, 8 May 2001.

ordinating meetings between the Secretariat and the Presidency, choosing instead to work more closely with Galloway and Keller-Noëllet.[20]

Despite this relative handicap, the Secretariat was able to influence the Portuguese to take up the question of creating specific legal bases for policies that had until then been adopted using Article 308 EC.[21] The Secretariat was interested in this both to: bolster the number of articles that might move to QMV, as it was politically impossible for the Member States to agree to transfer Article 308 EC itself to QMV; and to 'tidy up' the legal bases of EU policies. No Member State was pushing for this, and it would not have been on the agenda had it not been for the advocacy of the Secretariat.[22] Additionally, the subsequent discussions on the subject were very dependent upon the legal expertise of the Secretariat, as they possessed information on what the EU was currently doing under Article 308 EC that no Member State possessed. The final outcome, however, was disappointing for the Secretariat, with only one new legal base created for provisions on financial and technical co-operation with non-developing countries (Galloway, 2001, 109-111).[23]

During the French Presidency, the Secretariat played an even more limited role than during the Portuguese Presidency, being effectively cut out of the loop of the negotiations on most of the major points on the agenda. The main problem for the Secretariat as a whole was that the French attempted to run their Presidency from Paris and not from their Permanent Representation in Brussels, as is usual practice (Christiansen, 2002, 48). While a Presidency run from a national capital is often more concerned with national interests than common European interests, a Permanent Representation in Brussels is naturally used to working within the EU institutions and has close relations with other national representatives and officials from the Secretariat and the Commission. A Permanent Representation is therefore often more aware of what is acceptable among the other Member States, and is also more aware of the utility of using the Secretariat as a source of information and broker.[24]

---

[20] Interview with member of the Commission's IGC Task Force, Brussels, 26 April 2002.

[21] Interview with member of the UK negotiating team in the 2000 IGC, London, 22 February 2002.

[22] Interviews with member of the Finnish IGC negotiating team, Brussels, 8 May 2001 and 25 April 2002.

[23] Article 181a EC was inserted into the Treaties, which gave a specific legal base to these policies coupled with QMV. Galloway, 2001:109-111.

[24] The Dutch Presidency in the second half of 1991 during the 1990-91 IGC's end game was similar, with the Dutch attempting to run their Presidency from the Hague, ignoring the advice and knowledge of the Dutch Permanent Representation in Brussels, which had close contacts with the Council Secretariat. This resulted in Black Monday and the rejection of the

The Secretariat did work relatively closely with French Permanent Representative Vimont, and in issues where Vimont was responsible for conducting the negotiations, the Secretariat played its traditional role of trusted partner of the Presidency, gaining significant influence upon the outcome in the process.[25] This included the negotiation of flexibility and the extension of QMV (see below), both of which were primarily dealt with at the Preparatory Group level (Schout and Vanhoonacker in this volume; Gray and Stubb, 2001, 11).[26]

In most of the other issues, however, Paris attempted to control the negotiations and therefore for the most part did not draw upon the Council Secretariat for either assistance or guidance (Christiansen, 2002, 48).[27] The exception to this was the role of Deputy Secretary-General de Boissieu. De Boissieu's personal relationship with Chirac gave him privileged access to Chirac, and Chirac drew upon de Boissieu as a source of advice. For example, according to participants in the IGC, on the last evening of the Nice Summit, de Boissieu sat on the left hand side of Chirac and 'wrote' his script.[28] Several declarations, for example were written by Boissieu, including the declaration on the venue of European Council summits (Gray and Stubb, 2001, 21),[29] in which Belgium was compensated for having accepted fewer Council votes than the Netherlands (Galloway, 2001, 82-3).

While the Secretariat was unable to shape the agenda in most of the issues of the IGC, the Secretariat was nevertheless able to gain significant influence on the reform of the flexible co-operation provisions of the Treaties. During the French Presidency, the Secretariat wrote all of the draft articles on flexibility without much input or guidance from the Presidency, as the French did not fully understand the complex implications of the issue, according to par-

---

Dutch draft treaty. In the 2000 IGC, the Paris-based Presidency was also quite insensitive to developing areas of consensus, with the chaotic Nice Summit and the disappointing Treaty of Nice the somewhat predictable outcomes.

[25] Interviews with member of the Finnish IGC negotiating team, Brussels, 8 May 2001 and 25 April 2002; member of the Commission's IGC Task Force, Brussels, 26 April 2002.

[26] Interview with member of the Finnish IGC negotiating team, Brussels, 8 May 2001 and 25 April 2002.

[27] Interviews with member of the UK negotiating team in the 2000 IGC, London, 22 February 2002; member of the Finnish IGC negotiating team, Brussels, 8 May 2001 and 25 April 2002.

[28] Interview with member of the UK negotiating team in the 2000 IGC, London, 22 February 2002.

[29] Interview with member of the Finnish IGC negotiating team, Brussels, 8 May 2001 and 25 April 2002.

ticipants.[30] While the overall contours of agreement on revision of flexibility were both defined and broadly agreed upon by national delegates prior to the informal European Council Summit in Biarritz (Stubb, 2002, 118, 121), the Secretariat filled in the details, even ensuring that a deal would be reached by placating the fears of hesitant Member States. This was done by 'ring fencing' core areas of the internal market and economic and social cohesion, thereby putting them outside the remit of flexibility (Galloway, 2001, 134; Schout and Vanhoonacker, contribution to this volume). This made it easier for sceptical countries to accept the reforms of flexibility that would make it easier to use. Spain had in fact threatened to veto these changes if they did not explicitly exclude the internal market from the scope of flexible co-operation.[31] On aspects of flexibility such as the criteria, threshold for use, and voting, the Secretariat wrote the draft provisions, often together with Commission officials.[32] Further, the head of the Secretariat's Legal Service prevented the creation of a single cross-pillar flexibility provision, as he was concerned with the legal complications that a cross-pillar provision could have caused for the mixed nature of the Treaties (Stubb, 2002, 120; See also Galloway, 2001, 139-140).[33]

Turning to the extension of QMV, the French Presidency, together with the Secretariat, drafted numerous proposals that attempted to find texts that sufficiently took into account various national sensitivities, while at the same time trying to maximise the number of articles on the list to be transferred to QMV (Galloway 2001, 101-111). Because of the technical complexity of the issues involved, much of the time was spent on clarifying texts and refining successive drafts, especially in taxation, trade, and social policies. Yet with the available information, it is difficult to identify the concrete fingerprints of the Secretariat, and some participants interviewed argued that the Secretariat made a crucial mistake on the issue, as they put forward (together with the French Presidency) so many drafts with different formulas and lists that national delegates were overwhelmed and were unable to co-ordinate a national position on one draft with their respective capital before another pro-

---

[30] Interviews with member of the Finnish IGC negotiating team, Brussels, 8 May 2001 and 25 April 2002; member of the Commission's IGC Task Force, Brussels, 26 April 2002.

[31] Interview with member of the UK negotiating team in the 2000 IGC, London, 22 February 2002.

[32] Interview with member of the Commission's IGC Task Force, Brussels, 26 April 2002.

[33] The first pillar is supranational, whereas co-operation in the other two pillars is predominantly intergovernmental.

posal hit the table (Gray and Stubb, 2001, 12). They were therefore forced to start rejecting proposals out of hand.[34]

The Secretariat faired much better, with several of its 'pet projects' during the IGC end game. For example, during a lunch in the Val Duchesse informal Preparatory Group meeting on the 25th of November, the Secretariat presented several proposals that were accepted outright by delegates without discussion—in the words of one participant, "the Member States rolled over and took them without debate."[35] This was due to the lack of national experts at the lunch,[36] and to the perceived low political salience of several of the issues. Among the proposals accepted were provisions on the financial consequences of the expiry of the ECSC Treaty, Eurojust co-operation, a declaration on inter-institutional agreements, and reforms of the court of auditors. As seen above, the declaration on inter-institutional agreements was one of the priorities of Piris.

In the debates on the re-weighting of Council votes—arguably the most sensitive issue together with the size of the Commission—it was seen above that the Secretariat had a large state bias in the issue. Participants point out that the Secretariat was able to keep the issue wide open during the French Presidency. The rationale behind this was two-fold: to block the emerging consensus around the Commission's proposed simple dual majority option; and hope that if the issue would be resolved in the end-game, that the smaller states would be forced to swallow a simple re-weighting of votes favouring the larger Member States in exchange for being guaranteed the right to nominate a Commissioner.[37] Besides blocking the Commission's simple dual majority option, the Secretariat did not have significant influence upon the outcome in the issue – which ended in the messy horse trade of a triple majority system.

After the provisional text of the Treaty of Nice was finally agreed upon, the Secretariat had the job of tidying up the Treaty—a job that turned out to be quite significant, as the text of many draft provisions was highly ambiguous and needed to be clarified. One of the best examples of gaining influence through this relatively technical tidying up was in Article 66 EC, which deals

---

[34] Interview with member of the Commission's IGC Task Force, Brussels, 26 April 2002.

[35] Interview with member of the UK negotiating team in the 2000 IGC, London, 22 February 2002. Also member of the Commission's IGC Task Force, Brussels, 26 April 2002.

[36] Interview with member of the Finnish IGC negotiating team, Brussels, 8 May 2001 and 25 April 2002.

[37] Interviews with senior member of the UK negotiating team in the 2000 IGC, London, 21 February 2002; member of the Finnish IGC negotiating team, Brussels, 8 May 2001 and 25 April 2002.

with co-operation between departments of national administrations, and between these and the Commission. In Nice, the heads of state and government wanted to move the article to QMV, but they did not decide whether co-decision with the EP should apply for the Article, merely stating that the mechanism for Article 67 EC should be used. However, they overlooked the fact that Article 67 EC called for co-decision. In the process of tidying up the Treaty, the Secretariat inserted a declaration stating that the provision would switch to QMV in 2004 without co-decision, and then changed this to a legally binding protocol in the final Treaty text.[38] While the Secretariat based these changes upon legal arguments, it is not difficult to see it as an example of the Secretariat's interests in strengthening the Council contra other EU institutions.

Concluding, while the Secretariat gained significant influence in several salient issues, and much of the IGC's outcome came 'from the Secretariat's kitchen,'[39] the Secretariat was unable to successfully translate its expertise through the use of the 'power of the pen' and through giving advice as effectively as it had in previous IGC's. This was due to reservations on the part of the Portuguese Presidency to especially de Boissieu's assertive role, and due to the Paris-based French Presidency, which relied more on Parisian civil servants than on the expertise of the Secretariat.

The Commission

The Commission occupied a less opportune institutional position in comparison to the Secretariat for its attempts to gain influence upon the IGC agenda and outcome. In effect, the Commission had the same role as a national delegation, but with the further disadvantages of not having a vote and advocating an extreme policy position. The only options open to the Commission to shape the IGC agenda were offering both advice to Presidencies and assistance with the actual drafting process, and putting forward proposals in the IGC.

Investigating first the importance of being directly involved through consultations with Presidencies during the IGC, the Commission had quite good contacts with the Finnish Presidency. The Finnish Presidency was assisted by the Commission in its attempts to introduce a categorisation of different types of articles that could be transferred to QMV (Gray and Stubb, 2001, 16).[40] In subsequent negotiations, however, this approach was abandoned in

---

[38] Interview with senior British civil servant, London, 29 April 2002.

[39] Interview with member of the Commission's IGC Task Force, Brussels, 26 April 2002.

[40] Ibid.

favour of a case-by-case method, and the final outcome was closer to the least common denominator than to the Commission's approach (Gray and Stubb, 2001, 16).

The Commission had relatively poor relations with the Portuguese Presidency. Portuguese State Secretary for European Affairs de Costa saw the Commission as French dominated—especially Commission representative Barnier.[41] Relations with the French Presidency were, if anything, worse, as the French Presidency refrained from drawing upon the expertise of the Commission in the drafting process. At the highest level, Chirac had a very confrontational relationship with both the Commission and in particular President Prodi. This was particularly evident during the Nice Summit, with Chirac going out of his way to antagonise and side-line the Commission and Prodi in particular.[42]

In contrast to this, the Commission proved to be very influential in the discussions on the reform of the EU's judicial system, where the agenda-setting phase took place within an expert working party set up by the Commission, and the actual negotiations in the Friends of the Presidency group. The Commission was successful in garnering for itself the exclusive agenda-setting role for the working party, putting forward the set of questions that formed the basis of their discussions. The choice of national legal experts in the working party set the tone for the further negotiations, implying that they should be dealt with in a non-political and technical manner among what can be termed an empowered epistemic community.[43] The national legal experts shared common beliefs and norms, and a common policy project relating to which reforms of the EU's judicial system were necessary. Given their strong institutional position in the negotiations, and their legitimacy as expert actors (former ECJ judges for example), it could be expected that the outcome of the Friends of the Presidency discussions would be accepted by the IGC. The Commission also played a central role in the Friends of the Presidency Group.

Being negotiated in this forum had three effects. First, it privileged technical legal arguments over political arguments in the negotiations, giving the Commission significant potential influence in view of its extensive and authoritative expertise in dealing with EU law. Second, the Commission succeeded in its attempts to re-structure the rules of the game to create a privi-

---

[41] See above, page 381.

[42] Interviews with member of the UK negotiating team in the 2000 IGC, London, 22 February 2002; and senior member of the UK negotiating team in the 2000 IGC, London, 21 February 2002.

[43] For further discussion of epistemic communities, see Haas, 1992; Sebenius, 1992.

leged institutional position for itself, allowing it, for example, to set the agenda by providing the points to be discussed. Thirdly, and most significantly, the Commission could predict with reasonable certainty the negotiating outcome that would be reached by this epistemic community of legal experts, given that the group had shared policy goals regarding the need to ensure the effective functioning of the EU's legal system post-enlargement. These goals were perceived to be closer to the Commission's own interests than the outcome would be if it had been dealt with in political circles. If the negotiations had been handled by political actors, it is by no means certain that they would even have reached an agreement, as there were political actors in several Member States who were very critical of the ECJ's strong pro-integrative role, and who would therefore not be as motivated to undertake the necessary reforms to ensure the effectiveness of the judicial system.[44]

By creating a coalition of empowered 'believers' (Sebenius, 1992, 354) in the Commission's preferred outcome, this created an advantageous shift in the zone of possible agreements for the Commission from what it otherwise would have been had the issue been dealt with by political negotiators. The actual outcome did indeed reflect Commission preferences in most of the issues, although the Commission's proposed clarifications of Article 234 EC were not adopted (Commission, 2000c; Galloway, 2001; Gray and Stubb, 2001, 17-18; Working Party, 2000). Yet while the reforms of the judicial system were negotiated at the technical level, the amendments they agreed upon were not, but, "[...] may have a more significant impact on the development of the European Union than any of the other changes agreed in Nice" (Gray and Stubb, 2001, 17).

Turning to an investigation of Commission attempts to shape the agenda by submitting proposals, during the agenda-setting phase of the IGC, the Commission, under newly elected president Prodi, attempted to broaden the agenda by appointing a 'wise group' under the leadership of Jean-Luc Dehaene, which presented its report in October 1999 (Dehaene, 1999). This report was well outside what the Member States were interested in considering, with items such as the creation of a two-tiered treaty structure and the inclusion of defence questions in the IGC itself.[45] However, the report gave the Commission the opportunity to gauge the reaction of the Member States to these ideas, and the Commission's subsequent submission to the Finnish

[44] For developments in the 1990's, see Beach, 2001; Alter, 2001.

[45] Interview with member of the UK negotiating team in the 2000 IGC, London, 22 February 2002; See for example *Agence Europe*, No. 7582, 28/10/1999 for the very negative French reactions to the report.

Presidency was slightly more restrained, although it still argued for a broad IGC agenda (European Commission, 1999). Table 19.2 depicts the relative success and failure of the Commission's proposals during the IGC itself.

Table 19.2: The relative success or failure of major Commission proposals in the 2000IGC.[46]

Conf. nr.	Subject matter	Included in the Treaty of Nice
4701/00	Re-weighting of votes □ a simple dual majority	–
4701/00	Reform of the Commission □ strengthening of the President and individual accountability	+
4701/00	Extension of co-decision	(-)
4701/00	Article 133 EC – common trade policy □ extend QMV to all services, investment and intellectual property	(+)
COM(2000)109	Reform of the EU's justice system □ transfer routine cases to CFI while also clarifying the role of national courts in the preliminary reference procedure □ creation of a stronger enforcement mechanism	(+) –
4701/00, 4779/00	European Public Prosecutor	–
4701/00	Extension of QMV □ make QMV the general decision-making rule, with certain exceptions	(-)
4701/00, 4763/00	Creation of two-tiered treaty	–
4782/00	Article 7 EU – breach of democratic principles by Member State □ creation of an early warning procedure	(+)
4764/00	European political parties	+

If we first examine one of the most salient issues on the agenda, the Commission had a strong proposal on the re-weighting of Council votes; the proposal called for a simple double majority.[47] The intention was to take into account the population of larger Member States, while also giving assurances to smaller Member States through the use of simple majorities (Galloway, 2001, 71-72). This proposal had the support of a majority of Member States, but was unable to convince the French Presidency and did not influ-

[46] Note: + = fully incorporated; (+) = significant elements incorporated; (-) = only small parts incorporated; - = no influence.

[47] Put forward first in the Commission's Opinion (Commission, 2000a), and then officially submitted as CONF 4763/00.

ence the final outcome, both due to French insistence on a simple re-weighting of votes, and due to poor negotiating tactics on the part of the Commission (Gray, 2001; Dinan and Vanhoonacker, 2000-2001). Prodi, for instance, fell asleep more than once during the negotiation of the issue in European Council Summits.[48]

The basic problem for the Commission, however, was that most its proposals were far outside the zone of possible agreements. To the consternation of national delegates, the Commission was pushing its own hobby horses throughout the conference.[49] One of Barnier's pet projects was the creation of a European Public Prosecutor,[50] but the idea was from the start a no-flier despite repeated attempts by the Commission (Gray, 2001). Another proposal that the Commission continued advocating throughout the IGC was the split of the Treaties into constitutional and legislative parts[51]—another idea that provoked little interest among the Member States, who feared that a comprehensive revision of the Treaties would risk opening up a Pandora's box of compromises and cross-issue concessions built up over fifty years. French Minister for European Affairs Moscovici, for example, had already rejected the idea in October 1999 as being both "unrealistic", and "tantamount to overloading the IGC boat" (*Agence Europe* no.7582, 28 October 1999). Towards the end of the IGC, the Commission modified its position somewhat by stating that the IGC should create a group to undertake a revision at a later date—an idea that has influenced the agenda for the next IGC to be held in 2004 (*Agence Europe* no.7759, 15 July 2000; the Laeken Declaration). Prodi had also put forward the idea of moving the High Representative for CFSP from the Secretariat to the Commission in an attempt to unify the EU's external representation—this was also not discussed (*Agence Europe* no.7812, 4 October 2000).

Other Commission proposals were relatively successful, however. The Commission proposed changes to Article 7 TEU, which deals with the sanctions against Member States that breach basic democratic principles, thus

---

48 Interview with member of the UK negotiating team in the 2000 IGC, London, 22 February 2002.

49 Several of the Commission's ideas where taken up by the Portuguese Presidency in their discussion paper on possible issues to include on the agenda, but were never seriously discussed in the IGC. See CONF 4716/00. *Note de la Presidence - CIG 2000 : Eventuelle proposition d'inscription d'autres points à l'ordre du jour de la Conférence.* CONFER 4716/00, Bruxelles, 1er mars 2000.

50 CONF 4779/00. Interviews with member of the Finnish IGC negotiating team, Brussels, 8 May 2001 and 25 April 2002; member of the UK negotiating team in the 2000 IGC, London, 22 February 2002.

51 CONF 4763/00.

enabling the EU to establish an 'early warning' procedure (Galloway, 2001, 153-154). These Commission proposals were adopted in modified form. Another proposal dealt with European political parties, with the Commission proposing the inclusion of a provision in Article 191 EC that allows the EP or Council to establish regulations governing political parties at the EU level, which was included in the Treaty of Nice (Galloway, 2001, 126).

In the negotiations on the EU's common trade policy, one of the Commission's major priorities in the IGC, the Commission played a very influential agenda-shaping and mediating role.[52] The Commission had originally proposed an across-the-board transferral of all aspects of trade policy to QMV and EC competences, but this encountered resistance from especially France. Without the advocacy of the Commission, supported by the Finnish Presidency, the issue itself would not have been on the agenda (Schout and Vanhoonacker in this volume). The actual impact of the Commission in the issue will be discussed further below in the section on Commission brokerage.

Brokerage by Supranational Actors

The ability of the Secretariat and the Commission to broker key deals during the IGC was impaired, especially during the Nice Summit, as the French Presidency attempted to undertake all of the brokering roles itself.

From a theoretical perspective, we would otherwise have expected that given both the zero-sum nature of many of the most salient issues in the 2000 IGC and the deadlocked nature of the dispute on institutional questions would have created, *increased* opportunities for supranational actors to step in and employ various mediating strategies to alter actor perceptions of the issues and identify possible alternatives and compromises, thereby restructuring the negotiating situation from a zero-sum to positive-sum game (Hampson with Hart, 1995, 17-18; Tallberg, 2002).

The cleavages and potential compromises in the 2000 IGC were relatively obvious. Indeed, the basic contours of the compromise between large and smaller Member States had already been included in the protocol attached to the Treaty of Amsterdam.[53] Therefore, supranational actors had no relative advantages regarding privileged access to information on Member State preferences which would enable them to craft a compromise that other actors could not, due to their inability to see the zone of possible agreements.

---

[52] Interview with member of the UK's IGC negotiating team, London, 22 February 2002.

[53] Protocol 11 on the Institutions with the prospect of enlargement of the European Union.

Additionally, the French Presidency's conduct of the negotiations in the second half of 2000 was strongly partial to their own national interests, both as regards procedure and outcome. First, the French deliberately structured the negotiations in a manner that supported their own interests. For instance, in the negotiation of the re-weighting of votes, the French postponed the resolution of the issue until the later part of the Nice Summit in an attempt to put smaller Member States under pressure to cave in. The French also acted excessively partial as regards the outcomes that they advocated.[54] One example of this was their insistence upon a very small cap on the size of the Commission, which risked undermining one of the legs of a potential institutional compromise, where smaller Member States wanted assurances that they would be able to appoint a Commissioner in exchange for accepting a skewing of voting power towards the larger states. The combination of a partial Presidency, and a Presidency that attempted to undertake all of the brokering roles itself, created an environment where it was difficult for supranational actors to effectively intervene through brokerage—despite numerous indications that such brokerage would perhaps have created a less partial (and more efficient?) outcome.

The Council Secretariat

In contrast to previous IGCs, there were few examples of successful brokerage by the Secretariat in the 2000 IGC. One example was the compromise proposal on trade policy made by Piris, head of the Secretariat's Legal Service. Piris provided a legal formula in Article 133(6) EC which arguably no other actor except the Commission could have formulated in the Nice Summit. The formula excluded the sensitive areas of culture and shipping, thereby enabling France, Denmark and Greece to accept the final outcome.[55] Another example was the declaration on the venue for European Councils, written by de Boissieu during the Nice Summit. This declaration enabled Belgium to swallow being granted fewer Council votes than the Netherlands (Galloway, 2001, 82-3, 158).

The Commission

As with the Secretariat, the manner in which the 2000 IGC negotiations were conducted did not generate many opportunities for brokerage and mediation by the Commission. One of the basic problems for the Commission was that

---

[54] For an modified view of this, see Schout and Vanhoonacker, contribution to this volume.

[55] Interview with member of the UK negotiating team in the 2000 IGC, London, 22 February 2002. See also Galloway 2001, 106-109.

it was widely perceived to be excessively partial to its own interests, which were far outside the zone of possible agreements. Another problem was that while the Commission is usually viewed by smaller Member States as their ally, the Commission in the 2000 IGC did not have the trust of smaller Member States (Gray, 2001). This was due to the downfall of the Santer Commission in 1999, which substantially impaired the Commission's ability to draw upon the legitimacy of being perceived as the 'guardian of Europe,' and to the suspicions of many smaller Member States that top Commission officials were partial to a shift in power towards the larger Member States. Finally, Commission President Prodi was widely perceived to be a relatively ineffectual leader both within the Commission, and in the IGC negotiations, preventing him from playing a strong brokering role.

Despite these weaknesses, the Commission proved able to broker an important compromise in one very salient issue. In the deal brokered on amendments to the common trade policy (Article 133 EC), the Commission, together with the Finnish delegation, took part in intense, behind-the-scenes negotiations in the final hours of the Nice Summit. The main problem was getting the French on board, while also maximising the extent of the transferral of competences as desired by a majority of other delegations. Yet the complexity of the issue prevented other actors (except the Secretariat) from stepping in and brokering an outcome, as national experts in trade matters were not present in the Nice Summit.[56] The Commission brokered an outcome based upon the Finnish proposals,[57] coupled with the legal formula provided by Piris in order to get the French to accept the outcome.[58] Interestingly, in view of the aforementioned excessive partiality of the French Presidency, it is unlikely that the French would have accepted this outcome had they *not* held the Presidency, given that they preferred the no agreement outcome over the agreement in Nice on trade policy (Schout and Vanhoonacker, contribution to this volume).

In the negotiation of an extension of QMV in social security coordination,[59] the Commission *almost* successfully translated expertise into influence through brokerage. The Commission acted as a broker between Danish concerns and a majority of Member States, including the French

[56] Interview with member of the Commission's IGC Task Force, Brussels, 26 April 2002.

[57] Most centrally, CONF 4818/00.

[58] Interviews with member of the UK negotiating team in the 2000 IGC, London, 22 February 2002; senior member of the UK negotiating team in the 2000 IGC, London, 21 February 2002.

[59] Article 42 EC.

Presidency that wanted QMV and co-decision to be applied to the article. In very technical bilateral negotiations in the final weeks of the IGC between Danish representatives and the Commission, the Commission attempted to alleviate Danish sovereignty concerns (Laursen, contribution to this volume). The last draft put forward by the Commission was acceptable to Denmark, but the final deal was then blocked by the UK, as they had committed themselves to a no-agreement outcome in their IGC White Paper (Galloway, 2001, 103).[60]

Reviewing the Findings

The 2000 IGC was in many respects a worse case scenario for both the Secretariat and the Commission, particularly during the French Presidency. Both the Secretariat and the Commission had considerably weaker roles than in previous IGCs, and both the nature of the issues being negotiated and the relative simplicity of the negotiating situation opened for few opportunities for supranational influence. Yet both actors were able to influence outcomes in the IGC, although arguably on minor points. How was this possible? I will first summarize the findings regarding the impact of the contextual variables, and then turn to look at the process-related variables.

Contextual Intervening Variables

The level of Secretariat and Commission involvement (or more accurately, non-involvement) was strongly correlated with the ability of supranational actors to gain influence in the IGC. Both the Secretariat and the Commission had relatively weak positions, although the Secretariat maintained its influential drafting role. During the French Presidency, the impact of institutional role was best illustrated, for in those issues where the French drew upon the Secretariat and allowed it to play its traditional role, the Secretariat had considerable influence, and vice versa. The Commission's success in garnering for itself a privileged institutional position in the negotiation of judicial reform also clearly illustrates the causal impact of the institutional set-up. By gaining a central role in the discussions, and by creating an empowered epistemic community, the Commission gained considerable influence upon the reform of the EU's judicial system.

Turning to the impact of the nature of the issue being negotiated, table 19.4 illustrates the results for the level of political saliency of the issue. Ta-

[60] Interview with member of Commission's IGC Task Force, Brussels, 26 April 2002.

ble 19.4 shows no apparent correlation between the level of Secretariat influence and the political salience of the issue. While the Secretariat was able to both set the agenda and determine most of the outcome in low salience issues such as the status of inter-institutional agreements, it was unable to gain significant influence upon the outcome of the most sensitive institutional issues of the re-weighting of votes and the size of the Commission.

Table 19.4: Influence of Council Secretariat and Commission according to the level of political salience.[61]

	Issue	Overall influence of Council Secretariat upon outcome	Overall influence of Commission upon outcome
Low Political Salience	status of Inter-institutional Agreements	High	Medium
	internal reforms of the Commission	Medium	High
	reform of the Union's legal system	Medium	High
	political parties at EU-level	Low-Medium	High
Overall level of influence in low salience issues		Medium	High
Medium Political Salience	creation of separate legal bases for policies under Article 308 EC	High	Low
	fundamental rights	Low	High
	extension of co-decision procedure	Low-Medium	Low-Medium
	hierarchy of legal norms	Low	Medium
	flexible co-operation	Medium-High	Low-Medium
	venue for European Councils	Medium	Low
Overall level of influence in medium salience issues		Medium	Low-Medium

[61] Sources: Proposals of Commission and preferences of Secretariat compared with outcomes, and interviews with national civil servant, Brussels, May 2001 and April 2002; and two Commission officials, Brussels, April 2002.

High Political Salience	size of the Commission	Low	Low
	re-weighting of Council voting	Low-Medium	Low
	allocation of EP seats	Low-Medium	Low-Medium
	extension of QMV in politically sensitive areas (taxation, social policy, and JHA)	Medium	Medium
	changes to the common trade policy	Low-Medium	Medium-High
Overall level of influence in high salience issues		Low-Medium	Low-Medium

If we then control for issue technicality, in legally complex issues such as the creation of separate legal bases for Article 308 EC policies, together with flexible co-operation, the Secretariat was able to successfully translate its expertise into influence. In contrast, most of the salient institutional issues were relatively simple. For example, while there were numerous different vote re-weighting proposals on the table, it was relatively easy for national negotiators to determine who would win and lose in the various options considered—thereby making negotiators more reliant on their own calculators than the expertise and experience of either the Secretariat or Commission. More generally, the French Presidency was not as dependent upon expert advice and assistance as small state Presidencies, given the extensive legal and political resources available to the French government in Paris.[62]

Turning to the Commission, if we peruse the issues in table 19.4, it appears that the level of Commission influence varied according to political salience. While the Commission more or less wrote the outcomes on EU-level political parties and the internal reforms of the Commission, the Commission had no influence upon the outcome regarding the re-weighting of Council votes. If we then control for issue technicality, we see that in complex issues where the Commission had special technical expertise, such as common trade policy, they formed the outcome together with the Finnish delegation (see above). In the negotiation of several of the more complex sensitive articles were under consideration for a transfer to QMV, the Com-

[62] Interview with national civil servant, London, February, 2002.

mission was also able to translate its expertise into influence over the final outcome.

The basic handicap on the ability of the Commission to translate expertise into influence in complex issues was the appointment of Barnier as Commission representative to the Preparatory Group. Barnier, for instance, did not have the same grasp of the details of the issues as the national permanent representatives, who all had experience in dealing with technical EU issues through their participation in COREPER.[63]

The level of complexity of the negotiating situation was significant in that there was a relatively low demand for intervention in order to *find* an agreement, but given the strength of the divergences among governments, there was also a strong demand for brokerage in order for the parties to *reach* an agreement. The French Presidency attempted to supply this brokerage, with varying levels of success. In issues where there was a demand for brokerage by an expert actor, this created opportunities for supranational actors to intervene. This was most clearly seen in the brokerage of a deal on the common trade policy, where the Commission, Secretariat, and Finnish delegations reached a compromise agreement.

Process Intervening Variables

The context of the 2000 IGC created few opportunities for supranational actors to gain influence through agenda-shaping or brokerage. Neither actor proved very successful in their attempts at agenda-setting. The Secretariat was able to use managerial tactics to change the Finnish Presidency report in December 1999 that set the IGC agenda, but due to its weak institutional position in the Portuguese and French Presidencies, the Secretariat found itself unable to significantly affect the agenda thereafter except in a few isolated issues (e.g. flexibility and the extension of QMV). The Commission fared even worse, often due to tactical blunders, such as advocating extreme policy positions that were far outside of zones of possible agreement. Yet the Commission was able to gain significant influence on judicial reform due to the creation of an advantageous institutional forum.

Neither actor was able to supply brokerage except in a few isolated instances, due primarily to the manner in which the French Presidency conducted the negotiations. Crucial to the ability of the Commission and Secretariat to broker deals was their policy expertise in the issue being negotiated.

[63] Interviews with Commission official, Brussels, April 2002; national civil servants, London, February 2002.

Conclusion

This chapter has investigated how the context and conduct of the 2000 IGC affected the ability of the Council Secretariat and the Commission to translate their political resources into influence over the final outcome. The chapter first put forward a basic contingency model for supranational influence that detailed the hypothesised impact of the structure and conduct of the IGC negotiation process. After reviewing the preferences of the two institutions, their resources were detailed, showing that both the Secretariat and the Commission possessed substantial informational advantages vis-à-vis Member States. However, the two institutions varied in how the Member States perceived the acceptability of their interventions, with governments viewing the Secretariat as a valuable assistant to the negotiations, whereas the Commission was seen as being excessively partial to its own pro-integrative interests.

The empirical analysis demonstrated that the most significant factor in the 2000 IGC affecting the ability of supranational actors to shape the agenda was their level of involvement. The Secretariat was in several instances able to exploit its privileged institutional position in the drafting process to gain influence over outcomes. However, in contrast to earlier IGCs, the Secretariat was for the most part unable to exert influence because of the manner in which the French Presidency structured the negotiations. The Commission had an even weaker role, although its clever use of institutional politics enabled it to gain significant influence upon the negotiation of reforms to the EU's legal system. The creation of, first, a working party, and, subsequently, the Friends of the Presidency Group resulted in a group of like-minded experts who valued technical and legal arguments higher than political concerns, privileging the Commission vis-à-vis national governments, who were often unable to translate their politically-based sovereignty concerns into legalistic/technical arguments in the group. In contrast to this picture of unsuccessful Commission proposals, it can be argued that the Commission in many respects was following a longer-term strategy, with many of its proposals—especially in the final months of the IGC—aimed more at the forthcoming 2004 IGC than the 2000 IGC.

Neither institution was able to effectively broker agreements in the IGC, and this again was primarily due to the conduct of the negotiations by the French Presidency. Yet the Commission was able to broker a key deal in the common trade policy, translating its unparalleled expertise on the issue into influence. No other actor could have brokered in this instance, as the French were prevented from acting as a broker, given that the main cleavage in the issue was between their position and the position of a majority of other delegations. In the absence of Commission brokerage, the outcome would most likely have been no agreement.

Neither the Secretariat nor the Commission was able to gain significant influence upon the outcome, with supranational influence being primarily on the margins. Their lack of influence stemmed from several factors: the nature of the issues, with many zero-sum issues; the relative simplicity of the negotiating situation, with two main cleavages; and the manner in which the negotiations were conducted.

Yet supranational influence is contingent, and this lack of influence in the 2000 IGC can be contrasted with the parallel negotiations that also took place in 2000 on the EU's Charter of Fundamental Rights. Here we can clearly see the impact of the nature of issues, along with the institutional design of the negotiations, which granted the Secretariat many opportunities to translate its legal expertise into influence. The negotiations of the Charter dealt with complex questions of EU law—matters which required extensive insights into the legal workings of the case law of the ECJ on human rights. Yet the negotiations were conducted by representatives of governments, national parliaments, the European Parliament, and the Commission, assisted by the Council Secretariat (Galloway, 2001, 218-219). Given the asymmetry in legal expertise between the representatives and the Secretariat, negotiators were very dependent upon the advice and assistance of the Secretariat—advice that was not always neutral (de Búrca, 2001, 134-137; Christiansen, 2002).

Interestingly, the process whereby the forthcoming 2004 IGC is being prepared also gives the Secretariat significant opportunities to gain influence, whereas the Commission's relative decline in influence can be expected to continue. First, the Convention is composed primarily of politicians, who understandably lack the detailed knowledge of the workings of the Treaties and the case law of the ECJ that is necessary to carry out processes such as the constitutionalisation of the Treaties. Second, by giving the Secretariat a secretarial and drafting task for the convention, they obtain a relatively 'neutral' position from which to attempt to gain influence—in contrast to the Commission, who participates in a manner like other national delegates and the European Parliament. However, unlike the Commission, national delegates and representatives of the EP possess democratic legitimacy. Members of the convention will therefore be very dependent upon the expertise of the Secretariat, which generates numerous opportunities for the Secretariat to subtly influence the outcome. The Commission's interventions, in contrast, will be seen as in a manner similar to any other actor in the convention, with the disadvantage that they do not have any democratic legitimacy.

BIBLIOGRAPHY

Beach, Derek (2001), *Between Law and Politics: The relationship between the European Court of Justice and EU Member States*. Copenhagen: DJØF Publishing.

—— (2002), "The negotiation of the Amsterdam Treaty - when theory meets reality," in Finn Laursen (ed.), *The Amsterdam Treaty: National Preference Formation, Interstate Bargaining, Outcome and Ratification*. Odense: Odense University Press, pp. 593-637.

—— (2002), *Bringing Negotiations Back – supranational actors and the negotiation of intergovernmental conferences in the EU*. Ph.D.-dissertation. Odense: Odense University Press.

—— (2004) "The unseen hand in treaty reform negotiations: the role and influence of the Council Secretariat," *Journal of European Public Policy,* Vol. 11, No. 3, pp. 408-439.

Bercovitch, Jacob (1996a), "The Structure and Diversity of Mediation in International Relations," in Jacob Bercovitch and Jeffrey Z. Rubin (eds.), *Mediation in International Relations*. New York: St. Martin's Press, pp. 1-29.

—— (1996b), "Introduction: Thinking About Mediation," in Jacob Bercovitch (ed.), *Resolving International Conflicts – The Theory and Practice of Mediation*. London: Lynne Rienner Publishers, pp. 1-9.

—— and Allison Houston (1996), "The Study of International Mediation: Theoretical Issues and Empirical Evidence," in Jacob Bercovitch (ed.), *Resolving International Conflicts – The Theory and Practice of Mediation*. London: Lynne Rienner Publishers, pp. 11-35.

Carnevale, Peter J. and Sharon Arad (1996), "Bias and Impartiality in International Mediation," in Jacob Bercovitch (ed.), *Resolving International Conflicts – The Theory and Practice of Mediation*. London: Lynne Rienner Publishers, pp. 39-53.

Charlemagne (1994), "L'equilibre entre les etats membres," in *L'equilibre européen. Etudes rassemblées et publiées en hommage B. Niels Ersbøll*. Brussels: Edition provisoire, pp. 69-78.

Christiansen, Thomas (2002), "The Role of Supranational Actors in EU Treaty Reform," *Journal of European Public Policy,* Vol. 9, No. 1, February, pp. 33-53.

—— and Knud Erik Jørgensen (1998), "Negotiating Treaty Reform in the European Union: The Role of the European Commission," *International Negotiation,* Vol. 3, No. 3, pp.435-452.

Cox, Robert W. and Harold K. Jacobsen (1973), "The Framework for Inquiry," in Robert W. Cox, Harold K. Jacobsen et al. *The Anatomy of Influence – Decision Making in International Organizations*. London: Yale University Press, pp. 1-36.

Dehaene, Jean-Luc (1999), *The Institutional Implications of Enlargement: Report to the European Commission*. Brussels, 18 October 1999.

Dinan, Desmond and Sophie Vanhoonacker (2000-2001), "IGC 2000 Watch." Parts 1-4, in *ECSA Review,* Vol. 13, Nos. 2-4, 2000 and Vol. 14, No. 1, 2001.

Due, Ole (2000), "Regeringskonferencen og det judicielle system i EU," *EU-ret og Menneskeret*, Vol. 7, No. 2, June 2000, pp. 45-51.

Dupont, Christophe and Guy-Olivier Faure (1991), "The Negotiation Process," in Victor A. Kremenyuk (ed.), *International Negotiation: Analysis, Approaches, Issues*. San Francisco: Jossey-Bass Publishers, pp. 40-57.

Dyson, Kenneth and Kevin Featherstone (1999), *The Road to Maastricht: Negotiating Economic and Monetary Union*. Oxford: Oxford University Press.

Elgström, Ole (2001), "'The Honest Broker'? - The EU Council Presidency as a Mediator," Paper presented at the 4th Pan-European International Relations Conference, Canterbury, 8-10 September.

Europaudvalget (2000), "Europa-Kommissionen præsenterer ekspertrapport om todeling af EU-traktaterne," Info-note, bilag 152, 1999-00.

Finnemore, Martha and Kathryn Sikkink (1998), "International Norm Dynamics and Political Change," *International Organization,* Vol. 52, No. 4, Autumn, pp. 887-917.

Galloway, David (2001), *The Treaty of Nice and Beyond – Realities and Illusions of Power in the EU.* Sheffield: Sheffield University Press.

Gray, Mark (2001), "The European Commission and Treaty Reform," Speech given to Nuffield College, University of Oxford, May 2001.

—— and Alexander Stubb (2001), "The Treaty of Nice: Negotiating a poisoned chalice?" *Journal of Common Market Studies,* Vol. 39, Annual Review EU 2001, September, pp. 5-23.

Haas, Ernst B. (1990), *When Knowledge is Power: Three Models of Change in International Organizations.* Berkeley: University of California Press.

Haas, Peter (1992), "Introduction: Epistemic communities and international policy coordination," *International Organization,* Vol. 46, No. 1, pp. 1-35.

Hampson, Fen Osler (1995), *Multilateral Negotiations: Lessons from Arms Control, Trade, and the Environment.* Baltimore: The Johns Hopkins University Press.

Hopmann, P. Terrence (1996), *The Negotiation Process and the Resolution of International Conflicts.* Columbia: University of South Carolina Press.

Krasner, Stephen D. (1991), "Global Communications and National Power: Life on the Pareto Frontier," *World Politics,* Vol. 43, No. 3, April, pp. 336-366.

Kressel, K., Dean G. Priutt, and Associates (1989), *Mediation Research: Process and Effectiveness of Third-Party Intervention.* San Francisco: Jossey-Bass.

Laursen, Finn (2001), *Nice-traktaten: Baggrund, Kommentar, Perspektiver.* Copenhagen: Den Danske Europabevægelse.

——, ed. (2002), *The Amsterdam Treaty: National Preference Formation, Interstate Bargaining, Outcome and Ratification.* Odense: Odense University Press.

Lequesne, Christian (2001), "The French Presidency: The Half Success of Nice," *Journal of Common Market Studies,* Vol. 39, Annual Review, September, pp. 47-50.

McDonagh, Bobby (1998), *Original Sin in a Brave New World: An Account of the Negotiation of the Treaty of Amsterdam.* Dublin: Institute of European Affairs.

Metcalfe, David (1998), "Leadership in European Union Negotiations: The Presidency of the Council," *International Negotiation,* Volume 3, 1998, pp. 413-434.

Midgaard, Knut and Arild Underdal (1977), "Multiparty Conferences," in Daniel Druckman (ed.), *Negotiations: Social-psychological perspectives.* London: Sage Publications, pp. 329-346.

Moravcsik, Andrew (1999), "A new statecraft? Supranational entrepreneurs and international cooperation," *International Organization,* Vol. 53, No. 2, Spring, pp.267-306.

Petite, Michel (2000), "The IGC and the European Commission," in Edward Best, Mark Gray and Alexander Stubb (eds.), *Rethinking the European Union: IGC 2000 and Beyond.* Maastricht: European Institute of Public Administration, pp. 61-66.

Piris, Jean-Claude (1999), "Does the European Union have a Constitution? Does it need one?," *European Law Review,* Vol. 24, December, pp. 557-585.

Raiffa, Howard (1982), *The Art and Science of Negotiation.* Cambridge: Harvard University Press.

Sandholtz, Wayne (1992), *High-Tech Europe: The Politics of International Cooperation.* Berkeley: University of California Press.

Scharpf, Fritz (1997), *Games Real Actors Play: Actor-Centered Institutionalism in Policy Research.* Oxford: Westview Press.

Sebenius, James K. (1992), "Challenging conventional explanations of international cooperation: negotiation analysis and the case of epistemic communities," *International Organization,* Vol. 46, No. 1, Winter, pp. 323-365.

Simon, Herbert A. (1997), *Administrative Behavior: A Study of Decision-Making Processes in Administrative Organizations.* Fourth Edition. New York: The Free Press.

Stubb, Alexander (1998), *Flexible Integration and the Amsterdam Treaty: Negotiating Differentiation in the 1996-97 IGC.* Ph.D. dissertation, London School of Economics and Political Science.

—— (2002), *Negotiating Flexibility in the European Union.* Palgrave: Houndmills, Basingstoke.

Tallberg, Jonas (2001), "Responsabilité sans Pouvoir? The Agenda-Shaping Powers of the EU Council Presidency," Paper presented at the 4th Pan-European International Relations Conference, Canterbury, 8-10 September.

—— (2002), "The Power of the Chair in International Bargaining," paper presented at the 2002 International Studies Association Annual Convention, New Orleans, March 24-27.

—— (2003) "The agenda-shaping powers of the EU Council Presidency," *Journal of Common Market Studies,* Vol. 10, No. 1, pp. 1-20.

Wall, James A. and Ann Lynn (1993), "Mediation: A Current Review," *Journal of Conflict Resolution,* Vol. 37, No. 1, March, pp. 160-194.

——, John B. Stark and Rhetta L. Standifer (2001), "Mediation: a current review and theory development," *Journal of Conflict Resolution,* Vol. 45, No. 3, June, pp. 370-391.

Wehr, Paul and John Paul Lederach (1996), "Mediating Conflict in Central America," in Jacob Bercovitch (ed.), *Resolving International Conflicts – The Theory and Practice of Mediation.* London: Lynne Rienner Publishers, pp. 55-74.

Westlake, Martin (1999), *The Council of the European Union. Revised Edition.* London: John Harper Publishing.

Young, Oran R. (1967), *The Intermediaries: Third Parties in International Crises.* Princeton: Princeton University Press.

—— (1991), "Political leadership and regime formation: on the development of institutions in international society," *International Organization,* Vol. 45, No. 3, Summer, pp.281-308.

—— (1999), "Comment on Andrew Moravcsik, 'A new statecraft? Supranational entrepreneurs and international cooperation'," *International Organization,* Vol. 53, No. 4, Autumn, pp.805-809.

Zartmann, William I. (1991), "The Structure of Negotiation," in Victor A. Kremenyuk (ed.), *International Negotiation: Analysis, Approaches, Issues.* San Francisco: Jossey-Bass Publishers, pp. 65-77.

SECTION 3

INTERSTATE BARGAINING

CHAPTER 20

RE-WEIGHTING OF VOTES IN THE COUNCIL AND COMPOSITION OF THE COMMISSION: WHEN SIZE MATTERS[1]

INTRODUCTION

The IGC 2000 was slow to attack the two most controversial institutional issues, viz. the reweighting of votes in the Council and the composition and size of the Commission. This chapter will give an account of how these two issues were dealt with by IGC 2000.

Both issues to a large extent pitted the larger Member States against the smaller ones. Indeed, it was largely the larger Member States that called for a reweighting of votes in the Council in their favour, arguing that the future enlargement with many smaller states would require some adjustments. If a large group of small states with a minority of the Union's population could dominate, it would not be legitimate. It was also mainly the larger Member States that insisted on a smaller Commission which would lead to a situation where not all Member States would have a Commissioner of their nationality. They claimed a smaller Commission would be more efficient. But most small states attached great importance to nominating a Commissioner, seeing the Commission as a bulwark against a *directoire* of the large ones. They basically saw it as an issue of legitimacy.

In the following we will proceed chronologically, starting with the Portuguese Presidency during the first half of 2000, moving to the French Presidency during the second half, and finishing with the Nice summit in December, where these issues were decided upon after the longest summit in the EU's history. It was not only long, it was also very acrimonious. After all the settlement of these issues would determine influence in a future much enlarged EU.

The report of the three wise men, Dehaene, von Weizsäcker and Simon, issued in October 1999 had discussed the institutional issues. On the Commission the three authors said: "For understandable reasons most Member States do not accept the perspective of a Commission in which their country would not be represented. But the Commission is not, and must not become, an assembly of national delegates. It is a European institution of great originality, which has a crucial role to play in both decision making and man-

[1] The author would like to thank Berenice Lara Laursen for research assistance for this chapter.

agement. It therefore needs to remain effective, operational and well respected." The question of reweighting of votes was seen as "politically and symbolically important," but the group did not feel it had a mandate to make specific proposals (Von Weizsäcker, Dehaene and Simon, 1999).

In accordance with Article 48 TEU, the Commission produced an opinion in January 2000 prior to the start of the IGC in February. Concerning the Commission the opinion discussed two options: a Commission composed of fewer members than the future number of Member States, or a Commission made up of one national from each Member State. In the former case "a system of rotation that would treat all Member States strictly equally on the basis of a pre-set order" would have to be provided. In the latter case "there would at the same time need to be a major restructuring of the Commission" (European Commission, 2000a, pp. 13-14). But the Commission did not make a choice between the two options.

Concerning the question of weighting of votes in the Council, the Commission gave some useful historical background information and discussed basically two options: reweighting the votes of the Member States and double simple majority. Some changes were considered necessary. Successive enlargements had led to a decline in representativeness of a qualified majority vote (QMV) in terms op population from 67.70% in 1958 to 58.15% in EU-15. Based on an extrapolation the QMV in EU-25 would only represent 51.35% of the total Union population. Option one would require that the relative weight of the votes of the most populous Member States be increased. However, the Commission opted in favour of the double simple majority. A QMV would consist of a simple majority of Member States representing at the same time a majority of the total population of the Union. The argument in favour of such a solution was that it would lead to "a readable, simple and democratic decision-making process in the Council" (Ibid., p. 31).

In accordance with Article 48 TEU, the European Parliament was also consulted prior to the start of the IGC, but the resolution it passed contained no specific suggestions on the issues dealt with in this chapter (European Parliament, 2000).

The Portuguese Presidency

The Portuguese Presidency first produced a note on the Commission in March 2000. Basically it outlined the two options already discussed in the Commission opinion prior to the start of the IGC, a college consisting of a national from each Member State, or a college consisting of a fixed number of Commissioners regardless of the number of Member States of the Union.

It also asked some other questions relating to the Commission (CONFER 4727/00), and The IGC representatives had a first discussion of the issue on 28 March.

The IGC representatives had a first discussion of the issue of weighting of votes in the Council on 4 April 2000 on the basis of a document from the Presidency (CONFER 4728/00). The document gave some background information. The Protocol on the institutions annexed to the Amsterdam Treaty mentioned two possibilities: modifying the weighting of votes by reweighting or by dual majority. The protocol also linked the issue with that of Member States giving up the possibility of nominating a second Commissioner, suggesting the possibility of extra compensation for the large Member States losing a Commissioner in connection with enlargement. Further, Declaration No 50 from Amsterdam was mentioned. This Declaration stated that the Ioannina compromise would be extended until the first enlargement and that a solution for the special case of Spain be found.

The Ioannina compromise dates back to 1994 when the membership of Finland, Sweden and Austria was decided upon. The increasing size of the blocking minority was becoming a problem for some of the Member States, especially Spain and the UK. These two states proposed that the blocking minority should remain 23 as in EU-12 to allow for a blocking minority of two large and one small Member State (except Luxembourg) also in EU-15. While Norway was still a candidate, a blocking minority, based on an extrapolation of the existing system, would have created a blocking minority of 27. Such a blocking minority would require two large and two small Member States.

On 29 March 1994, in the Greek town of Ioaninna, the Council reached a compromise:

> If members of the Council representing a total of 23 to 26 votes indicate their intention to oppose the adoption by the Council of a Decision by qualified majority, the Council will do all in its powers to reach, within a reasonable time and without prejudicing obligatory time limits laid down by the Treaties and by secondary law ... a satisfactory solution that could be adopted by at least 68 votes (OJ No. C105, 13.4.94, p. 1)

According to Westlake, there was a "widespread but shortlived debate." But, "insiders saw [the Ioaninna Compromise] as a diplomatic device to enable a Member State government to retreat gracefully from a position which had become untenable" (Westlake, 1999, p. 94).

When it turned out that Norway would not join the EU the Ioannina Compromise was changed to read "Members of the Council representing a total of 23 to 25 votes" and "a satisfactory solution that could be adopted by at least 65 votes" (OJ No. C 1, 1.1.95, p. 1).

The so-called Spanish problem dated back to Spain's accession in 1986 when the country was given the choice of 10 votes in the Council like other large states and one Commissioner or eight votes in the Council and two Commissioners. Spain chose the latter arrangement, but would now according to the decision at Amsterdam lose one Commissioner. So Spain expected extra compensation in the Council.

The Presidency document included an annex with the current votes as well as population figures. In another annex these figures were extrapolated to EU-28 (see table 20.1)

At the time of an EU-15, a QMV was 62 votes out of 87, representing 71.26% of the votes and minimum 58.16% of total EU population of a little more than 375 million. A blocking minority was 26 votes, representing 29.89% of the votes and a minimum of 12.38% of the population. In EU-28 the percentages of votes would not change much if such extrapolation was used, but a QMV would only require 51.45% of the total population and a decision could be blocked by a group of small states representing only 11.88% of the population.

The Presidency document also mentioned that a QMV in EU-15 would require at least half of the Member States when deciding on the basis of a Commission proposal. For decisions not based on a Commission proposal, Article 205 TEC stipulates an additional requirement that a QMV must comprise two-thirds of Member States. Would it be acceptable in the future that a decision might be taken by less than half the States, the document asked. The essential requirements of a new system should be fairness, transparency and efficiency, it was stated. The document also asked whether the new system should be based on a purely political or a more objective approach.

In May, the Presidency produced another document on weighting of votes in the Council. It was discussed by the government representatives on 30 May. The document claimed that there was a "very broad agreement that any weighting of votes must reflect the dual nature of the Union, which is both a Union of States and a Union of peoples" (CONFER 4745/00). This meant that a QMV must represent a minimum threshold in terms of population to ensure its legitimacy. The discussion in March had shown "a rather clear trend in favour of a minimum threshold in the vicinity of 60%." On the second point, "most of the Member States also consider that any qualified majority should include at least half of the Member States of the Union, as has always been the case up to now," even if not specified as a rule.

Table 20.1: Extrapolation of current votes to EU-28 (1999 Eurostat population data)

Member States	Votes	Population (thousands)
Germany	10	82 038
Turkey	10	63 400
United Kingdom	10	59 247
France	10	58 966
Italy	10	57 612
Spain	8	39 349
Poland	8	38 667
Romania	6	22 489
Netherlands	5	15 760
Greece	5	10 533
Czech Republic	5	10 290
Belgium	5	10 213
Hungary	5	10 092
Portugal	5	9 980
Sweden	4	8 854
Bulgaria	4	8 230
Austria	4	8 082
Slovakia	3	5 393
Denmark	3	5 313
Finland	3	5 160
Ireland	3	3 701
Lithuania	3	3 744
Latvia	3	2 439
Slovenia	3	1 978
Estonia	3	1 446
Cyprus	2	752
Luxembourg	2	429
Malta	2	377
TOTAL EU 28	144	544 579

Determining a qualified majority

Total votes = 144	Votes	% Votes	Min. % Population
Qualified Majority	102	70.83%	51.45%
Blocking Minority	43	29.86%	11.88%

Source: CONFER 4728/00, 24 March 2000. 1998 data for Malta. Estimated figures for Turkey.

This new document included a hypothetical proposal from the Presidency. It was suggested to double the number of votes to broaden the scope for differentiation, and then subtract one vote from each Member State to introduce an element of reweighting, and finally allocate additional votes to the Member States that had to give up the right to nominate a second Commissioner. The result was a weighting starting with 23 votes for the Big Five (Germany, Turkey, UK, France and Italy), 19 votes for Spain and Poland and then down to three votes for the smallest three members (Cyprus, Luxembourg and Malta). This would give a total of 288 votes. A qualified majority of 206 votes would then represent a minimum of 58.18% of the population (CONFER 4745/00, Annex IV).

Another annex suggested how the population weight could be calculated in a dual majority system. In EU-28 Germany will have about 15% of the population. It was suggested to see this as 150 out of 1000. For France, with 10.8% of the population the figure then would be 108. The figure for the three smallest states, Cyprus, Luxembourg and Malta would be 1.

At the meeting on 30 May the representatives again discussed the issue of the size and composition of the Commission. This discussion took place on the basis of a note from the Presidency outlining three options. Apart from the two options discussed so far, the third option was a kind of compromise allowing the Commission to "consist of one national from each of the Member States after the first enlargement, while leaving the question of its definitive size after a second enlargement entirely open" (CONFER 4744/00). The same note also dealt with the question of introducing rules concerning the Commission asking for a vote of confidence from the European Parliament.

The Portuguese summarized the situation in a report to the Feira European Council meeting in June 2000. In annexes various possible solutions to the question of voting in the Council were reproduced. This included a possible reweighting of votes in favour of the most populated Member States going back to the Amsterdam negotiations in 1997. The proposal started with 25 votes for the Big five, 20 for Spain and Poland, and then falling gradually down to three for the smallest Member States. The total in EU-28 would be 311 votes. A QMV of 222 votes would represent 71.38% of the votes and as a minimum 58.18% of population (CONFER 4750/00, Annex 2.6). Another possible reweighting in favour of the most populated Member States was based on a doubling of existing votes and the adding five votes to the Member States losing a second Commissioner. This led to a scale from 25 to the largest over 21 to Spain and Poland down to four votes for the smallest Member States. This would give a total of 323 votes in EU-28. With a QMV set at 231 the minimum percentage of population would be 58.04% (CONFER 4750/00, annex 2.7).

More interestingly, the Feira report also reproduced a Swedish proposal based on an arithmetical approach.[2] The proposal was to give "each Member State a number of votes equal to double the square root of its population expressed in millions of inhabitants, rounded off to the nearest figure." (see fig.

[2] The Feira report does not say that this was a Swedish proposal, but when the French Presidency reproduced it in November it was called the Swedish proposal (CONFER 4796/00).

21.2). Such an approach would be "completely transparent" and it had the "advantage of adjusting automatically" to future enlargements (CONFER 4750/00, p. 23).

Table 20.2: Reweighting based on an arithmetical approach (Swedish model)

Member State	Votes
Germany	18
Turkey	16
United Kingdom	15
France	15
Italy	15
Spain	13
Poland	12
Romania	9
Netherlands	8
Greece	6
Czech Republic	6
Belgium	6
Hungary	6
Portugal	6
Sweden	6
Bulgaria	6
Austria	6
Slovakia	5
Denmark	5
Finland	5
Ireland	4
Lithuania	4
Latvia	3
Slovenia	3
Estonia	2
Cyprus	2
Luxembourg	1
Malta	1
Total EU of 28	204

Determining a qualified majority in a Union of 28 Member States

Total votes = 204	Votes	% votes	Minimum number (and %) of Member States	Minimum % of population
Qualified majority	146	71.57%	15 (50%)	58.18%
Blocking minority	59	28.92%	4 (14.29%)	12.08%

Source: CONFER 4750/00, 14 June 2000.

On the question of the Commission, the Feira report again basically outlined the two main options being discussed. It was claimed that most delegations considered that a college made up of one national from each Member State was "the only way of safeguarding the Commission's legitimacy in the eyes of the public." However, other delegations were of the opinion that such a solution "would be contrary to the Commission's very nature, as an independent, collegiate body whose Members do not represent States." The latter group also felt that such a large Commission would create problems of efficiency and consistency. And, admitted the Presidency, "It seems difficult to reconcile these two approaches at present" (CONFER 4750/00, pp. 12-13).

THE FRENCH PRESIDENCY

A first document on weighting of votes was presented by the French Presidency on 3 July 2000. The document discussed the underlying considerations of efficiency, legitimacy, transparency and political balance. It asked various questions, but made no concrete proposals (CONFER 47547/00).

A first document on the Commission from the French Presidency appeared on 11 July. It mainly dealt with the internal organization of the Commission, arguing that "it would not be worthwhile to resume the discussion" at that stage about the two main options outlined in the Feira report (CONFER 4757/00).

A second document on reweighting of votes from the French Presidency followed on 5 October. Significantly, it said that the issue of the weighting of votes was "one of the most sensitive points at the Conference which can be settled only within the framework of an overall agreement." It claimed that "a majority is emerging in favour of reweighting the votes sensu stricto, subject to achievement of an outcome which is politically acceptable to all parties," but it basically asked questions without putting forward proposals (CONFER 4781/00).

An informal meeting of the European Council took place on 13 and 14 October at Biarritz. It did not produce written conclusions. According to press reports, however, Biarritz showed that there were still fundamental differences in views. Indeed, over the dinner the confrontation between the large and small Member States became very clear (Lemaitre and Zecchini, 2000).

Afterwards the leaders explained some of their positions to the press. On both the size and composition of the Commission and the question of voting in the Council, Luxembourg's Prime Minister said that it was 10 against 5: 10 were for "one Commissioner per Member State" and 5 for a reduced Commission, and 10 were in favour of dual majority and 5 in favour of re-weighting of votes (*Agence Europe*, 16 October 2000). Juncker may have simplified, but there was clearly a small vs. large division on these two issues.

Juncker explained why he favoured one Commissioner per Member State by saying that a Commission where the large countries were not represented would have less political clout and clout would move to the Council. Similarly Swedish Prime Minister Göran Persson said that a Commission without a German or French Commissioner would not be 'egitimate.'And Austria's Chancellor Wolfgang Schlüssel explained that although a Commissioner does not represent his country in the Commission a Commissioner does act as a "bridge between the Commission and the public opinion of their country" (ibid.).

Germany faced a special situation. Chancellor Schröder explained that Germany "could live quite happily" with the formula of dual majority. What was not acceptable was an enlarged Union where Germany with 80 million inhabitants would have 10 votes while the 17 smallest countries with the same population would have 57 votes (ibid.).

A new document on weighting of votes submitted by the French Presidency on 9 November listed various proposals, including the Swedish square-roots proposal (CONFER 4796/00, annex V). It included the simple dual majority as proposed by the Commission (see table 20.3). In a double majority model the population weight could of course be set higher than 50%, and the first component could also be based on current weights or a reweighting of votes.

The Presidency document of 9 November also included an Italian proposal for a 'substantial' reweighting which would give 33 votes to the Big Four in EU-27 (Turkey not included), 26 to Spain and Poland, 14 for Romania, 10 for medium sized countries, from Netherlands to Portugal, down to three for the five smallest Member States (see table 20.4). The logic seemed to be more than a tripling for the big ones, a doubling for the medium-sized ones and less than a doubling for the smallest ones. The total in EU-27 would come to 330. With a QMV set at 234 votes, representing 70.91% of the votes, such a QMV could be reached by 12 states (less than half), but it would represent a minimum of 61.27% of the population (CONFER 4796/00, annex IV).

On 9 November the French Presidency also produced a new note on the size and composition of the Commission. The note suggested a discussion of four questions:

(1) the conditions for and timing of any changeover to a Commission consisting of one national from each Member State;

(3) the conditions for and timing of any changeover to a Commission with an upper limit;

(4) the principle and practical details of egalitarian rotation in the case of a Commission with an upper limit;
(5) the organisation of the college.

An annex suggested a new treaty article increasing the powers of the President of the Commission (CONFER 4797/00).

Table 20.3: 'Simple' Dual Majority (Commission Proposal).

Members of Council	Weighting A	Weighting B
Germany	1	170
United Kingdom	1	123
France	1	122
Italy	1	120
Spain	1	83
Poland	1	80
Romania	1	47
Netherlands	1	33
Greece	1	22
Czech Republic	1	21
Belgium	1	21
Hungary	1	21
Portugal	1	21
Sweden	1	18
Bulgaria	1	17
Austria	1	17
Slovakia	1	11
Denmark	1	11
Finland	1	11
Ireland	1	8
Lithuania	1	8
Latvia	1	5
Slovenia	1	4
Estonia	1	3
Cyprus	1	2
Luxembourg	1	1
Malta	1	1
Total EU 27	27	1000

Determining a qualified majority

	Minimum number (and %) of Member States		Weighting B	Minimum % of population
Qualified Majority	14 (51.85%)	*AND*	501	50.10%
Blocking minority	14 (51.85%)	*OR*	500	11.62%

Source: CONFER 4796/00, Annex I.

Table 20.4: 'Substantial' Reweighting (Italian proposal)

Members of Council	Weighted Votes
Germany	33
United Kingdom	33
France	33
Italy	33
Spain	26
Poland	26
Romania	14
Netherlands	10
Greece	10
Czech Republic	10
Belgium	10
Hungary	10
Portugal	10
Sweden	8
Bulgaria	8
Austria	8
Slovakia	6
Denmark	6
Finland	6
Ireland	6
Lithuania	6
Latvia	3
Slovenia	3
Estonia	3
Cyprus	3
Luxembourg	3
Malta	3
Total EU of 27	330

Determining a qualified majority

Total votes = 330	Votes	% votes	Minimum number (and %) of States	Minimum % of population
Qualified majority	234	70.91%	12 (44.44%)	61.27%
Blocking minority	97	29.39%	3 (11.11%)	17.40%

Source: CONFER 4796/00, Annex IV

A week later, on 16 November, the Presidency produced new notes on the Commission and the weighting of votes in the Council for a ministerial conclave on 20 November.

In the note on the Commission the Presidency now claimed: "Following discussions by Heads of State or Government at the informal European Council in Biarritz, a majority of delegations are prepared to consider the possibility of an upper limit on the number of Commission, at a time and subject to conditions which remain to be determined depending in particular on likely developments in the enlargement process." This of course was known as the French preference, but the Presidency duly did add: "Other delegations repeated their position of principle, namely that the Commission should include a national from each Member State" (CONFER 4802/00). The note went on to discuss again the conditions for and timing of the changeover to one Commissioner per Member State and later the conditions for and timing of the changeover to a Commission with an upper limit. In principle the first changeover was linked with enlargement. Should the next come a specific year, such as for instance 2010, or when the EU reached a certain number of members, such as 25 or 27? This note also had an annex on increasing the powers of the President of the Commission.

In the following document on weighting of votes of 16 November, the French Presidency said that although some delegations preferred a dual majority model like the one proposed by the Commission, it had emerged that "a large majority of delegations were prepared to continue discussion on the basis of a simple reweighting model, provided that the system—whatever it might be—still took account of the population and of the number of Member States" (CONFER 4801/00). The document therefore only presented three variants, a 'weak' reweighting coupled with a 'population safety net' of at least 58% of the total population of the Union, a moderate reweighting calculated in such a way that a QMV would comprise close to 58% of the population (a Swedish type B model), and a 'substantial' reweighting which would have the effect of producing a QMV of more than 60% of the population (the Italian proposal).

That the issue largely was one of the large versus the small states could also be read from the document. Many of the larger states favoured something like the Italian proposal. The problem with the Swedish proposals was that they were not compatible with the 'ad hoc' compensation written into the Amsterdam protocol (for the large ones losing a Commissioner). The smaller states wanted only a weak reweighting and several of them objected to the 'population safety net.'

A majority of the delegations did want the criterion requiring that a QMV should include half of the Member States.

In a 'Revised Summary' presented by the French Presidency on 23 November no figures were given for the votes (CONFER 4810/00). It had been prepared for a conclave in Val Duchesse (Brussels) on 25 and 25 November.

Concerning the Commission a final note was submitted by the French Presidency on 1 December. According to this note, "The Representatives' most recent discussions have shown that a majority of delegations are prepared to consider the deferred ceiling solution for the number of members of the Commission." The question then was, should the Nice Treaty set a limit now for a later date or postpone the decision till later through a so-called *rendez-vous* clause (CONFER 4813/00).

The note also discussed the idea of rotation. Two principles were suggested in an annex: "(a) the difference between the total number of terms of office held by nationals of any given pair of Member States may never be more than one, [and] (b) each successive college must be so constituted as to reflect satisfactorily the demographic and geographical range of all the Member States of the Union" (ibid.).

The draft Treaty proposal from the French Presidency on 6 December did not include concrete proposals for the weighting of votes in the Council. Concerning the Commission it proposed to change to a Commission with one Commissioner per Member State on 1 January 2005, and then to decide later what would happen after 2010. It also suggested an increase in the powers of the President of the Commission (CONFER 4816/00). This draft was distributed on the eve of the European Council in Nice. It was becoming amply clear that it was now left for the Heads of State or Government to try to reach a compromise on the difficult questions of the voting arrangements in the Council and the size and composition of the Commission.

The French Presidency put forward its first proposal on weighting of votes in Nice on Saturday 9 December in the morning. The proposal was to triple the number of votes for the Big Four to 30 votes and double the votes for most medium-sized and smaller Member States. Spain would move from eight to 28, more than a tripling (a tripling + 4!). Oddly enough, Poland with nearly the same population size as Spain would get 26. Luxembourg would move from two to three, less than a doubling (see Table 20.5). There was a certain inspiration in the proposal from the Italian proposal, but it was more generous towards Spain and a little less generous towards the Big Four, Germany, United Kingdom, France and Italy. Germany was kept on par with France, something referred to as 'clustering' during the IGC. In the first proposal the Netherlands and Belgium also stayed on par. French European Affairs Minister Pierre Moscovici explained that the logic of the proposal was "not purely demographic" (quoted by Sung, 2000a). In other words, it was political.

The first proposal was strongly criticised by the smaller states. Portugal's Foreign Minister Jaime Gama said that it would "humiliate or confiscate power from the small and medium-sized countries" (quoted from Sung, 2000a). Portugal's Prime Minister Antonio Guterres talked about an "institutional coup d'Etat," and Austrian Chancellor Wolfgang Schüssel said it was an "arbitrary and subjective proposal" (*Agence Europe*, 12 December, 2000). Also Sweden and Denmark, which were not the most outspoken among the small states, criticised it. Sweden's Prime Minister Göran Persson said: "The proposals keep the existing deadlocks. Nothing has changed" (quoted from Porter, 2000). The Danish Prime Minister Poul Nyrup Rasmussen called the proposal unacceptable and said: "There is too much imbalance between the large and the small states. The negotiations are going to be very hard" (quoted from Daley, 2000). But the big ones were not united. German Chancellor Gerhard Schröder criticised the proposal: "This is not the document on which we are going to find agreement" (quoted from Porter, 2000). In the afternoon the proposal was taken off the table and the Presidency started producing a new one.

A second proposal was presented on Sunday 10 December in the morning. Most small and medium-sized members would get an additional vote in this proposal, but the Netherlands would get two extra votes, thus creating a differentiation between Belgium and the Netherlands, while France and Germany stayed on par. Poland now moved up to the level of Spain, but strangely Lithuania was moved one vote down. Some of the smallest members got an extra vote, some did not. This proposal wasn't accepted either by the medium-sized and smaller members. Belgium was unhappy about the Netherlands moving ahead. Portugal still felt that Spain's voting weight was increased too much relative to Portugal's number of votes. Germany failed to get extra votes, but was now promised a new IGC in 2004 (James, 2000). A second population mechanism was also brought into play. A QMV should represent 62% of the population. This would allow Germany with two other large Member States to bloc a decision. Germany would also retain its 99 seats in the European Parliament, while other Member States would have to accept reductions. One observer referred to the emerging system as "a new system of Byzantine complexity that left Germany as first among equals" (Hughes, 2000).

The second proposal did not solve the problems which the smaller states saw. According to *The Guardian*: "In the most naked and bitterly contested of the power plays at the Nice summit, a crucial vote re-weighting deal stalled shortly before midnight after hours of furious haggling. President Jacques Chirac, the summit chairman, suspended the talks after Portugal, Finland and Belgium led a revolt of small countries angry at what they saw as a coup by the Big Four" (Black, 2000). Another report also mentions Austria, Greece and Sweden as members of a group of six smaller states strongly criticising the Presidency proposal (Sung, 2000b).

Table 20.5: Presidency proposals for voting weights in the Council and the final result.

	9 December Presidency proposal (SN 511)	10 December Presidency proposal (SN 522)	10 December Finnish proposal	11 December agreement (SN 533, Draft Treaty 12 December)
Germany	30	30	29	29
United Kingdom	30	30	29	29
France	30	30	29	29
Italy	30	30	29	29
Spain	28	28	27	27
Poland	26	28	27	27
Romania	12	13	15	14
Netherlands	10	12	14	13
Greece	10	11	12	12
Czech Republic	10	11	12	12
Belgium	10	11	12	12
Hungary	10	11	12	12
Portugal	10	11	12	12
Sweden	8	9	11	10
Bulgaria	8	9	11	10
Austria	8	9	11	10
Slovakia	6	7	8	7
Denmark	6	7	8	7
Finland	6	7	8	7
Ireland	6	7	7	7
Lithuania	6	5	7	7
Latvia	4	4	5	4
Slovenia	4	4	5	4
Estonia	4	4	5	4
Cyprus	3	4	4	4
Luxembourg	3	4	4	4
Malta	3	3	4	3
Total	321	339	357	345

Sources: SN 511, SN 522 and SN 533. Finnish proposal according to *Agence Europe,* No. 7860, 12 December. According to *Agence Europe* there was also a Portuguese proposal on 10 December. The final figures can also be found in the Treaty as published in OJ C 80 (10.03.2001).

Table 20.6: Council Votes in EU-27 (as of 1 January 2005 and onward) according to the Treaty of Nice

	Present votes	Future Votes	Population (mio.)	% of Union population
Germany	10	29	82,03	17.05
United Kingdom	10	29	59,25	12.31
France	10	29	58,97	12.25
Italy	10	29	57,61	11.97
Spain	8	27	39,39	8.19
Poland		27	38,67	8.04
Romania		14	22,49	4.67
Netherlands	5	13	15,76	3.28
Greece	5	12	10,53	2.19
Czech Republic		12	10,29	2.14
Belgium	5	12	10,21	2.12
Hungary		12	10,09	2.10
Portugal	5	12	9,98	2.07
Sweden	4	10	8,85	1.84
Bulgaria		10	8,23	1.71
Austria	4	10	8,08	1.68
Slovakia		7	5,39	1.12
Denmark	3	7	5,31	1.10
Finland	3	7	5,16	1.07
Ireland	3	7	3,74	0.78
Lithuania		7	3,70	0.77
Latvia		4	2,44	0.51
Slovenia		4	1,98	0.41
Estonia		4	1,45	0.30
Cyprus		4	0,75	0.16
Luxembourg	2	4	0,43	0.09
Malta		3	0,38	0.08
Total EU 27	87	345	481,18	100
Qualified majority of votes	62	258/255* (as well as a majority of members proposed by Commission, otherwise two-thirds of members)		Furthermore at least 62% of the Union population if a member state asks for control of this criterion
Blocking minority	26	88/91*		

Sources: Treaty texts and European Parliament, "Draft Treaty of Nice (initial analysis)," Brussels, 10 January 2001. Galloway, 2001, p. 88. The final version of the Nice Treaty was published in the *Official Journal of the European Communities* C 80, 10 March 2001.
* On the confusion about qualified majority and blocking minority, see the text of this chapter (see also *Agence Europe*, 23 December 2000; and Best, 2001).

Portugal's State Secretary for European Affairs, Francisco Seixas da Costa, said: "The Portuguese delegation has told the French presidency very clearly that the moment of truth has arrived. Without a change in the position of the presidency, an agreement cannot be reached" (quoted from Black, 2000).[3]

Saturday evening Finland made a proposal, limiting the votes of the Big Four to 29 and giving 27 to Spain and Poland. Slight increases were proposed for most smaller or medium-sized members (*Agence Europe*, 12 December, 2000).

After midnight the Presidency offered the medium-sized members one additional vote and reduced the large Member States' votes by one. Most of the smaller states accepted this proposal, but Belgium kept objecting. As a compensation Belgium was then offered 22 seats in the European Parliament instead of the 20 so far on offer. The argument in favour of such a solution was that Belgium was bilingual. But in order not to decouple Portugal and Greece from Belgium they too were offered 22 seats in the European Parliament. The Czech Republic and Hungary, not present at the IGC meeting of the Heads of State or Government, but with a similar size of population as Belgium stayed at 20 (*Agence Europe,* 12 December, 2000, and *Agence Europe*, 23 December 2000). Belgium was offered another 'sweetener': Gradually all meetings of the European Council would take place in Belgium (Sung, 2000b).

In the end the Belgians, too, gave in to the pressure. At 4:20 Monday morning an agreement was announced. The Belgian Prime Minister, Guy Verhofstadt, told the press that he had fought as hard as possible "for Europe, for smaller and medium-sized countries." He also said that the final deal was acceptable because the three Benelux countries would get 29 votes, the same number as the Big Four (Sung, 2000b).

The French Prime Minister, Lionel Jospin, made a point of "praising the efforts of Belgian Prime Minister, Mr. Verhofstadt, who, at the last moment, allowed an agreement among fourteen to become a complete agreement." Finland's Prime Minister, Paavo Lipponen, who said that "We will have to redo this treaty in the future," added, "Guy Verhofstadt is the hero of the evening. He fought as a true European" (*Agence Europe*, 12 December 2000).

If there is any logic in the figures, it is a political logic. The French Presidency tried to group the Member States in clusters of states. By maintaining that the four large ones should have the same number of votes France would

[3] According to *Agence Europe*, No. 7869, 12 December 2000, Portugal also put forward a proposal, but a full list of the proposed votes was not given.

remain on par with Germany. But the logic of clusters was not implemented consistently.

All kind of linkages and bargaining exchanges were brought into the negotiations. Portugal felt that Spain was treated too generously. And the treatment of the Netherlands upset the Belgians. Some of the countries that were upset got extra seats in the European Parliament, and Belgium was promised that future summits would take place in Brussels. Further, the decision that the Commission President in the future should be appointed by a qualified majority was also seen as a *cadeau* to Belgium, whose candidate Jean-Luc Dehaene had been vetoed when Jacques Santer got the job back in 1995 after Jacques Delors. Germany was mainly 'bought' by the stipulation that a QMV must also represent 62% of the population in the EU. Germany also got what some observers considered a relatively good solution for the European Parliament (Germany retaining 99 seats, while the three other large countries, France, UK and Italy, had to accept a reduction of 15 seats, from 87 to 72) (*Le Point*, 2000). The German proposal to have another IGC in 2004 was also accepted (*Les Echos*, 2000).

The re-weighting of votes in the Council that was agreed after prolonged negotiations can be seen in table 20.6, which also includes population figures.

Afterwards it turned out that there were some inconsistencies in the Treaty. For EU-15, the treaty had the weights in a protocol. The weights for EU-27 were in a declaration. In EU-15 there would be a total of 237 votes after entry into force of the new weights, if there had not been an enlargement by then. In the version of the treaty that appeared on 12 December, the QMV was set at 170 votes in such EU-15. In the context of enlargement there was, however, also a declaration on the qualified majority threshold and the number of votes for a blocking minority which said:

> "On 1 January 2005, when the new vote weightings take effect and insofar as all the candidate countries ... have not yet acceded to the Union, the percentage of votes constituting a qualified majority will be lower than the current percentage. The applicable percentage will increase until it reaches a maximum of 73.4%. When all the candidate countries ... have acceded, the blocking minority will rise from 88 to 91 votes" (SN 533/00).

During the end game Belgium succeeded getting two extra votes for Lithuania and one extra for Romania. This took the total in EU-27 from 342 votes to 345 votes. The figures in the quoted declaration had been based on an EU-27 with a total of 342 votes, and this was not changed. With a blocking minority of 91 out of 345, the QMV will be 255 votes, which corresponds to 73.9% (*Europolitique*, 20 December 2000).

After some intense negotiations in COREPER the figure for the QMV in EU-15 was changed from 170 to 169, corresponding to an increase of the blocking minority from 68 to 69. Especially Spain was against this change, since it would reduce its possibilities of blocking a decision in EU-15. With 68 votes Spain could form a blocking minority with one large and one small state, such as Italy and Greece for example. With 69 it would need a fourth coalition partner (Bocev, 2000)

But the final version of the treaty kept the QMV of 258 (out of a total of 345 votes) in EU-27, and the declaration underwent a subtle change:

> Insofar as all the candidate countries … have not yet acceded to the Union when the new vote weightings take effect (1 January 2005), the threshold for a qualified majority will move, according to the pace of accessions, from a percentage below the current one to a maximum of 73.4%. When all the candidate countries … have acceded, the blocking minority, in a Union of 27, will be raised to 91 votes, and the qualified majority threshold resulting from the table given in the Declaration on enlargement of the European Union will be automatically adjusted accordingly (SN 1247/01).

Interpretation: 73.4% would apply in say EU-25, but the blocking minority of 91 would apply in EU-27. In EU-27 the 73.4% level would actually require a blocking minority of 93 votes. But the French Presidency proposed to stick to 91 votes for the blocking minority in EU-27. Again, especially Spain was unhappy about this (Zecchini, 2000).[4]

Less controversial was that the Treaty of Nice also assigned a new number of seats in the European Parliament (see table 20.7). Here a differentiation between Germany and France had existed since a mini-reform in 1993. In the future Germany would retain its 99 seats, but the other Member States would have to accept reductions in their representation, except Luxembourg, which would retain six seats. But as mentioned Belgium, Portugal and Greece were offered two extra seats in the end game in Nice as bargaining exchanges for accepting the weighting of votes in the Council.

Concerning the issue of size and composition of the Commission, the Treaty of Nice only found a partial solution. From 1 January 2005 “the Commission shall include one national of each of the Member States.” When “the EU consists of 27 Member States”:

> The number of Members of the Commission shall be less than the number of Member States. The Members of the Commission shall be chosen according to a rotation system based on the principle of equality, the implementing arrangements for which shall be adopted by the Council acting unanimously” (SN 1247/01, p. 96).

---

[4] To follow up on this story, the Brussels summit in October 2002, when it was becoming clear that 10 of the candidate countries would accede to the EU on 1 May 2004, decided that in EU-25, with a total of 321 votes, a QMV would be 232 votes, i.e. 72.27%. The old weights would apply until 1 November 2004. In the interim period there would be 124 votes in total, with the QMV set at 88, i.e. 70.96% (*Tomorrow Europe*, February 2004, p. 10).

Table 20.7: Seats in the European Parliament (EU-27)

	Population (mio.)	Population as % of EU	Seats per Member State under the present system	Seats per Member State under the Treaty of Nice	Reduction in numbers	Reduction in %	Number of inhabitants per seat
Germany	82,04	17,05	99	*99*	0	0	828.667
United Kingdom	59,25	12,31	87	*72*	15	17,24	822.875
France	58,97	12,25	87	*72*	15	17,24	818.972
Italy	57,61	11,97	87	*72*	15	17,24	800.167
Spain	39,39	8,19	64	*50*	14	21,88	787.880
Poland	38,66	8,04		*50*			773.340
Romania	22,49	4,67		*33*			681.485
Netherlands	15,76	3,28	31	*25*	6	19,35	630.400
Greece	10,53	2,19	25	*22*	3	12	478.773
Czech Republic	10,29	2,14		*20*			514.500
Belgium	10,21	2,12	25	*22*	3	12	464.227
Hungary	10,09	2,1		*20*			504.600
Portugal	9,98	2,07	25	*22*	3	12	453.636
Sweden	8,85	1,84	22	*18*	4	18,18	491.889
Bulgaria	8,23	1,71		*17*			484.118
Austria	8,08	1,68	21	*17*	4	19,05	475.412
Slovakia	5,39	1,12		*13*			414.846
Denmark	5,31	1,1	16	*13*	3	18,75	408.692
Finland	5,16	1,07	16	*13*	3	18,75	396.923
Ireland	3,74	0,78	15	*12*	3	20	312.000
Lithuania	3,70	0,77		*12*			308.417
Latvia	2,44	0,51		*8*			304.875
Slovenia	1,98	0,41		*7*			282.571
Estonia	1,45	0,3		*6*			241.000
Cyprus	0,75	0,16		*6*			125.333
Luxembourg	0,43	0,09	6	*6*	0	0	71.500
Malta	0,38	0,08		*5*			75.800
Total EU 27	481,18	100		*732*			657.351

Source: European Parliament, 'Draft Treaty of Nice (initial analysis),' Brussels, 10 January 2001.

The number of members as well as the implementing arrangements for the rotation system should also be set by the Council acting unanimously. But two principles were laid out for the arrangements:

(a) Member States shall be treated on a strictly equal footing as regards determination of the sequence of, and the time spent by, their nationals as Members of the Commission; consequently, the difference between the total number of terms of office held by nationals of any given pair of Member States may never be more than one;

(b) Subject to point (a), each successive college shall be so composed as to reflect satisfactorily the demographic and geographical range of all the Member States of the Union (SN 1247/01, p. 97).

The changes "shall apply as from the date on which the first Commission following the date of accession of the twenty-seventh Member State of the Union takes up its duties."

Nice also strengthened the role of the President of the Commission. In the future the President may decide the internal organisation of the Commission and reallocate responsibilities among the Commissioners during the Commission's term of office. The President may also call on a member of the Commission to resign after obtaining the collective approval of the Commission.

Afterwards Peter Norman in *Financial Times* called Nice 'a horse-trading marathon.' It was, he said, 'a power play in which the five big members were determined to secure more clout" (Norman, 2000). Suzanne Daley in *New York Times* commented: "the leaders of the 15 countries which gathered in this Riviera city seemed unable to lift their heads above their own national political agendas" (Daley, 2000b).

Many of the leaders were disappointed. They left Nice feeling that next time it had to be done in a different way. British Prime Minister Tony Blair said: "…as far as Europe is concerned, we can't do business like this in the future. How we take these decisions has to be part of the agenda for the future" (quoted from Rafferty, 2000).

Many observers criticised the French Presidency for the confusion at the end of the negotiations in Nice. Peter Ludlow said:

> Prime responsibility for the disorderly proceedings, however, undoubtedly lay with Chirac. His misjudgements included: fixation with formal parity between Germany and the other three large states; the decision to give the Spaniards everything they wanted before the negotiations started, thereby destroying any rational basis for the reallocation of votes and skewing the arithmetic at every subsequent point in the proceedings; a serious underestimation of the determination of the small states to safeguard their position; and above all the apparent desire to be all things to all men (Ludlow, 2001).

Maybe one of the wisest remarks came from Luxembourg's Prime Minister Jean-Claude Juncker who said: "I think we are going to scale down our ambitions and then, in the great European tradition, call it a success" (quoted from Hughes, 2000).

BIBLIOGRAPHY

Agence Europe: *Europe Daily Bulletins* (Brussels), various dates.
Best, Edward (2001), "The Treaty of Nice: Not Beautiful but It'll Do," *Eipascope*, No. 1, pp. 2-9.
Black, Ian (2000), "Nice summit: Reweighting: Europe's big four pull rank on minnows: EU giants fight for voting dominance in bitter dispute," *Guardian*, December 11.
Bocev, Pierre (2000), "Les Quinze sont parvenus á un accord; Le traité de Nice enfin finalisé," *Le Figaro*, December 23.
CONFER 4727/00: Note from the Presidency. IGC 2000: The Commission, 24 March 2000.
—— 4728/00: Presidency Note. IGC 2000: Weighting of votes in the Council, 24 March 2000.
—— 4744/00: Note from the Presidency. IGC 2000: The Commission, 24 May 2000.
—— 4745/00: Presidency note. CIG 2000: Weightings of votes in the Council, 24 May 2000.
—— 4750/00: Intergovernmental Conference on Institutional Reform. Presidency report to the Feira European Council, 14 June 2000.
—— 4754/00: Presidency note. IGC 2000: Weighting of votes, 3 July 2000.
—— 4757/00: Note. IGC 2000: The Commission, 11 July 2000
—— 4781/00: Note. IGC 2000: Weighting of votes in the Council, 5 October 2000.
—— 4796/00: Working Document. IGC 2000: Weighting of votes in the Council, 9 November 2000.
—— 4797/00: Presidency note. IGC 2000: Size and composition of the Commission, 9 November 2000.
—— 4801/00: Note. IGC 2000: Weighting of votes in the Council, 16 November 2000.
—— 4802/00: Note. IGC 2000: Commission, 16 November 2000.
—— 4813/00: Note. IGC 2000: Size and composition of the Commission.
—— 4816/00: Projet de Traité de Nice. Conférence intergouvernementale sur la réforme institutionnelle, 6 December 2000.
Daley, Suzanne (2000a), "On Rocky Road to Reform, Europe Advances, but Not Far," *New York Times*, December 9.
—— (2000b), "European Union Reform: After 5 Days, a Yawn," *New York Times*, December 12.
European Commission (2000a), "Adapting the Institutions to make a success of enlargement: Commission Opinion in accordance with Article 48 of the Treaty on European Union on the calling of a Conference of Representatives of the Governments of the Member States to amend the Treaties," COM (2000) 34, Brussels 26 January.
—— (2000b), "Conduct of the IGC," http://www.europa.eu.int/comm/archives/igc2000/geninfo/index_en.htm#progress
European Parliament (2000), "Resolution of the European Parliament on the convening of the Intergovernmental Conference," http://www.europarl.eu.int/igc2000/offdoc/pdf/res03022000_en.pdf?redirected=1
——, Commission des Affaires Constitutionelles (2001), "Projet du Traité de Nice (première analyse)," PE 294.737. Bruxelles, 10 January.
European Union (1997), *Consolidated Treaties*. Luxembourg: Office for Official Publications of the European Communities.
—— (2001), *Treaty of Nice*. Luxembourg: Office for Official Publications of the European Communities. Also in *Official Journal* C80 (10.03.2001), Downloadable from http://www.europa.eu.int/eur-lex/en/treaties/index.html
Europolitique (2000), "Conférence Intergouvernementale: Le Coreper va tenter de clarifier le texte provisoire du traité de Nice," December 20.
Galloway, David (2001), *The Treaty of Nice and Beyond: Realities and Illusions of Power in the EU*. Sheffield: Sheffield Academic Press.
Hughes, David (2000), "The final curtain on a French farce," *Daily Mail*, December 11.
James, Barry (2000), "EU Nears Limited Accord Protecting Big Members," *International Herald Tribune*, December 11.

Le Point (2000), "Sommet de Nice; La France rate sa sortie," December 15.

Lemaitre, Philippe and Laurent Zecchini (2000), "Le sommet de Biarritz a été le theatre d'une explication animée entre les Quinze; Les grands pays placent les petits devant leurs résponsabilités," *Le Monde*, October 17.

Les Echos (2000), "Traité de Nice: la France a payé au prix fort la parité avec l'Allemagne," December 12.

Ludlow, Peter (2001), "The Treaty of Nice: Neither Triumph nor Disaster," *ECSA Review*, Vol. 14, No 1 (Spring), pp. 1-4.

Norman, Peter (2000), "Leaders have second thoughts as marathon runs its course," *Financial Times*, December 12.

Plechanovová, Bela (2003), "The Treaty of Nice and the distribution of votes in the Council: voting power consequences for the EU after the oncoming enlargement" European Integration online Papers, Vol. 7, No. 6. http://eiop.or.at/eiop/texte/2003-006.htm

Porter, Andrew (2000), "France puts its national interests before treaty deal," *The Scotsman*, December 10.

Rafferty, Neil (2000), "Blair claims victory for UK after deal is finally done at tetchy Nice summit," *Business a.m.* (Scotland), December 12.

Ross, George (2001), "France's European Tour of Duty, or Caution – One Presidency May Hide Another," *ECSA Review*, Vol. 14, No. 2 (Spring), pp. 4-7.

Smith, Brendan P.G (2002), *Constitution Building in the European Union: The Process of Treaty Reforms*. The Hague: Kluwer Law International.

SN 511/00: "Meeting Document. Subject: Elements for an overall agreement," Nice, 9 December 2000. Kindly provided by the Danish Foreign Ministry.

—— 514/00: "Mødedokument. Vedr.: Elementer til en samlet aftale," Nice, 9. december 2000. Kindly provided by the Danish Foreign Ministry.

—— 521/00: Konferencen mellem repræsentanterne for medlemsstaternes regeringer, "Arbejdsdokument Vedr.: RK 2000 – Formandskabets endelige kompromisforslag," Nice, 10. december 2000. Kindly provided by the Danish Foreign Ministry.

—— 522/00: "Protocol on the Enlargement of the European Union and Declaration on the Enlargement of the European Union to be included in the Final Act of the Conference (This Annex Cancels and Replaces pages 88-96 of CONFER 4816/00)," Nice, 10 December 2000. Kindly provided by the Danish Foreign Ministry.

—— 533/00: Treaty of Nice. Provisional text approved by the Intergovernmental Conference on institutional reform" 12 December 2000, http://www.euoffice.metu.edu.tr/abouteu/nice.pdf

—— 1247/01: "Treaty of Nice. This document contains the text of the Treaty of Nice in its definitive form, as finalized by the Legal/Linguistic Experts Working Party," Brussels, 30 January 2001. http://ue.eu.int/cigdocs/en/cig2000-EN.pdf

Sung, Grace (2000a), "It's each country for itself at EU summit," *Straits Times* (Singapore), December 11.

—— (2000b), "Small EU nations score win," *Straits Times*, December 12.

Tomorrow Europe (2000): "A multi-speed Europe," No. 21 (February).

Usher, John A. (2003), "Assessment of the Treaty of Nice – Goals of Institutional Reform," in Mads Andenas and John Usher (eds.), *The Treaty of Nice and Beyond: Enlargement and Constitutional Reform*. Oxford and Portland: Hart Publishing, pp. 183-206.

Von Weizsäcker, Richard, Jean-Luc Dehaene and David Simon (1999), "The Institutional Implications of Enlargement: Report to the European Commission. Brussels, 18 October. http://www.europa.eu.int/igc2000/repoct99_en.pdf

Westlake, Martin (1999), *The Council of the European Union*. London: John Harper Publishing.

Zecchini, Laurent (2000), "Les Quinze peinent a s'entendre sur l'interprétation du traité de Nice; Imbroglio politico-juridique sur la pondération dcs voix," *Le Monde*, December 23.

CHAPTER 21

QUALIFIED MAJORITY VOTING: A JOINT BUT FAILED SEARCH FOR EFFICIENCY BUILDING

Background to the Nice IGC

This chapter investigates the 2000 Intergovernmental Conference with a specific focus on the Council of Ministers and the IGC's dossier on the Council's modes for decision-making. Acknowledging that supranational influence is contingent upon both the context and actual strategies employed by supranational actors in an IGC (Beach, 2002; Christiansen, 2002), I focus on issues where the Member States' strategic positions were under review. The analysis will investigate the range of opportunities and constraints upon the proposals put on the IGC's table. I argue that the Nice IGC's outcome reflects a trend among Member States who already during the Maastricht reforms started to base their proposals on a non-agreed type measure: If each national interpretation of the EU's task to enhance its capacity to act is used and—more important—inherently accepted by the negotiating partners, any resulting Treaty no longer provides a coherent set of target objectives and criteria for evaluating and re-revising the EU legal constitution (Dinan and Vanhoonacker, 2000, 2001; Galloway, 2001).

The Intergovernmental Conference of 2000 focused almost exclusively on amending the institutional and procedural basics of the European Union in order to prepare it for enlargement by up to 12 new states. Past Intergovernmental Conferences (IGCs) had usually dealt with both substantive policy issues and some institutional issues. At the Nice IGC, the agenda was limited much more to institutional issues. This limiting of the negotiating agenda to a few basic questions regarding the institutional structure of the European Union made it clear from the outset that it would not be as easily possible to combine[1] the negotiations on the allocation of competencies in particular fields of public policy with those on institutional concessions in order to more efficiently 'fulfil' the rules on competencies. As in Maastricht and Amsterdam, loss of power was exchanged for reformed policies.

[1] On the concept of combining substance with institutional issues, with further references see Schumann (2001).

The mandate for negotiations in Nice was based on a two-tier cascade that had been formulated in Protocol No. 7 to the Amsterdam Treaty.[2] It dealt with three related issues, known as the Amsterdam 'leftovers' because the Treaty of Amsterdam in 1997 had failed to solved them. These were (1): the increased use of Qualified Majority Voting (QMV) in the Council, (2) the re-weighting of votes in the Council, and (3) the size and composition of the Commission.

In a declaration attached to this Protocol, the Governments of France, Italy and Belgium expressed the opinion that the Treaty does not correspond to the necessity to achieve essential progress in strengthening the organs of the European Communities, which is required by the mandate for negotiations. Those three countries[3] further made clear that a total revision focused on institutional issues would be "a necessary precondition for the conclusion of the first round of negotiations on enlargement."[4] Consequently, they expressed the opinion "that a considerable extension of the principle of qualified majority voting is an essential element to be considered."

To facilitate consensus among the 15 Member States, the European Council of Cologne, meeting in June 1999, thus decided to focus on a 'small solution' to the issue of 'leftovers' (Lehne, 1999; Kohler-Koch, 2000) of Amsterdam (as outlined in the Protocol and in a related declaration) to be tackled by the Intergovernmental Conference that was to be held by the end of 2000 under a French Council Presidency. According to the mandate that was finally agreed upon in 1999 in Helsinki, the Intergovernmental Conference 2000 was to review "the size and composition of the European Commission, the balancing of vote casting in the Council, the question of a possible extension of qualified majority voting in the Council, as well as further necessary amendments to the Treaty, as and when they appeared in the con-

---

[2] Before admission of the next—16th—Member to the EU, the number of the members of the Commission should have been limited to one person per state, if at the same time the balancing of the casting of votes in the Council of the European Union could have been adjusted (Article 1 of the Protocol). However, a comprehensive revision of the institutional basics of the European Union was planned only one year before the accession of the 21st Member State through a new Intergovernmental Conference (Article 2 of the Protocol).

[3] Originally, the Finnish Government intended to support the declaration as well. In its decision about the Treaty of Amsterdam from 19 November 1996, the European Parliament gave its consent to the declaration of the three countries and demanded to adjust the balancing of votes and the number of the Commissioners before each enlargement, and to limit the fields of application for unanimous decisions to decisions related to the constitutional structure of the EU.

[4] See the evaluation of the results of Amsterdam in *Integration*, 4 (1997) and in *Wirtschaftsdienst*, No. 1997/VII, pp. 375-385.

text of the implementation of the Treaty of Amsterdam or derived from the above-mentioned problems."

STARTING FROM A BROADLY SHARED CONSENSUS ON CHALLENGES AND OPPORTUNITIES

The objective of the Intergovernmental Conference 2000 thus led to a simple question: Should and can the European Union enter the 21st century as some kind of an ad-hoc coalition of organized particular interests or as a structured organization for the representation and execution of 'European Community interests'? The respective debate that was initiated to optimise the institutional and procedural design of the 'EU XXL' was not to be understood as an exaggerated exposure addressed to Brussels: In view of a dynamic community, from which the citizens expect to act with state-like instruments in almost all areas of public life, rules must be determined to provide a unique identity for the EU and its institutional components within the international system (de Schutter, Lebessis and Paterson, 2001). *Joschka Fischer*, in his Berlin-speech, emphasized the areas of conflict that were intensively and controversially discussed as key moving targets in the media and political science (Fischer, 2000; Joerges, Meny and Weiler, 2000).[5]

At first glance, the related question of enlargement was dominated by a concentration on the processes of economic transformation and adjustment, or approximation. Hence, the debate on the needs and options for reform of the distributive policies within the existing framework of the European Communities was closely linked to a hidden debate on the institutional and procedural legal aspects of related reforms, where the question of procedural rules in the fields of finance, budget, and cohesion policies of the EU/EC appear. No doubt, it makes a difference whether the basic regulations on financially intensive promotional programs have to be adopted unanimously, with qualified majority, in 'close cooperation', by co-decison with, assent or consultation of the European Parliament. Closely connected with enlargement questions was the discussion of whether institutional and procedural adjustments are necessary in order to secure or to improve the capacity of the European Union to implement policies in a more democratic, transparent and efficient way.

Finally, in relation to the surrounding international environment, the challenges of the EU have increased rather than decreased. However, with the end of the East-West confrontation, one of the 'legitimating-side-scenes' of the unification of Europe was lost. The scenarios of conflict and threat have

[5] See see as well: *Integration* 3 (2000), pp. 149-197.

been replaced by regional crisis, civil wars or wars of secession on the European continent, as well as in other regions outside Europe, where the EC/EU have contact, at least in terms of trade policy. In addition, the globalisation of the production of goods, services and risks, the oligarchic tendencies in the high technology sector and the world-wide competition of economic areas challenge the capacity of the European Union to act. Therefore, negotiations during the Nice Intergovernmental Conference focused on those parts of the EC/EU Treaty related to social and migration rights of third country citizens as well as the area of foreign trade policy, including securing efficiency of the procedural rules of the Common Foreign and Security Policy, with a specific interest in the Areas of Freedom, Security and Justice as well as the field of Judicial Cooperation in Civil and Criminal Matters and international aspects of European environmental policy.

To go from Where?
Institutional Needs and Options for Reform

The existing structures of the EC/EU of 1999 were still based on the logic of the Rome Treaties of 1957 and its six members, who acted in a relatively limited field of competencies and with wide common or shared interests towards third countries and organizations. Since the Rome treaties, the total number of Treaty articles dealing with specific competencies and decision-making rules—the *enumerative empowerments*—has grown considerably from 86 (EEC Treaty 1957) to 254 (Nice Treaty, 2000). Also, the increasing number of sectoral formats of the Council of Ministers (from four in 1958 to 23 in 1998) (Westlake,1995, pp. 164-167) as well as the extension of its administrative substructure, indicates that governmental actors have become more and more involved in using their Brussels networks extensively and intensively (Wessels, 2000, pp. 195-260).

As for the provisions governing the legal opportunities for the Council's potential efficiency, figure 21.1 shows the absolute proportion of the Council's internal decision making modes between 1952 until 1999. It can clearly be seen that the total number of rules providing for both unanimity and qualified majority voting (QMV) has increased considerably. Moreover, if we focus on the relative rates of the Treaty-based provisions in the Council (Figure 21.2), we also notice an over-proportional growth in QMV voting up to Amsterdam.

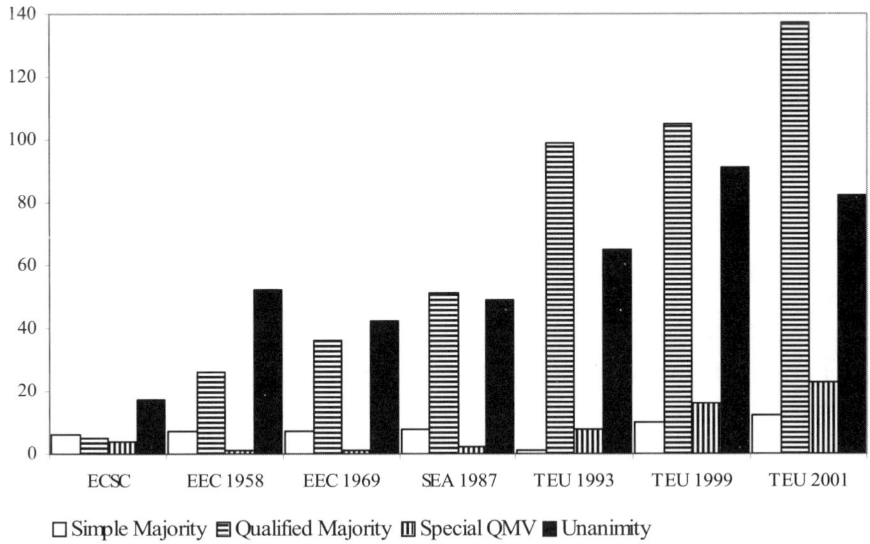

Sources: Original ECSC, EEC, EC and EU Treaties (by date of their entry into force).

Figure 21.1: Decision-making modes in the Council of Ministers 1952-2001 only EC Treaty area) in absolute numbers.

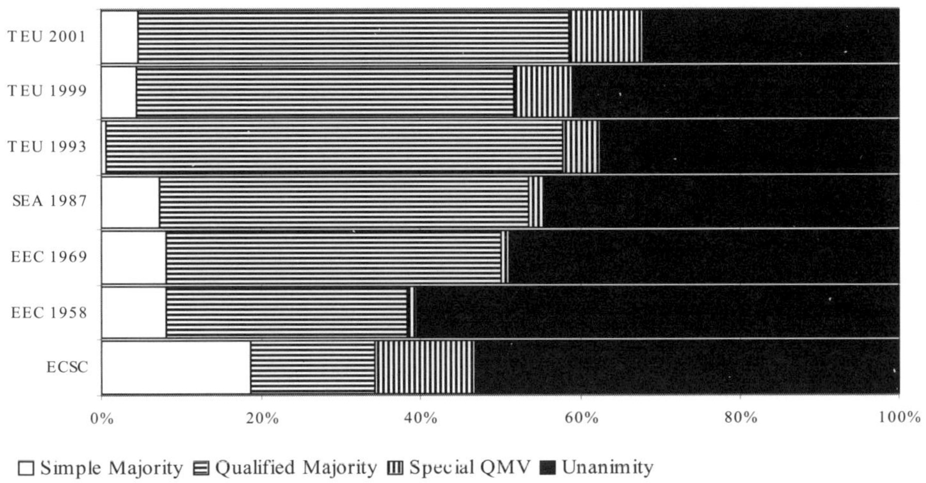

Sources: Original ECSC, EEC, EC and EU Treaties (by date of their entry into force).

Figure 21.2: Decision-making modes in the Council of Ministers 1952-2001 (only EC Treaty area) in per cent.

The Council's evolution is intimately tied to changes in the role of the European Parliament. Since 1979, the European Parliament augmented its role as a watchdog by making intensive use of its right to ask questions, by keeping a closer eye on EU expenditure (through the Committee on Budgetary Control) and by setting up temporary committees of inquiry. Since 1986/87, EC Treaty amendments have introduced important changes concerning the role and position of the European Parliament. On the basis of the positive experiences gained with the co-operation procedure since the entry into force of the SEA (1987), the Maastricht Treaty widened the procedure's scope and also created the so-called co-decision procedure. Herewith, the Parliament obtained the right to block a proposed legislative act without the Council having the right to outvote Parliament at the end of the procedure.

Understanding the slow but constant inclusion of the European Parliament into the EU system necessitates a perspective which departs from orthodox realism. Hence, the co-decision procedure could well be depicted as symptomatic of the 'general trade-off' between the 'problem-solving capacity' (Schimmelpfennig, 1996, p. 19) of EU decision-making on the one hand and parliamentary involvement on the other: "Expanding the legislative [...] powers of the European Parliament could render European decision processes, already too complicated and time-consuming, even more cumbersome" (Scharpf, 1994, p. 220). As for the roles provided by the treaties for the European Parliament, the relative proportion of its 'exclusion' from the EC/EU policy-making process has considerably diminished. However, in view of the absolute increase in Treaty-based decision-making procedures, the growth in consultation, co-operation and co-decision procedures is balanced by a small augmentation of 'non-participation' in the Council's rule-making process. The main reasons for this development are the dynamics of subsequent Treaty reforms widening the functional scope of European integration and co-operation into new areas. Of specific interest in this regard is the combination of both the respective powers of the Parliament and Council, which show a remarkable increase in procedural complexity over time. There is no typical procedure which clearly dominates the political system, e.g. general rules of QMV and co-decision.

Overall, we witness a strong centripetal trend towards 'institutional communitarisation': a push and pull of provisions towards the EC treaties or, within the treaties, towards supranational procedures,[6] or towards EC-like rules within the intergovernmental pillars of the Union[7]—even if it is with

[6] Qualified majority voting instead of unanimity; co-decision instead of co-operation for the EP.

[7] See article 34 TEU on JHA instruments and procedures as amended by the Treaty of Amsterdam.

many derogations, as in the Area of Freedom, Security and Justice (Title IV ECT)(Monar, 1998, pp. 320-335; den Boer and Wallace, 2000, pp. 493-519) and even if there occur, in terms of community orthodoxy, 'dirty' communitarisations (Wessels, 1997, pp. 117-135) and institutional anomalies.[8]

This character of Treaty provisions is reinforced by a specific legal feature: if we take a closer look at the treaties, we can identify a trend towards procedural ambiguity over time. Whereas the original treaties foresaw a restricted (clear) set of rules for each policy field, subsequent Treaty amendments have led to a procedural differentiation with a variety of rule opportunities. As a result, the Treaty provisions do not dictate a clear nomenclature of rules to be applied to specific sectors. Instead, since the SEA, Member States and supranational institutions can, in an increasing number of policy fields, select whether a given piece of secondary legislation—a regulation, a directive or another type of legal act—should be decided by unanimity, simple or qualified majority in the Council; according to the consultation, cooperation or (after Maastricht and Amsterdam) the co-decision procedure; without any participation of the European Parliament or with or without consultation of the Economic and Social Committee, the Committee of the Regions or similar institutions. In other words, different procedural blueprints and inter-institutional codes compete for application and raise the potential for conflict between the actors involved. From a national perspective, this growing variation of institutions and procedures entails a mixed set of opportunity structures for access and participation in the EC/EU policy cycle.

Options for actions that are related to specific institutions and fields of policy and respective opportunities for an efficient creation of policy within the legal community of the EC/EU should have followed all authorizations to act that are explicitly mentioned in the Treaty. The Treaty of Amsterdam, enacted in May 1999, specifically mentions a total of 222 authorizations to act with relevant rules for procedures, [i.e. rules for casting votes within the Council, rules for the functions of the Commission, and the participatory rights of the European Parliament, the Economic and Social Committee, the Committee of the Regions and other committees (Economic and Financial Committee, Occupational Committee, etc.)]. In 105 cases, it was stipulated that the Council may decide with the qualified majority of the weighted votes. However, even following the conclusion of the Treaty of Amsterdam, the Council was still forced to decide on 91 cases unanimously. Not only were cultural policy, the law on migration and the access to independent

[8] 'Institutional anomaly' was the term used by the Portuguese Council Presidency within the framework of the IGC 2000. See: Conference of the Representatives of the Governments of the Member States, Presidency Note on: IGC 2000: Possible extension of qualified majority voting - Articles which could move to qualified majority voting as they stand, *CONFER* 4706/1/00, Brussels, 11 February 2000.

economic activities decided upon unanimously, but also most of the decisions relating to Justice and Home Affairs, Common Foreign and Security Policy as well as the trade policy in the fields of services and protection of intellectual properties. Furthermore, the heads of states and governments constituted the risk of further self-blockades, which could show negative affects in the sense of 'output legitimisation' (Scharpf, 1975; Westle, 1989; Wessels, 1992, pp. 45-47) of the European Community in relation to the citizens, and which could be interpreted and efficiently abused as a structural weakness to act against third states and organizations (for instance in the framework of the WTO).

FIFTEEN TIMES SALADE NIÇOISE MAIN LINES OF THE NEGOTIATIONS ON MAJORITY VOTING

In deference to the rules on unanimity, the possibility of majority decisions reflects the awareness and necessity of the Member States to renounce national sovereignty in related policy fields permanently and to also implement "the adopted legal acts as a defeated minority—possibly against the will of the national parliament's majority—in order to ensure the capacity to act and the efficiency of acting" (Maurer, 1996, p. 32). The experience of an effective usage of qualified majority rules in the Council indicates that the extension of the fields of application for majority decisions does not lead to an increase of decisions on the basis of such procedure (Maurer and Wessels, 2003). In fact, majority decision-making functions more as a sword of Damocles, sweeping above the Council to increase the probability of decision-making in the 'shadow of voting'(Scharpf, 1997, pp.191-193; Golub, 1999, pp. 733-64).[9] The extension of the fields for application of decision-making by a qualified majority was already made in the last three Intergovernmental Conferences in 1986/1987, 1991/1993 and 1996/1999, and was declared as a goal of the majority of the Member States (Dehousse, 1999; Duff, 1997; MacDonagh, 1998; Petite, 1998). To emphasize this principle as much as possible would be to ensure the capacity to act as an enlarged union, because it could hardly be imagined how 27 states could decide unanimously only on distribution and regulation policies, which due to increasing socio-economic differences and resulting differences in interest, would lead to a tendency towards asymmetric distribution of costs and burden.

[9] On the concept of the majority vote see F. Scharpf (1997) and J Golub (1999).

In order to improve upon the poor outcome of the Treaty of Amsterdam (Jopp, Maurer and Schmuck, 1998, pp. 49-54)[10] the Commission and the German Federal Government referred to an approach which sought to transpose all the competencies of decision-making defined under the Amsterdam Treaty as unanimous decision-making, into decision-making with qualified majority. Exemptions to this rule were agreed upon according to a concrete catalogue of criteria ('rule-exemption-approach'). The principle of unanimity should have been applied under the following circumstances:

- decisions that are subject to ratification by the Member States;
- decisions with constitutional character that do not require an amendment of the Treaty, for example, institutional questions that concern the relative balance of power between the states (e.g. the question of languages, Article 219 EC Treaty), or decisions related to the authorization of the EU bodies to act in particular areas of policy according to Article 308 EC Treaty;
- decisions in the area of taxation and social security not related to the smooth functioning of the internal market;
- decisions related to military policy and defense.

Contrary to this strategy, another approach of organized analysis of particular cases already prevailed under the Finnish Council-presidency of 1999,[11] according to which any proceedings from the Treaty of Amsterdam must be reviewed for areas of decision-making requiring a qualified majority ('case-by-case-approach'). These cases should coincide with the following criteria:

- cases related to the European Internal Market where procedures for decision-making could be converted into decision-making with qualified majority without the need to amend the substantial provisions;
- authorizations for action, which cannot be fully transferred into QMV due to explicit concerns and particular interests of Member States;
- basic principles for actions in the areas of freedom, security and justice that have been incorporated into the EC Treaty;
- rules on assignments and appointments of representatives of particular EU institutions;
- 'institutional anomalies' i.e. rules of the Treaty which are already subject to the procedure of co-decision-making while still subject to the principle of unanimity, which is obligatory for decision-making within the Council.

Following the first sessions of the Intergovernmental Conference, which occurred on the level of personal representatives, the idea of subjecting the

[10] Finally, the Heads of States and Chiefs of Governments agreed in Amsterdam four fields of unanimity which were converted into decision-making with qualified majority.

[11] See Presidency Paper: Efficient Institutions after Enlargement. Options for the Intergovernmental Conference, Helsinki (Dok. No. 13636/99), 7 December 1999, p. 5; as well as in this context the remark of the Portuguese Presidency: Question of a possible extension of casting of votes with a qualified majority.

rules of the Amsterdam Treaty to review in each particular case, according to the above mentioned criteria, led to the identification of 25 areas of policy in which procedures for decision-making should be converted into decision-making with a qualified majority. In addition, by the end of April 2000, the Portuguese Presidency was able to address concrete proposals for the formulation of Articles 93 (fiscal harmonization), 42 (social security), 137 and 144 (social policy), 175 (environmental policy) and a new Article 188 b of the EC Treaty on financial aspects of development/cooperation where aspects relevant to unanimous decision-making were extracted or at least formulated in a more precise manner and were segregated from the rules of qualified decision-making.[12]

However, the approach for negotiations pursued by the Portuguese Presidency in the Council was also characterized by the fact that the criteria for review were heavily oriented toward a balance of interests among the Member States, rather than towards the abstract criteria seeking to secure the internal and external capacity of the Union to act. This capacity was expected to increase in its strategic importance, in view of the envisaged EU enlargement. The multitude of reservations of the Member States to sacrifice 'national sensitivity' options for a veto required the review of the mentioned particular cases.[13] Out of the total 76 EC- and 15 EU-rules of agreement which were subject to unanimity under the Amsterdam Treaty by December 2000, 49 were already made subject to negotiations,[14] and 31 of these under the French Council-presidency.

The negotiations became increasingly tense in November 2000 at the 18th meeting of the Representatives.[15] In the Area of Freedom, Security and Justice the delegates did not raise any principal objections against the move-

---

[12] See Presidency Note: Possible Extension of QMV, *CONFER* 4737/00, from 20 April 2000.

[13] Concerning the reactions of the delegations of the Member States with regard to the proposals of the Portuguese Presidency: *Agence Europe* No. 7710 from 5 May 2000. Opposition - for different reasons - by Member States to the Presidency's suggestions for extension of a qualified majority (especially concerning taxation and structural funds).

[14] See Presidency Note, Extension of decision-making with a qualified majority, *CONFER* 4753/00, 3 July 2000. Thirty-one authorisations to this act were identified for a complete move to decision making with a qualified majority as well as 8 provisions with regard to which decision- making with a majority should be applied only with regard to a few aspects of the respective provisions that provide authorisations to act. The list was extended in August to 43 (*CONFER* 4767/00 from 29 August 2000), in September to 46 (*CONFER* 47790/00 from 14 September 2000 and *CONFER* 4776/99 from 28 September 2000) provisions of the Treaty. The synthesis of the consultations from 1 December 2000 (*CONFER* 4815/2000) contains 49 provisions for transfer into decision making with a qualified majority.

[15] The following assessments refer to oral statements of three permanent representatives and of one state secretary who participated in the Intergovernmental Conference.

ment to majority decisions in respect to Article 65 EC Treaty (Judicial Cooperation in Civil Law Matters) and Article 66 EC Treaty (Cooperation between Government Offices). The representatives of Germany and France explicitly approved this as well. However, with respect to Article 65 of the EC Treaty, Sweden demanded that the section on Family Law be deleted. With respect to both core-articles 62 and 63 of the EC Treaty (policy on visa, external border regulations, internal border regulations, asylum, refugee and immigration policy), France insisted on the principle of unanimity, and the delegates initiated a declaration to the Treaty, which should have expressed that in 2004, under certain circumstances, the Council should move to a decision-making process with qualified majority.

In the field of social policy, during October 2000, a far-reaching approval of the Presidency for Article 137 EC Treaty was discernible, an approval aimed at a partial move to majority decision-making. However, it remained under dispute whether or not to shift to majority decision-making legal acts related to the representation and collective execution of employers and employees relations, because not only Great Britain but also Spain, Portugal, Ireland and Germany voted in favour of keeping the unanimity rule. Additionally, Great Britain and Denmark rejected the introduction of QMV with respect to Article 42 EC Treaty (Social Security in the context of the freedom of movement). Similar to what occurred in the Area of Freedom, Security and Justice, the chosen strategy for negotiations was oriented toward the analysis of a particular case that led to the loss of a coherent approach for reform. By favouring some kind of a 'pick-and-choose' mode, each competency for action indicated in the Treaty had been made subject to review from an add-up of 15 national perspectives.

In the field of tax policy (Article 93 EC Treaty), the British Delegation also declared its principle rejection of every move toward majority decision-making, making it abundantly clear that attempts of the Presidency to revise positions introducing amendments to the texts would be condemned to fail. Luxembourg and Ireland were hidden behind this British blockade, as well as Spain, Portugal and Sweden, all considered 'safe' partners in a coalition with Great Britain. In opposition to this position, Italy, Belgium, France, Finland and Germany, the Commission, as well as the European Parliament (which did not participate in the conference) declared interest in a more ambitious approach.

Particularly under dispute was the revision of the provisions on decision-making in the area of a common trade policy (Article 133 EC Treaty). In November the Commission distributed a proposal for a compromise based on a complete integration of the areas of services, intellectual property and investments with common trade policy and which was based on a decision-making process with a qualified majority. The various positions are outlined in table 21.1.

Table 21.1: Options for amendment of Art. 133 ECT.

Proposal	Support from
• Original proposal of the Commission European Commission (Option 1)	Italy, Belgium, Luxembourg, Finland, the Netherlands, European Parliament
• Proposal of the Commission with a negative list (isolation of areas for unanimous decisions)	European Commission, Italy, the Netherlands, Belgium, Finland, European Parliament
• 'Option 1 with braces' Compromise forwarded by the Commission	European Commission, Ireland, Portugal, Austria, Great Britain and Denmark
• Option 2 of the Presidency (positive list: isolation of areas for qualified majority	Spain, France
• Transition to qualified majority decisions with regard to Art. 133.5 ECT	Germany, Italy, Belgium, Finland
• Paris Proposal (Legal Adviser of the Council) for the protocol with procedural rules for WTO	Great Britain

Limitations were thus proposed concerning both substance and procedures, and it was foreseen that for specific cases, the establishment of a 'security net' would have allowed the Council to amend the mandate for negotiations, upon the initiative of the Commission, on the basis of unanimity. The original proposal of the Commission for a compromise envisioned a complete integration without any exemptions of those three areas into the trade policy, which were already under dispute in Amsterdam and thus withdrawn from the Commission itself, so that delegations of the Member States—freed from the conscience of the 'keeper of the Treaty'—were in a position to address proposals for distribution of institutional and procedural competencies on different levels. One month before the concluding round on the level of the Head of States and Governments, six different basic options were on the negotiating table:[16]

At an advanced stage of negotiations of Art. 133 ECT, the Presidency admitted numerous different options. Thus, France did not respect one of the essential functions of the Presidency in the Council: the accumulation of negotiations towards final options that could be discussed conclusively. Be-

[16] See in this respect *CONFER* 4776/00 from 29 September 2000; *CONFER* 4800/00 from 16 November 2000; with respect to the WTO-expertise the expertise of the legal advisers: SN 2705/00 from 10 May 2000 and SN 4849/00 from 25 October 2000 as well as *CONFER* 4753/00 from 3 July 2000.

cause of this 'organized anarchy' of positions, it was impossible to reach a satisfactory agreement at the final conference. The final proposal forwarded by the Finnish delegation[17] took into consideration the French concerns related to a too-far reaching 'supra-nationalization' of trade policy in the areas under dispute. On the positive side, the provisions in article 133 were extended to "the negotiation and conclusion of agreements relating to trade in services and the commercial aspects of intellectual property." However, there are a number of important exceptions, including trade in cultural and audio-visual services, educational services and social and human health services, and transport. Moreover, the IGC agreed to a blanket restriction on the use of QMV in external negotiations when the latter were concerned with questions for which the EC had not been given competence internally or where unanimity would be required internally. Trade policy on capital investments was thus excluded.

THE EU'S CAPACITY TO ACT 'IN THE SHADOW OF UNCERTAINTY'

The results of the Nice conference finally lead to 31 areas to be transferred into decision-making by a qualified majority after the enforcement of the Treaty. From that, nine provisions concern rules on appointment and approvals of agenda. Additionally, seven authorizations in the Treaty call for the EC/EU to act with respect to decision-making, using a qualified majority under the following conditions: Article 67 EC Treaty on procedures for asylum policy requires that the introduction of majority-decisions and co-decision procedures under framework agreements of the Council be decided earlier with unanimity. In other fields of immigration policy, QMV will be introduced only from 1st of May 2004. In Article 161 of the EC Treaty on structural funds and Article 279 on the EC's own resources, the transitional period will remain in effect until 1st of January 2007[18] and thus, given the decisions for the period 2007-2013 already decided upon at the Berlin European Council in 1999, in fact until 2013.

The quality of an enlarged European Union to act in its surrounding international environment (Maull, 1997, pp. 81-95; Wessels, 2000, p. 575-590) has been improved with the possibility to decide by QMV for the conclusion of agreements concerning trade in services and trade-related aspects of intellectual property (Article 133, Par. 5 EC Treaty) (Péraldi-Leneuf, 2001, pp.

[17] See *CONFER* 4818/00 from 8 December 2000.

[18] See the Memorandum of the Government of the Federal Republic of Germany to the Treaty of Nice: Memorandum to the Treaty of Nice from 26 February 2001, Berlin, 2001.

20-21). On the other hand, international agreements in the area of trade in cultural and audio-visual services, which fall under the area of education as well as under social security and healthcare, are subject to a mixed competence of the Community and its Member States (Article 133, Par. 6, sent. 2 EC Treaty). Consequently, these are further subject to the principle of unanimity. With regard to questions related to trade in intellectual property (patents, copyrights, trademarks) only an opening clause in favour of majority decisions has been stipulated, which requires a unanimous decision by the Council (Article 133, Par. 7 EC Treaty). These provisions are likely to weaken the central position of the European Commission as an international negotiating partner if particular EU Member States take advantage of the exemptions from the majority principle as a consequence of national reservations.

An overview on the extension of the field of an application for majority decisions reveals that Nice perpetuates the continuing trend (since 1958), at least in terms of quantity, of a reduction of unanimity requirements (see Figures 21.1 and 21.2).

At the Amsterdam IGC, numerous competencies for actions were newly established—first of all in the fields of Justice and Home Affairs—where the 'masters of the treaties' established original competencies with decision-making by unanimity. In Nice, a partially successful attempt was made to extend qualified majority decisions step-by-step, against a stronger fragmentation of already existing 'business rules'. Remarkable is the relatively high amount of new majority decisions with regard to appointments. To analyse how much of this is 'empty talk' is irrelevant. The introduction of majority decisions in these areas is to be understood first of all as a door handle for future package deal solutions. Hence, the occupation of the post of a General Secretary of the Council, of the head of EUROPOL, or of members of the Court of Auditors, directly concerns the question of the representation of Member States in EU bodies—staff-related questions are not treated 'by the way' in the Council of the European Union. One may imagine that in a European Union with 27 states, the increasing national staff needs of the EU's newcomers must be off-set against the readiness for compromise in other questions related to specific policy fields.

In the long run, as the Commission will have a larger staff available,[19] the provisions on appointment procedures and internal working structures will be reformed in the EC Treaty. These changes will take effect 1st of January 2005.[20] The question of the indirect legitimisation of the Commission by the

[19] See the extensive contribution of J. Monar in *Integration* 2001, No. 1.

[20] Art. 27 EC Treaty is strengthening the role of the President of the Commission who can decide on the areas of responsibility of the Commissioners, propose the vice-presidents and

European Parliament, which is closely related to the reform of the future working procedures of the Commission, is dealt with in Article 214 of the EC Treaty related to appointment procedures, now amended at the initiative of Belgium. This provision stipulates that the Council may appoint the President with a qualified majority and that the European Parliament is obliged to give its consent. In a second step, the Council, in cooperation with the appointed President, should create a list of candidates for the Commission. For this, again, the consent of the Parliament is necessary, whereby it is likely that the European Parliament will further apply its already twice-conducted procedure of individual candidate hearings. Only after the assent of the European Parliament is granted will the Council appoint the Commission with a qualified majority. These procedural rules are the fundamental breach of the institutional balance between Commission, Council and the European Parliament as a consequence of a 'significant reduction of intergovernmental elements' in one of the key provisions of the EU's multilevel system, which remains oriented toward a dynamic differentiation of institutions and policies (Krekelberg, 2001, pp. 223-229; Ludlow, 2001; Pescatore, 2001, pp. 265; Van Nuffel, 2001, pp. 329-387).

Council Rules and Council Behaviour

Legal provisions on the Council's (and the other institutions' mode of deliberating, negotiating and voting) do not determine actual voting behaviour. Thus, different expectations arise depending on the opportunity structure. The quantitative calculation is quite often criticized as an academic ivory tower exercise which does not take account of the limited number of 'real voting' cases and the different overlapping cleavages within the Council. Countries are not always in the same coalition of outvoted minorities. The prospect that QMV rules might be used is often said to be more important than their day-to-day application: What matters is that they encourage ministers and civil servants to act prudently. We know that about 9 to 10 per cent of all decisions were taken by qualified majorities in recent years, but the risk of blocked decision machinery is not negligible. Moreover, it is methodologically unacceptable to extrapolate past-behavioural trends of the present Union into an unknown future with 27 or even more members.

---

their tasks to the assembly and can appoint them. An introduction of different ranking Commissioners could be envisioned, whereby the Commission, rather than the Member States be responsible for their levels.

Table 21.2: Real voting in the Council, 1985-2000.

Cases	1985	1986	1994	1995	1996	1997	1998	1999	2000
Total Sum of Council Legal Acts	615	731	561	458	429	327	438	332	262
Number of Cases where 'Real Voting' occurred	+/- 70[21]	+/- 100[22]	64[23]	54[24]	45[25]	31[26]	No figures	31[27]	24
Percentage: Number of Cases of Voting/ Council Legal Acts	+/- 11.38	+/- 13.67	11,4	11,84	10,48	9,78	-	9,78	9,16

Source: Andreas Maurer, *Parlamentarische Demokratie in der Europäischen Union. Der Beitrag des Europäischen Parlaments und der nationalen Parlamente* (Baden-Baden, Nomos 2002), p. 81. Data are based on: for row one (Total Sum of Council Legal Acts): CELEX database; for rows two and three, see endnotes.

Scenarios of regional or 'socio-economic' coalitions establishing themselves as permanent blocking minorities seem less implausible than a scenario of flexible majorities along sectoral interests. Given a new kind of power game in a 27-member EU, some of the present members might also be inclined to establish more permanent coalitions. One issue for debate is the potential repercussions of the traumatic bargaining in the Nice IGC: Will the members of the Council build groups according to their size and perhaps create a per-

[21] Source: Answer to Written Question No. 1121/86 by James Elles to the Council of the EC; OJEC, No. C 306/42, 1.12.1986.

[22] Source: Answer to Written Question No. 2126/86 by Nicole Fontaine to the Council of the EC; OJEC, No. C 82/43, 30.3.1987.

[23] Source: Answer to Written Question No. E-1263/96 by James Moorhouse to the Council of the EU; OJEC, No. C 305/71-75, 15.10.1996, and: Answer to Written Question No. E-858/95 by Ulla Sandbaek to the Council; OJEC, No. C 213/22, 17.8.1995.

[24] Source: Commission Européenne (Secrétariat Général): Analyse des décisions adoptées à la majorité qualifiée en 1996, Bruxelles, 14 juillet 1997.

[25] Source: Ibid.

[26] Source: Monthly Summaries of Council Acts, January - December 1999, http://ue.eu.int/en/acts. Data for 1997 and 1998: Antwort des Rates auf die schriftliche Anfrage Nr. E-0917/00 von Christopher Huhne vom 24.3.2000 entnommen, Abl. der EG, Nr. C 26 E, 26 January 2001, p. 131.

[27] Own calculation on the basis of the Monthly Summaries of Council Acts, January-December 1999, http://ue.eu.int/en/acts.

manent cleavage into three groups of small, middle and larger Member States? In this regard, the population clause (Article 205.4 as amended by Article 3 of the Protocol on the Enlargement of the European Union) is also a specific case: Will Germany and/or larger countries apply the population criterion extensively? Even if it is not often used, such an instrument might create 'anticipatory reactions', as is often assumed with the indirect impact of the Luxembourg compromise. In cases where the potential use of this threshold is mooted informally, the Commission might shape its original proposals to accommodate the interests of an emerging blocking minority.

Clearly, the voting modalities do not point to a trend towards more supranational procedures. Intergovernmental reflexes have dominated at Nice, but not so much as to reverse former trends but rather, to limit their further increase. Treaty architects did not develop enough trust in Community institutions and rules to give up a final veto. Instead of accepting the 'veil of ignorance' and honouring their own commitments to the credible institutions, which they themselves had created, veto points remained. In the shadow of an uncertain future, they demonstrated reluctance and a lack of confidence in their own political collectivity.

FAILING COLLECTIVELY?

Overall, the extension of the field of application of decision-making with qualified majority lagged behind the general targeted objectives of all those who participated in the negotiations. As for the complaint that state 'A' or the group of states 'A, B and C' are singly responsible for the poor outcome of the negotiations, such position is not true. In fact, the Intergovernmental Conference was not dominated by conflicts in which solid blocks of proponents for integration and proponents of status quo acted. Rather, the Conference was dominated by the existence of different primary interests that were changing due to the specific policy environment. The concrete experiences and perceptions of policy outcomes in the vast field of the EU's legal order induced a mix of sectoral demands for more QMV or for less weighting. In addition, an evident segmentation of procedural authorizations in the area of trade policy and the Area of Freedom, Security and Justice, reflects two newer trends in the post-Maastricht European Union:

- First, the question of a more or less of 'integration' is no longer on the agenda of the participants of the Intergovernmental Conferences. Instead, competency norms are plucked to pieces so that the negotiators can consider developments of policy and particular cases, which were not predictable during the Intergovernmental Conference;

- Second, the legitimate actors for decisions increasingly assess the evaluation criteria for the institutional optimisation of the European Union as unilateral; a superior target perspective for the capacity of the European Union to act is increasingly rejected in favour of consciously articulated national interests.

As a result, all participants can and do assess the results of IGC negotiations as positive because important partial aspects of their objectives for reforms are considered and analysed according to a non-agreed type measure. The outcome of these 'composed puzzle reforms' such as these, however, looses credibility in view of the citizens, other states and organisations in the long run, when each national interpretation of the capacity to act on behalf of the Union is utilised rather than made subject of dispute, and the Treaty itself no longer provides any coherent target objectives and criteria for evaluation.

The Treaty of Nice was subject to severe criticism. Thus, it is placed in line with the list of institutional reforms conducted since the European Single Act. These agreements were at first blamed as being setbacks, minimal results or otherwise not acceptable. Only in the course of their implementation did the opportunities that these agreements provided to those who participated in the process of decision-making become evident. Consequently, nothing speaks against the assumption that in the future, the reforms of Nice will be evaluated in five or ten years as a positive push for further integration.

Like its predecessor and successors—the Single European Act of 1986, the Amsterdam Treaty of 1997 and the eventual Rome Treaty of 2003/4—the Nice Treaty has to be interpreted as but one 'grand bargain' decision (Moravcsik, 1997, pp. 513-553) among Member States along an uncharted path of European integration and co-operation. In this perspective, the Nice Treaty needs to be seen as a peak within a fluid landscape, moving with regard to time, and in terms of the functional, institutional and geographical dimensions of supranational integration and interstate co-operation and co-ordination. Member States—governments, administrations, parliaments, parties and other 'collective actors' (Haftendorn, 1990, pp. 401-423)—were and still are important, but they are no longer the only players in the game: Member State's preferences provide an input or a 'voice' (Hirschmann, 1970, p. 19; Weiler, 1991, pp. 2403-2483) on the basis of experience gained while traversing the landscape between the 'peaks' of intergovernmental conferences. We should therefore conceive Treaty revisions and amendments as initial 'offers' to actors working within the EU institutions. Placed within this multi-level and multi-actor framework for governance, these revisions create incentives and disincentives to use or to refrain from using Treaty articles; the revisions are legal empowerments that provide the skeleton of a 'living constitution' (Olsen, 2000; Olsen, 1996). Institutions and procedures provide arenas and rules for making binding decisions. Therefore, one could argue that Treaty-building has a significant effect on the subsequent day-to-day output of the EU and thus on the evolution of the system in general. Consequently, one has to consider the evolution of para-constitutional patterns within the integration process over the whole history of the EU. We should therefore expect to identify a post-Nice-implementation phase which will be defined by new decisions to create, amend or re-design the treaties.

Relations between Treaty reform and Treaty implementation are not unidirectional, however. Treaty reforms do not emerge from nowhere as a 'deus ex machina'. Rather, they represent reactions to foregoing developments and trends, reflecting both the complex day-to-day machinery at all relevant levels of policy-making as well as the reaction of socio-political actors who do not or only rarely intervene during the 'implementation' of a given set of treaties. Sometimes, Treaty foundations even simply formalise institutional developments which have occurred within existing Treaty provisions, through inter-institutional agreements, institutional rules of procedure and codes of conduct, or outside of the treaties, through bi- or multilateral agreements between EU members (Christiansen, 1998, pp. 99-121; Christiansen and Jørgensen, 1999). Treaty amendments also attempt to address institutional and procedural weaknesses identified during the implementation of previous adjustments to the rules of the game. Treaty revisions are thus endemic parts of the EU's process; they are not only independent variables affecting the nature and the evolution of the system but also become dependent variables themselves. Institutions and procedures—'formal rules, compliance procedures, and standard operating practices that structure the relationship between individuals in various units of the Polity and economy' (Hall, 1986, p. 19; North, 1990, p. 3; March and Olsen, 1989, p. 167)—are creations and creators at the same time. In this regard, more attention should be made to the way Member States, in negotiating and ratifying Treaty amendments, actually challenge their own politico-administrative systems. As long there is no (need for) unifying different national constitutions and their related interpretation in daily life, the effect of these challenges will continue to vary according to the nature of the political systems in the Member States.

An essential partial result of the Treaty of Nice included the "Declaration on the future of the European Union," according to which already in December 2001, the European Council of Laeken/Brussels adopted the concrete procedure for the preparation of the 2004 Intergovernmental Conference. It should also be mentioned that the voting rights and European Parliament seats fixed in the Protocol on the Enlargement of the European Union will again be proposed as part of the agenda of the post-Nice process, and the results of the Protocol will enter into force in June 2004 (European Parliament) and January 2005 (Council and Commission), respectively. As voting rights and seats in the European Parliament are connected with the readiness to move to majority decisions, it is possible that the next revision of the Treaty will again make the application of unanimity requirements a subject of discussion.

The design of the European Union, construed as a poly-centric (Schmitter, 1996, p. 132) and poly-archic (Pfetsch, 1998, pp. 293-317, pp. 295-301; Milner, 1997; Cohen and Sabel, 1999) multi-level-system, since Nice continues to be confronted with unpredictable needs and latitude for action due to internal and external influences (Maurer, 2000, p. 32.) In this context, the treaties constituting the European Union are, indicators of a constitutionally structured community system that—in respect to its authorizations to act that are sanctioned by primary law, its actual application of competencies, its institutions and its policy area related regulations—has not arrived at a *finalité politique* that is agreed upon by all partners. The Treaty of Nice is—and the outcome of the Convention is likely to be—a further benchmark of an evolutionary and dynamically constituted process of interstate and supranational policy-making.[28] which remains open-ended (Petite, 2000, pp. 887-903). As a vehicle for the further delay or even prevention of the South-East enlargement, the Treaty is definitely not suitable.

[28] The notion 'European Union as a process' goes back to the activities of a working team in the Centre for interdisciplinary Research Bielefeld, which from 1973 until 1980 under leadership of H. von der Groeben and H. Möller published six studies on the 'opportunities and limits of a European Union'. See von der Groeben and Möller 1980.

ANNEX

Articles in which qualified majority voting is or will be introduced

TEU Article 7	Fundamental Rights. A majority of 4/5 of Member States may decide that there is a serious breach by a Member State.
TEU Article 23.2	Appointment of CFSP special representatives.
TEU Articles 24.3 and 4	CFSP/JHA related international agreements, where QMV applies internally.
TEC Article 13	Anti-discrimination measures.
TEC Article 18	Measures facilitating the exercise of the rights of citizens to move and reside within EU territory. Will not apply to passports, identity cards, residence permits or social security provisions.
TEC Article 62.2a	Measures on the crossing of external borders. The Council will decide once agreement on border controls in place.
TEC Article 62.3	Nationals of third countries freedom of travel. QMV as from May 2004
TEC Article 63.1 a,b,c,d	Asylum. Following agreement on common rules and basic principles.
2 a	Refugees and displaced persons. As above.
3 b	Immigration. QMV as from May 2004.
TEC Article 65	Judicial cooperation in civil matters, but excluding aspects relating to family law.
TEC Article 66	Cooperation between national administrations. Possible QMV from May 2004.
TEC Article 67	Council 'will endeavour' to apply QMV and co-decision as soon as possible after May 2004 to other areas of visa, asylum, immigration and other policies related to free movement of persons.
TEC Article 100	Assistance to Member States in economic difficulties or confronted by natural disasters.
TEC Article 111.4	Representation at international level regarding EMU.
TEC Article 123.4	Measures for rapid introduction of Euro.
TEC Article 133	Trade in services.
TEC Article 137	Social provisions.
TEC Article 157	Measures supporting actions by Member States in industrial sphere.
TEC Article 159	Economic and Social Cohesion outside Structural Funds.
TEC Article 161	Reform of Structural and Cohesion Funds after 2007.
TEC Article 181a	Economic, financial and technical cooperation.
TEC Article 190.5	MEPs statute, excluding conditions relating to taxation.
TEC Article 191	Political parties at European level.
TEC Article 207.2	Appointment of Secretary General and Deputy.

TEC Article 210	Salaries, allowances and pensions in Court of First Instance.
TEC Article 214	Appointment of President of Commission and Commission.
TEC Article 215	Replacement of same in event of death or resignation.
TEC Article 223	Approval of Rules of Procedure of European Court of Justice.
TEC Article 224	Approval of Rules of Procedure for Court of First Instance.
TEC Article 225a	Approval of Rules of Procedure for Judicial Panels.
TEC Article 247	Appointment of Court of Auditors.
TEC Article 248	Approval of Rules of Procedure of Court of Auditors.
TEC Article 259.1	Appointment of Economic and Social Committee.
TEC Article 263	Appointment of Committee of Regions.
TEC Article 279	Financial Regulations concerning EU budget from 2007.

BIBLIOGRAPHY

Beach, Derek (2002), Bringing Negotiations Back into the Study of European Integration. Ph.D.-dissertation. Odense: University Press of Southern Denmark.

Christiansen, Thomas (1998), "Bringing Process Back in: The Longue Durée of European Integration," *Journal of European Integration*, No. 1, pp. 99-121.

—— (2002), "The Role of Supranational Actors in EU Treaty Reform," *Journal of European Public Policy,* Vol. 9, No. 1, pp. 33-35.

—— and Knud E. Jørgensen (1999), "The Amsterdam Process: A Structurationist Perspective on EU Reform," *European Integration Online Papers*, Vol. 3, No. 1.

Cohen, J. and C. Sabel (1999), *Directly Deliberative Polyarchy*, unpublished paper, Columbia Law School.

den Boer, Monica and William Wallace (2000), "Justice and Home Affairs. Integration through Incrementalism?," in Helen Wallace and William Wallace (eds.) *Policy-Making in the European Union.* Oxford: Oxford University Press, pp. 493-519.

Dehousse, F. (1999), *Amsterdam – The Making of a Treaty*. London: Kogan Page.

Dinan, Desmond and Sophie Vanhoonacker (2000-2001), "IGC 2000 Watch," *ECSA Review*, Vol. 13, Nos. 2-4, Vol. 14, No. 1.

Duff, A. (1997), *The Treaty of Amsterdam. Text and Commentary*. London: Federal Trust/Sweet and Maxwell.

Fischer, J. (2000), *Vom Staatenverbund zur Föderation – Gedanken über die Finalität der europäischen Integration.* Speech given at Humboldt-Universität, Berlin, 12th of May, Manuscript, pp. 3-5.

Galloway, David (2001), *The Treaty of Nice and Beyond - Realities and Illusions of Power in the EU.* Sheffield: Sheffield University Press.

Golub, J. (1999), "In the Shadow of the Vote?: Decision Making in the European Community," *International Organisation*, Vol. 53, issue 4, pp. 733-64.

Hirschmann, Albert O. (1970), *Exit, Voice and Loyalty: Responses to Decline in Firms, Organisations and States*. Cambridge, Mass.: Harvard University Press.

Haftendorn, Helga (1990), "Zur Theorie außenpolitischer Entscheidungsprozesse," in Volker Rittberger (ed.), *Theorien der Internationalen Beziehungen: Bestandsaufnahme und Forschungsperspektiven.* Opladen: Westdeutscher Verlag, pp. 401-423.

Hall, Peter (1986), *Governing the Economy: The Politics of State Intervention in Britain and France.* Cambridge: Polity Press, p. 19.

Joerges, C., Y. Meny and J. Weiler, eds. (2000), *What Kind of Constitution for What Kind of Polity ? Responses to Joschka Fischer.* Florence: EUI.

Kohler-Koch, B. (2000), "Regieren in der Europäischen Union. Auf der Such nach demokratischer Legitimität," *Aus Politik und Zeitgeschichte*, B 6, pp. 30-38.

Krekelberg, A. (2001), "Der Vertrag von Nizza – Grundlage für mehr Handlungsfähigkeit und Legitimität," *Integration* 2, pp. 223-229.

Lehne, S. (1999), "Institutionenreform 2000," *Integration* 4, pp. 221-230.

Ludlow, P. (2001), *The European Council at Nice: Neither Triumph nor Disaster*, Background Paper, CEPS International Advisory Council. 1-2 February.

MacDonagh, B. (1998), *Original Sin in a Brave New World. An Account of the Negotiation of the Treaty of Amsterdam.* Dublin: Institute of European Affairs.

March, James G. and Johan P. Olsen (1989), *Rediscovering Institutions: The Organisational Basis of Politics*. New York: Free Press, p. 167.

Maull, H. (1997), "Europa als Weltmacht? Perspektive für die gemeinsame Außen- und Sicherheitspolitik," in T. Jäger and M. Piepenschneider (eds.), *Europa 2020, Szenarien politischer Entwicklung.* Opladen: VS Verlag , pp. 81-95.

Maurer, A. (1996), "Reformziel Effizienzsteigerung und Demokratisierung – Die Weiterentwicklung der Entschei-dungsmechanismen," in M. Jopp and O. Schmuck (eds.), *Die Reform der Europäischen Union*. Bonn: Europa Union Verlag p. 32.

— (1998),"Die institutionellen Reformen: Entscheidungseffizienz und Demokratie," in Jopp, Maurer and Schmuck (eds.), *Die Reform der Europäischen Union*. Bonn: Europa Union Verlag, pp. 49-54.

— (2000), "Die institutionelle Ordnung einer größeren Europäischen Union – Optionen zur Wahrung der Handlungsfähigkeit," in Barbara Lippert (ed.), *Osterweiterung der Europäischen Union – die doppelte Reifeprüfung*. Bonn: Europa Union Verlag, p. 32.

— and W. Wessels (2003), "The EU matters: Structuring Self-made Offers and Demands," in W. Wessels, A. Maurer, and J. Mittag (eds.), *Fifteen into One? The European Union and its Member States*, MUP (in press).

Milner, H. (1997), *Interests, Institutions, and Information: Domestic Politics and International Relations*. Princeton: Princeton University Press.

Monar, Jörg (1998), "Justice and Home Affairs in the Treaty of Amsterdam: Reform at the Price of Fragmentation," *European Law Review*, No. 4, pp. 320-335.

Moravcsik, Andrew (1997), "Taking Preferences Seriously: A Liberal Theory of International Politics," International Organisation, No. 4/1997, pp. 513-553.

North, David R. (1990), *Institutions, Institutional Change and Economic Performance*. Cambridge: Cambridge University Press, p. 3.

Olsen, Johan P. (2000), "How does one get there? An institutionalist response to Herr Fischer's vision of a European Federation," *AREN Working Papers* No. 22.

— (1996), "Europeanisation and Nation-State Dynamics," *ARENA Working Paper* No. 3.

Pescatore, Pierre (2001), "Nice – aftermath," *Common Market Law Review*, No. 2, April, pp. 265.

Petite, Michel (2000), "Nice, traité existentiel, non essentiel," *Revue du droit de l'Union européenne*, No. 4, pp. 887-903.

—, M. (1998), "The Treaty of Amsterdam," *Harvard Jean Monnet Chair Working Papers* Series No. 2, http//www.law.Harvard.edu/Programs/Jean-Monnet/papers/98&/98-2.html.

Péraldi-Leneuf, F. (2001), "La réforme de la politique commerciale par le Traité de Nice (article 133): un difficile négoce," *La Gazette du palais*, No. 171-172, (20-21 June), pp. 20-21.

Pfetsch, F. (1998), "Negotiating the European Union: A Negotiation-Network Approach," *International Negotiation*, 3 pp. 293-317, pp. 295-301.

Scharpf, Fritz W. (1975), *Demokratietheorie zwischen Utopie und Anpassung*, Kronberg/Ts.

— (1997), *Games Real Actors Play, Actor-Centred Institutionalism in Policy Research*, Boulder, pp. 191-193.

Scharpf, Fritz W. (1994), "Community and Autonomy: Multi-level Policy-Making in the European Union," *Journal of European Public Policy*, No. 1-2, p. 220.

Schimmelpfennig, Frank (1996), "Legitimate Rule in the European Union. The Academic Debate," *Tübinger Arbeitspapiere zur Internationalen Politik und Friedensforschung*, No. 27, p. 19.

Schmitter, P. (1996), "Imaging the Future of the Euro-Polity with the Help of New Concepts," in G. Marksi, F. Scharpf, P. Schmitter, W. Streek, *Governance in the European Union*. London: Sage.

Schumann, D. (2001), "Die Bedeutung politikfeldübergreifender Koppelgeschäfte für die europäische Energiewirtschaft: Das Beispiel der Liberalisierung des Elektrizitätsinnenmarktes," *Diskussionspapiere* Nr. 01-2. Bochum: Ruhr-Universität.

de Schutter, O., N. Lebessis and J. Paterson, eds. (2001), *Governance in the European Union*, Luxembourg.

van Nuffel, Pieter (2001), "Le traité de Nice: Un Commentaire," *Revue du Droit de l'Union européenne* No. 2, pp. 329-387.

von der Groeben, H. and H. Möller, eds. (1980), *Die Europäische Union als Prozeß*. Baden-Baden: Nomos.

Weiler, Joseph H.H. (1991), "The Transformation of Europe," *The Yale Law Journal*, No. 8, pp. 2403-2483.

Wessels, Wolfgang (1992), Staat und (westeuropäische) Integration. Die Fusionsthese, in M. Kreile (ed.), *Die Integration Europas*, PVS-Sonderheft 23, pp. 45-47.

—— W. (2000), Die Europäische Union als Ordnungsfaktor, in K. Kaiser, H. Schwarz (eds.), *Weltpolitik im neuen Jahrhundert*. Bonn: Nomos, p. 575- 590.

—— (2000), *Die Öffnung des Staates. Modelle und Wirklichkeit grenzüber-chreitender Verwaltungspraxis 1960-1995*. Opladen: Leske and Budrich, pp. 195-260.

Westlake, Martin (1995), *The Council of the European Union*. London: Cartermill.

Westle, B. (1989), *Politische Legitimität - Theorien, Konzepte, empirische Befunde*. Baden-Baden: Nomos.

CHAPTER 22

ENHANCED COOPERATION: LOWERING THE RESTRICTIONS – AND CREATING THE BASIS OF A HARD CORE?

INTRODUCTION

Flexible arrangements have been a part of the European integration process since the 1950s. Transitional periods are examples of the use of flexible arrangements within the EU. These arrangements, however, have been practised outside the treaty framework. The Amsterdam Treaty introduced an institutionalization of flexible integration or closer cooperation.[1] The Treaty allowed for new possibilities to enter into and implement flexible arrangements that would be authorised by the Member States and maintained within the institutional framework of the European Union.

Prior to Amsterdam, ad hoc institutionalization of flexible integration had existed. The Maastricht Treaty involved flexibility arrangements in the case of Britain's self-exclusion from the Social Protocol and in the non-participation of Britain, Denmark and Greece in the EMU, the two first for domestic political reasons and Greece for reasons of non-qualification.[2]

The type of flexible integration introduced from the Maastricht Treaty and afterwards can, in general, be defined as an arrangement where "a subgroup of EU-member states decides to go ahead with further integration in certain areas without committing the non-participating EU-member states to necessarily join the subgroup, even at a later date" (Sutter, 2000, 42). This is a break with the predominant integration philosophy of a Europe of concen-

[1] Various concepts have been used to describe flexible integration: differentiated integration, hard core, variable geometry, closer cooperation, enhanced cooperation. This paper employs three such terms: 'flexible integration', 'enhanced cooperation', and 'closer cooperation'. 'Flexible integration' is the broadest term signifying all forms of differentiation. 'Enhanced cooperation' covers the institutionalised flexibility provisions in the Nice Treaty because this phrase is used in the Treaty itself. When referring specifically to the flexibility provisions in the Amsterdam Treaty "closer cooperation" will be used because that is the phrase used in the Amsterdam Treaty.

[2] Greece did not participate in the initial phase of the EMU due to lack of fulfilment of the qualifying economic standards. However, it was decided to bring Greece into the 'euro-zone' on January 1, 2001, one full year before the currency was introduced, because Greece succeeded in meeting all the Maastricht Treaty economic criteria. When Sweden joined the EU in 1995, it elected to stand outside the euro, but has no formal opt-out.

tric circles, meaning that some countries might move ahead but the others will catch up sooner or later.

At the 2000 IGC, the issue of flexible integration was linked to the larger issue of how to reshape the institutional framework and how to resolve the so-called 'Amsterdam left-overs'. The framework had to be updated and to obtain the institutional capacity needed to ensure a successful implementation of the Eastern enlargement of the European Union. A central concern raised in connection with the enlargement was that of the compatibility of deepening and widening. Would it be possible to pursue both, and was enhanced cooperation one of the proper tools for this?

This chapter focuses on the changes in the flexibility provisions introduced with the Nice Treaty. It first provides an analysis of the agenda setting stage and the negotiation process of enhanced cooperation in the IGC 2000. Second, it presents and examines the flexibility provisions institutionalised in the Nice Treaty. Third, the chapter evaluates the applicability of liberal intergovernmentalism. Finally, it discusses the impact that the institutionalization of flexible integration might have on the process of European integration.

Setting the Agenda of the 2000 IGC

The Feira European Council, held in June 2000, put flexibility on the agenda by stating that "the provisions on closer cooperation introduced in the Treaty of Amsterdam should form part of the Conference's future work while respecting the need for coherence and solidarity in an enlarged Union" (European Council 2000a). Prior to this decision to incorporate flexibility in the agenda, arguments had been made both for and against discussing the flexibility mechanisms on the IGC 2000.

The Surfacing of Flexible Integration on the 2000 IGC

The Finnish Presidency

In December 1999, the Finnish Presidency had chosen not to include the issue in its proposal to an agenda for the IGC 2000. The conclusion of the Finnish Presidency was: "In the consultations, a clear preference emerged for not including this issue [enhanced cooperation] on the IGC agenda" (European Council 1999). This was despite the fact that the Commission, in a report published two months earlier, had pushed for the inclusion of flexibility.[3] However, at this point the Member States did not focus on the issue and did not wish to enlarge the agenda. Only four Member States, the three Benelux countries and Italy, wanted flexibility on the agenda during the Finnish Presidency (Stubb 2002, 151). At this stage neither France nor Germany was pushing for the inclusion of flexible integration in the IGC 2000 agenda.

Even though there was no basis among the Member States for including enhanced cooperation on the agenda during the Finnish presidency, there was agreement on keeping the agenda open. The Portuguese Presidency was given the opportunity to "propose additional issues to be taken on the agenda of the Conference" (European Council 1999).

The Portuguese Presidency

During the first few months of the Portuguese Presidency, in the first half of 2000, the flexibility debate picked up speed. At this point the European Parliament in line with the Commission pushed for including flexibility on the IGC 2000 agenda (European Parliament, 23 February 2000) and a number of position papers were presented by some of the Member States in which they explained their attitudes towards enhanced cooperation. Italy, Belgium, Luxembourg and the Netherlands still argued for an inclusion, whereas the United Kingdom, Finland and Greece were opposed. Finland and the United Kingdom argued that the existing articles on flexibility were not yet operating and, therefore, there was no reason to make changes at this point (CONFER 4718/00; CONFER 4723/00). Greece saw the inclusion of enhanced cooperation as a problematic signal to send to the coming Member States because they might be hesitant about standing outside important parts of the cooperation and thereby not participating fully in the Community (CONFER 4719/00). Another reason for Greek reluctance may be the past experience of being excluded from participation in the initial phase of the EMU.

At the informal meeting on 14 April 2000 in Sintra, which was devoted to the subject of enhanced cooperation, Germany and Portugal argued—along with the already announced 'pro-inclusion' countries Italy, Belgium, the Netherlands and Luxembourg—that some or all aspects of flexibility needed

[3] The Commission had set up an advisory group consisting of Richard von Weizäcker, David Simon and Jean-Luc Dehaene to draft a report on the issues to be incorporated in the IGC 2000 agenda. In the report, entitled "The Institutional Implications of Enlargement", flexibility was emphasized as an important issue: "In a larger and more diverse Union, flexibility in the institutional framework is even more important than at present. Enlargement will increase diversity. This does not imply that Member States should be allowed to opt out of any policy they choose: the European Union would not survive if Member States were allowed to pick and choose among obligations of the Union. But it does imply that, in a more heterogeneous aggregate of Member States, some will wish to go further or faster than others."

to be addressed in the IGC (Stubb 2002, 110). By this time Finland had changed its position and also wished for the discussion of the issue at the IGC.

The informal meeting in Sintra helped establish flexibility in the IGC 2000 and the decision to include flexibility rested on a number of reasons. First, the idea of creating an *avant garde* group underlined the need to look into the clauses. German Foreign Minister, Joschka Fischer, proposed in May 2000 the possibility of a smaller group of Member States taking the position of an *avant garde*, which would push ahead integration (Fischer, 12 May 2000). Also French President, Jacques Chirac, called for the creation of a 'pioneer group' which "would blaze the trail, by making use of the new enhanced cooperation procedure defined by the IGC and forging, if necessary, cooperation in spheres not covered by the Treaty, but without ever undermining the Union's coherence and acquis" (Chirac, 27 June 2000). Both politicians talked about the possibility of breaking away from the framework of the existing Treaties if necessary.[4] These speeches intensified the fear of the Commission that cooperation between some integration 'enthusiastic' Member States would be initiated outside the Treaty framework if the provisions for enhanced cooperation were not changed.[5]

Therefore, a central aim of bringing flexibility on the agenda was to give the willing and able Member States the possibility of pursuing further integration within the institutional framework, first and foremost by making some of the Amsterdam flexibility clauses less restrictive.

Second, the enlargement of the European Union underlined the need for new tools for integration and drew attention to the possible difficulties of pursuing both widening and deepening. Would it be possible to pursue both in an enlarged Union? This question was also touched upon by the German Foreign Minister, Joschka Fisher, in his Humboldt speech: "Does the answer to the twin challenge of enlargement and deepening, then, lie in such a differentiation, an enhanced cooperation in some areas?" (Fischer, 12 May 2000).

Third, in the case of the second pillar, the progress of the European Security and Defence Policy (ESDP) created the wish to be able to put the breaks on the militarily non-aligned 'ESDP-sceptic' Member States (Stubb 2002, 107).

---

[4] The speeches by German Foreign Minister, Joschka Fischer, and French President, Jacques Chirac, cannot be taken as official national positions. However, they give a clear indication of the French and German position on including enhanced cooperation on the IGC 2000 agenda.

[5] The position of the Commission on flexibility was, as earlier mentioned, described in the report "The Institutional Implications of Enlargement".

Fourth, the approaches taken from the Member States on flexibility were based on different incentives. However, during the agenda setting stage both the 'euro-enthusiasts' and the 'euro-sceptics' saw a possibility of using enhanced cooperation as a "marketing trick, an issue which all Member States could sell at home as a negotiating victory" (ibid.).

Finally, flexibility was seen as a way to create epoch-making changes and "it gave the IGC 2000 a 'big idea', something that appeared to be more than just a rehash of the institutional 'leftovers'" (Gray and Stubb, 2001, 10).

Table 22.1: Member State positions and the position of the Commission and the European Parliament.

	Finnish Presidency	Beginning of Portuguese Presidency	End of Portuguese Presidency
For the inclusion of enhanced cooperation on the IGC 2000 agenda	Belgium (Stubb, 2002: 151) Italy (ibid.) Luxembourg (ibid.) The Netherlands (ibid.) The Commission (Report of the advisory group)	Belgium (CONFER 4721/00) Italy (CONFER 4717/00) Luxembourg (CONFER 4721/00) The Netherlands (CONFER 4720/00 and 4721/00) Portugal (Stubb, 2002: 151) The Commission (Report of the advisory group) The European Parliament (14094/1999)	Belgium (CONFER 4721/00) Finland (Stubb, 2002: 110) France (ibid.) Germany (ibid.) Italy (CONFER 4717/00) Luxembourg (CONFER 4721/00) The Netherlands (CONFER 4720/00 and 4721/00) Portugal (Stubb, 2002: 151) Spain (ibid.) The Commission (Report of the advisory group) The European Parliament (14094/1999)
Against the inclusion of enhanced cooperation on the IGC 2000 agenda		The United Kingdom (CONFER 4718/00) Finland (CONFER 4723/00) Greece (CONFER 4719/00)	The United Kingdom (CONFER 4718/00) Greece (CONFER 4719/00)

Sources: Stubb (2002) and official documents expressing Member State positions and the position of the Commission and the European Parliament. (Not all Member States gave any indication of their position on flexibility).

Despite, the lack of unity on including flexibility on the agenda and despite the fact that the motivations for doing this might differ, an agreement was reached. The end result of Feira was an inclusion of flexibility: "the provisions on closer cooperation introduced into the Treaty of Amsterdam should also form part of the IGC's work, while respecting the need for coherence and solidarity in an enlarged Union" (CONFER 4750/00). Moreover, flexibility would be adressed within all three pillars. Table 22.2 illustrates Member State positions and the position of the Commission and the European Parliament.

Negotiations on Enhanced Cooperation

The French Presidency made enhanced cooperation one of its main priorities and the issue was on the agenda of most of the formal meetings as well as some of the informal settings.[6]

A central question in the first part of the Presidency was whether enhanced cooperation outside the institutional framework could be allowed. The echoes of the Franco-German threat of creating an *avant garde* or pioneer group were reflected in the French Presidency notes by questions such as: "Can certain types of closer cooperation outside the institutional framework help to achieve the Union's objectives?" (CONFER 4758/00). This threat of some kind of future exclusion became a central motivation for the United Kingdom for engaging in the debate securing an acceptable outcome. This was in spite of the fact that in a joint proposal with Italy, Germany campaigned for a modification of the restrictions on enhanced cooperation to avoid cooperation outside the framework (CONFER 4783/00). The same concern was expressed by Belgium, Luxembourg and The Netherlands in a joint paper (CONFER 4787/00). In October, the United Kingdom and Sweden indicated a tacit approval of flexibility in general (Stubb, 2002, 116).

The Informal Meeting of Biarritz and the End Negotiations

The informal meeting of Biarritz was an important stepping stone on the road to Nice. At the meeting the Member States' four main issues in relation to flexibility were found: decision-making, number of member states required for starting a flexible arrangement, conditions and flexibility within the 2nd pillar (Stubb, 2002, 116).

---

[6] Archives, IGC 2000 (http://europa.eu.int/comm/archives/igc2000/geninfo/index_en.htm).

The issue of decision-making was related to the question of removing the emergency brake (ibid.) and the guarantee that, instead, a flexibility decision could be raised in the European Council. The United Kingdom was especially keen to have this guarantee. In the end, the emergency brake was removed in the first and third pillar.

Austria, Denmark, Finland, Greece, Sweden and the United Kingdom argued for the number of Member States required for starting a flexibility arrangement to remain half of the Member States (ibid.). During the negotiations a shift in preferences occurred and Austria, Finland and Greece changed their position in Biarritz. The generally 'euro-sceptical' countries Denmark, Sweden and the United Kingdom did not change their position until the final stages of the IGC when a clear majority accepted a 'critical mass' below half the member states—also after the enlargement of the European Union.

A number of conditions for flexible arrangements were negotiated the most important being that flexibility: should be used as a last resort, is not a substitute to qualified majority voting, is open to all willing and able Member States, should take place within the institutional framework and respect the *acquis* (CONFER 4786/00; 4798/00).

Flexibility within the 2nd pillar turned out to be the most difficult one. The difficulties were due to three reasons. First, the Treaty already contained the possibility of constructive abstention. Secondly, a number of Member States argued that the strength of the CFSP was unity. Finally, for domestic reasons Member States such as Denmark, Ireland, Sweden and the United Kingdom had difficulties accepting any changes on the 2nd pillar (Stubb, 2002, 117). In the end the subject was divided into Common Foreign and Security Policy (CFSP) and defence. A majority of the Member States supported flexibility provisions only in relation to the implementation of common positions and joint actions within the CFSP (ibid.). However, the issue was kept open until Nice but no further progress was made (Gray and Stubb, 2001, 17). Enhanced cooperation was one out of a few issues that was almost resolved before the Nice European Council.

THE FLEXIBILITY PROVISIONS IN THE NICE TREATY

The Nice Treaty provides a number of general conditions (Article 43, 43a, 43b, 44, 44a and 45) for all enhanced cooperation by inserting a new Title VII (TEU). These conditions are general enabling clauses and they define the over-arching framework for enhanced cooperation in all three pillars. Formerly, some conditions were spread out in the general conditions and integrated in the flexibility provisions under the 1st and 3rd pillar (Laursen, 2001, 35) and others were introduced for the first time.

The General Enabling Clauses

Some key changes can be seen in the general clauses. First, a new key condition is that a minimum number of eight Member States is required to initiate enhanced cooperation (Article 43(g) TEU). Second, the Amsterdam Treaty had stated that closer cooperation was "not to affect the competences, rights, obligations and interests of the Member States that do not participate therein" (Article 43(f) TEU, Ams. Article K.15). In the Nice Treaty, the word 'interests' was removed because it was not possible legally to define what the word contained (Article 43(h) TEU). Third, it is now stressed explicitly that enhanced cooperation can be allowed only as long as it does not undermine the internal market or the economic and social cohesion (Article 43(e) TEU). In the Amsterdam Treaty it had been stressed that closer cooperation should not put restrictions on intra-Community trade or distort competition (Article 11(e) TEF, Ams. Article 5A). Fourth, a provision saying that enhanced cooperation is not allowed to concern European Union citizenship has been removed, making it possible for a group of Member States to propose flexible solutions within this area if they wish to do so.

Finally, some principles already announced in the Amsterdam Treaty are reiterated such as those stating that enhanced cooperation must be a last resort and the provisions concerning financing.

The 1st Pillar

The most important change within the 1st pillar is the removal of the right of veto. In the Amsterdam Treaty, a Member State could oppose a request for enhanced cooperation, and the case would be referred to the European Council for decision by unanimity. In the Nice Treaty, it is still possible for a member to make a request for enhanced cooperation to be submitted to the European Council. Ultimately, however, the decision is taken by the Council by a qualified majority vote.

Member States seeking to initiate enhanced cooperation within the 1st pillar must make a request to the Commission, which then submits a proposal to the Council. The European Parliament has to be consulted and if the enhanced cooperation initiative lies within the policy areas covered by co-decision, the assent of the European Parliament is required. The Commission will ultimately have to decide if a Member States can join a flexible arrangement.

The 2nd Pillar

Enhanced cooperation in the 2nd pillar is limited to the CFSP, namely the common positions or joint actions, but does not cover defence questions.

The procedure for establishing enhanced cooperation resembles the normal CFSP procedure which "involves a qualified majority vote coupled with the right of veto" (Stubb, 2002, 131). Member States that initiate enhanced cooperation within the 2nd pillar will have to submit a request to the Council. The request will be sent to the Commission, which will render its opinion, and the European Parliament will be informed. The Council will decide by a qualified majority, which is valid only if at least 62 votes are in favour, and cast by at least 10 members (Article 23(2) TEU). In the 2nd pillar, it is still possible to refer a case to the European Council, thus remaining the right to veto.

In a situation where Member States wish to participate in an already existing enhanced cooperation, the Member States will have to address the Council and inform the Commission (Article 27(e) TEU). The Commission will issue an opinion to the Council, and the members of the Council, who already participate in the enhanced cooperation concerned, will decide by qualified majority in accordance with Article 23(2) TEU.

The 3rd Pillar

Also in the 3rd pillar as in the 1st the possibility of vetoing a request for enhanced cooperation by referring the case to the European Council is removed.

Member States wishing to initiate enhanced cooperation in the 3rd pillar have to address the Commission, which may submit a proposal to the Council. If the Commission refuses to submit a proposal, the initiative can be pursued by a group of at least eight Member States. In both scenarios the European Parliament is consulted. The Council will decide by qualified majority.

Member States that wish to join already existing flexible arrangements will have to notify the Council and the Commission. The Commission will give an opinion to the Council and the members of the Council who already participate in the enhanced cooperation, concerned will decide by a qualified majority vote.

Liberal Intergovernmentalism: Enhanced Cooperation in the 2000 IGC

Evaluating the Agenda Setting Stage

The phase covering the Finnish and the Portuguese presidency clearly shows that the national preference formations in relation to enhanced cooperation cannot be expected to be determined prior to entering the IGC 2000 process. Some Member States had no official position on the issue. Some Member States changed their position during this stage. Finally, some Member States showed preference consistency and maintained the same positive position on the inclusion of enhanced cooperation during the process. The latter group, however, consisted only of Belgium, Italy, The Netherlands and Luxembourg.

National Preferences – Not Always 'an Ordered and Weighted Set of Values'

Liberal intergovernmentalism will face some shortcomings when trying to explain this part of the process of the IGC 2000. As assumed within liberal intergovernmentalism there was not a well-defined bargaining space set by national preference formations of the 15 Member States. On the contrary, parts of the preference formation took place during the agenda setting stage. Moreover, at the end when enhanced cooperation was part of the agenda, the positions taken by the Member States on flexibility were based on different incentives. When reading the official position papers of the Member States (CONFER-reference numbers, see Table 22.2) it appears that during the agenda setting process, both the 'euro-enthusiasts' and the 'euro-sceptics' saw enhanced cooperation as a way to address future problems of European integration especially in relation to combining deepening with the already initiated geographic widening. This also makes it difficult to argue for an assumption of fixed preferences, because in such a situation the preference formation cannot be expected to be based on the same conceptualization and expectation and, therefore, the conceptualizing process and preference formation will be a part of the agenda setting.

In the case of enhanced cooperation, national preference formation and agenda setting were intertwined in a number of member states and, therefore, national preferences cannot always be expected to be "an ordered and weighted set of values" (Moravcsik, 1998, 24).

The national preference formation, the first stage of Moravcsik's analytical model, can be strengthened by introducing an agenda setting stage and by incorporating that: "EU negotiations do not take place in an environment characterised by almost perfect knowledge, but in an environment where uncertainty is the defining factor" (Friis, 1998, 59). The idea underlying this 'uncertainty assumption' is that "EU is an ongoing negotiation game" and that Member States are not only confronted by the shadow of the past in the form of old package deals which affect the present negotiations – but also the shadow of the present and the future (Friis, 1998, 60). The shadow of the present refers to the fact that Member States are engaged in several negotiations simultaneously and the shadow of the future relates to the forthcoming negotiations (ibid.). This notion of the process is also supported by Stubb, who describes an IGC negotiation as "an incremental learning process where the basic positions of the member governments illustrate[d] some continuity, but the specific positions of the negotiators fluctuate[d] with the dynamics of the negotiations" (Stubb, 2002, 144).

Despite the shortcomings, the first stage of Moravcsik's rationalist framework has some explanatory power, for example in relation to strategic assumptions on issue linkage. A reason for setting enhanced cooperation on the IGC 2000 agenda could be an underlying desire of some Member States for enlarging the agenda because such an enlargement would provide more material for negotiation. Including enhanced cooperation would make issue linkages easier which "may appear most advantageous where countries have highly asymmetrical interests in different issues" (Moravcsik, 1998, 65). This assumption can be taken as an acknowledgement of the fact that parts of the negotiations will be hard to predict and at the same time will link together the agenda setting stage with the stage of interstate bargaining.

Evaluating the End Negotiations and the Outcome on Enhanced Cooperation

Interstate Bargaining

Liberal intergovernmentalism does have explanatory power in relation to interstate bargaining on enhanced cooperation. The negotiations can be described as a coordination game with distributional consequences. Even though it can be difficult to predict what the content of these consequences might be, the negotiations indicate that most Member States feared that part of their future political and power capabilities would be dependent on the decisions made on enhanced cooperation in the Nice Treaty. This was the case both for the 'euro-enthusiasts' and the 'euro-sceptics'. An example was the United Kingdom, being in general a 'euro-sceptic' member, that feared being left behind in the integration process and therefore at a late stage engaged very actively in the negotiations trying to direct the outcome in its preferred direction. The same can be said about Ireland and Sweden who, together with the United Kingdom, blocked further progress in the negotiations on enhanced cooperation in the 2nd pillar. This also stresses the liberal intergovernmentalist assumption that Member States "(...) often dispute the precise nature of policy coordination, its speed and scope (...)" (Moravcsik, 1998, 51).

The agreement of the institutionalization of enhanced cooperation can be said to underline another central argument of Moravcsik's rationalist framework, namely, that the outcome found is preferred by all governments to unilateral or coalition alternatives. None of the governments, not even France or Germany, ended up working for the possibility of making enhanced cooperation outside the Treaty framework. However, enhanced cooperation opens up for future coalition formation within the Treaty framework, which in a theoretical perspective will be a challenge to Moravcsik's model.

Pooling and Delegation of Sovereignty

The institutional choices made in relation to enhanced cooperation involve both pooling and delegation of sovereignty. However, the pooling of sovereignty in the case of enhanced cooperation must be said to be more sophisticated than just to "(...) decide future matters by voting procedures other than unanimity" (Moravcsik, 1998, 67) in other words by qualified majority. Enhanced cooperation in the Nice Treaty does imply more qualified majority by the removal of the emergency brake in the 1st and 3rd pillar but also changes the frames for possible constellation of sovereignty pooling.

The delegation of sovereignty is minimal. The only formal delegation is in the 1st pillar, where the Commission in the end will decide whether a Member State can join an already existing flexible arrangement. Table 22.3 gives an illustration of the institutional choices by explaining the procedures for enhanced cooperation.

Table 22.2: The Procedures for Enhanced Cooperation in the Nice Treaty

	1st pillar	2nd pillar	3rd pillar
Initiating enhanced cooperation	The Commission submits a proposal. The EP is consulted, if the enhanced cooperation lies within the policy areas covered by co-decision, the assent of the EP is required. The Council will decide by a qualified majority vote.	The Commission renders its opinion. The EP is informed. The Council will decide by a qualified majority vote - at least 10 Member States. Possibility of referring a case to the European Council.	The Commission submits a proposal or a group of at least eight Member States submits a proposal. The EP is consulted. The Council will decide by a qualified majority vote.
Joining existing arrangements on enhanced cooperation	The Commission renders its opinion to the Council. The Commission decides.	The Commission renders its opinion to the Council. Qualified majority vote of the Member States already participating in the enhanced cooperation arrangement.	The Commission renders its opinion to the Council. Qualified majority vote of the Member States already participating in the enhanced cooperation arrangement.

Source: Based on Laursen 2001, 38.

Enhanced Cooperation – What will the Future Bring?

Simplified, the discussion of the expected consequences of the institutionalization of flexible integration can be described as taking place on a continuum with two poles. The one pole fears flexible integration to result in a slow dissolving of the Community and the failure of the European integration process. The other pole sees flexible integration as a strengthening and securing of integration.

A main challenge drawing on Moravcsik's theoretical framework is whether enhanced cooperation can be seen as institution building based on credible commitments. Governments will seek credible commitments and try to avoid 'incomplete contracting' (Moravcsik, 1998, 73). Pooling and delegation are solutions to this problem of incomplete contracting. The question is whether enhanced cooperation in the future can create problems of incomplete contracting and thereby undermine parts of the European integration process.

Models of Flexible Integration

It can seem as pure speculation to try to determine the use of the flexibility provisions in the future. However, different scenarios have been put forward in order to understand the possible future of the European Union. Lykke Friis distinguishes between three different models: hard core, à la carte and overlapping circles (Friis, 2001: 275). Table 22.3 illustrates the different types of integration and gives examples of existing flexibility arrangements.

Table 22.3: Different Models of Flexible Integration

Type	Definition	Examples
Multi-speed integration	The pursuit of common objectives is driven by a group of Member States that are able and willing to go further, the underlying assumption being that the others will follow later.	Transition periods. Convergence criteria for EMU.
Variable geometry	Unattainable differences solved within the integrative structure by allowing permanent or irreversible separation between a hard core and less developed integrative units.	Schengen cooperation after Amsterdam. WEU from Maastricht to Nice.
A la carte	Member States are able to pick and choose in what policy area they would like to participate.	Denmark and defence, EMU, 3rd pillar, Schengen, Title IV. Ireland and Schengen. United Kingdom and EMU, Social Charter, Schengen, Title IV.

Source: Based on Friis, 1997, 139; Laursen, 2003, 26; Stubb, 2002: 32-33.

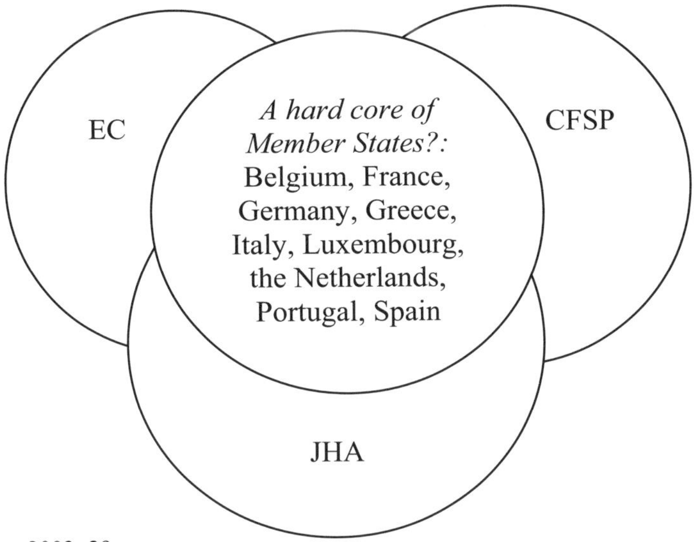

Source: Laursen 2003, 29.

Figure 22.1: The Eccentric Circles of EU

Which Model of Integration?

The argument presented by Friis is that neither the model of a hard core of Member States nor the model of à la carte, where the Member States can pick and choose, is likely to be seen in the future (Friis 2001, 275). The most likely model is the one where some Member States take part in all circles, while others choose to stay out of one or two of the circles (ibid.). This scenario is also termed variable geometry. Finn Laursen presents a similar model as to illustrate the current situation. He questions, however, in contrast to Friis, that a model of variable geometry will not end up creating a hard core of Member States (Laursen 2003, 29). Figure 1 illustrates this scenario by combining the idea of the integration process as eccentric circles that possibly end up creating a hard core.

To sum up, two main characteristics of the described institutionalisation of enhanced cooperation that might affect the future model of integration can be seen. First, flexible integration is no longer just a question of ability but also, and possibly even to a greater extent, a question of (political) willingness. Second, the institutionalisation of enhanced cooperation paves the way for flexibility within very different policy areas. Previous use of flexible integration has been used in relation to specific policy issues, for example in the case of Britain's self-exclusion from the Social Protocol. The break with the predominant integration philosophy of a Europe of concentric circles, meaning that some countries might move ahead but the others will catch up sooner or later, is evident.

CONCLUSION

The examination of the agenda setting stage demonstrates that the process leading to the inclusion of enhanced cooperation on the IGC 2000 agenda cannot be pictured as a simple aggregation of national preferences. The preference formation of the majority of Member States and the agenda setting were two parallel processes in the case of enhanced cooperation.

The end result of the negotiations on enhanced cooperation seemed to provide a satisfying solution to the 'euro-enthusiastic' as well as the 'euro-sceptic' Member States. This is in spite of the fact that applications of enhanced cooperation remain to be seen and, therefore, no one knows what kind of European integration process will emerge as a result of flexible integration.

The negotiation stage reflects that once enhanced cooperation was on the agenda, most Member States feared that part of their future political and power capacities would be dependent on the decisions made on this issue. This was the case both for the 'euro-enthusiasts' and to the 'euro-sceptics', which confirms Moravcsik's description of the negotiations as a coordination game with distributional consequences.

The flexibility provisions institutionalised in the Nice Treaty made it easier to initiate flexible arrangements especially by loosening the general restrictions, removing the emergency brake in the 1st and 3rd pillar and lowering the number of Member States required for initiating enhanced cooperation to eight. A key question raised by using Moravcsik's rationalist framework is whether these institutional choices will provide credible commitments in the future or will create a problem of incomplete contracting. Enhanced cooperation can be argued to be a possible undermining of the prospects for making credible commitments.

The question of how enhanced cooperation will influence the future development of the European integration process remains unanswered. A possible scenario is the creation of overlapping or eccentric circles where the participating Member States' decisions will depend on the policy area in question. However, it is reasonable to expect that a group of Member States will participate in all parts of the integration process creating a core of members. If flexible arrangements become a part of the European integration process, it is likely to be a difficult act of balance between mechanisms of integration and disintegration.

BIBLIOGRAPHY

Chirac, Jaques (2000), "Our Europe", speech at the German Bundestag, Berlin, 27 June.

CONFER 4718/00 "IGC. Reform for Enlargement," 16 February 2000.

—— 4719/00 "Memorandum from the Greek Government to the Intergovernmental Conference on Institutional reform of the European Union," 3 March 2000.

—— 4720/00 "Contributions from the Dutch Government – An Agenda for Internal Reforms in the European Union," 6 March 2000.

—— 4721/00 "Memorandum from Benelux," 7 March 2000.

—— 4723/00 "Contribution from the Finnish Government – Background and Objectives in the IGC 2000," 7 March 2000.

—— 4750/00 "Intergovernmental Conference on Institutional Reform. Presidency Report to the Feira European Council," Brussels 14 June 2000.

—— 4758/00 "Closer Cooperation. Presidency Note," 11 July 2000.

—— 4783/00 "Closer Cooperation" Germany and Italy, 4 October 2000.

—— 4786/00 "Enhanced Cooperation. Presidency Note," 18 October 2000.

—— 4787/00 "Memorandum from Benelux," 19 October 2000.

—— 4798/00 "Enhanced Cooperation. Presidency Note," 9 November 2000.

Dehaene, Jean-Luc, David Simon and Richard von Weizsäcker (1999), "The Institutional Implications of Enlargement." Report to the European Commission. Brussels: The European Commission.

Deubner, Christian (2000), "Harnessing Differentiation in the EU – Flexibility after Amsterdam. A Report on Hearings with Parlamentarians and Government Officials in Seven European Capitals." Working Paper, Forward Studies Unit, European Commission.

European Council (1999), "Presidency Conclusions. Helsinki European Council." Helsinki, 10-11 December 1999.

—— (2000a), "Presidency Conclusions. Santa Maria da Feira European Council." 19 and 20 June 2000.

—— (2000b), "Record of the informal meeting of the Biarritz European Council." 13-14 October 2000.

European Parliament (14094/1999), "Resolution of the European Parliament on Convening of the Intergovernmental Conference," 23 February 2000.

Fischer, Joschka (2000), "From Confederation to Federation – Thoughts on the Finality of European Integration", speech at Humboldt University, Berlin, 12 May.

Friis, Lykke (1997), *Europæisk stabilitet: EU's udvidelse med de central og østeuropæiske lande*. Copenhagen: Dansk Udenrigspolitisk Institut (DUPI).

—— (1998), "EU Enlargement and the Luxembourg Summit: A Case Study in Agenda-Setting," in Anders Wivel (ed.), *Explaining European Integration*. Copenhagen: Copenhagen Political Studies Press.

—— (2001), *Den europæiske byggeplads. Fra fælles mønt til forfatning*. Copenhagen: Centrum.

Galloway, David (2001), *The Treaty of Nice and Beyond. Realities and Illusions of Power in the EU*. Sheffield: Sheffield Academic Press.

Gray, Mark and Alexander Stubb (2001), "Keynote Article: The Treaty of Nice – Negotiating a Poisened Chalice?," *Journal of Common Market Studies*, vol. 39, no. (s)1, p. 5-23.

Laursen, Finn (2001), *Guide til Nice-traktaten. Baggrund, Kommentarer og Perspektiver*. Copenhagen: Den Danske Europabevægelse.

—— (2003), "The Danish 'No' to the Euro and its implications: Towards more Variable Geometry?" *CFES Working Paper*, no. 9. Odense: University of Southern Denmark.

Moravcsik, Andrew (1993), "Preferences and Power in the European Community: A Liberal Intergovernmentalist Approach," *Journal of Common Market Studies*, vol. 31, no. 4, pp. 473-524.

—— (1998), *The Choice for Europe. Social Purpose and State Power from Messina to Maastricht*. London: University College London Press.

Petersen, Nikolaj and Finn Laursen (1998), *Amsterdam-traktaten: Baggrund, Kommentarer og Perspektiver*. Copenhagen: Den Danske Europabevægelse.
Stubb, Alexander (2000) "Dealing with Flexibility in the IGC", in Edward Best, Mark Gray and Alexander Stubb (eds.), *Rethinking the European Union. IGC 2000 and Beyond.* Maastricht: European Institute of Public Administration.
— (2002), *Negotiating Flexibility in the European Union. Amsterdam, Nice and Beyond.* New York: Palgrave.
Sutter, Martin (2000) "Flexible integration, EMU and relative voting power in the EU," *Public Choice,* no. 104, pp. 41-62.
The Treaty on European Union and The Treaty establishing the European Community (2002). Official Journal of the European Communities (2002/C).
Wincott, Daniel (1995), "Institutional Interaction and European Integration: Towards an Everyday Critique of Liberal Intergovernmentalism," *Journal of Common Market Studies*, vol. 33, no. 4, pp. 597-609.

SECTION 4

THE PARALLEL PROCESSES

CHAPTER 23

THE EUROPEAN SECURITY AND DEFENCE POLICY: COMING OF AGE?

INTRODUCTION

The European Union (EU) gave birth to a new European Security and Defence Policy (ESDP) at the Nice summit, December 2000. In a separate report attached to the Presidency Conclusions, and which came in parallel to the new EU treaty, the EU announces its ambition to gain "an autonomous capacity to take decisions and action in the security and defence field" (EU, 2000a). The Nice Treaty (EU, 2000b, Article 17) itself states that the EU's foreign and security policy now includes the "progressive framing of a common defence policy," which amounts to a simple upgrade of the Maastricht Treaty's (EU, 1993, Article J.7) reference to "the eventual framing of a common defence policy, which might in time lead to a common defence."

According to Andrew Moravcsik (1998), this development is largely due to the opportunity statesmen have to pursue their ideologies in foreign policy whenever economic interests allow them. Charles Cogan rejects this type of contingency and argues that the ESDP represents an 'ineluctable' trend in Europe toward 'emancipation' and 'autonomy in defense' (2001, 134). Yet a third analyst, David Calleo, finds that the European security builds on culturally coherent power constellations, and warns that the EU may reach too widely and thus undermine the foundation of its policies, including the ESDP (2001). This chapter follows the latter argument and asserts that the ESDP represents a geopolitical phenomenon that Moravcsik grants insufficient explanatory weight, but which does not amount to an ineluctable trend.

The first section provides an overview of the ESDP as the Nice report defines it in terms of policies, institutions, capabilities, and allies. The second section traces the game played by major ESDP states, beginning with the situation created by the Amsterdam Treaty in 1997, continuing through the St. Malo declaration in December 1998 to the Helsinki summit in December 1999, and finally turning to the endgame before Nice. The third and final section examines the pertinence of the theory central to this book, Andrew Moravcsik's liberal intergovernmentalism, in light of geopolitical dynamics.

THE ESDP AT NICE

The 'Presidency Report on the European Security and Defence Policy' is short, consisting of about seven pages divided into eight sections. The report, however, is just a summary of more substantial agreements that are presented in seven annexes, some of which have appendices, totalling about thirty-five pages.

Table 23.1: ESDP Presidency Report: Overview

Introduction: political ambitions and summary of agreements	
Capabilities	*Annex I*: Military Capabilities Commitment Declaration *Appendix*: Achievement of Headline Goal: Review Mechanism for Military Capabilities *Annex II*: Strengthening of EU Capabilities for Civilian Aspects of Crisis Management
Institutions	*Annex III*: Political and Security Committee *Annex IV*: European Union Military Committee *Annex V*: European Union Military Staff Organisation
Allies	*Annex VI*: Arrangements Concerning Non-EU European NATO Members and Other Countries Which Are Candidates for Accession to the EU *Annex VII*: Standing Arrangements for Consultation and Cooperation Between the EU and NATO *Appendix*: Annex to the Permanent Arrangements on EU/NATO Consultation and Cooperation on the Implementation of Paragraph 10 of the Washington Communiqué

Source: EU 2000a.

The introduction states the overall ambition behind the ESDP: "to carry out the full range of Petersberg tasks as defined in the Treaty on European Union: humanitarian and rescue tasks, peace-keeping tasks and tasks of combat forces in crisis management, including peacemaking." The structure of the report then reveals the issues that the EU believes are necessary ESDP requirements: first a range of military and civilian capabilities (annexes I and II), then a range of institutions (annexes III to V), and finally good relations to third parties, or allies (annexes VI and VII). I will briefly examine each of these dimensions below.

ESDP ambitions

The level of ambition is defined by the so-called Petersberg tasks that were articulated by the Western European Union (WEU) in June 1992. At this point in time the EU had identified the WEU as its defence arm responsible for the elaboration and implementation of defence policy (EU, 1993, Article J.7). The WEU, by articulating the Petersberg tasks (WEU, 1992), took a first step in defining the type of defence policy the EU might have. In essence, the WEU had carved out a niche specialty for the EU: handling the crises that fall somewhere in the grey area between traditional foreign policy and defence.

The latter task of defence—which implies both territorial defence and the fighting of wars elsewhere—was reserved for NATO. This reservation still stands, as the report makes clear by stating that the EU will consider undertaking autonomous operations only "where NATO as a whole is not engaged" (EU, 2000a, 1). Moreover, the ESDP "does not involve the establishment of a European army" and "NATO remains the basis of the collective defence of its members."

The EU thus seeks to use the ESDP to complement its traditional crisis management policy by adding a military instrument. A traditional strategic actor would have sought to reinforce its military policy by adding other instruments, but defence policy in the EU does not signify such a turn toward strategic tradition. One might argue that the turn in time will come, but this, at least, is not the collective intention behind the Nice report. The EU should become better at handling other peoples' crises, and the EU should reinforce rather than abandon this mission.

Capabilities

The conduct of policy demands instruments or capabilities, and the EU has been challenged to define how many military forces it would need to mobilize. An answer was defined in December 1999 when the EU stated that the high-end of the Petersberg tasks peacemaking—demands a capability "to deploy rapidly and then sustain forces capable of the full range of Petersberg tasks as set out in the Amsterdam Treaty, including the most demanding, in operations up to corps level (up to 15 brigades or 50,000-60,000 persons)" (EU, 1999b, annex 1 to annex IV).

This chapter focuses on the defence dimension but it should be noted that the EU in annex II also defines civilian capabilities as a second capability leg of the ESDP. These involve the dimensions of police forces, justice, protection, and administration. At the Feira summit in June 2000 the EU articulated a headline goal for police forces, aiming to be ready by 2003 to deploy up to 5000 policemen, which is repeated in the Nice report (see Annex II; also Hansen and Klynge, 2001, chapter 4).

The appendix to annex I essentially examines the way in which the EU can continue inciting the development of the military forces that the EU needs. This 'review mechanism' begins with he Headline Goal and then is intended to result in

> …a method of consultation through which these goals can be met and maintained and through which national contributions reflecting Member States' political will and commitment towards these goals can be defined by each Member State, with a regular review of progress being made.

The review mechanism, which has since been baptized 'capability development mechanism,' is placed mainly in the hands of the Military Staff of the EU (see below). Military officers of different nationalities are here charged with the task of comparing distinct force catalogues: one, the Helsinki Headline Catalogue, which contains the forces needed to conduct various missions within the Petersberg range; a second, the Headline Force Catalogue, which contains the forces offered by member countries; and a third, the Helsinki Progress Catalogue, which enumerates needed capabilities. The EU has yet to establish a permanent mechanism but the basic idea is clear: use a type of military convergence criteria to incite countries to supply the forces needed for the ESDP.

Institutions

The organization of the ESDP begins at the summit with heads of state and then descends to the foreign ministers of the Council of Ministers. Defence ministers join their colleagues in cases of military crisis management. The real innovative steps have been taken below these political levels and fall into two categories.

A 'political pillar' has been constructed to offer decision-makers advice and enhance their operational control. This pillar includes a Political and Security Committee (PSC) (annex III), which is to survey the international situation, coordinate CFSP discussions within the EU, guide the development of military capabilities, prepare responses to particular crises for the Council, and be ready to exercise "political control and strategic direction" of an EU operation. The PSC is in fact the third layer of the political pillar because under the Council is the committee of permanent ambassadors (COREPER) through which the PSC must work. The PSC meets weekly to discuss ESDP affairs, and the Committee can draw on opinions and recommendations of the fourth layer, the EU Military Committee (EUMC). The EUMC (annex IV) is composed of the national Chiefs of Defence, represented on a day-to-day basis by their military representatives, and must, on the basis of consensus decision-making, provide military guidance for the EU.

A 'bureaucratic pillar' runs in parallel and is headed by the Council's Secretary General (currently Javier Solana) who is also CFSP High Representative. The only organizational innovation in this pillar at Nice is the establishment of an EU Military Staff (EUMS) (annex V) composed of approximately 130 national officers. Its task is to provide early warning, situation assessment, and strategic planning. Solana formally heads the EUMS but it also refers directly to the EUMC.[1]

Allies

The EU finally provides a blueprint for organizing relations to those countries or allies that can be expected to participate in EU sponsored operations, or which have an interest in influencing EU decisions.

In Nice the EU distinguished between candidates for accession[2] and non-EU European NATO members.[3] All countries were granted a number of minimum meetings with the EU on ESDP matters during each EU presidency, and were offered the opportunity to send officers to the EUMS. If a crisis erupts intensified consultations will take place. The EU guarantees the non-EU European NATO members an opportunity to participate in operational phases if the EU wishes to draw on NATO assets and capabilities, while other countries may receive an invitation if the Council so decides. Finally, those countries that end up participating in an operation will participate in a Committee of Contributors that will "play a key role in the day-to-day management of the operation."

Annex VII pursues this logic of consultation in the context of EU-NATO relations and provides for meetings between military staffs, Committees, and General-Secretaries on a regular basis. It also provides a road map for organ-

□□□

[1] The PSC, EUMC, and EUMS were all mentioned in the Cologne declaration of June 1999. They were then set up on an interim basis in early 2000 before being permanently established at the Nice December 2000 summit. These organs take over the planning functions of the WEU, which henceforth is fully marginalized within European security. The WEU will only contain some armaments cooperation, a defense clause (Article V), and a parliamentary assembly, although the latter is likely to whither.

[2] Bulgaria, Cyprus, Estonia, Latvia, Lithuania, Malta, Slovakia, and the Slovene Republic.

[3] The Check Republic, Hungary, Iceland, Norway, Poland, and Turkey.

izational relations in the context of crisis, outlining procedures for the EU calling on NATO assets and capabilities or for autonomous action. The appendix to annex VII outlines the EU view of the so-called Berlin Plus declaration of NATO, dating back to April 1999, which still serves as a framework agreement between the two organisations.

A number of developments have taken place since Nice affecting this relationship to allies. It soon became evident that political disputes between Greece and Turkey would be an obstacle to the implementation of the NATO-EU framework. Agreement took two years to cultivate, so that by December 2002 the two organisations could begin organizing their relations. Then, in December 2002 as well, the EU decided to invite ten countries to join the EU. Today the group of external countries is consequently reduced to five: Romania and Bulgaria as candidates; Turkey, Iceland, and Norway as NATO members. In addition, Romania and Bulgaria will become NATO members in the coming years, so the question of allied relations is substantially reduced and is now wholly focused on EU-NATO relations.

The EU deliberately kept the focus on European security in order not to duplicate or undermine NATO. External countries by implication meant European countries, which in turn caused Canada to be overlooked—the US hovering above it all as NATO leader. Canada was thus mentioned in the introduction to the report as one of several countries, including Russia and Ukraine, which could be "invited to participate." Moreover, consultations "will be stepped up in times of crisis" and Canada "will be of particular importance in the case of EU operations drawing on NATO assets and capabilities" (EU, 2000a, 6; see also Bolving, pp. 27-29).

ESDP overview

Table 23.2 sums up the discussion of the ESDP, as it was shaped at the Nice summit in December 2000.

Table 23.2: ESDP Components after Nice

Policy	Capabilities	Institutions	Allies
Petersberg tasks: humanitarian and rescue tasks, peacekeeping tasks, and tasks of combat forces in crisis management, incl. peacemaking. Strategy by heads of state; decisions by ministers	Military ambition: to be able to deploy up to 60,000 troops in area of hostility. Permanent force planning mechanism is under development Civilian ambition: broad involvement in policing and administrative reconstruction	'Political pillar' with Political and Security Committee (PSC) and Military Committee (EUMC) 'Bureaucratic pillar' headed by Secretary General with Military Staff (EUMS)	Regular consultations with candidate countries and NATO allies. NATO allies assured participation if the EU wishes to draw on NATO assets and capabilities. Support for Berlin Plus agreement.

Amsterdam to Nice

1996-1997 was perhaps a bad moment to revise EU foreign and security policy (CFSP) in light of the meagre track record of the CFSP, having come into effect in 1993, and the concomitant strengthening of NATO, which under US leadership had stepped into the Bosnian civil war, crafted a peace settlement, and provided forces to implement it. The end result was therefore not surprisingly that the Amsterdam Treaty, which went into effect in May 1999, only marginally strengthened the CFSP. By 1997 it appeared that the EU was destined to become a 'civilian actor' relying on occasional back-up from NATO and lacking the ability to realize the Maastricht defence ambition. The French-British agreement in December 1998 and pressure from the unfolding Kosovo crisis helped change the situation and by December 1999 the EU adopted the Helsinki Headline Goal. The question of defining the overall architecture of the ESDP then defined much of the year 2000, the end game before the presidency report, and the decisive last phase of agenda setting before the EU turned to the implementation of the ESDP.

Minor Advances in Amsterdam

The Amsterdam Treaty (EU, 1997) essentially made a few modest advances on the CFSP and largely left defence policy outside its framework. The

CFSP was strengthened in a number of respects. First, greater flexibility was introduced in CFSP decision-making. Qualified majority voting (QMV) now applied not only to the implementation of 'joint actions' but also to the adoption of a joint action itself *if* it follows from a 'common strategy' adopted by the European Council (EU, 1997, Article 23.2).[4] Moreover, flexibility was enhanced as member states now could abstain from joining CFSP decisions. This is known as 'constructive abstention' according to which members will not be obliged to accept a decision but allow it to move forward (EU, 1997, Article 23.1).

The CFSP was strengthened also by the appointment of a High Representative for the CFSP who henceforth represents the day-to-day nub of CFSP affairs, and is in this role strengthened in his dual capacity as Secretary General of the Council administration. The simultaneous creation of a post of Deputy Secretary General and a policy planning unit alongside the Council secretariat enhanced the ability of the High Representative/Secretary General (known as Mr. PESC) to run the administration and have it respond to his and the Council's initiatives. Besides now appointing a permanent representative, the Council also gained the ability to appoint 'special representatives' (EU, 1997, Article 18.5) in case the Council believed a more permanent (as opposed to rotating) representation was required in a particular context. These initiatives combined implied that the CFSP increasingly would be anchored in the Council structure rather than the Commission (see Forster and Wallace, 2000, 484-485).

These advances were checked by elaborate opt-out mechanisms, however. Constructive abstention and QMV were balanced by the possibility of deferring votes in cases where important 'reasons of national policy' are in play (EU 1997, Article 23.2). Likewise, QMV in joint action follows only once a 'strategy' has been adopted by unanimity and is in any case hostage to the same national security opt-out clause.

Advances in the defence area were very modest. Perhaps the most significant advance concerned the incorporation into the EU of the Petersberg tasks: "humanitarian and rescue tasks, peacekeeping tasks and tasks of combat forces in crisis management, including peacemaking" (Article 17.2). However, the relationship between the EU and the WEU remained unresolved (Article 17.1). Although the WEU was "an integral part of the development of the Union," it remained on the sideline and a future rapprochement required unanimity in the European Council.

The Amsterdam Treaty had thus delivered little of the improvements outlined in original agenda, and the defence arm, the WEU, was instead drawn

[4] Common Strategies adopted by the European Council were also a novelty introduced by the treaty.

closer to NATO, which granted the WEU access to its defence planning process and offered to plan for European contingencies. Jean Klein's (1997, 199) observation was thus not surprising, "we must recognize the fact that the CFSP is malfunctioning and that NATO represents the only remaining military structure in Europe."

Defence Break-Through

In the year following the conclusion of the Amsterdam negotiations, 1998, the EU achieved the political break-through that had eluded it for much of the 1990s. In fact, France and Great Britain crafted the break-through that was subsequently endorsed by all EU members. The two countries reached the agreement in December 1998 at St. Malo that the EU should be better capable of playing "its full role on the international stage" (Britain, 1998). More specifically (1998, paragraph 2): "the Union must have the capacity for autonomous action, backed up by credible military forces, the means to decide to use them, and a readiness to do so, in order to respond to international crises." In a stroke, the two countries had admitted that which was impossible at Amsterdam: defence, autonomy, and military forces fell within the CFSP.

This agreement was possible because both France and Britain had moved: France had become less hostile to NATO in the European security architecture, Britain less hostile to the prospect of European competences in security affairs. Their agreement was founded on the old Petersberg agenda and the idea that the EU should do something for which NATO was not ready: conflict prevention and crisis management. The Petersberg tasks thus continued to be at the heart of the EU defence question, but the tasks had also come a long way: in 1992 the WEU articulated these tasks to keep up with NATO in out-of-area debates; in 1997 the tasks were brought inside the EU; and in 1999, following the St. Malo agreement, the EU moved closer to developing the capacity to actually carry out these policies.

The spring of 1999 witnessed continued diplomatic efforts to spread the St. Malo momentum to the entire Union, which succeeded at the conclusion of the German presidency in June 1999. In the Cologne Declaration, the EU members declared (EU, 1999a, annex III), "we intend to give the European Union the necessary means and capabilities to assume its responsibilities regarding a common European policy on security and defence." Moreover, in an effort to defuse external concerns about EU self-sufficiency, they declared, "We want to develop an effective EU-led crisis management in which NATO members, as well as neutral and non-allied members, of the EU can participate fully and on an equal footing in the EU operations."

The Cologne Declaration was not only a statement of intent but also an agenda for continued EU work to be spearheaded by ensuing presidencies—Finland in the fall of 1999, Portugal in the spring of 2000, and then France in the fall of 2000. Two issues were particularly important: institutions and capabilities. The Cologne declaration had outlined three institutions, a Political and Security Committee (PSC), a military Committee (EUMC), and a Military Staff (EUMS), but had been silent on the precise contours of military capabilities, referring simply to 'necessary capabilities.' In the fall of 1999 France pushed to have the PSC operate at a very senior level, with senior ambassadors, which some countries, including Britain, resisted on the grounds that it would be too strong a measure of integration. In the end Britain agreed to a high-profile PSC because in return they gained a precise and serious military capability goal—the Helsinki Headline Goal (Howorth, 2001, 771-772).

The Finish presidency presented two capability reports presented as Annex I (military capabilities) and Annex II (civilian capabilities) to Annex IV (Strengthening the Common European Policy on Security and Defence) of the presidency report (EU, 1999b). Annex I to Annex IV contains the Headline Goal that subsequently has guided military planning within the EU:

> To develop European capabilities, Member States have set themselves the headline goal: by the year 2003, cooperating together voluntarily, they will be able to deploy rapidly and then sustain forces capable of the full range of Petersberg tasks as set out in the Amsterdam Treaty, including the most demanding, in operations up to corps level (up to 15 brigades or 50,000-60,000 persons). These forces should be militarily self-sustaining with the necessary command, control and intelligence capabilities, logistics, other combat support services and additionally, as appropriate, air and naval elements. Member States should be able to deploy in full at this level within 60 days, and within this to provide smaller rapid response elements available and deployable at very high readiness. They must be able to sustain such a deployment for at least one year. This will require an additional pool of deployable units (and supporting elements) at lower readiness to provide replacements for the initial forces.

The Helsinki summit also made it clear that the EU "should have the autonomous capacity to take decisions and, where NATO as a whole is not engaged, to launch and then to conduct EU-led military operations." In other words, autonomy was conditioned on NATO developments. This was fully in line with the agreement reached back in April 1999 at the NATO summit, but since then, at the Cologne summit, some observers had noted a slight move away from this condition because the Cologne Declaration is less explicit on the EU-NATO relationship. The issue was defused, however, November 25, when France and Britain jointly declared that NATO would remain the cornerstone of collective defence (*The Independent*, November 25, 1999).

End Game

Portugal and France shared the task of preparing the final ESDP report. Portugal focused on both military and civilian capabilities, as the established agenda dictated, and the Annex on ESDP contains four appendices, two of which deal with military and EU-NATO relations, two with civilian crisis management. Still, the main achievement of the Portuguese presidency concerned the interim establishment of the ESDP institutions—PSC, EUMC, and EUMS—described in the Cologne Declaration. With their establishment March 1, 2000, the institutions could gain operational experience before their official establishment at Nice in December.

With the establishment of these bodies, the Portuguese presidency also embarked upon the task of elaborating the Helsinki Headline Catalogue (HHC), which—as outlined in section one—contains the forces required by the EU to undertake a range of military operations, and which is inspired by, as the name indicates, the Helsinki agreement to undertake crisis management tasks including peacemaking. The HHC is confidential, but we know that its upper limit is that of Helsinki, 60,000 soldiers in a hostile zone for up to one year. Below this limit is a number of planning scenarios requiring mixed numbers of troops and infrastructure. The Portuguese presidency sought initially to make these scenarios as realistic as possible by naming the specific regions where the EU might take action (anonymous interviews with author). The naming of regions proved to be too sensible to the EU countries in light of their distinct interests and sensibilities, however, and the result was a fallback to the kind of parameter planning that the WEU had undertaken previously. The WEU Planning Cell operated (it has now ceased operating due to the EU superseding it) with generic planning dimensions: size of threat, distance for deployable forces, intensity of conflict, projected time, and cost (Collester, 2000, 375). The EUMS is likely using these parameters today. The WEU Planning Cell had developed a set of plans for operations of lower intensity, and the greatest task for the EUMS has therefore been to develop the high intensity plans, notably peacemaking.

Another aspect of the EUMS that must be noted concerns the level at which it operates. The EUMS, according to the Nice report, Annex V, must undertake 'strategic planning.' This is to say that the EUMS will do framework planning based on assessments of particular conflicts, and that it will not be responsible for operational planning, which concerns the specific military blueprint for action. Operational planning, which is the key to any operation, must therefore be 'imported' into the EU from either national headquarters, where only Great Britain and France have significant capacities, or from NATO whose Supreme Headquarters Allied Powers Europe (SHAPE) is fully trained and organized for the task. The restriction on the EUMS follows from the desire to avoid EU-NATO duplication: SHAPE continues undisputed while the EUMS resembles NATO's International Staff (see Nielsen, 2001). In consequence, the Nice report instructs the EUMS to draw on NATO expertise whenever necessary.

The French presidency took off July 1, 2000, and in many ways simply had to follow up on the roadmap from Cologne and Helsinki. The Nice Report, as the discussion also has made clear, reflects that which had been agreed to earlier. But still France had to craft a consensus to support the final report, which would then become the basis for 'ESDP implementation,' and France likewise had to continue the work on generating capabilities.

In the latter context, France had to move beyond the HHC and begin work on the Helsinki Force Catalogue (HFC), which implies motivating member states to commit forces to the potential operations of the HHC and then gathering these force contributions in one catalogue. For this purpose France hosted a Capabilities Commitment Conference November 20-21, 2000, which succeeded in gathering force contributions of 100,000 troops, 400 combat aircraft, and 100 warships. The resulting HFC is confidential, although unofficial estimates of national contributions exist (see e.g., ISIS, 2000, p. 3), but the total force is a composite of contributions from both EU and non-EU states. Since the EU aims to be autonomous if necessary, one must assume that at least 60,000 troops come from EU states along with a number of aircraft and warships. The CCC did not indicate whether force numbers are 'input' or 'output,' which is significant because an output indicates a force capable of sustaining itself, and which therefore consists of deployed troops, troops preparing for deployment, and troops resting, altogether a force of 180,000 troops (Wijk, 2000).

The need to fudge this issue is likely related to the coming challenge at Nice of agreeing to an ESDP report and having to bridge varying national positions, ranging from countries familiar with significant military engagements to countries with traditions of neutrality and only distant memories of the use of military force. Subsequent work on military capabilities has focused on filling in gaps—identified in a third catalogue, the Helsinki Progress Catalogue (HPC). A Capabilities Improvement Conference (CIC) was held in November 2001 and the EU has since then initiated a number of Action Groups consisting of countries willing to address particular capability gaps.

The stage was then set for final agreement in the early phases of the Nice summit, where the ESDP report was to be signed before the heads of states and governments addressed the new treaty. A tense moment erupted before calm again reigned: France suggested that the new EU force would be 'independent,' causing pro-Atlantic countries, Britain in particular, to protest. According to news reports, it took just eight minutes to settle matters and agree on the following declaration (*Financial Times* and *The Express*, December 9, 2000):

> "This does not involve the establishment of a European army. The commitment of national resources by member states to such operations will be based on their sovereign decisions. NATO remains the basis of the collective defence of its members."

The heads of states and governments subsequently played down this last minute row, as was to be expected, but the row is nevertheless a reminder that underlying national designs differ. Considering the meeting of military versus neutral traditions as well as the meeting between Atlanticism and Europeanism it is perhaps surprising that the ESDP emerged in the first place. This observation leads to an assessment of how the ESDP can be explained and whether Andrew Moravcsik's framework is appropriate.

EXPLAINING THE ESDP

State leaders play a key role in creating cooperation in contexts of high politics. The school of geopolitical theory normally advances this statement to demonstrate that state leaders respond to the international environment with its threats and incentives and change defence policy to optimise national security. Andrew Moravcsik has no problems agreeing that state leaders are central to high politics integration, but he takes issue with the primacy of geopolitics and instead argues that state leaders follow their ideologies to the extent that they are free of ties from domestic economic interests. The question I raise in this section is whether Moravcsik's view is adequate, and whether geopolitics should not be given greater emphasis.

Moravcsik's Framework

In *The Choice for Europe* Moravcsik (1998) argues that European integration happens because state leaders are pushed by societal, mainly economic interests to provide new solutions to negative externalities and because state leaders sometimes find themselves in a collective position that favours agreement at a European level. Thus, prodded by their grassroots, state leaders may agree to bring new issues into their common institutions, delegate power to supranational institutions, or pool decision-making power by allowing for decisions by majority vote.

Moravcsik sets up a test between geopolitical arguments and his own liberal-intergovernmentalist framework, reaching the unsurprising conclusion that his perspective is superior (1998, 474).

- Where geopolitics argues that economic interests are subordinated to geopolitical goals, Moravcsik finds that interests vary in nature.
- Where geopolitics argues that the timing of major policy initiatives coincide with external crises, Moravcsik finds that these initiatives are domestically timed.
- Where geopolitics argues that the major demands of states are geopolitical while concessions are economic, Moravcsik finds that major demands tend to be economic in nature.
- Where geopolitics argues that elites drive policy, Moravcsik finds that aggregated interests are at the root of policy.
- Finally, where geopolitics argues that elites in private meetings are concerned with geopolitical implications, Moravcsik finds that they are often talking about economics.

Moravcsik sets up the test himself and it may be in order to question his portrait of geopolitics. If, for example, statesmen in a geopolitical framework did not always subordinate economics to politics and instead argued that they have a different and subtler understanding of the way in which economics reinforce political power, the image becomes blurred. Moravcsik certainly cannot uphold, in that case, that every finding of economic primacy by definition entails a defeat of geopolitics.

Moravcsik allows that geopolitics may play a role, but then only when economic interests are uncertain or weak, and only in the shape of statesmen pursuing an ideology that they hold dear but which is more often than not in minority domestically (1998, 477). This limited concession will be challenged below in relation to three issues.

The Big Geopolitical Picture

Moravcsik essentially argues that economic primacy undermines geopolitics, but this argument may in itself be the consequence of a geopolitical context, the Cold War. During the Cold War European states were more or less free to focus European cooperation and integration on non-security issues, certainly once they experienced the pains of attempting to launch European defence integration in 1954-55. Subsequent integration focused on economics first of all, and the European Community and then Union based its success on a customs union and later a fully-fledged internal market. As long as the Cold War continued and as long as the US was committed to Europe's security there was no real reason to challenge this European focus. To be sure, increased superpower tensions in the 1980s sparked European efforts to create a distinct voice on nuclear issues via the WEU. But these initiatives were wholly conservative and aimed to re-establish the nuclear order—deterrence—and thus the framework that had allowed European integration to prosper. It is therefore not altogether surprising if Moravcsik finds that European leaders repeatedly linked high politics initiatives within the EC to economic issues—the bread and butter of European integration.

The CFSP emerged immediately after the geopolitical context changed dramatically, and the ESDP a few years later. This correlation is probably not coincidental: geopolitical theory certainly claims that the relationship is causal.

The CFSP was part of the Political Union that Germany and France put on the European agenda once the unification of Germany appeared inevitable – a geopolitical event par excellence. It was also a development that US policy-makers to some extent welcomed because they had their eyes focused on—in their view—major security challenges such as the Persian Gulf, where the US led a coalition against Iraq in early 1991, and the Soviet transformation into a more humble but perhaps also more frustrated Russia.

Another major initiative came in NATO in 1994-1996 when the Alliance agreed to craft a European Security and Defence Identity (ESDI) within it. The ESDI was greatly influenced by the war in Bosnia where Europeans were heavily engaged, albeit with very limited success, while the US stood aside and advocated a "lift the weapons embargo and strike with airpower" policy that provoked tense allied relations. This US policy was initiated by President Clinton very early in his presidency and was largely an outcome of electoral promises and positions. The ensuing debacle provoked a change: Clinton suggested an ESDI within NATO to promote the type of transatlantic cooperation that was missing. Later, when the European powers still could not gain control of the Bosnian situation, the US intervened and made possible the Dayton agreement of November 1995. Since the US did not wish to be an indispensable part to European crisis management, in light of European weaknesses, another NATO initiative resulted in the Berlin agreement of June 1996 to enhance the operational capacity of the ESDI (NATO, 1996).

It was essentially the inadequacy of this ESDI design in the crisis of Kovoso, 1998-1999, that provoked European countries to realize that a stronger European response was needed. To be sure, Britain was the country that moved first in the early fall of 1998, suggesting that it was now ready for greater EU security engagements, and it was then France along with Britain that crafted the St. Malo agreement of December 1998. Still, the translation of this bilateral agreement into an ambitious EU ESDP owes much to the

Kosovo crisis and its unambiguous display of a significant gap—in terms of both military capabilities and design for the intervention itself—that inevitably affected most, if not all, European allies.

The big geopolitical picture confirms that there is a strong relationship between external geopolitical events and policy initiatives in Europe. The relationship is not perfect in the sense that policies succeed and give birth to entirely new architectures. Policies may fail. But the strong relationship, including the Cold War context of his study, casts doubts on Moravcsik's claim to have undermined geopolitics.

National Interests and Flexible Coalitions

A second issue that lends credence to geopolitics is the increased use of flexibility within the CFSP and ESDP. Flexibility first became an issue in the run-up to the Amsterdam Treaty and has since been an inherent feature of EU negotiations and designs. This, I argue, is essentially because state leaders are preoccupied with their ability to control national security policy should collective efforts go in a 'wrong' direction. The growing importance of flexibility, as well as the controversy surrounding it in current negotiations, suggests that this concern is not a fleeting feature of a personalized ideology but a general political factor.

Multi-speed Europe was the subject matter of a paper presented by the German CDU-CSU in September 1994, and it drew wide attention because it was correctly seen as defining a new theme in European integration. The debate subsequently split those who believed in 'reinforced cooperation'—a semi-institutional avant-garde capable of driving the integration process forward—and the adherents of 'flexibility'—a more de-centralized model according to which states could opt in or out of varying issue areas. A 'Reflection Group' preparing the Amsterdam negotiations turned out to be prophetic by arguing that flexibility should be a 'last resort' option open in principle to everyone and always undertaken in respect for the *acquis communautaire* (Missiroli, 2000, 6). The Reflection Group's minimalist version prevailed for reasons of political disagreement.[5] Britain and Greece consistently opposed the idea of flexibility within security and defence affairs while others were ambivalent in light of the prospect that they might be left behind in a structure increasingly dominated by a 'CFSP directorate.'

[5] As Missiroli (2000, 7) notes, the issue was widely recognized as extremely sensitive and no less than twenty-two documents along with a number of "non-papers" were submitted on the matter by the negotiating governments.

In the end the debate over defence, security, and flexibility was postponed—flexibility was adopted in a minimalist version and did not apply to defence policy, of which the EU had none—because EU members focused on the EMU and feared that institutional overload would endanger the monetary "revolutionary step forward" (Forster and Niblett, 2001, 40).

The WEU-EU relationship therefore floundered. Britain was strongly opposed to the idea of bringing the WEU into the EU at this time. Britain favoured flexibility in its most de-centralized version and saw no need to create a structure, such as the EU-WEU, that might rival NATO. It was a policy crafted by 'tacticians' who 'abandoned' long-term thinking, concluded two observers (Forster and Wallace, 2001, 142). Still, Britain was joined in its opposition to WEU-EU integration by the neutral countries—Ireland, Austria, Sweden, and Finland—and combined they were able to defeat the coalition for integration that formed in March 1997 and which included France, Germany, Spain, Italy, and Luxembourg (see Klein, 1997, 195-196).[6]

With defence becoming a EU issue in 1999-2000, flexibility again became a key question. Greater flexibility was introduced into the CFSP at Nice but not at all into the new policy, ESDP. This did not imply that member states were ready to tie each other to a strong common defence policy. As was the case also during the Amsterdam negotiations, states use the principle of unanimity to control the development of a policy that is in its preliminary stages and has the potential to develop in contrasting—and undesirable—directions. Britain preferred de-centralised flexibility during Amsterdam to prevent the emergence of a hard core of pro-integrationist countries, such as the Franco-German couple, that with the creation of the ESDP possibly might 'hijack' this policy to advance their particular political conceptions of the EU.

The big EU countries are currently engaged in a process at the end of which they will have to reach an agreement on the type of flexibility on which the ESDP will be based. In an enlarged EU of 25 countries it is highly unlikely that unanimous defence decisions will be meaningful or even lead to action: hence the necessity of flexibility. If they do not reach agreement, it is possible that operations will be undertaken outside the EU framework—which the treaty allows as long as it does not undermine the EU itself—in completely flexible ad hoc coalitions. This path, however, will provoke significant resistance from countries that find themselves excluded from the informal *directoire* that will develop. Two illustrations follow.

□□□

[6] The coalition formed on the basis of a French-German proposal of December 1996.

Spain's rapprochement with NATO was in parts motivated by its hostility to ad hoc great power cooperation that tended to leave Spain out in the cold.[7] Spain had for instance been excluded from the Contact Group of big countries that formed in 1994 mainly to deal with war in the former Yugoslavia.[8] Italy managed to force its entry into this group via its EU presidency in 1996, but Spain opted for a different strategy: loyalty to the US. The strategy succeeded: Spanish candidates were selected in the following years for the positions as NATO Secretary General, EU Chief Representative in Bosnia, and EU special envoy to the Middle East (Niblett, 2001, 226).

Spain is also excluded from the so-called *quint*, which forms the second illustration. The quint consists of the US, France, Germany, Britain, and Italy and is a 'very discreet institution' rarely mentioned by officials and not recognized by EU member states (Gegout, 2002, 335). Moreover, as Gegout notes, the quint is not a coalition of the willing because other willing states cannot join, and still it regularly discusses CFSP issues. Excluded countries have reasons to express their dissatisfaction, which some of them have made public, and the quint represents precisely the kind of external flexibility that takes place because the CFSP-ESDP framework is complex and rigid. The countries of the quint have propelled this type of stealth cooperation because they wish to safeguard national autonomy, pointing to the conclusion emphasized in this section that flexibility, in one shape or the other, will continue to be crucial to the CFSP-ESDP for geopolitical reasons.

The US as an Engine of Change

According to geopolitical theory the structure of the international system plays a prominent role in the formation of regional security dynamics. At present the US occupies an undisputed position and it would therefore be logical to enquire whether the US has been a distinct source of the twists and turns that lead to the ESDP. The section on the 'big geopolitical picture' provided some of the answer, which is affirmative. A more substantial argument follows.

The modest advances achieved in Amsterdam by the EU are greatly indebted to US investments in NATO at a time when European states had run

□□□

[7] Spain had in fact been a strong proponent of European autonomy during the Maastricht negotiations in 1990-1991,which to a significant extent was due to the then-Socialist government's distrust of the US (see Holman 1996). Spain's rapprochement with NATO took place after a change of government in 1996.

[8] The Contact Group consisted of France, Great Britain, Germany, the US, and Russia.

out of steam in Bosnia. American involvement in the Dayton peace settlement of 1995 seemed to demonstrate the futility of 'autonomy,' and the key revisionist proponent, France, was engaged in domestic military reforms that led to a rapprochement with NATO. Thus, France and others demanded a greater 'voice' within NATO. This voice became possible with a new concept for organizing flexible NATO coalitions—Combined Joint Task Forces (CJTF) endorsed by NATO in January 1994[9]—a recognition of ESDI, for which "the Alliance's organisation and resources will be adjusted so as to facilitate" (NATO, 1994, paragraph 5).

In spite of NATO's vigour the architecture was still vulnerable to political turbulence. Was the US willing to follow through on its strategic leadership and articulate policies that take European points of view into account – or would the US rather be intoxicated by its success and Europe's failure at Dayton (see Hoffmann, 2000, 194)? If political disputes were again nurtured, it would invite efforts to bolster the EU—in terms of policy and institutions— to balance the US and NATO, also in spite of the obvious organizational powers of NATO. Political disputes were precisely what happened in 1998-1999 and these were in fact the root cause of the diplomatic constellations that produced the 'autonomous' defence option in the shape of ESDP.

At a time when European governments were generally focused on the European region and Yugoslav-style conflicts, the US looked beyond Europe and also beyond military crisis management. US Secretary of State Albright was particularly adamant that NATO needed to focus on threats to members' vital interests, irrespective of the nature of these threats (*Daily Telegraph* and *New York Times*, December 9, 1998). While Europe looked to the Balkans, the US looked to terrorist attacks on American embassies in Kenya and Tanzania, North Korean missile tests, all in August 1998, as well as a renewed air war over Iraq in October 1998. The compromise between European and American views is found in NATO's still valid Strategic Concept from April 1999 (NATO, 1999).

European governments were naturally capable of perceiving the American situation but they were also pulled back into the Balkans by the unfold-

[9] The CJTF concept was not new within the US armed forces where it had represented an effort to enhance interoperationability. In NATO the concept took on a slightly different meaning, not least because of the alliance's multinational setting. A 'task force' is defined as a group organized for a specific operation of a limited duration. It is 'joint' when two or more military services participate (army, navy, and air), and it is 'combined' when several nations participate. Out-of-area operations, the argument was, could be undertaken only by several countries at a time, and these countries were likely to offer disparate forces for the task. Concretely, CJTF work within NATO focused on developing headquarters that, apart from a permanent skeleton staff, would be able to operate with changing services and nationalities. These headquarters, moreover, would be geographically mobile, unlike NATO headquarters during the Cold War.

ing crisis in Kosovo during 1998. As General Wesley Clark (2001, 112), SACEUR at the time, recalls, European foreign ministers, including particularly the British and German, were determined in early 1998 to prevent another 'Balkan tragedy.' Plans for an air operation were ready in June 1998, and they came close to unleashing a series of strikes in October 1998. Richard Holbrooke, the Dayton architect, had been negotiating in parallel, however, and managed to have Serb President Milosovic sign an agreement. The agreement was eventually violated and NATO commenced a bombing campaign in March 1999. But Holbrooke's diplomacy, reminiscent of the Dayton debacle, had 'annoyed' European governments (Hoffmann, 2000, 194). France and Britain criticized the US for giving in too much in favour of the Kosovo Liberation Army (UCK), the Serbs' opponents, and for pushing too hard for a bombing campaign outside a diplomatic framework (*Information*, 30 January 1999). Again, the parallel to Euro-US disputes over Bosnia is obvious, and the US (along with the Contact Group of great powers) revealingly handed France and Britain the task of conducting peace negotiations in February-March 1999.[10]

It was in the midst of these diverging security perceptions that the St. Malo agreement came about. The ESDP was needed to make the EU more credible. Tony Blair was in no doubt about this dual motive in October 1998 (BBC, 1998; also Howorth, 2000). "Nothing must happen that in any way impinges on the effectiveness of NATO." However, Britain should be able to "put together an operation with, say, France, Belgium, Italy and Spain, in a way that meant we did not have to rely the whole time on the Americans." French President Chirac instead saw a promise to enhance the international profile of the EU "with a real foreign and defence policy" (*Libération*, December 5-6, 1998). Still, these diverging views did not prevent France and Britain from agreeing to a European defence initiative, which then resulted in the ESDP. France and Britain were midwives but the US lurked in the background as the father whose actions set its offspring onto a new course.

Conclusion

This chapter has examined the nature of the ESDP which the EU members agreed to launch formally at Nice, December 2000. The ESDP is an ambitious policy that complements the CFSP and builds on a policy goal of crisis management, new military and civilian capabilities, new institutions, and new relationships to allies and partners. Having provided an ESDP over-

---

[10] In addition, France took command of the 'extradition force' deployed to Macedonia in the fall of 1998 for the purpose of backing up OSCE observers in Kosovo.

view, the chapter traced the governmental negotiations that led to the ESDP, beginning with the Amsterdam treaty negotiations that were programmed at Maastricht but which failed to deliver the foreseen improvements. Amsterdam thus brought minor changes to the CFSP but the ESDP had failed to gather agreement. The Kosovo crisis coupled with a change of British policy were the immediate causes of the ESDP's unexpected emergence in late 1998 and early 1999. France, eager to promote a strong European polity, seized on the British change of tracks and other EU members saw the glaring lack of European capabilities in Kosovo and supported the initiative.

Does this development support the theoretical claims of Andrew Moravcsik? The third and final section provided a largely negative answer by pointing to a number of issues, crucial to the ESDP, that are geopolitical in nature. The first issue was the big geopolitical picture, according to which the emergence of both the CFSP and the ESDP happen in tandem with major geopolitical changes, just as Moravcsik's claim that European integration was dominated by economics limits itself to a supportive geopolitical context, the Cold War. The second issue was flexible integration which, since its appearance on the agenda in 1994, has become a fixed feature of EU politics, written into the CFSP and currently a disputed issue in the ESDP context. The final issue was the role of the US, whose strong investments in NATO have weakened the momentum behind the CFSP, just as its controversial campaign in Kosovo contributed to the forming of a distinct European security perspective—"we see security differently"—that previously had made itself felt in debates on NATO's strategic purpose.

Observers of the ESDP can use these conclusions to inquire theoretically whether and to what extent European integration is affected by geopolitics. Rather than relegating geopolitics to an appendix to liberal intergovernmentalism, it is now necessary to treat geopolitics as an independent source of insights into European integration and raise new questions. A key question is whether the EU is undergoing a transformation because greater geopolitical changes have led to the incorporation of security politics into the EU?

Closely related, they can also inquire about the apparent linear trajectory of the CFSP and now ESDP: will it continue? Is the underlying agreement on purpose and form strong enough to withstand the combined shock of enlargement and US security policy post-September 11? Enlargement will challenge the Petersberg consensus and the ability of institutions to function smoothly, and increase the challenge of coordinating disparate military and police forces. US policy is fully pursuing the logic of countering new threats that began under Clinton. Does the EU have the capacity to work with the US on strategic engagements aimed to combat asymmetrical threats while simultaneously building a crisis management capacity in Europe?

BIBLIOGRAPHY

BBC, "UK, Blair backs EU defence arm," 21 October 1998, http://news.bb.co.uk/hi/english/uk/newid_197000/197887.stm.

Bolving, Klaus (2002), "De 15, de 9 og de 6: ESDP og forholdet til tredjelandene," *DUPI report* 2002/07. Copenhagen: DUPI.

Britain (1998), "Joint Declaration issued at the British-French Summit, Saint-Malo, France, 3-4 December 1998," http://www.fco.gov.uk/news/newstext.asp?1795

Calleo, David P. (2001), *Rethinking Europe's Future*. Princeton: Princeton University Press.

Clark, Wesley K. (2001), *Waging Modern War*. New York: Public Affairs.

Cogan, Charles G. (2001), *The Third Option: The Emancipation of European Defense, 1989-2000*. New York: Praeger.

Collester, J. Bryan (2000), "How Defense 'Spilled Over' into the CFSP: Western European Union (WEU) and the European Security and Defense Identity," in Maria G. Gowls and Michael Smith (eds.), *The State of the European Union*. Oxford: Oxford University Press, pp. 369-389.

EU (1993), *European Union Treaty*. Bruxelles: EU Information Office.

— (1997), *Consolidated Version of the Treaty on European Union* http://europa.eu.int/eur-lex/en/treaties/dat/eu_cons_treaty_en.pdf.

— EU (1999a), *Presidency Conclusions, Cologne European Council, 3-4 June 1999*, http://europa.eu.int/council/off/conclu/june99/june99_en.htm

— (1999b), *Presidency Conclusions, Helsinki European Council, 10-11 December 1999*, http://ue.eu.int/Newsroom/LoadDoc.asp?BID=76&DID=59750&LANG=1

— (2000a), *Presidency Report on the European Security and Defence Policy*.

— (2000b), *Treaty of Nice*, http://europa.eu.int/eur-lex/en/treaties/dat/nice_treaty_en.pdf

Forster, Anthony and Robin Niblett (2001), "Concepts of European Order after the Cold War: In with the Old, Out with the New," in Robin Niblett and William Wallace (eds.), *Rethinking European Order: West European Responses, 1989-97*. London: Palgrave, pp. 27-57.

— and William Wallace (2000), "Common Foreign and Security Policy: From Shadow to Substance?," in Helen Wallace and William Wallace (eds.), *Policy-Making in the European Union*. Oxford: Oxford University Press, pp. 461-491.

— (2001), "The British Response: Denial and Confusion?," in Robin Niblett and William Wallace (eds.), *Rethinking European Order: West European Responses, 1989-97*. London: Palgrave, pp. 124-150.

Gegout, Catherine (2002), "The Quint: Acknowledging the Existence of a Big Four-US Directoire at the Heart of the European Union's Foreign Policy Decision-Making Process," *Journal of Common Market Studies*, Vol. 40, No. 2, pp. 331-344.

Hansen, Kenneth Schmidt, and Casper Klynge (2001), *EU og civil krisestyring*. Copenhagen: DUPI.

Hoffmann, Stanley (2000), "Towards a Common European Foreign and Security Policy?", *Journal of Common Market Studies*, Vol. 38, No. 2 (June), pp. 189-198.

Holman, Otto (1996), *Integrating Southern Europe: EC Expansion and the Transnationalization of Spain*. London: Routledge.

Howorth, Jolyon (2000), "Britain, France and the European Defence Initiative," *Survival*, Vol. 42, No. 2, pp. 33-55.

— (2001), "European Defence and the Changing Politics of the European Union: Hanging Together or Hanging Separately?," *Journal of Common Market Studies*, Vol. 39, No. 4, pp. 765-789.

International Security Information Service (ISIS) (2000), "States Pledge Resources for Crisis Management," *European Security Review*, No. 3, pp. 2-3.

Klein, Jean (1997), "Relations Franco-Allemandes et identité européenne de défense," *Stratégique*, Vol. 19, No. 4, pp. 185-199.

Missiroli, Antonio (2000), "CFSP, Defence and Flexibility," WEU Institute of Security Studies, *Chaillot Paper* 38, http://www.weu.int/institute/chaillot/chai38ex.htm

Moravcsik, Andrew (1998), *The Choice for Europe: Social Purpose and State Power From Messina to Maastricht.* London: UCL Press.

NATO (1994), "Ministerial Meeting of the North Atlantic Council/ North Atlantic Cooperation Council, NATO Headquarters, Brussels," 10-11 January 1994, http://www.nato.int/docu/comm/49-95/c940111a.htm

NATO (1996), "Final Communiqué of the Ministerial Meeting of the North Atlantic Council", 3 June 1996, http://www.nato.int/docu/pr/1996/p96-063e.htm

— (1999), "The Alliance's Strategic Concept approved by the Heads of State and Government participating in the meeting of the North Atlantic Council in Washington D.C.," http://www.nato.int/docu/pr/1999/p99-065e.htm

Niblett, Robin (2001), "Spain and European Order after the Cold War," in Robin Niblett and William Wallace (eds.), *Rethinking European Order: West European Responses, 1989-97*. London: Palgrave, pp. 207-24157.

Nielsen, Reimer (2001), *Den europæiske forsvarsdimension: baggrund og perspektiver.* Copenhagen: DUPI.

WEU (1992), *Petersberg Declaration, 19 June 1992*, www.weu.int/eng/comm/92-petersberg.htm.

Wijk, Rob de (2000), "Convergence Criteria: Measuring Input or Output?," *European Foreign Affairs Review*, Vol. 5, No. 3, pp. 397-417.

CHAPTER 24

THE CHARTER OF FUNDAMENTAL RIGHTS: NOVEL METHOD ON THE WAY TO THE NICE TREATY

INTRODUCTION

"...There is a need for a Charter of Fundamental Rights because the European Union has entered a new, more resolutely political phase of integration. The Charter is a major milestone for Europe as a political force, which is evolving into an integrated area of freedom, security and justice, simply as a consequence of citizenship. It is an indispensable instrument of political and moral legitimacy, both for the citizens of Europe in relation to politicians, administrations and national powers and for economic and social operators. It is an expression of the common values that are at the very core of our democratic societies".[1]

On 7 December 2000, the European Union Charter of Fundamental Rights was solemnly proclaimed in Nice at the summit of Heads of State and Government. This was a historic moment since, for the first time in the Union's history, a European document set out in a single text the whole range of civil, political, economic and social rights of European citizens and all persons resident in the EU. These rights were gathered in six sections: Dignity, Freedoms, Equality, Solidarity, Citizens' rights, and Justice. The principles which are at the heart of these sections are based on the fundamental rights and freedoms recognised by the European Convention on Human Rights (ECHR), the constitutional traditions of the EU Member States, the Council of Europe's Social Charter, the Community Charter of Fundamental Social Rights of Workers and other international conventions.

The aim of this chapter is to show how the Charter of Fundamental Rights was elaborated by a new body named Convention which is the forerunner of the Convention on the Future of Europe. The method used by this new body, the different positions adopted by Member States during the negotiations, and the outcome of this process with the first bill of rights for the Union are among the

---

[1] See Commission Communication on the Charter of Fundamental Rights of the European Union/* COM/2000/0559 final */.

main points covered by this chapter. The evolution of the Charter from a political declaration to a legally binding document is also subject of analysis.

The Protection of Fundamental Rights Prior to the Charter

Until the proclamation of the Charter, the European Convention on Human Rights (ECHR) was the main instrument of reference for the protection of fundamental rights in Europe. All EU Member States are part of the ECHR, and the European Court of Justice (ECJ) has often drawn inspiration and guidance from this legal instrument (Jones et al., 2003, 10).

The ECJ has also played a fundamental role in protecting fundamental rights by developing a jurisprudence that recognizes fundamental rights as 'general principles' of Community law. Fundamental rights as identified by the ECJ were based on the constitutional traditions of Member States and on the ECHR.

The protection of fundamental rights has for the first time been formally recognised by the Treaty of the European Union (TEU), which in Article 6 establishes the obligation of the EU to respect fundamental rights as guaranteed by the ECHR and as they result from the constitutional traditions enshrined within the Member States.

The fundamental rights provisions (Articles 6 and 7 of the TEU) are reinforced by the Treaty of Amsterdam which established that the Union is founded on "liberty, democracy, respect for human rights and fundamental freedoms, and the rule of law" and also provides the possibility of suspension of certain rights of a Member State in case of breach of one of these principles. The Amsterdam Treaty also provided in Article 49 TEU that the applicant countries must respect the principles set out in Article 6(1) TEU and stated in Article 46 TEU that the Court of Justice of the European Communities will ensure that the European institutions respect fundamental rights. As part of this fundamental rights protection, the provisions dedicated to the protection of fundamental rights by the Treaty establishing the European Community (TEC), notably the principle of non-discrimination on grounds of nationality, was extended by the Treaty of Amsterdam by broadening the grounds for non-discrimination to "sex, racial or ethnic origin, religion or belief, disability, age or sexual orientation," in Articles 12 and 13 of the Treaty establishing the European Community (TEC). The Treaty of Amsterdam also extended the jurisdiction of the ECJ to legislation related to the creation of an Area of Freedom, Security and Justice, which until then was only fragmentarily embedded within a few specific protocols. The system of legal protection established in the Treaty of Amsterdam presents serious weaknesses since it provided individuals only with limited access to the ECJ.

The Nice European Council decided to supplement Article 7 of the EU Treaty with a mechanism for preventing violations of fundamental rights. Furthermore, it established that the Council, acting by a four-fifth majority, and based on a proposal by one-third of all EU Member States, by the European Parliament or by the European Commission, may determine whether there is a clear risk of a serious breach of principles established by Article 6(1) TEU, and may address appropriate recommendations to that state.

More generally, the Community has actively pursued human rights protection in its external relations. The Union demands fundamental rights commitments from third states in connection with development aid and bilateral trade agreements, and ratification of the ECHR is a condition for EU membership.

The Need for a Bill of Rights at Union Level

The elaboration of the Charter is the culmination of a long process searching for the correct form of recognition of fundamental rights within the Union. However, the process never extended to the creation of a legal basis to provide for a general human rights competence. At the same time, the expansion of Community activity in a growing number of policy areas increased the necessity for the Union to define its human rights competences. Other motivations for the necessity of a Charter included:

1. The Charter puts fundamental rights at the heart of the EU construction, reinforcing the concept of EU citizenship and thus helping to establish the legitimacy of the EU. This is of particular importance in the context of the forthcoming enlargement of the Union since the Charter will be perceived as a commitment from the Union to promote the respect for human rights.
2. The Charter is a potent symbol of the transition from a system based on mainly economic interests to a mature political Union of Member States, and comes at a time when many would like to see the Union assuming a greater supra-national role.
3. EU citizens must be able to challenge the legality of acts of the EU institutions and of Member States when applying EU Law. A legally binding Charter will ensure that citizens are provided with a system of redress against acts of maladministration or the abuse of power across the whole range of EU activity.

4. For the first time a European legal instrument would gather together civil, political, economic and social rights. The Charter therefore makes rights visible to those it is intended to benefit and provides transparency and consistency to citizens, lawmakers and regulators.
5. Some Member States have expressed concern that the EU could not effectively protect rights enshrined in their national Constitutions. Incorporating the Charter will help to address these concerns and strengthen the principles underpinning the EU's legal system.
6. As the Union is increasing its competences and gaining new powers, a strong commitment to fundamental rights is needed. For example, granting legally binding value to the Charter is an essential component in the progressive establishment of the Area of Freedom, Security and Justice.
7. A binding Charter will help the Union to develop a more coherent Human Rights Policy not only internally but also externally, thereby addressing the criticism that the EU lacks coherence in its external fundamental rights policy.

The Content of the Charter: A Political Declaration

The Cologne mandate was very ambiguous on the subject of whether the Convention should draft a complete catalogue of fundamental rights or just a catalogue based on the specific competences of the Union. The Convention elaborated a complete catalogue of fundamental rights that comprised fundamental rights and freedoms, economic and social rights and the rights of citizens of the Union. The reasons for taking this decision were the following:

1. A reduced catalogue of fundamental rights would have sent the wrong signal at international level. As an example, even though assuming that the 'death penalty' is an issue that does not fall within the Union competences, if this article had not been included within the Charter, the role of the EU advocating the abolition of death penalty in international forums would have been highly questionable.
2. The difficulty of delimitating the competences of the Union. As an example, whereas the right to education primarily falls within the competence of Member States, Article 149 TEC gives the Community certain competences in this field.
3. To make the Charter valid through an extensive period of time thereby avoiding continuous modifications to the Charter in order to adjust to any change of the competences of the Union.

The result was an extensive document that gathers in a single text, and on an equal basis, the classic freedoms together with social rights. This makes the Charter the most modern document in the field of human rights. The text of the Charter is divided into a preamble and seven chapters including 57 articles and General Provisions. The Charter is also highly progressive since it includes a number of modern fundamental rights (right to protection of personal data, bioethics) and since it was drafted in a gender neutral way.

Impact of the Charter

For the first time, all the rights previously scattered throughout a variety of legal instruments were combined in a single document lending visibility and clarity to fundamental rights and freedoms. As stated in the preamble, the Charter helps to establish the citizenship of the Union and to create an Area of Freedom, Security and Justice. The Charter also strengthens certainty as to the law on the protection of fundamental rights, which in the past was guaranteed only by the case law of the Court of Justice.

Most of the rights are applicable to every person, irrespective of their nationality or residence. However, some of those rights are limited to EU citizens. The Chapter devoted to Citizen's rights considers specific situations affecting European citizens by reference to certain rights already included in the Treaties (freedom of movement and of residence, the right to vote, the right to petition), while at the same time introducing the right to good administration.

The general provisions (or so-called horizontal clauses) were key elements in order to achieve consensus and their role is fundamental as their purpose is: to establish links between the Charter and the European Convention on Human Rights (ECHR), and to determine the scope of the Charter. They state that the Charter applies to the European Institutions with due regard for the principle of subsidiarity and in no circumstances it may increase the powers and the duties conferred on them by the Treaties. The principles of the Charter also apply to the Member States (to the central authorities as well as to regional or local bodies) when implementing Community law. The obligation on Member States to respect fundamental rights when implementing Community law is not new and has already been confirmed by Court of Justice case law.

The Charter goes beyond the ECHR in the sense that it contains fundamental freedoms and economic and social rights derived from other international instruments as well as the common constitutional traditions of Member States. In this sense, the question of the accession to the European Convention on Human Rights cannot be seen as separate from that of the Charter and indeed one of the questions to be answered by the Convention on the Future of Europe.

Finally, the Charter is not only a potent symbol of compromise of the EU in the field of fundamental rights but also a signal of the political constitutional momentum which is gathering in Europe.

Building the Charter: The Core Elements of the Process

The Convention Method

On 3 and 4 June 1999 at the Cologne European Council,[2] the EU heads of State and Government, decided to "establish a Charter of Fundamental Rights of the European Union in order to make their overriding importance and relevance more visible to the Union's citizens." It was also decided to establish an ad hoc body to draft such a Charter. At the European Council in Tampere[3] on 15 and 16 October 1999, it was decided to compose this new body which was entitled the Convention. Finally, on 7 December 2000,[4] at the European Council in Nice, the three main institutions of the European Union (the European Parliament, the Commission and the Council) 'solemnly proclaimed' the Charter of Fundamental Rights of the European Union.[5]

Composition

The Convention was composed by: 15 representatives of the Heads of State and Government, 1 representative of the Commission, 16 members of the European Parliament and 30 members of the national Parliaments of the Member States.

[2] Cologne European Council 3 and 4 June 1999, Presidency Conclusions. http://ue.eu.int/Newsroom/LoadDoc.asp?BID=76&DID=57886&from=&LANG=

[3] Tampere European Council, 15 and 16 October 1999, Presidency Conclusions. http://ue.eu.int/Newsroom/related.asp?max=1&bid=76&grp=2017&lang=1

[4] Nice European Council, 7 and 9 December 2000, Presidency Conclusions. http://ue.eu.int/Newsroom/related.asp?max=1&bid=76&grp=3018&lang=1

[5] Charter of Fundamental Rights of the European Union, Solemn Proclamation, OJ C 364 18.12.2000 P001-0022.

Two representatives of the Court of Justice and two representatives of the Council of Europe enjoyed the status of observer. The Economic and Social Committee, the Committee of the Regions and the European Ombudsman were invited to give their views. There was also an exchange of vicws with the applicant countries.

The Convention was chaired by former President of the Federal Republic of Germany Roman Herzog. The Chairman was assisted by a drafting committee, the Praesidium, which was composed of three vice chairs and the representative of the Commission. It comprised, Gunnar Jansson, vice chairman representing the group of Members of national Parliaments, who was replaced by Pedro Bacelar de Vasconcellos (Portugal); Guy Braibant (France), the vice chairman representing the group of personal representatives Iñigo Méndez de Vigo, vice chairman representing the Group of Members of the European Parliament and Antonio Vitorino representing the Commission.

The Convention drafted the EU Charter of Fundamental Rights in nine months after 30 meetings. The composition of the Convention was very innovative since it brought together representatives of Member States, Commission, EP and National Parliaments within a single body.

Transparency

The method used for drafting the Charter can be classified as revolutionary since transparency was the rule as opposed to the secrecy which normally characterises negotiations at the Intergovernmental Conference (IGC). All proceedings were open to the public and all documents produced were published. The following features were among the most relevant:

- The public could have access to all the meetings.
- All documents related to the Convention were accessible via Internet.
- Special auditions were organised with the Economic and Social Committee, the Committee of the Regions and the European Ombudsman.
- There was a full day audition with the representatives of civil society.
- National Parliaments organised various hearings that helped to form the opinion of the respective national parliamentarians involved.
- Various hearings and panel discussions were organised for an exchange of views among members of the Convention, associations, citizens and non-governmental organisations (NGOs).
- The media coverage was extensive.

Working Methods

The Chairman proposed a work plan and undertook the preparatory work. Working groups were set up and the Drafting Committee, comprising the Chairman, three Vice-Chairs and a Commission representative, drew up a preliminary draft Charter in conjunction with the other members. The Convention met in Brussels and applied a full language regime (11 languages).

The Praesidium of the Convention and the task force assisting it, composed by staff of the Council Secretariat, played a key role in preparing the draft. The Praesidium drafts were quite ambitious and went well beyond the minimum common denominator.

The Member States' representatives formed a quite diverse group which included lawyers and politicians. They did not have mandatory obligations to follow since they were not given instructions from their national governments, but during the final stages of the drafting, Member State representatives were in close contact with national governments. The Members of the National Parliaments did not receive instructions from home country or specific guidelines to be pursued.

One of the more striking differences with the IGCs is the existence of dialogue with civil society. The relation was not perfect but did go beyond what was expected. There was only one formal consultation which was not very successful due to the lack of time and the very high expectations of network representatives. However, through informal means, civil society had an influence on the final draft of the Charter. Contributions were sent to the convention web page and civil society had informal meetings with members of the Convention. The openness of the sessions also facilitated the contact between members of the Convention and civil society. NGOs were able to influence the elaboration of the Charter, mainly through writing contributions and also by contacting the members of the Convention at their own initiative. As a result of this, the most active NGOs were clearly favoured and managed to include some of their proposals in the Charter.

Outcome

The method of consensus was applied and no votes were taken in this process. It was agreed that when the text of the draft Charter could eventually be subscribed by all the parties, it should be sent to the European Council. During the last meeting, all members of the Praesidium, each representing a different group, approved the text and only a few delegates spoke against it. This way of decision–making by consensus strengthened the legitimacy of the Charter. Heads of State and Government could have revised the draft text presented by the Convention. However, they preferred not to do so given the undisputed quality of the text, and considering that the text was the result of a lengthy political and democratic process. A revision of the text would therefore have threatened the fragile balance which had been achieved.

The Convention did not have to make a choice on the issue of legal status of the Charter since, due to the British opposition to a legally binding instrument, the Heads of State and Government decided to postpone the question of whether the Charter should be incorporated into the Treaties. Regardless of the uncertainty about the legal status of the Charter, the text was drafted as if it were to become legally binding.

The indisputable success of the Convention is based on the fact that it included new players that were not defending the interests of national governments, and it created the conditions for an effective debate.

The political relevance of the new document was emphasised by Professor Jürgen Meyer, member of the Convention, who stated that: "without codification of fundamental rights, the Community's legitimacy could increasingly be called into question. The proclamation of the Charter can therefore only be a first step, which has to be followed by the Charter's incorporation into the European Treaties."[6]

Role and Position of Actors

Member State positions

In this context, the following is a short overview of the position of several government actors and of the evolution of their position.

---

[6] A collection of documents with an introduction by Jürgen Meyer and Markus Engels: "The Charter of Fundamental Rights of the Union and the work of the Convention", p. 8.

Member State	Position
Finland	• Finland expressed concerns about the impact of a binding Charter on the level of protection of the Finnish Constitution. • The clarification of the relationship between ECJ and ECtHR was vital in this sense.[7]
France	• France abandoned its struggle to get the Charter incorporated into the EU Treaty because it had decided to sacrify its objective in order to get agreement on a more wide-ranging set of social rights.[8] • Prime Minister Lionel Jospin travelled to London to discuss the Convention's draft with Prime Minister Blair. The UK, being the main opponent to this process, stated that the Charter should remain as a political declaration. In exchange, France obtained an agreement to include a reference to the right of strike.[9]
Germany	• The Charter to be incorporated in the EU Treaty and be given a legally binding character as part of a EU Constitution to be negotiated in 2003.[10] • On the future status of the Charter, German Chancellor Gerhard Schröder, hoped that the Charter would be included in the Union's Treaty as an element of a kind of European Constitution.[11]
Italy	• A legally binding Charter should be part of the EU Constitution to be negotiated in 2003.[12]
Luxembourg	• Luxembourg did not have major objections to the Charter, while recognising that many legal issues remained to be solved.[13]
Portugal	• In favour of a binding Charter to be incorporated in the Treaties.[14]

[7] Record of meetings of the representatives of national parliaments and formal plenary meeting of the Convention on 20/21 March 2000.

[8] *European Voice* 29.09.00.

[9] Florence Deloche-Gaudez; Research and Policy Paper N.15: "The Convention and the Charter of Fundamental Rights: a Method for the Future?" November 2001.

[10] *Financial Times* 21.9.00.

[11] *Bulletin Quotidien Europe* N° 7895 3.02.01.

[12] *Financial Times* 21.09.00.

[13] Official from the Permanent Representation of Luxembourg to the EU.

[14] Member of the Convention which drafted the Charter, curent official at the Permanent Representation of Portugal to the EU.

Spain	• Prime Minister José Maria Aznar, was in favour of a Charter with binding nature and supports its future incorporation into the Treaties.[15]
Sweden	• Prime Minister Göran Persson, speaking on the future status on the Charter of Fundamental rights, asked for caution in order not to undermine other instruments such as the European Convention on Human Rights.[16] • The wording of the Charter of Fundamental Rights "is not sufficiently precise for incorporating it in the Treaty". According to Prime Minister Göran Persson, it would be preferable to sign up to the European Convention on Human Rights.[17]
UK	• Britain does not want the Charter to be more than a political declaration.[18] • The UK was the strongest opponent to the Charter project. Lord Goldsmith, representative of the British Government, signalled the approval of the Charter at the 17th meeting. At the end he announced that he would make an extremely positive report to Prime Minister Tony Blair and "strongly hoped" that the UK would accept the document.[19] • The UK was reticent about the ECJ interpreting Human Rights issues because of the possibility of the Court making an extensive interpretation of those rights. The UK was strongly in favour of accession to ECHR.[20]
Ireland, Denmark the Netherlands	• Against a binding Charter incorporated into the treaties.[21]

The main blocking Member States

[15] *El Pais* 12.10.10.

[16] Bulletin Quotidien Europe N° 7895, 3.02.2001.

[17] *Bulletin Quotidien Europe* N° 8074, 20.10.01.

[18] *Financial Times* 2.10.00.

[19] Florence Deloche–Gaudez: The Convention on a Charter of Fundamental Rights: a method for the future? Research and Policy Paper No. 15 November 2001, p. 6. Groupement d'Études et de Recherches Notre Europe.http://www.notre-europe.asso.fr/fichiers/Etud15-en.pdf.

[20] Member of the Convention which drafted the Charter.

[21] Press office of the European Parliament.

From a very early stage of the discussions, British representative Lord Goldsmith became the spokesman of the 'Charter sceptics.' Apart from the initial agreement achieved within the Convention on the Future of Europe, even today the British appear to be the main opponents of integrating the Charter as it stands within the future European Constitution. The conditions established by the British representative from the beginning were clear: first of all the Charter language must be closely aligned to that of the ECHR, and a list of limitations to the rights enshrined in the Charter had to be established having the same legal status of the rights themselves. From the British point of view, the case law of the European Court on Human Rights (ECtHR) had to be taken into account, however it was not absolutely necessary to take into account the ECJ's case law in fundamental rights. These views were strongly opposed by Germany, Italy and Luxembourg.

British representative Lord Goldsmith made also the proposal of dividing the Charter into two Parts: part A, to inform citizens of fundamental rights that they are guaranteed, and part B, establishing the legal explanations and restrictions to part A. This proposal was supported by the Danish and Irish representatives, but dismissed by the others. Commissioner Antonio Vitorino underlined that the proposal meant that the Charter would remain non-binding.

The discussions became extremely heated when the economic and social rights were at stake. The question on whether social and economic rights should be included appeared one of the most problematic. Opponents of the incorporation of these rights were concerned by the possibility that those rights would extend the competences of the Union and would represent a danger of higher national standards. The proponents argued that it was part of the mandate given in Cologne to include those rights. According to them, economic regulations need to be accompanied by minimum social standards and finally, the absence of these rights would send a wrong sign at international level. Lord Goldsmith did not want them to be included at all. On the other hand, the French representative, Guy Braibant, strongly underlined the significance of economic and social rights. Those two represented the most divergent positions in this topic. The Irish representative, Michael O'Kennedy, also opposed the inclusion of economic and social rights.

Candidate Countries' Positions

Candidate Countries had the status of observer during the negotiations of the Charter. Generally speaking, candidate countries largely agreed with the objectives of the Charter of Fundamental Rights and stressed the impact in promoting citizens' identification with the EU. They saw the Charter as a commitment of the European Union to explicitly proclaim the respect for human rights. During the works of the Convention Candidate Countries were mainly concerned about two points: they did not want a Charter which could add conditions to the *acquis* and they did not want the Charter to restrict the protection offered by the ECHR.

The following table illustrates the position of several candidate countries:

	Candidate Countries	
Cyprus	• The Charter will have positive and beneficial effects in the process of European integration. It will fit an obvious gap in the already broad spectrum of the activities of the Union. • The ECHR and the Charter should be consistent and complementary.	Permanent Secretary of the Ministry of Foreign Affairs Brussels, 12.06.00
Estonia	• In favour of provisional adoption of the Charter as a political declaration. • Rejection of the inclusion of economic and social rights.	Meelis Tigimae, Estonian representative in the Convention
Hungary	• Hungary is ready to accept the document in its form, as elaborated and adopted by the Member States, whether as a political declaration or a legally binding document included in the Treaties. • Necessary to avoid any inconsistency between the ECJ and the ECtHR.	Béla Szombati, Deputy Head of the State Secretariat for Integration of the Ministry for Foreign Affairs, Brussels, 19.07.00
Latvia	• The adoption of the Charter is a complementary step to the process of enlargement of the Union. • The Charter should complement and not compete with the legal system established by the ECHR. • If the Charter's scope will transcend the borders of a declaratory document, a very clear legal definition of Charter's application mechanism for its provisions will be necessary.	H.E. Mr. Andris Piebalgs Ambassador of the Republic of Latvia to the EU Brussels, 19.06.00

Poland	• In favour of a Charter as political declaration without excluding the evolution of some of its provisions into Community law (included into the Treaties). • The Charter should not create competition between the ECJ and the ECtHR.	Jerzy Kranz Vice Secretary of the Ministry of Foreign Affairs of Poland Brussels, 19.06.00
Slovak Republic	• Despite the fact that in the pre-accession period the Charter will be a fundamental political document having a declaratory nature in the associated countries, the Slovak Republic considers a clear resolution of the Charter binding status and enforceability as very important and paramount.	Audition with Candidate Countries on the Convention for the Charter of Fundamental Rights
Slovenia	• The Charter is the expression of the commitment of the European Union to explicitly proclaim the respect for human rights. • The Charter should be a non-binding legal document (declaration). • The EU should reconsider the possibility of acceding to the ECHR. This would be the best way to avoid the risk of the duplication of human rights standards.	Mitja Drobnic, State Secretary Brussels, 19.06.00
Malta	• Welcomed the Charter but expressed concerns about the overlap with the ECHR. • Against the prospect of the Charter being adopted as part of the acquis communautaire.	Michel Frendo, Maltese representative in the Convention
Bulgaria	• The Charter of Fundamental Rights should lead to a substantial improvement of the system for the protection of Human Rights. • The development of the area of freedom, security and justice goes together with the improvement of the protection of Human Rights and Fundamental Freedoms of the citizens of the Union. • The rights covered by the Charter, should not create new standards in the *acquis* of the Union and pose new requirements in the context of accession negotiations. • It would be useful to keep the clause stating that nothing in the Charter will restrict the protection offered by the ECHR. • The decision to elaborate a text with legal character is the right one, even if incorporation in the Treaty is not imminent.	H.E. Antoinette Primatarova, Ambassador of the Bulgarian mission to the EU Brussels, 19.06.00

Romania	• The Charter should spell out more clearly the addressees of the rights described therein, be it institutions or categories of individuals. • Concerned as regards the future relations between the ECJ and ECtHR. • Without providing appropriately for effective remedies in case of infringement of the rights enumerated, the Charter is likely to contain a political message alone, even if a particular strong one. • Welcomed the inclusion of economic and social rights.	Eugen Dijmarescu, Secretary of State Head of the Department for European Affairs within the Ministry of Foreign Affairs of Romania
Turkey	• Concerns that the ECHR system might be weakened. A new system competing with the ECHR should not be put in place. • The EU should accede to the ECHR. • The Charter should remain a non-binding document.	H.E. M. Nihat Akyol Ambassador of the Turkish Mission to the EU 19.06.00

As opposed to civil society representatives, Candidate Countries did not have a very significant role in shaping this process. They only had the opportunity to take part in an exchange of views as provided for in the Tampere conclusions: "an appropriate exchange of views should be held by the body or by the Chairperson with applicant States." In the end, they were just invited to present their contributions.

AFTER NICE: THE CONVENTION ON THE FUTURE OF EUROPE

The Laeken Mandate

Since solemnly proclaimed in Nice, the Charter has existed as a political declaration. While it had no express legal value, it has had an impact on the European Courts using it as an authoritative source in identifying fundamental rights.[22]

[22] The Community Courts have made reference to the Charter, at least 7 Advocate Generals at the ECJ have referred to the Charter when mentioning fundamental rights. As an example: Case C-491/01 R v Secretary of State for Health ex parte: British American Tobacco (Investments) Ltd and Imperial Tobacco Ltd (10 September 2002); Case C-112/00 Eugen Schmidberger Internationale Transporte Planzüge v Austria (11 July 2002); Case C-466/00 Kaba v Secretary of State for the Home Departement (11 July 2002) etc.

The Charter has also become an important reference document for newly drafted EU legislation in order to ensure the respect of fundamental rights.

Nice not only proclaimed the Charter, it also provided the mandate for the next IGC in 2004 which has to deal with:

- Clarification of the field of competences shared between the EU and Member States
- Status of the EU Charter of Fundamental Rights
- Simplification of the Treaties
- The role of national parliaments in the institutional structure of the Union.

On 14 and 15 December 2001, the European Council meeting in Laeken adopted a declaration on the future of the European Union and established a Convention to prepare for the new Treaty reforms at the next inter-governmental conference in 2004. The new Convention was entrusted with the specific aim of considering possible changes for the Treaties and working methods to prepare the Union to open up to the new members. The European Council gave the Convention the mandate to consider, among other things, "whether the Charter should be integrated within the Treaties and whether the European Community should accede to the ECHR". [23]

Creation of the Convention Working Group on the Charter

The question of the Charter cannot be treated in isolation from other questions that are being explored by the Convention on the future of Europe such as the reorganisation of the Treaties, the division of competences, the Pillar structure and the Union's legal personality. The final decision on the question of the Charter will not be taken in isolation but will very much depend on the choices to be made concerning these related questions.

Mandate

The Convention on the Future of Europe established a working group (WG), led by Commissioner Antonio Vitorino, to deal with the following questions: "If it is decided to include the Charter of Fundamental Rights in the Treaty: how

---

[23] European Council meeting in Laeken, Presidency Conclusions, 14.12 01. http://ue.eu.int/Newsroom/related.asp?max=1&bid=76&grp=4061&lang=1

should this be done and what are the consequences thereof? What would the consequences be of accession by the Community/ Union to the ECHR?"[24]

When looking at the proceedings of the WG, it is interesting to note the following features:

- The WG would not discuss the major political questions on whether the Charter should be incorporated or whether there should be accession to the ECHR. On the contrary, the WG worked "on the assumption that the two questions will meet a positive answer."[25]
- Incorporation and accession are seen as complementary. From the beginning, the WG stressed that these two aspects would not be addressed separately since they are considered as complementary and not as alternatives.
- The Charter is an acquis. The WG considered the content of the Charter, as negotiated by the previous convention, a common acquis to be maintained, while acknowledging that certain adjustments of purely technical nature would be necessary.

The WG had among its tasks to examine the different techniques for incorporation of the Charter, the precise legal effect and political profile to be conferred on the Charter, the question of replication of rights in the Charter and in the Treaties and the future structure of the Treaties. In relation to the question of accession to the ECHR, the WG had to examine the possible implications of this accession for the principle of autonomy of Community law, the form of legal basis provided for accession and possible alternatives to accession.

The mandate of the WG also includes a reference to two further questions which are connected with the protection of fundamental rights in the Union:

- Whether Article 230(4) TEC should be amended in order to extend the possibility of direct access of individuals to the ECJ or whether other alternatives should be considered.
- Extension of the competences of the ECJ in JHA matters.

Working Methods

The WG met seven times in Brussels. The working languages were English and French and access to the meetings was restricted to members of the Convention and collaborators only. This is different from the previous Convention where all meetings were public and the 11 official languages were applied. The group had

---

[24] Mandate of the Convention Working Group on the Charter. Doc CONV 72/02. http://register.consilium.eu.int/pdf/en/02/cv00/00072en2.pdf

[25] Document CONV 72/02, P2.

special hearings with representatives of the ECJ and the ECHR as well as the Directors-General of the legal service of the Commission, Council and European Parliament. Furthermore, there was an additional meeting with the "human rights" contact group where civil society was invited to present its views. Another important difference between the previous Convention and the present one is the formal involvement of Candidate Countries.

Member States' Positions

Negotiations regarding the Charter were most difficult. It is important to stress that in the beginning certain governments were still hesitant about the political question concerning the legal status of the Charter. The following table shows Member States' positions prior to the negotiations.

Member State	Position
Austria	• The Charter should be incorporated into the Treaty as a first step for a European Constitution. • In favour of accession to the ECHR.
Belgium	• The Charter should be part of the Constitutional Treaty. • The Union should accede to the ECHR.
Denmark	• In favour of incorporating the Charter into the Treaty. • The relationship between the EU and the ECHR needs further discussion.
Finland	• Reticent to incorporate the Charter into the Treaty. It is necessary to find a mechanism to make it visible in the Treaty. • One should be careful when defining the future legal status of the Charter, especially about the possible consequences for the EU and Member States' competences. • In favour of EC accession to the ECHR.
France	• The Charter should be at the heart of the future European Constitution. • Under certain conditions, citizens should have direct access to the ECJ.
Germany	• The Charter to be given legally binding value and to be incorporated into the Treaty as a first step for a European Constitution which integrates the Charter.
Greece	• The Charter must be incorporated into the EU Treaty and be legally binding.
Ireland	• As stated in Nice, the Charter must remain a political declaration. The EU must not establish two parallel systems for Human Rights

	protection. Furthermore, the protection of citizen rights must be reinforced within the Treaty.
Italy	• The Charter must be incorporated into the future European Constitution.
Luxembourg	• Fundamental Rights must be part of the Constitutional Treaty. • The Union should accede to the ECHR. However, the coherence of instruments must be guaranteed in order to avoid competing juridical orders and diverging jurisprudence.
Portugal	• The Charter must be legally binding.
Spain	• In favour of incorporation of the Charter into the Treaties and of giving individuals the possibility to accede to the ECJ for the protection of those Fundamental Rights.
Sweden	• Sweden had a reserved attitude on the future status of the Charter and urged to proceed carefully in order not to undermine the European Convention on Human Rights. • The Charter is not drafted in a sufficiently precise way to be incorporated into the Treaty.
The Netherlands	• A revised Charter must be integrated into the Community order. • The question of the status of the Charter comes together with the envisaged accession of the Union to the ECHR and therefore the question of the Strasbourg and Luxembourg jurisdictions.
United Kingdom	• In favour of maintaining the Charter as a political declaration. However, if it were to become a legally binding instrument, Britain was very anxious to: - Avoid potential conflict with the European Court of Human Rights - Avoid potential conflict with national legislation in the field of social rights.

The first discussions within the WG soon underlined that among the main concerns raised by participants were: whether the Charter would give new rights to individuals or new competences to the EU, relations between the Charter and the ECHR, and whether the horizontal clauses were sufficient. As in the previous Convention, from an early stage onward the British, followed by the Irish government, made clear that the Charter could not be integrated in a legally binding form. Both countries also felt that those 'new rights' recognised in the Charter, that were not already enshrined in the Treaties, should not lead to the creation of new competences.

Outcome

Surprisingly, subsequent to this initial reluctance, the WG managed to agree on the fundamental questions and presented its final conclusions on 22 October 2002.[26] The WG agreed on the following points:

- A legally binding Charter. The WG showed broad consensus in having a legally binding Charter, with a vast majority supporting the integration of the Charter into the Treaties.
- The form of integration. The majority of the WG supported the integration of the Charter in the first part of the Constitutional Treaty, although other alternatives were also considered such as to inserting a reference to the Charter in the Constitutional Treaty and then annexing the Charter in a different part of the Treaty.
- Not to reopen the substance of the Charter. While this compromise was agreeable to all partners, it was accepted that some technical adjustments of the general provisions or the so-called horizontal clauses were needed. Following this line, the WG proposed the following adjustments to the horizontal clauses with the objective of clarifying or restating what already existed in the Charter:
  - The Charter does not modify the division of competences between the Union and Member States
  - Articles in the Charter referring to an article in the Treaty should be interpreted according to those articles in the Treaty.
  - Fundamental rights derived from the constitutional traditions of Member States should be interpreted according to those traditions.
  - A new horizontal clause clarifying the division between rights and principles should be established.
- To give some kind of publicity to the explanatory notes of the previous Convention and as well as the current Convention.
- To maintain the preamble of the Charter as the preamble of the Constitutional Treaty.
- Accession to the European Convention on Human Rights (ECHR).
  - Members of the WG have unanimously agreed that the Union should accede to the ECHR.
  - It is necessary to create a Constitutional habilitation saying that the EU as such should be entitled to accede to the ECHR. The WG has not discussed the form, modality or content of the decision to accession. It is for the Council to decide

[26] Final Report Document CONV 354/02. http://register.consilium.eu.int/pdf/en/02/cv00/00354en2.pdf

by unanimity the modality of accession, possible reservations and the choice of protocols.
- Accession will not modify the division of competences. The EU can only accede to the ECHR within the limits of its own competences.
- Accession is totally complementary to having a legally binding Charter.
- Accession will not affect the individual positions of Member States in relation to the ECHR and protocols. The scope of accession only concerns EU Law and there will be no interference with national laws in relation to their special reservations, protocols etc.

Open Questions for the Future

Ideally, a future legally binding Charter should be complemented by accession of the Union to the ECHR. This will avoid any risk of inconsistency between the ECHR and the Charter. Accession is the best way to ensure consistency and to avoid divergent systems of protection. Both questions should not be presented as alternatives but as complementary.

Furthermore, no one disputes that the Union should have its own bill of rights and, at this stage the Charter of Fundamental Rights will unquestionably be the bill of rights of the Constitutional Treaty. The way of incorporating the Charter will very much depend on the final structure of the new Treaty. The Convention on the Future of Europe has already presented the first articles of the draft EU Constitution in which the Charter appears in Title II, Article 5.[27] The proposed text reflects the recommendation of the WG II and gives the Charter constitutional status by incorporating it in the Constitution, thereby making the Charter legally binding. The text also enables the Union to accede to the ECHR stating that "The Union may accede." A large number of amendments to these articles have been presented and most of them are in relation to the part of the Constitution in which the Charter should be placed. This could be considered as a largely symbolic question in the sense that the Charter will be legally binding either if included in the first part of the Constitution or if attached in a protocol. Having said this, a Charter incorporated in the first part of the Constitution gives a stronger message to the Citizens as to the importance that the Union attaches to Fundamental Rights.

However, besides the consensus achieved a few months ago within the WG, it seems that some questions are still open, as reflected in the last report issued on 3 February 2003 by the House of Lords on the future status of the EU Charter of

[27] Draft of Articles 1 to 16 of the Constitutional Treaty. Document CONV 528/03.

Fundamental Rights.[28] Among the 'open' questions are: the already classical argument of the Charter increasing competence of the Union, the legal and political complexity of acceding to the ECHR, access to justice and the necessity to reform Article 230(4) TEC in order to increase the possibility of individuals having access to the Court, the question of judicial remedies, (individuals must have access to effective remedies and incorporation of the Charter must be accompanied by effective remedies in order to make those rights meaningful) and the fact that the Charter contains a mixture of directly enforceable rights and principles of more aspirational character.

Today, the UK still appears the most reticent Member State to incorporate the Charter into the Constitution. Peter Hain, representative of the British government, in total disagreement with the drafting of Article 5 (his proposed amendments suggest the total deletion of Article 5) stated that: "We cannot accept the Charter of fundamental rights being an integral part of the Constitution as it stands"[29] and his alternate, Baroness Scotland stressed that the Charter as it stands is welcomed for a political declaration but cannot be integrated into the Constitution since it is 'ambiguous' and 'contradictory.' Considering the remarkable consensus achieved two months ago within the WG on the Charter, achievement of this consensus could be seriously hampered by the persistent British position on the topic. Even if decision making within the Convention on the Future of Europe does not take place by means of a veto or even by means of votes, it is clear that progress is blocked when a larger Member State is reluctant to move at the speed of the others.

[28] "House of Lords, Select Committee on the European Union: "The Future Status of the EU Charter of Fundamental Rights", Session 2002-03 6th Report.
http://www.parliament.the-stationery-office.co.uk/pa/ld/ldeucom.htm

[29] Suggestion for amendment of Article 5 by Peter Hein.
http://europeanconvention.eu.int/Docs/Treaty/pdf/5/Art%205%20Hain.pdf

BIBLIOGRAPHY

Arena (2001), Chartering Europe: The Charter of Fundamental Rights of the European Union, *Arena Working Paper Series*, No 13, May 2001 http://www.arena.uio.no/publications/wp01_13.htm

Búrca, Gráinne de (2001), "Human Rights: The Charter and Beyond"; *Jean Monnet Working Paper* No.10/01, Jean Monnet Program, New York University School of Law. http://www.jeanmonnetprogram.org/papers/01/013601.rtf

Church, Clive (2003), Introductory Notes: "How to implement the Charter and the Constitutional Structure", University of Kent, March 2003.

Convention on the Future of Europe http://european-convention.eu.int/bienvenue.asp?lang=EN&Content=

Council of the European Union, Fundamental Rights. http://ue.eu.int/df/default.asp?lang=en

De Schutter, Olivier (2002), "The questions to be decided – Protecting fundamental rights, and issue in the Convention on the Future of Europe". http://europa.eu.int/comm/justice_home/unit/charte/en/questions.

Deloche-Gaudez, Florence (2001), "The Convention on a Charter of Fundamental Rights: A method for the Future?" *Research and Policy Paper*, No 15 November 2001. Groupement d'Études et de Recherches Notre Europe.

Dutheil de la Rochère, Jacqueline (2000), "La Charte des droits Fondamentaux de L'Union européenne: quelle valeur ajoutée, quel avenir?," *Revue du Marché Commun et de l'Union européenne*, No. 443, décembre.

Eicke, Tim (2000), "The European Charter of Fundamental Rights – Unique Opportunity or Unwelcome Detraction. Liberty's Evidence to the inquiry of the House of Lords, European Communities Committee, Sub-Committee E (Law and Institutions) and formed the basis of its oral evidence given on 8 March 2000

European Commission, Fundamental Rights http://www.europa.eu.int/comm/justice_home/doc_centre/rights/doc_rights_intro_en.htm

European Parliament, Human Rights, Fundamental Rights http://www.europarl.eu.int/comparl/human_rights/default_en.htm

Heim, Matthew (2001), "The Charter of Fundamental Rights of The European Union; Recent Developments Following The Nice European Summit", *Challenge Europe On Line Journal* (April 2001), The European Policy Centre. http://www.theepc.be/challenge/top.asp?SEC=challenge

House of Lords (2002-2003), Select Committee on the European Union, "The Future Status of the EU Charter of Fundamental Rights", session 2002-2003 6th Report.

Jones, Hywel Ceri (2003), Matthew Heim and Cristina Pineda Polo, "A Charter of Rights for Europe", The European Policy Centre, *EPC Working Paper* 01.www.theepc.be

McCrudden, Christopher (2001), The Future of the EU Charter of Fundamental Rights, *Jean Monnet Working Paper* No.10/01, Monnet Program, New York University School of Law. http://www.jeanmonnetprogram.org/papers/01/013001.rtf

Meyer, Jürgen and Markus Engels (2002), A collection of Documents with an introduction, "The Charter of Fundamental Rights of the European Union". German Bundestag, Committee on the Affairs of the European Union, 2nd Enlarged Edition, Berlin October 2002.

SECTION 5

CONCLUSIONS

CHAPTER 25

EXPLAINING THE TREATY OF NICE: BEYOND LIBERAL INTERGOVERNMENTALISM?

INTRODUCTION

In this chapter we shall discuss how to explain the Treaty of Nice. In the introductory chapter we mentioned Andrew Moravcsik's approach, liberal intergovernmentalism (Moravcsik, 1993, 1998). This approach can structure an analysis of a treaty reform like the Treaty of Nice, but many authors, including contributors to this book, have also pointed to limitations in the approach (see also Christiansen, Falkner and Jørgensen, 2002).

Some of the criticisms concern the first stage, the formation of national preferences. According to Moravcsik, the main explanation of national preferences is that economic actors make demands to the politicians. These in turn supply solutions mainly to get re-elected. Moravcsik's explanation therefore downgrades the role of geopolitics, including ideas. Further, domestic institutions such as parliaments, party systems and public opinion do not play important roles.

Criticisms concerning the second stage include assumptions about the negotiation process which is based on the so-called Nash bargaining solutions (Beach, 2002). Such an approach downgrades the importance of specific institutional aspects of the negotiations, including the role of EU-level institutions, especially the Commission, the European Parliament and the Council Secretariat. Nor is there any particular role for Presidency entrepreneurship (see also Christiansen, 2002, and Beach, 2004).

Concerning the explanation of institutional choice in liberal intergovernmentalism, i.e. credible commitments, there have been fewer explicit criticisms. But scholars who question the rationality assumption of liberal intergovernmentalism will again ask about the role of norms and ideas at this stage, too (Wind, 1997; Risse, 2004; and Schimmelfennig, 2003)

Some might argue that liberal intergovernmentalism fared well when it came to explaining European integration from the Treaty of Rome in 1957 to the Economic and Monetary Union (EMU) part of the Treaty of Maastricht in 1993. This part was mostly about economic integration, where economic actors should be expected to play an important role. But Maastricht was more than EMU. It took a step towards political union, where the geopolitics of the end of the Cold War in 1989 was a very important event (Laursen, 1992).

In general one can argue that it was the bipolar system of the Cold War that created a situation in Western Europe that allowed the founding Member States of the EC to start economic integration (see also Rynning's contribution to this volume)

The post-Maastricht reforms, Amsterdam and Nice—and now also the draft Constitutional Treaty—must partly be seen as a response to the new situation in Europe after 1989. First some members of the European Free Trade Area (EFTA), then the former communist countries of Central and Eastern Europe (CEECs), started demanding membership of the EU. Would a much enlarged Union be able to function effectively? Further, the difficulties of getting Maastricht ratified in 1992-93 led to a new debate about the legitimacy of the process. The opinions of the wider public started to play a more important role. The permissive consensus of the early years was gone (Laursen, 1994). Institutional choice was now not only a matter of 'credible commitments' but also a question of legitimacy.

As long as integration in Europe was economic in nature, including the internal market and monetary integration, so-called 'output legitimacy' was sufficient. If the Communities made good decisions economic and political actors would be supportive (Lindberg and Scheingold, 1970). As long as integration was 'negative' integration, i.e. the abolishing of barriers, output legitimacy was sufficient. But as the European Communities (EC) moved towards 'positive integration', i.e. the development of common policies, the process became more politicized, and questions of transparency and democracy were now on the agenda. A concern for 'input' legitimacy emerged (Scharpf, 1999). The issue of the 'democratic deficit' was on the agenda of successive treaty reforms. The main result was the introduction of the co-decision procedure in Maastricht for internal market related legislation. This procedure made the European Parliament a co-legislator together with the Council of Ministers. The use of co-decision was subsequently extended by the Amsterdam and Nice treaties. This made the European Parliament an institutional winner in the most recent institutional reforms. This concern for input legitimacy goes beyond 'credible commitments' and can thus not be fully explained by liberal intergovernmentalism. Indeed, institutions and ideas do matter.

Explaining Differences

If, in line with liberal intergovernmentalism, we look at IGCs as 2-level games, governments have to be concerned about domestic ratification of an agreement negotiated at the EU-level (Putnam, 1988). In most Member States ratification is authorized by national parliaments, the two main exceptions being Denmark and Ireland, where ratification normally takes place through the use of referendums. In the case of the Treaty of Nice, Denmark avoided a referendum because an interpretation of the Treaty concluded that it did not extend the policy scope and would thus not fall under Art. 20 of the Danish Constitution, but Ireland did need a referendum. As we have seen Ireland had to go through two referendums to be able to ratify the treaty (see contribution by Tonra).

Given the fact that political elites tend to be more pro-European than the wider public a parliamentary ratification will usually be easier than ratification by referendum. However, it sometimes is the case that a parliamentary ratification runs into problems, as the British ratification of Maastricht did in 1992-1993. In the case of Nice the Labour government had a comfortable majority and ratification was fairly easy. Anyway, governments have to anticipate parliamentary reactions to the agreements they bring home. We have for instance seen this in the case of Spain and Nice (see Basabe's contribution to this volume). Despite the Aznar government's parliamentary majority, the government felt that it needed to return with a 'victory'. So even if criticism back home does not threaten ratification, governments have a wider concern to limit criticism and maintain a good image. A government with weak parliamentary support will be particularly sensitive to such concerns.

Various domestic institutional factors can play a role in preference formation.

One domestic-politics factor that had some impact on the Nice negotiations was the fact that during the French Presidency, France had cohabitation with a Gaullist president and a Socialist Prime Minister. This situation contributed to make it difficult for President Chirac to be a neutral president of the negotiations among the Heads of State and Government in Nice.

In a negotiation like the Nice negotiations, where formal EU institutions are changed, symbols and national prestige can play a great role. As we have seen France wanted to stay on par with Germany in the re-weighting of votes in the Council. Belgium compared itself with the Netherlands, Portugal with Spain, etc. Since leaders had to return to their national capitals and defend the outcome, they could not ignore these factors. As suggested in the chapter on Belgium, the Belgian leaders had to ask themselves how the reaction to front page news 'Netherlands – Belgium, 12-10' would be (see contribution by Kerremans in this volume).

On one of the issues on the Nice agenda, the extended use of qualified majority voting (QMV), liberal intergovernmentalism retains some explanatory power. Where Member States insisted on retaining unanimity they often did so for economic reasons. This was clearly the case when Britain resisted QMV for taxation and social policy issues. Austria wanted to retain unanimity for some issues related to environmental policy. This included water resources, an important concern in Austria, and energy, as there is strong opposition to nuclear energy in the country (see Kathrin Blanck's contribution). Denmark's insistence on unanimity for certain aspects of social policy was due to a fear that migrant workers and their dependants might undermine the tax base of the social welfare system. France's insistence on unanimity for the audiovisual and cultural sector was a defence of the French film industry as well as a defence of the French language. But countries favouring a large extension of the scope of QMV, such as Belgium, at least partly did so because of pro-European or federalist ideology. Interestingly, however, as mentioned by Bart Kerremans, the Belgians sided with the French on the cultural part of services, language being an important element of the Belgian federal system.

Other countries that favoured a much extended use of QMV included Italy, the Netherlands and Finland. In the Italian case, a pro-European ideology played a role. In the Dutch case, such an extension was promoted by the Foreign Ministry with some opposition from other Ministries. But the expectation was that other Member States would limit the extension, as indeed happened (see contribution by Luitwieler and Pijpers). That Finland too was in this group indicates that Finland, contrary to the two other Nordic EU Member States, has moved to a core position in European integration. But still Finland did want to keep certain budgetary decisions and defence outside QMV (see contribution by Antola).

That Greece defended unanimity for maritime transportation and structural policy fits in with liberal intergovernmentalism. On maritime transportation Denmark was an ally and on structural policy Spain and Portugal were allies of Greece (see contribution by Tsakaloyannis and Blavoukos). That Ireland defended national rights to determine taxation levels can also be explained by Moravcsik's approach (see contribution by Tonra). Ireland's low corporate tax had been an important element in the country's impressive economic growth in recent years.

Spain had a fairly long list of demands for unanimity: structural and cohesion funds, external borders (because of Gibraltar), taxation (low corporate taxes), social security, water resources (aspects of environmental policy). Also the United Kingdom had a long list. Apart from treaty reforms and enlargements, where there was wide support for retaining unanimity, the British wanted to retain unanimity for taxation, border controls (Schengen opt-out), social security, defence and 'own resources' (see contribution by Larsen). Liberal intergovernmentalism can explain most of this, but Gibraltar and defence take us into high politics where sovereignty issues dominate.

In the case of Member States having federal systems, Germany, Austria and Belgium, the regional governments did make some demands. As we saw in Christian Engel's contribution to this book it was the German Länder which formulated the demand for a declaration attached to the Nice Treaty about the post-Nice agenda, including in particular the question of delimitation of competences. Belgium and Italy joined Germany on this.

The German Länder also had some influence on Germany's policy on the scope of QMV. A couple of issues falling under the Länder's competence were affected. Germany insisted on unanimity for cultural support programmes (Art. 151(5)) and training and conditions of access for self-employed persons (Art. 47(2)). The threat of non-ratification—given the representation of the Länder in the Bundesrat—was sufficiently credible to secure that unanimity was retained for these two articles (see Christian Engel's contribution).

Other domestic political institutions have played various roles. All Member States have to coordinate IGC policies among ministries, and some do this more than others (see also Wessels, Maurer and Mittag, 2003). Demands for retaining unanimity in certain policy areas often came from the responsible ministries. Interest groups may have made demands, or the Ministries may simply have anticipated future problems, if QMV were to be introduced. In many Member States interest groups do not seem to have been very active in connection with the Nice negotiations (see for instance the contribution on Sweden by Karlsson and Svensson). But officials and politicians do anticipate possible demands.

In some Member States the European Affairs committees of the national parliaments have expressed their views and made demands to the governments (see also Maurer and Wessels, 2001). In the case of Denmark this process normally includes a negotiation mandate to the government, which was also the case for Nice.

The role of extreme right wing parties in some Member States was to have a special influence on the Nice negotiations. In the case of Austria, which had been exposed to sanctions from EU-14 when Jörg Haider's party (FPÖ) entered the Austrian government, this led the IGC to give high priority to getting Art. 7 TEU amended to avoid a similar case in the future. On the other hand Belgium had been a driving force in the decision to impose sanctions against Austria because the Belgian political elite feared their own extreme right party, the Vlaams Blok. We learn from Kerremans' contribution that the issue almost became a personal crusade for Louis Michel, the Belgian foreign minister. The issue also became a problem in Denmark, where it was exploited by EU-sceptical parties and groups in the euro referendum, which in turn affected the Danish determination to avoid a referendum on the Treaty of Nice. What we have seen then is that specific domestic events can reverberate through the whole EU system.

Although liberal intergovernmentalism seems able to explain much about the extension of the scope of QMV, the same approach faces greater difficulties for positions on other aspects of the Nice agenda.

Although there were cracks in the groups of large and small Member States the issues of re-weighting of votes in the Council and the composition of the Commission were very much small-vs.-large-Member-States issues, especially the question of the Commission.

These issues were about influence and relative power. Member States did compare themselves with other states of comparable size. They all approached the issue with a sense of fairness. Relative gains and losses did matter and the leaders were concerned about the domestic reaction to a bargain. Defining the 'national interest' in these matters did not depend on demands from interest groups. Politicians did not need the help of experts. It was simply a matter of maximizing future influence in an enlarged EU. Governments could easily calculate gains and losses. 'Realist' scholars can explain interests in this area without resort to complex theories.

Explaining the Bargaining Process

Concerning the bargaining process we have to ask about influence. Was it asymmetric interdependence that formed the basis? Some countries were more eager about enlargement than others. Which threats of veto or exclusion existed and were they credible? What influence did EU-level actors have?

Moravcsik mainly studied France, Germany and the UK. Is that sufficient? Shouldn't we at least include Spain in the case of Nice as well as the small Member States that formed a large coalition in support of retaining a member of the Commission and avoiding too much re-weighting of votes in the Council in favour of the larger members? It seems fair to say that just studying the three big ones would be inadequate for the Treaty of Nice.

Looking at the question of extended scope of QMV, the UK was an important 'minimalist' country insisting on unanimity on many issues and the UK power may have increased after the St. Malo bilateral summit with France in 1998 which started the development of ESDP, which in turn made the UK a more important actor in the EU (see chapter by Larsen). So threats of exclusion of Britain were less credible than they had been in the Single European Act (SEA) negotiations in 1985. And on most issues the UK had a number of allies. So the bargain on the scope of QMV was very much a lowest common denominator agreement as Moravcsik would expect.

The bargaining process on the Commission saw two coalitions facing each other. Neither side could use threats of exclusion. Both sides could use threats of veto. A compromise had to be found, one where both sides could claim to have won, but which in reality largely postponed the decision.

The bargaining process on the re-weighting of votes was the most difficult one. It cannot be explained without an analysis of the role played by the French Presidency. With France insisting on parity with Germany, Belgium could rightly expect parity with the Netherlands. The process was further complicated by the Spanish problem and the French decision to treat Spain well—possibly to have an influential southern ally in the future eastward-enlarged EU, but possibly also to silence a difficult negotiation partner (see Basabe's contribution to this volume). The French treatment of Spain had repercussions for the position of neighbouring Portugal. In the end veto threats from Portugal and Belgium had to be seen as credible. The two countries were partly bought off with more seats in the European Parliament, each getting 22 seats, while two future members of comparable size, the Czech Republic and Hungary got 20.

So the third ingredient in Moravcsik's interstate bargaining, linkage strategies, were used at the margin. But the narrow agenda limited the possibility of linkages.

Institutional Choice

Was institutional choice then because of 'credible commitments'? Yes, to some extent, it can be argued. To the extent that the concern was to have credible institutions after the impending Eastern enlargement such an explanation can be used. And there is no doubt that many Member States saw Nice as an enlargement treaty. At least the UK and the northern Member States clearly saw the treaty that way.

Especially the expanded scope of QMV can be explained by 'credible commitments'. So could the changed provisions on the Court of Justice and Court of First Instance, making sure that the judicial system will work in an efficient way in the future. The reform of the judicial system, interestingly enough, avoided politicisation and was largely handled by legal experts. Some may argue that the effort to reduce the size of the Commission could also be seen as a 'credible commitments' question, but others might argue that the larger Member States that insisting on a smaller Commission had a hidden agenda of decreasing the legitimacy of the Commission, making it easier for them to dominate the agenda setting through the intergovernmental European Council.

Nice was more than a question of credible commitments. It was also, as we have argued, about legitimacy. The extended use of co-decision—albeit limited to only six areas—can only be seen as a response to the 'democratic deficit.' The EP powers were also increased by giving the EP the power to bring actions before the ECJ concerning the legality of acts (Art. 230 TEC) and to seek an opinion from the ECJ concerning the validity of international agreements (Art. 300(6) TEC). Further, the EP can now take the initiative in charging a Member State with breach of fundamental rights (Art. 7(1) TEU) (see Neuhold's contribution to this volume). Increased influence for the European Parliament does not fit well with Moravcsik's 'credible commitments'.

Nor is it easy to see re-weighting of votes as a question of credible commitments. It was a question of relative power that enlargement forced on the agenda.

THE LIMITS OF LIBERAL INTERGOVERNMENTALISM

Overall it can be argued that liberal intergovernmentalism still retains a fair amount of explanatory power in relation to QMV when we study the case of Nice. But we have also seen some shortcomings. Some national preferences did have economic roots, but others were due to geopolitics and ideology. Pro-European ideology still plays a certain role in some Member States, including Belgium, Italy and possibly to a lesser extent Germany and the Netherlands, but now also to some extent Finland. In the bargaining process there were elements of asymmetrical interdependence and linkages were made to find compromises. But given the narrow agenda of the Nice IGC the use of linkage strategies was rather limited. Threats of exclusion may not have been used in the negotiations, but such threats may become more credible in the future because of the new provisions on enhanced cooperation. On the other hand the easier opportunity to use enhanced cooperation will reduce the credibility of threats of veto in the future.

Liberal intergovernmentalism is especially limited when it comes to the study of the role of the Commission, the European Parliamement and the Council Secretariat. The Commission has been involved in IGCs since the SEA negotiations in the 1980s. The European Parliament is not formally involved but has increased its informal involvement and had two observers who took part in the Preparatory Group in the Nice negotiations (see contribution by Neuhold). The Council Secretariat – to the extent it assists the Presidency – has been able to gain some influence through drafting some of the provisions. In the case of Nice these non-Member State actors were somewhat handicapped because of the way the French Presidency tried to control the process from Paris. This reduced the opportunity for third party entrepreneurship and brokerage (see contribution by Beach). Nevertheless, the Commission did have some influence on the reform of the judicial system, the strengthened internal role of the President of the Commission, article 133 TEC on commercial policy, article 7 TEU on the early warning system in cases of breach of democratic principles by a Member State, as well as the new provision on European political parties. The Council Secretariat also contributed to the compromise on the services part of commercial policy, required by France especially, and the declaration on the future venue of European Council meetings, a bargaining exchange to Belgium in the end-game in Nice.

Liberal intergovernmentalism is especially poor when we study the parallel process of ESDP. ESDP can first of all be explained by geopolitics. It was very much a response to the unfolding of events in ex-Yugoslavia, including disagreements with the USA on how to handle the crisis in Kosovo in 1998-99 (see Rynning's contribution to this volume).

Neither can the other parallel process, the Charter of Fundamental Rights, be explained by credible commitments. The concern for fundamental rights must be seen as a question of legitimacy as the process of European integration was becoming more political after the end of the Cold War (see the contribution by Pineda Polo and den Boer in this volume).

There is a further criticism. Liberal intergovernmentalism sees preference formation and interstate bargaining as sequential processes. In reality Member States do not always have clearly defined preferences when they go into interstate negotiations. This also implies a certain amount of uncertainty during the negotiations, which makes it impossible to define the bargaining space. Especially when new issues are placed on the agenda, like flexibility in the Amsterdam negotiations, can negotiations become a long learning process, where preferences are formed during the process (Stubb, 2002). Also during the Nice IGC we see that preferences in respect to 'enhanced co-operation' changed during the negotiations (see Olsen's contribution to this volume).

The limits of liberal intergovernmentalism can, thus, be found at both the level of national preference formation and at the level of interstate bargaining. At both levels there is a need to include institutions, such as political parties and parliaments at the national level and the Community institutions at the level of bargaining. The way IGCs have become 'institutionalized' must also be taken into account. Also ideas and individuals must sometimes be brought into the picture, be they national diplomats, like the Italian ones who have been involved in a number of IGCs and who have traditionally been fairly pro-European (see Bindi's contribution to this volume). Even representatives of the Member States taking part in European negotiations may go through a socialisation process. However, the nature of the issues, especially re-weighting of votes in the Council, and the way the French Presidency handled the endgame in Nice, made the Nice IGC a hard zero-sum bargaining game where 'national interests' triumphed.

Concluding Remarks

Due to the limited agenda and the focus on institutional issues, Nice may not be the best case study to test liberal intergovernmentalism. A longer process, such as the whole Amsterdam, Nice and Constitutional Treaty process, would give a better basis for a more extensive critique of liberal intergovernmentalism. It would be a real process, a moving picture, not just a snapshot (Pierson, 1996). It would not only study the 'summit' but also the 'valleys' in between (Christiansen and Jørgensen, 1999). One IGC would only be a peak in a wider landscape (see Maurer's contribution to this volume). Nice was about the Amsterdam left-overs. Nice itself started a post-Nice process, which has now produced a Constitutional Treaty. Whereas Nice was poorly prepared and rushed, the Constitutional Treaty process was well prepared by a Convention with a much wider input of ideas and a period of deliberation, not bargaining, before the final bargaining process in IGC 2003-04. During the Convention the power of arguments and ideas was decisive. And during the ensuing IGC the Irish Presidency played the role of a neutral policy entrepreneur, not the partisan role played by France in 2000 (Dür and Mateo, 2004b).

BIBLIOGRAPHY

Andenas, Mads and John Usher, eds. (2003), The Treaty of Nice and Beyond: Enlargement and Constitutional Reform. Oxford: Hart Publishing.

Aspinwall, Mark D. and Gerald Schneider (2000), "Same menu, separate tables: The institutionalist turn in political science and the study of European integration," *European Journal of political Research*, Vol. 38, pp. 1-36.

Beach, Derek (2002), Bringing negotiations back into the study of European integration: How negotiations affect the ability of supranational actors to gain influence in IGC's. Ph.D.-dissertation. Odense: Department of Political Science, University of Southern Denmark.

— (2004), "The unseen hand in treaty reform negotiations: the role and influence of the Council Secretariat," *Journal of European Public Policy*, Vol. 11, No. 3 (June), pp. 408-439.

Bond, Martyn and Kim Feus, eds. (2001), The Treaty of Nice Explained. London: The Federal Trust/Kogan Page.

Christiansen, Thomas (2002), "The role of supranational actors in EU treaty reform," *Journal of European Public Policy*, Vol. 9, No. 1 (February), pp. 33-53.

—, Gerda Falkner and Knud Erik Jørgensen (2002), "Theorizing EU treaty reform: beyond diplomacy and bargaining," *Journal of European Public Policy*, Vol. 9, No. 1 (February), pp. 12-32.

— and Knud Erik Jørgensen (1999), "The Amsterdam Process: A Structurationist Perspective on EU Treaty Reform," *European Integration online Papers* (EIoP), Vol. 3, No. 1.

—, Knud Erik Jørgensen and Antje Wiener, eds. (2001), The Social Construction of Europe. London: SAGE Publications.

Constantinesco, Vlad; Yves Gautier and Denys Simon, eds. (2001), Le Traité de Nice: Premières analyses. Strasbourg: Presses Universitaires de Strasbourg.

Dobson, Lynn and Albert Weale (2003), "Governance and Legitimacy," in Elizabeth Bomberg and Alexander Stubb (eds.), *The European Union: How Does it Work*? Oxford: Oxford University Press, pp. 156-173.

Dür, Andreas and Gemma Mateo (2004a), "Treaty-Making in the European Union: Bargaining, Issue Linkages, and Efficiency," *European Integration online Papers* (EIoP), Vol. 8, No. 18.

— and Gemma Mateo (2004b), "Explaining Bargaining Efficiency: A Comparison of the IGCs of 2000 and of 2003-04," *CFES Working Paper* No. 18/2004. Odense: Centre for European Studies, University of Southern Denmark.

Falkner, Gerda (2002), "Introduction: EU treaty reform as a three-level process," *Journal of European Public Policy*, Vol. 9, No. 1 (February), pp. 1-11.

Galloway, David (2001), The Treaty of Nice and Beyond: Realities and Illusions of Power in the EU. Sheffield: Sheffield Academic Press.

Gray, Mark and Alexander Stubb (2001), "Keynote Article: The Treaty of Nice – Negotiating a Poisoned Chalice?", *Journal of Common Market Studies*, Vol. 39, Annual Review (September), pp. 5-23.

Greve, Morten F. and Knud Erik Jørgensen (2002), "Treaty reform as constitutional politics – a longitudinal view," *Journal of European Public Policy*, Vol. 9, No. 1 (February), pp. 54-75.

Jupille, Joseph, James A. Caporaso and Jeffrey T. Checkel (2003), "Integrating Institutions: Rationalism, Constructivism, and the Study of the European Union," *Comparative Political Studies*, Vol. 56, No. 1-2 (February/March), pp. 7-40.

Kerremans, Bart (1996), "Do Institutions Make a Difference? Non-Institutionalism, Neo-Institutionalism, and the Logic of Common Decision-Making in the European Union," *Governance,* Vol. 9, No. 2 (April), pp. 217-240.

— (1998), "The Problem of Capacity and Control in an Enlarged EU Council," in Pierre-Henri Laurant and Marc Maresceau (eds.), *The State of the European Union*, Vol. 4, pp. 87-109.

Laursen, Finn (1992), "Explaining the Intergovernmental Conference on Political Union," in Finn Laursen and Sophie Vanhoonacker (eds.), *The Intergovernmental Conference on Political Union*. Maastricht: European Institute of Public Administration, pp. 229-248.

— (1994), "The Not-So-Permissive Consensus: Thoughts on the Maastricht Treaty and the Future of European Integration," in Finn Laursen and Sophie Vanhoonacker (eds.), *The Ratification of the Maastricht Treaty: Issues, Debates and Future Implications*. Maastricht: EIPA, and Dordrecht: Martinus Nijhoff, pp. 295-317.

— (2002), "Explaining and Evaluating the Amsterdam Treaty: Some Concluding Remarks," in Finn Laursen (ed.), *The Amsterdam Treaty: National Preference Formation, Interstate Bargaining and Outcome*. Odense: Odense University Press, pp. 639-655.

— (2003a), "Theoretical Perspectives on Comparative Regional Integration," in Finn Laursen (ed.), *Comparative Regional Integration: Theoretical Perspectives*. Aldershot: Ashgate, pp. 3-28.

— (2003b), "International Regimes or Would-be Polities?" in Finn Laursen (ed.), *Comparative Regional Integration: Theoretical Perspectives*. Aldershot: Ashgate, pp. 283-293.

Lindberg, Leon N. and Stuart A. Scheingold (1970), Europe's Would-Be Polity: Patterns of Change in the European Community. Englewood-Cliffs, N.J.: Prentice-Hall, Inc.

Maurer, Andreas and Wolfgang Wessels, eds. (2001), National Parliaments on their Ways to Europe: Losers or Latecomers? Baden-Baden: Nomos Verlagsgesellschaft.

Moravcsik, Andrew (1993), "Preferences and Power in the European Community: A Liberal Intergovernmentalist Approach," *Journal of Common Market Studies*, Vol. 31, No. 4 (December), pp. 473-524.

— (1998), The Choice for Europe: Social Purpose and State Power from Messina to Maastricht. Ithaca, NY: Cornell University Press.

Neunreither, Karlheinz and Antje Wiener, eds. (2000), European Integration After Amsterdam: Institutional Dynamics and Prospects for Democracy. Oxford: Oxford University Press.

Nielsen, Rasmus Leander (2003) "Nationale parlamentsvalgs betydning for den europæiske integrationsproces," Unpublished seminar paper. Odense: Department of Political Science, University of Southern Denmark.

— (forthcoming), "Why National Parliamentary Elections Matter on the Outcomes of European IGC's: A Finite Prisoners' Dilemma Model," *CFES Working Paper*. Odense: Centre for European Studies, University of Southern Denmark.

Peterson, John (1995), "Decision-making in the European Union: towards a framework for analysis," *Journal for European Public Policy,* Vol. 2, No. 1 (March), pp. 69-93.

— (2001), "The Choice for EU theorists: Establishing a common framework for analysis," *European Journal of Political Research*, Vol. 39, pp. 289-318.

Pierson, P. (1996), "The Path to European Integration: A Historical Institutionalist Analysis," *Comparative Political Studies,* Vol. 29, No. 2.

Putnam, Robert D. (1988), "Diplomacy and domestic politics: the logic of two-level games," *International Organization*, Vol. 42, No. 3 (Summer), pp. 427-460.

Risse, Thomas (2004), "Social Constructivism and European Integration," in Antje Wiener, and Thomas Diez (eds.), *European Integration Theory*. Oxford: Oxford University Press. Pp. 161-176.

Scharpf, Fritz (1999), Governing in Europe: Effective and Democratic? Oxford: Oxford University Press.

Schneider, Gerald and Mark Aspinwall (2001), The rules of integration: Institutionalist approaches to the study of Europe. Manchester: Manchester University Press.

Shepsle, Kenneth A. (1989), "Studying Institutions: Some Lessons from the Rational Choice Approach," *Journal of Theoretical Politics*, Vol. 1, No. 2, pp. 131-147.

Schimmelfennig, Frank (2003), The EU, NATO and the Integration of Europe: Rules and Rhetoric. Cambridge: Cambridge University Press.

— (2004), "Liberal Intergovernmentalism," in Antje Wiener and Thomas Diez (eds.), *European Integration Theory*. Oxford: Oxford University Press, pp. 75-94.

Smith, Brendan P.G (2002), Constitution Building in the European Union: The Process of Treaty Reforms. The Hague: Kluwer Law International.

Stubb, Alexander (2002), Negotiating Flexibility in the European Union: Amsterdam, Nice and Beyond. Basingstoke: Palgrave.

Sverdrup, Ulf (2002), "An institutional perspective on treaty reform: contextualizing the Amsterdam and Nice Treaties," *Journal of European Public Policy*, Vol. 9, No. 1 (February), pp. 120-140.

Wagner, Wolfgang (2003), "Why the EU's common foreign and security policy will remain intergovernmental: a rationalist institutional choice analysis of European crisis management policy," *Journal of European Public Policy*, Vol. 10, No. 4 (August), pp. 576-595.

Wessels, Wolfgang (2001), "Nice Results: The Millennium IGC in the EU's Evolution," *Journal of Common Market Studies*, Vol. 39, No. 2 (June), pp. 197-219.

Wolfgang Wessels, A. Maurer and J. Mittag, eds. (2003), Fifteen into One? The European Union and Member States. Manchester: Manchester University Press.

Wiener, Antje and Thomas Diez, eds. (2004), European Integration Theory. Oxford: Oxford University Press.

Wind, Marlene (1997), "Rediscovering Institutions: A Reflectivist Critique of Rational Institutionalism," in Knud Erik Jørgensen (ed.), *Reflective Approaches to European Governance*. Houndsmills: Macmillan Press, pp. 15-35.

CHAPTER 26

THE POST-NICE AGENDA: TOWARDS A CONSTITUTIONAL TREATY?

INTRODUCTION

The European Union (EU) has gone through a number of treaty reforms in recent years. The EU itself was formed by the Maastricht Treaty in 1992 (Laursen and Vanhoonacker, 1992 and 1994). It combined the pre-existing European Communities (EC) in reformed versions, including plans for Economic and Monetary Union (EMU), with two new pillars: Common Foreign and Security Policy (CFSP) and Justice and Home Affairs (JHA) cooperation. Further reforms followed through the Amsterdam Treaty negotiated in 1996-97 (Laursen, 2002). And in this book we have studied the Treaty of Nice negotiated in 2000.

From February 2002 until July 2003, a Convention on the Future of Europe prepared a new draft treaty referred to as a constitutional treaty (Laursen, 2003b). Starting on October 4, 2003, an Intergovernmental Conference (IGC) took up the considerations of the new EU constitutional treaty on the basis of the proposal from the Convention. The Italian Presidency hoped that the new treaty would be finalised by the end of 2003. But a meeting of the European Council in Brussels in December 2003 failed to conclude the negotiations during the Italian Presidency. The Irish then took over and they succeeded brokering an agreement in June 2004 (Laursen, 2004).

Why so many treaty reforms in recent years? The short answer is that since the end of the Cold War the EU has tried to adapt to a new situation in Europe. First three former members of the European Free Trade Association (EFTA), which used to be neutral during the Cold War, namely Austria, Finland and Sweden, joined in 1995. Then former communist countries of Central and Eastern Europe pressed for membership. From May 2004 the EU has 25 Member States. The old East-West division of Europe was over. But to get a much enlarged Union to work has required changes.

There have been two main issues: efficiency and legitimacy.

The discussion about legitimacy started after the Danish people rejected the Maastricht Treaty in 1992. The Irish people rejected the Nice Treaty in 2001. In both cases it took second referendums to get the respective treaties accepted. Three states, the UK, Denmark and Sweden, have political problems joining the single currency, the euro, even if the governments are in favour of joining. The proposition to introduce the euro was turned down in referenda in Denmark in 2000 and in Sweden in 2003. Another reason why there is a perceived problem of legitimacy is the fact that the turnout at elections for the European Parliament has been falling since direct elections started in 1979 (Bomberg, Cram and Martin, 2003)

The issue of efficiency goes further back. In the 1970s and early 1980s there was talk about euro-sclerosis. The Single European Act (SEA), which introduced qualified majority voting (QMV) to complete the internal market, was the response in 1986 to that debate.

But, as the EU enlarged in the 1990s, the question of efficiency remained on the agenda. Moving from 12 to 15 and then 25 members had implications for efficiency.

The response to the efficiency issue has especially been to increase the use of QMV in the Council. In all the treaty reforms mentioned, there were policy areas that were moved from unanimity to QMV.

The response to the legitimacy issue has mainly been to increase the involvement of the European Parliament in the legislative process. Maastricht introduced co-decision in some areas. Amsterdam and Nice increased the use of co-decision.

And still, after Nice the question remained: Was the Union ready to face the challenges? This was the background of the continued debate about the fundamental nature of the EU and its *finalité politique.*

That debate took a swift turn with the speech by Germany's Foreign Minister Joschka Fischer at the Humboldt University in Berlin in May 2000 already during the Nice IGC. Fischer, speaking in a personal capacity, suggested that in the longer run the EU should move toward a federation with a constitution (Fischer, 2000).

The geopolitical changes in 1989 led to a Europe united across old division lines. 11 of the EU members had introduced the euro by the time of Fischer's speech. After the meeting of the European Council in 1999 in Tampere, the EU seriously started working on the Area of Freedom, Security and Justice (AFSJ), including issues related to internal security. And sparked by the conflict in Kosovo, the EU developed a Common Security and Defence Policy (CSDP). Europe faced two projects that should be carried out in parallel: enlargement and increasing the Union's capacity to act.

In the long term Fischer saw "a very simple solution: the transition from a union of states to full parliamentarization as a European Federation." To those seeing problems with Europe's many "different peoples, cultures, languages and histories" Fischer said that a federation would respect such differences. European integration would take the "nation-states along with it into such a Federation." There should be "a division of sovereignty between Europe and the nation-state."

> The nation-states will continue to exist and at European level they will retain a much larger role than the Länder have in Germany. And in such a Federation, the principle of subsidiarity will be constitutionally enshrined (ibib., p. 9)

He was not sure that the gradual process of integration, known as the 'Monnet' method, would take the EU to such a federation. If a majority of Member States would not "take the leap into full integration and agree on a European constitution" then maybe a smaller group of member states could "take this route as an avant-garde" forming a "centre of gravity." Such an avant-garde could be an interim step towards a federation:

> Such a centre of gravity would have to be an avant-garde, the driving force for the completion of political integration and should from the start comprise all the elements of the future federation (ibid., 11).

The last step would be "a deliberate political act to re-establish Europe" in the form of a European Federation.

During the following weeks a number of Europe's leaders followed up on the discussion started by Joschka Fischer (see texts in Marhold, 2002). Some of the French leaders talked about a federation of nation-states, to emphasize that a European federation would be different from the more centralized USA.

The EU in a Comparative Perspective

Seen in a comparative perspective, the EU has gone further than any other integration scheme, such as ASEAN in South East Asia, NAFTA in North America, and MERCOSUR in the southern part of South America. It can be argued that the EU is becoming a multi-level polity with many federal traits (Laursen, 2003a). It is a case of deep integration, compared to shallow integration in other parts of the world (Haggard, 1995). It also means that the EU interferes much more with the daily lives of the citizens in the EU. Some observers estimate that about half of the legislation in force in the Member States is based on EU legislation. Others suggest higher figures.

Over time the functional scope of the EC/EU has increased, from coal and steel in the European Coal and Steel Community in 1952, to include nearly any kind of policy issue imaginable. At the same time membership has increase from six members in the 1950s to 15 in the mid-1990s and to 25 members from May 2004. The integration process in Europe has both increased policy scope and the geographical area covered by the process over time (Dinan, 1999).

Institutionally, the main difference between the EU and other integration schemes is the pooling and delegation of sovereignty that has taken place. Pooling refers to decision-making by majority voting in the Council and delegation refers to the decision to give 'supranational' powers to the European Commission and the European Court of Justice (ECJ). Andrew Moravcsik, in his monumental study *The Choice for Europe* (1998), argued that such pooling and delegation has taken place to create 'credible commitments'. He sees the EU as an international regime, and as such it can be compared with other international regimes and integration schemes. However, given the degree of pooling and delegation in the EU it can be said that the EU is very much a *sui generis* integration scheme.

In this way, the institutional capacity of the common institutions sets the EU apart from other integration schemes. Some scholars say that the EU is 'supranational'. Over time this dimension has been controversial. But the founding fathers were sceptical of purely intergovernmental organizations. They believed in strong common institutions, an independent Commission and ECJ, and majority voting in the Council. If we look at this dimension over time it is clear that the use of qualified majority voting (QMV) has increased (Laursen, 2001).

Political scientists have tried for years to come to grips with the European integration process. How can such expansion be explained? (Laursen, 1995). Early neo-functionalist theories put emphasis on 'spill-over' effects and unintended consequences. Moravcsik saw integration as a deliberate process controlled by rational governments driven by domestic demand for (economic) integration measures because of international interdependence.

From a rational perspective, the pooling and delegation of sovereignty can be seen as a way to overcome two fundamental problems of an international system of sovereign states: defection and distributional issues. Surveillance and enforcement mechanisms can help avoid defection or cheating and through common institutions issues of distribution can be dealt with through structural policies and various budgetary side-payments (Laursen, 2003a).

But the governments are caught in a two-level game. What they accept in the EU must be accepted at home. At the same time, in order to solve common problems brought on by international interdependence, they must reach agreements with their partners (Putnam, 1988).

At the outset of the integration process there was a feeling that citizens would accept it as long as they liked the decisions taken collectively (Lindberg and Scheingold, 1970). This notion has become known as output legitimacy (Scharpf, 1999). But as the EU became more intrusive, people started to be concerned about how decisions were made. This aspect has been called input legitimacy. The question of not only the role of the European Parliament, but also national parliaments, got on the agenda. So did the question of openness and transparency including access to documents. The fact that the Council legislated behind closed doors was criticised. It contributed to what was discussed as a 'democratic deficit'.

But can the EU become fully democratic? Some scholars put forward some doubt, saying that there is no European *demos* (Weiler, 1999). There is no European 'people', but several European peoples. There is no common European political space. Political debates are largely national. Media in Europe remain national, partly for language reasons. At the time of Nice the debates in the European Parliament took place in 11 official languages.

Another concept used in connection with this debate about legitimacy is that of 'identity.' National identities are very deep-rooted in Europe. The free movement of labour associated with the Treaty of Rome has not led to much migration. Most immigration has been from third countries outside the EU and it has given problems in many Member States because of a deep-rooted sense of national identity. The 'shift of loyalty' towards European institutions that Ernst Haas talked about in the 1950s, when he studied the ECSC, has not happened to any important degree (Haas, 1958).

The more optimistic response to the debate about identity is that we all have multiple identities and that one can perfectly feel both, say German and European, at the same time. To quote Thomas Risse, "the European polity does not require a 'demos' that replaces a national with a European identity, but one in which national and European identities co-exist and complement each other" (Risse, 2004, p. 169).

Can a European identity be fostered? The answer is yes in principle, but it takes education, communication and political leadership. According to social constructivists, interactions do affect identities (Christiansen et al., 1999, 2001). Discourse and ideas do matter. Political leaders can be norm entrepreneurs.

So the question of getting an efficient and legitimate EU is more than an institutional issue. Social constructivists studying the formation of collective identities have a contribution to make. So do classical studies about the formation of security communities (Deutsch et al., 1957) as well as some neo-functionalist studies looking at utilitarian and affective support for integration and 'actor socialization' (Lindberg and Scheingold, 1970).

THE POST-NICE AGENDA

As they left Nice, the leaders called for "a deeper and wider debate about the future development of the European Union." They went on to mention the following points on the agenda of that future post-Nice debate:

1. How to establish and monitor a more precise delimitation of competences between the European Union and the Member States, reflecting the principle of subsidiarity.
2. The status of the Charter of Fundamental Rights of the European Union proclaimed in Nice.
3. A simplification of the Treaties with a view to making them clearer and better understood without changing their meaning.
4. The role of the national Parliaments in the European architecture.

The Declaration also talked about "the need to improve and to monitor the democratic legitimacy and transparency of the Union and its institutions, to bring them closer to the citizens of the Member States."

Nice therefore decided that a new IGC should be convened in 2004 to discuss these issues. This IGC started on October 4, 2003, earlier than originally expected and finished in June 2004.

Nice was clearly not the end of the road. The nature of the EU was still very much on the agenda. What kind of Union is it? What kind of Union should it become?

The meeting of the European Council at Laeken in December 2001 accepted the idea of preparing IGC-2004 through a Convention. Such a method had been used with success to produce the Charter on Fundamental Rights in parallel with the Treaty of Nice negotiations in 2000. In the Declaration of Laeken on the Future of the European Union the leaders claimed that the EU is a success story and asked a number of questions about the future development of the EU. The EU faced "twin challenges, one within and the other beyond its borders." Internally the institutions should "become more democratic, more transparent and more efficient." Internationally, 'now that the Cold War is over and we are living in a globalised, yet highly fragmented world, Europe needs to shoulder its responsibilities in the governance of globalisation' (Belgium, EU Presidency, 2001).

The Convention's Draft Constitutional Treaty

The Convention on the Future of Europe had former French President Valéry Giscard d'Estaing as chairman and was composed of 15 representatives of the Heads of State or Government of the Member States (one from each Member State), 30 members of national parliaments (two from each Member States), 16 members of the European Parliament and two Commission representatives. Candidate countries were also involved (without votes). A Praesidium was composed of the chairman, two vice-chairmen (Giuliano Amato of Italy and Jean-Luc Dehaene of Belgium) and nine members drawn from the Convention.

The novelty of the Convention method was the relatively high involvement of members of parliaments (MPs) from the Member States as well as many members from the European Parliament (MEPs). The idea was to have a more open process with more debate, and hopefully get a more legitimate outcome.

The Convention, which had a total of 105 members, held 26 plenary sessions of two days. It went through stages: listening (February-July 2002), study (September-December 2002), proposals and editing (January-July 2003). The study phase included the work in 13 Working Groups. During the final phase, the Praesidium played a decisive role (de Poncis, 2003; Duhamel, 2003, Beach 2003). In the end the Convention produced a consensus draft (CONV 850/03; European Convention, 2003). Five members refused to accept this draft. Instead they produced a minority report (CONV 773/03).

At the meeting of the European Council in Thessaloniki, Greece, 19-20 June 2003 Giscard d'Estaing presented a Draft Constitution (CONV 724/03). The final version was presented to the Italian President of the European Council in Rome on 18 July 2003 (CONV 850/03)

The draft constitutional treaty includes a number of changes. The following were among the most important ones:

1. The Union shall have *legal personality* (Art. 6).
2. The Union shall recognise the rights, freedoms and principles set out in the Charter of *Fundamental Rights* (Art. 7). These rights were listed in Part II of the draft constitutional treaty.
3. The limits of Union competences are governed by the *principle of conferral*. Competences not conferred upon the Union in the Constitution remain with the Member States (Art. 9).
4. The Constitution, and law adopted by the Union's Institutions in exercising competences conferred on it, shall have *primacy* over the law of the Member States (Art.10).
5. The Union shall have *exclusive competences* in the following areas: competition rules within the internal market, monetary policy (for the Member States which have adopted the euro), common commercial policy, customs union, the conservation of marine biological resources under the common fisheries policy, and for the conclusion of a number of international agreements (Art. 12).
6. The Union shall have *shared competences* in the following areas: internal market, area of freedom, security and justice, agriculture and fisheries (excluding the conservation of marine biological resources), transport and trans-European networks, energy, aspects of social policy (defined in Part III of the constitutional treaty), economic, social and territorial cohesion, environment, consumer protection and common safety concerns in public health matters (Art. 13).
7. The Union shall adopt measures to ensure *coordination of the economic policies* of the Member States. This included employment policies (Art. 14).

8. The Union may take *supporting, coordinating or complementary action* at the European level in these areas: industry, protection and improvement of human health, education, vocational training, youth and sport, culture and civil protection Art. 16).

The Draft Constitution also contained a so-called flexibility clause which was largely a repetition of the existing Art 308 TEC (ex. 235): "If action by the Union should prove necessary (...) to attain one of the objectives set by this Constitution, and the Constitution has not provided the necessary powers, the Council, acting unanimously on a proposal from the Commission and after obtaining the consent of the European Parliament, shall take the appropriate measures" (Art. 17).

Concerning CFSP, the Draft Convention said "The Union's competence in matters of common foreign and security policy shall cover all areas of foreign policy and all questions relating to the Union's security, including the progressive framing of a common defence policy, which might lead to a common defence" (Art. 15). This is what is already in the EU treaty (Art. 17 TEU, ex. J.7). We notice this competence is not mentioned among shared competences. Despite abolishing the pillar structure of the Union, CFSP remained apart from the rest. The Draft Convention had a section on specific provisions for implementing common foreign and security policy (Art. 39). It talked about "the development of mutual political solidarity" and "achievement of an ever-increasing degree of convergence." Normally, "decisions relating to the common foreign and security policy shall be adopted by the European Council and the Council of Ministers unanimously." However, in some cases "the European Council may unanimously decide that the Council should act by qualified majority."

Specific provisions for implementing a common defence policy were based on unanimity (Art. 40). This too was in line with existing rules. ESDP shall "provide the Union with an operational capacity." This is new in the treaty, although in principle decided at the Helsinki summit in December 1999. The Union may engage in "peace-keeping, conflict prevention and strengthening international security in accordance with the principles of the United Nations Charter." These are the missions know as Petersberg tasks, inserted into the treaty by the Amsterdam Treaty. But the draft treaty mentioned the possibility of Member States "whose military capabilities fulfil higher criteria and which have made more binding commitments to one another" establishing what was referred to as "structured cooperation." The Draft Convention further mentioned the possibility of "closer cooperation" as regards mutual defence. If a Member State participating in such closer cooperation "is the victim of armed aggression on its territory, the other participating States shall give it aid and assistance by all the means in their power, military or other, in accordance with Article 51 of the United Nations

Charter" and "in close cooperation with" NATO. This was new. Nice specifically excluded defence from closer cooperation. The Constitutional Treaty opened the way for an *avantgarde* or 'hard core' of Member States developing a defence policy including collective defence *à la* Article 5 of NATO (or Article V of the Western European Union).

When it comes to the institutions, the Draft Convention wanted to limit the membership to the European Parliament to 736. "Representation of European citizens shall be degressively proportional, with a minimum threshold of four members per Member State." The composition of the EP would have to be decided before the EP elections in 2009—by unanimity (Art. 19). The implication is that the Nice composition would be used until then. The EP is strengthened by having to elect the President of the European Commission, albeit on a proposal from the European Council (Art. 26). This opens the way for more parliamentary democracy in the Union, but controlled by the Member States. In a way it is mainly window dressing. The Member States are trying to stay in control.

One of the most debated novelties was the proposal for a permanent European Council Chair: "The European Council shall elect its President, by qualified majority, for a term of two and a half years, renewable once" (Art. 21). This president "may not hold a national mandate." The exact job description of this future President was very controversial.

In the Council of Ministers, QMV would become normal practice: "Except where the Constitution provides otherwise, decisions of the Council shall be taken by qualified majority" (Art. 22). Interestingly, it was proposed that "such a majority shall consist of the majority of Member States, representing at least three fifths of the population of the Union" (Art. 24). This would abolish the cumbersome system of weights adopted by Nice. This was a controversial change. Especially Spain and Poland opposed this redefinition of QMV. They wanted to retain the Nice weights.

Various Council formations were proposed: General Affairs Council, Legislative Council, Foreign Affairs Council, and further formations to be decided. The Foreign Affairs Council would be chaired by a new Foreign Minister. The presidency of other formations "shall be held by Member State representatives within the Council of Ministers on the basis of equal rotation for periods of at least a year … taking into account European political and geographical balance and diversity of all Member States" (Art. 23).

The Commission would retain the exclusive right of initiative in legislation. According to the draft it would be limited to 15 so-called European Commissioners, including the President and the Foreign Minister. There would further be non-voting Commissioners from the remaining Member States (Art. 25). This would allow all Member States to have a Commissioner, but in some cases without a vote. This proposal was especially controversial. A number of smaller states were against this change, insisting that each Member State must have one voting member of the Commission. Also the Commission was in favour of each Member State having a Commissioner with voting rights (COM(2003) 548 final).

The Foreign Minister would be appointed by the European Council by qualified majority, with the agreement of the President of the Commission. He/she would be one of the Vice-Presidents of the Commission and would chair the Foreign Affairs Council. This arrangement was referred to as 'double-hatting.' The new post might increase the Union's visibility internationally, but would the incumbent have a foreign policy?

"The Commission, as a body, shall be responsible to the European Parliament." The old possibility of the EP passing a censure motion, which would force the members of the Commission to resign, was retained.

The terminology of the legal acts of the Union would change. What used to be a regulation would become a European law. A directive would become a European framework law. Non-legislative acts of general application would become known as European regulations (Art. 32). European laws and framework laws would in the future also be used in the Area of Freedom, Security and Justice (Art. 41). But they were excluded for CFSP (Art. 39).

The Draft Convention had a section on the Democratic Life of the Union. The Union is founded on the principle of representative democracy: "Citizens are directly represented at Union level in the European Parliament. Member States are represented in the European Council and in the Council of Ministers by their governments, themselves accountable to national parliaments, elected by their citizens" (Art. 45). This suggested a double kind of legitimacy.

The principle of participatory democracy was mentioned. The Union institutions were encouraged to involve citizens and representative associations in their work. Under transparency the participation of civil society was also mentioned. Further, a new citizens' initiative was introduced: "No less than one million citizens coming from a significant number of Member States may invite the Commission to submit any appropriate proposal on matters where citizens consider that a legal act of the Union is required for the purpose of implementing the Constitution" (Art. 45).

Transparency of proceedings was prescribed. The draft treaty made it clear that the Council of Ministers shall meet in public "when examining and adopting a legislative proposal" (Art. 49).

A Protocol on the application of the principles of subsidiarity and proportionality gave national parliaments a special role in supervising the compliance with subsidiarity: When reasoned opinions on a Commission proposal's non-compliance with the principle of subsidiarity represent at least one third of all votes allocated to the Member States' national Parliaments and their chambers, the Commission shall review its proposal. The stipulation mentioned votes, because chambers of a bicameral parliamentary system would have one vote each, but the national parliaments of Member States with unicameral parliamentary systems would have two votes.

ENTER THE MEMBER STATES[1]

The IGC started on 4 October 2003 in Rome during the Italian Presidency. The big question then was, to what extent would the Member States reopen the compromises found during the Convention? Would they mess it up? Or would the IGC be able to agree on the draft Constitutional Treaty from the Convention without too many changes?

When the IGC opened it was clear that some Member States were not ready to accept the draft from the Convention. The proposed new definition of a QMV, viz. at least 50% of the states, representing at least 60% of the EU population, was not acceptable to the Spanish and Polish governments, which wanted to retain the formula of the Treaty of Nice which gave them more formal influence.

Some countries had problems with the extended use of QMV. In particular the British had some so-called 'red lines', i.e. non-negotiable items. These focused upon Common Foreign and Security Policy (CFSP), taxation, budget sources and financial frameworks, social security and criminal justice. The British also wanted further clarification concerning the incorporation of the Charter of Fundamental Rights.

The question of the composition and size of the Commission was still an issue. Most small Member States wanted to retain a voting Commissioner from their country in the future.

The French and German governments were among the few that had no problems with the proposed Constitutional treaty. They were pressing the other states for a speedy conclusion of the negotiations. In general the original six Member States of the European Communities were the most favourable towards the Convention's proposal. The new Member States from Central and Eastern Europe largely sided with other small Member States like Austria, Finland and Portugal insisting on retaining a voting member of the Commission in the future.

Prior to a ministerial conclave in Naples 28-29 November the Presidency put forward proposals on 25 November (CIG 52/03 and CIG 52/1/03). One of the issues discussed in Naples was whether the preamble should include a reference to Christianity. The proposal was supported by Poland and some

---

[1] This and following sections rely on Laursen, 2004.

other Catholic countries and Christian Democratic political parties, but opposed by France, the Nordic countries and some Socialist and Liberal political parties. Another issue discussed was defence. Real progress was made on this issue in Naples. This included structured cooperation and a mutual defence clause. The former should be based on objective parameters and the latter should not prejudice the specific character of the security and defence policy of certain member states and be compatible with NATO.

On December 9 the Presidency published its proposals to the IGC meeting of Heads of State or Government, 12-13 December in Brussels. One document, CIG 60/03 Add 1, contained concrete proposals on a number of issues. The Presidency considered that it had taken into account the different views of the delegations and that this document constituted a balanced package. The other document, CIG 60/03 ADD 2, addressed the more sensitive political issues. They should constitute the focus of the discussions on 12-13 December (see also CIG 60/03). The sensitive issues were: the preamble (question of reference to Christianity), composition of the Commission (reduction or one member per member state?), definition of QMV (double majority or the Nice formula) and scope of QMV (taxation, etc.) as well as minimum threshold for seats in the European Parliament (should the proposed minimum of four seats be increased to five or six?).

But the summit in Brussels in December 2003, which the Italian Presidency had hoped would conclude the negotiations, failed to reach an agreement. Afterwards the mood was sombre. Some blamed the poor handling of the summit by the Italian Prime Minister Silvio Berlusconi. Others blamed Spain and Poland for their intransigence on the definition of a QMV. But meeting the press afterwards most heads of state or government said that it had been a collective failure.

However, both the German Chancellor Gerhard Schröder and French President Jacques Chirac now talked about the possibility of a smaller group of Member States going ahead if the 25 could not agree. If the IGC were to fail definitely in 2004, said Chancellor Schröder, "Then two-speed Europe would be the logical consequence. We do not want this, but we are prepared to do so." President Chirac referred to his speech to the German *Bundestag* in 2000, where he had talked about the possibility of a 'pioneer group.' "I continue to think that it is a good solution, because it will give impulsion and set an example. I think this will allow Europe to go faster, further and better", he said (*Agence Europe*, 15 December, 2003).

After the failure in Brussels in December 2003 it was up to the Irish Presidency to try to rescue the negotiations during the first six months of 2004. The Irish set out slowly and carefully. They consulted with all Member States to seek an agreement to restart the negotiations. The Irish stressed that a restart would presuppose a political willingness to find a compromise.

In March 2004 the IGC was restarted. The change of government in Spain after the elections on 14 March was one of the factors that increased the chances of success. The election followed shortly after the terrorist bombing attack in Madrid on 11 March. The meeting of the European Council on 25-26 March confirmed that the 25 European leaders would work to reach a compromise "no later than the June European Council" scheduled for 17 June (*Financial Times,* 27-28 March, 2004). In a document to the summit the Irish Presidency concluded: "The Presidency's assessment is that there is a strong case for bringing the Intergovernmental Conference to an early conclusion, and that there is reason to believe that an overall agreement acceptable to all delegations is achievable if the necessary political will exists" (CIG 70/03, 24 March 2004).

As expected the new Socialist government under Rodriguez Zapatero moved Spain to a more pro-EU line. This isolated Poland on this issue. So the Poles also indicated willingness to compromise.

Let us mention here that it was on 20 April that British Prime Minister Tony Blair told the House of Commons that the Constitutional Treaty would be put to a referendum in Britain. Obviously frustrated by the domestic debate he said, "It is time to resolve once and for all whether this country, Britain, wants to be at the centre of European decision-making or not" (*Financial Times 2*, 25 March 2003). Whatever the exact reason for the British u-turn, it forced the other Member States to listen even more to the British 'red lines' in the end-game. But it also started the potentially fatal process of many referendums to authorize ratification.

The Irish Presidency succeeded getting an agreement at the summit in Brussels, 17-18 June 2004. This followed shortly after the elections to the European Parliament, where the turn-out had been extremely low.

On the 16th of June the Presidency presented two documents to the IGC. One contained a set of texts which the Presidency considered would find consensus in the framework of the final agreement (CIG 81/04). The other contained proposals on outstanding issues (CIG 82/04). The first one included text on Council configurations (pre-established groups of three Member States for a period of 18 months), the EU Foreign Minister, budget procedures, own resources (unanimity), financial frameworks, judicial cooperation in criminal matters (possibility of transferring draft framework law to the European Council), defence policy (permanent structured cooperation, incl. QMV, and "closer cooperation on mutual defence"), QMV in the field of CFSP (basically for implementing decision, with the possibility of referring the decision to the European Council for a decision by unanimity), decision-making in the area of the Common Commercial Policy (normally QMV, but unanimity for cultural and audiovisual services as well as trade in social, education and health services), social security (possible referral to the

European Council), taxation, enhanced cooperation and a number of other issues. It included a preamble that did not contain a reference to Christianity. Further, the text included simplified procedures for amending the constitution, viz. the possibility of the European Council by unanimity deciding to move some policy area from unanimity to QMV, referred to as a *passerelle*, (with the exception of defence) and the possibility of changing internal policies of Part III through unanimity in the European Council, i.e. avoiding an IGC. The text also included a protocol on Denmark making the Danish opt-outs from 1992 part of the new treaty.

The document with compromise proposals from the Presidency included a definition of the QMV of 55% of the states representing 65% of the population thus increasing both elements by 5%, but a Blocking minority should also include at least four states. This meant that three big states, such as Germany, France and the UK, would not be able to bloc a decisions supported by all the other Member States. The minimum number of seats in the European Parliament was raised to six. The Commission would have one member per Member State until 2014 when it would be reduced to 18 members. The document further included proposed texts for economic governance, especially for the Member States that have introduced the euro, multiannual financial framework (unanimity) and explanations relating to the Charter of Fundamental Rights.

The final solution on QMV reached in Brussels on 18 June 2004 was at least 55% of the states, comprising at least 15 of them, and representing at least 65% of the EU population. The further stipulation about the blocking minority was retained: A blocking minority must include at least four states (CIG 84/04, p. 7). This applies to decisions based on a proposal from the Commission. In cases of decisions not based on proposals from the Commission, e.g. some decisions within CFSP, JHA and EMU, "the qualified majority shall be defined as 72% of the members of the Council, representing Member States comprising at least 65% of the population of the Union" (Council of the European Union, 2004a).

According to a protocol the new QMV would enter into force from 2009. Further, a declaration included an Ioannina-type stipulation. If Council members representing at least three quarters on the Member States or three quarters of the EU population required to form a blocking minority state their opposition then the Council will continue to discuss the issue during a "reasonable time" with a view to answering the concerns expressed by these states (*Agence Europe,* 21 June, 2004). The declaration should apply from the entry into force of the new QMV in 2009 until 2014 after which "the Council may adopt a European decision repealing it" (Declaration on Article I-25, in Council of the European Union, 2004b). What had started as a simple formula for a QMV gradually got more complex during the IGC.

The small states eventually accepted a compromise on the size of the Commission. The new Commission from November 2004 would have one Commissioner per Member State. So would the next Commission (2009-2014). But from 2014 the Commission would be reduced to two-thirds the number of Member States and equal rotation would be introduced, "unless the European Council, acting unanimously, decides to alter this figure" (CIG 84/04, p. 4).

The minimum number of seats in the European Parliament was set at six. The maximum was set at 96, meaning three less for Germany, which currently has 99. The total membership was increased from 736 to 750.

The British 'red lines' were to a large extent accepted by the IGC. Some areas where the draft from the Convention had foreseen QMV were moved back to unanimity. (This included own resources, multi-annual financial framework, indirect taxation and company taxation). The British threat of veto was credible. The Irish Presidency was very inventive in finding language that would reassure those fearing to be outvoted on important issues. In some cases this included the emergency break of sending an issue to the European Council or further negotiations to try to reach consensus (social security for migrant workers). In some cases closer cooperation was mentioned as a possibility in case no consensus could be found (judicial cooperation in criminal matters). In the end this made the Constitutional Treaty adopted by the IGC a more complex document than the one adopted by the Convention. From an efficiency point of view these changes constituted steps backwards (Grevi, 2004).

Let's finally take note of the fact that the demand from Catholic countries, especially Poland and Italy, to have a reference to Christianity in the preamble, was not accepted by the IGC. France, Belgium and the Nordic countries were strongly against such a reference.

Afterwards the Irish Taoiseach and European Council President Bertie Ahern presented the new treaty as "fundamental progress." "We are all winners," he said. British Prime Minster Tony Blair said he had "won a victory for the United Kingdom and Europe." He welcomed the strengthened role of national parliaments and said that the treaty ensured the United Kingdom of a right of veto in sensitive areas such as taxation, social security, foreign policy and defence (*Agence Europe*, 21 June, 2004). Chancellor Gerhard Schröder talked about a "truly historic" decision. Prime Minister Jean-Claude Juncker from Luxembourg talked about a "qualitative breakthrough" and said that the constitution was "good for Europe, as it makes the Union more transparent, more democratic because of the increased powers of the European Parliament and more effective" (ibid.).

The new Polish Prime Minister Marek Belka said that the Constitution was a "great success as we have assured Poland a strong position in the EU, stronger than that provided for at Nice, even if this seemed impossible." He added that "the greatest success we have achieved concerns the introduction of the Ioannina mechanism, which establishes population thresholds still more favourable for Poland." He did regret, however, that the preamble did not include a reference to Christianity (ibid.).

THE REFERENDUM TRAP

All 25 Member States now had to ratify the proposed Constitutional Treaty according to national rules. About 10 of these decided to have a referendum, including Spain (20 February 2005), Portugal, Luxembourg, the Netherlands (1 June 2005), Poland, France (29 May 2005), Ireland, the United Kingdom, the Czech Republic, and Denmark

Future research will have to ask why 10 countries decided to have a referendum. Experience shows that referenda are rather unpredictable (Hug, 2003). Voters often see a referendum as a mid-term evaluation of the incumbent government. We know that the Danes voted No to the Maastricht Treaty in 1992 and the French barely accepted it later the same year. In 2001 the Irish voted No to the Treaty of Nice. The Danes and the Swedes have voted No to take part in the single currency, the euro, in 2000 and 2003 respectively. Voters do clearly not always follow the advice of the government in power. There was therefore a high statistical risk that one or more Member States would vote No to the Constitutional Treaty. No doubt it would take a tremendous amount of national political leadership to pull the required Yes votes through.

Yet, at least eight states that did not need to have a referendum decided to have one. Ireland and Denmark may have had constitutional constraints requiring a referendum.

As is well-know by now, the French voters rejected the Constitutional Treaty on 29 May and the Dutch followed on 1 June. In the meantime about 10 countries had ratified the Constitutional Treaty, Spain after a referendum in February, and the other Member States through parliamentary votes. The European Council meeting later on 16-17 June called for a reflection period and the fate of the Constitutional treaty is now rather uncertain.

It seems likely that the Treaty of Nice will have a longer life than expected. One possible future scenario is a Nice-plus treaty, a situation where parts of the Constitutional Treaty are rescued through smaller treaty reforms.

BIBLIOGRAPHY

Beach, Derek (2003), "Towards a new method of constitutional bargaining? The role and impact of EU institutions in the IGC and convention method of treaty reform." Paper presented to the Danish Society for European Research, Aalborg, 27 September.

Belgium, EU Presidency (2001), "The Future of the EU: Declaration of Laeken." Downloaded from www.eu2001.be

Bomberg, Elizabeth, Laura Cram, and David Martin (2003), "The EU's Institutions," in Elizabeth Bomberg and Alexander Stubb (eds.), *The European Union: How Does it Work?* Oxford: Oxford University Press, pp. 43-68.

Christiansen, Thomas, Knud Erik Jørgensen and Antje Wiener, eds. (1999), "The Social Construction of Europe," Special Issue of *Journal of European Public Policy*, Vol. 6, No. 4.

—, Knud Erik Jørgensen and Antje Wiener, eds. (2001), *The Social Construction of Europe.* London: Sage.

COM (2003) 548 final: Commission of the European Communities, "*A Constitution for the Union.*" Opinion of the Commission, pursuant to Article 48 of the Treaty on European Union, on the Conference of representatives of the Member States' governments convened to revise the Treaties. Brussels, 17 September, 2003.

CONV 724/03: The European Convention, "Draft Constitution, Volume I – Revised text of Part One," Brussels, 26 May 2003.

— 773/03: Contribution by Mr. David Heathcoat-Amory, Mrs. Irene Belohorska, Mr. Jan Zahradil, Mr. Jens-Peter Bonde, Mr. Peter Skaarup, members of the Convention and Mr. Esko Seppanen, Mr. John Gormley, Mr. Per Dalgaard, Mr. William Abitbol, alternate members of the Convention: "Minority report – The Europe of democracies", 30 May 2003.

— 850/03: The European Convention, "Draft Treaty establishing a Constitution for Europe," Brussels, 18 July 2003.

Council of the European Union (2004a), *Draft Treaty Establishing a Constitution for Europe as approved by the Intergovernmental Conference on 18 June 2004.* Volume I. Luxembourg: Office for Official Publications of the European Communities.

— (2004b), *Draft Treaty Establishing a Constitution for Europe as approved by the Intergovernmental Conference on 18 June 2004. Protocols. Declarations.* Volume II. Luxembourg: Office for Official Publications of the European Communities.

De Poncis, Étienne (2003), *Vers une Constitution européenne. Texte commenté du projet de traité constitutionnel établi par la Convention européenne.* Paris: Éditions 10/18.

Deutsch, Karl, et al. (1957), *Political Community and the North Atlantic Area: International Organization in the Light of Historical Experience.* Princeton, N.J.: Princeton University Press.

Dinan, Desmond (1999), *Ever Closer Union: An Introduction to European Integration*, 2nd ed. Basingstoke: Palgrave.

Dobson, Lynn and Albert Weale (2003), "Governance and Legitimacy," in Elizabeth Bomberg and Alexander Stubb (eds.), *The European Union: How Does it Work?* Oxford: Oxford University Press, pp. 156-173.

Duhamel, Olivier (2003), *Pour l'Europe: Le texte integral de la Constitution expliqué et Commenté.* Paris: Éditions du Seuil.

Edwards, Geoffrey and Alfred Pijpers, eds. (1997), *The Politics of European Treaty Reform: The 1996 Intergovernmental Conference and Beyond.* London and Washington: Pinter.

European Convention (2003), *Draft Treaty Establishing a Constitution for Europe.* Luxembourg: Office for Official Publications of the European Communities.

European Council (2000), "Presidency Conclusions. Nice European Council Meeting 7, 8 and 9 December."

European Union (2001), *Treaty of Nice*. Luxembourg: Office for Official Publications of the European Communities. Also in *Official Journal* C80 (10.03.2001), Downloadable from http://www.europa.eu.int/eur-lex/en/treaties/index.html

Fischer, Joschka (2000), "From Confederacy to Federation – Thoughts on the finality of European integration." Speech at the Humboldt University in Berlin, 12 May.

http://www.auswaertiges-amt.de/www/de/infoservice/download/pdf/reden/redene/r000512b-r1008e.pdf
Giscard d'Estaing, Valéry (2003), *Valéry Giscard d'Estaing présente la constitution pour l'Europe*. Paris: Éditions Albin Michel.
Goldstein, Leslie Friedman (2001), *Constituting Federal Sovereignty: The European Union in Comparative Context*. Baltimore and London: The Johns Hopkins University Press.
Grevi, Giovanni (2004), "Light and shade of a quasi-Constitution: An Assessment," *EPC Issue Paper* No 14 (23 June).
Haggard, Stephen (1995), *Developing Nations and the Politics of Global Integration*. Washington, D.C.: The Brookings Institution.
Haas, Ernst (1950), *The Uniting of Europe: Political, Social, and Economic Forces 1950-1957*. Stanford: Stanford University Press.
Hug, Simon (2003), *Voices of Europe: Citizens, Referendums, and European Integration*. Lanham: Rowman & Littlefield.
Hughes, Kirsti (2003a), "The Battle for Power in Europe – Will the Convention Get it Right?" CEPS/EPIN Working Paper, February.
Hughes, Kirsti (2003b), "A Dynamic and Democratic EU or Muddling through Again? Assessing the EU's Draft Constitution," EPIN Working Paper No 8 (July).
Laursen, Finn (1994), "The Not-So-Permissive Consensus: Thoughts on the Maastricht Treaty and the Future of European Integration," in Finn Laursen and Sophie Vanhoonacker (eds.), *The Ratification of the Maastricht Treaty*. Dordrecht: Nijhoff, pp. 295-317.
— (1995), "On Studying European Integration: Integration Theory and Political Economy," in Finn Laursen (ed.), *The Political Economy of European Integration*. The Hague: Kluwer, pp. 3-29.
— (2001), "EU Enlargement: Interests, Issues and the Need for Institutional Reform," in Svein S. Andersen and Kjell A. Eliassen (eds.), *Making Policy In Europe*. 2nd ed. London: SAGE, pp. 206-228.
—, ed. (2002a), *The Amsterdam Treaty: National Preference Formation, Interstate Bargaining and Outcome*. Odense: Odense University Press.
— (2002b), "Vers un traité constitutional?" *L'Europe en formation*, No. 1, pp. 29-40.
—, ed. (2003a), *Comparative Regional Integration: Theoretical Perspectives*. Aldershot: Ashgate.
— (2003b), "The Convention's Draft Constitutional Treaty: Towards a more federal EU?" *L'Europe en formation*, No. 2, pp. 59-76.
— (2004), "Enter the Member States : an Analysis and Evaluation of the Intergovernmental Conference 2003-2004," *L'Europe en formation* No 4, pp. 31-52.
— and Sophie Vanhoonacker, eds. (1992), *The Intergovernmental Conference on Political Union: Institutional Reforms, New Policies and International Identity of the European Community*. Dordrecht: Martinus Nijhoff.
— (1994), *The Ratification of the Maastricht Treaty: Issues, Debates and Future Implications*. Dordrecht: Martinus Nijhoff.
Lindberg, Leon N. and Stuart A. Scheingold (1970), *Europe's Would-Be Polity: Patterns of Change in the European Community*. Prentice-Hall, Inc, Englewood-Cliffs, N.J.
Marhold, Hartmut, ed. (2002), *Le nouveau debat sur l'Europe*. Nice: Presses d'Europe.
Moravcsik, Andrew (1998), *The Choice for Europe*. Ithaca, NY: Cornell University Press.
Putnam, Robert D. (1988), "Diplomacy and domestic politics: the logic of two-level games," *International Organization*, Vol. 42, No. 3 (Summer), pp. 427-460.
Risse, Thomas (2004), "Social Constructivism and European Integration," in Antje Wiener and Thomas Diez (eds.), *European Integration Theory*. Oxford: Oxford University Press, pp. 159-176.
Scharpf, Fritz W. (1999), *Governing in Europe: Effective and Democratic?* Oxford: Oxford University Press.
Tsoukalis, Loukas (2003), *What Kind of Europe?* Oxford: Oxford University Press.
Weiler, J.H.H. (1999), *The Constitution of Europe*. Cambridge: Cambridge University Press.

INDEX